D0992370

HISTORY OF
EAST AFRICA

HISTORY OF
EAST AFRICA

Edited by
D. A. LOW
and
ALISON SMITH

VOLUME III

CLARENDON PRESS · OXFORD
1976

KRAUSS LIBRARY
LUTHERAN SCHOOL OF THEOLOGY
AT CHICAGO

Oxford University Press, Ely House, London W. 1

GLASGOW NEW YORK TORONTO MELBOURNE WELLINGTON
CAPE TOWN IBADAN NAIROBI DAR ES SALAAM LUSAKA ADDIS ABABA
DELHI BOMBAY CALCUTTA MADRAS KARACHI LAHORE DACCA
KUALA LUMPUR SINGAPORE HONG KONG TOKYO

ISBN 0 19 821680 7

© *Crown Copyright, 1976*

*All rights reserved. No part of this publication may be reproduced, stored in
a retrieval system, or transmitted, in any form or by any means, electronic,
mechanical, photocopying, recording or otherwise, without the prior permission
of Oxford University Press*

*Printed in Great Britain by William Clowes & Sons Limited
London, Colchester and Beccles*

JKM Library
1100 East 55th Street
Chicago, IL 60615

PT
365
·H5
v. 3

PREFACE

IT is now seventeen years since the three volumes of the Oxford *History of East Africa*, then a pioneer project in the historiography of Africa, were first planned. Paradoxically the very fact of its early conception has had much to do with its long gestation.

Before 1960, even although the end of the colonial era was clearly imminent, the idea that it would be completed and rounded off before the third and final volume went to press would have seemed fanciful. At that time, also, source material was largely limited to published official statements, newspapers, and legislative assembly debates; little work had been done on the assembling of oral evidence. Post-graduate work on history within East Africa itself was in its infancy, and there were no East African historians with higher degrees.

Naturally, perhaps, the first reaction to the quickening pace of events was to try to keep up with them, to present after all the completed story within the original time schedule. The first political chapters of the present volume were submitted in 1964, less than a year after Kenya became independent, and only a few months after the first revolutionary upheaval had toppled the first successor government in Zanzibar. Long before all the first drafts had been received, these chapters in the light of rapid post-independence events had become out of date; and, while other causes of delay have been many, it is fair to say that the rapid succession of changes in perspective has been especially important. During the past seven or eight years a whole series of historical questions applied to the theme of decolonization have been asked, sometimes in part answered, often modified or cast aside. The earliest accounts tended to concentrate on constitutional developments and on official and metropolitan policies. Then there was an emphasis on the history of nationalism. Later it seemed that nationalist energies must be redefined in more precise and differentiated terms; and that, in tracing the antecedents of the successor states, more attention needed to be given to other elements in their legacy—the heritage of governmental structures, for instance, or of patterns of political authority. Developments in East Africa, moreover, took on a sharper significance when seen against the backcloth of the whole wider African scene: the war in Algeria, the turbulence of the Congo, or the course of events in Central Africa since the breakdown of Federation and Rhodesia's UDI. In the light of all these rapidly changing perspectives, it became clear in 1968 that there would have to be a fresh stocktaking, a re-appraisal, before the third volume could be given anything approaching a definite form.

As this was done, it became apparent that in several respects a decade after the last of the erstwhile British East African territories became independent was no bad moment from which to make a preliminary review of the last phase of the colonial period. There was now becoming available a body of source material which, although still far from complete, was far more balanced in its coverage in that substantial evidence from the African side now included the first instalments of autobiography. Much fuller official documentation, too, was already coming to light in the shape of local administrative records, both those of the central secretariats and those of provincial and district centres. The extension of quantitative data moreover was giving far greater precision to the measurement of economic and social change, more especially when set against post-independence development; while a number of new studies, by economists, political scientists, and social anthropologists, as well as historians, were adding fresh dimensions and a new richness to our understanding of the period of terminal colonialism.

The editors and contributors are nevertheless very conscious that this can be no more than the most temporary and provisional of syntheses. Historical perspectives in Africa still change at a bewildering pace. The concepts of 'levels' and 'arenas' may well soon prove as blunt and unserviceable research tools as 'tribalism' and 'nationalism' seem today. Despite the richness and variety of source material as compared with that available only a few years back, there still remain moreover important categories untapped: British official papers subject to the thirty-year-rule restriction; official material similarly restricted in East Africa; besides a considerable wealth of private papers. Where the discussion may have led by the end of another decade and thereafter is anyone's guess. Very soon our snapshot may well have a sepia hue to it. The sober binding of the Clarendon Press should not induce any misplaced faith in finality of judgement.

Although the scope of this volume is in the main confined to the period since the Second World War, there are some exceptions. A number of contributors have felt it necessary to pick up the threads of their chapters a few years earlier to maintain continuity with the previous volume. Besides this, there were one or two topics which could not easily be divided between the second and third volumes; the present one accordingly includes a number of chapters which look back over the whole span of the colonial era: legal institutions, the impact of western thought, the role of the immigrant communities.

The general project of an East African History goes back over twenty years, having been first suggested at a conference of the governors of the then three British East African territories in 1952. As described in the Preface to the second volume, it has been financed out of Colonial (later Commonwealth) Development and Welfare funds on the grounds that a contribution to the building up of teaching and historical research within East Africa could suitably be ranked with more practical forms of aid as a productive long-term investment. The reception accorded to the first two volumes (both have been reprinted) and the growth in the East African university institutions of distinguished schools of historical research have fully vindicated the faith of the promoters. We should emphasize however that the editors' discretion has been complete and that no official responsibility has ever either been claimed or exists for anything which appears here.

The first volume, edited by Roland Oliver and Gervase Mathew, was published in 1963; the second, covering the colonial period down to the end of the Second World War, and edited by Vincent Harlow and Elizabeth Chilver with the assistance of Alison Smith, in 1965. Already before that volume appeared the death of Vincent Harlow, and the departure from Oxford of Elizabeth Chilver to become principal of Bedford College, London, deprived the third volume of two of those originally planned as editors. The third, David Walker, of Exeter University, put in much valuable work on the planning and vetting of the economic chapters before he was forced to give up owing to ill-health. Meanwhile Dame Margery Perham took on the main burden of editorship, and piloted the volume through the most critical phase of political re-appraisal before she too was obliged to give up on medical advice. During a considerable period while the position was being reviewed thereafter, Jack Gallagher, then Beit Professor of Commonwealth History at Oxford, generously held a watching brief. Finally, the project was re-activated under the joint editorship of Anthony Low, then Professor of History in the School of African and Asian Studies at the University of Sussex, and Alison Smith of Queen Elizabeth House, Oxford.

Movement to new posts, and other events, have also caused a number of changes in the originally planned team of contributors. Amongst these the heaviest blow was the death, early in 1969, of George Bennett, who had contributed generously, both as author and as adviser, to this as well as to the second volume of the history.

The reader will quickly be aware of one notable gap. The direct contribution of East African historians to the present work is a very small one. The original cause of this, as will have been clear from the foregoing, is that at the time the volume was first planned trained historians from East Africa were not yet available. When it came to providing for its completion, practical difficulties, and in particular the emphasis on a close personal co-operation between contributors by way of periodic seminars in Oxford and Sussex, caused the imbalance to remain unremedied. The editors are under no illusion that this has its drawbacks; increasingly the history of East Africa will be written, as it is already being written, by East Africans. But they are not without hope that the present set of essays, written for the most part by people who, although expatriates, had as teachers and research workers a close involvement with East Africa during the critical period of history about which they have here written, will have a value and a unity of its own.

Acknowledgements are many. The Institute of Commonwealth Studies at Oxford has, throughout the long history of the project, been unfailing in help and encouragement and in administering the funds which financed it; to its Librarians in particular, Margaret Robins and R. J. Townsend, we owe a special debt of gratitude. The Librarian and staff of Rhodes

House, and the Library of the old Colonial Office in its subsequent manifestations, have been patient and sympathetic to our needs. Individuals who have given valuable specialist advice include E. A. Brett, Arthur Hazlewood, Kenneth Ingham, R. Cranford Pratt, P. Robson; besides which must be recorded the generous advice of most of the contributors themselves and more especially of George Bennett, Cyril Ehrlich, F. B. Welbourn, and Christopher Wrigley. Miss Levinson, Mrs. C. Newbury, Mrs. P. Simmons, Mrs. S. Hopkins, Mrs. P. Robson, and Ieuan Griffiths have given assistance with statistical compilations, bibliography, and maps. We should also like to thank Miss Yvonne Wood and Mrs. D. Hopkins for much secretarial and typing help.

Two debts are outstanding. One is to the late Sir Andrew Cohen, who as governor of Uganda in 1952 was one of the first to look ahead and foresee the role that could be played by scholarly and responsible historical work in the process of state-building and development in Africa; and one of whose last acts, only a few weeks before his untimely death in 1968, was to secure financial provision from the Ministry of Overseas Development where he was Permanent Secretary to bring the project to a successful conclusion. The second is to Dame Margery Perham, who as a friend and scholar has watched over the fortunes of the history from its first inception. If others supported the proposed history as a service to political growth, to her it owed its conception as a work of scholarship. Successive editors and contributors have constantly looked to her for encouragement and advice. She was the main editor of this third volume during the most difficult period; it can be said without hesitation that without her it would never have been completed.

D. A. L.
A.S.

1973

CONTENTS

LIST OF ABBREVIATIONS
in references

Brit. J. Pol. Science	*British Journal of Political Science*
CO	Colonial Office
EEMO	European Elected Members' Organization
FO	Foreign Office
FOCP	Foreign Office Confidential Print
H. of C.	House of Commons
IBRD	International Bank of Reconstruction and Development
IO	India Office
J. Af. History	*Journal of African History*
J. Mod. Af. Studies	*Journal of Modern African Studies*
KWN	*Kenya Weekly News*
Leg Co	Legislative Council

(For abbreviations of political parties, associations, etc. see Index.)

LIST OF MAPS

INTRODUCTION: TOWARDS THE NEW ORDER 1945–1963

D. A. LOW AND J. M. LONSDALE

IN 1945 East Africa was under British rule. Many pressures exerted in the inter-war years had prevented it from passing irrevocably under the control of its small European population. But there were still a few who looked to Kenya's future as a 'white man's country'; and European unofficials exercised a large influence over its neighbours too. Within less than twenty years there was revolutionary political change. By 1963 independence had come to all four of the territories of East Africa, Tanganyika, Uganda, Kenya and Zanzibar, as part of the vast process in which dependencies of Europe have emerged as the Third World. It is difficult to discern an equivalent revolution in their economy and society. Their tripartite caste structure was as yet little modified by the upward mobility of Africans in the political and administrative fields. Europeans still controlled large-scale production; Asians still serviced industry and agriculture by craftsmanship and trade; most Africans remained peasant farmers. Nor are the processes of change within African society itself easily susceptible of theoretical analysis. A nationalist historiography, for instance, must confront the lack of territorially organized national movements prior to the decades covered in this volume. In sharp contrast to other parts of the Third World, there was no significant span of time during which nationalist groups and their ideologies might have affected the patterns of mobility or the boundaries of community. The nationalist impetus had to depend, instead, upon the successful meshing by tiny literate minorities—rarely possessed of independent means or professional status—of their own aspirations with the groundswell of discontents among the rural and urban populations. And these cannot be described straightforwardly as peasantry and proletariat, nor yet the élites as a bourgeoisie. A Marxist analysis, therefore, which would stress not the achievement of independence but the unfinished business of class conflict, is as difficult to formulate. For the historical experience of these years is too rich in variety. Its more obvious aspects, the imperial recession or the nationalist upsurge, may be the easiest to delineate in the pages which follow; but in future perspectives they may be of least importance. Deeper processes may prove to be of more enduring significance. This chapter will try to explore the complex moral and social dimensions of individual and corporate innovation in change, and to draw together some of the threads which underlie the more detailed histories of the countries concerned. It will end with a brief overview of the politics of the final phase of East African decolonization.

Imperial recession

The ending of British rule was, as in other parts of the world, a synthesis of imperial decision and nationalist pressures. Its East African application was, however, not a simple replay of other peoples' experience. It came, of course, in the wake of Britain's leading decision to relinquish empire in Asia, and then in West Africa and the Caribbean. But in most British minds these precedents offered no guide to the future of East—or Central—Africa: on the contrary, their European and Asian minorities made these areas entirely different.[1] However much their local African nationalisms might draw strength from the success of similar movements elsewhere in Africa and in other parts of the world, for much of the period under review the imperial authorities could not accept what the nationalists had to assert, that the Third World was one. This British attitude was grounded in traditional sentiment; it was much reinforced by the strategic requirements of the Cold War, and by the new economic importance attached to Africa in assisting the post-war reconstruction of Britain. The local European population was the most reliable collaborator in both military and economic purposes. This global metropolitan perspective—and it was the view from the defence and economic ministries rather than the Colonial Office[2]—shaped the local political framework in two decisive ways. First, inter-territorial organizations were created as the sturdier successors of the instruments of wartime co-ordination.

[1] D. A. Low, *Lion Rampant: essays in the study of British imperialism* (London, 1973), ch. 6, provides an outline account.
[2] Illustrated perhaps by the absence of maps on the Secretary of State's room walls until Lyttelton took over in October 1951: Viscount Chandos, *The Memoirs of Lord Chandos* (London, 1962), p. 346.

Secondly, the careful contrivance of 'partnership' or 'multiracialism' was erected against the claims of African nationalism. It followed that governmental intervention against this growing force was much more determined than in the West African colonies.

The official hardness of heart owed much to the fact that eastern Africa overlooked the Indian Ocean, on the further shores of which the certainties of Empire were giving way to the diplomacies of Commonwealth. The Second World War had seen this empire on the march; no contingents had been more ubiquitous than those from India. The Indian Ocean's eastern gateway had also witnessed the empire's most crushing defeat, at Singapore in 1942. The consequences of military unpreparedness against the Japanese were painfully demonstrated in the losing battles by Dutch and French to re-establish themselves in Indonesia and Indochina, and by Britain's long fight against the communist guerrillas in Malaya. Nearer at hand, by 1948 India, Pakistan, Ceylon, and Burma were all independent, the last having slipped almost unnoticed out of the Commonwealth. And in June of that year Britain abdicated from her Palestine Mandate. Yet the eastern Mediterranean, once the route to India, retained immense strategic importance; the Suez military base must now take over from the Indian sub-continental barracks the task of guaranteeing to Britain her access to Persian Gulf oil. But in 1951, barely two years later, no force was used at Abadan in defence of the Anglo-Iranian oil company against Mussadiq; and the Canal base itself was soon to be under Egyptian siege following the Wafd government's abrogation of the Anglo-Egyptian treaty of 1936. Suez, far from being its nerve centre, became a 'concentration camp' for a large proportion of the British Army.[1] The strategic artery of late-Victorian empire was at risk; the Imperial General Staff looked to its flanks, to Cyprus (after the loss of Palestine) and the Arab lands on the one hand and, on the other, to East Africa, which had owed its British connections in part at least to its position as an outlying picket on the way to India.[2] In 1947 acres of Suez stores had been

---

[1] In the words of John Strachey, onetime Secretary of State for War, *Hansard*, 5th series, H. of C., 524, c. 2477, 11 Mar. 1954.

[2] Ronald Robinson and John Gallagher, with Alice Denny, *Africa and the Victorians* (London, 1961).

shipped to Mackinnon Road, inland from Mombasa.[1] Then in 1950 British and French military discussions in Nairobi had stressed the need to maintain a southerly air route across equatorial Africa. Wider talks in the following year, again in Nairobi, had involved the other colonial powers and South Africa; these had been more concerned with the defence of Africa itself.[2] Kenya, with its naval and air facilities, was pivotal to both designs. In contemplating the next, the planners were no doubt re-fighting the last war. Then, the three mainland territories of East Africa, besides providing base facilities for the Middle East theatre, had raised twenty-nine battalions of King's African Rifles; these, with units from Britain, West and South Africa, had helped to drive the Italians out of Somalia and Ethiopia; they had also operated against the Vichy French in Madagascar and the Japanese in Burma; one battalion did garrison duty in Egypt and Palestine.[3] Thereafter, men from East Africa were called upon to help to fill the yawning gap in imperial manpower caused by the departure of India. A Kenya battalion saw service in the Malayan Emergency (it was followed by a similar unit from Central Africa), and in the 1950s East African Pioneers replaced Egyptian labour in the Suez Canal base.

British East and Central Africa stood, then, at the western end of the great Indian Ocean arc which reached east to Singapore, and on the southern fringe of the Middle East. However much the relative importance of these two spheres might shift in imperial strategies, East Africa's supporting role would remain unchanged. Eastern Africa also occupied much the same position on the African continent. Within all these three interlocking zones of British influence it was seen as a firm base which underpinned the more flexible and realistic policies pursued elsewhere in Britain's readjustment to the post-war world. To some metropolitan minds and interests this readjustment looked uncommonly like retreat. Old habits of behaviour demanded

---

[1] Elizabeth Monroe, *Britain's Moment in the Middle East* (London, paperback edn., 1965), pp. 157–8; Negley Farson, *Last Chance in Africa* (New York, 1950), p. 64.

[2] J. M. Lee, *African Armies and Civil Order* (London, 1969), p. 28; Eric A. Walker, *A History of Southern Africa* (London, 1964 imp.), p. 824; also Admiral R. L. Conolly, 'Africa's Strategic Significance', in C. Grove Haines (ed.), *Africa Today* (Baltimore, 1955), p. 58.

[3] Lt.-Col. H. Moyse-Bartlett, *The King's African Rifles* (Aldershot, 1956), Part v.

that however much the area of direct British authority might contract, the degree of British influence in the world ought to remain as far as possible unimpaired. Yet by the early 1950s it was already apparent from the Asian experience that British influence would be most strongly rooted through a flexible accommodation to local nationalisms. The rupture between Holland and Indonesia, the catastrophe of French arms at Dien Bien Phu, were clear enough illustrations of the alternative which the British themselves had so nearly had to face in India. India's republican membership of the Commonwealth had, after all, gone against the grain of both the existing British conventions of association and extreme opinion within Congress. A decision which proved to be the turning-point in the evolution of the post-war Commonwealth, and of critical significance to later British policies in Africa, might so easily have turned in the opposite direction. As late as 1946 Congress had been committed to secession, in reaction to its thirty years of recurrent conflict with the Raj. There were many reasons for Nehru's reversal of this stand; none was more important than his desire to hedge his non-alignment against the threat of isolation in an uncertain and potentially hostile world.[1] In Indian eyes the friendship offered by the Commonwealth connection was composed of many intangibles; the British could persuade themselves that it was valued for their own palpable military presence in the area, as Nehru himself seemed to acknowledge in his understanding of the British position in Malaya.[2] And in Ceylon, at the centre of Britain's Indian Ocean arc, the two policies of accommodation to nationalism and retention of military potential had coincided; Britain continued to enjoy the use of the Trincomalee naval base until 1957. In the British view of South Asia as a whole, the presence of bases provided insurance in a world of local nationalisms; but it was a successful nationalism which ensured the local security of the base.

The same combination of conciliating nationalisms when necessary and falling back upon prepared military positions where possible—a conditioned reflex rather than a long-term policy—was practised by the British when facing the changing circumstances of the Middle East and Africa. Eastern Africa was

[1] Michael Brecher, *Nehru: a political biography* (London, 1959), pp. 317, 413-18.
[2] Ibid., p. 581.

directly involved in both spheres; in British minds the boundary between them lay along the northern frontiers of Uganda and Kenya.

We have indicated how Kenya was by 1947 already involved in the extension of the military options available to the British in the Middle East. The way in which this process interlocked with the momentum of local nationalisms must now be outlined, for it was to be paralleled in sub-Saharan Africa. In both spheres the story unfolded against a triangle of forces. In the Middle East the triangle was formed by Egypt, the country in which Britain had the greatest interest and whose nationalism was accordingly the least tractable; by the Sudan, representative of areas of lesser British interest; and by Cyprus—supplemented by Kenya—the secondary position available after the first, Egypt, had become untenable. Anglo-Egyptian relations had been chronically bad for decades, crossed by the twin conflicts over Britain's military requirements and the status of the Sudan. British dealings with Sudanese political leaders had been conditioned by a competition with Egypt for their future affection.[1] Britain's agreement in 1953 to a three-year transitional period before self-determination was her final and, it appeared, successful throw in the game. This same reliance upon peripheral Middle Eastern nationalisms as potential counterweights to the latent influence of Egypt at the centre was apparent in Britain's readiness to depart from the former Italian possessions of Libya, Eritrea, and Somalia; and her hesitation over progress in British Somaliland reflected her desire to conciliate the more ancient nation of Ethiopia. Once the British government had accepted that the Suez base was more of a liability than an asset, and once the Free Officers had taken power in Egypt, it was even possible to predict an era of good feeling in Anglo-Egyptian relations.[2] Yet old military habits of thought died hard. Egypt was once again alienated when Britain consolidated her alliance with the states on the Middle East's northern periphery by joining the Baghdad Pact in 1955. But the disconcerting way that even a contracting military potential could jeopardize the friendly relations, by which alone Empire could safely be replaced, was more dramatically shown in the

[1] For details see L. A. Fabunmi, *The Sudan in Anglo-Egyptian Relations* (London, 1960); M. Al-Rahim, *Imperialism and Nationalism in the Sudan* (London, 1969).
[2] Monroe, *Britain's Moment in the Middle East*, pp. 175 sqq.

armed resistance which now flared on the island colony of Cyprus. In 1950 the Colonial Secretary had claimed that 'in our Colonial Territories the movement for political and constitutional advance never checks, never pauses.'[1] Four years later, with the British army withdrawing to Cyprus from Egypt, a junior minister declared the contrary, that in view of its strategic importance the island could 'never' expect to be fully independent. This slip, which came out in reply to questioning, heralded the onset of the Cyprus emergency.[2] In relation to their wider setting, there was much resemblance between EOKA and Mau Mau.

Britain's choices in Africa

The parameters of British policy in Africa were well illustrated by a series of events in 1948. Against the menacing background of the Berlin crisis, the year witnessed the Christiansborg riots in the Gold Coast, Malan's victory over Smuts in the South African elections, the acceptance in official British circles of the desirability of federation in Central Africa[3] and, on 1 January, the institution of the East Africa High Commission for the co-ordination of inter-territorial services. As British authority and influence were challenged in the west and south, measures were being taken to consolidate them elsewhere.

In 1940 black troops from the Gold Coast had fought side by side, as good comrades indeed, with whites from South Africa in the Abyssinian campaign. By 1951 South Africa was denouncing the Gold Coast's progress towards self-government.[4] For Britain, some foresaw a future need to choose between association with the white supremacist south or the emergent 'Gold Coast democracy'.[5] But for the British government this was a choice

---

[1] James Griffiths, *Hansard*, 5th series, H. of C., 477, c.1380, 12 July 1950.

[2] For the government's embarrassment over the statement see Chandos, *Memoirs*, p. 436. An equally momentous statement on Uganda was to be made in similar unguarded circumstances. See p. 73 sqq. below.

[3] Claire Palley, *The Constitutional History and Law of Southern Rhodesia, 1888–1965, with special reference to imperial control* (London, 1966), p. 333.

[4] Walker, *History of Southern Africa*, pp. 824–5; see also Gwendolen M. Carter, *The Politics of Inequality: South Africa since 1948* (London, 1948), p. 202, for the influence of the Gold Coast and Mau Mau upon the 1953 South African general election.

[5] P. N. S. Mansergh, *The Multi-racial Commonwealth: proceedings of the Fifth Unofficial Commonwealth Relations Conference, held at Lahore, Pakistan, March 1954*

between sentiments; to the national interest the nationalisms of West and South Africa were almost equally risky. It is true that after the 1948 riots the Gold Coast moved swiftly towards independence; to protests from a Kenya settler in 1951 the Colonial Secretary, James Griffiths, replied: 'And what was the alternative, man? Bloody revolution, that's what it was.'[1] The Indian government had risked this alternative three times in as many decades. It was a measure of the force of the Indian example no less than of the comparatively smaller British stakes in West Africa that the Labour government would not take similar risks in Accra. The principle of the devolution and eventual transfer of power, which had been translated so reluctantly from the white to the brown empire, was now to be applied without further argument to the black African dependencies; but only to the western ones, at least for the time being. It was difficult to argue that the people of the Gold Coast shared, with the white Dominions, the traditions and culture of Britain; but neither, now, did the ruling circles in South Africa. In the political and economic fields indeed, the Gold Coast seemed to be the more reliable. Many of the Gold Coast élite had graduated from British universities, and even the London School of Economics seemed preferable to the former theological seminary of Stellenbosch. The Gold Coast's Cocoa Marketing Board continued to earn dollars for the Sterling Area. South Africa, by contrast, withdrew from the Area's dollar pool; the Nationalist government had to recall Smuts' gold loan to Britain; British capital, nervous of take-overs, ceased if only for a time to flow to South Africa. It found fresh outlets in the Rhodesias.

This trend of events in the south played a major role in converting the Attlee government to reluctant support of federation in Central Africa. The scheme appeared to hold clear economic advantages. And had not Cripps, Britain's new Chancellor of the Exchequer, given as his opinion to the African Governors' Conference in 1947 that 'The whole future of the sterling group and its ability to survive depends . . . upon a quick

(London, 1955), quoted in idem, *The Commonwealth Experience* (London, 1969), p. 357; see also Margery Perham's letter to *The Times*, 4 Aug. 1950 and her article, 'The British Problem in Africa', *Foreign Affairs* (July 1951), both reprinted in her *Colonial Sequence, 1949 to 1969* (London, 1970), pp. 20 sqq., 26–39.

[1] Sir Michael Blundell, *So Rough a Wind* (London, 1964), p. 83.

and extensive development of our African resources'?[1] Any political scruples were countered by the fear that, without federation, Southern Rhodesia might take up the option offered in 1923 and join the Union; already one-fifth of its white voters were Afrikaners, and some observers thought they might dominate the country within a decade.[2] In bundling protesting Africans into the federation while simultaneously refusing to hand over to the Union their fellows in the three High Commission territories, Britain was but repeating her nineteenth century encirclement of the Boers. Nkrumah's nationalism—if it could not be Danquah's—was less alarming than Malan's; that of Sir Godfrey Huggins was positively to be welcomed.

This discrimination between nationalisms, of whatever colour, could be rationalized by a modern form of the old prejudices over racial competence in government. Lugard's appreciation of the Fulani as 'born rulers . . . incomparably above the negroid tribes in ability'[3] is well known. Later comparisons were also made, always unfavourable to eastern Africans, most of whom (and it was no coincidence) were perceived as a working class. Whereas a British official in the Gold Coast for instance, remarked how in 1948 his official colleagues were all, 'in varying degrees, good nationalists', there can have been few such in East and Central Africa at that time. Apart from the difficulty in choosing between rival nationalisms there, white and black, the Negro peoples of West Africa seemed to belong to 'a quite different stock from the Bantu of Central Africa, and they seemed to be of higher calibre . . . these people were no more like the Central Africans than we are like the Eskimos.'[4] And in eastern Africa itself the 'Hamitic hypothesis', that there was 'a positive correlation between the amount of Hamitic blood in a people's veins and the degree of their political evolution',[5] still enjoyed currency in European circles; there is evidence to suggest that it may have conditioned Kenya's official mind when

[1] Rita Hinden, *Common Sense and Colonial Development* (Fabian Colonial Bureau, London, 1949), p. 9.
[2] Chandos, *Memoirs*, p. 387.
[3] Margery Perham, *Lugard: the years of authority, 1898-1945* (London, 1960), p. 47.
[4] Sir Kenneth Bradley, *Once a District Officer* (London, 1966), pp. 148 sqq.
[5] B. A. Ogot, 'Kingship and Statelessness among the Nilotes', in J. Vansina, R. Mauny, and L. V. Thomas (edd.), *The Historian in Tropical Africa* (London, 1964), p. 284.

it faced the claims of 'negroid tribes'.[1] Those with closer experience of the Hamitic Somalis were more impressed with the fact that they were virtually ungovernable;[2] nevertheless, the peoples to whom the British had ceded independence in North-East Africa were either Hamites (Cushites more properly speaking) or Arabs, most markedly so in the Sudan. Racially as well as strategically, this area was conceived as part of the Middle East, not Africa, or *Afrique noire* as the French unapologetically called it. Historical perspective has obediently decreed that the transition to independence of Ghana, not its earlier achievement in the Sudan, should mark the start of sub-Saharan Africa's path to freedom.[3]

Such rationalizations conspired with the strategic argument to foster the belief that the tides of nationalism could be checked within geographical compartments. This reluctance to admit the force of precedents elsewhere could be more demonstrably justified by the presence or absence of a local 'political class'.[4] The Gold Coast élite was recognized as such by the British, the handful of African literates in East and Central Africa was not.[5] The political class was there provided by the local Europeans and, as was more grudgingly acknowledged, by the leaders of the Asians.

The immigrant groups have also been described by a former official as 'economic man incarnate'.[6] And in British business circles the political implications of colonial Africa's new economic importance appeared to be plain enough. In 1948 Colonel Ponsonby, MP, Chairman of the Joint East Africa Board, stated that

up to a year or two ago the policy was 'Africa for the Africans'. . . . Now the opposite course is being pursued. In order to increase the world's production of raw materials, the word has gone out, 'Full

[1] See the discussion of the incidence of 'Mau Mau' among Masai whose 'pure strain' had been diluted by Kikuyu blood, in *Historical Survey of the Origins and Growth of Mau Mau*, by F. D. Corfield, Cmnd. 1030 (1960), pp. 208–9.

[2] Sir Richard Turnbull, 'Djibouti: last French dependency in Africa' (review article), *Geographical Journal*, 135, 2 (June 1969), 240.

[3] And in the largest territory in colonial Africa, Nigeria, there is little doubt that British sympathies with the Muslim North played a disproportionate part in influencing the structure of the federal government.

[4] J. M. Lee, *Colonial Development and Good Government* (London, 1967), *passim*.

[5] Chandos, *Memoirs*, p. 389.

[6] N. S. Carey Jones, *The Anatomy of Uhuru* (Manchester, 1966), p. 73.

speed ahead,' which means that the natives gradually must continue
to come less and less under the rule of the chief and more and more to
be a part of an active European organisation. . . . This is probably
best for the African in the long run, but the Government must say so
quite frankly and not wrap it up in pious hopes about Africans taking
over the management or becoming the owners of great enterprises . . .[1]

Neither British political party could have accepted the full logic
of this argument at any time in the past twenty years. Both
Labour and Conservatives flatly refused to concede to Huggins
and Welensky the amalgamation of the two Rhodesias.[2] There
was nevertheless more than a streak of this kind of thinking in
the Central African Federation scheme as finally adopted.

And East Africa's Groundnut Scheme was hailed by the
Economist of London as an example of 'the sort of economic
planning which is needed to change the face of the colonial
empire'.[3] Apart from the fact that its disastrous failure subsequently vindicated the advocates of increased African peasant
production, the scheme had three features which bear directly
upon our argument. First, its scale; the British government
invested no less than £36 million in an attempt to coerce
mechanically the barren scrubs not only of Tanganyika but
also—had the original plans materialized—of Kenya and
Northern Rhodesia, into producing edible fats for the metropolitan housewife. Secondly, overall responsibility lay with the
British Ministry of Food, with the United Africa Company as its
agent, not with the territorial government or the Colonial Office.
Finally, one of the chief attractions of the selected areas was the
paucity of Africans upon them.[4] And the logic of this large-scale
economic development did appear to carry over into the politics
of regional co-ordination. As the Groundnut Scheme opened, so
London published its revised proposals, 'Colonial 210', for the
composition of the East African Central Legislative Assembly.
In deference to settler protest, these marked a significant retreat
from the equality of racial representation originally proposed.

[1] In a letter to *The Times*, 31 Mar. 1948.
[2] Even then it must be remarked that Britain was as much concerned for the
control of the strategic mineral copper as for the welfare of the Africans who mined
it.
[3] The *Economist*, 1 Mar. 1947.
[4] S. Herbert Frankel, *The Economic Impact on Under-developed Societies* (Oxford,
1953), pp. 141–53.

The arguments for administrative co-operation between the three mainland East African territories had been greatly strengthened by their recent wartime experience; and the Labour government insisted that it was thinking in terms of continued administrative efficiency only, and not about political federation. But the controversy over the East African Assembly had shown how contentious was the attempt merely to provide a constitutional basis for the operation of the common services. Had there been a stronger local political will for closer union, as among the whites of Central Africa, had East Africa had the same economic potential, it is very possible that the global priorities of military strategy and economic reconstruction would have prevailed against the lengthy Colonial Office tradition of territorial autonomy. It was not until late in 1950 that the Secretary of State publicly concluded that it would be best to pursue constitutional change 'separately in each territory rather than on a general East African basis', and even then with the qualification, 'for the time being at any rate'.[1]

The second colonial occupation

The Colonial Office tradition of territorial autonomy did indeed come much closer to political reality after the Second World War. Although the scale of British economic planning was now global, the institutional sinews of development remained firmly embedded in each territory. In this as in other contexts the Groundnut Scheme was an aberration, for the close interrelationship between economic and political development was now the topic of Empire.[2] Some political change was recommended by the conventional canons of business efficiency. The general concept of representative government as a successor to 'administration', and its specific application by Sir Philip Mitchell to Kenya in the 'membership system', are cases in point.[3] But there was also a new awareness that the rank and file as well as the captains of the colonial economies must be associated, if only at the local or district level, in the making and implementation of policy. From the first, all administrative

---

[1] James Griffiths, *Hansard*, 5th series, 482, c.1167, 13 Dec. 1950.
[2] Lee, *Colonial Development and Good Government, passim.*
[3] See chap. ii below.

officers had known that without African co-operation nothing would ever get done; there was now much more to do. From the late 1940s there was a great intensification of government activity throughout British Africa; in contrast to earlier years, and to the recent war period when territories were drained of staff, this access of official energy amounted to a second colonial occupation. It had a variety of causes.

Its origins lay in the 1930s when the world depression generally and the West Indies riots in particular crystallized a new set of attitudes to Britain's dependent Empire. The Colonial Development and Welfare Act of 1940 codified the growing opinion that Britain must play a much more active role in promoting the welfare of her colonial peoples; it broke with the old convention of territorial self-sufficiency in finance. The conception of purposeful state action was then applied in Britain—an expedient during the war, the prime tool of the Labour administration's social engineers thereafter—and subsequently exported to the dependencies. Innovatory paternalism, the leverage required before a people internalized the desirability of change for themselves, received a powerful new ideological support. It was buttressed in the colonies by two further considerations. First, large human and economic investments were held to be necessary before Africans would be 'fit for self-government'. Secondly, and more negatively, it was believed that as Africans became 'detribalized', so governments would in any case be obliged to assume the social welfare functions formerly performed within the tribes.[1]

What chiefly distinguished this post-war period from earlier years was the availability of development funds. For the most part these were provided by the territorial governments, which enjoyed buoyant revenues until the sustained boom in primary commodity prices finally ended in the mid-1950s. The metropolitan Colonial Development and Welfare funds were perhaps more important for their institutional than for their directly economic contribution. They were granted in aid of Ten-year Development Plans devised by the local bureaucracies, not by

---

[1] A. Creech Jones, 'British Colonial Policy, with particular reference to Africa', *International Affairs*, 27, 2 (Apr. 1951), 178, 182. The formulation foreshadowed that of Karl Deutsch in his 'Social Mobilization and Political Development', *American Political Science Review*, 55, 3 (Sept. 1961), 492–514.

Whitehall. Further, such grants were conditional upon the recognition of trade union rights within a colony.[1] And the Secretary of State's 1947 circular on local government stressed the need to secure full benefits from development moneys at least as much as further political education; local governments had to be 'efficient', not 'democratic' merely.

All levels of activity in the colonial world were now much more firmly interlocked. Great Britain's own needs had, for instance, prompted the transfer to Africa of the long-term bulk-purchasing contracts which had long featured in her trading relations with the old white Commonwealth.[2] And the local contracting parties, the commodity marketing boards, gave to territorial governments an immense discretion in economic affairs. At the same time the territorial governments in Africa were, for all the signs of imperial recession elsewhere in the world, intervening increasingly in what had hitherto been local concerns. They did so in the name of the efficiency which would raise African production, protect African land from erosion or Africans themselves from disease, and in search of the democratic supports without which no project, however expert, could be implemented. It was here, at the local rather than at the territorial or global levels, that the decisive strains appeared in the colonial relationship as it applied to East Africa.[3]

It was no accident that East Africa's most ambitious rural development scheme—apart from the special case of land consolidation in Kikuyuland—was prosecuted in the Sukuma area of Tanganyika's Lake Province, the territory's experimental laboratory for local government reform.[4] But it was no accident either that what may well have been the precipitating crisis in Tanganyika's early achievement of independence also occurred

[1] B. C. Roberts, *Labour in the Tropical Territories of the Commonwealth* (London, 1964), pp. 187-8.

[2] P. H. Ady, 'Britain and Overseas Development', in G. D. N. Worswick and P. H. Ady (edd.), *The British Economy, 1945-1950* (London, 1953), p. 558.

[3] By contrast with, say, Algeria and the Belgian Congo, both of them cases where the involvement of metropolitan politics and metropolitan sensitivity to world opinion were of much more direct consequence. See Crawford, 'Decolonization in Africa', in L. H. Gann and Peter Duignan (edd.), *Colonialism in Africa, 1870-1960*, vol. ii (Stanford, and London, 1970), pp. 467-79.

[4] G. Andrew Maguire, *Toward 'Uhuru' in Tanzania: the politics of participation* (London, 1969); for the flavour of official enthusiasms at the time see Elspeth Huxley, *The Sorcerer's Apprentice: a journey through East Africa* (London, 1948), pp. 176-81.

in Sukumaland.[1] The political history of Uganda and Kenya in these years likewise centred upon their local crises, in Buganda and Kikuyuland. These were exceptional in their intensity only, typical in that their origins lay in great measure in the frustration of local interests by an increasingly purposeful territorial government. For the complementary halves of the Colonial Office policy—to raise the level of efficiency in African production while widening the incidence of popular participation in development—only too often fell into mutual opposition on the spot.

The district teams of administrative and technical officers pursued efficiency, the African councils with whom they worked took up their stand upon the bruised principle of participation. It was partly that officials found economic development a more concrete, more congenial task than political education, partly that there were many more officials, of the technical variety especially, than ever before.[2] The understaffing of the colonial service was a perpetual cause of concern to parliament, but it was deficient only when measured against the new range of government duties. The perspective from below was rather different. Just as measurable numbers of Africans were acquiring the necessary professional skills, so their contribution and their ambition was engulfed by the swelling numbers of expatriate officers, by raised levels of technical knowledge, and by a tendency for the planning of quite parochial schemes to vanish into the higher reaches of government. If this new generation of secondary-school-leavers and graduates felt themselves insufficiently recognized, the older intermediary leadership of chiefs and mission teachers was being actively displaced, not only in the local arena of the district council, but in the parochial ones within it, the chiefdoms. Before the war this intermediary leadership had enjoyed very considerable control over the political resources and rewards available at both levels, for the colonial governments had occupied a comparatively small portion of the political space which lay beyond the centre. But the central governments were now attempting to penetrate the remotest corners of their political territory. Their officials, most of whom were those same new Africans already mentioned, made

---

[1] For the 'Geita crisis', see Maguire, *Toward 'Uhuru'*, pp. 196–234.
[2] Lee, *Colonial Development and Good Government*, pp. 35 sqq., 86, 144.

direct demands upon individual family heads, in breach of the previous unspoken contract with the parochial intermediaries. If the one were to achieve an autonomous political role or the other to regain its lost political ground, both sets of African leadership, together or in competition, would have to parallel the new intensity of government themselves by linking up the parochial, district, and territorial levels of authority and their associated arenas of political competition.

Individuals in a turning world

At this point it becomes important to explore further what was happening at the local levels rather more generally. Indeed if the drama of these years is to be portrayed in the round we must begin with the fact that the experience of the last two decades before independence was as much that of men as individuals as of men in their more corporate capacities. It is only possible here of course to be illustrative, but our purpose will be served by being at once quite particular and quite general.

Mpuga and Kihara, it is reported, were two somewhat ordinary Amba villagers. Their homeland lay below the western slopes of Mount Ruwenzori right upon the western edge of Uganda.[1] In the past their people had lived in villages, each of which had very largely been an independent political unit. In the first half of the twentieth century, however, they had found some of the people with whom they intermarried becoming subject to the dominion of the 'Congo', while they themselves became part of a 'county' of neighbouring Toro, which was one of the kingdoms of the British 'Protectorate' of 'Uganda'. They became subject indeed to a Toro 'county chief' and to three Toro 'sub-county' chiefs placed under him. Ineluctably the Amba found themselves submitting to this new political superstructure and even, through those Amba who became 'parish' and 'sub-parish' chiefs at its base, participating in it. As a consequence during a few short decades the world in which they lived under-

---

[1] This section is based on Edward H. Winter's three publications, *Bwamba: a structural-functional analysis of a patrilineal society* (Cambridge, 1956); *Bwamba Economy*, (East African Studies No. 5, Kampala, 1955); and *Beyond the Mountains of the Moon: the lives of four Africans* (London, 1959). The biographical portraits are drawn from the last.

went a political transformation. No longer was it an almost isolated entity. Its 'scale' enlarged to an extent which was unique in its history.[1] In the recent past an Amba village had simply been part of the Amba social system. Now it was being linked in a myriad of ways to all sorts of other systems. Cultivation, moreover, was now increasingly not just for subsistence or for local exchange. In the 1920s the overarching British administration had introduced the cultivation of coffee into Bwamba country for the world market, and in the 1930s cotton as well. The most conspicuous symbol of the vast new world to which Amba society was now being actively linked had come in 1938 with the opening of the road around the north end of the mountains to Fort Portal, the capital of Toro.

In some ways Mpuga and Kihara were a little more prosperous than their neighbours. In the mid-1950s, when it was reckoned that annual incomes were around the Sh. 120 mark, Kihara earned roughly Sh. 250 (mostly from selling coffee and cotton), while Mpuga had about Sh. 350 (since he occasionally secured a paid job). They were nevertheless still primarily involved in those things which preoccupied most other Amba—dealing with their wives, arguing with their neighbours, coaxing their children, worrying about sickness, busying themselves with their cultivation, going off to market. Kihara himself was a serious, but in certain respects disappointed, man. In the early years of British rule his father had held a prominent position locally, and he himself had once worked as a sub-parish chief under Toro overlords. His promotion, however, had been blocked because he had never learned to read and write. His neighbour Mpuga had been a church teacher. More recently he had been an employee at the locally established though short-lived Yellow Fever Research station. By all accounts he was a staunch Christian. He believed, for example, that the biblical account of the creation of the world was strictly factual. He had not of course dismissed the beliefs in local powers and local spirits which were still held by the majority of his fellow countrymen, for how could he know that they did not coexist with the God of whom Christianity spoke, and that in certain specific circumstances their influence might not be more efficacious? He

[1] Godfrey and Monica Wilson, *The Analysis of Social Change* (Cambridge, 1945), esp. chaps. ii and vi.

was convinced, however, that Christianity was the gateway to the larger world which was now pressing in upon him, and he was quite clear that to be like Kihara and remain a 'pagan' was to allow the opportunities which that new world had to offer—as Kihara himself had discovered—to pass him by. He was faced even so by a serious problem. Because he had three wives living in his household, the representatives of the Christian Church told him he was 'living in sin'. He himself did not see it that way, but because the Church did he could not participate in its activities as fully as he would have wished. Like a great many other East Africans at this time he was thus caught in a vortex, and was finding it difficult to make his way out of it.

Personal adjustments were nevertheless being made, even in very unpromising circumstances. Towns were growing very rapidly in East Africa by the 1950s. It was estimated for example that while in 1943 Dar es Salaam, Tanganyika's capital, had some 43,000 people, fourteen years later it had grown to 129,000. Here for numbers of ordinary people the physical environment was very largely new; so was their work situation; so was their style of life.

Hasan [J. A. K. Leslie noted of an inhabitant of Dar es Salaam in 1956] is a youngish man in his thirties, of some dignity and personality, though perhaps inclined to give himself more airs than his elders would allow him. . . . He lives in Buguruni where he built in 1950, and has his own house, a low-roofed three-roomer, whitewashed and with painted doors and lintels, all in a little need of redoing. There are two lodgers, both young men like himself, each with one room and paying 10 Shs. a month to him. . . . He was born near Kitunda, that is beyond Mbezi to the north, in a bit of bush where houses are scattered and few. Some of his family are still there, but both parents are dead. . . . He worked for the military in Dar es Salaam during part of the war; once he was a Public Works Department daily paid labourer on the roads; several times he had periods of up to a year with various Europeans as laundryman and houseboy . . . [Recently] he has had a death in the family, which meant a whipround among fellow-tribesmen and relatives both here and in the home village a few miles out on the Kawe road; whether he made something on balance out of the funeral, or whether it meant that he came into a bit of property I do not know. Anyhow he has taken out a Shs 20. licence to be a trader at the Shark Market and he buys tables and chairs from local artisans, cash down, and sells them on the never-

never in the Shark Market, making a margin for himself. He says it is a good living.[1]

These eventualities were being experienced not just by individuals but by whole societies, and some of them developed a sophisticated language in which to discuss them. Five hundred miles north-west of Dar es Salaam, and perhaps four hundred miles eastwards of Bwamba country, where the boundary between the British territories of Kenya and Tanganyika reached down to the eastern shore of Lake Victoria, lay Kuria country.[2] Up to the late 1920s, it had seen little European administration. But by about 1930 schools, Christian missions, technological improvements in agriculture, external trade, and closer British administration had come to it, and by the 1950s their impact was beginning to be very intense. The Kuria, it seems, were not an especially religious people. Nevertheless ritual actions and requirements, it has been stated, 'figure very large in their life and in the planning activities', and in these were to be found 'a tight cluster of ideas and symbolic actions', in which 'the ideas of life, well-being and "straightness"' were involved but in which there was also a correspondence sought between 'the ordered growth of natural things and that of people in society'. By the 1950s, however, 'straightness' and 'ordered growth' were becoming increasingly difficult to sustain. Increasingly Kuria were being confronted by what they called *chomba*—by that which was introduced, modern, non-Kuria, and non-African. By *chomba* they meant in the first place any area or place of development: Nairobi, Mombasa, Mwanza, Kisumu, the tea estates of Kericho and so on. Even neighbouring Kisii and Migori were called *chomba* when mentioned in this context. It was also the place from which the Europeans and Asians had come; and to which Kuria migrant labourers now went. *Omochomba*, a '*chomba* person', was the term originally applied to the Arabs who had come to the country, and then to the Europeans and Asians who followed them.

Most often it was used with the derogatory, indeed inhuman, prefixes, *iri/ama*, rather than with the personal ones, *omo/aba*. By

---

[1] J. A. K. Leslie, *A Survey of Dar es Salaam* (London, 1963), pp. 138–9.
[2] This section is based on M. J. Ruel, 'Religion and Society among the Kuria of East Africa', *Africa*, 35, 3 (1965), 293–306, and on an unpublished typescript on the Kuria which Dr. Ruel has generously allowed us to use.

amachomba, '*chomba* things', Kuria came to mean all people of alien culture—including those Kuria who associated with it—mission converts, European employees, chiefs, headmen, and even the elders who sat in the new councils and courts. All were seen as inhuman, alien, and threatening; and in naming them *chomba* the Kuria conceptualized their disdain for, and fear of, the whole new world which was now impinging upon them. The opposition between 'traditional Kuria' and '*chomba* things' was not however just conceptual. There was practical opposition as well—to the building of roads, to the erection of a dispensary, to the recruitment of labour. Fairly distinct cultural classes, moreover—'traditionalists' and 'new Kuria'—were now appearing in a society which previously had been both homogeneous and markedly conformist. More seriously, a kind of social hiatus had opened up in Kuria society in which traditional forms of organization and social status had disappeared before they had been fully or effectively replaced.

The explosive invasion, that is, which for men like Kihara and Mpuga away in Bwamba country had brought periodical tension and strain, or for Hasan in Dar es Salaam had involved some swift-footed readjustments, was here bringing conflict and cleavage. Sometimes it even opened chasms. In one form or another the Kuria experience was widely shared amongst the peoples of East Africa.[1] On occasion indeed the breakdown in pre-existing patterns of social organization occurred with extraordinary swiftness. In 1935, it has been reported, 'the traditional rituals celebrated by the lineages and chiefdoms [of the Nyakyusa peoples down near the north end of Lake Nyasa in south-western Tanganyika] formed a coherent system. They were directed towards the shades and the heroes.' 'By 1955 [however] the ritual cycle was nowhere celebrated in full; what remained were "bits and pieces" of ritual none of them fully intelligible without reference to the complete cycle.'[2] Sometimes the disintegration could be very disruptive indeed. In 1952 a lifelong observer, Dr. L. S. B. Leakey, described the effect upon Kikuyu marriage and socialization patterns (and so much that went with these things) of the flow of migrant labour to Nairobi and the 'White

---

[1] See e.g. J. H. M. Beattie, 'Bunyoro through the Looking Glass', *Journal of African Administration*, 12, 2 (Apr. 1960), 85–94.

[2] Monica Wilson, *Communal Rituals of the Nyakyusa* (London, 1959), p. 211.

Highlands'.[1] Other observers, of the Luo, for instance, of Kenya's Nyanza province, reported similarly. Particularly where there was large-scale migrant labour, families were left without their male head. Wives found themselves in an uncertain position. Elderly parents suffered neglect. Boys were left free to roam around as they wished. Girls lacked the protection their fathers could provide. Social obligations were fairly easily reneged upon; and disputes festered.[2]

'*Comba iri ni ijire.*' 'The Europeans arrived.' So said, not just the Kuria (though the term is the same as theirs), but the Meru of Mount Kenya; and the ensuing sense of malaise could often be acute. Sometimes it brought internal conflict. 'You are not as we were', a Meru elder remonstrated with a young literate fellow-tribesman, 'you always quarrel, and the reason is that you do not respect your elders.' In the old days, another inveighed,

the young initiates were told to behave properly; the elders were expected to do the actions of elderhood and not of childhood. The only man to suffer in those days was the one who did not want to do like the others. We say that if our chief *munene*—the Mugwe, would come back, we would not like to be dominated by the present state of affairs, *comba iji iri ku nandi*.[3]

On so many occasions indeed the buttresses of society, both social and ideological, looked as if they were about to collapse. Despite the attempts of men like Jomo Kenyatta,[4] or Kabaka Daudi Chwa of Buganda,[5] back in the 1930s to make re-adjustments, existing value-systems seemed to be singularly inadequate to meet the exigencies of the changing milieux. The Mugwe (the chief ritual figure of the Meru), Father Bernardi has recorded, was by the 1950s 'a failing prophet', 'a figure of the past', 'as an institution [the Mugweship had] lost its significance with the people and its influence on the social structure.'[6] The integrity of existence looked to be falling apart.

[1] L. S. B. Leakey, *Mau Mau and the Kikuyu* (London, 1952), pp. 74-7.
[2] M. G. Whisson, *Change and Challenge: a study of the social and economic changes among the Kenya Luo* (Nairobi, 1964).
[3] B. Bernardi, *The Mugwe: a failing prophet* (London, 1959), pp. 170, 174-5.
[4] See J. Kenyatta, *Facing Mount Kenya* (London, 1938).
[5] Kabaka Daudi Chwa, 'Education, Civilization and Foreignization', in D. A. Low, *The Mind of Buganda* (London, 1970), pp. 104-8.
[6] Bernardi, *The Mugwe*, p. 182. For further examples of the general phenomenon discussed here see *inter alia* John Beattie and John Middleton, *Spirit Mediumship and Society in Africa* (London, 1969), pp. xxix, 161, etc.

The positive response

The great fact was, however, that for all the stresses and strains, it was in East Africa only very occasionally that substantial disintegration occurred.

Some people deliberately sought to resist innovation. The Masai, for instance, and some other pastoralists, like the Samburu, maintained their deep disdain for outsiders throughout. Having adjusted themselves reasonably successfully to the sparse ecology of their homeland areas, they found little in the outsiders' contrivances to attract them. Status in such societies was generally ascribed, so that there was not much personal benefit to be had from education, or from financial success, or from entering a modernized élite. The pastoralists' pre-eminence in war had given them a cultural prestige amongst some of their neighbours which had led to a widespread adoption of certain pastoralist values.[1] Now however some of these neighbours found themselves obliged to break ranks, enter the modern cash economy, and start to adapt—in the case of the Arusha of northern Tanzania largely because of a sharp population increase and a consequent land shortage.[2] Even so there was never a breakdown—the mechanisms of social control could, it seems, be adapted in time.[3] In a multitude of ways indeed the response of most Africans to the radical changes to which they found themselves subject was at once flexible and fertile. Hardly any of them went the way of the North American Indian, the Australian aborigine, or the South African bushman.[4] Very few turned their faces to the wall. But then those who had developed a full subsistence agriculture and were not deprived of their land were relatively well-placed to maintain their footing. Amongst the Kuria, for example—for all their clear-sightedness about the threat to the ordered growth of their society—there were steady

[1] P. H. Gulliver, 'The Conservative Commitment in Northern Tanzania: the Arusha and Masai', in Gulliver (ed.), *Tradition and Transition in East Africa: studies of the tribal element in the modern era* (London, 1969), pp. 223–42. Paul Spencer, *The Samburu* (Berkeley, 1965).

[2] P. H. Gulliver, 'The Arusha; economic and social change', in Paul Bohannan and George Dalton (edd.), *Markets in Africa* (New York, 1965), pp. 250–84.

[3] P. H. Gulliver, *Social Control in an African Society* (London, 1963).

[4] This large subject does not as yet appear to have been systematically considered. One starting point would be C. D. Rowley, *The Destruction of Aboriginal Society* (Canberra, 1970).

readjustments,[1] especially where their political units retained their 'traditional' boundaries.[2] Amongst the Basoga,[3] the Tiriki,[4] and a great many others, there was similar accommodation. Time and again, moreover, this process of adaptation moved with the half dozen or so positive ingredients which were usually in the offing.

Few were of greater importance than the continued vitality, despite all sorts of vicissitudes, of the economy and society of the rural areas.[5] These things might undergo 'development' and change. Their continuance might be seriously threatened. But by and large men were not chased from their hearths. And even when they were it was often feasible to rebuild them in similar form elsewhere. Perhaps of particular importance was the persistence of the previously elaborated social structures. The clans to which men belonged remained in being. 'The very vagueness of its functions may have permitted the clan to become a symbol of important values,' it has been said. It 'stood to the people as a recurrent reminder of the basic verities of their heritage and of their membership in some large community.'[6] At the same time, although men's consciousness of their subjecthood within a rulership, or of their personal progression through an age-grade organization, might now present them with novel problems, for the most part the scaffoldings by which the social order was upheld seem to have borne remarkably successfully the strain which the enlargement of scale brought about. Rarely were they so brittle as to break.

A prime consideration here was the striking openness of most East African societies. For a start, many 'tribes' had never been hard and fast communities:[7] the inflow and outflow of people amongst them—and not just at their edges—had been marked.

---

[1] Ruel, 'Religion and Society among the Kuria', loc. cit.

[2] For a discussion of this phenomenon in India see L. I. and S. H. Rudolph, *The Modernity of Tradition* (Chicago, 1967).

[3] See especially Lloyd A. Fallers, *Law without Precedent: legal ideas in the courts of colonial Busoga* (Chicago, 1969).

[4] Walter H. Sangree, *Age, Prayer and Politics in Tiriki, Kenya* (London, 1966).

[5] See W. Allen, *The African Husbandman* (Edinburgh, 1967), especially chaps. xi–xiii, xviii, xxii.

[6] Elizabeth Colson, 'African Society at the Time of the Scramble', in L. H. Gann and Peter Duignan (edd.), *Colonialism in Africa*, vol. i (Cambridge, 1969), p. 55.

[7] Ronald Cohen and John Middleton, *From Tribe to Nation in Africa: studies in incorporation processes* (Scranton, 1970).

One thinks, for example, of the merging frontiers of the Masai people, of Rwanda migrants turning themselves into Ganda, or of the readiness of the Nyamwezi to assimilate strangers.[1] Equally, it had long been common practice for the institutions of one people to be adopted by another—age-set organizations, for example, had spread on both sides of the Rift Valley region, as had rulership in Alur country westwards of Lake Albert.[2] Such contacts could lead moreover to the adoption of major social values—witness the spread of Masai-like *laibon* through the Kalenjin peoples;[3] and there could be a wide dispersion too of religious movements such as that of the Yakany in the regions west of the Nile.[4] Since for most people the processes of adaptation were as much a matter for those in the spirit world as for those whom one could see and touch, the issues here were essentially religious issues; and despite all the vicissitudes of the time the widespread assumption that there were matters here of quite fundamental importance was scarcely ever shaken. If the existing conceptions seemed to be inadequate, then the new ones that were on offer were carefully investigated. If these also seemed to have their drawbacks, the quest was rarely abandoned: most usually it now moved into its most creative and adaptive phase. If the world was out of joint—so it seemed that people were saying—that was no reason for renouncing it: the need for them to wrestle with their destinies was all the more vital.[5]

The new aggregations

There were two broad processes that we may consider here with which these constructive forces seem to have worked. In

[1] Julian H. Steward (ed.), *Contemporary Change in Traditional Societies*, vol. i (London, 1967), pp. 164, 286; A. I. Richards (ed.), *Economic Development and Tribal Change* (Cambridge, 1954); R. G. Abrahams, *The Political Organization of Unyamwezi* (Cambridge, 1967), pp. 151–5.

[2] See e.g. A. H. J. Prins, *East African Age-Class Systems* (Groningen, 1953) and Robert LeVine and Walter H. Sangree, 'The Diffusion of Age-Group Organisation in East Africa: a controlled comparison', *Africa*, 22, 2 (Apr. 1962), pp. 97–110; and for the Alur, Aidan W. Southall, *Alur Society* (Cambridge, 1956).

[3] Robert A. Manners, 'The Kipsigis of Kenya', in Steward, *Contemporary Change*, i. 262 sqq.

[4] John Middleton, 'The Yakan or Allah Water Cult among the Lugbara', *Journal of the Royal Anthropological Institute*, 93, 1 (1963).

[5] See *inter alia* Beattie and Middleton, *Spirit Mediumship and Society*, and David B. Barrett, *Schism and Renewal in Africa: an analysis of six thousand contemporary religious movements* (Nairobi, 1968), *passim*.

the first place, they frequently found concrete expression within the multiple forms of aggregation which were occurring in East Africa during the colonial period. They also found expression in developments in the new religion, Christianity.

Modern tribalism is often characterized as a means to reduce the outside world to a manageable size; but here we would emphasize its positive side.[1] Not only did Africans frequently manage their world with some success, but in order to do so they enlarged rather than diminished the range of their social relationships. In the past, many East African societies had been essentially small-scale, yet they commonly shared with their neighbours some cultural or linguistic affinity. These clusters we may call latent societies; now they were increasingly becoming actual. To take three examples only: the Luo-speaking peoples were becoming the Luo people, Nyakyusa-speakers the Nyakyusa people, Lango clans the Lango people.

These processes of social aggregation altered the self-image of quite large communities in relation to the outside world in general; but the myriad initiatives which went to extend the boundaries of community were taken by individuals, and for specific purposes. As people engaged in an increasingly varied range of new occupations, so they needed a wider range of associates on whom they could rely or whose assumptions they could understand. Farmers who took new crops to market; small traders who found that two men's social circles more than doubled the opportunities which were available to one; teachers who were posted to a school beyond the neighbouring ridge; workers who stepped, uncertain, off the bus that took them to town—all needed to establish their acceptability beyond the knowable bounds of kin. These fluid social boundaries— generally expanding but contracting sharply on occasion—did not enclose mere operational groups or contestants. They also defined social arenas, that is, spheres with generally recognized (if not always honoured) rules of right behaviour and a set of cultural referents which might serve both as points of departure

---

[1] For many of the insights and case studies which inform this section see Gulliver, *Tradition and Transition in East Africa*, and especially Gulliver's introduction; Cohen and Middleton, *From Tribe to Nation*; and June Helm (ed.), *Essays on the Problem of Tribe* (Seattle, Wash., 1968)—especially the paper by Elizabeth Colson.

for deviant factions and as rallying points for larger unities. Indeed, the peoples who mastered the new situation with the greatest confidence seem often to have been those—like the Ganda, or the Kikuyu, or the Chagga—whose cultural distinctiveness was most assiduously fostered.[1]

It is true that even in the nineteenth century, along with the social disruption and economic diversification which had occurred in these parts, there had been aggregation as well.[2] What made this process so much more rapid, substantial—and its outcome perhaps more durable—in the twentieth century was the super-imposition of vastly larger political structures by the colonial powers. These actively influenced the expansion of social scale in two quite distinct ways. First, each administrative level—in East Africa typically the 'district'—not only transmitted the external demands which prompted peoples to aggregate with their neighbours, but gave them, if often unintentionally, the political resources which helped them to do so: the district councils which were instituted in order to give to the framework of administrative planning the underpinning of popular consent and the lubricant of a local rate; district appeal courts whose ruling came to affect judgements in the smaller units, the chiefdoms; co-operative unions created to market the cash crops whose geographical distribution so often justified the designations 'coffee district', 'cotton district'; and in some places a standardized district vernacular—used in pulpit or council chamber, if not in the home—originally designed to promote economies of scale in education. The control of these and other local political resources became the first object of competition among men who were concerned for the well-being of their society. New social aggregations thus merged with new

[1] Our understanding of the relationships between different levels and arenas of political authority and competition has been refined by the following works in particular: F. G. Bailey, *Tribe, Caste and Nation* (Manchester, 1960); idem, *Politics and Social Change* (Berkeley, and Bombay, 1963); Fredrik Barth (ed.), 'The Role of the Entrepreneur in Social Change in Northern Norway', *Arbok for Universitetet I Bergen, Humanistisk Serie* (1963), No. 3 (Bergen, 1963); Marc J. Swartz (ed.), *Local-Level Politics* (Chicago, 1968; London, 1969); Martin Staniland, 'Single-party Regimes and Political Change: the P.D.C.I. and Ivory Coast Politics', in Colin Leys (ed.), *Politics and Change in Developing Countries* (London, 1969), pp. 135–75; and Bernard S. Cohn, 'Political Systems in Eighteenth Century India: the Banaras Region', *Journal of the American Oriental Society*, 82, 3 (July–Sept. 1962), 312–20.

[2] e.g. amongst the Nandi. See vol. i of this *History*, p. 309

politics,[1] and political arenas developed both to govern access to the rewards offered by the administrative system, and to check its demands.

There were several levels of authority in the world of colonial East Africa. The lowest which concerns us here we may for convenience label the parochial level—in Tanganyika the chiefdom, in Kenya the location, the county in Uganda. Above this stood what may be defined—again somewhat arbitrarily—as the district level; and above this again the provincial. The district was always a substantial entity, the province rarely so, either in terms of administrative concentration or of African community. The two levels higher still, the territorial and the inter-territorial or regional, represented in 1945 planes of regular social intercourse or responsibility for only a handful of East Africans. But—and this was the second contribution of the overarching colonial institutions to the processes of social aggregation—such levels did provide a stable frame of reference within which African societies might place both themselves and a much wider range of neighbours, or rivals, than previously. As societies gained new instruments of internal articulation, so also they came to be in greater need of solidarity against forces external to them.

Although from above the parochial units might appear to be sub-units beneath the district levels, they often in fact had an autonomy of their own; and within them important aggregations were occurring. Following their incorporation into Tiriki location, for instance, the Tiriki clans of Western Kenya became transformed under their chief Hezron Mushenye into a single society, self-consciously distinct from its neighbours.[2] Reporting upon the Sebei, a small cluster of Kalenjin-speaking groups to the north of Mount Elgon, Walter Goldschmidt remarked upon a similar development:

The word Sebei refers to a group of formerly independent but closely interrelated tribes living on the northern and north-western slopes of Mount Elgon (and on the plains below) in Eastern Uganda. The term has come into use in modern administration parlance and these

---

[1] For further examples see Audrey Richards (ed.), *East African Chiefs* (London, 1960), e.g. on the Soga, p. 93; Goran Hyden, *TANU Yajenga Nchi: political development in rural Tanzania* (Lund, 1968).

[2] Sangree, *Age, Prayer and Politics, passim.*

people now identify themselves as Sebei. Etymologically, *Sebei* (variously Sabei, Sapei, etc.) is a corruption of Sapin (the name of one of the tribes that constitutes modern Sebei).[1]

Similarly the Luguru, to take an example from eastern Tanganyika, were becoming increasingly conscious of themselves at this time as Luguru. Like the Tiriki and the Sebei they were a parochial unit, both within the larger cultural region of related peoples to which they had long belonged, and at the administrative level of Morogoro District within which they were now incorporated. In the past the clan and the still smaller unit, the lineage, had been the principal groupings in which their social relations had operated; they had had no tribe-wide organization nor any concept of 'tribal' unity. The distinctions between Luguru and the Kaguru and Nguru to the north, and the Kutu and Zaramo to the east had, moreover, been very uncertain. By the 1950s, however, the Luguru were becoming a more cohesive entity: and when some of them moved to other areas, so the census counts showed, they described themselves as Luguru who were living outside the Luguru area.[2]

Larger-scale district units were being activated as well. At a time of uncertain change the possibility of aggregating within a wider latent system so as to create a larger actual system was often seized upon as the most effective mode for meeting the new challenges. The common terms for these, 'district tribes' and 'tribal districts', well illustrated the close relationship between social and administrative levels and arenas. But in the kingdom areas, where larger political entities had existed before the creation of the colonial bureaucratic structures, similar developments were also occurring; peripheral areas were now being increasingly tied in with the larger kingdoms as in Ankole;[3] or, as in Busoga, formerly separated state structures within a single cultural region were being newly amalgamated.[4] The whole process created social and cultural bases which possessed the triple merits of matching with many peoples' pre-existing social networks; of seeming firm enough to face the more concrete

---

[1] Walter Goldschmidt, *Sebei Law* (Berkeley, 1967), p. 7.
[2] R. Young and H. A. Fosbrooke, *Land and Politics among the Luguru of Tanganyika* (London, 1960), pp. 39 sqq.
[3] Richards, *East African Chiefs*, pp. 156 sqq.
[4] Lloyd A. Fallers, *Bantu Bureaucracy* (Cambridge, n.d.).

demands of the larger political superstructures, colonial and then national; and of enjoying legitimacy in the eyes of those who commanded the apex of these superstructures—at least while the latter were still Europeans. Thus it was that corporate groups like the Luhya, Gusii, and Kamba in Kenya; the Chagga, Haya, and Zaramo in Tanganyika; the Acholi, Teso, and Gisu in Uganda, and many more besides, now became substantially more than their component parts.[1] Not all such aggregations were effected smoothly, and the relationship between parochial and district units often differed considerably through space and over time. But where, as in the instances just quoted, the district arena substantially encompassed the parochial, it provided both a polity and a focus of identity for several hundreds of thousands of people who had previously seen themselves as principally involved in much smaller groups. Important tribal units were coming into existence to comprise the major elements in the East African scene.

The most substantial of them were those that comprised aggregations of provincial dimensions, specifically Buganda, Kikuyu, and Sukuma. While their actual articulation varied, it was no coincidence that they each became the scene of the most serious political crises which the three mainland administrations encountered in the decade or so before independence. These societies had a solidity which in East Africa was without parallel.[2] And—a point to which we shall return—they were also distinguished by the standing discrepancy between the provincial size of their African arenas and the district-level institutions upon which the British mainly concentrated.

At the territorial level the situation was different. Here the colonial rulers had created a relatively formidable structure of political, economic, and even cultural power. Here was the apex of an array of modern institutions—courts, schools, public works departments and so on, as well as the command of police,

---

[1] See for instance the chapters on the Gisu by J. S. La Fontaine and on the Chagga by Kathleen M. Stahl, in Gulliver, *Tradition and Transition*.

[2] See, e.g. D. A. Low, *Buganda in Modern History* (London, 1971), Introduction; C. G. Rosberg and J. Nottingham, *The Myth of Mau Mau* (New York, 1966); Maguire, *Toward 'Uhuru'*. Aggregation on this scale was sometimes sought by others, e.g. the Kalenjin and Mijikenda of Kenya, see Gulliver, *Tradition and Transition*, p. 23; Manners, 'Kipsigis', in Steward, *Contemporary Change*, i. 323–7.

central prisons, and troops.[1] Given the concern of African political leaders to establish African control over the destinies of East Africa's peoples, it was inevitable that these should become the target for their strivings, particularly when they saw that aggregations upon this scale would provide the means for establishing their own people's equality with the other peoples of the world, many of whom were formed into internationally-recognized independent nation-states, often of no greater size. By the same token, the comparatively slender political resources of the regional level invited relatively less attention from African politicians.

But lest it should be felt that this way of looking at what was afoot was alien to the peoples of East Africa themselves, it is worth considering a report by two foreign observers upon the perspectives of a small community in Kisii country in Western Kenya in the mid-1950s.[2]

The social universe as Nyansongans see it [they wrote] is made up of units of increasing size and inclusiveness from the family to the nation, all of them referred to by the same term, *egesaku*, and all composed of a group of men who recognize a common patrilineal ancestor and occupy a common territory. *Egesaku* in its most general sense thus means 'lineage', although it can refer to the group of father and sons in a single homestead, a lineage at one of four levels between family and clan, a clan, one of the seven Gusii 'tribes', the Gusii people as a whole as contrasted with other ethnic groups (each one of which is also termed *egasaku*), or a nation such as Kenya, the United Kingdom or the United States. Each unit within the Gusii ethnic group is spoken of as *egesaku* when considered as a separate entity, but when considered as one of several segments of a larger social unit, it is called *enyomba*, 'house'. Thus each social unit is thought of as sub-divided into 'houses', a pattern based explicitly on the polygamous extended family . . .

It was precisely indeed because there were people who could see their socio-political positions in these terms that there were such remarkable positive responses to the larger aggregations

---

[1] If only because of their post-imperial significance these institutions deserve more study than they have received.

[2] Robert A. and Barbara B. LeVine, *Nyansongo: a Gusii community in Kenya* (New York, 1966), p. 18.

which were evolving. Whilst such an outlook did not preclude some concentration upon one particular 'level', if this seemed necessary, it effectively postulated an ever-enlarging series of social universes within which men could perceive themselves. At the same time it recognized that there were distinctions between coexistence and aggregation. An *egesaku* might persist as an *egesaku* (as, given the peculiar heterogeneity of its peoples, Bukedi District in Uganda, for example, saw before independence).[1]

Sometimes the developing process of aggregation would itself provoke opposition from a peripheral group: thus the Sebei insisted that they should be separated from Bugisu District in Uganda,[2] and the Konjo of Mount Ruwenzori, who by the time of Uganda's independence had become bitterly opposed to being incorporated in neighbouring Toro, resorted to arms.[3] An *egesaku* might also, however, turn itself into an *enyomba*—a component part of a larger whole. Since, moreover, the whole concept was explicitly based upon the workings of the polygamous extended family, it encompassed one further feature as well. Gusii recognized that polygamous wives along with their offspring were prone to quarrel. Accordingly they took steps to keep them physically apart. Yet for many operational purposes they also saw them as being ideally linked together in successive pairs.[4] In this way such an outlook encompassed the tendency towards internal division within a single *egesaku* or *enyomba*—within, that is, any social entity—which (if we may take three examples from Uganda) could be seen, at a parochial level, in the division between Mukirane and the splinter group in Ruwenzori who in 1963 refused to countenance violence;[5] in the division at a district level between the Iseera and the

---

[1] F. G. Burke, *Local Government and Politics in Uganda* (Syracuse, 1964).

[2] Uganda Government, *Exchange of Despatches between His Excellency the Governor and the Secretary of State for the Colonies concerning the Creation of Sebei District* (Entebbe, 1962).

[3] Uganda Government, *Report of the Commission of Inquiry into the Recent Disturbances amongst the Baamba-Bakonjo People of Toro* (Entebbe, 1962); Martin R. Doornbos, 'Kumanyana and Rwenzururu: two responses to ethnic inequality', in Robert I. Rotberg and Ali A. Mazrui, (edd.) *Protest and Power in Black Africa* (New York, 1970), pp. 1088 sqq.

[4] LeVine, *Nyansongo*, pp. 67 sqq.

[5] Kirsten Alnaes, 'Songs of the Rwenzururu Rebellion: the Konzo revolt against the Toro in Western Uganda', in Gulliver, *Tradition and Transition*, pp. 249, 261.

Ngoratok in Teso District;[1] and more generally at the territorial level between Bantu and Nilotic. It was precisely because that way of looking at all these processes was in terms of the replication, at a number of successive levels, of some locally familiar principles[2] that there was both a ready adaptation to the multiple demands of a rapidly changing environment, and so much vehemence, not only about the newly emerging forms of co-operation, but over the new axes of conflict as well.

The spread of Christianity

The other phenomenon of these years with which the constructive forces seem to have worked was the spread through much of East Africa of Christianity. Although many avowed Christians held on to their old anchorages in pre-existing religious practices, there was surprisingly little syncretism. It looks as if the new religion spread in ways that indigenous cults had ordinarily done; along kinship routes, in response to particular small-group tensions—all much like a bush fire; taking on, moreover, particular local emphases (much as previous cults had, and concurrent ones were still doing). Christianity's diffusion was now, however, on a much larger scale than that of even the most wide-ranging of these other movements, such as the Chwezi cult in southern and western Uganda.[3] If by western standards its local resources might still seem exiguous, in East African terms they were clearly formidable. It was not just that its material resources were larger. Even the smallest of its missionary societies generally possessed a directing strategy of an order that no indigenous cult could mount. It mobilized, trained, and posted its evangelists in a far more systematic way. It did not, moreover, have to create its own rituals or its own doctrines as most of the cults had to do,

---

[1] Uganda Government, *Report of the Commission of Enquiry into the Management of the Teso District Council* (Entebbe, 1958).

[2] The Lugbara of north-western Uganda provide another example. Amongst them, it is reported, '*suru* has the meaning of a group of people who consider themselves and are considered by others to form a group because they share a territory and have ties between them based on common ancestry. . . . Thus *suru* refers to major lineages and sections, clans, subclans and subtribes. The term is also used in a wider sense as the *suru* (peoples, tribes) of Madi or Europeans . . .', John Middleton, *The Lugbara of Uganda* (New York, 1965), p. 39; while Dr. Anne King tells us that her informants discussed the two World Wars in terms of *Suru germani* and *Suru britishi*.

[3] See Luc de Heusch, *Le Rwanda et la civilisation interlacustre* (Brussels, 1966).

for it had its own long-matured stores of tradition to draw upon. In addition, for all the narrowness which some of its expositors displayed, its concern for the human state *vis-à-vis* both society and the divine could be profound. Its written scriptures for instance provided, as it seems many people found,[1] immense stores of guidance for all sorts of human situations. Furthermore, it displayed a capacity that no cult possessed to comprehend the new world into which so many people were moving at such breakneck speed. In particular it offered a value-system, an ideology, a vision of the true end of man, that could claim to interpret the greatly enlarged frame of existence with which the peoples of East Africa were increasingly forced to come to terms. Given that there was no such indigenous conspectus; that in this period, outside certain restricted areas, it had no substantial competitor; that it was vigorously preached; and that through its associated school-system it provided the main point of entry into the higher-level roles which were rapidly opening up within the developing new order, it is hardly surprising that it attracted large numbers of new adherents.[2]

There were at the same time sustained efforts to develop its African character. If the intellectual and social resistance to its adoption was—by Indian standards for example—inconsiderable, there was soon a keen intellectual and social desire to relate it to African conditions. Nowhere was this more true than in the evangelical revival movement which spread through many of the Protestant churches during this period: it was, for all the alien analogies which might be adduced, emphatically an African movement.[3] More specifically there were some who came to feel that only if they broke with the mission churches and created churches of their own could a satisfactory nexus

[1] Barrett, *Schism and Renewal in Africa*, pp. 127 sqq.

[2] On Christianity in East Africa see, e.g., R. A. Oliver, *The Missionary Factor in East Africa* (London, 1952); Lloyd W. Swantz, *Church, Mission, and State Relations in Pre and Post Independent Tanzania 1955–1964*, Program of Eastern African Studies, Syracuse University, Occasional Paper No. 19; Monica Wilson, *Communal Rituals*, chaps. xii–xiii; J. V. Taylor, *The Growth of the Church in Buganda* (London, 1958), Part ii; Edward H. Winter and T. O. Beidelman, 'Tanganyika: a study of an African society at national and local levels, Part ii, Ukaguru: the local level', in Steward (ed.), *Contemporary Change*, i. 166–88; Sangree, *Age, Prayer and Politics*, chaps. v–vi. On the cults see David J. Parkin, 'Medicine and Men of Influence', *Man*, 3, 3 (1968), 424–39, and references there cited.

[3] Max Warren, *Revival: an enquiry* (London, 1954); Winter and Beidelman, 'Ukaguru', in Steward, *Contemporary Change*, i. 181–2.

between the needs of their society and the Christianity they had made their own be secured. The real significance of such men, we may suggest, lay not in their numbers; as compared with those who stayed in the mission churches these have tended to be exaggerated. Rather it was that they were frequently the first to give expression to the key issues of Africanization, of African independence, of 'a place of one's own', which the nationalist politicians only took up later.[1] It is arguable indeed that the political developments in East Africa at this time should in a very real sense be seen as no more than the political expression of a larger endeavour which related to men's place in the world generally.

That the cleavage with the mission churches was not more widespread was partly because those who moved into them in the decades immediately preceding independence still found the new experience all-engrossing; while upon other fronts there was probably just enough sensitivity to African proclivities for fresh dispositions—for example the new welcome in the 1950s for the Revival in Uganda, or the consecration of African bishops there and elsewhere—to be made in time.

All these issues were plainly of immense importance. No feature of people's thinking (as revealed by a survey of opinion in the cosmopolitan Buhaya district in north-western Tanzania shortly after independence) seems to have been more substantial than their belief that their 'fate is in the hands of God'.

The local word that is expressing their opinion on this question is *omugisha*—blessing. It has always been a common belief in Buhaya that a human being needs *omugisha*—blessing by the supernatural powers—in order to succeed.

Almost nine out of ten respondents said as much. God might be conceived of in different ways—as the Christians conceived of Him or otherwise. But that the order which He, or at all events one or other manifestation of the divine, had determined was the one with which before all else men had to

---

[1] F. B. Welbourn, *East African Rebels* (London, 1961); F. B. Welbourn and B. A. Ogot, *A Place to Feel at Home* (London, 1966); Sangree, *Age, Prayer and Politics*, chap. vii; Barrett, *Schism and Renewal*; T. O. Ranger, 'The African Churches of Tanzania', *Historical Association of Tanzania*, Paper No. 5 (Nairobi, n.d.).

make their peace seems to have been a view which was widely held.[1]

Leaders and the well-being of society

In most areas the leadership in the two enterprises we have just considered—the elaboration of larger politico-cultural entities, and the adoption of Christianity—lay with the members of a new élite. They constituted indeed the two chief processes by means of which it evolved. Where there was already a pre-existing élite within a particular society there was sometimes an uneasy relationship with the newcomers: very often, however, the new men were the old élite's sons. Characteristically most of them had been at mission schools and had thereby secured a literary education. They generally included those who were leaders in the churches—priests, pastors, evangelists, school-teachers. They numbered as well those who entered most warmly into elaborating the new political and cultural insti-tutions, both by entering the district or parochial administration, and by developing new extra-governmental activities, including some secular cultural ones. Most strikingly these men tended to develop a new style of life—in clothes, in house-patterning, in work roles, in their preoccupation with the education of their own and their kindred's children, and in a new sensitivity to extra-parochial, extra-local issues. In Tanganyika such people were widely linked by their common use of Swahili. In many places they were linked as well by their common experience of a particular mission school. By mid-century they were in most areas immediately recognizable as the district élite.[2]

Two features were crucial to their position. First, however distinct they may have become from their rural background, the tendrils by which they were attached to it possessed a quite remarkable elasticity. And secondly in the virtual absence in East Africa of anything which could as yet be called a national élite—of the kind which in many West African countries had long been present—such people had a peculiar special signifi-cance not just in their own local areas but, potentially at least, as

[1] Hyden, *TANU Yachenga nchi*, p. 215; but see also *inter alia* John Middleton, *Lugbara Religion* (London, 1960).
[2] Winter and Beidelman, 'Ukaguru', in Steward, *Contemporary Change*, i, *passim*; L. A. Fallers, *The King's Men* (London, 1964), esp. chaps. iii and iv; Middleton, *The Lugbara*, pp. 91–2.

the source from which those who would take the lead on a yet larger plane would be drawn.

Of vital importance here was the phenomenon of what, if we may adopt the Kikuyu term, we may call the *muthamaki* tradition amongst so many of the peoples of East Africa—the tradition which acknowledged the existence of 'prominent men'.[1] Its foundations lay in the fact that few East African societies had previously had any rigid social stratification. Where there was at the same time little hereditary fostering of specialized skills, there was very often room for men with particular personal skills to prove themselves as leaders and pioneers, more especially *vis-à-vis* those outside the local society.[2] When, in the first half of the twentieth century, that which was originally right outside the local society came to impinge increasingly upon it, this tradition came to express itself in new terms. Jomo Kenyatta had revealed his own relationship to it back in 1942 when he had published a small pamphlet entitled *My People of Kikuyu and the Life of Chief Wangombe* (a turn-of-the-century Kikuyu *muthamaki*). As the twentieth century advanced there was an efflorescence of this previously established tradition. That meant both that there were men who felt free to provide leadership for excursions into the new openings which the new century brought to East Africa, and more especially that political leaders with a traditionally legitimized authority were available when the political situation suddenly started, as it did in the less than two decades covered by this volume, to change very rapidly. In the first category one can name William Nagenda, the Balokole leader from Buganda, Bishop Mathew Ajuoga of the Church of Christ in Africa, Bishop Obadiah Kariuki of the Anglican Church in Kikuyu country, or a Muganda farmer such as Leonard Basudde. In the second one thinks of Hezron Mushenye, Chief of Tiriki; of Tom Mboya, a highly effective trade union leader when he was still in his mid-twenties; of Oginga Odinga with his Luo Thrift and Trading Corporation; of Eridadi Mulira, the Uganda schoolmaster

---

[1] See, e.g. H. E. Lambert, *Kikuyu Social and Political Institutions* (Oxford, 1956), pp. 105–6; Peter Marris and Anthony Somerset, *African Businessmen* (London, 1971), chap. ii.

[2] Such a person was called a 'laiguenan' amongst the Samburu, an 'ntwale' amongst the Nyamwezi, an 'opi' amongst the Lugbara. Spencer, *Samburu*, p. 181; Abrahams in Cohen and Middleton, *From Tribe to Nation*, p. 104; Middleton, *The Lugbara*, pp. 40–1.

who became a politician and newspaper publisher; and of several of those many who became active in agricultural co-operatives before moving into politics more centrally— George Magezi, for instance, and Felix Onama in Uganda, or Paul Bomani and Nsilo Swai in Tanganyika. In addition to Kenyatta himself one thinks as well of Milton Obote, of Julius Nyerere, and even of that startlingly dramatic figure 'Field-Marshal' Okello.[1]

It must be remembered that substantial numbers of the new élite managed to find considerable personal fulfilment from participating in the parochial, district, and Christian arenas into which they moved. Paulo Kavuma for example, sometime Katikiro of Buganda, was no anxious, uncertain, disenchanted man, despite the trauma of his time in that office in the early 1950s. Though the winds of fortune beat upon him, he never lost his inherent composure; and as behoved a long-experienced former chief clerk to the British Resident in Buganda, he was an efficient bureaucrat as well. Always, moreover, a staunch Muganda according to his own personal lights, he remained a man who was calmly proud of the way he believed he had served his people (and he always seemed to fit a western-tailored suit better than anyone else in Uganda). Kosia Shalita stood likewise. Living as bishop in a former missionary's house where he had once been a house-boy, and looking back upon his time as pastor of so many churches at once that only he could be expected to remember their number, he had, in the aftermath of a year of study at Wycliffe Hall, Oxford, become the principal Protestant figure in his own and a couple of neighbouring districts in south-western Uganda. As father of a large family he was a much respected figure, unpretentious, active, a reconciler who was always unquestioningly serene in his personal religious

---

[1] On Ajuoga see Welbourn and Ogot, *A Place to Feel at Home*; on Mushenye see Sangree, *Age, Prayer and Politics, passim*; on Mboya see his own *Freedom and After* (London, 1963); on Odinga his own *Not yet Uhuru* (London, 1967); on Magezi and Onama see Crawford Young in E. A. Brett and D. G. R. Belshaw, *Public Policy and Land Development in East Africa* (Nairobi, 1972); on Bomani see Maguire, *Toward 'Uhuru', passim*; on Swai see Anton Nelson, *The Freemen of Meru* (Nairobi, 1969), *passim*; on Obote see Cherry Gertzel, *Party and Locality in Northern Uganda, 1945–1962* (London, 1974); on Nyerere see Judith Listowel, *The Making of Tanganyika* (London, 1965); on 'Field-Marshal' Okello, see his own *Revolution in Zanzibar* (Nairobi, 1967). Information upon Nagenda, Kariuki, Basudde, and Mulira is from personal recollections. See also Marris and Somerset, *African Businessmen, passim*.

faith. There were others like him; the schoolmaster James Aryada, for instance, first of his small tribe (the Samia of the Uganda–Kenya border) to go overseas—again to Oxford, but in his case for a mathematics degree. As compared with that of most of his compatriots his style of life was clearly élitist. His kinship links however were strong. He was at his happiest, moreover, when he had a piece of chalk in his hands and a roomful of boys in front of him. But he also displayed a shrewder knowledge of all levels of school education than anyone else in Uganda, and could talk about them with unassuming authority.[1]

There were men like this not only in Uganda but in the other territories as well. Tribal state, Christian church, and school, all provided for some of those who worked within them both their major commitment and a steady contentment.

So much indeed was this the case that when numbers of other men of lesser serenity saw a threat to the order within which they moved, they tended to react in a highly protective manner; one thinks here of the defiant actions of Kabaka Mutesa II of Buganda through much of the 1950s and 1960s, or of those African clergymen who would have no truck with africanizing their vestments—because they saw here the symbol of a great betrayal—and clung tenaciously to liturgies which by this time, even in the original, were patently archaic. The assured ones may have been a minority. Certainly there were acute conflicts afflicting many a parochial or district situation, both internally and in relation to the colonial government superimposed upon them. The split between the Iseera and Ngoratok in Teso District in northern Uganda is but one example of the first, the Meru land case of the second.[2] What seems so often to have accompanied them was a keen desire to take part in some grouping with a cause to advance, so as to thrust aside the atomizing propensities of the changes which were occurring. In Kamba country in the 1950s even the British administration could mobilize a popularly acceptable movement against sorcery when this became widespread;[3] while as independence neared, not only Legio Maria, the breakaway movement from

---

[1] Information upon all the examples quoted in this section is from personal recollection.

[2] *Inquiry into . . . Teso District Council*, loc. cit.; Nelson, *Freemen of Meru*.

[3] J. C. Nottingham, 'Sorcery among the Akamba in Kenya', *Journal of African Administration*, 11, 1 (1959), 2–14.

the Roman Catholic Church in Kenya, but the Kamcape movement in south-western Tanganyika, and a series of movements among the Mijikenda peoples of the Kenyan coast all sought to provide through religious renewal both individual security and the renovation of society.[1] The chief appeal at this time of the independent churches was precisely indeed that they offered some people what Welbourn and Ogot have neatly termed 'a place to feel at home'; while the sudden alarm which shot through Kipsigi country on the eve of independence in Kenya exemplified the convulsion that a threat of alienation could effect.[2] Such concerns pervaded the Bataka movement in Buganda in the 1950s, the Luguru rioters in 1955, and the Geita disturbances in 1958.[3] They were close to the centre too of the precipitation towards violence upon the slopes of Mount Ruwenzori in the Rwenzururu movement in the early 1960s, and in Nairobi in the early 1950s,[4] as they were of course to Mau Mau generally. And as Mau Mau—or for that matter the Bataka movement in Buganda—showed, they were especially prevalent where the sense of political, economic, social, and cultural deprivation was most acute. This was particularly the case where, as with the Kikuyu, an enterprising and unhidebound people constantly found itself being confined to what the régime above it saw to be the norm for Bantu Africans in the first half of the twentieth century—that of a labouring proletariat. Amid the torrent of unco-ordinated change, and within the plethora of all these separated movements, there were those whose focus was narrow or who believed that life was concerned with more things than politics. But there were nevertheless increasingly those who saw the chief threat to their individual and social integrity in outside forces—in particular in the persistence of the alien colonial régime in East Africa, most fearfully because it supported the privileged position which the domiciled European population had attained, and

---

[1] Audrey Wipper, 'Prophets, Priests and Protests' (University of California Ph.D. thesis 1968), chap. v; R. G. Willis, 'Kamcape: an anti-sorcery movement in south-west Tanzania', *Africa*, 38, 1 (1968), 1–15.

[2] Manners in Steward, *Contemporary Change*, i. 327–9.

[3] *Inquiry into ... Disturbances in Uganda ... 1949*, loc. cit.; Young and Fosbrooke, *Land and Politics, passim*; Maguire, *Toward 'Uhuru'*, chap. vii.

[4] Doornbos in Rotberg and Mazrui, *Protest and Power*, pp. 1088 sqq.; Rosberg and Nottingham, *Mau Mau*, chap. vii.

the powerful economic hold which the domiciled Asians had secured.

Political levels and arenas

If ever they were to present an effective challenge to the alien régimes, those Africans who did see the issues in these political terms would have to learn how to influence the various levels of authority in East Africa. They would have to do more: to deploy the assets they accumulated within East Africa at still wider levels if they wished to bring additional pressure to bear upon the Imperial government. At the 'global' level, East African politicians made use of the United Nations forum, most effectively those from Tanganyika for whom access to this level was formally provided through the Trusteeship Council and its three-yearly Visiting Missions. The 'African' or continental level also had its uses which, after the All African People's' Conference of 1958, confounded the myopic belief of many colonial administrators in the political impermeability of territorial frontiers. More immediately important was the 'regional' or inter-territorial level, for which the Pan-African Freedom Movement for East and Central Africa (PAFMECA) was founded in the same year. It faced in two directions. It attempted to represent Eastern Africa as a group within the continental, African arena. But at the same time, like the Imperial government, PAFMECA used its authority to mediate between contenders at a lower level, most notably between the Nationalist and Afro-Shirazi Parties in Zanzibar.[1] It was on the 'territorial' level however—once again in replication of the imperial authority—that African nationalism mainly concentrated. Until the 1950s Africans had been permitted to exercise power only at the still lower levels which we have called 'parochial', and it was here that they acquired their political expertise. Organized nationalism was thereafter the means through which Africans converted the supports which they had accumulated at these subordinate levels into resources which

[1] PAFMECA began as a regional grouping within the framework of the All African People's' Conference. Its first meeting at Mwanza in Tanganyika in September 1958 was attended by African leaders from Tanganyika, Kenya, Uganda, Zanzibar, and Nyasaland. There were later meetings in Moshi in 1959, in Mbale in 1960, and in Nairobi in 1961. See Richard Cox, *Pan-Africanism in Practice* (London, 1964).

could be staked against the expatriate power-holders at the territorial level. And it was as the hold of the colonial governments relaxed that the territory became increasingly available to Africans as an arena for their own political competitions.

The political processes involved were here, as everywhere, made up of a complex interplay between the needs of societies and the desires of men. East Africa experienced, however, a particular stimulus to this widening of political activity which was perhaps peculiar to the colonial world—namely, an increasingly irreconcilable discrepancy between arenas and levels. The concerns and rivalries, that is, which preoccupied the subject peoples tended to diverge ever more insistently from those political institutions which the colonial power had either ratified or created to deal with them.

It is important to remember that this divergence had been continuous throughout the colonial period, at the parochial level particularly, where every demand for the subdivision of a chiefdom, for the establishment of additional village headmen— or, conversely, for the recognition of a senior chief—was evidence that some Africans at least thought that the existing institutions prejudiced their chances in parochial competition. In successfully pressing any of these demands a group climbed to a higher political level. Such competitive level-climbing could also occur at the district level, especially where cultural or linguistic discontinuities between groups served as symbols of confrontation for the African actors, and justification to their white rulers for the creation of a new district. In this way, as we have seen, the Kalenjin-speaking Sebei peoples of Mount Elgon both came together in a new grouping and secured their own district in order to deny administrative advantage to the Bantu Gisu, more than ten times their number, who by a similar process of aggregation had come to dominate the district which they had formerly shared. To the south of the same mountain, the Bukusu were able to use a much slighter cultural variation from their fellow Bantu-speakers in Kenya's North Nyanza district in order to define a separate district which would ensure for them the more exclusive enjoyment of their large maize revenues. When 'Elgon Nyanza' was created for the Bukusu in 1956, and Sebei District in 1962, two parochial-level aggregations had climbed to the district level.

In these and in similar cases, then, discrepancies between arenas and levels were overcome by adjusting the levels. The terms of formal access to the structures of power were revised, and with them the balance of resources available for competitive activity. To the colonial authorities, such readjustments were consistent both with a philosophical predisposition towards matching the scale of government with what was thought to be the proper scale of African society, and with the maintenance of overall control. They did not affect the fundamental concordat of colonial coexistence by which, in return for acceptance of its monopoly of power at the territorial level, the alien government allowed a degree of autonomy to its native supporters at the lower levels. As long as the political ambitions of African leaders and their followings were focused primarily upon parochial-level rewards such as chiefships—which often conferred access to district-level power through *ex officio* membership of a district council—or upon the satisfactions available to the district élites, so long did each colonial territory maintain a comparative political stability. This is not to imply that before, say, the 1940s all African social arenas were encapsulated in chiefdom or, at most, district. On the contrary, large numbers of Africans played a part in various other arenas associated with their employment, trade, or religious affiliation, which could extend much further afield, even at times beyond the limits of their colonial territory.[1] But such arenas were only fitfully the scenes of political activity, either because the rewards which they offered were too uncertain to support any structured and enduring competition between Africans themselves, or because— in direct contrast with the situation pertaining at the parochial and district levels—political contests between Africans and the colonial authority could not be long sustained, for lack of any mutually accessible set of intermediary political institutions. When one or both of these conditions ceased to apply, the monopoly of the rulers at the territorial level was very soon challenged.

We may identify three historical processes as the collective cause of such a change, in which new political arenas crystallized

---

[1] For instance, the migrant labour experiences of the Rwanda, the Luo or Nyakyusa; or the Kikuyu settlers on Mount Kilimanjaro; or the Somali cattle-traders throughout East Africa; or the independent churches which came in to southern Tanganyika from further south.

out of those social arenas which bridged the gap between the local and territorial levels of power, and in so doing critically curtailed the colonial governments' room for readjustment.

The first process, the colonial governments' penetration of the myriad localities at the parochial and district levels, was, as we have suggested, greatly accelerated during the 'second colonial occupation'. While the funds and powers transmitted through these levels were greatly increased, their autonomy, never absolute, was further reduced, at the parochial level especially. The growing number of agents of improvement, the instructors of every kind, were often insensitive to the moral pressures of local politics; and their goodwill might have to be won by breaking local ranks, especially in those periods when the government was focusing its hopes upon individual 'better farmers'. The chiefs, or at a higher level the white district commissioner or African district secretary-general, were no longer the only keepers of the gates which opened on to other levels; and against the press of traffic the gates could no longer be kept closed.[1]

This situation underlined what was already apparent to many Africans, particularly in Kenya—the failure of what has been called the 'politics of local focus',[2] in which the main prizes had been district-level office whose prime obligations had been to secure a more advantageous allocation of resources from the central government and the curtailment of central powers. It was no accident that the community which leant most heavily upon the central government, the white settlers, was also the most agile in jumping levels, able to influence policy equally in their district councils in the Highlands, in the Standing Finance Committee of Kenya's legislature, or in Britain's House of Lords. By the post-war period, not a few Africans saw clearly that interests which remained tied to local levels were unlikely to be well served, and determined to act accordingly.

---

[1] For a case study of comparable developments in the Southern Rhodesian context, see *Report of the Mangwende Reserve Commission of Enquiry* (Salisbury, 1961), on which is based J. F. Holleman, *Chief, Council and Commissioner* (Assen and London, 1969).

[2] J. M. Lonsdale, 'Some Origins of Nationalism in East Africa', *J. Af. History*, 9, 1 (1968), 119–46; but see also the discussion of 'fourth-phase political institutions' in D. A. Low, 'Political Parties in Uganda', reprinted in *Buganda in Modern History*, London, 1971), pp. 167–266.

The second of the processes which we are considering here was the sharpening during the post-war period of the long-standing rivalry between two groups who were readily identifiable within most of the district élites of East Africa. On one side were those to whom government officers often referred as the district establishment—the chiefs, the older generation of schoolteachers, the more senior district councillors, many of whom had served in some branch or other of government earlier in their careers. These men's district-level power was in most cases a consequence of their parochial leadership which, in turn, they commonly owed to their formal intermediary role between parochial society and such 'territorial' institutions as the administration, the missionary societies or (as co-operative society officials) the statutory crop-marketing boards. Their rivals were as heterogeneous in origin—younger teachers, independent traders, traditional leadership groups which had since been displaced— and alike only in their shared sense of exclusion from formal power. Some of these men were preoccupied with long-standing parochial-level intrigues. But, increasingly, there was an 'unofficial' district élite whose primary social and economic networks were at the district level—often in the local township— and whose major interest lay in the decisions of the district licensing authority or in the district council's allocation of school building contracts. Some of these men found that district-level power was denied them for lack of a parochial base; such an impasse could be a powerful reason for canvassing the existence of a new 'district tribe', greater than its component chiefdoms.[1] Others managed to secure election to the district council and tacit recognition as the established opposition.

Whether or not they were councillors, the unofficial district élite tended to have a much more pressing interest than did the district establishment in testing the political potential of association with actors in other district arenas, and to be more realistic in their perception of the limitations of local-focus politics. Both dispositions now accentuated the district rivalries from which they had taken their origin. For if, as we have just

---

[1] As in the case of Luhya, a name coined by district-level opponents of the chiefs of Wanga, Maragoli, Tiriki, and so on, to distinguish the 'district tribe' from its parochial components. See J. M. Lonsdale, 'Political Associations in Western Kenya', in Rotberg and Mazrui, *Protest and Power*.

suggested, the district establishment's power sprang from its members' simultaneous occupation of roles at different levels, then its maintenance required that those levels be kept apart, with intercommunication limited to the official networks which they themselves controlled.[1] But political associations—even those whose membership was circumscribed by the district arena—aspired to become an alternative means of bridging the gap between levels; and political parties thereafter appeared to hold over the district establishments the ultimate threat of closing the gap altogether by compressing the various levels into one nation.

Much of nationalism's inspiration, and certainly the incidence of the nationalist parties' early support, can be traced to the internal district rivalries which ensued. But the nationalisms of East Africa gathered weight and mass as part of a third process. This involved the continuing drama of social change in directions dictated largely by the colonial economies, but with a critical new element. There was a growing awareness by those Africans who were most committed to change, that they were now pressing hard against the limits of that 'improvement' which had previously made change bearable for many and welcome to the few.[2] For an increasing number of people, the aspirations of nationalism filled the gap between expectation and fulfilment which the colonial governments were also striving to bridge through the developmental policies of the second occupation.

The constraints on improvement were apparent to rural producers and urban wage-earners alike. While producer prices did indeed rise almost continuously from the early years of the Second World War until the mid-1950s and many new areas were therefore brought into production, it is nevertheless probable that opportunity ceased to expand for the more ambitious farmers in older centres of production such as Chaggaland or Bugisu or southern Kikuyu. Population pressure made the further extension of a man's holding costly and contentious, if indeed it was still possible. Declining soil fertility or inability to find the capital with which to pay labourers limited

---

[1] For a theoretical discussion of this point see F. G. Bailey, *Stratagems and Spoils* (Oxford, 1969), pp. 144-82.

[2] See J. Iliffe, 'The Age of Improvement and Differentiation', in I. N. Kimambo and A. J. Temu (edd.), *A History of Tanzania* (Nairobi, 1969).

the returns from the land which was available. Amongst all classes of producer it seemed possible to detect a rather general sense of unease as they appreciated the likelihood of fundamental changes in the generally egalitarian pattern of rural life.[1] Rural opposition to specific government measures—these were based during the 1950s upon the desirability of an increase in social differentiation which was regarded as in any case inevitable— was like an occasional eddy indicative of the much deeper groundswell beneath. But at the same time the growing, in some places clamant, interest in co-operative marketing organizations or in obtaining credit, fertilizer, or technical advice, all of them services supported or provided by government, was a potential political resource of great value to any organization which promised African control over government's decisions.

In the rapidly growing towns, African distress was more immediate than in most rural areas; workers' discontent reached a peak in the late 1940s, with general strikes in 1947 at Mombasa and along the lines of rail in Tanganyika, when other workers followed the lead given by the Dar es Salaam dockers.[2] More needs to be known about how conditions varied for different categories of worker, but all were adversely affected by wartime and post-war price inflation, the pressure of increasing numbers of job-seekers upon a relatively static labour market, and an inadequate—in Dar es Salaam's case even a contracting—stock of urban housing. Under some circumstances at least, workers were acting together as a working class. And the 'territorial' political consciousness which this activity projected (save in Uganda where so many African workers were of immigrant origin) was further sharpened by the tendency of strikers' demands to be settled in negotiation with government officials or government-appointed tribunals, rather than with often ineffectual employers' organizations; and in the 1950s by governments' close involvement in the developing machinery of industrial relations.[3]

---

[1] C. C. Wrigley, *Crops and Wealth in Uganda* (Kampala, 1959), p. 80.

[2] J. Iliffe, 'A History of the Dockworkers of Dar es Salaam', *Tanzania Notes and Records*, 71 (1970), 119–48.

[3] For government involvement see ibid., pp. 133–4; Mboya, *Freedom and After*, p. 32. For trade unions more generally, William H. Friedland, *Vuta Kamba: the development of trade unions in Tanganyika* (Stanford, 1969); Roger Scott, *The Development*

If the beginnings of a territorial African community could be most visibly detected in the trade unions, the tribal unions which grew alongside them preserved within this community the principle of segmentation.[1] These tribal unions strove to meet all the individual and social hazards of migrant labour—death far from home, the abandoned wife, the unchaste daughter; but also to promote the welfare of the 'tribal' community in education, in employment opportunity, or on the sports field—highly political activities all. Tribal unions were rarely strong organizations; their existence did nevertheless indicate that for some peoples their rural, district, social arenas now substantially encompassed town and plantation as well. And there were two specific elements in the wider environment, aside from the normal differences of opinion over ways to advance social welfare, which demanded that this enlarged social arena should also be a field of political activity. First, the urban authorities tended to regard tribal affiliation as the natural constituency for the representation of resident African opinion. Tribal unions could thus attempt to control access to formal urban office, whether this was membership of a social centre's committee of management or a seat on the municipal council. Secondly, the rivalries which split the district élites were projected on to the urban and even more the national levels by governments' application there of the selection procedures used at the district level. In 1945, for instance, two up-country chiefs were success-fully used as intermediaries in a strike at Mombasa.[2] More remarkable was the extent to which African officials were the first representatives of their community at the territorial level. The first three African members of the Tanganyika Legislative Council were all chiefs; their counterparts in Uganda were officials of their kingdom or other local governments. And at the inter-territorial level even Kenya, which accorded to chiefs much less importance than its neighbours, sent as one of its first members in the Central Legislative Assembly the Luo chief, Paul Mboya.

of Trade Unions in Uganda (Nairobi, 1966); and postgraduate theses on the Kenya trade unions at the University of Sussex by R. J. Sandbrook and by Margaret Kiloh.

[1] For these, see David Parkin, Neighbours and Nationals in an African City Ward (London, 1969).

[2] Rosberg and Nottingham, Myth of 'Mau Mau', p. 209.

The leaders of organized nationalism therefore not only had to move between political levels; in so doing—as many had already learned in the district arenas—they faced direct competition with African officials who had reached up from their generally parochial bases to the territorial level of representation and beyond.[1] In this competition the nationalists—who were recruited rather more often from the unofficial district élites than from the establishments—were handicapped by the discrepancy in size between the political arena and the levels of authority into which it was divided. The arena was the colonial territory, or at least the jointly rural and urban environment which now supported the life of most 'district tribes'. But the decisive institutions of authority remained at the district level, at the disposal of the district establishments. It was not until the late 1950s that direct elections to Legislative Council in all the territories superseded indirect methods of selection based upon the district and eliminated this discrepancy; or rather, with civil servants debarred from party-political activity, reversed it to the nationalists' advantage.[2]

Patterns of nationalism

The relative strengths of local government institutions clearly had an important influence upon the course of nationalism in each of the territories (and, subsequently, upon the character of the post-independence régimes). A scale can be constructed on which Tanganyika's local government system was the least and Uganda's the most strongly developed in the post-war period.[3] Tanganyika's district administrations found it difficult to adjust the elaborate and very personalized native authority system which had been handed down from the time of Sir Donald Cameron's governorship. Where early experiments in conciliar forms were essayed, as in Sukumaland, they were crippled by

[1] In Tanganyika the government for a time placed some reliance upon a territorial-level convention of chiefs as a counterweight to the nationalist politicians; see chap. iii below.

[2] For striking examples, see Gertzel, *Northern Uganda, passim.*

[3] For information on local governmental developments see Stanley Dryden, *Local Administration in Tanzania* (Nairobi, 1968); Burke, *Local Government and Politics in Uganda; Report of Local Government Commission of Enquiry* (Nairobi, Govt. Printer, 1967).

their complexities. While Tanganyika's start in representative local government had some need of the stimulus provided by the Creech Jones despatch of 1947, Kenya's district councils could well have served as the model for that despatch, in their representative qualities at least, if not in the extent of their powers. Some of them had been inaugurated as early as 1925. Chiefs had been accustomed to sharing these local forums with unofficial councillors right from the start; by the late 1940s many councils had a majority of elected members, a nucleus of experienced men who could serve as paid local government officials, expanding revenues and some power to spend them to local advantage. In Uganda such councils were a somewhat later growth, but they soon overhauled Kenya's in terms of power, largely because the Buganda kingdom's government and Lukiko (council) provided the model to which they all aspired to rise. A brief reference to the careers of three national leaders will serve further to illustrate the differences between the territories.

Paul Bomani's career in Tanganyika provides an outstanding example of the politician's special skill in using the resources of different arenas in order to exercise power at several levels.[1] He helped to organize the Sukuma cotton-growers in their villages and the traders in Mwanza town; he helped to found the co-operative federation which spanned all Sukumaland and thereby provided one arena for what was formally five districts or forty chiefdoms. His nomination to the Tanganyika Legislative Council in 1954 recognized and reinforced his local position. But peculiar to Tanganyika was the apparent absence of any selection process at the local level prior to Legislative Council nomination and, correspondingly, the virtual inability of the administration—save in the exceptional area of Kilimanjaro—to offer any real political prizes at the district level. In consequence, there were no significant mediatory institutions to soften any clash between the Tanganyika African National Union (TANU) when it entered the political arena, and the territorial government. It was already 1960 when local governments which approximated to those in Kenya were set in train in Sukumaland; not only did Bomani as the local Member of Legislative Council advise upon their constitution, but the majority of TANU's

[1] Maguire, *Toward 'Uhuru'*, passim.

KRAUSS LIBRARY
LUTHERAN SCHOOL OF THEOLOGY
AT CHICAGO

candidates, many of them without previous local government experience, were elected unopposed in the wake of the party's landslide victory at the national level.

In western Kenya, by contrast, a whole generation of Luo politicians found local government office more attractive than any prizes offered by the Kenya African Union. Oginga Odinga's early political career, in some ways similar to Bomani's, differed from the Sukuma leader's in having to confront this obstacle.[1] When he first entered Legislative Council in 1957 he did so as the elected representative of the district opposition, victorious over the champion of the district establishment (and Kenya's first African Minister), Apolo Ohanga.

Milton Obote's entry to the Uganda legislature later in the same year was the outcome of a different pattern again.[2] He was the choice of his Lango District Council, sitting as an electoral college. The Lango council had already witnessed something like a transfer of power from one establishment generation to the next (to whom they were not infrequently related), which had emerged as the established opposition with the opening of a local branch of the Uganda National Congress. During this period the districts were arenas of much greater consequence than the territory: they even controlled the appointment of chiefs, a power which, although it was to be short-lived, was much in excess of any enjoyed by Kenya's African district councils, let alone Tanganyika's.

It cannot be claimed that these three experiences are to be taken as archetypes of the relationship between local-level politics and the developing nationalism of their respective territories; there was too wide a variation between districts in all three territories for that. It is not easy however to imagine the circumstances of any one of these contests being replicated in either of the neighbouring territories.

Yet for all the many territorial differences, the politics of East Africa during the period of growing nationalist opposition to colonial rule did have one common characteristic. Political allegiance, whether to the territorial governments or to their

---

[1] For Odinga's career, see *Not Yet Uhuru*; B. A. Ogot, 'British Administration in the Central Nyanza District of Kenya, 1900–1960', *J. Af. History*, 4, 2 (1963), 249–73; Cherry Gertzel, *The Politics of Independent Kenya* (Nairobi and London, 1970).
[2] See Gertzel, *Northern Uganda*, ch. 4.

opponents, became much more jealous in its demands upon individuals' thoughts and energies.[1] This was partly because the political stakes were much higher than before, in that nationalists appeared to offer not only independence but an entirely new way of life. It was also a direct result of the new interplay between different levels and arenas, where so much political activity was concerned with exploring unfamiliar ground or with testing alliances which, perforce, had to be struck with strangers. Uncertainty naturally bred suspicion of anything other than total commitment to a political leader and his cause and helped to give to East Africa's, as perhaps to all nationalisms, much of their forward impetus.

The formulae of partnership

The political field on which in East Africa this rising African consciousness encountered the general thrust of imperial policy was governed by the local rules of multi-racialism or partnership. The contest centred upon the relative degrees of influence which the several racial communities should exercise in government and so, more critically, over the whole social and cultural fabric of existence. Communal fears were in no way diminished by the Imperial government's long refusal to commit itself to any policy on the timing and direction of constitutional change. As a matter of principle British governments, of whatever political hue, were reluctant to interfere in what they felt should be the organic development of a colony. In the affairs of East and Central Africa, the explosive possibilities latent in the divergence between their inherited policies of imperial trusteeship towards Africans and local responsibility for Europeans demanded an abnormal reticence. And Conservative governments, in power from 1951 until after the last of the East African territories achieved independence, had compelling party reasons for imprecisions of statement, as was shown by the growth of the settler lobby after 1959, when equivocation between the 'West African' and

---

[1] This applied to Europeans as much as to Africans, as may be seen not only in such a well-known incident as the reception of Blundell as a traitor by the settlers on his return to Nairobi after the 1960 Kenya Constitutional Conference, but in the more general sharpening of animosities in small upcountry communities, largely composed of officials, between those sympathetic and those opposed to African nationalism.

'South African' traditions of policy could no longer be maintained.[1]

It was in this context that the partnership concept was so attractive to British policy-makers. It was flexible and imprecise, as the old doctrine of native paramountcy which it supplanted was not. Partnership could be interpreted either as an end in itself, as, in effect, the preservation of privilege for the European minorities upon whose strategic loyalty and economic dynamism the imperial government placed such reliance; or it could be taken as a means for negotiating the difficult transition to majority rule.[2] If the latter, then in its various stages it might imply the partnership of senior and junior—like the Central African rider and horse; collaboration subsequently between equals; and, finally, an unequal partnership again but with the former roles reversed. The concept and the rhetoric remained the same.[3] But for all its conceptual flexibility, partnership was an artificial political system, responsive less to politicians' rhetoric than to a slide-rule; a slide-rule moreover which measured the communal pressures upon a colonial government to a degree that it never would have done upon an African one.[4] Partnership had, then, two flaws. The first was that the majority of the local Europeans (in Kenya certainly) and virtually all Africans, at least until the later 1950s, took it to be an end which as things turned out it could not be; and the mutual mistrust which this belief engendered compounded the second, which was that as a means for easing the passage of white privilege (and thus of imperial control) its inherent stress upon communal difference and minority interests inhibited the creation of a well-structured successor régime.

For rather more than a decade after the end of the war, the colonial governments continued to use the perspectives of the social engineer. Their sequence of priorities was to foster the

---

[1] David Goldsworthy, *Colonial Issues in British Politics, 1945–1961* (London, 1971), pp. 306–9, 364–72; Dan Horowitz, 'Attitudes of British Conservatives towards Decolonization in Africa', *African Affairs*, 69, 274 (Jan. 1970), 9–26.

[2] Cf. W. P. Kirkman, *Unscrambling an Empire* (London, 1966), p. 55.

[3] Creech Jones, 'British Colonial Policy, with particular reference to Africa', loc. cit., p. 180; and compare the discussion on the concurrent concept of administrative partnership in David E. Apter, *The Political Kingdom in Uganda* (Princeton, 1961), pp. 223–4.

[4] Cranford Pratt, '"Multi-racialism" and Local Government in Tanganyika', *Race*, 2 (Nov. 1960), 37.

economic growth which was needed to underwrite the more equal society in which, in turn, a lasting political partnership between the races might prosper. They set their face against any political pressure which appeared to threaten this careful and always incomplete structure. East African governments regulated the political arena with a force and frequency sanctioned neither by general principle nor by the precedents of British West Africa, where African politicians were but rarely imprisoned and their parties were never banned. In Kenya, not only was war levied against large sections of the Kikuyu people, but African political organizations at the national level were outlawed for six years from 1953. In Tanganyika some TANU branches were closed, and the African Congress was denied registration. In Uganda too, African parties were banned in the 1940s and again in 1959, and the strong separatist drive of the kingdom of Buganda was more than once halted. Government action against immigrant political opinion was rare, and taken only against individual newspaper editors or owners—Indians who were too friendly, Europeans who were too rude to Africans.[1]

The racial disparity in these restraints upon political expression reflected in the late 1940s the official preoccupation with economic development and, in subsequent years, the difficulties in changing the political arrangements under which continuing European and Asian investment had then been encouraged. The practice of representative government, as it developed in the British colonial territories, had had two purposes: to secure the co-operation of the colonial community as a whole and to harness the commercial expertise of specific interest groups; but in East Africa the economic priorities of the day lent a preponderant weight to the second objective, and so to the representation of the immigrant minorities. As representative principles took hold, moreover, so the colonial government's capacity to act authoritatively to determine the rules and rewards of the political arena at the territorial level was weakened by its need to hold its own there as a competitor on its own

---

[1] For examples in Kenya see Felice Carter, 'The Asian Press in Kenya', *East Africa Journal*, 6, 10 (Nairobi, 1969), pp. 30–4; idem, 'The Kenya Government and the Press, 1906–60', *Hadith*, 2 (Nairobi, 1970), 243–58; George Bennett and Carl Rosberg, *The Kenyatta Election: Kenya 1960–1961* (London, 1961), p. 96.

account. The political history of the 1950s certainly seemed to justify the fears expressed earlier by metropolitan critics, that the conjunction of multi-racialism and representative government would give to the immigrant communities, as the currently 'senior' partners, additional political resources which would unnecessarily complicate, if not prevent, any future revision of the terms of partnership.[1]

The similar fears entertained by Africans were compounded by the impact of the second colonial occupation. While the Kenya government, for instance, appointed a leading settler to the quasi-ministerial post of Member for Agriculture, it doubted whether Africans were competent even as peasants;[2] such doubts in Tanganyika had argued for the mechanized Groundnut Scheme. It was not until midway through the 1950s that governments began to act on the belief that prosperous African farmers could be raised up as the professional and political partners of the white settlers. Until then the African partners-presumptive had been pre-eminently the agricultural and veterinary assistants and, to a lesser extent, the schoolteachers who graduated from Makerere College. But however much these might participate in the second occupation, especially in the campaign against soil erosion,[3] they did so as the skirmishers of a visibly European army. Although Europeans generally and some Asians were being co-opted into government,[4] Africans were now finding themselves governed as never before.

While a few percipient settlers, even at the peak of their post-war confidence, foresaw that the Imperial government might later regard them as merely the economic midwife for a political revolution in which they would have little place, Africans could not be so certain.[5] Their campaigns to secure firm assurances from London on political advance were launched

[1] As was foreseen by Uganda's wartime governor Sir Charles Dundas: see Apter, *The Political Kingdom*, p. 221 sq.; for criticisms of Creech Jones' policies on this score, Goldsworthy, *Colonial Issues*, pp. 19 sqq., 155 sqq.

[2] M. P. K. Sorrenson, *Land Reform in the Kikuyu Country* (Nairobi, 1967), p. 55.

[3] A condition which seemed to some Europeans proof of peasant incompetence. Robert Chambers, *Settlement Schemes in Tropical Africa* (London, 1969), p. 22.

[4] Most obviously so during the Kenya Emergency, not only at the War Council level but also on the ground, with young white settlers mobilized in the Kenya Regiment or employed as assistant district officers and (with some Asians) in the Police Reserve.

[5] George Bennett, *Kenya: a political history* (London, 1963), p. 106 sq.

within the separate territories. But, in contrast to West Africa where British colonies were not contiguous, there was also in East African decolonization an inter-territorial flow of political currents. This may best be charted by watching the course of what we call the 'symbolic formulae' of multi-racial representation in the colonial legislatures and executives.[1]

The key indicator was the composition of the legislatures, and here there were three basic formulae. There was 'primacy', either European primacy, as when in Kenya and Tanganyika the white unofficials had a clear majority over those of other races, or African primacy in the years immediately preceding independence. There was 'parity', also European or African, when the members from one community balanced the other two (or three in the case of Kenya with its Arab members). And finally there was 'equal representation', briefly in Uganda in the 1940s and in Tanganyika a decade later, when each community had the same number of representatives. These permutations could be modified almost indefinitely by adding in the balance of unofficials on the executive councils or by counting heads among assistant ministers.

After the promise of the late 1940s—with the 1947 Local Government Despatch revealing London's nervous preparedness for a torrent of post-war change—the formulae of representation from the African viewpoint worsened quite perceptibly, until by the early 1950s the terms of partnership appeared to have congealed into a pattern from which Africans might never emerge as the senior. There was a retreat from equal representation in the inter-territorial Legislative Assembly. Governor Twining's proposals for African parity in Tanganyika's legislature were diluted into equal representation. In Uganda Sir John Hall's rhetorical declaration in 1946 that 'Primarily, the development . . . must be by the African, for the African,'[2] (which was based upon the old native paramountcy doctrine and the self-evident primacy of peasant production), had been superseded by 'partnership', whose virtues were pressed even

---

[1] The symbolism of the period extended beyond these formulae into government statements. The sequence in announcing a territory to be 'multi-racial', 'non-racial', 'predominantly African', and 'primarily African' is one example of what Tanganyikan officials referred to as magical cantrips (witches' spells). Appendix 2 summarizes the mathematical progression of these formulae.

[2] Kenneth Ingham, *The Making of Modern Uganda* (London, 1958), p. 228.

upon this most 'West African' of the East African territories by
the Colonial Secretary, James Griffiths, in 1951. And in the background were the preliminaries of Federation in Central Africa.
By 1950, six years after the first African had entered any of the
territorial legislatures, there was European parity on the unofficial benches in Kenya and Tanganyika, African parity in Uganda.

The gap between the last two narrowed when, in 1952 and
1954 respectively, Uganda first instituted and Tanganyika
enlarged its Executive Council. By comparison with their
unchanged legislatures the former retreated, the latter advanced,
each to arrive—among the unofficial members of their Executive
Councils—at equal representation, 2:2:2 being the formula for
balancing the races. Mathematical juggling was relatively
simple in these two territories, where all the unofficial legislators
were still nominated by the governor. In Kenya, where the
settler representatives were elected and experienced, it was quite
different, as the Secretary of State discovered in 1951. European
parity was at that time secured by the formula 11:4:5:2 for
Europeans, Africans, Asians, and Arabs respectively. Following
Kenyan African demands, Griffiths agreed to increase African
representation to six, while the rift between Muslim and Hindu
argued for another Asian member too. But in order to preserve
European parity—even though he was careful not to accept this
as a permanency—Griffiths increased the unofficial European
membership to fourteen;[1] a concession of two to Africans had
occasioned a European advance of three. It is small wonder that
few Africans trusted the calculus of partnership.[2] In the
nationalist view, the terms of partnership would never change
unless they were given a jolt and the symbolic formulae unhinged.

Towards a new order

The first African jolts were administered not by territorial
nationalist movements but in convulsions within two strategic

---

[1] Statement on Kenya Constitution (Discussions) in *Hansard*, 5th series, H. of C.,
488, cc.408–10, 31 May 1951.
[2] A point graphically illustrated in Vicky's *Evening Standard* (London) cartoon
'Bingo!', showing a bemused Kaunda sitting while the figures of Macleod (with his
concealed playing-card), Sandys, Welensky, Lords Beaverbrook and Salisbury
cavort with their successfully completed cross-racial voting cards during the 1961
negotiations on the Northern Rhodesian constitution: Kenneth Kaunda, *Zambia
Shall be Free* (London, 1962), facing p. 91.

localities which had long been close to crisis—Kikuyuland and Buganda. It is true that at the time of the Kikuyu convulsion there was already in existence in Kenya the most powerful political movement in East Africa, the Kenya African Union, and that it was not confined to Kikuyuland. But the Kenya government was genuinely confused between the identities of KAU and 'Mau Mau', and of one thing it was certain: 'Mau Mau' was a Kikuyu affair. And it was in reaction to 'Mau Mau', not KAU, that Kenya Africans were first admitted to a limited partnership in government. For all his refusal to see 'Mau Mau' as anything other than a reversion to barbarism, the new Conservative Secretary of State, Oliver Lyttelton, saw that African confidence in government was the only alternative there to rule by force; he made it clear moreover that the settlers could not continue to wield sole political power. And so by the terms of the 'Lyttelton constitution' of March 1954 the partnership principle was extended from the legislature to the new Council of Ministers. European parity was retained there in the formula 3:2:1, but that 1 was portentous: the first African in East Africa had a ministerial portfolio.[1]

Two months later, discussions of still greater import opened on Namirembe Hill in Kampala.[2] These aimed at the resolution of the crisis which had blown up in Buganda in the previous year over the kingdom's internal administration and its external relations with the rest of Uganda. Both problems had been amplified by the multi-racial mould prescribed both for Uganda and East Africa as a whole which, so an unguarded remark by Lyttelton implied, might one day emulate the newly launched Central African Federation. Only after there had been some solid confirmation that Uganda would after all develop as an African state were Buganda's problems resolved, temporarily as it subsequently proved. But the profound difference of view on this point between Uganda's governor and the Colonial Office meant that Lyttelton's assurance, that Uganda's future was to be 'primarily as an African state with proper safeguards for minorities', had to be drawn from him, as his questioner Eirene

---

[1] The importance of the symbolism in the formula is seen clearly in Blundell's account of the negotiations. See *So Rough a Wind*, pp. 144–59, and for Lyttelton's view, Chandos, *Memoirs*, p. 406 sq., and *Hansard*, 5th series, H. of C., 525, cc.880–5, 22 Mar. 1954.

[2] For a full discussion see Low, *Buganda in Modern History*, chap. 4.

White put it, 'accidentally by intervention in debate'.[1] Well might the Secretary of State have refrained from including this declaration in his earlier statement on the Kabaka's deportation: it marked the initial breach in the partnership line drawn about East and—ultimately—Central Africa. It remained for the Namirembe conferences to unhinge the symbolic formulae of partnership. By late 1954 it was agreed for Uganda not only to allow an overall African majority in a legislature which still retained a semblance of multi-racial balance on its unofficial benches, but to remove all trace of arithmetical elegance from the unofficial side of the Executive Council. There equal representation was to be supplanted by African primacy with the decisive ratio of 5:1:1.

By early 1956, when these reforms were implemented, the initiative in change had veered back to the region's two ruling minorities, the Zanzibar Arabs and the Europeans in Kenya. During the two years from 1954 influential sections among them, led by Sheikh Ali Muhsin and Michael Blundell respectively, reached the conclusion that their continued survival depended upon their transforming their communities from a closed caste into the élite among a non-racial political class.[2] The Arab initiative was the more determined of the two. It was also, until a month after independence, successful.[3] What is important here is that the Arab Association deliberately abandoned the protection of communal representation under Zanzibar's own version of the multi-racial formula and, in direct opposition to the British constitutional proposals of 1955, went for a common roll. Blundell's much more hesitant steps in the same direction succeeded only in splitting European opinion, but this was a prerequisite for any further political movement;[4] and in the end, his wedge of liberal opinion was to prove Macleod's most valuable lever in the constitutional conference of 1960.[5]

---

[1] *Hansard*, 5th series; H. of C., 521, cc. 1268–9, 2 Dec. 1953.

[2] For Blundell's thoughts on the problem see *So Rough a Wind*, pp. 148, 160, 178 especially. See also *Round Table*, (Sept. 1956), 405–8.

[3] Michael F. Lofchie, *Zanzibar, Background to Revolution* (Princeton, 1965), especially pp. 127–80; and chap. iv below.

[4] As was quickly recognized by the Labour MP, James Johnson, in commenting upon Lyttelton's constitutional proposals. *Hansard*, 5th series, H. of C., 525, c.884, 22 Mar. 1954. See also Margery Perham, letter to *The Times*, 31 Dec. 1954, reprinted in *Colonial Sequence, 1949 to 1969*, p. 100.

[5] See Macleod's review of Blundell's memoirs, in 'Blundell's Kenya', *The Spectator*, No. 7082 (20 Mar. 1964), p. 366.

All these developments kept the East African terms of partner-ship in motion, decisively so in the case of Uganda. They did little to question the continuation of imperial control. The United Nations Visiting Mission of 1954 had suggested a target of 20 to 25 years for Tanganyika's self-government. Nyerere accepted this estimate. While government rejected it in principle, subsequent remarks by the Colonial Secretary left little doubt as to the real objection: the timetable was too short.[1] As it turned out, even the lower of these estimates was cut by two-thirds. For the upward thrust of Tanganyikan nationalism was to coincide with, and provide the first East African test of, a new realism towards the African residue of Empire—now its emotional core—which was forced upon Britain by fresh crises in the eastern Mediterranean.

The Suez invasion of November 1956 was designed to secure very specific western interests in Egypt. But in the minds of the colonial powers, Nasser was also the personification of all the perils immanent in decolonization. The French joined the invasion to stop up the back door of the Algerian revolution; Belgium's foreign minister foresaw 'a long series of retreats' for the west, the British prime minister feared the reaction of Africa (personified in a Nigerian Muslim chief) 'if Nasser were allowed by the world to seize his spoil and keep it.'[2] Radio Cairo's broadcasts were already the bane of the East African govern-ments; its *Sauti ya Uhuru* (Voice of Freedom) attempted to give the impression of originating from a mobile transmitter in the Mount Kenya forests. And in the background was the fear of a Russian penetration of Africa via Egypt. Had not the 1955 Simonstown Agreement described southern Africa's defences as lying 'not only in Africa but also in the gateways to Africa, namely in the Middle East'?[3] The upshot of the invasion, however, changed all this. Under the thermo-nuclear umbrella, the next year's Defence White Paper sounded the retreat.[4] Compulsory military service in Britain was to be ended within three years, and the strength of the armed forces to be almost halved. Colonial garrisons were to be reduced, even if East

[1] *Speech by the Rt. Hon. Alan Lennox-Boyd, . . . at a Luncheon in the Karimjee Hall, Dar es Salaam . . . October 28th 1957* (Government Printer, Dar es Salaam), p. 4.

[2] Sir Anthony Eden, *Full Circle* (London, 1960), pp. 458, 443.

[3] *Exchange of Letters on Defence Matters between the . . . United Kingdom and the Union of South Africa, June 1955*, Cmd. 9520 (July 1955).

[4] *Defence, Outline of Future Policy*, Cmnd. 124 (Apr. 1957).

Africa was still indicated as a base for the defence of the Persian Gulf. In July 1957 the new prime minister, Harold Macmillan, in some little-noticed passages of a speech at Bedford, talked of the need to accommodate African nationalism in terms very similar to his 'Wind of Change' oration of 1960.[1] It would be wrong to conclude that the British government had decided to relinquish the remainder of its African empire. Not only was the withdrawal from Cyprus a sensitive enough reversal of policy for the moment,[2] but it lent added military importance to Kenya, where the building of barracks for a brigade of the British strategic reserve began in 1958. But Suez did help to crystallize a growing acceptance—in Whitehall if not in Africa—of Britain's diminishing capacity for guiding the social and economic developments by which colonial policy had hitherto been measured. And in 1955 the East Africa Royal Commission's report[3] had shot away even the economic case from under the privileges of the local guarantors of the imperial interest, the Kenya settlers. The official powers of guidance would now have to be harnessed increasingly to the motor of African nationalism—once it had generated sufficient momentum to become not merely a rival but a potential successor to the settlers.

And it was now that Tanganyika, seen conventionally as the territory least well-equipped to fend for itself, began to set the pace. There, TANU's hotly debated decision in January 1958 to contest rather than boycott the forthcoming elections enabled the party to demonstrate that political power took little account of even the most carefully contrived of multi-racial constitutions. The new legislature might have equality of representation, 10:10:10, on its unofficial benches, but almost all the new members, of whatever race, owed their presence to TANU support. The multi-racial United Tanganyika Party was as empty as its Swahili acronym, *utupu*, had proclaimed. Though the assurance seemed revolutionary enough at the time, the new

---

[1] The speech did later achieve some notoriety, but for a different reason—the first use of the phrase, We (or you) have 'never had it so good'. See Harold Macmillan, *Riding the Storm, 1956–1959* (London, 1971), pp. 350 sqq; and for comparisons between the two speeches, Horowitz, 'Attitudes of British Conservatives', loc. cit., pp. 15 sqq.

[2] Goldsworthy, *Colonial Issues*, pp. 306–16, 365.

[3] *East Africa Royal Commission Report*, chairman Sir Hugh Dow, Cmd. 9475 (London, HMSO, 1955), chap. xviii especially.

governor, Sir Richard Turnbull, was only stating the obvious when in October 1958 he opened the new Council session by declaring that at independence the country's government would be 'predominantly African'.[1] What was genuinely revolutionary was the speed at which Tanganyika now moved towards that goal. TANU's electoral victory was won against the background of European fears of violence, and perhaps some African fears too. At times in Tanganyika, as in comparable periods elsewhere, nationalist élite and colonial government seem to have joined in a tacit defensive alliance against those uncertainties of rapid change by which they, no less than ordinary individuals, were beset.[2] In the districts it seemed that TANU's local cadres were strong enough to disrupt the processes of rural administration, but were disturbingly deficient in the disciplines required of a potential party of government. Officials contemplated the possibility of an Emergency with a good deal of pessimism. There were very few police; in contrast to Kenya virtually every tribe would have become involved; it would be like Cyprus, without the Turks. The governor had therefore to act quickly, to help to convert a crumbling colonial order into a stronger nationalist one.[3] Two important elements in former policy and the chief issues of political contention—the multi-racial local councils and vigorous land utilization schemes—were fundamentally modified, but accelerated constitutional advance was the only political resource now available to augment the authority of TANU over its followers; the Tanganyika government had little option but to put to the test the thesis being increasingly accepted by Blundell in Kenya that the only solid safeguard for the immigrant minorities could be the goodwill of the majority, not the constitutional devices of multi-racialism. It was able to move ahead rapidly since Tanganyika was not split as were both Uganda (between Ganda and non-Ganda) and shortly Kenya as well (between KANU and KADU).

[1] *Address by His Excellency the Governor at the Opening of the 34th Session of the Tanganyika Legislative Council on Tuesday, 14th October, 1958* (Govt. Printer, Dar es Salaam, 1958).

[2] Cf., Maguire, *Toward 'Uhuru'*, pp. 234, 253–6; and Tom Mboya's article in the *Observer*, (14 Dec. 1958), reprinted in *The Challenge of Nationhood* (London, 1970), p. 38.

[3] For a well-informed guide to Turnbull's relations with the nationalists see Judith Listowel, *The Making of Tanganyika* (London, 1965), pp. 340 sqq., 348–57.

By the middle of 1959 Kenya was isolated.[1] The general position taken at the Chequers conference of January 1959 between the Secretary of State and the East African governors— that nationalism should be subject to imperial restraint for a further decade[2]—had been cut away. Power could not be held for that long in suspense.[3] Tanganyika did not, like Kenya, have its Hola camp or Uganda's trade boycott, or Nyasaland's full-blown Emergency, but the lesson seemed clear; the perils of going too fast were as nothing to the perils of going too slow— even if the Imperial government had a somewhat exaggerated impression of the current fragility of colonial authority.[4] Kenya's isolation was magnified moreover as one looked out beyond East Africa. Ghana had been independent for two years already, Nigeria would be in 1960, and so also would be Somalia on Kenya's borders. Still more startling changes in French Africa culminated in a rush of independences in 1960. The Belgians then announced their imminent withdrawal from the Congo; and de Gaulle's determined handling of Algeria demonstrated both the possibility of resolving the problems of settler Africa and the bitter consequences of leaving them until too late. At a deeper level, Britain's economic interests now seemed to depend more upon the future of Europe than of Empire. So, fortified by his election victory in 1959, Macmillan travelled to Africa early in 1960 and reiterated in Accra and Cape Town what he had said three years earlier at Bedford. This time people took notice. Kenya's constitutional conference was already in session at Lancaster House; after a month's negotiation Macleod announced that a new legislature with an African majority would be elected early in 1961, with African 'parity' among the unofficials in the Council of Ministers being obtained with the

---

[1] As was recognized by the Colonial Editor of *The Times* (27 Jan. 1959), in the second of a series of three articles, 'African nationalism spreads apace'. This view he repeated on the following day to a gathering of 250 members of the civil service, the professions, and industry, organized by the Royal African Society: *The Africa of Today and Tomorrow* (London, 1959), p. 26 sq.

[2] Chequers conference reported in *The Times*, 26 Jan. 1959, under the headline 'Nationalism sweeps East Africa: urgent need for a Colonial Policy'; Blundell's account, *So Rough a Wind*, p. 261 sq., is corroborated in Roy Welensky, *Welensky's 4000 Days* (London, 1964), p. 139.

[3] Cf. Margery Perham, *The Colonial Reckoning*, p. 79 sq.

[4] Goldsworthy, *Colonial Issues*, pp. 361 sqq.; Macmillan, *Riding the Storm*, pp. 734, 737.

formula 4:3:1 (the one being an Asian). For all the maintenance of this multi-racial façade—and it was intended to last for some years—it was clear at last that in Kenya the direction now lay towards African predominance. Within weeks of the end of the conference the African deaths at Sharpeville seemed to provide in South Africa tragic confirmation of the alternative.

Tanganyika went on to achieve independence in 1961, Uganda in 1962. Before Kenya's turn came in 1963, the global and territorial levels of British policy had one last opportunity to interact. For the final timing of Kenyatta's release from restriction in August 1961 owed something at least to the British need for political calm around the Kenya base from which troops were then operating to defend imperial interests in the Persian Gulf state of Kuwait.[1] A local nationalism was once again being conciliated in order to preserve a continuing military capability elsewhere; the strategic priorities demonstrated in this case were a clear indication that the imperial camp was about to be struck in this part of Africa. With it went the devices of multi-racialism, whose winding up was made visible in the buying out of many white farmers in Kenya and the offer of British citizenship to Asians. In the British view, if these commitments were the price of disengagement it was not, at the time, expensive. For Africans they marked merely the start of a search for the political, not symbolic, formulae which might foster a new social order.

---

[1] Patrick Keatley, *The Politics of Partnership* (Harmondsworth, Middlesex, 1963) p. 388 sq.

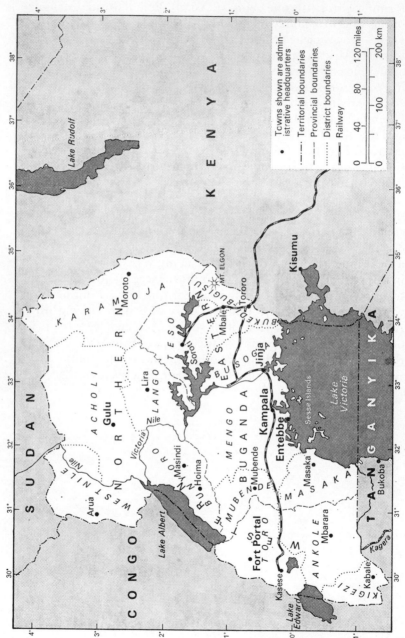

MAP I. UGANDA: GENERAL AND ADMINISTRATIVE, 1956–7.

I

KINGDOMS, DISTRICTS, AND THE UNITARY STATE: UGANDA 1945–1962

CHERRY GERTZEL

UGANDA at the end of the Second World War was a predominantly African country with few of the racial conflicts that beset neighbouring Kenya. Both immigrant communities were small and limited in political influence. The 33,767 Asians[1] played a prominent role in commerce and controlled much of the country's retail trade. The 3,448 Europeans were for the most part in government service, business, or employed by the missions. With the exception of a handful of planters in Western Province there was no settled European population. Uganda in this respect followed the pattern of the West African territories rather than that of her East African neighbours. Sir John Hall, governor from 1944 until the end of 1951, based his policies on the principle that the country should be developed primarily by Africans and for Africans.

The African population, which in 1947 was about five million, was highly pluralistic. Its major ethnic groupings were the Bantu-speaking peoples of the southern half of the protectorate and the Nilotics of the north and related peoples in Karamoja and Teso districts. Cutting across these ethnic cleavages were deep religious divisions between Protestant and Roman Catholic (and to a less extent Muslim) which, having their origins in the religious conflicts of the 1890s,[2] remained a powerful force in the twentieth century. Economically there was also a considerable variation between different parts of the protectorate, particularly the Bantu south and the Nilotic and Nilo-Hamitic north.

The most striking economic and political contrasts were, however, between the kingdom of Buganda and the rest of the

[1] Uganda Census of 1948. There were also 1,488 Goans, 1,475 Arabs, and 643 Coloured listed in the census.
[2] See volumes i and ii of this *History*.

country. Buganda, rich in history and past achievements, continued to stand out distictively from all other districts of the protectorate. The homeland of the largest single tribal group (the Ganda accounted for 17 per cent of the total African population), a province by itself, it was also the most economically advanced region in the protectorate. The regular rainfall, the fertility of the soil, the ready availability of immigrant labour,[1] the railway to Kampala, and past protectorate policies had all contributed to its great agricultural wealth. Buganda's farmers led Uganda in the production first of cotton and then of coffee,[2] and greatly benefited from the incidence of high coffee prices after the war. Nor was it only in agriculture that Buganda had the advantage. The availability of raw materials, the ready market, and the transport facilities led to the concentration of business and industrial development around Kampala and Jinja. Industrial and commercial development were consequently, in the early 1950s, concentrated in the southern part of the protectorate, and particularly in Buganda.

Educationally Buganda enjoyed considerable advantages. Early missionary concentration there had given the province more schools and other educational facilities than the other districts. There were many more educated Ganda than any other tribal group, and the greater educational facilities helped to preserve the imbalance. In 1951 Buganda had 58,046 of the total of 173,000 primary school children in the whole country; and 1,036 children in senior secondary schools compared with 876 in the rest of the country.[3]

Politically the Uganda Agreement of 1900[4] assured Buganda a much greater measure of internal autonomy than the other districts, including the Western Agreement Kingdoms, enjoyed.

---

[1] African immigrant labour had for many years moved into Buganda from Ruanda-Urundi and Tanganyika, the Sudan and the Congo, and from other districts of Uganda, particularly West Nile. See A. Richards (ed.) *Economic Development and Tribal Change* (Cambridge, 1954).

[2] C. Wrigley, *Crops and Wealth in Uganda* (East African Institute of Social Research, Kampala, 1959).

[3] See *African Education in Uganda*, being the Report of a Committee set up by His Excellency the Governor (the de Bunsen Committee) to study and make recommendations on the future of African Education in the Uganda Protectorate (Entebbe, Govt. Printer, 1953).

[4] See D. A. Low and R. C. Pratt, *Buganda and British Overrule* (Oxford, 1960), Part i.

Her traditional institutions, safeguarded by that agreement and adapted and developed to meet the needs of the twentieth century, emphasized her separate political identity. At the head of her government stood the Kabaka, the hereditary ruler who symbolized the identity of the kingdom; beneath him his three Ministers,[1] his Lukiko (reformed in 1945 to include an indirectly elected element, but still dominated by the land-owning class) and a graded hierarchy of chiefs who were economically as well as politically dominant. The Ganda retained an intense pride in their institutions and a consciousness of an independent identity which had led them in the past to reject any close association with the rest of the country. This separatist sentiment explained Ganda leaders' continued ambivalent attitudes in 1945 towards membership of central government institutions, particularly the Legislative Council.

There was a considerable ignorance in the post-war years in Buganda of what was happening elsewhere in the Protectorate. The attitudes of the Ganda were to a large extent formed by their experience of the immigrants who flocked in from other districts and who were usually from the poorest elements of their communities. Intensely self-assured, the Ganda believed in their superiority over other tribes, particularly the non-Bantu.[2]

The Ganda contribution to political and constitutional discourse in Uganda had over many years been considerable. In the immediate post-war years there was also a greater popular political involvement in Buganda than in other districts. Ganda politics remained characteristically focused upon rivalry for office within the kingdom; but a growing rural discontent aroused by economic and political grievances had by the end of the war increased popular opposition to the chiefs, expressed largely through the old Bataka Party. These grievances had led to serious political disturbances in January and February 1945, and later to the assassination of the then Katikiro, Martin Nsibirwa, soon after his reinstatement by the protectorate authorities.[3] The disturbances were contained but populist

---

[1] The Katikiro, or Chief Minister; the Omuwanika, or Treasurer; and the Omulamuzi, or Chief Justice.

[2] See, e.g., A. Richards, *Economic Development and Tribal Change*, pp. 221–2; E. Huxley, *The Sorcerer's Apprentice* (London, 1949), p. 264.

[3] See volume ii of this *History*. The crucial grievance concerned land transfers, to which the Ganda were opposed.

political activity increased after 1945, in reaction particularly to the protectorate government's marketing and prices policies. Suspicion of British intentions was also increased by that government's plans for an East African High Commission, first announced in 1945 and subsequently modified in a second White Paper in 1947.[1] These proposals revived earlier Ganda fears that they would be forced into an East African Federation that would subordinate them to the Kenya Europeans. Popular political and economic discontent resulted in increasing opposition to the Ganda leaders who supported the British and provoked demands both for the transformation of the Lukiko into a popularly chosen body and for the popular election of chiefs. Factional intrigue led to an alliance between a section of the chiefs anxious to unseat those in power in the Buganda government and the small farmers in the countryside.

Two organizations articulated these grievances in the 1940s: the Bataka Party, founded in 1945 by James Miti and (closely associated with this) the Uganda African Farmers' Union (UAFU) formed in 1947 by I. K. Musazi, who had been active in Buganda politics since the 1930s. Both rapidly attracted considerable support at village level for their stand against both the Buganda and the protectorate governments. The Bataka Party, particularly well organized at *miruka* (parish) level, was by 1948 holding well-attended regular monthly meetings throughout the countryside, at which its leaders attacked government economic policies and demanded political reforms. They exploited the growing network of communications spreading out from the new African urban area of Katwe, growing up on the edge of Kampala, to establish links throughout the countryside.[2] The Luganda vernacular press, which had no counterpart in the rest of the country, was a further means of communication.

In September 1949 this political movement erupted into a second wave of violence when riots broke out, which were put down only after considerable destruction of property.[3] Both the Bataka Party and the UAFA were proscribed as a consequence

---

[1] *Inter-territorial Organization in the East Africa*, Col. 191 (London, HMSO, 1946). *Inter-territorial Organization in East Africa; revised proposals*, Col. 210 (London, HMSO, 1947). See chap. ii below.

[2] *Report of the Commission of Inquiry into Civil Disturbances in Uganda during April 1949*, Chairman Sir D. Kingdon (Entebbe, Govt. Printer, 1950).

[3] Ibid.

of their implication in these riots; but political feelings remained intense.

It was understandable, given her greater economic development, that Buganda should produce a political movement before any other part of the country. The 1949 riots demonstrated both the intensity of the agitation and its successful organization. This activity was directed, however, not against the protectorate government but against the Lukiko. Ganda politics at the grass-roots level were consequently in 1949 tribal and inward-looking rather than nationalist in orientation. They were also at all levels intensely chauvinistic, concerned with Buganda's identity, as the Lukiko's refusal to nominate a member to sit on the Legislative Council in 1950 showed.[1]

The protectorate government failed to recognize the depth of popular African resentment in Buganda against particular policies and therefore the need for radical change. Cautious steps were taken to increase the elected element into the Ganda councils, but no idea was entertained of the root and branch change in the Lukiko or the Buganda government demanded by the Bataka Party.

The protectorate government adopted a highly cautious attitude also towards the question of political change in the central government. First, the emphasis was on economic rather than political development. Second, the governor, Sir John Hall, argued that political change must start with local rather than central government. He proposed, in order to correct the imbalance between Buganda's institutions and those of the other districts, to build up a new level of Provincial Councils, on which gradually considerable powers and responsibilities would be devolved by the protectorate government. These Provincial Councils would act as electoral colleges for the Legislative Council. Hall was thus proposing something like a federal system of government.[2] The difficulties in the way of such a policy arose from the fact that no such Provincial Councils then existed; and although provision was made for them by the African Local Government Ordinance of 1949 they were given no legislative

[1] For these years see particularly Low and Pratt, *Buganda and British Overrule*, and David Apter, *The Political Kingdom in Uganda* (Oxford, 1961).

[2] See Sir John Hall's dispatch to the Secretary of State, 29 Aug. 1947, and the Secretary of State's reply, 47234/1/47 of 13 Jan. 1948 (both printed). Also Apter, *Political Kingdom*, p. 231.

powers. The existing District Councils, based (with certain exceptions) on the tribe as the administrative unit, were moreover for the most part reluctant to submerge themselves into a provincial authority. The Provincial Councils when established did not, as a result, become bodies of any great significance.

The first Africans nominated to the Legislative Council in 1945 were officials: one of the Ganda ministers nominated by the Kabaka; one of the Katikiros to represent the Western, and one of the Secretaries-General to represent the Eastern Province.[1] When African representation was increased to eight in 1950 the members were still officials, chosen by the new Provincial Councils.

Sir Andrew Cohen and the concept of a unitary state

This approach to political development was radically altered, however, with the arrival of Sir Andrew Cohen as governor in January 1952.

Cohen, before his appointment, had been Head of the African Division in the Colonial Office, where he had been a major influence in shaping post-war policies for political advance in West Africa and the colonial territories generally. Once he took up residence there his vigorous mind and easy informality quickly transformed the official atmosphere in Uganda. His arrival also brought a radical change in governmental policy about the appropriate pace and direction of political development. He was determined to push the country as quickly as possible along the road to self-government. Within a short time he had visited all parts of the protectorate, talking extensively with a wide range of officials and non-officials. Within a short time also he had begun to tackle existing economic and political grievances, with the result that the government quickly became 'the most aggressive and positive force for change',[2] the objective of which was the establishment of a strong, unified Uganda.

The three major prongs of Cohen's proposals had been outlined within eighteen months of his arrival. First he abandoned the system of Provincial Councils and recognised the district as the basic unit of local government. The government proposed

---

[1] Uganda Legislative Council *Debates*, 23 Oct. 1945. A fourth African was appointed for the Northern Province when it was reconstituted in 1949.
[2] Apter, *Political Kingdom*, p. 261.

to introduce a more representative and responsible local government system at district level, based upon the report produced
by C. A. G. Wallis, who carried out an inquiry into local government during 1952[1]. Considerable responsibility for local services
was to be transferred to the District Councils, and more autonomy conceded in genuinely local matters.

The vital assumption underlying Cohen's policies was that
Uganda must develop as a unitary state, in which no part of the
country should dominate any other. This view was clearly
enunciated in the protectorate government's memorandum on
the Wallis Report, which fully endorsed

the view put forward by Mr. Wallis . . . that the future of Uganda
must lie in a unitary form of central government on parliamentary
lines covering the whole country with the component parts of the
country developing within it according to their own special characteristics and, where they exist, according to the Agreements. The
Protectorate is too small to grow into a series of separate units of
government, even if these are federated together. . . .[2]

Cohen thus rejected earlier official thinking based upon the
devolution of power to the provincial level. Instead he conceived of a strong central government in which all districts
including Buganda would be represented. This concept had
implications for the whole country; but particularly it challenged
the separatism that had characterized Buganda's attitudes
towards the rest of the protectorate.

Second, he announced a significant increase in African participation in the central government institutions. Soon after his
arrival Cohen had appointed six unofficials—two Africans, two
Europeans, and two Asians—to the Executive Council. Following this change he proposed in 1953 to increase membership of
the Legislative Council from 32 to 56, of whom 28 would be
representative members. Of these, 14 would be African, one
elected by each of the district councils outside Buganda, and

---

[1] Government Memorandum on the *Report by Mr. C. A. G. Wallis of an Inquiry
into African Local Government in the Uganda Protectorate* (Entebbe, Govt. Printer, 1953).
The preparations for local government reform had almost certainly been set in
motion before Cohen's arrival, but he was bound to have been concerned with them
while in the Colonial Office, and once in Uganda he was closely associated in all
stages of the inquiry.

[2] Ibid, para. 7.

three by the Lukiko; the other 14 would consist of seven Asians and seven Europeans nominated by the governor after consultation with the respective communities. A cross-bench was also proposed, of officials and unofficials of all races, chosen for their individual contribution to the Council, and free to speak and vote as they chose except on matters of confidence.[1]

Third, Cohen (with the Kabaka's support) proposed significant reforms in the Buganda government. The government recognized that Buganda, by virtue of the 1900 Agreement and her size, occupied a special position within Uganda, and was prepared to accord to the kingdom both the position of a 'native state' within Uganda and the powers appropriate to a government at the provincial level. In a joint memorandum on constitutional development issued by the governor and the Kabaka in March 1953 it was agreed that responsibilities for certain departmental services would be transferred to the Buganda government, and the necessary financial adjustments made. It was also agreed that 60 of the 89 members of the Lukiko would be elected, by a system of indirect elections at the *miruka* level, and that the Kabaka would in future consult a Lukiko Commitee before selecting his ministers. Three additional ministers would also be appointed. Finally, Buganda acknowledged that she was an integral part of Uganda, which would be developed as a unitary state.[2] The 1953 proposals thus involved a crucial change of direction, that might not be achieved without difficulties.

Buganda's size and dominant economic and political position posed obstacles to her easy incorporation into a single united state whose poorer units she might be asked to assist. It was thus essential for the success of Cohen's proposals that the Ganda should co-operate in their implementation. The governor hoped to win that co-operation by the transfer of additional powers to the Buganda government, and by recognition of the kingdom's provincial status. But by giving Buganda these additional powers he created a further imbalance between the kingdom and the districts inimical to the growth of a unitary state.

[1] The reconstituted Legislative Council met in February 1954, with the fourteen African representative members in their places. *Correspondence relating to the Composition of the Legislative Council in Uganda* (Entebbe, Govt. Printer, 1953). See pp. 88–93 below for a discussion of their part in the Council.

[2] *Memorandum on Constitutional Development and Reform in Buganda* (Kampala, 17 Mar. 1953). The Buganda reforms were published in August.

The Ganda reaction to the concept of a unitary state

The Ganda in fact approached Cohen's proposals with suspicion. To the extent that the changes in the Lukiko necessarily weakened the position of chiefs and officials, and increased the powers of the elected representatives, they were likely to be popular with the radical elements. The changes in the Legislative Council were not, however, enthusiastically received. The Ganda still did not regard themselves as part of the protectorate, and their reluctance to do so was demonstrated by the Lukiko's refusal to nominate the Ganda members of the enlarged Legislative Council. In the event the young Kabaka, Mutesa II, who had on a number of occasions since his accession in 1942 supported the protectorate government against the Lukiko, again acceded to their request and nominated the three members. An immediate crisis was thus avoided. The future development of Cohen's unitary government depended, however, upon the Kabaka's co-operation; and the latter's own uneasy position in Buganda, where his loyalty to the British had made him suspect, made the situation fragile and tenuous. In the middle of 1953 this situation first worsened, and subsequently radically deteriorated, as a result of a political crisis sparked off in London, which quickly turned Buganda's initial hesitation into open opposition to Cohen's plans.

The Buganda crisis of 1953–55 was begun by a chance remark by the then Secretary of State for the Colonies, Oliver Lyttelton, about the possibility of a future federation of the East African territories.[1] This remark and the publicity it received in the Kenya press revived Ganda fears of an imposed federation; and the Buganda ministers wrote to the governor expressing their concern. Although Sir Andrew Cohen gave public reassurances in the Legislative Council that there would be no imposition of a federation against Ganda wishes, the Kabaka himself had by that time also engaged in the debate. In a letter to the governor he argued that the assurances given to his ministers were inadequate. He went on to ask that Buganda affairs should be transferred from the Colonial Office to the Foreign Office, and

---

[1] The crisis is best documented in Low and Pratt, *Buganda and British Overrule*, pp. 317–49, and also in D. A. Low, *Buganda in Modern History* (London, 1971), chap. 4.

that a timetable for Buganda's independence should be set in motion.

In a series of meetings between the Kabaka and the governor which subsequently took place at Entebbe, the former went further to reject the policy of a unitary state and to ask for the separation of Buganda from the rest of the country. He also refused to give the assurances then demanded by Cohen, and in line with the 1900 Agreement, that he would not publicly oppose the government's policies for Uganda's development as a unitary state, insisting that he could give no such assurances without first consulting the Lukiko. As a result the governor, in November 1953, withdrew British recognition from him as Kabaka and deported him to Britain. A state of emergency was declared, and troops were deployed around Kampala.

The events that followed, which dramatically demonstrated the identification of the Kabaka with Buganda nationalism, have been analysed in detail elsewhere.[1] There was no outbreak of violence such as had occurred in 1949, not least because of the precautions Cohen had taken. Instead the countryside lapsed into a sullen silence. The Ganda were stunned by this treatment of the Kabaka. Earlier popular dissatisfaction with Mutesa for his support of the protectorate government was forgotten. Instead his deportation was seen as an affront to the whole kingdom, and to Ganda pride and ambition. It was the Ganda nation that had been affronted; the Ganda therefore could accept neither the deportation nor the suggestion put soon afterwards that they should elect another Kabaka. An alternative was proposed, however, by a small group of younger professional Ganda, who had only recently been elected to the Lukiko. This group, seizing the initiative, persuaded that body to send a delegation to London to appeal to the Secretary of State for the Kabaka's return.

Although their appeal was rejected two important developments resulted from this visit. First the Secretary of State, defending the governor's actions in the House of Commons, made the important announcement of policy that Uganda would be developed 'primarily as an African country, with proper safeguards for minorities'. Second, it was agreed that discussions should be held between the Ganda and the protectorate govern-

---

[1] Ibid., and Low and Pratt, *Buganda and British Overrule*, loc. cit.

ments on the constitutional relationship between the kingdom and the government, under the chairmanship of Professor Sir Keith Hancock.[1] Out of these discussions, called the Namirembe Conference, which took place in Kampala between July and September 1954, and which were in themselves an event of great political significance, emerged the Buganda Agreement. It was signed the day after Mutesa's triumphal return in October 1955.[2]

In theory the 1955 Agreement turned Buganda into a constitutional monarchy. The Katikiro was in future to be elected by the Lukiko, which would also submit a list of names from which he in turn would choose his five ministers. The Kabaka's government would be responsible to the Lukiko. The Kabaka, therefore, was to be removed from the business of government. All sixty of the representative members of the Lukiko were to be elected under the system introduced in 1953. The *saza* chiefs became responsible solely to the Buganda government; and an Appointments Board (appointed by the Kabaka) assumed responsibility for the selection and control of chiefs and other Buganda government officials. Responsibility for additional services, including junior secondary education, rural health services and some agricultural services, was transferred to the Buganda government. The three additional ministers were appointed. At the same time Buganda recognized that she belonged to the protectorate: Article 1 declared that Buganda should continue to be an integral part of Uganda, and under Article 7 she agreed to send elected representatives, their number increased to five, to the Legislative Council. Buganda's representatives were to be directly elected in 1961, if not before. The protectorate government undertook to review the system of elections to Legislative Council before 1957 (and in 1956 it was agreed that direct elections should be held in 1958). It was agreed that there should be no further fundamental constitutional changes before 1961.

---

[1] The proposal that these constitutional discussions should take place originated with Cohen, who persuaded Lyttelton to appoint Hancock to the task.

[2] Originally the government had ruled that the Kabaka should not return until after the agreement had been signed. But the finding of the Chief Justice of Uganda, in Buganda's appeal against the government's right to deport the Kabaka, that although they possessed the right they had acted under the wrong article, weakened their position and led to the concession that he should return first.

The agreement therefore gave Buganda what amounted practically to internal self-government. 1955 was consequently a crucial watershed in Uganda politics. Buganda's relationship with the centre henceforth much more closely approximated to a federal position. To this extent the principle of a unitary state, although it remained the government's stated objective, had been significantly modified. Immediately after the Kabaka's return this fact was, however, pushed into the background.

As a result of the Namirembe settlement important changes had also been announced in the central government.[1] These were introduced in the early part of 1956. As a result Africans made up half the membership of the Legislative Council; and a ministerial system was introduced by which the Executive Council included seven unofficial Ministers, five of whom were African. The central government thus became predominantly African, and Uganda took a long step closer to the objective of a self-governing state. The Ganda members took their places in the Legislative Council beside the other African representatives.

This was not, however, the beginning of a new era of co-operation, for those in power in Buganda were still reluctant to associate themselves with the central government. The 1955 Agreement had not essentially altered the political structure inside Buganda; but the crisis had had the effect of increasing the Kabaka's personal power. Events soon suggested that he was far from being the constitutional monarch of the agreement. In practice there was a striking increase in royal prerogatives and royal influence. Whatever the reality of his relationship with his ministers, it was widely believed that no important decision could be taken without his agreement.[2] He had the overwhelming support of the rural populace, for whom loyalty to the Kabaka was the dominant influence. At the centre, in the Buganda government, he had the support of the neo-traditionalist leadership which had seized power during the deportation crisis. The latter established a powerful alliance with the Kabaka, and so with the Buganda populace which entrenched them in power.

[1] H. E. the Governor's address to the Great Lukiko, 14 Nov. 1954 (Entebbe, Govt. Printer, 1954).

[2] *Report of the Uganda Relationships Commission*, Chairman Lord Munster (Entebbe, Govt. Printer, 1961), para. 64. See also A. I. Richards, Epilogue, in L. Fallers (ed.) *The King's Men* (Oxford, 1964); *Desecration of my Kingdom*, by the Kabaka of Buganda (London, 1968); Low, *Buganda in Modern History*, ch. 5.

They had the support of the chiefs and a majority of the Lukiko. They were led by Michael Kintu, made Katikiro in 1955, and Amos Sempa, the Omuwanika. It became clear soon after the Kabaka's return that this dominant group were determined to maintain Buganda's traditional independence, and so would oppose any political change that invaded the kingdom's autonomy or their own power.

This was demonstrated first by the neo-traditionalists' rejection of the political parties that had appeared by 1955[1]. During the crisis the former had co-operated with the first political party to be formed, the Uganda National Congress (UNC); and the election of four UNC leaders to the Legislative Council by the Lukiko in 1955 was an indication of some tacit agreement. This rapprochement quickly came to an end, however, once the parties began to assert themselves in the Lukiko. Party members elected to the Lukiko then received rough treatment. In September 1956 E. M. K. Mulira, the leader of the Progressive Party, was charged in court with an attempt to bring the Buganda throne into disrespect because he had announced in public that under the 1955 Agreement the Kabaka was a constitutional monarch and could not expel or confirm members of the Lukiko. The leader of the Democratic Party was not permitted to take his seat in the Lukiko because he was a member of one of the East African High Commission organizations. By these and other actions the conservative neo-traditionalist element demonstrated their continued control of Buganda against political party rivals.

Second, the Buganda government and the Lukiko began to hesitate again about participation in the central government. Suspicion of the centre increased as the African representative members of the Legislative Council adopted an increasingly nationalist attitude, and questioned the separate treatment accorded to Buganda.[2] As self-government came closer this raised a new issue: that of relations between Buganda and the rest of the country in an independent Uganda. Fearing their subordination in a unitary state, the Ganda neo-traditionalists hesitated further. At the end of 1957, when two of the Ganda representatives resigned from the Legislative Council, the

---

[1] See pp. 80, 86–8 below for the formation of the parties.
[2] See pp. 89 sqq. below.

Buganda government refused to replace them.[1] From this point both the Lukiko and the Buganda government became increasingly hostile towards the protectorate government, and explicit in their rejection of the unitary state. The successive stages of this rejection stood out clearly. In March 1958 the Lukiko refused to proceed with direct elections for Buganda's Legislative Councillors until Buganda's position *vis-à-vis* a future central government, and the role of the Kabaka, had been decided. In May, when the Lukiko had already raised the idea of a federal government, the Lukiko Constitutional Committee announced that the Kabaka should be Head of the State of Uganda. In December the Lukiko forwarded a memorandum to the Queen requesting her to terminate the agreement. The re-election of Michael Kintu as Katikiro, following Lukiko elections in January 1959, confirmed the continued strength of the neo-traditionalists in the Buganda government and Buganda's refusal at this stage to co-operate with the rest of the country within a unitary state.[2]

By 1959 new political pressures upon the protectorate government from the districts outside Buganda had, however, changed the situation at the centre. By this time the new African representatives in the Legislative Council had become a vocal and successful opposition to the government. These developments, which demonstrate the manner in which the rest of Uganda had responded to Sir Andrew Cohen's proposals for a self-governing, unitary state, must now be considered.

Political change outside Buganda, 1952–1959

A suitable starting point from which to consider these political developments outside Buganda is the inquiry into local government carried out by Mr. C. A. G. Wallis in 1952. Up to that year there appeared to be little popular awareness of events beyond the level of the district. In the districts from which immigrant

---

[1] This was on the grounds that the governor, by appointing a Speaker to the Legislative Council, had departed from the 1955 Agreement that there would be no major constitutional change before 1961. The governor, Sir Frederick Crawford (who had succeeded Cohen in 1957), disagreed, his view being upheld by the Privy Council to which the Buganda government appealed.

[2] These events are best followed in Low, *Buganda in Modern History*, chaps. 6 and 7. See also the *Uganda Argus*, particularly the issues for 17 and 26 July, and 17 Dec. 1965; 5 Feb. 29 Mar., and 22 May 1958.

labour travelled to Kampala there must have been a considerable knowledge of Buganda itself. Parties of chiefs had also visited districts other than their own. Otherwise inter-district contacts were limited. Before 1952 there had been very little discussion outside official circles in the districts about the future political development of Uganda as a whole.[1] After 1952, however, the districts were drawn increasingly into the debate on constitutional change. Cohen's visits to different parts of the protectorate gave a larger number of people the opportunity to express their views on central government policies. When Wallis visited each district to discuss local government development with the standing committee of each district council his inquiry also raised questions concerning the future development of the central government. The government's local government proposals based on Wallis's report were subsequently discussed with the councils twice in 1954.[2] In 1954 also, Professor Hancock, in addition to his major discussions in Buganda, found time to visit the Western Kingdoms briefly to discuss their constitutional position, and to assist Bunyoro and Ankole leaders to formulate their ideas for constitutional change. In 1956 a senior civil servant toured the country to discuss the question of direct elections with the district councils, whose views were put to an informal committee of Legislative Council members in Kampala.[3] In 1959 the Wild Committee, set up to consider constitutional issues, toured each district.[4] All this promoted a new awareness of the centre.

Two new institutional links between the districts and the centre provided additional means of communication. The first was the Uganda National Congress (UNC); the second the African representative members of the Legislative Council, elected by the district councils.

---

[1] Of the chiefs however Wallis said in 1952, 'All the Standing Committees made it plain that they are bent upon reaching the status of a native state . . . and they believe that they will eventually supplant the Protectorate government . . .' Wallis *Report*, para. 12.

[2] Leg Co *Debates*, 23 Nov. 1953, p. 44, and 13 Apr. 1954, p. 7.

[3] Sessional Paper No. 4 of 1957–8. In 1956, when African representative members of Legislative Council objected to the decision to hold direct elections in Buganda alone in 1958, the governor appointed this committee to discuss the implications of direct elections for the whole country. See p. 91 below.

[4] The Wild Committee was set up in 1959 to consider the question of direct elections on a common roll in 1961, and related constitutional issues. See p. 94 below.

The UNC was founded in 1952 by the Ganda politician
I.K. Musazi and by Abu Mayanja, a young Muganda then an
undergraduate at Makerere College.[1] Its organization was based
largely on Musazi's earlier Federated Partnership of Uganda
African Farmers (FUAF) established in 1951, itself the successor to the UAFU. There were non-Ganda at the party's
first meeting, but the leadership was predominantly Ganda and
overwhelmingly Protestant. Nevertheless the leadership was
nationalist in its outlook, and conceived the UNC as a nationalist
party; its objectives were summed up in the slogan 'self- government now'.

The party's early strength emerged in Buganda, where it
appealed to the same economically and politically discontented
elements that had earlier supported the Bataka Party and the
UAFU, and where a network of branches was soon established,
many of them growing out of the FUAF. These branches had
few paid-up members but many sympathizers. The leaders
failed, however, to establish a working headquarters organization. The party lacked the funds and the full-time officials needed
to establish a viable, effective, party machine.

The UNC was at that stage potentially a country-wide party.
Musazi and Mayanja travelled frequently to the districts outside Buganda in 1952 and 1953, and in a number of places were
able to establish branches with an enthusiastic local leadership:
in particular in Lango, Toro, Teso, Acholi, Bugisu. Branch
chairmen travelled the districts. The UNC was unable, however,
to establish centralized control of its branches; and while it was
country-wide in its scope it did not produce a country-wide mass
movement. This failure can be attributed to three different
factors: the impact upon the UNC of the Buganda crisis of 1953
to 1955; the divisions within the party leadership; and the
emphasis placed upon local issues by branch leaders at district
level.

Although the deportation of the Kabaka was a tribal rather
than a national issue it was one on which the Ganda response
was unequivocal. The UNC could not therefore ignore it if they
wanted to keep a popular following in Buganda. Very quickly
therefore the UNC supported the demands for the Kabaka's

---

[1] For the UNC see M. Lowenkopf, *Political Parties in Uganda and Tanganyika*
(London, MA thesis, 1961); also Apter, *Political Kingdom;* D. A. Low, *Political
Parties.*

return. This assured them of popular support, but only by turning inwards into Buganda and so losing their pan-Ugandan focus. The popular support, moreover, did not survive because by 1955 the UNC had lost any claim to leadership of the Ganda populace to the neo-traditionalists and the Kabaka. The UNC thus lost its popular base in Buganda, although its national headquarters remained in Kampala. After 1955, moreover, the neo-traditionalists made it increasingly difficult for the party to function in Buganda.

The party suffered in a different way from the succession of personal disputes that from 1953 disrupted the central executive. These, which were primarily between the younger and more educated Ganda leadership and Musazi, led to a series of party conflicts, and in 1957 to the withdrawal of the younger element to form the United Congress Party when they failed to dislodge him from his office. This internal feuding minimized the executive's capacity to organize, and UNC branches consequently functioned with little direction from Kampala.

UNC branches in the districts, although they consistently raised nationalist issues such as self-government at their meetings, were on their part forced by circumstances to take up district issues and grievances. Thus in Busoga branch leaders challenged the government on local land grievances. In Bunyoro the UNC supported the 'Young Turks' ' move to make the Omukama a constitutional monarch and give greater power to a representative Rukurato. In Toro the UNC on the other hand opposed the proposals for the Queen Elizabeth National Park and backed the Omukama and Rukurato in their efforts to acquire a greater status for Toro. In Lango and Acholi they took up local grievances against chiefs and administration. This emphasis upon local issues increased the tendency for UNC branches to operate as independent autonomous units, since in no two districts were the immediate party objectives the same. As a result, although the UNC had a country-wide expression, it did not have a country-wide organization. This was demonstrated by the reactions to the protectorate government's land tenure proposals of 1955[1], which were vehemently rejected by every

---

[1] Following the recommendations of the East Africa Royal Commission 1953–5 the Uganda government put forward proposals for the introduction of individual land tenure in all districts. The proposals were published to elicit public views, but they were quickly withdrawn.

district except Kigezi (in Western Province). Although popular opposition to these proposals was country-wide, and although the UNC, in all districts where it was established, was prominent in that opposition, there was no country-wide campaign against the proposals. Each district acted independently.

The development of the UNC outside Buganda (and of the other parties when they followed) was closely linked with the local government system, which provided an important focus for political activity at district level. The provincial administration had, in the 1940s, made a cautious but genuine attept to democratize the African local governments in which the chiefs had hitherto been completely dominant.[1] A four-tier set of councils modelled on the Teso system had been gradually introduced into all districts at parish, sub-county, county, and district level, all including elected non-officials as well as the official members. At the *miruka* level the non-officials were elected by acclamation by the local taxpayers. Above this level each council acted as an electoral college for the council above. It was possible therefore for the unofficial elected by acclamation in his village to find his way to the district council through this process of indirect election; and a number did. The district council was not of course new. But whereas before the war it had been a council of county chiefs, by 1949 it included in all districts elected non-officials.

These councils had no statutory responsibilities. The provincial administration, moreover, retained a firm paternalistic control over them and their standing committees (of which the district commissioner was chairman). Nevertheless they were participating, through their standing committees, in the administration of their districts. The lower councils, moreover, had some important functions; in Teso, for example, the *miruka* councils adjudicated land disputes. Most important, lower councils (in contrast to those in Buganda) participated in the choice of chiefs (which later assumed greater significance). In addition they provided a focus for political activity. On the one hand the *saza* chiefs wished to acquire greater status and powers

---

[1] These developments can be followed in the Annual Reports of individual districts. See also Entebbe Archives, Notes on Native Administration and Political Development in Northern Provinces, 14 June 1947; and Leg Co *Debates*, 23 Nov. 1953, for an account of the development of the council system in the Eastern Province by the then Provincial Commissioner, T. Cox.

for themselves within the local government structure, and in several districts began to campaign for the appointment of a Paramount Chief.[1] On the other hand, the elected non-officials had begun by 1950 to chafe at their own lack of power, to question the dominant position of the *saza* chiefs, and to demand increased authority for the councils.

The lower councils in some districts, particularly in northern Uganda, attracted a good deal of local attention among peasant cultivators. In Lango in the late 1940s, for example, the village councils were reported as meeting every Sunday 'regardless of whether they have anything to discuss'. And the district commissioner at Lira in 1948, finding it difficult to deal with the elected members on the district council, considered that 'a lot has been sacrificed to the democratic principle' and that it was 'time efficiency and common sense had a look in'.[2]

The indirect elections provided an opportunity for hitherto unrepresented groups to establish a foothold for themselves in the district council, the only institution which at that time provided for popular political representation. This was all the more significant where there were strong internal cleavages within the district. In Ankole, for example, the Iru welcomed the elections as a means of participating in a local government that had hitherto been dominated by the Hima ruling class. Clan rivalries in Acholi and Bugisu, tribal rivalries in Bukedi, were channelled into competition for council representation. Perhaps most significant for future political developments, where strong religious cleavages existed within the district, they too stimulated competition for places in the councils.

By 1951 the elected members on the district councils were more representative of the peasant cultivators and the small traders and shopkeepers than their predecessors had been. In Lango District, for example, the leader and several members of the Lango branch of the UAFU had become councillors. These men brought new kinds of question to the council, particularly on economic grievances such as the monopolist position of the Indian cotton buyers and ginners. They challenged both the

[1] Wallis *Report*, para. 12.

[2] Ministry of Regional Administration Archives, C 183/3, District Commissioner, Lira, 14 Dec. 1948. By 1950 most district councils had a membership of at least 70. For a visitor's account of councils in Ankole and Teso, see Huxley, *Sorcerer's Apprentice*, pp. 200–1, 250.

adequacy and the dominant position of the chiefs, whom they insisted should be chosen from among the more educated section of the community. They also began to demand executive powers for the councils. The desire to participate in district affairs began consequently to exceed what the administration considered legitimate.

Where the UNC established a branch these councils, both at district and at lower levels, offered its district leaders a political forum. In certain districts the new UNC branch officials were already unofficial councillors. Whether this was the case or not they set out to find a local man at parish or divisional level who could put their case in the village council, raise local grievances and challenge the administration and the chiefs.[1] As a result, although the branch had few paid-up members, it acquired small groups of supporters and sympathizers scattered about the district who, having established themselves in the councils, used them as a political forum. The UNC branch was thus typically a small coterie of men, at the district headquarters, who maintained personal and informal contacts with groups of supporters throughout the district, and encouraged activity within the local councils. At the district level the group consisted of the more educated men in the community: some were teachers, others clerks and traders. At village level its supporters were the cultivators and small shopkeepers. These leaders and their supporters took up local issues and grievances, such as the use of unpaid labour by the chiefs, local government rules about famine granaries, or forest reserves. While they sometimes held large public rallies, the greater part of their activity took place in the market place and the parish councils.

This pattern of activity was particularly characteristic of the Northern Nilotic districts of Lango and Acholi, where the UNC had its most active branches. It was also to be found in parts of Eastern Province. In the Western Province, however, the local UNC leadership was less successful in building any grass roots organization, although it acted as a local pressure group within the district councils.[2]

---

[1] See, for example, Lango District Archives, Administrative Officers' Touring Reports, by County, 1950–60, *passim*.

[2] The evidence for the Nilotic districts is taken from fieldwork carried out in Lango and Acholi and interviews with early UNC leaders in those districts. Cherry

Thus in the mid-1950s a new kind of political activity was beginning to emerge at district level which was no less significant because restricted in its scope. This had certain similarities with the populist agitation that had grown in Buganda in the 1940s: it reflected dissatisfaction with the chiefs and with administrative control. But there were certain crucial differences. First, popular involvement was less intense. Outside Buganda, political agitation was not uniform and in some districts can have involved only a small section of the rural population. While the councils had produced a forum for debate on local matters, there was no organization of the peasantry similar to that built up by the Bataka Party in Buganda. Poorer communications, the absence of urban centres, the absence of the same intense economic grievances, the slower economic development, all help to explain this difference in scale. Second, the political agitation that began in this way was not inward-looking in orientation. The hostility towards the chiefs was in one sense a struggle against the richer men in the community. But this and the struggle with the administration were potentially nationalist in orientation. The UNC leaders who took up local issues were also nationally orientated. Thus in 1954 the Lango District UNC leaders condemned the idea of a multi-racial government as 'entirely abominable to the people of Uganda', and demanded a wholly African parliament in 1955.[1] A majority of councils similarly rejected multi-racial government. Third, there was no secessionist talk outside Buganda.

After a good deal of debate at both national and district level the protectorate government's local government proposals became law in January 1955.[2] The District Councils (District Administration) Ordinance transferred increased responsibilities for local services, particularly in agriculture, health and education, to the district councils; provided that those councils that wished might introduce direct elections of their unofficial members; and established an Appointments Committee elected by the council, which assumed responsibility for the appointment

Gertzel, *Party and Locality in Northern Uganda 1945–1962* (London, 1974). Evidence for other districts is taken from District Annual Reports (unpublished) and from Lowenkopf, *Political Parties*.

[1] Lango District Council files, Report of Meeting of UNC, Lira, 11 Dec. 1954.

[2] The legislation had been ready at the beginning of 1954, but was delayed at the request of the African representatives to enable them to scrutinize it. See p. 90 below.

of staff, including chiefs.[1] The Senior Executive Officer of each council was elected by the council. The councils thus acquired a good deal more power and patronage than they had previously enjoyed.

Not all districts adopted the ordinance; and, in those that did, no two adopted the same pattern: the local government franchise, the method of election, the chairmanship of the council, varied greatly from one district to another.[2] Nevertheless in all districts the district council assumed increased importance, and became a highly competitive arena. One result was that between 1955 and 1960 elected councillors actively sought further to enlarge their powers at the expense of the officials and the provincial administration. In all districts a good deal of energy was consequently absorbed during these years in the contest for power at district level.

The African representative members of Legislative Council, all of whom were *ex officio* members of their district councils, fully supported the demands for increased powers at district level. They carried the campaign into the Legislative Council where, for example, in 1958 they vigorously but unsuccessfully objected to the withdrawal of powers of appointment from the Appointments Committees.[3] These issues in the first instance however concerned district leaders, and the campaigns established an intermediary leadership between district and centre, a district political élite, small in numbers but wielding considerable influence.

It was at the district level, moreover, that the foundations of competitive party politics were laid. By 1956 the UNC was no longer the only party in the field. Two others had by this time been formed. The first was the Progressive Party (PP), formed in 1954 in Kampala by that small group of educated Protestant

---

[1] This power of appointment was withdrawn in 1958, against strong protests from Legislative District Councillors, on the grounds that there had been too much political interference in appointments. See Leg Co *Debates*, 5 May 1958. See also *Report of the Commission of Inquiry into Management of the Teso District Council* (Govt. Printer, Entebbe, Mar. 1958).

[2] Toro, Busoga, and Bukedi, for reasons of internal politics, refused to adopt the Ordinance, and remained under the 1949 legislation. The details will be found in the *Uganda Gazette*, 1955 and 1965, *passim*. Three councils, Madi, Teso, and Kigezi, immediately introduced an electoral college, or a special electoral college was set up at that level.

[3] Leg Co *Debates*, 5 May 1958.

Ganda who, as members of the 1953 Lukiko, had played such an important part in the Namirembe discussions. This party, which represented Protestant schoolmasters, richer farmers and merchants in Buganda, was formed as a reaction to the alleged communist sympathies of the UNC and against the dominant position of the neo-traditionalists in Buganda. Although it campaigned for support in the districts, and subsequently sponsored several candidates in the 1958 elections, the party did not emerge as a significant political force either in Buganda or in the rest of the country.

The second party, also formed in Buganda, was to become of much greater national significance. This was the Democratic Party, which grew out of the long-established religious divisions between Protestants and Roman Catholics. In 1955 Protestants controlled the leadership of both the UNC and the PP; they also enjoyed the dominant position in the Buganda government. Roman Catholics in Buganda began to fear that this Protestant ascendancy would be carried over into independent Uganda. They and the Roman Catholic hierarchy were also perturbed at the UNC's apparent communist leanings.[1] When the Catholic bishops failed to persuade the Anglican Bishop of Uganda to co-operate in the formation of a Christian Democratic party they supported Ganda Catholics in the formation of the DP. Although the party insisted that it was restricted neither to Catholics nor to Ganda, its original support was primarily from that grouping. It had little formal organization before 1958, relying instead on the Catholic Action organization to mobilize Catholic support in the districts, as it did at district level in response to local Catholic fears of discrimination by Protestant-dominated district councils. This activity increased as those councils assumed greater powers: and thus the Democratic Party was drawn increasingly into district politics, and particularly where, as in Kigezi District in Western Province, or Acholi in the north, there was a serious cleavage between Protestant and Catholic. By 1958, when Benedicto Kiwanuka, a Ganda

---

[1] See, for example, *A Communist Build Up in Africa* (1956), written by Father Tourigny, National Director of Catholic Action, Kampala. 'The religious authorities strongly disapprove of adhesion of Catholics to Congress although no direct condemnation has been issued yet by the hierarchy. The establishment of a UNC office in Cairo was one factor that stimulated this fear.' Quoted in Lowenkopf, *Political Parties*. See also Low, *Buganda in Modern History*, chap. 6.

Catholic lawyer, became president of the party, there were DP supporters in most councils; and in 1959 they won the Acholi District Council elections.

Finally the enhanced position of the district administrations and the increased political activity at that level increased the sense of district identity at a time when Buganda was asserting her right to a special status. UNC councillors in Lango had as early as 1955 used the district council to raise objections to specific protectorate government policies, particularly the question of multi-racial government raised by the appointment of an Asian minister in 1956. All councils, however, and both parties, grew increasingly suspicious of the autonomy enjoyed by Buganda. As the Ganda neo-traditionalists between 1957 and 1959 intensified their demands for a special status, the districts demanded greater powers for themselves. Only the Western Kingdom of Toro demanded a federal status; elsewhere, notwithstanding the growing demands for a district constitutional head who might meet the Kabaka (and other rulers) as an equal, the preference was for a unitary state. But there was nonetheless an increasing suspicion of Buganda, typified by the Lango District Council's answer to the Lukiko's proposal that the Kabaka should be King of Buganda. In a resolution passed in June 1958 that council, while deploring the Buganda Lukiko's behaviour because it produced a 'wide gap of hatred among the tribes', asserted that 'we shall maintain the wish to achieve a unitary state of self-government which shall not compel us to be under any hereditary ruler whether we like it or not.'[1] This reinforced the view of their own representative in Legislative Council, and generally of all that body's non-Ganda members.

The concept of a unitary state: the response of the Legislative Council, 1954–1959

Communication between the districts and the centre was maintained in the 1950s less by party leaders than by the African representative members who took their seats in the Legislative Council in February 1954.[2] They took a little time to find their feet in this new setting, but a helpful and fruitful relationship was established with the Asian and European rep-

[1] Lango District files, Report of meeting, June, 1958.
[2] See pp. 71–2 above.

resentatives within the new Representative Members' Organization that was set up. Although the Ganda had hitherto led the political debate in Uganda, it was not the Ganda members of the Legislative Council who assumed the most prominent role: that went to the non-Ganda, of whom the hard core soon appreciated the use to which they could put this forum to criticize government policies. By 1956 the leadership had been assumed by George Magezi of Bunyoro, John Babiiha of Toro, and Cuthbert Obwangor of Teso, all men with a strong district following. They owed their position not to any party affiliation but to their role as district representatives. At the same time, while they pressed the claims of their districts they, and the other representatives, were able to adopt a common front on national issues, such as the question of elections, and so provided parliamentary opposition to the government. One other newcomer to the council must also be mentioned: Milton Obote from Lango. Obote, having been working in Kenya for several years, where he had participated actively in Nairobi politics, returned to Lango in 1956. Although closely involved in UNC politics in Lango, he avoided being drawn into the district arena, awaiting his chance to move to the centre. At the end of 1957, when Lango's representative (who had been remarkably quiet in the Council) was persuaded to retire, he took his place. Within a short time he had assumed a prominent position in the legislature. The African members' first intervention occurred over the proposed local government draft legislation which was tabled in April 1954: they persuaded the government to delay the bill to allow further consideration of its contents by a committee of the Council, and for discussion with the districts. As a result the Dreschfield Committee, chaired by the Attorney-General, and including most of the African representative members, spent several weeks in 1954 touring the districts, discussing the draft legislation not only with the standing committees but also with councillors and at public meetings. Their inquiry led to several significant changes in the draft legislation, all of them giving the district councils greater authority.[1]

It was these legislative councillors also who expressed the opposition outside Buganda to the special treatment accorded to that kingdom. Immediately after the Kabaka's deportation in 1953

[1] Leg Co *Debates*, 13 Apr. 1954, and 12 Jan. 1955.

there had been signs of sympathy in other districts for him and Buganda; and it was perhaps only Buganda's reluctance to co-operate with the rest of the country that prevented the deportation from becoming a national issue. Members of the Legislative Council and the district councils did, however, object, as the Dreschfield Inquiry found, to the exclusion of Buganda from the proposed local government legislation of 1954. They were suspicious of this separate treatment; and when the terms of the Namirembe Agreement were published, and when these were followed by the 1955 Agreement, they directly challenged the degree of autonomy which was granted to Buganda.

The African representatives challenged three of Cohen's constitutional proposals: the appointment of an Asian minister, the introduction of direct elections in Buganda in advance of the rest of the country, and the decision that there should be no further fundamental constitutional changes until 1961. The appointment of an Asian minister raised the question of multi-racial government, to which there was general African opposition in the district councils as well as in Kampala. On this Cohen refused to give way, and in the end the criticism died down. In the event, however, the African members subsequently won their point that a common roll was the best protection of minority interests, and no overt representation for non-Africans was ever introduced.[1] They also challenged the decision to proceed with direct elections in Buganda and not the whole country, and the decision to halt further constitutional changes until 1961. As they pointed out, this had been agreed upon in the Namirembe negotiations, at which they had not been represented; and they demanded recognition of their right to participate in negotiations about the future of the country.

In January 1956 a motion demanding direct elections for the whole country was rejected by the Chief Secretary as 'inappropriate'.[2] This was followed in April by a statement from the governor, in which he attempted to meet these criticisms but proposed no changes in the constitutional timetable: direct elections would be held in the first instance in Buganda in 1957, and in the whole country in 1961. Instead of easing the situation this aroused strong opposition in the district councils, and from

---

[1] Leg Co *Debates*, 30 Sept. 1957.
[2] Leg Co *Debates*, 11 Jan. 1956.

the UNC spokesmen as well as from the legislative councillors. The latter, more united than they had been when they first entered the Legislative Council, were adamant in their rejection of this separate treatment. Having accepted the goal of a unitary state proposed by Cohen, they demanded uniform political treatment for the districts and Buganda. They were determined that direct elections should be held in the whole country; and, influenced by the recent constitutional proposals in Kenya, insisted that Uganda was more than ready for them. To forestall a collision in the Legislative Council the governor proposed, and the members accepted, that an informal Committee of Councillors, parallel to but separate from the joint committee of Buganda and protectorate government officials already set up to consider Buganda's elections, should also consider the proposals. The government subsequently accepted this committee's recommendations that direct elections for the next Legislative Council should be held in 1958 in all districts that wished to have them; and that the life of the Legislative Council should be extended to allow the necessary arrangements to be made.[1] In a visit to Uganda in October 1957 the Secretary of State announced that direct elections would take place throughout the protectorate in the following year.

This was an important victory for the African representative members. The decision undoubtedly owed not a little to Cohen's desire to push ahead with constitutional development as swiftly as possible, but by the time it was made he had been succeeded by Sir Frederick Crawford, and the successful conclusion of the inquiry owed as much to the African members' assertion of their right to participate in the decision-making at the centre. From this date onwards a new, more nationalist, tone could be discerned in their speeches and statements. Their acceptance of the concept of a unitary state, their rejection of any suggestion of special representation for non-African communities, and their demands for a timetable for self-government, all reflected this tone. Their major concern was not that self-government would not be forthcoming, but that the protectorate government would retreat from its policy of a unitary state, and that Buganda would be left in the dominant position.

---

[1] Sessional Paper No. 4 of 1957–1958; Leg Co *Debates*, 30 Apr., 7 Aug., and 30 Sept. 1957.

Their attitude was not in doubt: as Magezi put it, they wished to close the gap between Buganda and themselves,[1] and in the following two years they explicitly challenged the inconsistencies in government policy which, while directed at the establishment of a unitary state, yet conceded Buganda autonomy. In May 1958, in a reasoned but vigorous attack on the protectorate recognition of special status for Buganda, Milton Obote (who had taken his seat only two months earlier) raised the crucial question. Arguing that the development of the Kabaka's government as a provincial rather than a local government was inconsistent with the development of a unitary state, he asked:

If the government is going to develop this country on a unitary basis how on earth can (it) develop another state within a state? Does the government really think that when self-government comes to this country the State of Buganda will willingly give up the powers it has got now to join with other outlying districts or provinces? I do not think so. Already we have got troubles about the position of the Buganda government. It is a state within a state and the government must therefore make it perfectly clear that this country is not going to be developed on a unitary but on a federal basis.[2]

In November 1958 the first direct elections were held for the Legislative Council. Since Buganda refused to participate and Karamoja had been excluded in the original proposals, and since Bugisu and Ankole also, for reasons of internal politics, had refused to introduce direct elections, they took place in only ten districts. In those ten districts, however, the elections were highly successful, with enthusiastic campaigning and high polls.[3] Over the country as a whole 85 per cent of the registered voters voted; in Kigezi the figure was well over 90 per cent. Three parties put up candidates—the UNC, the PP, and the DP. Although candidates in most cases had a party affiliation, only in Lango was there anything of a party campaign where the UNC was particularly active and organized. In each district, notwithstanding party affiliations, the election was essentially between individuals.

[1] Leg Co Debates, 7 Aug. 1957, p. 36.
[2] Leg Co Debates, 6 May 1958, p. 79.
[3] A Report on the First Direct Elections to the Legislative Council of the Uganda Protectorate, by C. P. S. Allen, MVO, OBE, Supervisor of Elections (Entebbe, Govt. Printer, 1958).

Of the candidates elected four were affiliated to the UNC, one to the DP, and the others were Independents. Immediately after the Legislative Council elections, however, in December 1958, seven of the representative members, led by George Magezi of Bunyoro (who resigned his rather tenuous connections with the UNC) and William Rwetsiba (one of the two indirectly elected Ankole members) formed a new party, the Uganda People's Union (UPU). The UPU drew its support from the Western Kingdoms and parts of the Eastern Province; the UNC from the north and the east. By the end of 1958 therefore the non-Ganda were organized into three parties, the UNC, the DP, and the UPU, which derived support from the country as a whole, and all of which were represented in the Legislative Council.

The year 1958 marked an important watershed in Uganda's political development. The elections had aroused a good deal of popular interest and enthusiasm. The representatives in the Legislative Council could now rightly claim that they enjoyed a popular mandate and a popular base. The locus of power there-fore moved more definitely to the Council: the initiative moved to the African members. Buganda, however, remained outside the Council, and showed herself increasingly hostile to the African members, as the latter intensified their pressures upon the protectorate government to hasten the pace of political change.

The constitutional debate, 1959–1961

Although in 1959 the initiative had moved to the African members, the protectorate government did not appear willing to be hurried. While the final goal of self-government was not in doubt, the timing was. Sir Frederick Crawford, faced with Buganda's refusal to co-operate either with the protectorate government or with African leaders, appeared less anxious to hasten forward than his predecessor had been. A three-cornered debate therefore developed, from 1959 until 1961, between the non-Ganda (led by their Legislative Council members), the Ganda, and the protectorate government, on two issues: the pace of constitutional change; and the concept of a unitary state as enunciated by Cohen in 1953.

The first question was discussed by the Constitutional Committee set up after the 1958 elections. This committee (known as the Wild Committee) was permitted by its terms of reference to consider, in addition to the proposal for direct elections in 1961, a wide range of related constitutional questions, including the size and composition of the legislature and the future form of government. Although it was chaired by a senior civil servant, ten of the fifteen members were Africans, and of these the seven elected members of the Legislative Council played the most important role in its deliberations. The committee heard evidence during 1959 from all the district councils, as well as from the political parties and members of the public. Its majority recommendations undoubtedly reflected majority opinion throughout the country outside Buganda.

The Wild Report, published in December 1959, recommended that direct elections on a common roll, on what amounted to a universal franchise, should be held as soon as possible and no later than 1961. It rejected any special representation of non-African communities on the grounds that a common roll was the most effective means of safeguarding the minorities. It recommended also that the legislature should be enlarged to 82 members. A majority of the committee (including all the African elected councillors) also recommended the introduction, after the next elections, of a Council of Ministers chosen by the governor in consultation with the leader of the majority party and presided over by the latter as Chief Minister. On the future form of government the report found that a majority of people throughout the country preferred a unitary state. It proposed, however, that after the elections a conference of elected representatives and others should consider this issue, with the assistance of a constitutional expert invited for the occasion.

This therefore was the position that the greater part of the country had reached in 1960. On the pace of constitutional development they wanted internal self-government the following year, elected by people voting on a universal franchise on a common roll. And they wanted a unitary state. That this reflected widespread views, and not only those of the Legislative Council, was confirmed later that year when, in June 1960, at a meeting of Katikiros and Secretaries-General in Kampala, no one supported the Katikiro of Buganda's proposal for a federal constitution.[1]

Buganda's attempt on that occasion to win support for a federal position indicated how far she had gone in the opposite direction. Following her withdrawal from the Legislative Council in 1958, the Buganda government had refused in 1959 to participate in the Wild Committee unless questions concerning Buganda's future position were agreed upon her own terms. While the Lukiko discussed both withdrawal from the protectorate and the establishment of a federal government, in December 1959 the Buganda government announced that Buganda's aim was a federal government.

The Ganda objected to the Wild Committee for the same reason that they had refused to enter the Legislative Council, had feared a federation in 1953, and twenty years earlier had opposed the idea of closer union: their intense fear that Buganda would lose her political identity as part of a larger state.[2] The strength of this feeling was demonstrated by the emergence of a populist movement reminiscent of the Bataka movement of the late 1940s. The Uganda National Movement was formed in February 1959 by a group of relatively little-known Ganda, some of whom were acknowledged associates of the Kabaka and the neo-traditionalists. They were opposed to the constitutional committee and the proposed Education Bill then under debate. They were soon joined by most of the Ganda party politicians, including E. M. K. Mulira, Dr. Muwazi and Godfrey Binaisa, who had come to the conclusion that only by joining the neo-traditionalists could they hope to achieve political influence. Only the DP, under Benedicto Kiwanuka, refused to join. The movement's leaders failed to obtain support outside Buganda, but in March they successfully launched a boycott of non-African trade within Buganda. This spread rapidly through the countryside and within a short period had forced the greater number of Asian traders out of the rural areas. Intimidation and violence, the destruction of buildings, and slashing of coffee-trees became widespread. The protectorate government declared

[1] Low, *Buganda in Modern History*, p. 207.

[2] The immediate reason given by Buganda was her argument that direct elections on a common roll raised the question of citizenship which should be left until after independence. On the more general issues see D. A. Low, *The Mind of Buganda: documents of the modern history of an African kingdom* (London, 1971).

Buganda a disturbed area, and proscribed the movement; it reappeared immediately in a new guise.[1] Although six of its leaders were arrested and deported at the end of May, the movement maintained its momentum. Without leadership, a popular organization functioned throughout the countryside with some 200 so-called 'mayors' collecting funds and issuing instructions in the villages. The boycott was completely effective.[2]

The protectorate government believed the Buganda government was implicated: the Katikiro made no formal call to stop the disorder until April, by which time the initiative lay completely with the movement and two ministers were financial contributors to the vernacular paper which supported the boycott.[3] The Kabaka's government found it 'extremely difficult' to make a 'complete' condemnation of the movement.[4] In July, however, after pressure from the protectorate government and the threat to cut financial assistance, the Kabaka addressed a special meeting of the Lukiko, calling for an end to the violence; and the Buganda ministers called on the chiefs to exert their influence to restore order in the countryside. Gradually the disturbances ceased, although sporadic violence continued and parts of the kingdom remained a disturbed area until the middle of 1960. But the movement demonstrated the strength of the neo-traditionalists in Buganda, and the popular support behind the official opposition to any constitutional reforms that encroached upon Buganda's autonomy.

Faced with the situation, the protectorate government reaffirmed its resolve to lead Uganda to self-government by appropriate stages. In his speech opening the Legislative Council in February 1960 the governor announced that the British government had accepted the Wild Committee's recommendations for direct elections on a common roll as early as could be arranged in 1961, as well as for a majority of non-official ministers in the Executive Council. They did not, however, agree to a universal franchise, or to responsible government, which they believed

---

[1] First as the Uganda Freedom Movement, then the Uganda Freedom Convention, and finally the Uganda Freedom Union.

[2] *Uganda Argus*, 16 Feb. and 2 Mar. 1959. F. Welbourn, *Religion and Politics in Uganda 1952–1962* (Nairobi, 1965). 'Epilogue' by A. Richards in Fallers (ed.), *The King's Men*; Low, *Buganda in Modern History*, pp. 156–8.

[3] Quoted by Richards, *King's Men*, pp. 371–2.

[4] *Uganda Argus*, 9 July 1959.

would at this stage be premature. The Executive Council would continue to be advisory to the governor, who would still preside.[1]

On the question of a unitary state the governor now appeared to hesitate. As early as October 1957 the Secretary of State (when he announced that direct elections would be held throughout the country in 1958) had publicly affirmed the British government's intention that the prestige and dignity of the rulers should be preserved in any future constitutional arrangements.[2] Re-affirming this pledge in February 1960, Sir Frederick Crawford announced the government's intention of setting up a commission to inquire into the question of the relationships of the various parts of Uganda with the centre. Clearly the form of the future government was now open for discussion.

This decision, as well as the knowledge that direct elections were now in the offing, provoked a new phase in party activity. The African elected members, deeply offended at the government's rejection of the majority recommendations in the Wild Report, and alarmed at the apparent capitulation to the Buganda government, responded by merging their separate organizations to form a new party. In March 1960 the UNC and UPU members formed the Uganda People's Congress (UPC), with Milton Obote as President and George Magezi as Secretary-General.[3] A final split in the UNC in August 1959 had left Obote and Abu Mayanja (now returned to Uganda) in charge of the 'Obote wing' which retained the support of all UNC branches in Northern and Eastern Uganda. When Mayanja became a minister in the Kabaka's government in Janary 1960 Obote was left in control of the only effective wing of the UNC. The UPC was thus the lineal descendant of the UNC, inheriting its nationalist mantle as well as a good deal of local grass-roots support built up by district leaders, especially in Lango and Acholi. The extent of this support had been demonstrated in Lango as recently as January 1960, when the UNC had won an overwhelming victory in the first fully direct elections to the Lango District Council.[4] The UPC also inherited the UPU's

[1] Leg Co *Debates*, 23 Feb. 1960.
[2] Leg Co *Debates*, Oct. 1958.
[3] *Uganda Argus*, 10 Mar. 1960. The sole DP legislative councillor, Mr. G. Oda, remained outside, although he co-operated within the Elected Members' Organization.
[4] The UNC won 38 seats, the DP one seat. One seat went to an Independent.

following in the Western Kingdoms. Although this was based more on the personal leadership of the former UPU members of the Legislative Council than on a long-established district organization, it was no less significant in its extent, as local government elections in Bunyoro and Ankole later that year also demonstrated.[1] The UPC thus brought the non-Ganda districts together.

By 1960 the DP, although it had only one member in the Legislative Council, had also expanded its activities at district level and had begun to establish a more militant national organization. Its success in the Acholi District Council elections in 1959, and subsequently in Ankole and later Kigezi, demonstrated that it too had grass-roots support outside Buganda.[2] It also retained a minimum but significant Catholic support within Buganda, which gave it a more genuine countrywide following than the UPC.

Both parties were, however, constrained at this point in their efforts to develop a centralized party machine by the earlier political developments at district level. The political rivalry within the new district councils had after 1955 in a number of them produced serious local tensions. In Teso in 1958, for example, factional cleavages between north and south seriously interfered with the work of the Appointments Committee and the selection of district officials, including chiefs. The protectorate government intervened to transfer power over appointments from the Appointments Committee to an Appointments Board directly under the control of the governor.[3] In Bugisu and Bukedi there were serious riots in 1960 which could be traced back to internal cleavages and resulting opposition to the chiefs.[4] All councils were also seeking greater powers for themselves, symbolized by the demands for a constitutional district head. Although only Toro and Bugisu supported the idea of a federal state before the Munster Commission in 1961, every district was anxious to improve its status and its bargaining powers in relation to Buganda.

---

[1] In Bunyoro the UPC won 29, the DP 11 seats; in Ankole the DP 36 seats, UPC 28.
[2] In Kigezi in January 1961 both parties won 24 seats.
[3] Report of the Commission of Inquiry into the Management of the Teso District Council March 1958 (Entebbe, Govt. Printer, 1958).
[4] Report of the Commission of Inquiry into Disturbances in the Eastern Province, 1960 (Entebbe, Govt. Printer, 1960).

Local politicians had built up their support at district level on the basis of their position over such issues, and to the extent that they were associated with either the UNC or the DP at the district level they committed their branches to a particular line of action. Thus when the UPC and the DP began consciously to organize throughout the country, both parties, if they wished to retain and increase grass-roots support, were constrained to support the local branch leadership in the stand it had taken on district issues. The district leaders were to this extent in a strong bargaining position. The central leadership of both the UPC and the DP successfully established itself over the whole country, and began to co-ordinate the party at the national level. But in doing so it had to work through a district leadership, and therefore to support that leadership on specific issues. The district branches were consequently able to retain a good deal of independence of action.

Although political activity outside Buganda increased greatly at this point, events in Buganda continued between 1960 and 1961 to dominate the political scene. The growing support for the political parties outside Buganda increased Ganda neo-traditionalists' unwillingness to co-operate with the rest of the country. In August 1960 the Buganda government boycotted the registration of voters, with the result that only 4 per cent of those qualified put their names on the registers. Violence flared up again in the Ganda countryside; and an ugly demonstration against politicians and political parties took place in the Lukiko, when demonstrators invaded the chamber and ejected members thought to have supported the registration of voters.[1] The DP, and particularly its president, Benedicto Kiwanuka, were the special target of attack since that was the only party that had resisted the boycott, and the only party active in Buganda. At the same time talks in London between a Buganda Constitutional Committee and the Secretary of State failed to produce any agreement. The Buganda government insisted that the future form of government must be settled before any elections were held; the Secretary of State insisted that elections and the Relationships Commission should proceed. The tumultuous welcome given to the Kabaka on his return from London in September demonstrated the popular support for both him and

[1] *Uganda Argus*, 28 Aug. 1960.

the neo-traditionalists' cause. And in October, in reply to the Secretary of State, the Lukiko forwarded a long, carefully argued, memorandum to the Queen announcing their wish to terminate the Uganda Agreement.[1] Although in the following two months the Buganda government appeared to alter its views, and the Kabaka himself counselled patience, on 31 December 1961 the Lukiko, under the influence of the extreme neo-traditionalist element, declared Buganda's secession from Uganda.[2]

The Lukiko's declaration of secession made no difference to the relationships between the two governments, except that the Lukiko no longer submitted its resolutions for the governor's approval, and the protectorate government maintained that they had no legal effect. The governor ignored the secession. In January Lord Munster and his colleagues began their inquiry. In March, notwithstanding Buganda's refusal to participate, the general election took place for 82 seats for a new national assembly.

The 1961 election was undoubtedly a party election.[3] Although seven parties put up candidates, only the UPC and the DP covered the whole country, and the election was a straight fight between them. Neither party had a country-wide machine, but both opened branches in most towns in the protectorate; and all candidates had the support of their party's district branch. There was a good deal of campaigning, although most candidates favoured small meetings rather than large rallies. Within Buganda the UPC put up candidates in only 7 of the 21 constituencies (in addition to the three Kampala seats), and did not campaign intensively. The DP, which contested all the Buganda seats, suffered considerable intimidation and opposition, which prevented all save 3 per cent of the registered voters from going to the polls. But that 3 per cent won them the election. The UPC won a majority of the votes, 494,959 against the DP's 415,718. But the DP's victory in Buganda, where they won 20 of the 21 rural constituencies, gave them 43 seats against the UPC's 35. Of the nine specially elected members chosen by the new Legislative Council sitting as an electoral college, six were DP

---

[1] Quoted in full in Apter, *Political Kingdom*, Appendix.

[2] *Uganda Argus*, 1 Jan. 1961.

[3] *A Report on the General Election to the Legislative Council of the Uganda Protectorate held in March 1961* by R. C. Peagram, Supervisor of Elections (Entebbe, Govt. Printer, 1961).

and three UPC. Benedicto Kiwanuka thus took his party into the government, becoming Leader of the House, and in July Chief Minister. Obote became Leader of the UPC Opposition, whose greater parliamentary experience enabled them vigorously to attack the new government.

The Report of the Relationships Commission, which had proceeded with its inquiry over the same period notwithstanding Buganda's refusal to co-operate, was published in June.[1] The commission rejected the possibility of secession for Buganda. Recognizing, however, that the kingdom already enjoyed what was virtually a federal relationship,they recommended that this continue. Uganda should become a single democratic state with a strong central government with which Buganda should have a federal relationship. If the Lukiko were directly elected, Buganda should be allowed the option of indirect elections for the National Assembly. The Western Kingdoms should be given a semi-federal relationship which entrenched the position of their rulers. The report also recommended that a referendum should be held on the 'lost counties'—the areas in dispute between Buganda and Bunyoro—before independence.[2]

The Munster recommendation offered the Kabaka's government a way out of an impasse which they had by this time recognized. Buganda had received no backing for her secessionist stand either from the other kingdoms or from other countries which she had approached. In June 1961, moreover, the protectorate government had issued the report on its inquiry into Buganda finances, which indicated clearly the financial difficulties into which that government had sunk.[3] Moreover, from early 1961 the Kintu government found itself under fire within Buganda, both from political party leaders and from a new populist organization—*Mwoya gwa Gwanga*—to implement secession or resign. Finally the Buganda government was deeply opposed to the DP and to the thought of Kiwanuka, a *mukope* (peasant), in power in Entebbe. This last situation pointed the way to a rapprochement with the UPC, who were equally anxious to find a means of toppling the DP government, and whose leaders

---

[1] *Report of the Uganda Relationships Commission, 1961*, Chairman Lord Munster, (Entebbe, Govt. Printer, 1961).
[2] See pp. 104–5 below.
[3] The Watts Report, 1961 (mimeo).

had been notably discreet in their approach to the problems of the Agreement Kingdoms and the rulers. Thus, notwithstanding Ganda opposition to political parties, Obote and the UPC, equally anxious with the Kabaka to eject the DP from power, were able to reach a rapprochement with Buganda.[1] Obote agreed to support Buganda's constitutional demands—particularly for indirect elections to the National Assembly—in return for the kingdom's return to the centre and acceptance of a single central government. Thus Buganda took her place in London for the September constitutional conference.

Self-government and independence, 1961–1962

The conference[2] reached swift agreement on the Munster recommendations for the structure of the future government: the Legislative Council would, at internal self-government, become a unicameral legislature of 82 elected members, directly elected (save from Buganda) on a universal suffrage. Nominated members would disappear, although the nine specially elected members would be retained. The Cabinet would be drawn from the majority party, presided over by the leader of that party as prime minister and responsible to the National Assembly. Under the internal self-government constitution, which would come into effect on 1 March 1962, the governor would act on the advice of the prime minister, except in the exercise of his reserve powers. The date for full independence was agreed as 9 October 1962.

There was less agreement on the Munster recommendations concerning the relationship between the kingdoms, and particularly Buganda, and the central government. Kiwanuka and the DP strongly resisted the proposal that Buganda should be permitted to elect her members to the National Assembly through the Lukiko. The understanding reached between the Kabaka's government and the UPC, however, ensured the conference's majority support for the Munster proposals, in spite of Kiwanuka's and the DP's strong objections to indirect elections. Buganda obtained virtually all she asked. The conference agreed that she should be in a federal relationship with the centre, and that the constitution should define her exclusive legislative

[1] *Uganda Argus*, 18 and 19 Sept. 1961.
[2] *Report of the Uganda Constitutional Conference, 1961*, Cmnd. 1523 (London, HMSO, 6161).

powers, which would include all matters concerning the kabakaship and her traditional institutions. Provision was made for a Buganda police force and for a High Court of Buganda. Provided that the Lukiko was directly elected, Buganda's twenty one representatives to the first National Assembly should be indirectly elected.

The conference left several crucial issues unresolved, including the question of the future head of state and of the 'lost counties'. Nevertheless the constitutional proposals opened the way for Buganda to participate once again in the central government. The first step was taken in February 1962, when direct elections were held to the Lukiko, in which the DP was overwhelmingly defeated by a new Ganda movement, the *Kabaka Yekka*.

Kabaka Yekka (KY) had been formed in the middle of 1961. At that time all loyalist Ganda had been intensely concerned at the failure to secure guarantees for the future safety of Buganda and the kabakaship. The Lukiko's secession move had failed, and both the neo-traditionalists and the politicians had demonstrated their inability to provide an alternative. The March 1961 elections had not only shown the support in the rest of the country for the political parties; they had put the DP and the Roman Catholics into power. The opposition to the political parties left a political vacuum in Buganda. Faced with this situation, a group of Ganda not immediately connected with either the Kabaka's government or the leading politicians decided to organize a new movement to fill that vacuum. At a meeting in Kampala in June the organizers' appeal for support from all Ganda who had not taken part in the March elections and who supported the Kabaka as the 'only ruler of Buganda' won an immediate response; and *Kabaka Yekka* ('Kabaka Alone') came into being.[1]

The movement brought together the many strands in the Ganda leadership: the neo-traditionalists in the Buganda government (which gave the movement its support for the elections); the leaders of the former National Movement, some of whom were now openly seeking to oust the Kabaka's ministers from office; and all the Ganda politicians, including Mulira

[1] Richards, 'Epilogue', loc. cit. C. Gertzel, 'How Kabaka Yekka Came to Be', *Africa Report*, Oct. 1964; I. R. Hancock, 'Patriotism and Neo-traditionalism in Buganda: the Kabaka Yekka movement, 1961–2', *J. Af. History*, 11, 3 (1970), 419–34.

Luyimbazi Zake, Godfrey Binaisa, and Abu Mayanja, who saw this as the compromise necessary to ensure Buganda's participation in the national scene. In December the movement announced the formation of an alliance with the UPC, who agreed not to put up candidates for the Lukiko elections. The February election was therefore a straight fight between KY and the DP in which KY won an overwhelming victory, taking 65 of the 68 seats.

For the politicians who aligned themselves with the traditionalists in KY the issue was primarily that of unity, which was the essential prerequisite for independence and for political stability. The past popular antagonism both to the central government and the political parties meant that only through an alliance such as that between KY and UPC could the Ganda be drawn back into the mainstream of political events. For the Ganda voters, however, the issue was undoubtedly the kabakaship and loyalty to the throne, against a DP characterized as its enemy. The victory for KY was in this respect a further victory for the neo-traditionalists. The new Lukiko was therefore still Ganda-oriented; and for this reason it posed possible difficulties for the future integration of Buganda with the rest of the country.

The KY victory determined the composition of the new government formed after the national elections in April. Obote's UPC won a comfortable victory over the DP outside Buganda; the alliance secured them a further 21 seats. In May 1962 therefore Obote was sworn in as head of a UPC–KY government which had a majority of 34 over the DP in the National Assembly.[1]

In the year between the first constitutional conference and independence Uganda leaders faced a number of issues that had been left undecided by that conference and the solutions for which were not easily found in time for the second constitutional conference in June 1962. The first and most intractable concerned the 'lost counties'—that area which had been transferred from Bunyoro to Buganda in the 1890s in return for the latter's support of the British Administration against the Omukama Kabarega. The Nyoro had never accepted the finality of that transfer; and a deep sense of bitterness had remained at the continued refusal of the protectorate government to return the

---

[1] The final position in the National Assembly after the election of the specially elected members was: UPC, 43; KY, 24; DP, 24.

disputed area, as well as at the treatment of Nyoro in those counties by the Ganda. The Munster Report urged the necessity of reaching a solution before independence; and recommended a referendum in at least those two counties in which the Nyoro were in an overwhelming majority. Buganda's refusal to accept this procedure made it impossible, however, for the September Conference to reach any agreement, and the Secretary of State had compromised by appointing a Commission of Inquiry: a decision which displeased both Ganda and Nyoro, although for different reasons. (The UPC's apparent support for Buganda on this issue lost it both its seats in Bunyoro in the 1962 election.) Nor did the recommendaton of the Molson Report (published in May after the elections)[1] that the two predominantly Nyoro counties should be returned to Bunyoro provide a solution, for Buganda obstinately refused to accept it. At the second constitutional conference in June 1962, faced with an impasse that the UPC could not break, the Secretary of State therefore announced that there would be no immediate transfer of territory; that the administration of the two counties would be transferred to the central government; and that not less than two years after independence a referendum would be held in those counties in which the electorate would be given the opportunity to express their choice as to which administration they preferred. Uganda therefore moved to independence with the issue unresolved.[2]

A number of other claims upon the central government were dealt with before the final June Conference agreed to the independence constitution. The Western Kingdoms (led by Toro) won their demand for full federal status. This defined more precisely the kingdoms' full control over their own traditional institutions, particularly the office of ruler. The District of Busoga, accorded the title of Territory, was granted a similar status.[3] The claim of the Sebei for a separate district of their own, apart from Bugisu, was accepted,[4] whereas the Baamba-Bakonjo

---

[1] *Report of a Commission of Privy Counsellors on a Dispute between Buganda and Bunyoro'* Cmnd. 1719 (London, HMSO, 1962).

[2] *Report of the Uganda Independence Conference 1962*, Cmnd. 1778 (London, HMSO, 1962). Both Buganda and Bunyoro dissented from this decision.

[3] Constitution of Uganda (Statutory Instrument No. 2175 of 1962) Schedules 2-5.

[4] *Exchange of Dispatches between His Excellency the Governor and the Secretary of State for the Colonies concerning the creation of Sebei District* (Entebbe, Govt. Printer, 1962).

claim to a separate district was rejected, thus leaving a source of serious difficulty for the future.[1] Generally, in the final settlement the districts improved their status and their powers as local government authorities. Those districts which wished to do so were permitted to establish the office of constitutional head; and were allowed to style up to four of the chairmen of district council committees as ministers. The Local Administrations Ordinance of February 1962, which provided for local government in the independent state, therefore acknowledged the significance of the district as the political base, and the district at independence enjoyed significant political resources.

---

[1] *Report of the Commission of Inquiry into the Recent Disturbances amongst the Baamba-Bakonjo People of Toro* (Entebbe, Govt. Printer, Oct. 1962).

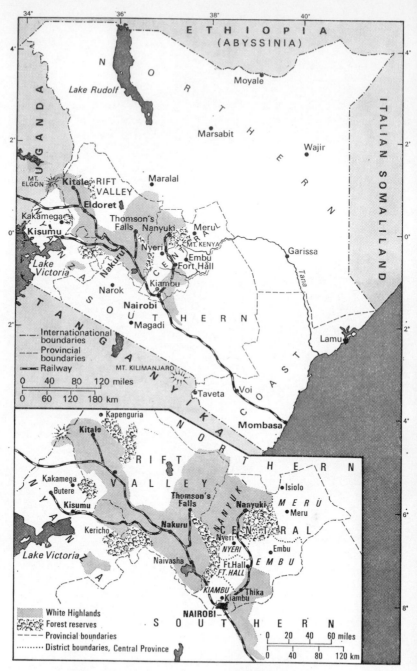

MAP 2. KENYA: GENERAL AND ADMINISTRATIVE, 1956-7.

II

KENYA: FROM 'WHITE MAN'S COUNTRY' TO KENYATTA'S STATE 1945–1963*

GEORGE BENNETT AND ALISON SMITH

WITHIN twenty years of the ending of the Second World War, Kenya—along with almost all the British-ruled territories in tropical Africa—was to become an independent state, with a government which in a real measure owed its inception to the choice of some five million mostly peasant African people. But in 1945 the most sanguine revolutionary would hardly have foretold this.

In Kenya as elsewhere change was in the air, but it did not appear as the kind of change initiated from below. There were wider visions of the possibilities of government action on the economy, of the extension into the colonial field—embodied in the Colonial Development and Welfare Acts of 1940 and 1945— of the state initiative which had characterized the conduct of the war, and which would banish for ever the spectre of famine and economic depression. There was at the same time a more purposeful emphasis on constitutional advance, but it was constitutional advance at a pace to be carefully regulated from above: gradually widening representation on the local

* The original draft of this chapter was received from the late George Bennett in 1965. By 1968, when the revision of the volume was undertaken, it had inevitably become outdated in its approach, particularly on account of the further evidence and important new publications then available; but the author's hopes of embarking on a far-reaching recasting of the draft were cut short by his untimely death early in 1969. The task of revision accordingly fell upon myself. In undertaking it I have been greatly helped by the advice of others more deeply versed in Kenya politics than I—in particular Dr. Cherry Gertzel, Dr. John Lonsdale, and Professor Keith Sorrenson—as well as by George Bennett's own notes (including especially press references) and other writings. Of the latter, the later chapters of his short *Kenya: a political history* (London, 1963) gave much useful detail of political manoeuvring and constitutional change which it has therefore been possible to omit from this revision, thus making room for a more analytical assessment. I would like to hope that it still retains something of the stimulating and vigorous approach of his own original text. The chief responsibility for its shortcomings remains my own.—A. S.

legislature; the building up of responsibility through local government; a cautious extension of approved trade unionism. These gradualist principles were soon hustled out of recognition.

But in Kenya the revolution was a double one. It involved not only the speeding up beyond all expectation of the process of devolution, but the radical re-structuring of power within the colonial territory. The old metropolitan preoccupation of the inter-war years with avoiding at all costs outright settler rebellion crumbled under the pressure of African protest and demand, and of new and wider stategic imperatives in a period when the balance of world power was dramatically changing. The 'white man's country' of European settler imagination gave place to an African state—a prospect which as late as 1948 Kenya's first post-war governor had dismissed as fantastic, 'as practicable a proposition as it would be to set up in the United States an entirely autonomous, self-governing Red Indian Republic'.[1]

Kenya's five million inhabitants included not only widely differing indigenous societies, from the pastoralists of the semi-desert regions to the densely settled agriculturalists of the Central Province and Nyanza and the urban workers of Nairobi and Mombasa, but also powerful and articulate immigrant minority groups of Europeans and Asians. Among the African agriculturalists the raising of the inter-war ban on African production of profitable cash crops, such as cotton, coffee, and pyrethrum, had opened the way for the limited expansion of a new class of well-to-do African farmers, both in the highlands and the rich agricultural lowlands of Nyanza Province.

There were indeed signs at the end of the war—more evident than elsewhere in East Africa—that the political ground was moving. Kenya was unique in British East Africa in having had, even before 1939, some overt African political activity directed towards the centre of power. As early as 1929 an African political body, the Kikuyu Central Association (KCA), had put forward a demand for an eventual African majority on the Legislative Council.[2] A number of leading KCA members were detained on

---

[1] Speech at Nakuru, Nov. 1948, quoted in Electors' Union Memorandum 65/EU/49, EEMO/EU Box 1/3, Rhodes House, Oxford.
[2] *Historical Survey of the Origins and Growth of Mau Mau*, Commissioner, F. D. Corfield, Cmnd. 1030 (London, HMSO, 1960), p. 42. Cp. Letter from Kenyatta to *Manchester Guardian*, 26 Apr. 1930, printed in *Government and Politics in Kenya*, ed. Cherry Gertzel, M. Goldschmidt, and D. Rothchild (Nairobi, 1970), p. 197.

the outbreak of war, but had been released in 1943. In October 1944 the first African member, the Kikuyu Eliud Mathu, was nominated to the Legislative Council,[1] and a fresh political group, the Kenya African Union,[2] was formed to support him. There was also a spectacular expansion of the African press. In the Independent Schools movement, which was most active in the Central Province, there was a massive African educational initiative that was giving concern as well as commanding respect. It was widely realized, moreover, at least in official circles, that the return to civilian life of the many who had served in the forces, particularly overseas, would bring enhanced expectations; and that these would encounter some very considerable economic problems, including the over-use and consequent exhaustion of land, and the shortage of housing to cope with the influx of population to the towns.[3] Nairobi's African population grew from 40,000 in 1938 to more than 95,000 in 1952; already by 1948 half of Kenya's African wage labour was non-agricultural.[4]

---

[1] Eliud W. Mathu, 1910– . One of the first pupils at the Alliance High School, Nairobi, then a teacher; at Fort Hare 1933–4; Exeter University College 1938–9; Balliol College, Oxford 1939–40; Principal of Kikuyu Kar'inga School, 1943; nominated Member of Kenya Legislative Council 1944–57; Member of Executive Council 1952.

The changes in the composition of the central legislature and executive during the period covered by this chapter, which are numerous and complicated, have been tabulated in Appendix 2. Mbiyu Koinange claims that Mathu was selected because the colonial government was piqued by his own stratagem of approaching the Colonial Secretary (Oliver Stanley) direct. The appointment was in theory made on the basis of voting by the Local Native Councils, which showed a substantial majority for Koinange. *The People of Kenya Speak for Themselves* (Kenya Publication Fund, Detroit, 1955), p. 8.

[2] Formed under this name in October 1944, it changed its name under government pressure to the Kenya African *Study* Union a month later; but reverted to the original title at its second Annual Delegates' Council in February 1946. The KCA was believed to number about 7,000 members at the time of its proscription in 1940. Corfield *Report*, p. 48. Koinange says that KAU (the date is not clear) had 150,000 members in 50 branches, Koinange, *People of Kenya*, p. 10.

[3] *Report of the Sub-Committee on Post-War Employment of Africans* (Nairobi, Govt. Printer, 1943), pp. 5–6. Some 97,000 Kenyans served in the East African fighting forces. Among those deeply influenced in their political views by service overseas were Waruhiu Itote and Bildad Kaggia. In March 1948 the government estimated that there were 22,000 people in the African locations of Nairobi who could not possibly find proper accommodation, 4,000 of these being completely homeless. Legislative Council *Debates*, 20 Mar. 1948, col. 314.

[4] *Report of the Committee on African Wages*, Chairman F. W. Carpenter (Nairobi, Govt. Printer, 1954), Table III, p. 9.

The outward political scene

Nevertheless to the outside world the dominant picture was one of prosperity, and of the apparent continuance of the European pre-eminence which had from the beginning characterized the country's political life. The European settlers had not, indeed, gained all that they had hoped out of the altercations of the 1930s,[1] but their enthusiastic participation in the management of the economy during the war had greatly strengthened their position in practice. As members of the Agricultural Production and Settlement Boards, they had contributed largely to the great boost in agricultural output. Their hold on the reserved 'White Highlands' seemed unchallengeable, and in the three years following the end of the war some 8,000 white immigrants came out to join them, actively encouraged by the British government. Their centre, Nairobi, had become the effective capital of East Africa, while the leadership of their party, the Electors' Union,[2] by a business man, Alfred (later Sir Alfred) Vincent, indicated the growing importance of the commercial element among them. They held twelve of the nineteen unofficial seats on the Legislative Council.

This was the situation which Sir Philip Mitchell inherited when he was appointed as governor by the Conservative Colonial Secretary, Oliver Stanley, in 1944. Mitchell had already a distinguished record in East Africa: he had been Sir Donald Cameron's right hand man on 'native administration' in Tanganyika, and had spent five years as governor of Uganda; during the war he had for a time been responsible for co-ordinating the needs of the Middle East from East Africa. More immediately he came from the governorship of Fiji. His aims were closely in tune with the current metropolitan ethos, in some ways even more closely when in 1945 a Labour government came into office. He believed firmly in the primacy of the economic base, in tackling the agrarian problem and in consolidating Kenya's wartime prosperity by internal administrative action and external co-ordination—in particular by continuing the inter-territorial economic co-operation of the war years. From his Fiji experience

---

[1] See chap. vi in the second volume of this *History*.
[2] Formed in 1944, this in effect superseded the Convention of Associations of the inter-war period.

he brought—for the first time as a theory to East Africa—the concept of multi-racialism as a positive principle of government. Further, he was anxious to combat the caprice and frustrations of colonial government through the Legislative Council by introducing something like ministerial responsibility, with unofficials in charge of groups of departments. It would then no longer be possible for these to oppose in debate measures which they had shared in discussing and formulating. This would also end the cumbrous system whereby all branches of administration were channelled through the Chief Secretary.

There was no room in Mitchell's thinking for any broadly-based popular initiative in these developments. It was his firm conviction that

the great mass of the people in this region are still in a state of ignor-ance and backwardness, uncivilised, superstitious, economically weak to the point of near helplessness, and quite unable to construct a civilised future for themselves, to 'pull themselves up by their own bootstraps'.[1]

Only by 'a radical transformation of the subsistence society in which the masses are still enmeshed' could the situation be gradu-ally changed. He did of course recognize the existence of individ-uals and groups more politically mature, 'distinct from the great backward masses of ignorant tribesmen'. It was to the co-operation of these that he looked in his plans for multi-racial government at both the inter-territorial and the territorial level, but only so long as they accepted the gradualism implicit in his own doctrine of trusteeship. Eventually, as two recent historians of nationalism in Kenya have put it, he argued that

as individual Africans achieved the economic status of the Europeans, so they would begin to identify themselves as fellow-members of the new community of 'all civilised men' . . . It was held that the pos-sibility of advancement into this new status would give the African masses a continuing stake in the new community.[2]

---

[1] Philip Mitchell, *African Afterthoughts* (London, 1954), pp. 219-21.

[2] Carl Rosberg and John Nottingham, *The Myth of 'Mau Mau': nationalism in Kenya* (London, 1966), p. 203. Controversial as it is, this is the most important single re-interpretation of the history and politics of Kenya during the colonial period yet to appear. The debt of this chapter to it will be evident.

Mitchell's measures to implement his policies were the occasion of what at the time appeared as the dominant political
issues of the immediate post-war years. The Europeans, with
the most effective political voice, reacted to them broadly as
might have been predicted. His proposals for the reorganization
of the administration,[1] published in 1945, brought from them
on the whole a warm response, particularly when Major
Cavendish-Bentinck, long the chief advocate of European immigration, was not only nominated to the key post of Member for
Agriculture but also given the responsibility for European
settlement, which was a central item on Mitchell's economic
programme. On the other hand the first proposals for formal
inter-territorial co-operation, put forward in the same year,[2] met
with a storm of European protest; this was because they proposed
basing representation on the principle, which had obtained in
Fiji, of equality between the region's three racial groups. Most
repugnant to the European representatives was the equal
position allotted to the Asians; and although some were for a
measure of African advancement in this less politically-charged
inter-territorial arena, Vincent sought to bargain their agreement for the promise of an unofficial European majority on
Kenya's own Legislative Council. In the end, despite the
welcome given to it by the non-European representatives, the
principle of equal representation was modified in a revised set of
proposals published in 1947[3]—a fact interpreted on all sides as
a victory for the European community. At Mitchell's own
suggestion, moreover, the officials transferred to the Central
Assembly were not replaced on the Legislative Council, thus
leaving that body with an unofficial majority. On the other hand,
African nominated representation was increased (with European
agreement) to two in 1947, and to four in the following year.[4]

Meanwhile, the long-standing issue of taxation gave the European members the opportunity to comment on the governor's
schemes for African development and the rehabilitation of the

---

[1] *Proposals for the Reorganization of the Administration of Kenya*, Sessional Paper No.
3 of 1945 (Nairobi, Govt. Printer, 1945).

[2] *Inter-territorial Organization in East Africa*, Col. 191 (London, HMSO, 1945).

[3] See *Inter-territorial Proposals in East Africa, Revised Proposals*, Col. 210 (London,
HMSO, 1947). These proposed that the Kenya contingent to the Central Assembly
should consist of two Europeans and two non-Europeans only.

[4] See Appendix 2.

eroded reserves. In 1946 a report by a fiscal commissioner, Sir Wilfrid Woods, although made at their request, had advised against the ending of European income tax;[1] and in fact had commented, as previous enquiries had done, on the heavy burden of poll tax borne by Africans. In the debate on the report in September 1947 the European representatives reiterated their refusal to pay for African development. Beneath the racial abuse with which the debate was bespattered lay a restatement of the basic denial—long entrenched in separate education finance[2] and more recently in separate hospital finance for each community, and expressed in many other ways—that Kenya was a single political community. The sequel was the appointment of a fresh committee, this time presided over by a civil servant lent by the South African government, which, while it recommended a graduated wealth tax for Africans to replace the poll tax, also took the view that European taxation was too high and should be reduced.[3]

In these controversies the nominated representatives of non-European interests, and in particular Archdeacon Beecher and the nominated African member Eliud Mathu, took a generally independent line. In 1947 Mathu himself, moreover, raised another issue, that of finger-printing, which illustrates both the strong emotions which a racial question such as this could arouse, and the extent to which the assumption of European social predominance was beginning to be questioned. He demanded the abolition of the *kipande*, the employment registration card with its owner's fingerprints which since 1920 African men had been obliged to carry outside the reserves. The government met the request to the extent of proposing—with the agreement of the European though not of the Asian members of the Legislative

---

[1] *A Report on a Fiscal Survey of Kenya, Uganda and Tanganyika*, by Sir Wilfrid Woods (Nairobi, Govt. Printer, 1946), pp. 82, 86.

[2] In a parliamentary reply in the House of Commons in 1954 the following figures for annual primary education tuition expenditure were given:

	£ s. d.
per European child	49 6 0
per Asian child	18 4 0
per African child	3 0 0

In each case about one-third of the cost was met from school revenues. *Hansard*, 5th series, House of Commons, 529, c. 401, 23 June 1954.

[3] *Report of the Taxation Enquiry Committee, Kenya*, Chairman R. P. Plewman, (Nairobi, Govt. Printer, 1947).

Council—that the system, instead of being abolished, should be extended to all races. But the public reaction among the Europeans was so vehement that in the end a loophole was provided —discriminatory in effect if not in form—by waiving the finger-print requirement for those who could sign their own name unaided, and supply two photographs of themselves.[1] This in turn provoked a storm of African indignation and accusations of bad faith which were supported by at least one European member, Derek Erskine.[2] The end of the incident, ironically enough, was the re-introduction of the original provision for universal registration; but not before the whole controversy had led to a marked increase in racial antagonism.

On this and other topics the African representatives[3] in the Legislative Council spoke forcibly. On the nomination of Cavendish-Bentinck, on taxation and—with some reservations—on the inter-territorial proposals, Mathu himself was notably outspoken. Outside the council he was even more so; at Kakamega, for instance, in 1947, he was claiming that only the Africans were the true and rightful inhabitants of Kenya, which was theirs of right.[4]

Such was the outward appearance of Kenya politics during the two or three years following the end of the war. But how far in reality did the proceedings in Legislative Council, or the preoccupations of the European press, reflect the fears and aspirations of the main body of Kenya's peoples?

The growth of African politics

One thing very quickly became clear. During these post-war years the European representation of African interests could no longer keep pace with the rising temper of politics. Archdeacon Beecher, the missionary in whom this representation had been

[1] Kenya Leg Co *Debates*, 24 July 1947, cols. 129–30; 16 Aug. 1949, cols. 187–90; *Report of a Commission of Inquiry appointed to Review the Registration of Persons Ordinance, 1947* (Nairobi, Govt. Printer, 1950).

[2] Later Sir Derek Erskine. He followed up his protest by resigning from the Legislative Council.

[3] The others were F. W. Odede (Luo), W. W. Awori (Luhya), and B. A. Ohanga (Luo).

[4] Leg Co *Debates*, 18–25 July 1945; 24–26 Sept. 1946. *East African Standard*, 18 July 1947.

vested since 1943, was a man of integrity and generous sympathies.[1] It was he who was chiefly responsible for securing the increase of the nominated African members to four in the new
Council of 1948. He readily welcomed and put forward the
views of African correspondents. But, although he expressed the
hope that the post of Member for Agriculture would one day be
held by an African, he welcomed Cavendish-Bentinck's appointment; he was on the committee which came out with the recommendation for reduced European taxation; and he was deeply
involved in the politically sensitive issue of African education,
including that of providing government assistance and supervision for the independent schools—notably in the Central
Province—which had long been one of the main growing points
of African political consciousness.[2]

Mathu's own position was not without ambiguity. He was
indeed supported by the Kenya African Union (KAU)—the
legitimized successor to the pre-war Kikuyu Central Association
—which in particular threw its weight behind the demand for
increased, and elected, African representation on the Legislative
Council. This underlined the recognition by leading African
politicians that the central organs of power were now the
essential focus of political action. But although its first committee,
formed in 1944, was of varied regional origin,[3] KAU itself was
still not at this time in any sense the united voice of Kenya nationalism.

It was even now only in the Central Province that the concern with territorial politics had become paramount. Detailed

[1] L. J. Beecher (1906–) had come to Kenya in 1927 as a CMS missionary to
teach in the Alliance High School. He had been appointed as representative of
African interests in the Legislative Council in August 1943. For further details of
his career see G. Bennett, 'Imperial Paternalism: the representation of African
interests in the Kenya Legislative Council', in *Essays in Imperial Government*, ed.
K. E. Robinson and A. F. Madden (Oxford, 1963).

[2] He headed the important committee which reported on these questions in 1949,
and urged both further government financial support and closer supervision. See
African Education in Kenya (Nairobi, 1949). Eliud Mathu was also a member of the
Committee. The Electors' Union commended the report to its members as being
'in fact more a law and order measure than a social service one'. Electors' Union
Newsletter, 21 Aug. 1950, 79/EU/50, EEMO/EU Box 2/1, Rhodes House, Oxford.

[3] It included Harry Thuku, James Gichuru, F. M. Ng'anja (Kikuyu) Albert
Awino (Luo), Francis J. Khamisi (Coast), John Kebaso (Gusii), J. Jeremiah (Taita)
Simeon Mulandi (Kamba), Harry Nangurai (Masai), and S. B. Jackayo (Luhya).
Rosberg and Nottingham, *Myth of 'Mau Mau'*, p. 214.

research has shown that this was not simply because the Kikuyu were more directly influenced by settler politics and more deeply affected by the land issue, or because Kikuyu politicians were more vocal and importunate. In Nyanza also there were ambitious and politically active individuals and groups, but the basic social structure and the relative harmony between that structure and government policies made it possible right into the 1940s for these to find sufficient scope within the local arena. In consequence the efforts of KAU to spread its influence in the Nyanza region for some time met with no great success. Those seeking to attract economic opportunities or government resources to their own localities, and to exercize political leadership, still found it most profitable to act through rather than against officially-sponsored institutions.[1]

Even in the Kikuyu area, moreover, KAU was only the most orthodox and most articulate point of protest in a widening and deepening general discontent. Here there was the long-standing and special grievance over land. But there were other more widespread sources of friction. There was the fact that the overall growth in the country's prosperity had not been shared by the population as a whole; a growing disparity between African and European incomes was accentuated by the increasing African dependence on wage earnings. By 1951, it is claimed, 32·5 per cent of African real income was earned outside the African economy, yet the average African *per capita* income of some £3 per annum was only one quarter of that in Uganda.[2] There were the difficulties encountered by Africans—now extending beyond Kikuyuland—in starting up their own economic enterprises; these difficulties, it is true, were often due to lack of experience and insufficient initial capital, but even apart from this the pioneer entrepreneurs felt that they met with little positive official encouragement.[3] Above all there was the friction, for which there is now abundant evidence in much of East Africa, involved in the

[1] For a discussion of this thesis see John Lonsdale, 'Some Origins of Nationalism in East Africa', *J. Af. History*, 9 (1968), 119–46; and 'The Emergence of African Nations', *African Affairs*, 67, 266 (1968), 11–28.

[2] These comparisons are made by Carl Rosberg and John Nottingham in *Myth of 'Mau Mau'*, pp. 203–4. See also *Report of the Committee on African Wages* (Nairobi, Govt. Printer, 1954), pp. 32–3.

[3] Oginga Odinga gives a vivid account of his experiences in starting up various businesses, and in particular the Luo Thrift and Trading Corporation, in the 1940s in his autobiography, *Not Yet Uhuru* (London, 1967), pp. 76–94.

intensified government action to tackle agrarian problems.[1] Such action was, as we have seen, central to Sir Philip Mitchell's conviction that economic reform was the essential precondition to political progress, but its effects did not always match the hopes of the administration. The new practices enjoined— cattle culling, contour-ridging, mulching—were not invariably constructive or profitable in practice. In any case, at a time when discontent was already rife, they brought African farmers and the colonial government into an unprecedented degree of direct confrontation; they involved the presence of growing numbers of technical staff unfamiliar with the local societies among whom they worked; and sometimes they imposed upon local traditional authorities responsibilities of a kind that their office was unable to bear. Moreover, when government-sponsored schemes did prove profitable—as for instance the Kerugoya and Karatina dried vegetable factories set up during the war in the Central Province—there was reluctance to allow them to be turned over to African control.[2] Above all, African farmers felt bitterly that reforms in farming practice were largely irrelevant while the basic injustices of the land apportionment—the reserves and the White Highlands—remained inviolate.[3] For the first time a broad sector of the African peasantry was becoming resentful and open to the possibilities of political change as a means of reaction to practical grievances.

Discontent found expression in a variety of ways. There was the simple passive resistance of the agriculturalists to the con- servation measures enjoined upon them. A network of local unofficial 'Land Committees' came into being for the protection or recovery of African-claimed land. The tone of proceedings in the official African representative bodies, the Local Native Councils,[4] became increasingly outspoken. New associations

---

[1] Lonsdale, 'Origins of Nationalism' loc. cit.; Lionel Cliffe, 'Nationalism and the Reaction to Enforced Agricultural Improvement in Tanganyika during the Colonial Period', in *Socialism in Tanzania*, ed. L. Cliffe and J. S. Saul, 2 vols. (Dar es Salaam, 1973).

[2] Rosberg and Nottingham, *Myth of 'Mau Mau'*, pp. 235–7; Koinange, *People of Kenya*, pp. 21–2.

[3] See especially M. P. K. Sorrenson, *Land Reform in the Kikuyu Country* (Nairobi, 1967), pp. 521–5. Sorrenson points out that the land grievance was exacerbated by the return to the reserves of many squatters squeezed off European farms, and of landless Kikuyu from other areas.

[4] Odinga, *Not Yet Uhuru*, pp. 107–8, 90–4.

were formed, both secular and religious, with strong political overtones. Notable among the former was the 'Forty Group', an association based on the Kikuyu ex-service men of the group circumcised in 1940, many of whom had seen service outside Kenya, which actively encouraged anti-conservation and trade union activities,[1] but which was also credited with some indiscriminate hooliganism; while the latter included a number of sects such as that whose members called themselves the *Dini ya Jesu Kristo*. These last, rejecting all alien teachings and usages, wore skins and pledged themselves to deliver Kenya from the Europeans, and were embroiled with the police in a violent encounter in the Fort Hall District in December 1947.[2] What was perhaps most disturbing to the colonial administration was the explicit questioning of European authority in the Kikuyu independent schools—the institutions which had embodied the most constructive and imaginative response to colonial rule.[3]

A significant feature for the harnessing of this generalized opposition with the forces of nationalism was the strengthening of links between the forces of rural and urban discontent. Chege Kibachia, a Kikuyu from Kiambu, had led the successful Mombasa dock strike of 1947 which had resulted in the foundation of the African Workers' Federation. He himself was arrested and deported shortly afterwards, but the impetus which he had given to labour organization and action lived on to surface, first in the East African Trade Union Congress—which was refused registration by the government on the grounds of its communist connections—and later in the officially approved Kenya Federation of Registered Trade Unions which was subsequently to form a political base for Tom Mboya.[4] There was also, to an extent probably not recognized by the administration, a mushrooming of minor and often ephemeral newspapers in a variety

---

[1] Rosberg and Nottingham, *Myth of 'Mau Mau'*, p. 240; G. Delf, *Jomo Kenyatta* (London, 1961), p. 142; Waruhiu Itote, *'Mau Mau' General* (Nairobi, 1967), pp. 37–8.

[2] Rosberg and Nottingham, *Myth of 'Mau Mau'*, p. 327. See also the clash in April 1950 at Kolloa, in which the *Dini ya Msambwa* were involved. *Report of the Commission of Inquiry into the Affray at Kolloa, Baringo* (Nairobi, Govt. Printer, 1950).

[3] See John Anderson, *The Struggle for the School* (London, 1970), especially chap. viii; and chap. vii in the second volume of this *History*, pp. 367–71. Anderson argues that the directly revolutionary role of the schools was much exaggerated.

[4] Rosberg and Nottingham, *Myth of 'Mau Mau'*, pp. 208–10; Odinga, *Not Yet Uhuru*, pp. 108–9.

of languages which helped to spread activist views. Oginga Odinga has described in his autobiography how one of his ventures, the *Ramogi* Press, made it their policy to print such papers, even at uneconomic rates, as their contribution to the mobilization of political feeling.[1] The urban element was one of the factors affecting the development of the formally recognized political body, KAU, itself. It was particularly in Nairobi that the older, proscribed, KCA in fact survived; increasingly activist in character, it became identified closely with KAU, and eventually dominated the more moderate wing of the latter body. By 1951, for instance, KAU had adopted something of an international outlook; it sent representatives—Fred Kubai and Mbiyu Koinange—to help the Meru of Tanzania in the land case which they carried to the United Nations.[2]

It will be seen, then, that the African members of the Legislative Council, and in particular their spokesman Eliud Mathu, could at best represent only a fragment of the political ferment that was brewing. Mathu was a Kikuyu, and the political body with which he was associated was largely Kikuyu in outlook; he was also a nominated member. He reflected in some measure the deepening divisions within Kikuyu society itself, partially symbolized in the split between the extremist and the moderate wings of KAU. For if the unrest which was soon to manifest itself in the Mau Mau uprising was ultimately directed at the central national arena, most of its immediate venom would be expended on those Kikuyu who at the point of cleavage threw in their lot with the administration and the establishment. These most obviously included the district élite: chiefs and headmen, government teachers and the like; but those who had stuck to the more moderate courses of reform could also be compromised. Mathu was one of these. He was for a time a member of the board concerned with the resettlement of landless Kikuyu—the return of whom to the reserves was a major factor in the political unrest; in 1947 he drew up a memorandum in which he sought to warn the government of the extent and character of subversive activity;[3] in 1949 he was a member of the Beecher Committee on

---

[1] Rosberg and Nottingham, *Myth of 'Mau Mau'*, pp. 208–10; Odinga, *Not Yet Uhuru*, p. 82.
[2] Anton Nelson, *The Freemen of Meru* (Nairobi, 1967), pp. 34, 44.
[3] Leg Co *Debates*, 9 Jan. 1948, coll 759.

African education. The first African member, in 1952, of the Executive Council, he continued to be a member of the Legislative Council throughout the Mau Mau Emergency until he was displaced in the 1957 elections.

The growth of African political activity during this period, its range, its conflicts, and its limitations, is more vividly illuminated by the return in 1946 to the Kenya scene of Jomo Kenyatta, after fifteen years' voluntary exile in Europe. During that time Kenyatta had visited the Soviet Union, had studied social anthropology under Malinowski at the London School of Economics, and had worked and lectured in wartime Britain; moreover, in taking part in the pan-African movement centred in Manchester he had been in contact with Kwame Nkrumah, George Padmore, and others. He had also written a book, *Facing Mount Kenya*.[1] This work is of interest not only as the first analytical anthropological study by an African of his own people, but also as a political document. It reflects bitterly on the sequel to the hospitality shown by Kikuyu to early European travellers, and on the restrictions on African movement and the inadequate help given to African farming. But perhaps the most interesting section in this context, not least because of its connection with the independent schools movement, is that which discusses the effects of western education. Despite the western emphasis in theory on character-formation, Kenyatta argued, the failure in practice to link African education to the relationships and values of the peoples upon whom it was imposed had in fact tended to destroy the main basis upon which this character-forming could be built. The practical benefits of western learning were not in doubt; but only by carrying through the necessary process of modernization in their own way, and without destroying their own social bonds, could African societies be helped to 'create a new culture which, though its roots are still in the soil, is yet modified to meet the pressure of modern conditions.'[2]

Kenyatta on his return immediately threw himself into his country's politics. His hint that he might be nominated to the Legislative Council was met with the cool response, consonant with Mitchell's own views on the pace and method of constitutional development, that he should make a beginning by seek-

---

[1] H. H. Kenyatta, *Facing Mount Kenya: the tribal life of the Gikikuyu* (London, 1938).
[2] Ibid, p. 125.

ing election to the Local Native Council of his home area. Never-theless he *was* appointed, in March 1947, to the African Land Settlement and Utilization Board, and so was in the midst of the agrarian improvement drive which was a major source of popular discontent. The government, it seems, did not find his contribu-tions very helpful, and he resigned in June 1949;[1] on the other hand he was studiedly cautious in his reactions to the threats of the 'Forty Group' against anyone supporting soil conservation measures. In June 1947 he was elected President of KAU, and it may have been from this point that KAU at length became acceptable to the militants of the proscribed KCA, with whom Kenyatta had certainly been in touch since his return in the previous year.

Meanwhile he had a month earlier taken over control, from Mbiyu Koinange,[2] of the Teachers' Training College at Githung-uri, the nerve-centre of the Kikuyu independent schools. In a strike at Kiambu in September 1947 there were reports that in-timidation through oath administration was being used to raise money for the college.[3] Whether or not this was true—Kenyatta replied that he was insisting that the fund-raising should be voluntary—it is certain that the practice of oathing, which was to figure so grimly in all accounts of Mau Mau, was spreading rapidly among the Kikuyu in these post-war years.

The oath was a long-established instrument of social control among the Kikuyu. It had been widely used by the KCA before the war, both to secure the commitment of its followers and to raise the organization's funds. Now it was employed to try to build up, by overriding recognized cleavages of economic

---

[1] Corfield *Report*, p. 50 note 15. There are a number of reports of his active efforts to stimulate agricultural non-co-operation in EEMO/EU Box 38 A/1, Rhodes House, Oxford.

[2] Mbiyu Koinange was the son of Koinange Mbiyu, who as one of the most influ-ential and respected chiefs in southern Kiambu during the inter-war years, had eventually and reluctantly moved over from co-operation with the administration to full association with the nationalist cause. Sent by his father to be educated in America, he returned in 1938 and was one of the first African candidates for member-ship of the Legislative Council (see p. 111, n.1 above). He was thereafter contin-uously prominent in KAU politics and educational enterprise, but also on occasion in efforts— such as the Kenya Citizens' Association—directed towards inter-racial co-operation. Rosberg and Nottingham, *Myth of 'Mau Mau'*, (see index); Anderson, *Struggle for the School*, pp. 122–8.

[3] For a European view of Kenyatta's activities at this time see Corfield *Report*, pp. 50, 66.

interest and kinship, a unified and solidly-based populist movement.[1] What was new about it in this period was its secrecy and the scope for intimidation which this entailed. Yet at least for some time the element of voluntary and whole-hearted commitment seems to have been much stronger than that of fear. A crucial part in the development of oathing was played by an administrative issue involving a group of Kikuyu settled at Olenguruone, on the southern edge of the Mau plateau. They were in origin a miscellaneous group of landless farmers whom the government in 1941 established on a stretch of land acquired from the Masai, and had been incensed by a fundamental misunderstanding as to the terms on which some of the land was held and therefore of the degree to which the government could dictate the agricultural use that was made of it. They bound themselves to resist administrative pressure by an oath which held them together through more than three stubborn years; and when at length in 1950 they were forcibly evicted, they carried with them throughout the Kikuyu reserves the sense of unity and purpose in opposition which the oath and its supporting songs had forged among them.[2] It is claimed that until the Emergency was already in force there were only two main types of oath: the first was simply a promise of co-operation and commitment, of the non-betrayal of the movement's members or secrets, the second, only taken by—in some cases imposed upon—a much smaller number of adherents, specifically included the commitment to violence. It is said that the latter came into use only in the middle of 1952, when the resort to force became accepted as inevitable. Both these oaths—like those employed in other societies and circumstances—involved rituals whose striking, and sometimes contra-natural, features impressed their overwhelming binding power upon the taker.

But the terms of the oaths were geared to Kikuyu experience and aspirations, and the very features which strengthened the movement's hold in the Central Province were a hindrance to its extension further afield. To a considerable extent Jomo Kenyatta had at first been successful in arousing enthusiasm

---

[1] For the development of oathing and its significance see especially Rosberg and Nottingham, *Myth of 'Mau Mau'*, pp. 241–62; Donald Barnett and Karari Njama, *Mau Mau from Within* (London, 1966), pp. 117–24, 130–4.

[2] Rosberg and Nottingham, *Myth of 'Mau Mau'*, pp. 248–59. Cp. Corfield *Report*, pp. 296–7.

among the inhabitants of the Nyanza Province, and in making contact with those leaders who were no longer satisfied with the politics of the local arena. But it was largely a personal achievement, and was increasingly prejudiced by the Kikuyu character of the movement which he represented and of the sanctions by which it was sustained. In Nyanza the oath had never played the social role that it did among the Kikuyu. The independent schools movement, although it had arisen there very much earlier than in the Central Province, had never acquired a similar political impetus, and the same was largely true of the Luo and Luhya independent religious sects. And the 'nationalist' leaders among the Luo were as yet untried men only just beginning to find their political feet, in contrast to the seasoned politicians of Nairobi and the Central Province whose experience dated from the pre-war years.[1]

In the latter part of 1948 and the beginning of 1949, for reasons which are a little obscure, there was some subsidence of the agitation which had become widespread in Kikuyuland. At KAU meetings Kenyatta was making speeches that earned the commendation of the *East African Standard*, blaming the Africans for many of their troubles and urging them to action to raise their own standard of living.[2] In Kikuyu country he attacked their propensity for land litigation, the embezzlement practised by their officials, the dishonesty of traders, the failure to take advantage of the new freedom to grow tea or coffee and to take soil conservation measures. Nevertheless the European community did not cease to press for Kenyatta's deportation, on the grounds that he was responsible for subversive propaganda.[3]

At this point two fresh issues arose which renewed tensions. The first was the publication in September 1949 of the *Kenya Plan* of the European Electors' Union. Worried by pronouncements on Africa in the governing Labour Party in Britain, the

[1] Anderson, *Struggle for the School;* Lonsdale, 'Origins of Nationalism', loc. cit.; B. A. Ogot, 'British Administration in the Central Nyanza District of Kenya, 1900–1960', *J. Af. History*, 4, 2 (1963), 266–70.

[2] *East African Standard*, leading articles, 6 July, 9 Oct. 1948. George Bennett draws attention to this in 'Kenyatta and the Kikuyu', *International Affairs* (Oct. 1961), p. 480. George Ndegwa, the Secretary of the KCA, may have been misled by this lull in applying in June 1948 for the registration of the association's newspaper *Muigwithania*. His frankness cost him a year's imprisonment. Corfield *Report*, p. 54.

[3] Resolution of Electors' Union, 11/12 Mar. 1948. EEMO/EU Box 38 A/1, Rhodes House, Oxford.

Union asked in the *Plan* for an unequivocal statement that European settlement was a permanency, and that the maintenance of British leadership would be 'paramount'.[1] The *Plan* also showed the growing concern among Europeans over the United Nations influence on Tanganyika, and called for the incorporation of that territory 'within the empire' and for the creation of a new British East African Dominion under European leadership. The African press reacted strongly to the call for a halt to constitutional change, and Mathu, who had long been pressing for an African appointment to the Executive Council, said that the *Plan's* implementation would be tantamount to the declaration of political war.[2]

So violent was the non-European reaction on all sides that it had the effect of drawing together African and Asian leaders in a temporarily close alliance. KAU and the East African Indian National Congress in April 1950 held a joint meeting of protest and passed a motion of no confidence in European leadership.[3] One speaker was Makhan Singh, an outspoken Sikh communist. He had formed, and had become general secretary of, the East African Trade Union Congress, whose president was Fred Kubai, a leader of the Forty Group.

The resulting hardening of the lines of division became apparent over the second issue—the celebrations in March 1950 for the fiftieth anniversary of Nairobi and for the royal charter granting city status to the capital. Nairobi, with its housing problems, its residential segregation, and its strongly European-dominated municipal government, stood for much that was hateful to Africans and Asians; on top of this there were rumours that the city was to be extended to incorporate for white settlement a large slice of the Kikuyu reserve. Nevertheless even up to this stage there were leaders on the moderate wing of KAU who were prepared to play a part in the celebrations; and when the East African Trade Union declared a boycott, a press communiqué

---

[1] The main points of the *Plan* were detailed in the *East African Standard*, 9 Sept. 1949, p. 11. It was issued without previous consultation with the European Elected members, to whom it was a considerable embarrassment. The European press in East Africa was lukewarm, and *Rhodesia and East Africa* went so far as to describe its publication as a 'major blunder'. Oxford Colonial Records, EEMO/EU, Box 1/3, Minutes, Jan. 1948–Dec. 1949.

[2] Letter in *East African Standard*, 7 Oct. 1949.

[3] *Kenya Weekly News*, 19, 26 May 1950.

was issued denouncing it—although this was only after bitter internal conflict, and was subsequently repudiated by Kenyatta. During the celebrations attempts were made on the lives of the two leading KAU members—Tom Mbotela, the vice-president of KAU,[1] and Muchohi Gikonyo, a city councillor—who had taken part in them, for the latter of which attempts Fred Kubai was later arrested and tried. Meanwhile in May a general strike had taken place in Nairobi when legal action had been taken against him and the East African Trade Union's secretary, Makhan Singh, as officers of an unregistered and therefore illegal organization. From this point onwards it seems that the urban and more militant elements steadily gained the upper hand in KAU. Kubai, after being acquitted of the attempted murder of Gikonyo and released in February 1951,[2] brought into that body the main political force of African workers from the proscribed labour union and, in the Nairobi KAU branch elections the following June, these finally swept the moderates from office. On the same occasion Kubai made a demand for independence within three years.[3]

By contrast, even the next cautious step in Sir Philip Mitchell's programme of constitutional advance had brought an uncompromising reaction from the European side. In October 1950 he had announced proposed increases in African and Asian representation on the Legislative Council;[4] but his efforts to bring the various racial groups together to discuss these changes failed to make any headway. Despite a carefully balanced policy statement by the new Colonial Secretary, James Griffiths, in December,[5] Mitchell failed to dislodge the Asians and KAU from their demand for a common electoral roll for all races, or the Europeans from their refusal to budge from the interpretation of 'parity' represented by the existing formula—that is, of an

---

[1] Mbotela (who was of Nyasa, not Kenya, origin) had been appointed vice-president only in the previous October. He was in fact assassinated in November 1952.

[2] Makhan Singh was not released until October 1961. His own account of these events is published in *History of Kenya's Trade Union Movement to 1952* (Nairobi, 1969).

[3] For the above, see Rosberg and Nottingham, *Myth of 'Mau Mau'*, pp. 265–70. Cp. Corfield *Report*, pp. 55–6, 83–4, 255–6.

[4] Leg Co *Debates*, 24 Oct. 1950, cols. 12–13; Rosberg and Nottingham, *Myth of 'Mau Mau'*, p. 229. For the detailed course of developments over the next eighteen months see Bennett, *Kenya*, pp. 127–9.

[5] *Hansard*, 5th series, House of Commons, 482, cc. 1161–71, 13 Dec. 1950.

equality of representation between the Europeans on the one side and all non-Europeans on the other. It was at this time that the slogan 'parity or partition' indicated the direction in which at least one section of European thinking was moving.[1] In May 1951 James Griffiths himself visited Kenya and met representatives of all groups, including Kenyatta and Mbiyu Koinange. He also received a formal memorandum from KAU demanding *inter alia* twelve elected instead of four nominated African representatives (i.e. African parity with European unofficials), equal representation on the Executive Council, and an eventual common roll.[2] On his return, however, he announced that major changes would be deferred until after a constitutional conference to be held within a year of the election due in 1952. While there would be some slight modifications (the size of the Legislative Council would be increased, the margin of the unofficial majority narrowed, and an African appointed for the first time to the Executive Council) to take effect in 1952, the existing balance of the forces was to remain broadly unaltered.[3]

Mau Mau

His pronouncement, while satisfactory to neither side, was less unacceptable to the European than to the African leaders. But before any conference could be held, a phase of violence had intervened. From about the middle of 1952, soon after the final retirement of Mitchell from the governorship of the colony, the rate of murders and cattle-maiming and arson incidents—which had already for some time been disquieting to the administration—in the Central Province rose alarmingly. There were also attacks on mission schools and a church was desecrated. Rumours were made public of a plot to massacre all the Europeans in the colony. Most of this happened during the three months' interregnum following Mitchell's departure in the last week of June, and at the end of August a delegation of senior officials went to London to seek special powers to deal with the situation. The

---

[1] *East African Standard* and *Kenya Weekly News*, 9 Feb. to 9 Mar. 1951, *passim*.

[2] The Memorandum is printed as Appendix B to the Corfield *Report*, pp. 292–5. At this time there were 11 European, 4 African and 5 Asian elected members, and one Arab.

[3] For the above, see Rosberg and Nottingham, *Myth of 'Mau Mau'*, pp. 229–33; Corfield *Report*, pp. 59, 292–5; *Hansard*, 5th series, H. of C., 488 cc. 408–10, 31 May 1951. For details of the changes in representation, etc., see Appendix 2.

climax came in early October with the murder in broad day-light outside Nairobi of Senior Chief Waruhiu, a strong Kikuyu supporter of the administration. Finally, on 20 October, a State of Emergency was proclaimed by the new governor, Sir Evelyn Baring. It was not to be lifted for seven years.

The first six months of the Mau Mau rising, apart from a number of isolated murders, were spent mainly in the building up of forces on both sides. Units of the King's African Rifles were recalled from other parts of East Africa; a battalion of the Lancashire Fusiliers was flown in from the Suez Canal Zone; the local territorial forces were called up and they and the police were expanded. Meanwhile thousands of Kikuyu took to the forests on the slopes of Mount Kenya and in the Aberdare range. Estimates vary, but it seems that at the height of the Emergency in mid-1953 they may have numbered some 15,000.[1] The second phase of hostilities brought a more positive and concerted offensive against guard posts and 'loyalist' villages, and there was a period when responsible European leaders could express real concern over the possible outcome of the struggle.[2] By early 1954, however, the security forces had decisively gained the upper hand; there followed a long period during which the forest groups were progressively isolated by the concentration of the people of the reserves into large fortified and strictly controlled villages, and were worn down by the bombing of their camp sites. By 1955 it was possible to withdraw troops from the Kikuyu reserves, and to carry the offensive into the forests themselves, and this continued until the Emergency was finally ended in 1959—although even at that time some hundreds of Mau Mau adherents still remained in the forests. By the end of it all, the political and economic scene, not only in the Central Province but throughout Kenya, had been transformed.

It is difficult in retrospect to ascertain how far back and how widely warnings were given or taken seriously by the colonial administration as to the danger of a rising. As early as 1947 there was a circumstantial intelligence report of a plot to murder all the Europeans in the territory, and it was in the same year that Mathu gave his account in the Legislative Council of secret

---

[1] Rosberg and Nottingham, *Myth of 'Mau Mau'* p. 297. cf. Odinga, *Not Yet Uhuru*, p. 117.

[2] Michael Blundell, *So Rough a Wind* (London, 1964), p. 153.

oathing meetings. In 1950, in connection with other oathing ceremonies, an association named as 'Mau Mau' had been proscribed by the government. In November 1951 there had been massive agrarian disobedience in Fort Hall, and three months later an outbreak of arson in Nyeri.[1] Yet the scale of violence that mounted during the latter part of 1952 seems to have taken at least some of the senior levels of government by surprise. When Mitchell had left the country in June, he was apparently unaware of any widespread subversive activity, and found in Kikuyu country nothing but 'smiling faces and happy, cheerful people'.[2]

The question has been asked, whether there was in fact a real long-term threat to peace and security. It had been argued that the final resort to violence was provoked by the Emergency, rather than the cause of it; that only the arrival of troops, the arrest of political leaders, and the imposition of harsh emergency measures (including the forced repatriation of squatters) drove the Kikuyu into open revolt. With this is linked the question of the personal involvement of Jomo Kenyatta, who was arrested along with other leaders on the outbreak of the Emergency, and was subsequently tried and convicted on a charge of 'managing Mau Mau'.

To the second question at least, it seems likely that no clear answer is possible. Even amongst those who were themselves in the thick of the movement assessments vary.[3] It is indeed inconceivable that Kenyatta was not broadly aware of what was going on, even in the most extremist sections of the nationalist movement. Moreover, he made it clear on many public occasions that he did not rule out the use of force at some point to attain its ends. But it by no means follows that he himself advocated violence in this form or at this time. Such evidence as there is, together with the political skill demonstrated by Kenyatta after his subsequent return to power, suggest rather that he was keenly alive to the importance of keeping the movement on as broad an inter-tribal front as possible, and only tardily and reluctantly fell in with the Kikuyu militancy which seemed likely to undermine a wider

[1] Corfield Report, pp. 74 sqq.
[2] Mitchell, African Afterthoughts, pp. 254–61.
[3] Compare, for instance, those in Rosberg and Nottingham, Myth of 'Mau Mau', and Itote, Mau Mau General.

unity of purpose. At the end of 1950 he took part in the early meetings of a short-lived Kenya Citizens' Association formed belatedly to try to re-open an informal inter-racial dialogue; and as late as October 1951, after the militants had gained control of the Nairobi branch of KAU, he was still insisting on multi-tribal representation.[1] Between this time and his arrest, however, as he was repeatedly called upon to speak out against Mau Mau, his public utterances became more studiedly ambiguous.[2] It would seem that by this time his main concern was to avoid alienating himself from the movement, whatever form it might take.

The appeal to force, however, as Kenya's earlier history confirms, was never far below the surface in a settler-dominated society, and it is hard to imagine any circumstances in which it could here have been avoided. On the one side there was a nationalist movement with at least a determined militant wing dedicated to the use of violence, a very considerable section of the Kikuyu population dissatisfied with the government and bound by oath to obedience in the nationalist cause, and an increasing supply of arms, stolen, or smuggled from Ethiopia. On the other side, a tough settler minority believed that surrender to the nationalist demands would mean immediate political suicide. Even if, as is claimed, the more drastic secondary 'ngero' oath, specifically binding to violence and law-breaking, became current only on the eve of the Emergency, its introduction at some point would seem to have been a foregone conclusion.

The development of the oath—of which fresh forms were continually devised as the Emergency persisted—as a central instrument of controlling and strengthening the nationalist movement may have been necessary for cementing Kikuyu unity: but for the time being it confirmed the separation between the Kikuyu and the nationalist movements elsewhere in Kenya. A decision was taken early in 1954 to send out emissaries to enlist the help of neighbouring peoples,[3] but if these were sent they met with little practical response. Except among the Embu and

---

[1] Rosberg and Nottingham, *Myth of 'Mau Mau'*, pp. 267–71. For an account of Kenya Citizens' Association and its aims by its president, Derek Erskine, see EEMO/EU Box 33/1, Rhodes House, Oxford. It was formed in the first instance by Mbiyu Koinange.

[2] Corfield *Report*, pp. 94–5, 102–4, 137–8; *Kenya Weekly News*, 8 Dec. 1950.

[3] Odinga, *Not Yet Uhuru*, p. 118.

Meru and to some extent the Kamba, with broadly similar social institutions and some grievances in common, Mau Mau did not spread to the rest of the territory—although the presence of troops and the enforcement of emergency measures certainly affected the overall political climate. What is more important is that the stress upon oathing underlines the continuing cleavages, at all events in the earlier stages of the Emergency, among the Kikuyu themselves. For all its essential concern with the rejection of colonial status, the struggle proved to be in large measure in fact an embittered continuation of the rift which had opened during the preceding years—and which was made worse by the administration's emergency measures—between the militants on the one hand and the 'establishment' Kikuyu on the other. The casualties among government forces, given as something less than 1,000 killed, were far outnumbered by those of their opponents, estimated at more than 11,000—to which must be added the grim figure of more than 1,000 executions[1]: but it is believed that the civilian victims of the latter numbered not much less than 2,000. By comparison with these figures the attacks on European farms, despite the inevitably high publicity given to them, pale into insignificance.[2] The most dramatic and

---

[1] The figures of executions in connection with the Emergency, which were given in reply to persistent questioning by Mr. Fenner Brockway and others in Parliament, are as follows:

From 20 Oct. 1952 to 19 July 1955   909
From 20 July 1955 to 31 Dec. 1955   79
From 1 Jan. 1956 to 31 Mar. 1956   27

Total 1,015

Less than one-third of the charges were of homicide, the commonest being the possession of firearms and 'consorting with terrorists', which between them accounted for more than half. *Hansard*, 5th series, House of Commons, 551, cc. 145–6, 25 Apr. 1956.

[2] Up to the close of the active phase of the Emergency at the end of 1956, 32 European civilians had been killed and 26 wounded. On African casualties on the government side it is hard to reconcile the divergent estimates, of which those given below are samples:

		F. Majdalaney*				Corfield Report**		
killed	security forces	534	2360		101	1920		
	civilians	1826		3743	1819		4305	
wounded	security forces	465	1383		1469	2385		
	civilians	918			916			

State of Emergency (London, 1962), p. 221.   **p. 318.

(Footnote continued on next page)

tragic illustration of the nature of the movement as in large part a civil war among the Kikuyu is provided by the attack in March 1953 on the village of Lari, when upwards of 100 of the inhabitants, including the ex-chief Wakahangara and 26 of his family, were massacred. The background to this incident has since been made clear. Wakaharanga's own *githaka* lands at Tigoni, a few miles away, had been alienated in the 1930s for European settlement; by agreeing to accept in exchange land at Lari claimed by other Kikuyu *mbari*, Wakahangara had aligned himself decisively on the side of the administration. The attackers were not, as was popularly supposed at the time, regular Mau Mau forces, but the rival faction within Lari itself.[1]

Organization within the resistance movement was never highly developed. Its most effective approach towards co-ordination was probably that exercised through the Nairobi Central Committee of the KAU, which continued to meet secretly in the capital after the organization itself had been proscribed, and which called itself the War Council. This was linked with a number of district committees in Nairobi, and through them arranged for the transmission of recruits and supplies to the forest fighters. Its work seems to have been effectively disrupted, however, when in April 1954, in 'Operation Anvil', the government screened and passed through detention camps virtually the whole male Kikuyu population of Nairobi, upwards of 25,000 men.[2] Meanwhile there were attempts to set up corresponding organizations within the forests, first a 'Kikuyu Defence Council', and later, early in 1954, the 'Kenya Parliament', which functioned until the following year. But such accounts as there are of the proceedings of these bodies seem to bear witness rather to the enormous difficulties of achieving any degree of effective overall planning than to the success of the leaders in solving them, although the three 'Land Freedom Armies' operating in the field showed resource and resilience as individual guerrilla

Non-African casualties were as follows:

			Europeans		Asians	
killed	security forces	63		95	3	29
	civilians	32			26	
wounded	security forces	102		128	12	48
	civilians	26			36	

[1] Sorrenson, *Land Reform*, pp. 100–1.
[2] Rosberg and Nottingham, *Myth of 'Mau Mau'*, p. 302.

units.[1] In practice after 1955 all attempt at general co-ordination appears to have broken down. One reason for this was almost certainly the fewness among the forest fighters of men with any high degree of military training, of political experience or indeed of secondary education—largely perhaps because these were predominantly the 'have nots' of Kikuyu society, those lacking the benefits of association with the establishment. It is clear that the prolonged sense of isolation among their more illiterate and superstitious companions was one of the heaviest strains that the handful of more qualified men and women in the forests had to bear. Another reason was the activities of the *komerera*—the fringe element of outright and uncontrolled thuggery which is inseparable from most forms of irregular warfare. According to later accounts, these *komerera* were responsible for some of the most apparently inexplicable and insensate killing episodes.

What did the movement hope to achieve? That it had a carefully worked out political programme from the beginning is incompatible with the interpretation of the rising as something largely spontaneous and un-premeditated. Possibly it was no more than, as has been subsequently claimed, the invoking of the 'imperial factor'—the forcing of Kenya's issues back into the forefront of the metropolitan consciousness. Certainly the accounts of those who were involved in the one serious attempt at peace negotiations, in March 1954, give no more than a blurred picture.[2] The emphasis of the forest fighters' demands was on the old grievance of the 'lost lands' and on the recent and acute one of the release of the imprisoned political leaders; to which was added the general and overriding concern for Kenya's independence under African leadership. But it is noteworthy that the demand was emphatically made for Kenya, not for the Kikuyu; the same insistence on overall Kenya nationalism was apparent in the title and the deliberations of the 'Kenya Parliament' of the forests. A second striking feature was the stress— along with the requirement that 'loyalists' should be disarmed and the new fortified villages dismantled—on the need for recon-

---

[1] Rosberg and Nottingham, *Myth of 'Mau Mau'*, pp. 272–4, 300–1; Barnett and Njama, *Mau Mau from Within*, Part II, *passim;* Odinga, *Not Yet Uhuru*, pp. 117–119; Corfield *Report*, pp. 259–61.

[2] Rosberg and Nottingham, *Myth of 'Mau Mau'*, p. 264; Barnett and Njama, *Mau Mau from Within*, pp. 330–1, 349–53; Itote, *Mau Mau General*, pp. 108–209.

ciliation, for healing the cleavages caused by the conflict of loyalties.

Who, finally, were the 'loyalists'? The hard core were, by and large, those who had established themselves by co-operation with the administration—government-appointed chiefs and head-men, teachers at the recognized schools, pastors of the regular churches and their adherents, tribal police; and also, significant-ly, the richer landowners. It does not follow that these factors fully account for the fact that they included also very many Kikuyu Christians, both of the regular and the independent churches, who did not directly stand to lose by the threat to the régime, but who were genuinely shocked and repelled by the nature and violence of the movement.[1] It would however be very difficult to assess at any time the strength of 'loyalism'; even in the most apparently successful days of the movement the forces on the government side included hundreds who had taken Mau Mau oaths, just as at a later stage 'rehabilitated' forest fighters were effectively enlisted to fight against their erstwhile comrades. In the latter days it seems certain nevertheless that, beneath the massive return to co-operation prompted by the plain fact of the government's overwhelmingly superior power, the great majority of the Kikuyu had swung irrevocably to the acceptance of radical political change as inevitable and desirable.

From the Emergency to the First Lancaster House Conference, 1954–1960

There is no doubt that in the minds of many Europeans at the time the impression was that the trend towards wider African political powers had been set far back by the Mau Mau Emer-gency. KAU and all other national political associations had been banned. In the heat of the Emergency, indeed, a government announcement had declared that 'the Kenya Government can never again allow such an association as the Kenya African Union.'[2] The task of restoring peace and order from the brutalities and insecurities of the Emergency was, like the two successive world wars, something which had drawn the

---

[1] Sorrenson, *Land Reform*, pp. 107–9, quoting in particular a study of the social composition of the Githunguri Kikuyu Guard carried out by J. D. Campbell, the district officer in charge of it.

[2] Broadcast by Acting Chief Native Commissioner, 8 June 1953, quoted in *Opportunity in Kenya*, Fabian Colonial Bureau Research Series No. 162 (London, 1953), p. 3.

administration and the European farmers together in self-help schemes and security planning. The settlers' leader, Michael Blundell, had been one of the small War Council which from March 1954 became its nerve-centre. Sir Patrick Renison, who in 1959 succeeded Baring as governor, in May 1960 referred to Jomo Kenyatta as 'the leader to darkness and death' and gave the impression that his return to political life was unthinkably remote.[1] There was, meanwhile, the forthright pledge given by the Colonial Secretary, Alan Lennox-Boyd, in October 1954, that the Europeans were in Kenya to stay, and that they 'would have the full force of Her Majesty's Government behind them': he 'believed in British emigration to Kenya'.[2]

Yet even as these apparently confident notes were sounded on the Europeans' behalf, strains of the counter-theme were becoming clearer and stronger. While the Emergency was still at its height in 1954 Oliver Lyttelton, the Conservative Colonial Secretary, had visited Kenya and had told the Europeans that they could not 'expect to hold all the political power and to exclude Africans from the legislature and from the government.'[3] In an interim constitution which he announced in March 1954 the 'membership' system was replaced by full ministerial responsibility. Both Asians and Africans were to have an effective voice in government, an African for the first time holding a ministerial post (the portfolio for Community Development). At the same time an assurance was given that a review would be undertaken of the ways and means of introducing direct elections for the African seats.[4]

They were introduced in the event before the next elections, which took place in 1956/7. Early in 1955 a civil servant, Mr. W. F. (later Sir Walter) Coutts was appointed to advise on methods of the selection of African members, and in the following year the government accepted his proposals for direct elections,

---

[1] Speech by Sir Patrick Renison, 9 May 1960 reported in *The Times*, 10 May 1960. Baring too had promised in 1954 that Kenyatta would not be allowed to return.

[2] *East African Standard*, 8 Oct. 1954, It should not be inferred however that the whole settler community was consistently opposed to African political advance. From at least 1956 there was a section of European opinion actively in favour of increasingly multi-racial government.

[3] Lord Chandos, *The Memoirs of Lord Chandos* (London, 1962), p. 398.

[4] *Kenya, Proposals for a Reconstruction of the Government*, Cmd. 9103 (London, HMSO, 1954). See also Blundell, *So Rough a Wind* pp. 165–7. The detailed changes are given in Appendix 2.

although these were to be on a narrow qualitative franchise and there were to be special restrictions on voting by the Kikuyu, Embu, and Meru.[1] Less than a year later the 'Lennox-Boyd Constitution' increased the number of African directly-elected members from eight to fourteen, while in January 1960 the Lancaster House Conference pointed the way to a total and rapid transition to African majority rule.[2]

The successive stages in this dramatic and yet bloodless shift of political power may be traced in the growing strength and political skill of the African opposition: strength as popular opinion rallied behind them, political skill in using the formal structures of colonial bureaucracy and parliamentary government not merely to accommodate but to achieve their objective of independence. But before doing this it is worth considering the role of the executive. For this was not a simple contest for power between the European immigrant community and the African majority of Kenya's people. In retrospect it could be held that the most significant factor during the five years from 1953 to 1958 was the greatly enlarged sphere of government action,[3] which not only spelt out a number of far-reaching lessons to the metropolitan government in Whitehall and Westminster, but also ultimately determined the resources inherited by the successor state. The immediate post-war period, under the impulse of Mitchell's energy, had already seen a considerably greater government initiative in administration. But whereas the total Kenya public expenditure had risen from £8·6 million in 1946 to £28·2 million in 1952, the cost of the Emergency alone was reckoned at some £55·6 million down to June 1959; while during the same period the annual expenditure had reached the figure of £43 millions.[4] Included in this there was the Swynnerton Plan for land consolidation and agricultural reform, launched in 1954 at a cost of £5 million, by which government action achieved a

---

[1] *Report of the Commissioner Appointed to Enquire into Methods for the Selection of African Representatives of the Legislative Council*, Commissioner W. F. Coutts (Nairobi, Govt. Printer, 1955); Sessional Paper No. 39 of 1955/6 (Nairobi, 1956).

[2] *Kenya, Proposals for New Constitutional Arrangement* (Lennox-Boyd Constitution), Cmnd. 309 (London, HMSO, 1957). Negotiations following the elections for the non-African seats in September 1956 had resulted in the number of African elected members being increased from six to eight.

[3] For an illuminating analysis of this see Cherry Gertzel, *The Politics of Independent Kenya* (Nairobi, 1970), pp. 20–31.

[4] Kenya *Annual Reports*, 1946, 1952, 1959.

very considerable restructuring of Kenya rural society,[1] and so helped to make possible the maintenance of a deep underlying political continuity into independence. All of this was reflected in an intensifying of administration and development that was unparalleled in the history of British colonial territories. The number of adminstrative posts, for instance, rose from 184 in 1951 to more than 300 in 1960, the total number of employees in the agricultural, veterinary, and land departments from some 600 to nearly 4,000 in the same period, while the regular police force doubled to 12,000.[2]

It seems likely that the scale of this intensification in administration and its cost entered in to thinking in Whitehall and Westminster as one of the factors which prompted towards rapid decolonization. It became more evidently politic to look forward realistically towards identifying an element to which power could in due course be transferred. Moreover, it was already being proved that the very scale of government intervention in the economy could be used to influence effectively the pattern of political and social development. The concentration of more than a million Kikuyu, Meru, and Embu into 854 villages within the fifteen months June 1954 to October 1955 was an operation unprecedented in British African history. The land consolidation measures simultaneously set in motion, and more or less linking up with the Swynnerton Plan, were deliberately employed to encourage the potentially 'loyalist' elements among the Kikuyu, and to create what it was hoped would be a stable and reliable middle class of farmers.[3] Similarly, although the formation of African political parties was again permitted in June 1955, these were still restricted to a district basis, and were forbidden altogether to the Kikuyu save for a 'loyalist' advisory council; while an emphasis on 'loyalty' and 'rehabilitation' also figured prominently in the qualifications for the first African franchise introduced on the Coutts recommendations of 1955. In the event, the political tempo increased at a rate far quicker than could have

---

[1] See chap. vi below.
[2] Gertzel, *Independent Kenya*, p. 25.
[3] Sorrenson, *Land Reform*, Part II, gives a fascinating account of these policies. He makes the point, however, that the administration wisely refrained from the expedient of rewarding the loyalists at the direct expense of Mau Mau adherents, and believes that the programme did help to heal Kikuyu divisions 'not merely between loyalists and rebels, but also between those who were gaining and losing land through litigation'. Part III, p. 250.

been anticipated by the adminstrative officers who contrived the consolidation operation. The consolidation itself, after the first impetus of change, proved less far-reaching than the blueprints had indicated.[1] Nevertheless, although the political élite that emerged over the five or six years before independence was not of course limited to those who had reaped advantages from the land changes in the Central Province, their presence was to be an important element in the political and economic structure of the successor state. So too, in a smaller degree, was the steadily renewed predominance of loyalist Kikuyu in civil service posts.

Yet in the most central arena the Emergency and the administrative action that followed influenced the pattern of African politics in a different sense. For a critical eight years the Kikuyu lost their pre-eminence in national politics. The course of developments within the Kenya nationalist movement during these years must now be reviewed.

The declaration of the Emergency had not immediately caused KAU to be proscribed; and even after this was done, in June 1953, there continued to be African representation on the Legislative Council. Inevitably, however, with heightening tensions this representation tended to become muted and ineffective.[2] Walter Odede (who had been nominated as a member in 1947) was arrested in March 1953 and detained for the rest of the Emergency, so that the greater part of the KAU leadership as publicly accepted was in detention. The drama of Kenyatta's long trial, moreover, could not fail to create the belief that not merely Kikuyu violence, but Kenyan nationalism as a whole, was at stake in the rising, and thus to deflect African interest from proceedings in the legislature. When it became once more the focus of political aspiration the initiative had passed to other activists, and more particularly to the Luo. This was signally marked in the 1957 elections—the first in which Africans voted—when, owing to the virtual exclusion of the Kikuyu from participation, they were not represented among the eight

[1] Colin Leys, 'Politics in Kenya: the development of peasant society', *Br. J. of Pol. Science*, 1 (1971), 307–37.

[2] Mathu, the only African member of the Executive Council, said that he and his five African colleagues on the Legislative Council accepted the emergency powers, but felt that they had been 'placed in political cold storage'. *The Times*, 25 Oct. 1952.

now directly elected African members on the Legislative Council.

It was thus to Luo leaders that there fell the task of organizing political action during this critical phase. At the same time their local influence throughout the country increased; by 1957, 90 branches of the Luo Union had been opened in various parts of Kenya.[1] Two of these leaders in fact deliberately sought to build up bases of power that extended beyond Nyanza Province. Tom Mboya, who had become Acting General Secretary of the Federation of Registered Trade Unions in 1953, and who returned late in 1956 from studying industrial management in Britain and establishing widespread links in North America, built up the union movement for this purpose;[2] C. M. G. Argwings-Kodhek, Kenya's first qualified African barrister, proposed to form a 'Kenya African National Congress'—though this only avoided proscription by re-naming itself the 'Nairobi District African Congress'. By contrast the third outstanding Luo politician, Oginga Odinga, concentrated on building up as a basis for his offensive on the centre of power a strongly entrenched position in his own home district of Central Nyanza.[3]

Already by the time of the debate, early in 1954, on the proposed Lyttelton Constitution, a gap was becoming apparent between these leaders and the nominated African members of the Legislative Council. The latter at first rejected the proposals for limited multi-racial government, but ultimately accepted them; B. A. Ohanga, although only with much hesitation, accepted the post of Minister for Community Development. Both Odinga, however, and Tom Mboya's Federation of Labour continued to reject them, and Ohanga's acceptance of a ministry was met by a storm of protest in Nyanza.

The elections of 1957, in which African voters for the first time took part, proved a turning point.[4] The franchise, it is true, was a narrow qualitative one; even when fully operative it would

[1] Odinga, *Not Yet Uhuru*, p. 131. It is not quite clear from the context to what date this statement refers.

[2] T. Mboya, *Freedom and After* (London, 1963), pp. 65, 78–80.

[3] Odinga, *Not Yet Uhuru*, pp. 128–40; Ogot, 'British Administration in Central Nyanza', loc. cit., pp. 272–3.

[4] For a short-term analysis of the 1957 election see G. F. Engholm, 'African Elections in Kenya, March 1957' in *Five African Elections*, ed. W. J. M. Mackenzie and K. E. Robinson (Oxford, 1960), pp. 391–459; see also G. Bennett and C. G. Rosberg, *The Kenyatta Election: Kenya 1960–1961* (London, 1961), pp. 33–5.

cover only some 30 per cent of the adult population, and at this time a large proportion of Central Province potential voters were still disqualified. Moreover, whether from distrust, lack of interest, or unfamiliarity with the requirements of the complex franchise qualifications, only about one-third of those eligible were in fact registered. Political associations, on their restricted district basis, remained embryonic. Only ten were registered, and Ardwings-Kodhek's NDAC could claim fewer than 400 paid up members. Nevertheless the perception and determination of the nationalist leaders now brought militant nationalism, supported by an effective wider popular will, for the first time to the centre of the political stage. Six of the eight existing African members of the Legislative Council were displaced, including Eliud Mathu, who was defeated by the Meru Bernard Mate; B. A. Ohanga, the Member for Community Development, whom Odinga defeated in Central Nyanza; and the nominated member for Nairobi, whose seat was won by Tom Mboya, contesting it also against Ardwings-Kodhek.

The newly elected members set themselves forthwith to make the most of their position. On the one hand they used it to challenge the strength of the administrative bureaucracy as it grew in power, 'the stiffest hurdle along their chosen path', as the Minister for African Affairs described it.[1] On the other, they used it to obtain for the first time the nation-wide platform which was denied to them by the continued ban on national political parties. One of their first actions was to form themselves into an African Elected Members' Organization. While their numbers did not yet allow them to prevail in the legislature on any given issue, they could and did give their views the widest possible publicity, both in Kenya and in Britain. It was this, and not participation in government, that they regarded as their business; they accordingly consistently refused, with one exception, to accept ministerial office over the next four years, regarding all constitutional arrangements as temporary and expendable until the attainment of African majority rule.[2]

An external influence of great importance during these years was the precedent set by Ghana; Ghana attained independence

---

[1] Leg Co *Debates*, 20 May 1957, col. 997. Quoted by Cherry Gertzel, *Independent Kenya*, p. 27.

[2] *Kenya Weekly News*, 6, 13 June 1958; Odinga, *Not Yet Uhuru*, pp. 161–4, 180–1.

three days before the 1957 elections; and soon afterwards Mboya invoked the Ghanaian example when calling for the boycotting of the Lyttelton Constitution. Collections were taken in Ghana to assist the defence in a defamation case when seven of the African members were sued for criminal libel for denouncing as 'stooges, quislings, and black Europeans' those of their colleagues who had accepted office or membership of the 'special seats' established under the Lennox-Boyd constitution of December 1957.[1]

This constitution, the last of the transitional stages before a decisive African majority was reached, was propounded by Alan Lennox-Boyd (who had followed Oliver Lyttelton as Colonial Secretary in July 1954), after lengthy discussions with all parties in the colony in October 1957. While conceding to African elected members parity with Europeans (14 each) it sought to maintain a slight brake on the shift of power by the device of 'special seats', to be filled by the Legislative Council—with its overall European predominance—voting as an electoral body. It was against the remaining vestige of privilege implied in these special seats that the African members took up their stand.

However, the unanimity on the central objective of securing an African elected majority did not extend far on other topics. Kenya's administrative history had long tended to entrench— where it did not create—local separateness; this tendency was now reinforced by the conditions for political activity imposed by the government. The African elected members on many matters had interests that were narrow and competitive. They were not subject to any party discipline, and each was perforce concerned with building up his own constituency support.

The most conspicuous division, it is true, that between the two Luo leaders, Odinga and Mboya, was a personal rather than a regional one.[2] This was evidently in part a difference in age, temperament and personal style; but it had other overtones. It reflected a suspicion, shared by others besides Odinga, of Mboya's Western contacts and sympathies—sharpened when there were some signs that Mboya might be willing to assume the mantle of the imprisoned Kenyatta; to this was added the contrast in

---

[1] *Guinea Times*, 21, 31 May 1958. Nkrumah is also reported as having advised Mboya in March 1958 on the subject of Kenyatta, 'Never let go of your martyrs'. *KWN*, 5 Sep. 1958.

[2] Odinga, *Not Yet Uhuru*; Mboya, *Freedom and After, passim*.

political strategy between Mboya's all-Kenya trade unionism and Odinga's concentration on the local base in Nyanza.

But besides rivalry of personalities there were differences in wealth and opportunity between the different areas. The coast, represented by Ronald Ngala, was economically far behind the other main agricultural regions, and its people tended to be apprehensive of the influence of the large immigrant labour element from the interior amongst them. The Central Province, both historically and in consequence of the capital input arising from the Emergency, was better off than Nyanza, and was also much more sensitive on land issues; there was, finally, considerable jealousy between the richer agricultural peoples, both Kikuyu and Luo, and the pastoralists—chiefly those linked historically with the Masai—who came to describe themselves as the Kalenjin.[1] This last was to form the basis of the main division during the prelude to independence, that between the Kenya African National Union (KANU) and the Kenya African Democratic Union (KADU). In September 1958 the members for the Kipsigis and the Tugen respectively, Taita Towett and Daniel arap Moi, proposed a Convention of United Kenya Parties which would 'aim to preserve the legitimate conservatism and traditions of the Kenya tribes and their tribal integrities'. On this basis they went on to form local organizations among the Elgeyo, Marakwet, and Nandi as well as the Kipsigis and Tugen.[2] In their fears that the larger, richer, and more organized Luo and Kikuyu might dominate the future, and in particular might secure the main benefits from any freeing of land in the White Highlands, they were joined by representatives of the smaller groups and the peoples of the coast. The European members, both by sympathy and by immediate political interest, were on the side of those who wished to entrench minority rights, whether regional or ethnic. Odinga claims that the decision not to allocate to Nyanza Province one of the six new African seats established by the Lennox-Boyd Constitution of 1957 was due to European fears of the influence of the 'Nyanza clique'.[3]

[1] This characteristic process of political and social aggregation, at once generated from below and promoted by policies and development from above, is analysed by Low and Lonsdale in the Introduction to this volume. See pp. 25–9 above.

[2] *KWN*, 5 Sept. 1958.

[3] Odinga, *Not Yet Uhuru*, pp. 153–4.

In April 1959 Lennox-Boyd outlined in the House of Commons the conditions of the British government for a transfer of power, and promised a constitutional conference to be held before the Kenya general election in the following year.[1] Although the formation of nation-wide all-African parties was still forbidden, it was a logical extension of the support invoked by the pastoralists and their allies for the rights of minority groups that at this time they were prepared to co-operate with non-Africans; the formation of their first regular nation-wide organization, the Kenya National Party (KNP) was announced by an Asian, and its multi-racial character (which it retained, however, for only four months) assured it of registration under the government's regulations.[2] The more radical group, in contrast, determined to challenge these regulations by claiming again the right of Africans to organize on a national basis. Early in August a forcefully-worded policy statement appeared, signed by six of them—Odinga, Kiano, Oguda, Mate, Mboya, and Kiamba; under the name of the Kenya Independence Movement (KIM) it demanded both the fixing of a date for independence and the release of Jomo Kenyatta.[3]

Just as Kenyatta's return to the Kenya political scene in the late 1940s illuminates much of the political development of those years, so his changing image—although still in detention—ten years later reflects the broadening current of nationalism in the 1950s. He had, as we have seen, largely failed before the Emergency to create unity behind his own leadership outside his Kikuyu homeland. And as late as June 1958 it was possible for one of the elected African members to speak in the Legislative Council of Kenyatta and his imprisoned associates as leaders who had failed—whose careers had 'foundered like ships in a sea'. But in the same debate Odinga caused a stir by referring to the detainees as 'still the political leaders',[4] and this was the turning point. The next major milestone was the death in March 1959 of a number of detainees at a camp at Hola, an ugly episode

---

[1] *Hansard*, 5th series, House of Commons, 604, cc. 561–8, 22 Apr. 1959.
[2] Leg Co *Debates*, 23 July 1959, cols. 219–20.
[3] Odinga, *Not Yet Uhuru*, pp. 168–71. See Gertzel, Goldschmidt, and Rothchild, *Government and Politics in Kenya*, pp. 198–9, for the text of the statement.
[4] Leg Co *Debates*, 17 June 1958, cc. 2406, 2409; Odinga, *Not Yet Uhuru*, pp. 156–9.

which affected attitudes in Britain as well as in Kenya.[1] Strengthened by the widespread indignation over this incident, the Luo politicians were before the end of the year seeking to outbid each other in praise of the imprisoned leader. The Mau Mau forces were being described as gallant freedom-fighters and in Accra Dr. Kiano, a Kikuyu elected member—even though elected only by those with 'loyalty' certificates—was comparing Kenyatta to Kwame Nkrumah. The Kikuyu movement was in retrospect being incorporated into a wider national consciousness, and Kenyatta himself was being embodied in an all-Kenya mythology.[2] By the time that the promised conference opened at Lancaster House early in 1960 no African group could have declined to join in the clamour for Kenyatta's release and return to political life.

The Lancaster House Conference was a response primarily to sustained African pressure, threatening a continued boycott of the Legislative Council until constitutional talks were promised. But the Colonial Secretary's path was made easier by some measure of European co-operation. The Europeans, immediately after the 1957 elections, had closed their ranks to deal with the first confrontation with African Elected Members. In April 1959, however, Michael (later Sir Michael) Blundell resigned as Minister of Agriculture in order to lead a multi-racial New Kenya Group in the Legislative Council, and this subsequently became the basis for his own political party (NKP). At the opposite extreme Group Captain L. R. ('Puck') Briggs replied to the manifesto of the Kenya Independence Movement by forming the United Party, committed to a regionally segregationist pattern of government and to the reduction of the Legislative Council to purely advisory functions. The forming of divisions on the African side, and now Blundell's share in promoting a conference, were bringing corresponding divisions in European attitudes.[3]

---

[1] Documents relating to the Deaths of Eleven Mau Mau Detainees at Hola Camp, Kenya, Cmnd. 778 (London, HMSO, 1959); Report of the Committee on Emergency Detention Camps (Nairobi, Govt. Printer, 1959). Iain Mcleod later wrote that the Hola affair, along with the Nyasaland riots in the same year, was a turning-point in his thinking on Africa. See 'Trouble in Africa', Spectator, 31 Jan. 1964.

[2] KWN, 19 Dec. 1959. In November 1959 Baring spoke in the Legislative Council of the danger of a cult of Kenyatta. Debates, 4 Nov. 1959, col. 9.

[3] Blundell, So Rough a Wind, pp. 246–52; Susan Wood, Kenya: the tensions of progress (London, 1960), pp. 45–56.

Looking back, these groupings seem puny enough. The quotation which gives the title to Blundell's autobiography is apposite:

> We shall be winnowed with so rough a wind
> That even our corn shall seem as light as chaff,
> And good from bad find no partition.[1]

It is abundantly clear that no multi-racial system of government embodying even the most modest degree of entrenched minority rights could in practice have survived. It is equally clear that there was even less chance of a European electorate forcing through a reversal of the prevailing currents setting in Kenya towards African majority rule. The function of multi-racialism was, as it turned out, to afford a valuable mechanism by which the total reversal of political roles could be carried out without any overt breach in the political order.

Yet in the political climate of 1958–9 these things were less obvious. With the closer adminstrative control and the continued prosperity despite the Emergency, the number of Europeans in the country was greater than ever before. There were at least some leading African politicians who were ready to co-operate in a degree of either multi-racialism or regionalism, or both.[2] More important, there was the situation in Central Africa, which to white opinion was more relevant than that in Ghana: African representation had just been effectively reduced in the Federal Assembly, while in Southern Rhodesia the election of June 1958 had brought the defeat of the Liberal, Garfield Todd. Moreover, it was less than six years since Lennox-Boyd had given his pledge about the future of European settlement in Kenya, and only a few months since he had repeated that the British government's responsibility to all the inhabitants of Kenya of all races and communities would not be abandoned 'in the foreseeable future'.[3]

In fact, the speed with which the Kenya situation was transformed cannot be explained without some reference to the rapid evolution in the colonial policies of the Conservative

---

[1] Shakespeare, 2 *Henry IV*, IV. i.

[2] See e.g. Blundell, *So Rough a Wind*, pp. 244–6; and the brief episode of the multi-racial Kenya National Party, Wood, *Kenya*, p. 51.

[3] Press Conference at Nairobi, 8 Nov. 1957, on the announcement of the 'Lennox-Boyd Constitution'.

government in London. There are indications that the prime minister, Harold Macmillan, had been contemplating a major shift in colonial policy for some time past;[1] the key factor in this seems to have been the appreciation prompted by developments in Ghana that nationalism was likely to become as irresistible in Africa as it had proved in India, the strategic reappraisal following Suez, and the heavy expenditure involved in metropolitan aid and control. But it was only with victory in the 1959 elections that he felt strong enough to carry through the implications of this; the succession of Iain Macleod to Lennox-Boyd at the Colonial Office registered the decision that the urgent task was to identify a political body to which power could be handed over, not eventually but as quickly as possible. Such a body could no longer be the Kenya Europeans. The Emergency was brought to an end in November 1959 by the new governor, Sir Patrick Renison, who had succeeded Baring a few weeks earlier. The four-year-old recommendation of the East Africa Royal Commission for the ending of the reservation of the White Highlands was belatedly accepted. It was essentially the Ghana solution, not the Rhodesian one, which was to be prescribed for Kenya.

This was the background to the Lancaster House Conference held in January 1960.[2] The objective set out in Macleod's opening speech was 'a nation based on parliamentary institutions on the Westminster model and enjoying responsible government'; and while the representatives of Blundell's party (the most conciliatory of the European groups and that most numerous at the conference) held out for a continuing measure of multi-racialism, Macleod made it clear that his chief concern was simply to bridge as smoothly as possible the inevitable transition to eventual common roll elections. The outcome was an African majority on the Legislative Council which, for all the reservations on behalf of community interests for the time being, made the longer-term movement towards complete African control a foregone conclusion. It was symptomatic that although demands

---

[1] For a discussion of this question see D. Horowitz, 'Attitudes of British Conservatives towards Decolonization in Africa', *African Affairs*, 69, 274 (1970), 9–26. Also relevant are two articles by Iain Macleod, 'Blundell's Kenya', *Spectator*, 20 Mar. 1964; and 'Britain's Future Policy in Africa', *Weekend Telegraph*, 12 Mar. 1965.
[2] The antecedents and course of the First Lancaster House Conference are discussed in Bennett and Rosberg, *Kenyatta Election*, pp. 17–26. Cp. Odinga, *Not Yet Uhuru*, pp. 176–81; Mboya, *Freedom and After*, pp. 115–16, 125–8.

that Kenyatta should attend were refused, Mbiyu Koinange, his sometime close associate and alleged confederate in Mau Mau activities, was eventually admitted as a legal adviser;[1] and that the United Party representatives, who were most vehement in denouncing Koinange's presence, could do no more than stage a token abstention of a single afternoon from the discussion in protest. The more general European reaction was reflected in the thirty pieces of silver flung at Blundell's feet at Nairobi airport on his return, and in a sharp fall on the Nairobi stock exchange.

The final phase

Although the African representatives went to the Lancaster House Conference as a single group, with the member for the Coast, Ronald Ngala, as chairman, and the Luo Tom Mboya as secretary, their co-operation was—apart from the main issue of elective majority rule—superficial and temporary. Despite some cross-currents largely arising from the personal animosities which played continually around the personality and ambitions of Tom Mboya, it was not many months before the two main African parties which were to fight the 1961 election crystallized broadly along the lines of the previous divisions.[2]

A conference of political leaders held at Kiambu on 27 March 1960 was attended by delegates from thirty African political organizations. In the months that followed, however, such associations either disappeared or were merged in the two main national parties. Popular political participation was widespread and intensive. But, although the image evoked was generally that of an incipient two-party system along orthodox British party lines, any such analogy was far wide of the mark. What was ostensibly at stake was who could claim to speak with the voice of Kenya nationalism; at a PAFMECA meeting at Moshi shortly before the Lancaster House Conference the debate had been as to whether KNP or KIM should go to London as the

[1] This was preceded by five days of negotiation, ended by a face-saving device whereby the British government agreed to issue a blank pass, on which the African delegates might write Koinange's name for entry to Lancaster House, though not to the conference chamber. Odinga, *Not Yet Uhuru*, pp. 177–8.

[2] Bennett and Rosberg, *Kenyatta Election*, is the main source for the account of the election that follows.

true nationalist party.[1] Behind this issue lay the fundamental divergences of interest already described—whether the successor political power should be monolithic or should be circumscribed in the interests of ethnic and regional minorities. In particular, fears and jealousies over land had been aggravated by the Kenya government's acceptance, at the end of 1959, of the Royal Commission's recommendation that the reservation of the White Highlands should be brought to an end. For the next three years the members of the dominant Luo–Kikuyu alliance fought steadily—though not without much factious division—to establish a monolithic national party, broadly based among all Kenya's peoples, under the leadership of Kenyatta; its opponents were able to do no more than stage a series of rearguard actions.

After the Lancaster House Conference delegates from thirty of the district associations decided to form a mass organization, to be known as the Kenya African National Union (KANU). Its colours and symbols were to be those of the KAU of the past, and the continuity was further stressed by the choice of Kenyatta as president (though the government at first made the withdrawal of his name the condition of registration), and of James Gichuru to act in his absence. Odinga was vice-president and Tom Mboya, by virtue largely of his strong trade union network, was general secretary. Its anxiety to preserve a genuinely national front was shown by the election of Ronald Ngala, the vigorous member for the Coast, who was then absent in the United States, as treasurer; Ngala, however, on his return refused the KANU treasurership, and in June headed the representatives of the Coast Peoples' African Union in joining the pastoralists' alliance, which took the name of the Kenya African Democratic Union (KADU).

Against their KANU opponents, and the powerful Luo and Kikuyu regional interests which dominated them, it is remarkable that the Kalenjin and their allies were able to hold out as long as they did. They were heavily outnumbered by the KANU-dominated groups which included between 60 per cent and 75 per cent of the electorate; they had far poorer resources with which to campaign; and with only one or two exceptions they had no one to match the Luo and Kikuyu leaders in political

---

[1] Richard Cox, *Pan-Africanism in Practice* (London, 1964), pp. 28–31; *Tanganyika Standard*, 17 Sept. 1959.

experience. Moreover, minority and regional rights are inherently a poor theme around which to build up a mass movement. In this case, for instance, it meant co-operation with the Somali National Association, and thus a measure of support for an ethnic group whose main objective was ultimate secession from Kenya. It also meant a degree of inter-racial co-operation, which in the long run was probably even more damaging. In February 1961, at the first of the two general elections that followed the Lancaster House Conference, KANU won 67 per cent of the votes, and 19 of the 32 open seats. At the second, in 1963, the KANU victory became in effect absolute.

Yet up to the election of May 1963 KADU continued to be a major force on the political scene. The high-water mark of its influence was reached in January 1962, when the second Lancaster House Conference agreed on a regionalized constitution and a coalition government.[1] But the party's lease of life was thus prolonged for two reasons only. The first was that its moderate and multi-racial character for a time acted as a protection. It enjoyed the support of the administration and of the liberal wing of the European element; this enabled it, when KANU followed up its first election victory by refusing to take office unless Kenyatta were released, to run a minority government for the next two years, and thereafter to take part in a coalition until the next general election. The second reason was the persistence of deep rifts within KANU, combined with deficiencies in the party's internal organization.

Some of these rifts were personal, centred in particular around the continued rivalry between Mboya and Odinga. Odinga had spent the greater part of 1962 in a wide round of travels and contacts which included Egypt, Yugoslavia, China, Japan, and the Soviet Union, collecting funds and arranging student scholarships.[2] Mboya by contrast continued to be suspect as a tool of Western imperialism; there were stories that in 1961 he was involved with the administration, along with the Kikuyu

---

[1] *Report of the Kenya Constitutional Conference*, 1962, Cmnd. 1700 (London, HMSO, 1962). According to Mboya (*Freedom and After*, p. 86), 'the brains behind most of KADU's arguments and papers' on regionalism were those of prominent New Kenya Party leaders. A Swiss constitutional lawyer was employed as a consultant. The constitution was published as L. N. 718/1963 (Independent Instruments No. 1968/1963).

[2] Odinga, *Not Yet Uhuru*, pp. 184–92.

James Gichuru and the KADU leaders Ngala and Muliro, in a design to keep Kenyatta out of office.[1] Thus the quarrels turned mainly on the issue of proving loyalty to the absent Kenyatta; but even Kenyatta's release in August 1961, and his assumption of the presidency of the party, did not immediately end them.

The release of Kenyatta brought to an end the main justification for maintaining KADU in power as a minority government. It accordingly also provided an occasion for a final effort to bring the parties together in a single national movement.[2] Such a united movement was keenly desired by Kenyatta himself. But preliminary talks between the two groups quickly broke down. No formula for dividing up the ministries satisfactory to both sides could be found; the KADU leaders expressed fears for their lands and distrust of Kenyatta's leadership; and in the end Kenyatta was left to take on the presidency of KANU alone. Although at the ensuing second Lancaster House Conference a coalition government was with some difficulty formed, the insistence at that conference on the KADU blue-print for regionalism underlined the wide gap between the parties. It soon became clear that the coalition's short period of office was to be merely one of skirmishing before the general election to be held the following year.

During this period KANU's internal dissensions still seemed to be a substantial obstacle to the party's aspirations. In June 1962 Mboya as Minister of Labour in the coalition government had to deal with a series of strikes which many believed to be fomented by his fellow-ministers. In August a Luo United Movement (LUM) was launched with the blessing of his father-in-law, Walter Odede, and a meeting in Nairobi of trade unionists, many of them Luo, went so far as to attack Kenyatta's leadership. Only a re-affirmation by Mboya of his loyalty to Kenyatta checked the possibility that the LUM might break away altogether from KANU. There was in fact a breakaway— a more serious one—by the Kamba under Paul Ngei. Ngei had been in detention with Kenyatta at Lodwar; since his release in 1961 he had taken a much more extreme position over the issue of the European lands than was welcome to the responsible

---

[1] Odinga, *Not Yet Uhuru*, pp. 199–200, 211–13.
[2] Clyde Sanger and J. Nottingham, 'The Kenya General Election of 1963', *J. Mod. Af. Studies*, 2, 1 (1964).

leaders of KANU, and now the Kamba found a further cause for dissatisfaction in the representations submitted to the commission for delimiting the new regions to be set up. They wanted the Kamba to have their own regions separate from both the Kikuyu and the Masai.

In the end, although some of KANU's dissidents in Nyanza did join, Ngei was unable to hold them, and his African People's Party (APP) soon revealed itself to be no more than a sectional one of the Kamba.[1] Nevertheless, the Kamba secession proved to be the final shock needed to destroy any KANU complacency that remained after the 1961 victory. Kenyatta determined to take the party structure in hand, and in this he was helped by the observations made by Odinga on the latter's visit to West Africa in 1960, when he had studied Sekou Touré's party organization in Conakry. A new treasurer, Joseph Murumbi, who had been acting secretary of KAU just before the Emergency, improved KANU's headquarters 'out of all recognition', and proceeded to tighten up the party's organization generally. Despite some disputes over the nomination of candidates both groups in the party planned the election campaign together. Outside financial support came from the governments of Ghana, Ethiopia, Algeria, and Egypt, and from TANU in Tanganyika.

In contrast, KADU's inherent weaknesses were now made manifest. The support given to KANU by Kenya's neighbours strikingly showed the dangers of association with actual or potential irridentist movements, particularly the Somali. Co-operation with the Kamba proved difficult, for Ngei remained a nationalist at heart, and refused to come out with a clear pledge in support of KADU's policy of regionalism. Indeed, more generally, KADU found itself unable to maintain throughout the election the tribal alliances on which it essentially depended; clashes arose, for instance, over the detailed recommendations of the commission set up in 1962 to determine regional boundaries,[2] and these resulted in some defections to the KANU ranks.

[1] G. Bennett, 'Political Realities in Kenya', *World Today*, 19, 7 (July 1963), 294–301.
[2] *Report of the Regional Boundaries Commission*, Cmnd. 1899 (London, HMSO, 1962). There were clashes in the neighbourhood of Maseno between Luhya and Luo in February 1963, and the threat to detach the township of Kitale from the Rift Valley Region sent the northern Masai over to the KANU ranks.

The 1961 election had produced a decisive victory for KANU; that of May 1963 witnessed a landslide.[1] Their share of the vote, indeed, was about the same as before—two thirds of the total. But KADU and their allies were unable to field enough candidates to constitute even a potential majority. KANU secured 68 out of the total 112 seats, while a further four Independents declared themselves for KANU immediately after the election. KADU won 32 seats, and Paul Ngei's APP eight.

When, on 1 June 1963, Kenyatta became Kenya's first prime minister on the attainment of internal self-government, his government had every appearance of a broad national base. His ministers included a Kamba, a Kisii, a Maragoli, a Taita, and a European of South African origin; his parliamentary secretaries another European, an Asian, and a Masai. Old KAU leaders, and men tried with Kenyatta in 1953, were balanced with the new KANU men who had gained prominence in their absence.

During the six months that remained before the date of final independence on 12 December 1963, KANU consolidated its position and the opposition fell into further disarray. The uneasy co-operation between KADU and Paul Ngei's APP broke up in September, when Ngei, finding himself excluded from the opposition's delegation to the final pre-independence conference in London, crossed the floor with his seven Kamba followers. At the conference KANU claimed an electoral mandate to modify the 'regional' constitution which had been agreed upon in the previous year; and, although in Nairobi KADU supporters retaliated with a threat to form a breakaway KADU state, the bluff was called. A final agreement on 20 October—the eleventh anniversary of the declaration of the Emergency—between the British and the Kenya governments strengthened the powers of the central government over the police and the public service commission, and made the regional powers alterable by a two-thirds majority in a national referendum.[2] Although KADU formally boycotted the final session of the conference, Ngala on his return to Nairobi announced the shelving of the KADU

---

[1] Sanger and Nottingham, 'Kenya Election of 1963', loc. cit.

[2] *Kenya Independence Conference, 1963*, Cmnd. 2156 (London, HMSO, 1963). See also H. W. M. Okoth-Ogendo, 'Constitutional Change in Kenya since Independence', *African Affairs*, 71, 282 (1972), 9–34.

secession plan, ostensibly in reliance on the government's promise to implement the regional constitution.[1] In the next few weeks a number of Kalenjin leaders crossed the floor of the National Assembly to join the victorious ruling party.

At independence some 1,500 forest fighters came out from the forests of Mount Kenya and laid down their arms. They symbolized both the strength and the weakness of the government which Jomo Kenyatta headed. It was in many ways a more securely based government than had been in power when he had returned to Kenya as one of five million unenfranchised Africans seventeen years before. It had secured the independence from Britain which the Europeans had once dreamed of for their 'white man's country'. It had been voted into power by an overwhelming majority of the adult population of the country. It had at its disposal an administration more highly qualified and more powerful in relation to the population than had ever been the lot of any British ex-colonial territory save India. But the forest fighters did not only symbolize the government's authority and their acceptance of it. They stood also for still unsatisfied demands. The major part of Kenya's economy and administrative structure had been built during the colonial period around the contribution of the immigrants; European business men, farmers, and civil servants, Asian traders, clerks, and craftsmen. Now the landless wanted a speeding up of the settlement schemes started in 1962 in the former 'White Highlands'; those with some training, or eager to acquire it, were impatient for the Africanization of the public services; but meanwhile a mounting pool of unemployed looked for the livelihoods which economic and political uncertainties had made it more difficult to earn.

In the future the local and regional jealousies which had so long complicated the progress of Kenya's African nationalism would not vanish. They would however be partially submerged in the re-assertion of important continuities with the patterns of colonial Kenya's political and social structure. Many, but by no means all, of the European farmers would have departed. But there would still be some big estates, and a limited number of

---

[1] By a series of amendments (Acts Nos. 28 and 38 of 1964, Act No. 14 of 1965) the regional constitution was in the event virtually dismantled within 18 months of independence.

fairly rich farmers—the ranks of the latter swelled by the effects of land consolidation in the Central Province; by contrast there would still be the vast majority of primarily subsistence farmers, and an increasing number of landless and unemployed. Nairobi would continue to be the commercial and financial centre of East Africa, attracting a fair volume of foreign aid and trade, and generating a prosperity now shared by Africans as well as Europeans—but not shared very widely. Those who could command the centre of political power would continue to be the masters and allies of a civil service singularly well-versed, for Africa, in the arts of planning and of administrative control, and strongly reinforced with foreign expertise. Not without reason has Kenya been seen as an outstanding example of the neo-colonial pattern of change in Africa.[1]

---

[1] Leys, 'Politics in Kenya', loc cit., p. 309.

MAP 3. TANGANYIKA: GENERAL AND ADMINISTRATIVE, 1956–7.

III

SOCIAL ENGINEERING, MULTI-RACIALISM, AND THE RISE OF *TANU*: THE TRUST TERRITORY OF TANGANYIKA 1945–1961

MARGARET L. BATES

THE achievement of independence by Tanganyika on 9 December 1961, the first of the British East African territories to reach this status, surprised the country's own political leaders and would have seemed impossible sixteen years earlier. At the end of the Second World War Tanganyika was less advanced than Kenya or Uganda when measured by economic or educational criteria; size and lack of communications made administration and development difficult, while the government's devotion during the inter-war years to the ideal of 'Native Administration' meant that it had concentrated on politics and administration at very local levels. In contrast to Kenya and Uganda, Tanganyika possessed no political movement with a substantial impact at the territorial level until well after 1950, or at least so it appeared to the government and European observers.

By 1945 the African Association—the single territory-wide African political organization then in being—had begun to move into the political arena, its spread of influence made easier by the general use of Swahili as a lingua franca and by the increased mobility of African civil servants after the war.[1] To the central government however it seemed to represent only a handful of Africans, and for several years most decisions were taken without any regard for its opinions. At local levels its branches had more weight, principally because the first government steps for change and recognition of African political participation occurred there. Government policy was in fact to create the very conditions and institutions through which a nationalist movement could operate: elected councils at various levels, co-operatives, trade unions, a greatly expanded educational structure. The pace of

---

[1] For further discussion of the African Association see p. 167 sqq. below.

change was at first extremely slow; as late as 1954 even nationalist leaders were still speaking of independence in twenty years' time, and the government was protesting that this was moving much too fast.

The territorial political climate in 1945 was largely determined by government policies and ideas, with some small influence to be assigned to individual British settlers and, very occasionally, an Indian businessman or African chief. Low literacy rates and the lack of a vernacular press handicapped the formulation of African territorial opinion. Public opinion as usually thought of represented a small group of persons, centred mainly in Dar es Salaam and communicating in English. The large majority of Africans were outside this network; so were most of the European settlers who were not British. Early political discussions at a 'territorial' level were restricted to a group largely consisting of colonial civil servants and their social circle. Tanganyika in the late 1940s was essentially a group of disparate political communities and interest groups held together through the government administrative structure. With the constitutional changes of the 1950s and the rise of the nationalist movement local, group, and territorial politics began to coalesce into a national pattern.

In the early post-war period, however, the government had tended to regard political reform largely as a dependent variable, and had concentrated on what it saw as more basic social and economic change. Tanganyika's post-war planning had begun with reports submitted in 1940 by the Central Development Committee and in 1943 by the Central Education Committee. Wartime experience affected these first ideas; economic co-operation with Kenya and Uganda was close, and had revived the idea of an East African federation in both East African and British minds. The British settlers in Tanganyika had worked closely with government officials during the war and favoured such an idea. They also wanted more extensive white settlement, and a much greater emphasis on economic development. On the second point at least they were at one with government officials, many of whom believed that Tanganyika had been allowed to stagnate economically during the inter-war period. Their attitude was also generally compatible with new ideas prevailing in the Colonial Office. Sir Wilfrid Jackson, who had become governor in 1941, began discussions on a new constitution as early as 1943, but the major problems of the territory were viewed as primarily those which required money, technical expertise and investment of time.

The pattern of change envisaged for Tanganyika in the late 1940s was built around a series of interconnected policies. An economic development plan emphasized creation of a basic economic infra-structure for the territory, concentrating on road-building, increased production of export crops, and the extension of water supplies. Closer co-ordination with Kenya and Uganda was to create a larger and more promising area for development. A moderate increase in schools was to provide trained Africans for the lower echelons of the civil service and the Native Administrations, the tribally-based local governmental structures for which Tanganyika had become famous. Basic changes in some social policies would remove the grosser forms of racial discrimination against Africans and assist in the gradual westernization of African society. At the same time, reform of the Native Administrations and of the Legislative Council would make these bodies more efficient and increase African participation in policy-making. Changes in the international agreement by which Great Britain administered the Tanganyika Territory, made possible after signing of the United Nations Charter, would give the British government the requisite authority to achieve these objectives.[1]

This general programme was one of social engineering, in which changes were to be brought about by a paternal Tanganyika government, working in general alliance with sympathetic settlers, businessmen, missionaries, and members of the small westernized African community. Its implementation involved a substantial shift from prewar premisses about the preservation of African societies, premisses which were deeply ingrained in the whole structure of government in Tanganyika and also in the minds of the very officials whose job it was to bring about change. The programme paid little attention to the timing of change, and as noted its objectives were formulated largely without consultation with the African population. The

---

[1] The final text of the Trusteeship Agreement according to which Great Britain administered Tanganyika appeared in United Nations *Treaty Series*, viii, 1947. For discussion of British relations with the UN see pp. 174–6 below.

programme was cognizant of the possible impact of international events, although it proved later to have substantially underestimated this factor.

The first development plans were cautious in the extreme. On the financial side, the territory benefited from three circumstances not of its own making: the general change in imperial attitudes which made financing for many projects available from Colonial Development and Welfare funds; the British decision to use for Tanganyikan development the funds accruing from the sale of German-owned properties in the territory; and the phenomenal rise in the price of sisal brought about by the Korean war. It was not until the 1950s that these had much local impact. The first large-scale economic project in Tanganyika, the Groundnut Scheme of 1947, was largely outside the control of the Tanganyika government and its results for the Territory were very mixed. Tanganyika's economic boom before independence took place mostly in the later 1950s; development plans were constantly revised, as funds, personnel, or equipment became available, and planning priorities often changed from month to month.[1]

All the programmes demanded trained manpower, largely unavailable in Tanganyika. The British administrative cadres, as elsewhere, were markedly under establishment at the end of the war; by 1950 they had begun to increase rapidly despite continuing difficulties of recruitment. Ironically, African officials in the Native Administrations, who had exercised initiative and authority during the war years, now found their role diminished. The Liwali of Bagamoyo, who had administered that district without any British officers in most of 1944 and 1945, was now supervised by three administrative officers and a growing technical staff. As British staff increased, the ordinary African found his own life much more closely affected by officials than had previously been the case.

Expansion of the administrative and technical services, and the Groundnut Scheme, brought larger numbers of Europeans

---

[1] Cf. *A Ten-Year Development and Welfare Plan for Tanganyika Territory, Report by the Development Commission*, (Dar es Salaam, Govt. Printer, 1946); *Revised Development and Welfare Plan for Tanganyika 1950–56*, (Dar es Salaam, Govt. Printer, 1950). For the Groundnut Scheme in Tanganyika, see *The Future of the Overseas Food Corporation*, Cmd. 8125 (London, HMSO, 1957) and Alan Wood, *The Groundnut Affair* (London, 1950); and chapter vii below.

into the territory. Settlers also arrived to take up farms, especially in Northern Province, while private investment in sisal, tea, and other industries introduced additional European personnel.

By 1952, the estimated European population was over 25,000, far above earlier figures. It was, moreover, extremely heterogeneous; there were substantial numbers of Greeks and Germans, and many other nationalities were represented. Many of these Europeans did not have a 'permanent interest' in Tanganyika, as Governor Twining phrased it, for they were in Tanganyika for a period of years but did not contemplate permanent settlement for themselves or their families. Their numbers were always much smaller than those of the Europeans in Kenya; they were widely scattered geographically and despite attempts to obtain political power their base for doing so was weak.

The problems of planning were particularly shown in such areas as transportation, agricultural development, and education. Railway engines and rolling stock ordered in Britain in 1947 were not delivered until three or four years later, while costs of road-building increased astronomically. Agricultural change depended upon a greatly increased demonstration staff and extension work for which both British and African personnel were inexperienced, while the territorial policy of enforcing agricultural change through the Native Administrations was widely resented by Africans and became a serious point of friction with the administration.[1]

A ten-year plan for African education, announced in 1947 when approximately 7·5 per cent of Tanganyikan children attended school, aimed at a general attainment of literacy, but at very little training of Africans to university or advanced technical levels. Projected figures for Tanganyika students to attend Makerere College remained substantially lower than those for Kenya and Uganda. Only six students entered the college in 1946, and the total entry for Tanganyika students up to 1953 was exactly 207. Although it had been hoped to have all eligible children in primary school by 1956, a review of progress in that year disclosed that first-year enrolments were less than one half of that target, and that only one child in ten continued beyond the fourth year. Territorial planning after 1955 concentrated on middle and secondary education, but Tanganyika at

[1] See pp. 169-71 below.

independence depended largely on the skills of youngsters who had reached the middle schools before that date.[1]

However gradual this educational development, it contributed to the changing pattern of Tanganyikan society. A larger and more westernized group of Africans, emerging from Makerere and the leading secondary schools, was interested in territorial problems and became increasingly vocal about African aspirations. Migration to Dar es Salaam and other towns (Mwanza, Tabora, Dodoma) created the first urban concentrations and their accompanying problems, although Dar es Salaam itself in many ways remained, right up to independence, a Zaramo community. In 1947 Dar es Salaam had its first serious strike, a spontaneous demonstration by dockworkers, and trade unions began to appear. Other African associations increased in activity and importance, both in the towns and in rural areas where African co-operatives, churches, and tribal associations frequently played a major role. In Uchagga, Usambara, and Unyakyusa new forms of tribal patriotism appeared, which substantially affected both the Native Administrations and political planning at the centre. The African Association could draw for membership upon a larger and more sophisticated African community.

Government policies frequently aided the emergence of these new groups. In the rural areas, co-operative development was pushed as a major matter of policy, and other improvement societies were encouraged.[2] Trade unions were assisted by the Labour Department, and a new Department of Social Welfare (later Social Development) was created which was concerned with everything from communal well-digging to making films in Swahili. More extensive educational opportunities for women were made available, and in several instances native courts were persuaded to change local customs which seemed unduly discriminatory. The first measures to abolish discriminatory racial laws came in 1947, when the word 'native' was removed from most legislation, and civil service positions were made no longer entirely dependent on race. Until 1954, however, when

---

[1] *A Ten-Year Plan for the Development of African Education* (Dar es Salaam, Govt. Printer, 1947); Tanganyika, Report of the Education Department, 1955. See also J. E. Goldthorpe, *An African Elite: Makerere College Students 1922–1960* (Nairobi, 1965).

[2] By 1954, Tanganyika had the largest number of co-operative societies in the colonial empire. There were 243 societies with 196,775 members.

strong pressure to abolish racial discrimination was undertaken as part of its multi-racial political programme, government actions in this field were piecemeal and contradictory. In 1949, for instance, the schools were so segregated that the Director of Education was the only point of contact for quite separate African, Indian, and European education structures. A segregationist approach to land tenure was still required by law. Changes were more often those of terminology than of substance; the practical separation of the races was largely achieved in Dar es Salaam by zoning based on development covenants, although the language of race disappeared from the law. The government spoke of race relations as good, but from the African point of view there were few changes in the prevailing social pattern which placed Europeans in the most important positions, Asians in the middle, and Africans at the bottom.

Government initiatives in constitutional and political change, 1945–51

Government plans for political change in Tanganyika started with the premisses that a reform of local and central government structures was overdue, that some connection must be worked out between the two levels of government, and that Africans must increasingly if gradually be associated with the process of decision-making. Government was interested in the entry of Africans into the public services, in the introduction of some representative principle in the Native Administrations and in the Legislative Council, and in efficient forms of local government. These long-term objectives were reasonably clear, but the means had to be worked out. There seems never to have been a clear-cut sequence of thinking about levels of administration as there was in Uganda, and the focus of change shifted from the centre to local levels and back again. The pattern of district councils which existed in both Kenya and Uganda was not accepted in Tanganyika until 1955; in the decade before that much experimentation occurred. The differing types of local administration, based on tribal usage, which had previously been accepted as desirable were now perceived to be disadvantageous for coherent territorial development, but there seems to have been considerable disagreement within the Tanganyikan administration itself as to acceptable substitute mechanisms.

The governor, Sir Wilfrid Jackson, wrote to the Colonial Office in 1944 stressing the desirability of seizing the initiative in political matters and underlining the necessity of providing for African membership on the Legislative Council.[1] In 1945 an Order in Council increased the size of the Council to 29 members, 14 of them to be appointed unofficials. The order did not specify membership by race, but in practice the four new unofficial seats were to be African; the unofficial side of the Council was thus divided evenly between Europeans and non-Europeans. Chiefs Kidaha Makwaia from Sukumaland and Abdiel Shangali from Uchagga were the first appointed African members. Other African appointments waited several years, the government maintaining that it had difficulty finding Africans whose knowledge of English was adequate for the Council's work. This gave Africans a link to central government which had previously been entirely lacking, and showed African leaders a path by which they might increasingly influence governmental decisions. From the beginning African members of the Council regarded their role as a representative one, even though the sympathies of the chiefs sometimes lay with the government.

Once this step was taken government initiatives for the next few years concentrated on local government. The Provincial Commissioners' Conference, reactivated in 1944, considered native administration reform, and some changes had already been made before March 1947 when the Secretary of State for the Colonies, Arthur Creech Jones, issued his circular dispatch on the democratization of local government. This principle was entirely acceptable to the administration in Tanganyika, but democratizing in accordance with local tradition meant a continuation of the extremely varied patterns of existing Native Administrations. It was also discovered that the objectives of Africanization, democratization, and efficiency often conflicted. Councils of elders, created to advise chiefs, proved in a number of instances to be stunningly ineffective, while the new tasks assigned to native treasuries and native courts could only be undertaken with the assistance and training provided by an

---

[1] Jackson to Colonial Office, 16 Oct. 1944, Tanzania National Archives (TNA) Secretariat Minute Paper (SMP) 16431. Jackson, whose term of office lasted from 1941 to 1945, played a major role in territorial development which has not yet been fully explored.

increased European personnel. Popular reaction also varied. In Uhehe the government found itself pushing reform well ahead of the local population, while in Uchagga and Usambara change was felt to be long overdue and demonstrations against the Native Administrations had already occurred.[1]

Despite these difficulties, Tanganyika after 1947 became a showcase for experiments in local government as it had been in native administration. In areas where a tribal authority did not exist, the pre-war system of appointed *liwalis* as administrative officials was expanded, often with councils of elders or lineage heads to whom were added representatives of the 'young men' of the community. In Sukumaland, a widespread and complicated network of councils (more than 900) was created, as part of the Sukumaland Development Scheme, a comprehensive attempt at development in the political, economic, and educational fields. The scheme was based politically upon the Sukuma tribe and its pyramid of local councils, but its economic base, the growing of cotton, called for the inclusion of neighbouring non-Sukuma peoples. The unwieldy conciliar system seemed to appeal more to the European than the African mind; politically, the scheme was not very workable although it produced some valuable economic results. After several years of considerable government effort the project was overtaken by new schemes for local government, especially that of county councils, and also by a growing African nationalism.[2]

In Uchagga a different picture emerged. In 1946 the government regrouped the nineteen existing Chagga chiefdoms into three divisions under new chiefs, and introduced some popular representation on divisional councils. To its surprise there was considerable local opposition to this move, from young men who felt the reforms did not go far enough, and the resulting five-year agitation for a constitutional conference and the election of a paramount chief drew territorial attention and imitation by other tribal groupings.

The Chagga had seized the political initiative from the British authorities and begun to create their own political

---

[1] For developments in Uchagga see below.

[2] *Development of African Local Government in Tanganyika*, Col. 277 (London, HMSO, 1951); J. Gus Liebenow, jun., 'Responses to Planned Political Change in a Tanganyikan Tribal Group', *American Political Science Review*, 50 (June 1956); G. Andrew Maguire, *Toward 'Uhuru' in Tanganyika* (Cambridge, 1969).

institutions. Their treasury, however, was frequently in financial difficulties as it undertook more extensive programmes each year; the local demand for education was almost insatiable and well beyond government capacities to meet; the Paramount Chief, Marealle II, was deposed several years later for a series of unpopular actions including the attempt to make his office hereditary, and replaced by an officer responsible to the council. There was, furthermore, no attempt to relate Chagga patterns of government to those of the country at large.[1]

The administration was, in fact, still trying to decide where the boundary lines between local and central government lay. Here there was considerable confusion between attempts at administrative devolution, turning over to local bodies responsibility for some central government services, and the development of autonomous local institutions with their own spheres of activity. In 1950 administrative officials were advised that native authorities, hitherto regarded as integral parts of central government, were to be regarded as separate entities.[2] At a somewhat less local level the problem was more difficult. In June 1949 the government created the Lake Province Council, a multi-racial appointed body whose job it was to advise the government and to administer some local projects financed with central government funds. It had no statutory basis or independent powers, and it was unclear where it fitted into financial, administrative, or political patterns. In 1950 a similar council was created in the Southern Highlands and, under strong European settler influence, it baulked at undertaking development projects or administering local programmes until it was allotted its own financial resources. These provincial councils, however, proved to be a second experiment which was overtaken by changing events and ideas, and they only marked time until their disappearance several years later.

The mobilization of African discontent

Government initiatives were, in the early 1950s, challenged by the establishment of effective African and European political

---

[1] P. H. Johnston, 'Chagga Constitutional Development', *Journal of African Administration*, 5, 3 (July 1953); G. K. Whitlamsmith, *Recent Trends in Chagga Political Development* (Moshi, 1955); Kathleen M. Stahl, 'The Chagga', in P. H. Gulliver (ed.), *Tradition and Transition in East Africa* (London, 1969).

[2] *The Development of African Local Government in Tanganyika 1950–57*, mimeograph (Dar es Salaam, 1957).

groupings, and political debate on a much wider scale began to occur.

The principal forum for African activity was the African Association. Formed late in 1929, it had been established by African civil servants, teachers, and other members of the small group of western-educated Africans; it had a variety of social, educational, and political objectives. In the 1930s it had a number of branches throughout Tanganyika and in Zanzibar, often centred around government *bomas*. Its claim to speak for Africans was disputed at that time by the African Commercial and Welfare Association, a society formed in Dar es Salaam mainly by African traders, businessmen, and urban workers. There seems to have been a considerable shifting of membership between the two groups. The leaders included Joseph Kimalando, who had been active in Chagga politics and who had taken part in demonstrations against the Chagga coffee rules in 1937; Ramadhani Ali, a Mzaramo trader and business man who had tried to have the TCWA recognized as a co-operative union; the Plantan family of Dar es Salaam, descendants of a South African soldier who had served with the Germans; and Erica Fiah, a Muganda who founded in 1936 Tanganyika's first African newspaper *Kwetu*. Ultimately, it was the African Association which survived. It had expressed its political views from time to time, beginning with its opposition to closer union in 1930.[1]

In March 1945 the association held its third territorial conference at Dodoma, and devoted a substantial proportion of its discussions to political questions. While it expressed its general gratitude for the liberal and humane attitudes characteristic of Great Britain, it took the administration to task for unsatisfactory educational and agricultural policies, strongly opposed white settlement and closer union, asked that trade unions be encouraged, supported the mandate, and urged that government salary scales should not be based on colour. One

---

[1] The early years of the African Association are documented, although quite incompletely, in the Tanzanian National Archives. I have here drawn particularly on an unpublished honors thesis by Christopher St. John, 'The Rise of Tanganyikan Nationalism', submitted at Harvard College in 1967; I am most grateful to Mr. St. John for allowing me to consult this. See also chapters by John Iliffe and A. J. Temu in I. N. Kimambo and A. J. Temu (edd.), *A History of Tanzania* (Nairobi, 1969). These works now largely supersede the earlier articles on TAA by Ralph Austen and George Bennett which appeared in the *Makerere Journal* in 1963.

conference resolution, entitled Brotherhood (*Umoja*) particularly foreshadowed later African political views:

... it shall be the duty of each and every African to do away with all tribal, religious, sectarian, economical, political, cultural, educational, territorial and other differences, and to work wholeheartedly to foster and promote a sense of solid brotherhood of Africans. .... Africa is one country, and Africans are one nation, no matter where they live or where they are born.[1]

Subsequently conferences of the association were held at Dar es Salaam in 1946 and in Zanzibar in 1947, when there was a quarrel between island and mainland groups and the association split, the Zanzibar group continuing as an independent entity. In May 1948 the mainland group prefixed 'Tanganyika' to its name, and the majority of its activities after that date were political in nature. By the late 1940s the TAA was submitting memoranda to the Committee on Constitutional Development and the UN Visiting Mission. Its branches were however still largely autonomous, and their views as well as their pace of activity depended a good deal on particular personalities. The African Association in Dar es Salaam, which saw itself as the national headquarters, was constantly trying to increase its influence and control the branches, but was handicapped by distance, lack of communications, and lack of personnel. The absence of an African press was particularly serious; *Kwetu*, after a very difficult period in the late 1940s when it was published erratically, seems to have ceased publication in 1951. A few district or mission publications existed, but the most widely read newspaper was the Nairobi *Baraza*, with the result that literate Tanganyika Africans often knew far more about events in Kenya than in their own territory. Communications depended largely on personal contacts, frequently kept up through the transfer of civil servants from one post to another.

By 1950 a large proportion of educated 'detribalized' Africans were members of the association. 'Old boys' of Makerere or Tabora were often among its leaders; there was also an influential group of the more progressive chiefs, including those who sat on Legislative Council. A third element, less influenced by western

---

[1] TNA/SMP 10856, v. 4, p. 47.

education or by contacts with the administration, were Muslim businessmen and traders. Coastal Swahili groups, as well as Muslims from Ujiji or Tabora, played a much larger part in the development of African politics than they have usually been accorded by observers working mainly in English, but historians working in Swahili are now beginning to set the balance more truly.[1] TAA however lacked a mass base, until the association found in African grievances exactly what it needed for popular appeal. It built on discontent of several different kinds.

The Chagga disputes of the late 1940s were publicized throughout the territory; the Kilimanjaro Chagga Citizens' Union, which led opposition to the government reforms, included TAA members and frequently functioned almost as a local TAA branch. Its programme urging the abolition of government chiefs, the introduction of voting, the appointment of independent magistrates, and the election of a paramount chief, became something of a model for Native Administration reform throughout the territory.[2] TAA members were active in other disputes concerning the role of chiefs and government plans for tribal administrative change. Their participation in protest activities in Upare, in Bukoba, and in Sukumaland is particularly well known.

A second major focus of African discontent was agricultural regulation, now being more strictly enforced as development plans were implemented and more technical staff arrived. The government's agricultural policy involved three kinds of compulsion. In many areas there were famine relief orders which required African cultivators to grow certain food crops; these had been proved both necessary and beneficial in the past, given the uncertain rainfall pattern of Tanganyika, but they were perceived by Africans as designed to supply Europe in the food crises after the Second World War. A second type of compulsion required the following of specific agricultural practices: tie-ridging, burning of cotton plants, etc.; while the third required cattle dipping, and in certain areas cattle culling, to control disease and soil erosion. Some of the agricultural practices were

---

[1] See especially S. A. Kandoro, *Mwito wa Uhuru* (Dar es Salaam, 1961). I am grateful also for information to this effect given to me by August Nimitz of Indiana University.

[2] For material on the KCCU and Chagga politics in general see p. 166 fn 1 above.

of doubtful validity, certainly when applied on a very large scale, while any interference with cattle was a guaranteed trouble-maker among the many tribes for whom cattle occupied a specially venerated position. The form of enforcement was also highly unpopular. Offenders were charged with violating native authority rules and tried by the native courts; the role played by subsidiary African staff such as stock guards and agricultural demonstrators made corruption and intimidation possible.

Government agricultural plans were not only formulated without consulting Africans; there was very little explanation of their utility or purpose. The farmer in Southern Province who was ordered to tie-ridge to preserve water, when his major farming problem was too much rainfall and his crops rotted in the fields, not unnaturally saw the regulations as a means of ruining him. Schemes were burdensome in other ways; at the height of its operation the Uluguru Land Usage Scheme demanded that African farmers work three days a week on terracing. In 1955 grievances in Uluguru exploded into riots and demonstrations against the government, threatening the whole structure of government administration in the area.[1] Governor Twining admitted, some years later, that agricultural policy had been one of the major mistakes of his governorship.[2]

The impact which these grievances could have on politics and development was particularly shown in Lake Province. All three types of compulsion were found there, along with another major agricultural grievance: the system of ginning and marketing cotton, which was entirely in Asian hands. Cotton production increased dramatically in the province after the Second World War, and in 1949 Paul Bomani founded the Lake Province Growers' Association to attempt to change this marketing structure. The association met with opposition from government, which feared its intervention in the affairs of the native administrations, especially in Sukumaland, but membership grew so

[1] For the Uluguru disturbances see Roland Young and H. A. Fosbrooke, *Land and Politics among the Luguru* (London, 1960); American title, *Smoke in the Hills*. For agricultural grievances in general, see Gorän Hydén, *TANU Yajenga Nchi: political development in rural Tanganyika* (Lund, 1968); Lionel Cliffe, 'Nationalism and the Reaction to Enforced Agricultural Improvement in Tanganyika during the Colonial Period', in *Socialism in Tanzania*, ed. Cliffe and Saul (Dar es Salaam, 1973); John Iliffe, *Agricultural Change in Modern Tanganyika*, Historical Association of Tanganyika Occasional Paper No. 10 (Nairobi, 1971).

[2] Interview with Sir Edward Twining, London, August 1959.

rapidly in the early 1950s that this policy had to change. By 1955, with the establishment of the Victoria Federation of Co-operative Unions, the bulk of the cotton crop had come under African control and the union was the largest single business in Tanganyika. Meanwhile, the enforcement of agricultural regulations had become increasingly difficult, and government fears were intensified by the activities of the Sukuma Union, a society of younger, educated, men founded in Mwanza in 1945, and the Mwanza branch of TAA, which was now expanding its membership and activities throughout Sukumaland. In the early 1950s the Mwanza branch was the most active in Tanganyika, and it provided much of the impetus for large-scale territorial organization.[1]

The most dramatic grievance was that concerning the Meru land case, which more than any other single issue mobilized African opinion against the government. In 1952 a group of Meru farmers petitioned the Trusteeship Council of the United Nations to halt their forcible removal from farms in the Sanya corridor area of Northern Province. The farms had been scheduled to become European holdings in accordance with the Arusha-Moshi Lands Commission report of 1947, but there had been major delays in implementation, and the 1951 Visiting Mission to Tanganyika had challenged government action because the normal practice of allowing Africans the choice of staying on the land or receiving compensation for it had not been followed. A Trusteeship Council recommendation that the order be reconsidered was turned down by the Tanganyika government although it already had considerable reservations about the wisdom of encouraging racially segregated land-holdings, and it later found Meru removal from the farms, as a result of passive resistance by the people, impossible to carry out.[2]

Although the Meru petition did not achieve completely successful results at the United Nations, discussion of the case

---

[1] A detailed and extremely interesting account of native administration, co-operatives, and the growth of nationalism in Lake Province is contained in Maguire, *Toward 'Uhuru'*. For the TAA see also Kandoro, *Mwito wa Uhuru*.

[2] For the Meru case in the UN see p. 176 below. For the various viewpoints on this issue see *Report of the Arusha-Moshi Lands Commission*, Commissioner, Mark Wilson (Dar es Salaam, Govt. Printer, 1947); *The Meru Land Problem* (Dar es Salaam, Govt. Printer, 1952); Kirilo Japhet and E. E. Seaton, *The Meru Land Case* (Nairobi, 1967); Anton Nelson, *The Freemen of Meru* (Nairobi, 1967).

was widespread throughout Tanganyika, and African fears of European seizure of land became acute. Petitions submitted to the United Nations, even from areas where there had never been any land alienation for white settlement, discussed land alienation as the outstanding African grievance. One result was a heightened distrust of government intentions, and an opposition to government schemes which it was feared might lead to a European take-over of land. Multi-racial local councils were opposed, several years later, because they might provide Europeans with a forum for land regulation. Among the Meru themselves, the repercussions of the case brought an increased willingness for agricultural change and strengthened a newly-formed coffee co-operative.

Such major instances of confrontation were well-known through the growing information network of TAA and its sympathizers; money to support the Meru case before the UN came from all over the territory. A similar pattern of economic grievances and expanding local political associations, co-operatives, and other voluntary groups, could be found in many other regions. Coffee and co-operative politics played a major role in Bukoba, Uchagga, and Unyakyusa. Tribal unions designed to bring together modernizing elements were active in these areas and in Upare and Usambara, where they presented a major challenge to the Native Administrations. Often the tribal union was another name for the local branch of TAA, and among all of these groups there was a considerable overlapping membership. In contrast to Uganda, where many Africans gained their initial political experience in the district councils, Africans in Tanganyika were trained in the co-operative movement, in voluntary associations, and in the branches of TAA.[1]

Since Tanganyika was primarily a rural country rural griev-ances were of particular importance; they were well-known in the towns through migration and the activities of the tribal unions. It was frequently the town-dwellers who helped to organize protests and who began to press the government for specific reforms. Mwanza, Dodoma, Arusha, and Ujiji were all

---

[1] Sources for this paragraph are extremely varied. They include annual reports of the provincial commissioners, the Department of Agriculture and the Department of Co-operative Development; interviewing by the author in 1956 and 1960.

deeply involved in the problems of the surrounding countryside. All these towns also were experiencing urban problems, especially acute in Dar es Salaam and Tanga: housing problems including zoning, food supplies, tribal rivalries, unemployment, social disruptions of all sorts. African attempts at starting small businesses frequently ran foul of government regulations. The towns were, furthermore, very much under government control, with no mediating Native Administration.

The Tanganyika government was relatively late in discovering urban problems; it tended to believe that all Africans belonged in the countryside and that town-dwelling was an aberration. There were, for instance, constant problems in the administration of Dar es Salaam, including much moving of government offices, because the capital city was administered as a part of the large surrounding district.[1] Attempts at trade union organization fared somewhat better, for the government was in principle committed to the encouragement of trade unions. In Dar es Salaam and Tanga dockworkers and domestic servants began to organize, but major trade union growth was relatively late in occurring, becoming important only after the formation of the Tanganyika Federation of Labour in 1955.[2]

Two other major grievances were shared by all Africans: the difficulty of obtaining an education, and the social discrimination against Africans which continued to exist. The latter problem particularly rankled for it was seldom admitted by non-Africans. Official restrictions had indeed begun to disappear, but irksome and humiliating discriminations continued, and there were few Africans among the leadership group at independence who had not personally suffered.

In the early 1950s TAA had thus found the basis for creating a mass African protest movement, but it was still searching for the leadership and organizational structure to enable it to build a coherent national programme.

[1] A good history of Dar es Salaam remains to be written, but some useful information is contained in M. J. B. Molohan, *Detribalization* (Dar es Salaam, Govt. Printer, 1957), which despite its title is an administrative survey of Dar es Salaam district; J. A. K. Leslie, *A Survey of Dar es Salaam* (London, 1963); 'Dar es Salaam: City, Port and Region', *Tanzania Notes and Records*, 71 (1970), and TNA materials on such groups as the Zaramo Union.

[2] For relations between the trade unions and the nationalist movement, see p. 190 below. Cf. also William Friedland, *Vuta Kamba: the development of trade unions in Tanganyika* (Stanford, 1969).

External political influences

The events so far described had been influenced by two factors external to the territory: the status of Tanganyika as a trust territory of the United Nations, and British government attempts to bring about closer administrative and economic co-operation in the East African territories.

Great Britain had agreed in January 1946 to place the mandated territory of Tanganyika under the new trusteeship system of the United Nations. She did so with reluctance, influenced almost entirely by the international political climate at the end of the Second World War. At the San Francisco conference in 1945 British proposals for the trusteeship system had been almost exactly those of the old League of Nations mandate system, but the growth of anti-colonial feeling internationally made these impossible of acceptance. The trusteeship system created in Chapter 12 of the United Nations Charter introduced several changes disliked by the British government; among these were the provisions that national representatives would sit on the Trusteeship Council, and that Visiting Missions would be sent to each trust territory every three years.

The trusteeship agreement for Tanganyika marked a certain cautious advance on the terms of the mandate. While many of the provisions designed to protect the local population were retained, two changes were very much the result of mandate experience. Article 4 stipulated that Tanganyika must play its part in the maintenance of international peace and security, and made the United Kingdom responsible for the defence of the territory, while under Article 9 the grant of equal rights for United Nations members was subject to the interests of the people of Tanganyika and to reciprocity. The Administering Authority undertook to develop free political institutions and to safeguard natural resources. The agreement avoided reference to 'Africans' or 'natives' except with specific reference to native law and native land, following the language of the Charter in speaking of 'inhabitants'.

The draft agreement was considered by the Executive Council in Tanganyika, and the Chief Secretary, Sir Rex Surridge, and the senior unofficial member of the Legislative Council, Sir Charles Phillips, were in London for many of the negotiations.

Phillips introduced a motion approving the trust agreement in the Legislative Council in July 1946, but found his fellow unofficials unready for discussion. While there was some irritation at lack of local consultation, unofficial members and European interest groups in the country apparently agreed that trusteeship for Tanganyika was an imperial necessity, while African and Asian groups favoured trusteeship primarily as a means of protecting their own status. There was not however much local debate in Tanganyika. In Kenya, in contrast, the question was the subject of two days' debate in the Legislative Council, European unofficials opposing the agreement and other races favouring it.[1]

From 1948 Tanganyikan affairs were discussed yearly by the United Nations, in a climate increasingly critical of colonialism.[2] The British government proved to be highly sensitive to international publicity, often much more so than the Tanganyikan administration itself. The report of the first Visiting Mission in 1948 was regarded in Tanganyika as moderate and even helpful, but was badly received in the United Kingdom, where Lord Listowel referred to the United Nations as fifty-eight backseat drivers. Later mission reports had a varied reception; that of 1951 was welcomed as doing a careful job while that of 1954 was regarded with exasperation and even fury by Tanganyikan officialdom but was highly acceptable to the African nationalist movement.[3]

The first major issue which arose between the Trusteeship Council and the Administering Authority concerned the question of East African closer union, which the council believed might contravene Article 5 of the trust agreement. The British government initially considered the matter to be outside the council's jurisdiction but after 1950 it shifted its

---

[1] For final text of the Trusteeship Agreement, see United Nations *Treaty Series*, viii, 1947. British drafts issued publicly appeared as Cmd. 6840 and Cmd. 6935, (London, HMSO, 1946). For East African discussions of trusteeship, *Tanganyika Standard*, 16 Feb., 27 July, and 10 Aug. 1946; Kenya Legislative Council *Debates* (2nd series) 24, cc. 127–75.

[2] B. T. G. Chidzero, *Tanganyika and International Trusteeship* (London, 1961) considers relations between the UN and Tanganyika to 1959.

[3] There were five Visiting Missions to Tanganyika, in 1948,1951, 1954, 1957, and 1960. Their reports, together with related documents including British government comments, were published as Supplement 3 to the appropriate annual Trusteeship Council *Official Records*. The 1954 report particularly is discussed below.

position and reported to the council on inter-territorial co-operation, even agreeing to allow the visiting missions direct access to the East African High Commission in Nairobi. Opinion in the council was divided and it cannot be said that it ever took a clear stand for or against the union arrangements. It had however been largely presented with a *fait accompli*, since final decisions about the High Commission were made in 1947 as the council was just beginning its activities.

The second serious issue to reach the council was the Meru land case. The council heard an oral petitioner from the Meru, Kirilo Japhet, and urged the Tanganyika government to reconsider its decision to evict the Meru farmers (a resolution much more condemnatory of the Administering Authority failed to receive the necessary two-thirds vote for passage in the General Assembly). The Tanganyikan government refused to accept the Trusteeship Council's recommendation and became in subsequent years much more critical of council activities. But the Meru case demonstrated to Africans the possibility of using the United Nations as an international forum and as a pressure point for grievances. Petitions were sent to the council from all over the territory, and the Meru example of sending a representative to New York was followed by other political groups after 1954.[1]

By 1954, the Trusteeship Council was urging acceptance of a timetable for political advance. United Nations activities of almost any kind constituted a challenge to the gradual development originally planned for Tanganyika, but the international situation forced Britain to modify her position. It is notable that when the first steps toward elections in Tanganyika were approved in 1955, announcement of the decision was made in New York before it was heard of in Dar es Salaam. It was already apparent that the United Nations would substantially affect both the timing and the substance of political change in Tanganyika.

A second imperial decision affecting Tanganyika was the establishment in 1948 of the East Africa High Commission, reviving many of the ideas and controversies of the inter-war period. Proposals for inter-territorial organization were first

---

[1] The T/PET 2/ series issued by the Trusteeship Council contains a number of extremely interesting items about Tanganyika politics in this period.

published in June 1945; they suggested a permanent High Commission, consisting of the governors of Kenya, Uganda, and Tanganyika, and a series of executive departments to supervise existing common services (posts, customs, etc.) and to control such other matters as railways, aviation, defence, industrial licensing, income tax, marketing boards, and broadcasting. To this administrative unification there was to be added a central legislature which included unofficial representatives from the three territories.

The paper had a mixed reception in Tanganyika; even settlers who were generally favourable disliked the automatic assumption that the commission's headquarters would be in Nairobi and that the governor of Kenya would be its permanent chairman. One of the first African members of the Legislative Council, Chief Kidaha Makwaia, opposed the idea of interterritorial organization in his maiden speech, although the proposals were not formally debated at this point. Revised proposals in 1947 were debated at length; they somewhat diminished the authority of the executive departments and the Central Legislative Assembly, while specifying a method for selecting assembly members which differed from territory to territory and which ensured a European majority.

This latter point in particular made the scheme unacceptable to Tanganyika's Indian community. Europeans in the Legislative Council favoured the proposals, while the two African chiefs who were then council members abstained from voting on the motion of approval. Urban African opinion certainly opposed the idea of closer union; the chiefs explained their abstention by noting that the proposals had been published in Swahili only two weeks before the council debate, leaving no time for consultation up-country. Their position illustrated the extent to which they regarded themselves as members of the administration. This vote was the only one in Tanganyikan history in which straight racial voting prevailed.[1]

All segments of Tanganyikan opinion were very wary of the High Commission and its activities, for it was believed to show a Kenyan bias. Negotiations for railway unification in 1948 were a

[1] *Inter-territorial Organization in East Africa*, Col. 191, (London, HMSO, 1945) and Col. 210, (London, HMSO, 1947); Legislative Council *Proceedings*, First Extraordinary Meeting, 1947, pp. 17–35, 36–47.

particular point of contention; at a later stage commission decisions on industrial licensing, income tax, roads, and even tsetse research came under attack. This dislike of the commission was shared by many Tanganyikan officials. In 1951 the Southern Highlands Provincial Council discussed rail and road services, and on a free vote official and unofficial members alike were unanimous in condemning the commission's activities.

The commission in the next few years made a concentrated attempt to remove some grievances, mostly in allowing greater administrative devolution. Nevertheless this suspicion of Kenyan motives was a constant thread running through all the discussions about East African co-operation, and it was probably as widespread at independence as it had been sixteen years earlier. It was most strongly felt by Africans, who equated Kenyan influence on the commission with Kenya settler influence. Commission activities were, also, largely concerned with problems of economic development, and while they offered new opportunities for Tanganyika they also limited the freedom of action of the Tanganyika government and its control of the process of development.

Sir Edward Twining and multi-racialism

A considerable impetus to change had appeared in June 1949 with the arrival of Sir Edward Twining as governor. His predecessor, Sir William Battershill, had been ill for some months, so that major decisions had been postponed. Sir Edward was a bluff, vigorous, man ready to push for more rapid advance in all fields, and his enthusiasm and dynamism soon permeated the whole territory. His governorship was a time of major experiment, and his name became largely synonymous with the policy of multi-racialism which he advocated strongly and pushed consistently. His role in Tanganyika, despite later differences with the nationalist movement, was both vital and important.

Sir Edward announced in December 1949 the appointment of a Committee on Constitutional Development, composed of all unofficial members of the Legislative Council plus the Attorney-General (Charles Mathew) and the Member for Local Government (R. de Z. Hall).[1] The committee was charged with examining all aspects of constitutional and political change, and it worked for eighteen months, travelling widely and collecting political testimony throughout the territory; it recorded its disappointment that it found as much political apathy as interest. Its unanimous report, submitted in May 1951, concentrated mainly on political problems as seen from the centre. It regarded some measure of administrative devolution as necessary, and urged the creation of representative structures on a regional rather than a provincial basis, with county councils possible at more local levels. While it seemed to be moving toward two- or three-tier local government as in the United Kingdom and some other British colonies, the committee did not consider at all the lowest tier of government, the Native Administrations. Members of the committee, the large majority non-African, were both uninterested in and uninformed upon questions of African local government.

The committee's fundamental recommendation was that equal racial representation should be established among the unofficial members of the Legislative Council, the suggested ratio being seven Africans, seven Europeans, and seven Asians; it turned down the offer of an unofficial majority as premature. Its proposal for political multi-racialism, of equal representation of numerically unequal racial groups, was accepted by Governor Twining and adopted as the keynote of his governorship. His own initial suggestion to the committee had been for a different type of parity; he had proposed a council which would be half-African, half non-African, but this had created an outcry among the European community and had been rejected by the committee.[2]

The European community in Tanganyika at this point made a bid for political power. The community in the early 1950s had grown rapidly in size but its interests were varied, for there was

---

[1] The 'membership system', adopted in 1948, had grouped government departments under 'members' who were directly responsible to the governor, and who sat on Legislative Council by virtue of this office. It was designed to ease the responsibilities of the Chief Secretary. The title 'minister' appeared in 1957.

[2] *Report of the Committee on Constitutional Development* (Dar es Salaam, Govt. Printer, 1951). Twining's original proposal, locally known as the 'cockshy' was included in the six volumes of committee papers deposited in the Secretariat Library, Dar es Salaam. A summary appeared in the *Tanganyika Standard*, 3 Dec. 1949.

no geographic or economic point of concentration. As a result of the Open Door provisions of the mandate and trust agreements, the community was nationally and culturally diverse; co-operation did not come readily to Greek tobacco-farmers in Iringa, small South African farmers in Kilimanjaro, and British produce exporters in Dodoma. Apart from a few areas around Kilimanjaro, European farms were not in separate blocs but tended to be surrounded by African holdings, while the capital invested in sisal, coffee, and tea was often Indian as well as European. The European grouping had neither the economic nor the social cohesion found in the European community in Kenya.[1]

The Tanganyika Europeans did, nevertheless, make a serious attempt to organize themselves, and to influence government policy. A preliminary association had come into being in 1946 as the Northern Province Secretarial Bureau, a body uging greater European immigration, security of land tenure, and closer co-operation with Kenya. Originally appealing particularly to the South African farmers of West Kilimanjaro, it had become progressively the Northern Province Council and then, in 1949, the Tanganyika European Council (TEC), widening its geographical base and attempting to represent all Tanganyika Europeans. In discussions on inter-territorial organization and constitutional change, however, the group ran into serious problems. Many Tanganyika Europeans, especially those living in the Southern Highlands and Tanga provinces, were unhappy with the racial exclusiveness of the TEC, and they also disliked tendencies of the Northern Province to work closely with the Kenya Europeans.

For several years after its founding the council was closely organized and very vocal about the course of Tanganyikan politics. It made strong representations to the Constitutional Committee in the European interest, and it waged a campaign up-country to defeat Twining's original proposals on representation. When the committee produced its own tripartite formula in 1951 the TEC was violently opposed, but differences within

[1] One of the neglected areas in Tanganyika history is research on the European community. Apart from elementary census data and a series of impressions based on personal contacts little is known about the community. Such sub-groups as Greeks and Cypriots, Swiss in the Tanga area, Italian and Swedish missionaries seem well worth study. The various Indian communities similarly demand an historian.

its own ranks weakened its ability to oppose effectively the political multi-racialism suggested. In 1952 it was forced to an acceptance of the tripartite formula and this killed TEC; but in the three preceding years it had effectively modified the governor's proposals and slowed down his timetable for increasing African political participation. TEC history indicated a lack of leadership in the European community, although Europeans remained active in politics and several TEC members later worked with the nationalist movement.[1]

The philosophy outlined in the Constitutional Committee's report was one of cautious advance toward modern political institutions, and the tripartite representation formula was the most controversial change suggested. Immediate elections were not urged, although the committee accepted the idea of elections in principle; members were dismayed by the communal politics they saw in Kenya, and they sought to avoid following Kenya's example. Even the most extreme European opposition to equal racial representation was swayed by this desire for racial harmony. Equal representation was formally accepted by the Colonial Office in June 1952; even before that date major government policies were re-examined in the light of this principle. In urging multi-racialism upon all sections of the community, the government began to consult public opinion more consistently, using as its liaisons the Tanganyika Unofficial Members' Organization and, after the appointment of Chief Kidaha as its first African member in April 1951, the Executive Council.

The concept of multi-racialism challenged previous ideas of racial separatism and exclusiveness; it also, to the government, involved a greater acceptance of modernization, or perhaps more accurately, westernization, on British models. The Local Courts Ordinance of 1951 took the first steps toward the separation of

---

[1] There is an interesting internal history of TEC, though it is tangential to a discussion of Tanganyikan politics. The paragraphs above are based on the *TEC Bulletin* and on material in the organization's archives, seen in Arusha in 1952.

I have not attempted to discuss here the activities of the Indian (later Asian) Association. Its internal rivalries were highly complex and little known to outside observers. With the advent of elections it played a role in selecting candidates and in deciding to co-operate with TANU. It may be noted that, in the eyes of many TEC members, the Indian community gained most when the idea of equal racial representation was accepted.

administrative and judicial structures and began to move away from a concept of jurisdiction based on race. The Local Councils Ordinance of 1953, which replaced the Native Authority Ordinance, went much further. The basic principle of multi-racial local government was accepted although, as the Member for Local Government stressed when African opposition appeared in the Legislative Council, it would not be *imposed* against local wishes. The ordinance manifested a major break with earlier orthodoxies; there was very little that could be called traditionally African about the structure of the local councils, although *ex officio* traditional membership was possible, and the local chief often became president of the council. With the disappearance of the terminology of Native Administration, its basic principle, the use of traditional political institutions and personnel, also began to atrophy. That the government was still in a transitional stage in its own thinking was shown by the African Chiefs Ordinance of 1953, which was designed to protect the position of chiefs and gave them substantial responsi-bilities for law and order, and by the Local Government Memorandum of 1954, which continued to speak of 'African Local Government in a multi-racial society'. But the trend was unmistakeable and led the government, several years later, to a direct confrontation with African nationalists over the question whether local government *must* be multi-racial; by 1957 the government was saying unequivocally yes.

The general approach of multi-racialism was carried further in 1952 and 1953 by the report of Professor W. J. M. Mackenzie of Manchester University, who enquired into a number of questions raised by the Constitutional Development Committee. Professor Mackenzie suggested that equal racial representation in the Legislative Council implied common roll elections in the near future in some constituencies, and he believed that this would be entirely acceptable to all elements of opinion in Tanganyika. This was a surprising statement in view of consider-able opposing testimony received by the Constitutional Develop-ment Committee, but Professor Mackenzie proved to be right. There was remarkably little discussion in Tanganyika about the principle of common roll elections, although the elaborate voting system later introduced by the government was disliked by many.

In dealing with electoral qualifications and especially with what might be done to surmount the problems of nationality and citizenship in a trust territory, Professor Mackenzie suggested the acceptance of residential criteria. In areas not yet ready for direct elections he proposed the use of local councils as electoral colleges for African members of Legislative Council. Regionalization, which he found highly artificial in Tanganyika, was to be abandoned. The provinces would be retained as administrative entities while he urged that county councils should be the sole unit for local government.[1]

In May 1954 the creation of the new Legislative Council was announced, with 31 officials and 30 appointed unofficials, the latter being chosen to represent the eight administrative provinces and Dar es Salaam, with three members for 'general interests' which were, apparently, the Arab community, the sisal industry, and the Bukoba district. The Council became bilingual, an important point for many African members, as standing orders permitted the use of Swahili and provided for simultaneous interpretation. The council procedure also became, for the first time, notably parliamentary.

This nominated Council had however a relatively short life. It had hardly met for the first time when in March 1955 the government announced its intentions of moving toward elections, probably in 1958. Ideas of electoral colleges were abandoned; direct voting was to be tried everywhere. To support multiracialism, inter-racial voting was required. Each voter would have three votes and must use them to vote for one Asian, one African, and one European. Other franchise requirements remained to be worked out.[2]

[1] *Report by the Special Commissioner Appointed to examine Matters arising out of the Report of the Committee on Constitutional Development* (Dar es Salaam, Govt. Printer, 1953). Professor Mackenzie's report contains much technical detail but also some extremely interesting ideas and discussion about governmental structure in a country emerging from colonialism. His recommendation for a franchise based on residence rather than citizenship was designed to solve a problem the government had recognized in the early 1920s but refused to tackle, the fact that under British law no procedure for naturalization existed in a mandate or trust territory. After passage of the British Nationality Act of 1948 it was possible for Tanganyikan residents to become British citizens, but not Tanganyikan citizens. The residence requirement was adopted by the franchise committee several years later; in the 1960 Legislative Council there were some ten nationalities represented.

[2] United Nations Trusteeship Council *Official Records*, 15th session; Leg Co *Debates, 31st Session*, 1956–7, p. 10.

County councils did not, in the event, prove satisfactory. One, the Southeast Lake County Council, was created in mid-1955, but it was very shortly found that the area to be covered (eight administrative districts) was too large, and that friction with both Native Administrations and Lake Province Council remained. Local councils had been created in Mafia and Newala and in some of the larger towns; despite operating difficulties, they seemed to offer a better basis for development. A report by C. A. G. Wallis of the Colonial Office in October 1955 strongly urged concentration on a district level; this recommendation was, more than a year later, finally followed. The councils were to be multi-racial in composition, although the exact racial ratio might vary from council to council.[1]

The acceptance of district councils as local government units, and the inauguration of the new Legislative Council, completed, from the government point of view, the long search for appropriate political structures. It had also apparently been decided that government could not be decentralized, for all major decisions remained with Dar es Salaam. Efficient government however continued to be sought; the number of trained personnel had markedly increased and the staffing of native administrations had changed out of all recognition. Africans were also beginning to enter central government in positions of higher rank; the Lidbury Report in 1954[2] had removed some of the salary inequalities which were so disliked by African (and Asian) government personnel, and the first African district officer was gazetted in 1955. Most of the technical services also opened their ranks although training requirements meant that African recruitment proceeded much more slowly. The Commissioner of Police began to Africanize higher ranks, a point of major importance since Tanganyika did not create tribal police but opened all areas of the territory to central police operation; in 1955 the police budget, for the first time, exceeded that of the provincial administration. It is notable that several services not directly under control of the Tanganyikan administration,

---

[1] C. A. G. Wallis had previously reported on local government in Uganda and may have been influenced by his experience there. It cannot be said that County Councils were given much chance.

[2] *Report of the Commission on the Civil Services of the East African Territories and the East Africa High Commission*, Chairman Sir David Lidbury, 2 vols., (London, Crown Agents, 1954).

especially the judiciary and the army, were relatively late in moving Africans into positions of major responsibility.[1]

The philosophy of multi-racialism, however, extended far beyond the question of politics *per se*. After 1954 the educational structure was reviewed; although the government continued to speak about 'European-type' schools it moved consistently if slowly toward educational integration. Land policy underwent a series of revisions, with the acceptance of the criterion of the best use of land adumbrated by the East Africa Royal Commission of 1953–5.[2] Substantive action to remove social discrimination against Africans also took place. In 1955 the most popular law in years finally made it legally possible for Africans to buy European liquor. Inter-racial social contacts were encouraged. Lady Twining's Tanganyika Council of Women, founded in 1951, was especially active. At its most extreme this posture of inter-racial parity became slightly ridiculous. One social club in Dar es Salaam thus set its membership requirements on the same 1:1:1 basis as the membership of the Legislative Council. Nevertheless, race relations in Tanganyika were no longer negative as they had been earlier; the races were pushed together by Governor Twining, and forced to see each other and co-operate. In this respect the policy of multi-racialism paid dividends.

Julius Nyerere and the Tanganyika African National Union

On 7 July 1954, the transformation of the African Association into the Tanganyika African National Union was announced in Dar es Salaam. This change was in many ways a formality, given the association's activities already chronicled. It marked however the public announcement by Tanganyika Africans that they intended to work for the complete removal of the British administering authorities; it also marked the

---

[1] See, for instance, government staff lists in the late 1950s. The army had only junior African officers at the time of independence, and the highest African judicial official was a resident magistrate.

[2] *Report of the East Africa Royal Commission 1953–55*, Cmd. 9475 (London, HMSO, 1955). See Appendix 1 below. The policy urged by the commission was regarded by the 1954 Visiting Mission and by African nationalists as not sufficiently protective of African interests. Although in the late 1950s government policy began to impose more stringent conditions on occupancy of land by non-Africans, a full reassessment of Tanganyikan land policy was not undertaken before independence.

arrival in the public eye of Julius Nyerere, president of the new union.

Nyerere was a Mzanaki from Musoma district, son of a minor chief, who had been educated at Tabora and Makerere. In 1949 he received a government bursary to attend Edinburgh University, one of the first Africans to be sent overseas for higher education. He took a degree in the social sciences and returned in 1952 to become a teacher at St. Francis School, Pugu. His political activities with the African Association in Dar es Salaam however soon put him at odds with school officials, and he became, as he described himself, a full-time 'political agitator'. As President of TANU he became the chief spokesman and organizer of the independence movement, proving himself to be extraordinarily competent in both roles.[1]

TANU's programme had six major points of action: (1) preparation for self-government; (2) rejection of tribalism and the achievement of a united nationalism; (3) establishment of a democratic form of government; (4) establishment of African majorities on all bodies of government; (5) removal of all forms of racialism; and (6) encouragement of and co-operation with trade unions, the co-operative movement and other sympathetic groups such as tribal unions.[2] The major challenge to government policy lay in the strong rejection of multi-racialism and the stress upon Tanganyika as an African country. Officials were however even more concerned about possible TANU tactics. Although Nyerere pointed out that the union wished to achieve its aims by constitutional methods, the old fears about threats to the Native Administrations and to law and order up-country were intensified with the creation of the new organization.

The government had already issued in August 1953 a memorandum prohibiting membership in political organizations by government servants. It advised native authorities to follow its lead, and many missions did so as well. The result was to make overt membership in TANU or similar organizations impossible for all chiefs and for a very large proportion of educated Africans. The following year the passage of the Societies Ordinance, a very

---

[1] There is as yet no full biography of Nyerere and for most details of his early life we are dependent on government press releases. His later activities with TANU are chronicled in all the major works on Tanzanian politics: see among these J. Listowel, *The Making of Tanganyika* (London, 1966) and Kandoro, *Mwito wa Uhuru*.

[2] *The Tanganyika African National Union Constitution*, 1954.

widely-drawn measure, gave the governor control of all associations, permitting him to refuse or revoke their registration, and enabling officials to examine their records.[1] TANU branches were thus denied registration, especially in Sukumaland where none at all were permitted, and political activities were driven underground. In other areas TANU membership spread rapidly and rather untidily, and by 1956 Nyerere claimed 100,000 members. Party organization was taken in hand by a series of secretaries-general (Stephen Mhando, E. A. Kisenge, and Oscar Kambona) but despite their efforts much so-called TANU activity was locally inspired, sometimes by non-members, and it remained outside the control of Dar es Salaam, an irritant to government and to TANU itself.

The possibilities for independent initiatives came particularly in the widely-spreading activities which were not in a strict sense political, and which illustrated its growing role as a national movement. A Youth League and a women's section were created; a series of independent schools for those students denied places by the government were set up; considerable adult education work was undertaken. The TANU programme to eliminate various social evils was taken extremely seriously by some Youth Leaguers and local workers, who ordered villagers to clean streets, banish prostitutes, and occasionally usurped the position of the courts in judging offenders. Overlapping membership between TANU and local tribal unions and labour unions also sometimes brought TANU into local disputes. All of these activities reinforced government belief that TANU was subversive, as did several up-country incidents with which its members were associated. The most serious of these were the Uluguru disturbances already referred to, which did indeed destroy the existing structure of the native administration. Responsibility here was however uncertain; there were TANU members among the Africans protesting against the enforcement of agricultural regulations, but they were not the instigators of the incident. The deputy chief of the Luguru, Patrick Kunambi,

---

[1] 'Membership in Political Associations', Government Circular 1 Aug. 1953; Societies Ordinance, No. 11 of 1954. TANU believed that the provisions of the ordinance, particularly those concerning finances, were used by some district commissioners to harass it. The ban on civil servants joining political organizations seems to have originated with the Colonial Office in London. A number of colonies such as Kenya passed laws similar to the Societies Ordinance.

who was responsible for enforcement, was himself a founder member of TANU.[1]

There were also some divergences of opinion within the top ranks of TANU in Dar es Salaam, as the organization sorted out its own opinions and tactics. Observers have tended to disregard these differences and to view Julius Nyerere as the determinant of TANU policy, but this exaggerates his power. TANU decision-making was usually collective, with its Central Committee and National Executive Committee playing major roles. Nyerere was usually able to influence policy but his will did not always prevail. One effect of the Societies Ordinance, indeed, was to keep out of active TANU leadership men who might have been his rivals; many of them were however sympathizers and sometimes advisers in the background. This was true even of some of the chiefs, although many of them had now been bypassed by younger men who regarded them as too conservative and tribally oriented.

TANU's popularity was increased by the recognition accorded to it by the UN Visiting Mission in 1954, and Nyerere's visit to the Trusteeship Council in February 1955 both impressed delegates there and brought him an enhanced prestige at home. On his return he spoke to an open-air meeting of 10,000 people in Dar es Salaam. These actions and TANU's general policies made him increasingly unpopular with Sir Edward Twining. The governor, appointed to a second term in 1955 and ready to convene the new parity Legislative Council, found the political initiative slipping away from him. He did not appoint Nyerere to the new Legislative Council, although a TANU sympathizer such as Bomani was there. For the next three years, therefore, TANU tended alternately to criticize or ignore the Council, and its activities centred on organizing work in the countryside, on public meetings and on further trips to the UN.[2]

---

[1] Most of the material in this paragraph is based on personal experience and interviewing in Tanganyika, 1956 and 1960. The *Tanganyika Standard* reported many of these activities.

[2] TANU during this period is most extensively discussed in an unpublished thesis by Martin Lowenkopf, submitted at London University in 1961. I am grateful to Mr. Lowenkopf for allowing me to read this. Reasonably good coverage of the movement, at least in Dar es Salaam, was maintained by the *Tanganyika Standard*. See also Julius K. Nyerere, *Uhuru nu Umoja: Freedom and Unity: a selection from writings and speeches 1952–1965* (Oxford, 1967); Margaret Bates, 'Tanganyika' in Gwendolen Carter (ed.), *African One Party States* (Ithaca, N. Y., 1962); E. M.

In February 1956 28 of the 30 unofficial members of the Legislative Council signed the manifesto of a new United Tanganyika Party, designed to support government policies on multi-racialism and in the economic field. The president of the group was I. C. W. Bayldon, the senior unofficial member of the Council and a founder of the Southern Highlands Union which had opposed the TEC on racial policies. Its executive secretary was Brian Willis, who had been a Conservative Party organizer in the United Kingdom. The patron of the party was very much Governor Twining, and the UTP was never able to rid itself of the aura of association with government. It organized and campaigned extensively in the next two years, attracting some support from all racial groups.[1]

From early 1956 both parties were campaigning for the elections, due in two stages in 1958 and 1959. The franchise requirements were generally regarded as favouring UTP, for they were clearly designed to support a multi-racial political community, with Africans in only a slight majority in most constituencies. This was achieved by economic and educational qualifications (£150 annual income, or successful completion of middle school, Standard 8) which enfranchised all Europeans, most Asians, and a very small minority of Africans. TANU, urging a universal franchise, regarded as derisory a registration roll of 59,317 voters in a population estimated at 10 million. This strict franchise limitation, and the provision that each voter must vote for three candidates—one from each racial group—were viewed by many Africans as so prejudicial to their aims that they favoured boycotting the election entirely.[2]

The official position of TANU on racial questions had earlier been expressed by Nyerere in speaking to the Trusteeship Council. The future Tanganyika would be racially hetero-geneous but nationally homogeneous; all citizens would be accorded equal rights, but their due share of responsibility

Barongo, *Mkiki wa Siasa Tanganyika* (Dar es Salaam, 1969); William H. Friedland, 'Cooperation, Conflict and Conscription: TANU-TFL relations 1955-64', in Jeffrey Butler and A. A. Castagno (edd.), *Boston University Papers on Africa: transition in African politics* (New York, 1966).
    [1] The party manifesto appeared in the Dar es Salaam *Sunday News*, 26 Feb. 1956.
    [2] *Report of the Committee Appointed to Study Government's Proposals Regarding the Qualifications of Voters* . . ., Government Paper 1, (Dar es Salaam, 1957); Stephen Mhando, *TANU and the Vote* (Dar es Salaam, 1956).

should be exercised by Africans in accordance with democratic principles, and TANU remained an African organization.

After some months of discussion the TANU annual conference at a crucial meeting in Tabora in January 1958 decided that TANU would participate in the elections. This course meant backing Asian and European candidates if TANU was to have any chance of controlling the unofficial side of the Legislative Council; the African share of 10 of the 30 seats would otherwise leave them very much in a minority position. Since the nomination procedure was largely a racial one, TANU could only endorse or oppose candidates already nominated; in the spring of 1958 it began this procedure, considerably to the surprise of some of the non-African candidates. Nyerere tried at the time to open TANU to inter-racial membership but in this he was unsuccessful.[1] A group of TANU members led by Zuberi Mtemvu left the party on this issue of racial co-operation in the elections, and formed the African National Congress on a platform of Tanganyika for Africans only. In the elections however they proved singularly unsuccessful and were never a challenge to TANU.

The years 1957 and 1958 were ones of considerable tension, with a number of disturbances and protests occurring. In Dar es Salaam TANU worked closely with the Tanganyika Federation of Labour, supporting several strikes and a long-drawn-out beer boycott. The influence of the unions increased during this period although TANU clearly remained the major maker of political policy. Many TANU leaders viewed the unions as junior partners and only a branch of the party, but favoured using economic as well as political weapons to oppose the government. Trade union leaders such as Rashidi Kawawa and Michael Kamaliza became TANU leaders as well.[2]

The most serious unrest occurred in Geita District, where African opposition to the creation of a multi-racial district council developed over a period of months into demonstrations, rioting, and a large public march to Mwanza. The initial demonstrations were apparently spontaneous and the men who

---

[1] Lowenkopf's thesis discusses the TANU meeting in Tabora. Sophia Mustafa's *The Tanganyika Way* (London, 1961) is a lively participant's account of the electoral campaign and the general atmosphere of Tanganyika at the time.

[2] See William Friedland, 'Cooperation, Conflict and Conscription', loc. cit.

became leaders only joined TANU later. A visit to the area by Nyerere and Bomani led to a major public demonstration of support for TANU, even though Nyerere, under a government ban which prohibited him from making public speeches, remained silent throughout the trip.[1]

One government initiative during this period was, apparently, a revival of an old idea that a House of Chiefs might be created as the second house for a Tanganyika parliament. The governor called together in May 1957 a Convention of Representative Chiefs, suggesting that they consider the place of chiefs in the political structure of Tanganyika and warning them against the political party composed of detribalized people, full of ideas from outside the territory, which did not have the interests of Tanganyika at heart.[2] It was rapidly clear however that the time for such an appeal was past; later meetings of the group showed the chiefs to be trying to accommodate themselves as gracefully as possible to the new nationalist winds.

A major crisis for TANU arrived in the summer of 1958, when Nyerere was indicted in Dar es Salaam on charges of criminal libel, the result of comments in the party newsletter *Sauti ya Tanu* alleging discrimination by several district officials, including the district commissioner in Geita. The government feared violence and TANU a prison sentence for Nyerere which would greatly handicap the party just before the first election. The trial ended with a conviction, but Nyerere was fined rather than being sent to gaol.[3]

This circumstance has usually been attributed in Tanganyika to the newly-arrived governor, Sir Richard Turnbull, who moved very quickly to ease the political situation. One current interpretation, indeed, suggests that he and Nyerere worked together in this instance. Evidence on this point is lacking, but it is clear that Turnbull managed almost immediately to win the liking and co-operation of TANU leaders. He was not identified with the policy of multi-racialism and was unwilling to support it longer; he was also impressed with the absolute necessity of TANU–government co-operation if internal disorder was to be

---

[1] The Geita disturbances are discussed in detail in Maguire, *Toward 'Uhuru'*.

[2] *First Convention of Representative Chiefs in Tanganyika 10th–16th May 1957*, 1957.

[3] The *Tanganyika Standard* for the summer of 1958 covers both the Geita disturbances and the Nyerere trial.

avoided. The Geita disturbances in particular reminded the Tanganyika government exactly how weak its military and police resources were; a compromise was necessary. Turnbull achieved this, and the administration and the party proceeded, during his governorship, to work in tandem.

In the September 1958 elections TANU-supported candidates won in all constituencies; in February 1959 they were mostly returned unopposed. In the new Legislative Council an Elected Members' Organization (TEMO) was formed to act as a parliamentary opposition, grouping together TANU, European members led by Derek Bryceson, and Asian members headed by Amir Jamal. This organization had a remarkable success in welding together the members of the three racial groups, who shared each other's constituency work and hammered out policies in co-operation with the TANU Executive. Although technically in opposition, TEMO influenced government policy considerably, as in its strong urging that Sir Ernest Vasey of Kenya be appointed Minister for Finance. After March 1959 executive responsibilities were also undertaken, with five TEMO members being appointed to the new Council of Ministers.[1]

From this point events moved very swiftly indeed. After the Conservative Party's victory in the United Kingdom elections, the Secretary of State (Ian Macleod) was urging rapid progress towards independence. In December 1959 Turnbull announced that new elections would be held with a wider franchise, and on a basis which would create a Legislative Council with an African majority and some reserved seats for Asians and Europeans. In September 1960 TANU won 70 out of 71 Legislative Council seats, and Tanganyika moved to *madaraka*—responsible government—with Nyerere as Chief Minister. With very rapid subsequent negotiations and a final constitutional conference in Dar es Salaam in March of the following year, Tanganyika reached independence on 9 December 1961.

Tanganyika at independence

Tanganyika thus reached independence more quickly than her leaders had predicted even four years earlier. The reasons

---

[1] *Report on the First Election of Members to the Legislative Council of Tanyanyika* mimeograph, 1959); Tanganyika Elected Members' Organization, *Minutes*.

why this occurred included the organizational strength and leadership of TANU, the absence of major internal political cleavages such as tribal rivalries, and British government decisions about imperial defence and strategy which accorded little importance to Tanganyika. International publicity and pressure at the United Nations undoubtedly influenced the pace of events, and the threat of internal disorders after 1958 seems to have been the final influence on changes in policy.

In the last years before independence some major problems of the country were by-passed; others had not yet become evident. Great Britain had planned and left behind a certain economic, social, and political infrastructure. But the new African government brought a different set of ideas and priorities to its task. Many British policies it saw as inappropriate to an independent Tanganyika, and twenty years of institution-building it felt to be largely irrelevant. Tanganyika would react against the experience of British rule as much as it would build upon it.

The first problem to be faced by the new government involved the crisis of loyalties. The administrative structure of British government, which had been the major unifying force, no longer commanded African respect despite its new African officials. To the countryman the government was alien, and on independence he expected much of it to disappear. The erosion of loyalty to the British had meant problems in tax collection, for instance; in some areas in 1960 it was down to 18 per cent. As the legitimacy of government declined, a loyalty to TANU had to a certain extent taken its place. But the party itself was very new, its most rapid expansion having occurred in the last two years. It had many members whose political socialization was incomplete; they had never voted, and had indeed followed TANU because of quite specific local grievances and with little knowledge of territorial issues. Many were illiterate. The populist strain in TANU, which made authority difficult up-country, has been emphasized. The task of building a sense of nationality and of nationhood could begin only at independence, and it was of fundamental importance.

A second major problem was the general lack of experience in new jobs and new roles. The cadres of trained Africans were very small; in December 1961 there were 1,170 Africans in senior and middle grade posts in the civil service, out of a total of 4,452 posts. Africans taking these posts left leadership gaps in local government and co-operatives, and the top leadership of TANU itself went *en masse* into government. Political leaders had, at most, three years' experience in the Legislative Council and two years in executive positions. For the country as a whole, parliament and local councils remained imported, feeble institutions; local government did not really exist, for all important decisions remained in Dar es Salaam. There was, furthermore, no country-wide legacy of popular control of government. The British example had been one of paternalism, and of faith in the government as the principal agent of progress. The British had also left behind a number of manifestations of arbitrary government: laws providing for control of all organized groups, making collective punishment possible, permitting the rustication to remote districts of political dissidents or other troublemakers, specifying agricultural practices, requiring marketing through co-operatives.

New policies had thus to be worked out. Control of defence, external affairs, and finance were taken by the TANU government only at independence. TANU had some slight experience in international affairs through its contacts with the United Nations and through PAFMECA which it had founded in 1958,[1] but it had hardly thought about questions of strategy and defence and had not developed many ideas about economics, despite some tentative discussions of socialism. Relations with the chiefs, with local administrations, with minority communities, needed attention. And some unpopular policies of the past had probably to be accepted: taxation, for instance, and agricultural regulations.

Tanganyika's political resources to meet these problems included the widespread feeling of goodwill and euphoria throughout the country, together with a certain singleness of purpose. TANU was popular and was organized throughout the country. It was also an open party, with room for new ideas and new personnel, and there seemed to be no major divisions of opinion within it. Tribal feeling did not present the difficulties that it did in Kenya and Uganda; racial antagonisms had been

[1] Pan-African Freedom Movement for East and Central Africa.

muted. Economic neo-colonialism, as known in the Congo, did not exist, and the British had not left a heritage of ill-feeling. The country had faith in its leadership, and in Julius Nyerere a prime minister of integrity, ability and charisma. But it is not surprising that his motto and that of TANU had become not only *uhuru*, freedom, but *uhuru na kazi*, freedom and work.

IV

THE END OF THE ARAB SULTANATE: ZANZIBAR 1945–1964

ALISON SMITH

As in Uganda the dominating factor in the development of politics during the colonial period was the special status of Buganda, so in Zanzibar the central element was the presence of the Arab sultanate.

The sultanate, like the kingdom of Buganda, was bound to Britain in a treaty relationship. Its position was more substantial in that its authority covered the whole of the Zanzibar Protectorate; it was more precarious in that it was identified with an alien immigrant minority. The Arab overlordship was tied up with a plantation economy which had entailed substantial dispossession, and was associated historically with the slave trade which had once supplied its labour. The plantations continued seasonally to employ a considerable migrant labour force, while alongside these migrants there were the landless labourers of Zanzibar town and the squatters of the clove and coconut plantations. Thus to a much larger extent than elsewhere in East Africa the quarter of a million inhabitants of the two islands—Zanzibar proper and Pemba to the north—were stratified on economic lines. In the event, class divisions, hardening along lines of racial self-classification, were to prove the decisive factor in determining the shape and future of the protectorate's independence. But it was a near thing. The sense of territorial identity seemed sufficiently strong, the patterns of race and class sufficiently fluid, for the Arab aristocracy, rather than trying to safeguard itself by constitutional devices, to trust in its ability to retain power on a full popular common roll vote. At the moment of independence, on 10 December 1963, it almost seemed that its faith was justified.

In addition to the authorities cited, the author would like to acknowledge the help she has derived from notes and press references prepared (in connection with another chapter in an earlier plan of the volume) by the late George Bennett. Like that on Kenya, this chapter should have been his.

In 1945 the members of the Arab élite, besides holding the greater part of the land on the two islands, [1] were still the chosen instruments of British administration—as nominated members of the Legislative Council, and as the more senior subordinate officials in the central and local government. Minor government posts, together with most commercial activity, were in the hands of the Asian community. Those Zanzibaris of African, or mainly African, descent, formed the peasant and worker classes.

But Zanzibar society was more complex and fluid that this bare statement would suggest. This was especially true of the 45,000 Arabs who in 1945 constituted some 17 per cent of the population. They included the often long-established and wealthy families of Omani origin, and also poorer Arabs—often small traders—from the Hadramaut as well as more recent immigrants from Oman. They included, moreover, a substantial element which twenty years earlier had been content to identify itself as 'Swahili', and most 'Arabs' were in fact of more or less mixed descent. This meant that the 'Arab' society was by no means wholly closed; to join it was indeed a widely-held aspiration. [2] On the other hand it was far from being economically secure, for most of the Arab clove-plantations were in fact heavily mortgaged to Asian creditors. [3] The 15,000 Asians (5·8 per cent) were, apart from the few Europeans, the most distinct and self-contained element of the population. But they were divided among themselves: 3,800 Hindus, 4,600 Sunni Muslims, and 6,300 Shias. The African sector for its part, comprising 75 per cent of the total, was divided between those of comparatively recent mainland origin and those—about three-quarters—who had been long settled on the islands as a landholding peasantry and who, in virtue of a somewhat fanciful and remote Persian connection with the coast, called themselves 'Shirazi'. The Shirazi shared with the mainlanders some practical grievances

---

[1] See Michael Lofchie, *Zanzibar, Background to Revolution* (London, 1969), pp. 85–8. Lofchie's study, despite an emphasis on the Arab aspect, is by far the most comprehensive account of Zanzibar politics during this period, and the short account that follows is heavily indebted to it. A more recent account by the same author is 'The Zanzibari Revolution: African protest in a racially plural society', in *Protest and Power in Black Africa*, edited by Robert Rotberg and Ali Mazrui (New York, 1970).

[2] Ibid., pp. 73–6; P. Lienhardt, 'Behind the Zanzibar Mystery', *New Society*, 6 Feb. 1964.

[3] Lofchie, *Background to Revolution*, pp. 106–26.

against Arab rule and overlordship, but they also shared with the Arabs a long history of mainly peaceful symbiosis and a certain contempt for the often slave-descended Africans of more recent mainland origin. Some of them moreover were competitors with the latter in the labour market. The precise balance in these sentiments varied as between the two islands; the Shirazi of Pemba, the northern island, had suffered less from dispossession and were correspondingly richer, and were also more widely related to the Arabs by marriage, than those in the island of Zanzibar.[1] It was essentially the Pemba Shirazi who were to hold the balance of power during the last phase before independence.

The Zanzibar economy, despite efforts at diversification, was tied to the clove plantations which covered Pemba and some of Zanzibar island, and which at this time produced some four fifths of the world output. And it was primarily over issues arising directly or indirectly out of clove production and clove prices that unrest from time to time troubled the islands. Before the war the effects of the world depression and Arab indebtedness had led to bitterness and sometimes violence between Arab landholders and their Asian creditors. In 1948 discontent over wages in relation to rising prices led to a serious strike by African dock labour which for the first time showed signs of racial undertones.[2]

Nevertheless, up to the last ten years of the colonial era the prevailing atmosphere was one of easy-going tolerance and public security. There seems to have been no economic hardship of the degree that sharpened political unrest in Kenya. The edges of social and economic alignment were often blurred. Ali Muhsin, who became the leader of the main Arab-led party, was of Shirazi descent on his mother's side, while his chief opponent, the African harbour-worker and boat-owner Abeid Karume, was married to an Arab wife.[3] A large majority of the people of the islands, Arab, African, and Asian, shared at least the elements of a common attachment to Islam, and a very real common

[1] John Middleton and Jane Campbell, *Zanzibar: its society and its politics* (London, 1965), pp. 35–6.
[2] Reports of the disturbances are given in *The Times* and *East Africa and Rhodesia*, 4–14 Sept. 1948, and briefly in the Zanzibar *Annual Report* for 1948 (Zanzibar, Govt. Printer, 1949).
[3] Cyril Dunn in the *Observer*, 21 July 1957.

loyalty to the sultanate, represented until 1960 by the respected figure of the elderly Seyyid Khalifa.[1] In some ways the more conspicuous lines of cleavage ran between the main body of 'His Highness' subjects' who acknowledged this loyalty, and the fringe elements—Hadramauti Arabs, many of the Asians, and mainlander Africans—who did not.[2]

None of these factors altered the essentially privileged position enjoyed by the Arab community in the distribution of power; but they left a good deal of room for manoeuvre, and for a time they even made the idea of a restored though 'constitutional' sultanate—an independent state under Arab leadership but based on genuine Shirazi African support—seem a practicable possibility. It was an idea shared by a British colonial administration which, from 1945 onwards, was committed to an ultimate if decorous progress towards self-government. It was implicit in the designation of the senior British adminstrator as 'Resident', and at least until 1960 the officials who held that office tended to think and act in an appropriate spirit. As late as 1951 Sir Vincent Glenday, on the eve of his retirement, assured the Arab Association that Zanzibar would be developed as an Arab state.[3]

The Arab Association was one of a number of bodies based upon the various racial groups that went back to the pre-war period. But it is not easy to discern in them at that time anything that could be interpreted as nationalist objectives. The Arab Association, founded in the early 1920s to press for compensation for losses from slave emancipation, became during the 1930s primarily pre-occupied with defending Arab landowners' interests against Asian creditors. African and Shirazi Associations

---

[1] Seyyid Khalifa-bin-Harub-bin-Thwaini-bin-Said. Born 1879, succeeded to throne 1911, after the abdication of Sultan Ali. He was the seventh descendant of Seyyid Said, and reigned for almost 49 years.

[2] It is interesting that in 1957 Abdul Rahman Mohamed ('Babu'), at that time Secretary to the Nationalist Party, helped to produce a pamphlet, *History of the Zanzibar Nationalist Party*, in which the classification of Zanzibar's population does not include the African mainlanders. Lienhardt, 'Zanzibar Mystery', loc. cit.

[3] T. Mayhew, 'Zanzibar Elections 1957', MSS. Afr. 3, 1361, Rhodes House, Oxford. According to a leading Arab politician, this assurance was explicitly stated to have been given with the authority of the Secretary of State. Institute of Current World Affairs, DER-24, 10 Sept. 1954. The last four Residents were Sir Vincent Glenday, 1946–52; Sir John Rankine, 1952–4; H. S. (later Sir Henry) Potter, 1954–60; Sir George Mooring, 1960–3.

were formed in 1934 and 1939 respectively, but while they ful-
filled some of the functions of incipient trade unions, their
activities were mainly confined to welfare matters and without
political impact.[1]

After the Second World War, however, the Arab Association
quickly assumed a different and more militant character. One
element in this was no doubt the increasingly assertive voice of
the Arab world, soon generously relayed to East Africa by Cairo
radio, which extended its beamed programmes to Africa in July
1954. Perhaps more potent was the Arabs' realization that they
could afford to lose no time if they were to make good a claim
to the leadership of an independent Zanzibar before this could
be challenged by the African majority. The opening shots in the
ensuing campaign were fired in 1954 in the shape of a series of
fiercely anti-colonialist articles published in the Arab Association's paper, *Al Falaq* ('the Dawn').[2] To these the administration
replied by arresting and trying for sedition the whole executive
of the Arab Association: but the principal result was merely to
unite with the activists those who had up to then been moderates,
in a general Arab boycott of all participation in government
which lasted for more than eighteen months.

In 1955 a more far-seeing step was taken by the Arabs when
some of the more influential amongst them adopted and identified themselves with a small local peasant party which called itself 'the National Party of the Subjects of the Sultan of Zanzibar'.
It originated in the village of Kiembe Samaki, which three years
earlier had been the scene of one of the island's rare episodes of
violence. A group of local farmers, already resentful over the
expropriation of their land to extend the airport, had risen in
protest against a government campaign for anthrax inoculation
—an incident which is notable as the one Zanzibar instance of a

---

[1] The African Association did however demonstrate its connections by affiliating
on its formation to the Tanganyika African Association (TAA), and in 1939 it was
host to a conference of TAA branch presidents. There was also an Indian Association,
formed as early as 1910, while a Muslim Association was formed after the partition
of the sub-continent. But these do not figure effectively in the political developments
after the Second World War.

[2] March 1954. The 25-year-old editor of *Al Falaq*, Ahmed Lemke, had spent
twelve years in Egypt and had been imprisoned there for two years for communist
revolutionary activities. He came of a wealthy Zanzibar landowning family.
Institute of Current World Affairs, DER-23 10 Sept. 1954; Lofchie, *Background to
Revolution*, pp. 140–5.

theme so conspicuous in mainland politics.[1] This merger drew upon the widespread personal loyalty to the Sultan ('subjects' excluded most mainland and other immigrants), and also upon the genuine degree of common interest between the Arabs and some of the Zanzibar farmers. The moving spirit in bringing it about was Ali Muhsin Barwani, a young Arab from a wealthy landowning family who held an agricultural diploma from Makerere and whose nationalist visions drew both on the heritage of Islamic culture and on his reading of the history of nineteenth-century Europe. In 1956 Ali Muhsin became the party's unofficial leader and its title was shortened to the Zanzibar Nationalist Party (ZNP). Events were to show however that it was no mere projection of the Arab Association, and it remained almost to the end substantially more than a purely communal organization. One of its first moves was to take up the demand already made by the Arab Association for common roll elections.[2]

The British administration, comfortably embedded within its long-standing habit of co-operation with the more conservative elements of the Arab élite, found it hard to perceive or comprehend the new political currents. Although in 1946 the administration had taken the initiative in proposing the introduction of elected members into the Legislative Council, this had been envisaged largely as a gentle extension from the principles of nominated representation, and it was felt that anything in the nature of a common roll would aggravate rather than diminish communal tensions. The administration regarded the *Al Falaq* articles as the work of an extremist minority from whom the moderate majority could easily be detached by firm action, and they were shocked by the strong general Arab reaction of non-co-operation, by the insistent demand for common roll elections, and by the murder in November 1955 of the single Arab Legislative Councillor who defied the boycott.[3] Nevertheless, they

[1] *Report on the Civil Disturbances in Zanzibar on 30 July 1951*, by Sir John Gray (Zanzibar, Govt. Printer, 1951).

[2] Ibid., pp. 143–54. Ali Muhsin's background is described in the *Guardian*, 10 Oct. 1960. See also Institute of Current World Affairs, DER-23, 10 Sept. 1954. For an early comment on the ZNP's broad-based support, see *Tanganyika Standard*, 9 Nov. 1955. The Arab Association, in a policy manifesto of June 1955, had cited the abolition of communal voting in Ceylon in 1928.

[3] Sheikh Sultan Ahmed el Mugheiri, a retired police inspector, who was well aware of the risks he ran in continuing to attend the Council's meetings.

persevered with their own more modest proposals for constitutional advance, which were announced in October 1955 by
the new Resident, H. S. (later Sir Henry) Potter. The main
features of these were the enlargement of the unofficial side of the
legislature (still however nominated), unofficial representation
on the Executive Council, and the appointment of an advisory
Privy Council.[1] At the same time, on the recommendation of
W. F. Coutts, a senior Kenya official who was invited to the protectorate in 1956 to advise on the question, common roll elections
—on a very limited franchise—were scheduled for 1957.[2] Upon
this the Arab Association ended its boycott. Significantly, the
Coutts proposals were modified before being accepted to confine
the franchise to subjects of the Sultan, instead of including all
British 'protected persons'.[3]

In one respect the British administrators were right in their
assessment that nationalist politics in Zanzibar were still very
narrowly based. The African and Shirazi Associations, although
formed in the 1930s, had remained for the most part welfare and
social organizations only. The educational advantage enjoyed
by the Arabs meant that very few Africans had any secondary
schooling, while of those who did many were excluded from the
political arena when in 1953 the administration took steps to
enforce the regulations—until then largely disregarded—debar-
ring civil servants from engaging in politics. Their compliance,
and the apparent conservatism of Zanzibar African politics
generally during the next five years, can be readily explained by
their very real fear, brought out by the *Al Falaq* trial and its
sequel, that an independent Zanzibar would be a Zanzibar permanently dominated by the Arab minority. It led the Africans
and Shirazi, conscious of their own weakness and lack of organization, at first even to oppose the proposal for common roll
elections. It was principally the exhortations of the administra-

---

[1] *Constitutional Development, Zanzibar*, Sessional Paper No. 9 of 1955 (Zanzibar,
Govt. Printer, 1955). The proposals were shelved in the light of the Coutts Report.
A useful summary of these and other constitutional developments during the period
is given in Samuel G. Ayany, *A History of Zanzibar: a study in constitutional development* (Nairobi, 1970).

[2] *Zanzibar Protectorate, Methods of Choosing Unofficial Members of the Legislative
Council*, Commissioner, W. F. Coutts (Zanzibar, Govt. Printer, 1956). Coutts had
just completed a report recommending direct African elections in Kenya.

[3] *The Times*, 18 June 1956. Most mainlander Africans were thus excluded.

tion, nervous of Arab domination, that effectively swelled their numbers on the voters' roll.[1]

However, once the fact of the elections had to be faced, the African and Shirazi Associations met the challenge by joining together in an electoral alliance; in the event the rival ZNP failed to win even one of the six seats for which the first elections were held, in July 1957.[2] There followed a sharp rise in racial tensions. African squatters were evicted from Arab-owned plantations; Afro-Shirazi co-operative consumer stores forced hundreds of small Arab shopkeepers out of business; old-established Afro-Shirazi dock labourers found themselves displaced by Nationalist Party labour on the Zanzibar waterfront. One feature of the election campaign was the emergence as a national figure of Abeid Karume, whose credentials as an election candidate his opponents had rashly tried to impugn. He came triumphantly out of the enquiry to find himself a popular hero, and resoundingly defeated Ali Muhsin in the fight for the constituency of Ngambo, the African and Shirazi quarter of Zanzibar town.

Nevertheless, contrary to the forecasts of some observers, the elections did not immediately herald the emergence of a united African–Shirazi anti-colonial front.[3] The largest number of votes—just over two-fifths of the total of 35,000—went to candidates without explicit party affiliations.

Indeed, despite the election results, it was the ZNP that for the time being regained the overall political initiative and the reputation for being the party of radical reform. In 1958 Ali Muhsin secured the support of President Nkrumah of Ghana. Through its general secretary, Abdul Rahman Mohammed— usually known by his nickname 'Babu' (grandfather)—the party had contacts with the communist world. Babu also visited

---

[1] Mayhew, 'Zanzibar Elections, 1957', loc. cit. The British official in charge of the election register claimed that his exhortations had tripled the number of those who registered. *Observer*, 21 July 1957.

[2] Lofchie, *Background to Revolution*, pp. 175–8; J. C. Penny, 'Notes on the Election in the Protectorate of Zanzibar', *Journal of African Administration*, 10, 3 (1958), 145–52. The votes cast were: for candidates officially sponsored by Afro-Shirazis, 13,052; by ZNP, 7,761; for Independents, 14,548.

[3] e.g. Mayhew, 'Zanzibar Elections, 1957', loc cit., *The Times*, 22 July 1957; *Observer*, 21 July 1957. For the unrest, see *Report of a Commission of Enquiry into Disturbances in Zanzibar during June, 1961*, Chairman, Sir Stafford Foster-Sutton, Col. 353 (London, HMSO, 1961), pp. 2–3.

Britain and used the professional advice of the Labour Party to good effect in building up a formidable network of local organizations: voluntary associations, welfare centres, youth clubs, besides his own foundation of trade union support.[1]

This last was of considerable importance. In 1953 union membership in Zanzibar was still only 527. By 1957 it had jumped to 3,800, and in 1959 seven of the larger unions combined to form the Zanzibar and Pemba Federation of Labour (ZPFL), affiliated to the ICFTU, and with a membership of largely urban labour. Over against this Babu successfully mobilized the agricultural workers and some Shirazi dock-workers into the only slightly smaller Federation of Progressive Trade Unions, formed two years later, and affiliated to the WFTU until 1962, which until the last months before independence was enlisted in the ZNP camp. (By 1961 membership was estimated at 9,000.) Moreover, a battery of supporting newspapers, including no less than five dailies, helped to advance the ZNP cause.[2] All these moves sought to emphasize the overall Zanzibari character of the party, as against any more narrowly racial designation, while at the same time they were financially supported by its solid base in the wealthiest sector of the protectorate's economy.

In consequence of its effectiveness the ZNP's progress was watched with approval and encouragement by socialists overseas (the *Daily Worker* continued to back the party right up to the next election).[3] And when the British administration and the African mainland politicians—the latter under the auspices of the PAFMECSA organization—intervened in an effort to bring about peace and co-operation between the party and its Afro-Shirazi opponents, and succeeded temporarily in arranging a truce, it was the ZNP which emerged as clearly the dominant element in the resultant 'Freedom Committee'.[4]

[1] Clyde Sanger in the *Guardian*, 10 Oct. 1960; R. Segal, *Political Africa* (London, 1961), p. 474; Lofchie, *Background to Revolution*, pp. 225–6.

[2] *Zanews* (Swahili), circulation *c.* 1,000; *Kibarua* (Swahili), 400; *Worker* (English) 400; *Umma* (Swahili), 1,000; *Sauti ya Wananchi* (Swahili), 500. Besides these there were *Mwongozi* (Swahili, English and Arabic) weekly, 1,000; *Adal Insaf* (Gujerati, English, and Swahili), weekly, 500; and *Al Falaq* (Arabic and English) fortnightly, 500. See Lofchie, *Background to Revolution*, p. 211. For trade-union membership, see Zanzibar Labour Department Reports, 1946–60.

[3] *Daily Worker*, 11 Jan. 1961.

[4] Lofchie, *Background to Revolution*, pp. 172–3.

The poor showing of the African and Shirazi Associations, despite the fact that their electoral alliance was shortly ratified by the formation of a joint party,[1] can be explained partly in terms of lack of political experience and resources, but more fundamentally in the difference of aim between its mainlander African supporters and many of their Shirazi allies. The fear of promoting Arab rule made the former hesitant to act forcefully against the administration; the latter disliked the anti-Arab direction given to the party, and increasingly came to respect its rival as being in fact the more effective anti-colonial organization.[2]

In these circumstances the shallow unity of the Afro-Shirazis soon came under strain. It had never been fully accepted by the Shirazi of Pemba, who were suspicious of the mainland Africans and contemptuous of the worker background of the party's leader, Abeid Karume; their own successful candidates, Mohammed Shamte and Ali Sharif, had indeed joined the party only after the election. These, and some Zanzibar Shirazis, now turned away from the main body. Following the expulsion in December 1959 of Ameri Tajo, an Islamic theologian from Zanzibar and an influential Shirazi member of the Legislative Council, Mohammed Shamte and Ali Sharif joined him in forming the Zanzibar and Pemba People's Party (ZPPP).[3] From that moment until independence this almost wholly Shirazi party, whose strength was in Pemba, held the balance of power.

The effects were soon to be demonstrated as other developments combined to throw the political situation into flux. At the end of 1959 the Resident, Sir Henry Potter, was succeeded on his retirement by Sir George Mooring. Mooring came from Nigeria and his appointment, coinciding with the Lancaster

---

[1] At first named the Afro-Shirazi Union (ASU). After the party split in 1959 the main rump became the Afro-Shirazi Party (ASP), and it was this body that was concerned in the next four years' campaigning.

[2] It has been pointed out however that the expressed policy of both groups was very fluid. At the end of 1959 Karume was demanding 'Uhuru now', while the Shirazi leaders were counselling patience. Jane Campbell, 'Multi-racialism and Politics in Zanzibar', *Political Science Quarterly*, 77, 1 (1962), 82–3.

[3] This party was foreshadowed in the short-lived *Ittihad ul'Umma* (The People's Party) formed in late 1956 by Mohammed Shamte and Ali Sharif, but disbanded before the 1957 elections when it failed to obtain Zanzibar Shirazi support. Lofchie, *Background to Revolution*, pp. 172–3.

House Conference on Kenya, was widely interpreted as a break with the old aristocratic Arabist tradition of Zanzibar administration. The break was further marked by the appointment of Sir Hilary Blood as a Special Commissioner to make fresh proposals on constitutional advance.[1] In fact these proposals—for a fully elected unofficial majority in an enlarged Legislative Council with a ministerial system under a chief minister[2]—were accepted by all the political leaders; but both the enquiry and the preparations for the election (which was postponed from July 1960 to January 1961 to allow for the implementation of the report) showed the lines along which political divisions were hardening. The key election issues were those of loyalty to the sultanate and of the qualifications needed for recent immigrants to acquire Zanzibar citizenship. Yet even now the scales were very evenly balanced. While some of the ZNP representations to the Blood Commission (such as that for a bicameral legislature) had tended to reinforce Arab influence, the party's insistence on immediate independence, full adult suffrage, and non-racialism enabled it to castigate its opponents as racial groupings sheltering under the deliberately-prolonged protection of the imperial régime. The Afro-Shirazi Party (ASP) for its part could point accusingly at the ZNP's communist leanings, indicated by 85 student scholarships in Cairo, Moscow, and Peking. Preparations for the elections took place in an atmosphere of rising tension which caused the Resident to threaten a ban on all political meetings unless racial animosity abated.

In the event the ZNP won nine of the 22 seats and 35·8 per cent of the total vote. Its strong financial support and vastly improved organization, represented by 120 local centres and provision for 8,000 pupils in 120 schools, had dramatically retrieved the party's fortunes. Even so, it would have yielded to the ten seats and 40·2 per cent of votes gained by the Afro-Shirazi Party but for the three constituencies (17 per cent of votes) secured by the newly-formed ZPPP. The sequel however showed the division of opinion within the ZPPP itself. While two of its leaders carried

[1] 'It was thought that Sir Henry did not really approve of elections. . . . But he was succeeded by Sir George Mooring, and a fresh breeze blew in with the new Resident from Nigeria. In its slipstream came Sir Hilary Blood, a one-man constitutional commission.' *Guardian*, 10 Sept. 1960.

[2] *Report of the Constitutional Commissioner Zanzibar 1960*, Sir Hilary Blood (Zanzibar, Govt. Printer, 1960).

the main body of the party over into alliance with the ZNP, the third, Ali Sharif, resigned to rejoin the ASP, thus completing the stalemate.[1] To break the deadlock a fresh election—with the creation of an extra seat to prevent a similar result—was fixed for the following June.

Even this, for which the ZNP and ZPPP campaigned together, failed to produce a wholly unequivocal result. It was preceded by a period of rising party and racial feelings. The ASP had been taken aback by the degree of their opponents' success in January. The death of the Sultan Seyyid Khalifa at the end of 1960 had broken something of the old spell of loyalty and toleration, and there were allegations of a plot in which his successor's family were involved, and of the conduct of the campaign by ZNP on a racial and religious basis. These were countered by objections to the support that ASP by now was receiving from the mainland —finance, Land-Rovers, and TANU speakers. Newspaper propaganda on both sides rose to fever pitch. When the election took place, it set off a week of rioting in which 68 Arabs were killed and some 400 people injured.[2] The results of the poll gave the ZNP and ASP ten seats each; only by its alliance with the ZPPP (three seats) was the ZNP able to form a government, and it was to the ZPPP leader, Mohammed Shamte, that Ali Muhsin felt obliged to offer the post of chief minister.

Over the next two years, while the coalition government continued in office, the balance of political forces remained ostensibly unchanged. But beneath the surface the sources of power were shifting. A major factor here was that although the ASP had won only 10 of the 23 seats, they had polled an absolute majority—just over 50 per cent—of the total vote.[3] Another factor was the dramatically quickened pace of Tanganyika's advance to independence following the recognition of TANU's electoral victory in 1959. At the same time there was a growing rift in the ruling ZNP–ZPPP coalition between the right-wing

---

[1] For details of the January 1961 elections see Lofchie, *Background to Revolution*, pp. 199–201.

[2] *Guardian*, 2, 3, 5 June 1961; *Sunday Times*, 4 June 1961; Foster-Sutton *Report*, pp. 8–13.

[3] Detailed figures, and an interpretation of the results, are given in Lofchie, *Background to Revolution*, pp. 202–11. The ASP had a considerable overall majority in Zanzibar, but the other parties an overall majority in Pemba.

(mainly Muslim) and the radical (explicitly Marxist) elements.[1] In mid-1962 ten ZNP leaders were charged with a number of sabotage incidents attributed to the action group of the ZNP's Youths' Own Union. They included Babu, who had already been convicted of publishing seditious statements in the ZNP journal (*Zanews*) which he edited; and when he was sentenced to fifteen months' imprisonment, the leaders of the party in the government raised no protest. On his release Babu put forward his own list of candidates for the next election;[2] when it was turned down he promptly resigned and left for the mainland. He returned however before the election to form, with two other defecting members of ZNP, his own left-wing *Umma* ('the masses') party—though this did not immediately field any candidates. Together these factors—the growing evidence of popular support for the ASP, the quickened political tempo on the mainland, and the apparent tendency of the ZNP to be dominated by its right-wing elements—completed the development which some had mistakenly claimed to have taken place five years earlier: the explicit alignment of the African majority party with the main current of politics on the East African mainland. The colonial metropolitan government, anxious here as elsewhere to identify a clear national party to which to hand over power, sought to make constitutional progress conditional upon internal agreement,[3] to which end PAFMECSA in July 1962 once again tried to bring about a reconciliation between the two Zanzibar parties. But to no real effect. Although a brief agreement was reached the ZNP, not without reason, suspected the PAFMECSA mediator, Mbiyu Koinange from Kenya, of being something less than neutral; in September their suspicions seemed confirmed when the UN Committee on Colonialism

---

[1] Lofchie, *Background to Revolution*, pp. 227–58.

[2] Ibid., p. 259. Babu strenuously opposed the practice of choosing candidates according to the prevailing racial element in the constituencies for which they were to stand.

[3] *Report of the Zanzibar Constitutional Conference 1962*, Cmnd. 1699 (London, HMSO, 1962). It seems that the Colonial Secretary, Reginald Maudling, was at the time much more preoccupied with the parallel conference on Kenya; and that he sought rather arbitrarily to apply this Kenya recipe to the very different problem of Zanzibar. Contrary to the view widely put about by the revolutionary government, there is no evidence that either the British government or the Zanzibar administration at this time particularly favoured an Arab-led government.

adopted a Tanganyika-sponsored motion for immediate elections and independence. [1]

The timing of the next election became, in fact, the central issue between the two parties. Although both were committed to a rapid advance to independence, the ASP, confident of their electoral strength, insisted that this should be preceded by an election, since they feared that otherwise the minority government would entrench itself in power. In the end, after further inconclusive constitutional discussions, [2] the elections were fixed for July 1963, just a fortnight after the establishment of internal self-government.

For these elections the demand of the ASP for full adult suffrage had been conceded. [3] They were therefore baffled and frustrated by the result, which very closely resembled that of the election two years earlier: on a 99·3 per cent poll the ruling coalition was again victorious, with 18 out of 31 seats, the balance once again being held by the Shirazi ZPPP with six seats. It seemed that after all the ruling aristocracy, with the support of a considerable body of the Shirazi, had prevailed even on the test of a full popular vote.

But whereas the close results of the 1961 elections had represented genuine ambiguities in the political scene, that of 1963 no longer corresponded acceptably to the real weight of popular opinion. This time a clear overall majority of votes (54·3 per cent) went to the ASP, their large majorities in Zanzibar being however nullified by the failure to win more than two of Pemba's 14 seats. Even in Pemba the ZNP majorities were much reduced. [4] To secure its evidently frail position the ruling coalition, still headed by Mohammed Shamte as prime minister, set about entrenching its power in an authoritarian régime that would survive independence: but this in fact still further alienated popular support. Steps were taken to staff the government, notably the rural administration, with ZNP supporters of proven

---

[1] Richard Cox, *Pan Africanism in Practice: PAFMECSA 1958-1964* (London, 1964), pp. 62–3. The earlier PAFMECSA intervention of November 1958 (see p. 204 above), on the other hand, seems to have been entirely uncommitted.

[2] *The Times*, the *Guardian*, 25 Feb.–1 Mar. 1963.

[3] While the ASP failed in their bid to postpone self-government until after the elections, they had succeeded also in securing the promise of outside arbitrators and military forces to supervise the elections, and of some modification of constituency boundaries.

[4] Lofchie, *Background to Revolution*, pp. 217–20.

loyalty. Provision was made for the proscription of all political opposition. Most rashly of all, the African mainlanders in the police force, who had formed its most experienced and efficient rank and file, were summarily dismissed.[1]

Zanzibar became independent on 10 December 1963. Just one month later, revolution swept away both the governing coalition and the Arab sultanate which Britain had protected for more than a century. In Zanzibar, as throughout the rest of East Africa, a government which could with some reason claim the support of the majority of the indigenous people was in control.[2]

Yet the revolution was not primarily the work of the party which had up until then ostensibly represented the majority's rights. The ASP had reacted to the ZNP victory of the previous July with all its old hesitations and squabbles, and had failed to make any impact on the latter's strong-arm measures. The real potential for resistance lay rather in what had once been a section of the ruling ZNP itself—that part which had broken away under Babu's leadership to form the Umma Party. Babu's political leadership and organizing power were as formidable to the ZNP in opposition as they had been valuable in support. He had carried with him the main body of the workers from the FPTU, and was subsequently able to combine these with the larger Zanzibar and Pemba Federation of Labour under a National Labour Committee. Behind this was mobilized the All Zanzibar Journalists' Organization (AZJO), which effectively enlisted mass support for Umma with scorching newspaper-attacks on the government.[3] Behind this again were the insecurities, hopes, and fears of the landless workers who made up so considerable a part of the population. Zanzibar nationalism was at length powerfully and irreversibly redefined in terms of the interests of these groups, expressed essentially in racial terms. The bid for an Islamic territorial nationalism under predominantly Arab leadership had failed.

[1] Lofchie, *Background to Revolution*, pp. 265–8; Ayany, *History of Zanzibar*, pp. 129–31.

[2] The main participant account of the revolution is in J. Okello, *Revolution in Zanzibar* (Nairobi, 1967). It is also extensively described in the contemporary issues of *The Times, Guardian*, and *Observer*. See also Lofchie, 'Zanzibari Revolution', loc. cit.

[3] Ayany, *History of Zanzibar*, pp. 131–2.

The catalyst in bringing together the still disparate forces of the ASP and Umma was supplied by a relative outsider, almost a soldier of fortune—the Luo John Okello—who used a small personally-enlisted force, in which Umma supporters were prominent, to topple the vulnerable ruling régime. On the night of 11–12 January 1964 Okello's men seized the police armouries at Ziwani and Mtoni, and after distributing weapons from these, gained control of Zanzibar town within a few hours, after which there was no effective further resistance. Nor was there any British attempt at intervention. Probably the most critical element in the support Okello received was that of the many dismissed mainland police who had not been repatriated to the mainland. But his hour was short. In the reorganization which followed the successful rising, the militants of Umma at length joined with Abeid Karume and the radical elements of the ASP to thrust him aside and forge the most dramatically socialist régime in East Africa. This régime continued to maintain its separate identity and to develop its close communist contacts, even within the political union which was formed three months later to create the new state of Tanzania.

V

DAYSPRING MISHANDLED?
THE UGANDA ECONOMY 1945–1960

DENNIS LURY

THERE was substantial growth in Uganda from 1945 to 1960 by any of the generally used criteria. Despite this growth there was considerable dissatisfaction in 1960 with the state and structure of the economy. The main reasons for this disquiet were two. In the first place, the advance had not been a steady one. It had been concentrated in the years 1949 to 1955, and the expectations then engendered drained away in the following years as the impetus ebbed, and what happened seemed to be only the results of earlier plans, rather than the consequences of new initiatives. Secondly, and perhaps more disturbingly, the growth had apparently occurred without any really significant change in the character of the economy and—against a world background of falling primary product prices and restrictive commodity agreements—it was widely believed that substantial structural changes were necessary for longer term development.

One of the main purposes of this chapter will be to consider the questions that arise in such a context. What was the nature of the expansion that took place and how had it occurred? Would there have been a more rapid rate of growth over the period as a whole if government had adopted different policies? Could there have been greater structural changes in the economy? Discussion of government economic policy will be prominent because government was relatively unfettered by countervailing

The author would like to acknowledge his general debt to discussions with Professors W. T. Newlyn and P. Robson (who were Economic Advisers to the Uganda Government when he worked there) and to the group of economists at Makerere College then led by Professor D. Walker. None of them has any responsibility for anything in this chapter, but he would like to recall that two specific points —that relating to the comparison of peasant and experimental yields (pp. 223–4) and that of the pre-war producer/marketing situation (p. 234)—were first emphasized by Professor Newlyn.

economic power and did not suffer from lack of resources (partly as a result of its policies, of course).

The growth of the economy

The population of Uganda grew during these fifteen years by over 2 million to about 6·7 million by 1960.[1] Non-Africans were little more than 1 per cent for most of the period—they numbered about 90,000 (1·3 per cent) in 1960.[2] About 85 per cent of the African working population were farming,[3] their activities ranging from nomadic pastoralism in Karamoja to commercial farming in Buganda. They produced the cotton and coffee which dominated Uganda's exports. The senior positions and most of those in the middle grade in industry, commerce, and government were occupied by non-Africans. The number of Africans recorded in 1960 as employed in professional posts was less than 1,000, whereas the corresponding number of non-Africans was about 5,000.[4]

The national income figures are summarized in Table I. They are as good (or as bad, if one prefers) as those for most developing countries at the time. The total gross domestic product figure includes a crude estimate of the value of subsistence production based on estimates of population, production, and rural prices. The monetary series is better, but there is no reliable index to convert it into real terms. The three price series given are conflicting but it does not appear that any likely combination of price changes would alter the broad pattern of a rapid rise to 1955, both in total income and income per head, and of stagnation thereafter.

The importance of cotton and coffee exports over the entire period is clear from Table II. From 1950 their annual value averaged about £35 million—over three-quarters of total exports

---

[1] Uganda Government *Statistical Abstract 1963* (Govt. Printer, Entebbe, 1964), Table UB2 and extrapolation.

[2] Ibid.

[3] This assumes the African working population consists of men and women aged 16–45, and takes no account of the fact that a number of people have more than one occupation.

[4] East African Statistical Dept., Uganda Unit, *Enumeration of Employees 1960* (Entebbe, 1961), Tables 21–3. Excludes education, medical and miscellaneous services, where occupational classification was very poor: excludes employers and self-employed.

TABLE I
INCOME INDICATORS

	Gross Domestic Product £m.		Price indices		
	Total	Monetary	European (Dec. 1951 = 100)	Kampala African (Jan. 1957 = 100)	Imports (1954 = 100)
1946		21·4			
1948		30·3	79		
1950	83·5	54·3			
1952		88·3	104	91	
1953		76·3	112	157*	
1954	130·7	93·0	117	132	100
1955	142·2	102·3	122	109	98
1958	146·8	106·3	136	102	97
1960	151·8	110·5	138	93	102

* Bad harvest.

SOURCES: (a) Total and Monetary GDP 1954–60: *Statistical Abstracts*, 1960 and 1963, Tables UN1 and UN2. (b) Total GDP 1950: estimated from 1959 figure assuming the 78 per cent increase from 1950 to 1959 given in East African Statistical Unit—Uganda Unit, *The Gross Domestic Product of Uganda 1954–1959*, para. 86. (c) Monetary GDP 1946–1953: H. W. Ord, 'The Growth of Money Incomes in East Africa', *East African Economics Review*, 9, 1 (June 1962). The basis is a little different from the subsequent official series, mainly in the treatment of public corporation inter-territorial transactions. The orders of magnitude of changes over the combined series are not seriously distorted by this. (d) Kampala Price Indices: Figures for June, *Statistical Abstracts* 1957 and 1963, Section UO. (e) Uganda Imports Index: *Statistical Abstracts* 1960 and 1963 Section UD.

—but to maintain these receipts about three times as much coffee had to be exported in 1959 and 1960 as in 1950 and in 1951.

Before 1939 it had been the fortunes of cotton that had dominated economic developments.[1] After the first three post-war years, during which the war-time emphasis on food production spent its force, a campaign to increase cotton-planting lifted the quantity of cotton exports in 1949 back to the level of the late 1930s. The quantity of cotton grown and picked in subsequent years increased only slightly. After 1950 and 1951, when top prices for cotton were paid and its export brought in about £30 million in each year, export proceeds from cotton and its products settled down to about £20 million a year. But during this period coffee became as important as cotton. The value of coffee

[1] See chap. viii, 'The Uganda Economy', by C. Ehrlich, in Volume ii of this *History*.

TABLE II

UGANDA EXPORTS

	Total £m.	Outside E. Africa £m.	E. Africa £m.	Cotton Qu. m.lb.	Cotton Value £m.	Cotton Price £/lb.	Coffee Qu. 000 cwt.	Coffee Value £m.	Coffee Price £/lb.
1946	10·5	8·9	1·6	87·7	5·6	0·064	628	1·8	0·026
1948	15·7	13·5	2·2	69·7	7·5	0·108	755	3·2	0·038
1950	31·0	28·7	2·4	139·3	16·7	0·111	637	8·3	0·117
1952	50·8	47·2	3·6	151·2	30·0	0·198	789	12·3	0·140
1953	37·9	33·4	4·6	133·7	16·8	0·125	714	11·5	0·144
1954	45·7	40·6	5·1	157·3	20·9	0·133	693	13·5	0·174
1955	46·7	41·9	4·8	122·5	16·4	0·134	1489	20·1	0·121
1958	50·2	45·4	4·8	155·0	18·1	0·117	1574	20·8	0·118
1960	48·3	41·6	6·7	132·0	14·9	0·113	2336	17·0	0·065

SOURCES: (a) Columns 1–3, D. A. Lury, 'The Trade Statistics of the countries of East Africa 1945–64', *East African Economic and Statistical Review*, 14 (Mar. 1965). Figures exclude specie and re-exports. (b) Columns 4–9; (exports outside East Africa) *Annual Trade Reports for Kenya, Uganda and Tanganyika* (for 1946–8); *Statistical Abstracts*, 1957 and 1963, Section UD (for 1950–60). Prices from 1950 onwards calculated from original data, not from rounded figures given in previous columns.

exports more than doubled in the ten years to 1960; and from 1957 to 1960 cotton and coffee exports overseas both averaged £19·5 million a year.

At a very general level, therefore, resources for development in Uganda can be traced to increased participation in the international division of labour through the trading of cotton and coffee on the world market.

Nearly all the coffee was grown in Buganda and most of the cotton in Buganda and Eastern Province, and there were accordingly sizeable disparities in regional incomes. In 1959, over one-half of African income went to Buganda and over one quarter to Eastern Province.[1] Nine out of every ten non-Africans, with their much higher average incomes, also lived in these regions, and naturally the results of increased prosperity were much more obvious there. Farmers put roofs of corrugated iron and then of tiles on their houses, cemented their floors, and began to build with bricks. Africans participated widely in a lively transport industry, particularly in the operation of 'private' taxis. Kampala, Jinja, and Mbale became substantial towns and, although they retained residentially their historical non-African character, about 130,000 Africans were living in or around them in 1959.[2] This number represented a more than doubling since 1945, but it was of course still only a small proportion of the total African population. What were the characteristics of the agriculture the vast majority continued to practise?

Agriculture

Most Ugandans were peasant farmers engaged in cultivating two- to four-acre holdings with a hoe, producing food crops mainly for their own consumption, and one or two crops specifically for sale.[3] Daily labour input was normally of the order of three to four hours.[4] Longer hours were worked at planting

---

[1] East African Statistical Department, Uganda Unit, *The Gross Domestic Product of Uganda 1954–1959*, (Entebbe, 1960), p. 36.

[2] For a description of African town life, see A. W. Southall and P. C. W. Gutkind, *Townsmen in the Making*, (East African Studies No. 9, Kampala, 1956).

[3] For a general description see C. C. Wrigley, *Crops and Wealth in Uganda* (East African Studies No. 12, Kampala, 1959).

[4] 'Every person . . . should see that he puts not less than six hours in his work every day.' The Katikiro (Chief Minister) at the opening of the Lukiko, 1946. *Uganda Herald*, 4 Sept. 1946. But cf. 'The average peasant works from three to four hours a day,' *Report of the Agricultural Productivity Committee* (Entebbe, 1954), p. 31.

(including land-breaking) and harvesting times, and the amount of work that could be handled by the household at these peak periods set the level of activity for the rest of the year. The broad division of labour on the homestead was that the men cleared the ground, built the huts and stores, and concentrated on the cash crops. The women helped in building, for example by carrying materials; assisted in the cultivation of cash crops (weeding the cotton): and were entirely responsible for the cultivation of food crops. They fetched water and firewood, prepared food, looked after the children and worked considerably longer than the men.[1] A small proportion of the men followed a craft or trade (carpenter, smith, shopkeeper, potter) in addition to farming.

The area of land cultivated per head seems to have remained fairly constant during the period at about one and a third acres.[2] Double cropping (that is, two crops a year—for example, cotton following millet) and mixed planting (for example growing cotton and beans together) are common in Uganda, and there is therefore considerable double counting in this figure: if this is removed, the area under cultivation at any one time was probably about 0·8 acres per head.

It was possible for this type of holding to be reproduced as population grew and the number of households increased, for four main reasons. First, there were unused areas in 1945 which could be opened up, either through official resettlement schemes, as in Western Province, or through natural expansion, as in

---

[1] This division of labour did not apply on those farms in Buganda where migrant labour was employed. Nevertheless although there is little reliable quantitative information for all Uganda, Winter's conclusions, drawn from a detailed study of the Bwamba, are likely to be of fairly wide application: 'The man's productive efforts are determined by the number of women whose labour is at his disposal . . . a man with only one wife is underemployed . . . most of the women are cultivating an optimum acreage given [the] productive goals and preference for leisure.' Once again, however, it is necessary to add the rider that the 'underemployment' of the male was not so great at times of planting and harvesting, so that the potential labour limit, considering the farming system throughout the year, was more restrictive than these quotations imply, especially in areas where annual crops predominated and there was some conflict between the requirements of food and cash crops. E. H. Winter, *Bwamba Economy* (East African Studies No. 5, Kampala, 1955). See also J. L. Joy, 'Mechanical Cultivation in Acholi', in *Symposium on Mechanical Cultivation in Uganda* (Kampala, 1960), pp. 14–16 and 21, and L. A. Fallers, *Bantu Bureaucracy* (Cambridge, 1956), p. 78.

[2] Agricultural Department, *Revised Crop Acreage Estimates 1945–1956* (Entebbe, 1958), and subsequent Agricultural Department Annual Reports.

Buganda. Secondly, the Department of Tsetse Control, set up in 1947, reclaimed 7,000 square miles which had become fly-infested 10 to 20 years earlier.[1] Thirdly, soil conservation practices improved considerably, particularly in Kigezi where terracing was remarkably successful. The fourth development was more intensive use of the soil. Under the system in use the farmer required, in addition to the land actually in cultivation at any one time, more land 'in resting' so that he could work a rotation with fallow. The period of fallow needed to restore the land varies from place to place, but it was clear that the time actually allowed at the end of the period had fallen below what had been previously regarded as necessary.[2] The resulting overcropping was not accompanied by widespread adoption of any of the proposed remedies to retain the fertility of the land (use of manure, planting of grasses instead of waiting for natural regeneration). This fourth development therefore seemed likely to be self-defeating in the long run.

For these reasons land was available on which the existing type of holding could be reproduced. As already remarked, fertility was likely to fall on land obtained by reducing the fallow period, but much of the other land freshly taken into cultivation was sound. Although there is little reliable information, there are no indications of significant changes in yields averaged over the country as a whole; and since the proportion of the holding under food crops did not alter, food production *per capita* remained at about the same level during the period.

For cotton and coffee the area under cultivation in Buganda increased by about 40 per cent, as did its population. In the main cotton-growing areas outside Buganda (Busoga, Mbale, Teso,

---

[1] The fly began to encroach again in 1956 and heavy expenditure was required for control.

[2] The ratios of fallow to cultivation pre-1939 were 8:3 in elephant grass areas and 4:1 in short grass areas. See *A Report on Nineteen Surveys done in Small Agricultural Areas in Uganda with a view to Ascertaining the Position with regard to Soil Deterioration* (Entebbe, 1958). But by 1960 'the land could not be cropped safely for more than three years in five'. J. D. Jameson and R. K. Kirkham, *Empire Journal of Experimental Agriculture*, 28 (1960), 111. See also *The Economic Development of Uganda*, Report of a Mission organized by the International Bank for Reconstruction and Development (IBRD) (Baltimore, 1962), p. 119: 'Cultivators are advised by the Agricultural Department to adopt a six-year rotation consisting of three years of consecutive cropping followed by three years' rest.'

Lango, Acholi, and West Nile) the area under cotton increased by about 10 per cent and the population by about 25 per cent. Thus the increase in cotton and coffee cultivation can be mainly attributed to a growing population following a broad pattern of farming already laid down.[1]

The main change in the traditional practice was the switch in Buganda from cotton- to coffee-growing. The reasons for this seem plain. An acre of coffee yielded an average of 1,180 lb. of dried coffee cherry (*kiboko*) and an acre of cotton yielded about 500 lb. of seed cotton. The coffee acre required only 80 man-days' labour per year compared with 140 for cotton. Thus if prices to growers for *kiboko* and seed cotton were equal, the advantages of coffee were obvious. In fact, from 1953 the price paid for *kiboko* was *higher* than that paid for seed cotton (sometimes twice as high). Further, a coffee plot was a tangible asset that could be passed on to the next generation. Since the staple food crop of the Ganda, the plantain (*matoke*) is a perennial not an annual crop, there were no prejudices against tree-type crops to overcome; and the disadvantage of the waiting period of three to four years before the first crop would be harvested was mitigated by planting supplementary food crops among the young trees. In view of these advantages it is not surprising that coffee displaced cotton. The transition was facilitated by the number of migrant labourers in Buganda. They were employed in coffee cultivation, some farmers employing such labour on a considerable scale in relation to the size of their holdings. Other migrant workers 'normally domiciled around the borders of Buganda—moved into Buganda during the cotton season and hired land for the sake of growing cotton, returning to their original country at the end of the season'.[2]

Except for this one change in the pattern of cultivation, easily explicable in its context, the basis of the Uganda economy remained much the same, new households following existing patterns, and the improved position of the economy derived mainly from the high prices obtained overseas for cotton and coffee during a part of the period.

[1] It is thought that the *orders of magnitude* of these comparisons—obtained from census data and the still more dubious acreage figures in *Revised Crop Acreage Estimates 1945–1956* and subsequent reports—are correct.
[2] D. E. B. Kibukamusoke, 'Competitive Effects of Coffee on Cotton Production in Buganda', *Empire Cotton Growing Review*, 39, 2 (1962), pp. 106–13.

Although this replication was a natural process, it would not have occurred so readily but for some government technical assistance. As already noticed, the Agricultural Department's campaign in 1948 to increase cotton cultivation helped to stimulate production after the war. Some of the land newly cultivated was available because of the activities of the Department of Tsetse Control. Resettlement schemes were introduced. The Empire Cotton Growing Association research station at Namulonge reorganized the distribution and multiplication of seed and developed new varieties giving a higher lint out-turn: its analysis of the association of a higher yield with an early date of planting led to the Agricultural Department's long-continued drive for early planting. This brought the median date of planting back three weeks to the beginning of July. A copper dressing to prevent blackarm disease was developed and added 'an estimated 8 per cent to the total annual (cotton) crops.'[1] The yield of cotton per acre in Uganda as a whole, however, showed little change as these improvements were merely sufficient to offset the falling off involved in the transfer of cotton-growing from Buganda to generally less fertile areas. Although certain improvements were firmly adopted by the farmers (so that, for example, in some areas in Kigezi terracing came during this period to be talked of as if it had been part of the traditional practice), other good husbandry techniques were maintained only by the continual persuasion of agricultural extension workers. For example, the quality of Bugisu coffee fell rapidly when close supervision was removed.[2]

If rapid and continuous development was to be the aim, however, there were dangers in depending upon export returns from two primary products. Further, at some time in the future, this process of muliplying traditional holdings would come to its limits. The difficulties of wider development would have to be faced sooner or later, and it was clearly desirable to take advantage of the favourable circumstances to prepare for the changes that would be required. How far was government in a position to make a substantial impact on agricultural technology?

---

[1] *Report of the Commission of Inquiry into the Cotton Ginning Industry of Uganda* (Entebbe, 1962), p. 16.

[2] *Report of the Commission of Inquiry into the Affairs of the Bugisu Co-operative Union Ltd.* (Sessional Paper No. 14 of 1958), para. 36.

First, impracticable possibilities must be excluded from consideration. Peasant agriculture is a conservative activity, and the period dealt with here is but fifteen years—less than a generation. Given the feelings about the land, there were obvious limitations to the type of change that a colonial government with failing powers could hope to guide through. Although much of the best land in Buganda had been held in individual title from the beginning of the century, and a start to granting individual titles was made in Western Province in the 1950s, any large-scale grouping of holdings was out of the question. Further, opportunities for bringing together private capital—which was of course mainly in non-African hands—and the land were limited by legal and political barriers; and even in Buganda, where the long history of individual title might have been thought to have prepared the way, feelings about land ran high. There were bitter protests, for example, about the use of land at Namulonge for the official research station into cotton-growing.

Attempts were made to introduce tractors but they were not successful. The Agricultural Department set up a Special Development Section in 1949 to investigate mechanical means of cultivation. The initial experience was promising, showing considerable reductions in costs, and provision was made therefore to spend more than £1 million from the African Development Fund on mechanization. But the money was not spent, since, it was later claimed, 'the conditions in which tractor operating costs become prohibitive are not uncommonly found in Uganda . . . attempts to incorporate tractors into existing small-scale peasant farming systems will be normally doomed to failure.'[1]

Continued propaganda for ox ploughing had little effect, and the use of draught animals scarcely spread outside Teso. In Ankole, where it might well have been adopted owing to the large number of cattle, farmers contended that 'an ox, once it has worked, is valueless for dowry or slaughter.'[2]

Little progress was made in getting mixed farming adopted although, once again, the Agricultural Department tried hard

[1] 'Some Generalizations about Social and Economic Factors Affecting the Success of Farm Mechanization applied to Uganda', *Symposium on Mechanical Cultivation*, p. 139. Only £123,000 out of the £1,015,000 earmarked by government in its development plans for the development of mechanized farming was used.

[2] Agricultural Department Annual Report, 1956.

through its advisory services to arouse interest. The number of livestock increased rapidly—faster than population—and increased production of meat led to some specialization. Nevertheless the management of herds was generally not treated economically: cattle continued to be wanted primarily as status symbols, as a store of wealth, and for dowry payments.

One theoretical way of increasing total effort in some areas would have been to re-distribute work so that the men had more to do. A change of this nature had occurred in Buganda and Eastern Province at the beginning of the century, when men undertook cultivation of cotton for the first time: but the imposition of colonial rule had then just changed some of their previous activities; they needed money for taxes, and with cotton receipts could buy exemption from traditional labour dues to chiefs and the community. There was little a colonial government could now do directly about altering the way in which work was divided: neither could it do much to make marriages more secure and thus increase a woman's interest in her husband's returns and her willingness to help with the cash crops.

But one policy which might have had a similar effect would have been to pay greater attention to research work into food crops and into investigating farming systems as a whole, rather than to concentrate upon individual export crops in isolation; the Agricultural Department started to give increasing emphasis to these aspects only in the late 1950s. Another step that could have been taken would have been to avoid the distinction regularly drawn between cash and food crops. This rigid distinction—and its associated policy of district self-sufficiency—was in any case holding up the general development of specialization between regions and individuals.

In 1954 the governor, Sir Andrew Cohen, set up an Agricultural Productivity Committee to produce a plan for raising 'agrarian productivity and standards of farming'. The committee included senior officials of the Agricultural and Veterinary Departments and it endorsed the existing policy of trying to increase production by intensive methods, by raising yields per acre rather than by extending the area under cultivation.[1] The

---

[1] For an early statement of official policy see Agricultural Department Annual Report, 1948.

committee accepted that the latter policy would have led to increased production (though only in the short term, in their view) but argued that it would be 'thoroughly unsound as it will have the effect of extending to valuable reserves of land the inefficient traditional farming methods.'[1] This view had not prevented the drive in 1948 to increase the area under cotton already mentioned—a drive combined with a sharp increase in the price to the grower and the introduction of bonus payments to African local governments which were tied to production in their areas. The implicit assessment of future needs against current requirements by the committee was unduly vague and non-quantitative for such an important issue. Nevertheless it was accepted as a basis for policy until 1961. It was then tacitly shelved, a forceful drive to get more land under cotton was mounted and successfully increased the acreage planted by about one-third, without any substantial reduction of the acreage under other crops.[2] There are some grounds for believing, therefore, that a policy of extension of cultivation could have led to the increase in cotton production which would have kept up the momentum of development in the short term. Even if considerable weight is given to the conservation argument, an extra two or three hundred thousand acres put under cotton would have been negligible relative to the area under cultivation or in reserve. There would have been difficulties—for example, pressure through chiefs would not have been as effective as it would have been earlier—but, given appropriate price marketing policies, such a policy would have had a substantial chance.

Official discussion about raising yields was carried on in somewhat naïve terms. It made great play with the difference between the yields obtained on experimental plots and those apparently obtained by the farmer, stating that by following a few simple rules the farmer could double his yields. The argument was faulty because general farming could not hope to equal the yields obtained under the special experimental conditions. Further, the actual official comparisons used an estimate of peasant yields which was almost certainly too low since it divided

[1] *Report of the Agricultural Productivity Committee*, p. 39.
[2] There were of course other factors: coffee returns were expected to fall and the cotton price to keep firm. Further, owing to disastrous weather, the crop finally harvested was one of the smallest ever.

an accurate production figure by an acreage estimate that was too high. The changes in practice required to obtain the increased yield—such as, for example, early planting—could not be fitted into the existing labour sequence without considerable effort. This was not properly appreciated until the farming system as a whole was studied.

Many economists have considered that the way to improve and transform peasant agriculture is to mount a large extension programme, although it is generally recognized that one of the difficulties in doing this quickly is the shortage of trained extension workers. The Agricultural Productivity Committee recommended a considerable expansion in agricultural education but only 'a measure of expansion' in field activities. What was perhaps the best opportunity in the period for obtaining resources for a considerable stepping up of extension work was therefore missed.

One aspect of government agricultural policy that was criticized strongly, particularly by the East Africa Royal Commission, was the insistence on district self-sufficiency. The need for this was proclaimed by the Agricultural Productivity Committee[1] and maintained by the governor, Sir Andrew Cohen, in his comments on the report of the Royal Commission.[2] There had been no recent serious food shortages in Uganda—although there were several in living memory—and this was regarded as evidence of the desirability of the existing system. Crops classified as cash and food—for example cotton and millet—frequently formed part of a satisfactory double crop rotation. From the earliest days, colonial administrators had often attempted to secure a measure of self-sufficiency in food, and this attitude was supported by some agricultural economists whose approach may be summed up:

In Africa the desire to be largely self-sufficient in foodstuffs is very strong—much stronger than the economists who pay little attention to the realities of high risk–low capital situation seem prepared to admit when they, on Adam Smith lines, criticise administrators.[3]

---

[1] *Report*, p. 42.

[2] *Despatches from the Governors . . . commenting on the East Africa Commission 1953–1955 Report*, Cmd. 9801 (London, 1955), p. 111.

[3] J. R. Raeburn, 'Some Economic Aspects of African Agriculture' *East African Economics Review*, 5, 2 (Jan. 1959), 45. The reference to 'Adam Smith lines' could be

Nevertheless, whilst these are compelling arguments against a precipitate move towards a free market, some slackening of control could well have been allowed as the transport and distribution systems improved. There was little need for dogmatic enforcement everywhere and market forces could have been allowed to take over as much as possible, thus leading to increased specialization. Although the extent to which these regulations were effective varied over time and space, the failure to ease the processes of exchange removed one of the main forces that could have helped the transformation from 'cultivation to farming' which, among others, the Agricultural Productivity Committee was itself urging.

Pricing and marketing of cotton and coffee

To concentrate on the technological questions of production, however, is to ignore the key economic problems of price and marketing policies. In Uganda, throughout the period, the pricing and marketing of cotton and coffee were controlled by the government through Statutory Marketing Boards, and government frequently intervened in the disposal of other crops also (for example maize). The basic procedure for cotton and coffee was to guarantee a price for the season, though this was not consistently done for coffee when the external market fluctuated greatly. The fixed price was paid to the growers by the processors, who were then remunerated on a cost-plus basis, incorporated in the price paid to them for the processed cotton and coffee finally purchased by the Marketing Boards.

The price to the growers was considerably affected by the heavy export taxes placed on cotton and coffee, and also by the building up, and subsequent running down, of Price Assistance Funds. In considering the operation of this latter arrangement it must be remembered that the size of the Price Assistance Funds at any one time was not the result of government policy alone: it was affected by the price received for the commodity when it actually came on the world market, and government could not foresee this accurately. Thus the additions to and subtractions from the Price Funds were often considerably greater or less than forecast in the original estimates.

queried: after all, Smith defended the Navigation Acts on the grounds that 'Defence is more important than Opulence.'

The effects of this marketing and tax policy on the income of growers are summarized in Table III.

TABLE III

COTTON AND COFFEE: PAYMENTS TO GROWERS AND
DEDUCTIONS, 1945–60

	Cotton £000	Coffee £000	Total £000
Payments to growers	135,254	96,618	231,872
Export taxes	43,537	24,691	68,228
To Price Assistance Funds	38,112	9,494	47,606
Of which, transferred to Development Funds	24,200	625	24,825

SOURCE: D. A. Lury, 'Cotton and Coffee Growers and Government Development Finance in Uganda 1945–60', *East African Economics Review*, 10, 1 (June 1963).

During these fifteen years the amount kept back from the growers was extremely large and was equal to about half the payments actually made to them. Admittedly some of this retained income was transferred in the first instance to Price Assistance Funds and regarded by the growers as 'theirs', but before long half of it was transferred to government development funds and, in a last squeeze, a further £5 million was borrowed from the Cotton Fund for government expenditure. These are total figures referring to the whole period. During the early years the with-holdings were at a much higher rate: in 1951 they amounted to over £25 million whilst payments to growers were under £14 million. From 1953 the policy of building up surplus funds by paying below estimated break-even market prices was abandoned and producer prices were based on 'the best estimate possible of the world price at the beginning of each season'.[1]

The sum of nearly £25 million transferred from the price support funds to development funds may be regarded as a disguised export tax: as being an adjustment between the two methods of levy in accordance with Sir Andrew Cohen's view that it would have been preferable 'to have drawn off the major

[1] *Despatches from Governors*, Cmd. 9801, p. 118.

part at any rate of any surplus in export tax payable into general revenue rather than by allowing surplus funds to accumulate'.[1] On this basis 'tax' levies on growers amounted to £93 million on total incomes of £348 million, or 27 per cent: this percentage is again an average, and the actual annual figures varied from about 50 per cent during 1948–52 to about 15 per cent in 1959–60. The average rates for cotton and coffee were different, being 31 per cent for cotton and 21 per cent for coffee.

How did this tax policy distort the pattern of production? It is convenient to look first at cotton against coffee, and then at cotton and coffee together against (a) other crops and (b) leisure.

It is unlikely that the different rates of tax on cotton and coffee affected significantly the substitution of coffee for cotton since the differences in tax on the two crops appear small in relation to the advantages to coffee in Buganda discussed earlier. In fact, coffee could probably have been taxed more heavily than cotton without seriously altering the rate of substitution. But it may be noted that the balance of taxation was certainly inconsistent with the Agricultural Department's greater emphasis on cotton than coffee.

The effect of export taxes on the allocation of resources between cotton and coffee as against other crops is harder to assess. If the policy of district self-sufficiency is to be taken as given, the remaining scope for re-allocation was limited. Because of this policy there was in many areas no alternative marketable crop; and where there were alternatives, marketing uncertainties appeared large. An indication of what could have happened if markets for alternative crops had been generally available is given by the sudden doubling of maize cultivation when a high guaranteed price was available for it in 1953 as a result of a crop failure in Kenya. If higher prices had been paid to growers for cotton and coffee the policy of self-sufficiency could not have been maintained. This was, indeed, advanced as one reason for keeping prices down.[2] This argument for the pricing policy clearly does not hold if self-sufficiency is rejected.

[1] Ibid.
[2] 'If too much money was allowed to go out on cash crops, food crops would be neglected, and also possibly other economic crops which commanded a lower price but were of great value to the general economy of the country.' Sir John Hall, 'Some Aspects of Economic Development in Uganda', *African Affairs*, 51, 202 (1952), 133.

Speculation as to the extent that higher prices would have brought forth greater total effort from the existing growers is rather on the level of guesses about 'what song the Syrens sang', but some points may be listed. First, even after levies, payments to growers rose rapidly in the period 1945 to 1952, the last year in which the policy of building up surplus funds applied (export taxes of course continued throughout the whole period). The figures are given in Table IV. Although import and other prices were rising, they were not rising at this rate and there was a substantial gain in real incomes.

TABLE IV

COTTON AND COFFEE PRICES AND PAYMENTS TO GROWERS 1945–52

	Price: Seed cotton cts. per lb.	Payments to growers £000	Price: Robusta kiboko cts. per lb.	Payments to growers £000
1945/6	18	2,576	15	1,109
1946/7	20	2,956	17	759
1947/8	22	2,399	19	1,578
1948/9	30	7,376	21	1,049
1949/50	33	7,334	25	2,033
1950/1	45	10,372	40	3,610
1951/2	50	11,929	50	4,331
1952/3	50	10,374	70	5,731

SOURCE: Agricultural Department annual statements.

Provincial commissioners were reported as agreeing, in 1951, that 'in some areas . . . cash income is acquired so easily that there is little, if any, incentive to increase production or the quality of production or even to work at all.'[1] Such an assessment seems to indicate moral indignation rather than economic analysis; but there were in fact widespread reports from observers in the field that a considerable amount of cotton was being left unpicked. In view of the shortage of goods, and of the slowness of changes in consumption patterns in rural areas, it is possible that—at least in the very short term—a rise in price would have

---

[1] *Uganda Herald*, 14 Aug. 1951.

evoked less work. It is true that the rise in cotton price from 1947/8 to 1948/9 was matched by an increase in acreage, but the larger area planted may have been due as much to the widespread central and local government drive to press farmers to grow more cotton since subsequent rises in prices did little to increase the acreage planted, even if we exclude Buganda to allow for the switch to coffee there. The problem, however, is one of assessing not merely the effect on existing growers, but the demonstration effect on potential growers, particularly those outside Buganda. Again, in the short term, the rises in price from 1948 to 1952 (although these were not so substantial in real as in money terms) had little effect, the area planted outside Buganda remaining at about 1,100,000 acres each year.

Although for the grower at the time of the levy there was little difference between money taken for export taxes and money put to Price Assistance Funds, the reasons for, and the effects of, the deductions were not of course identical. Both served to reduce current pressure of demand and to provide reserves which could be injected into the economy when export prices fell back. But a major aim of the funds was stabilization, and although no detailed analysis was made of what 'stabilization' implied, it was intended to cover a fixed intra-seasonal price and longer-term price and income stability.[1] The possible conflict between price stability and income stability was not explored in public pronouncements. Many of the senior colonial administrators had experienced in the 1930s the drastic fall in commodity prices, and the resulting decline in the economies and revenues for which they were responsible had bitten deeply into their minds. Particularly between 1945 and 1950, policy was much influenced by expectations and fears of a world-wide slump in the near future—a steep decline in export prices leading to a decline in incomes. The use of Price Assistance Funds to slow down the local effects of the expected fall in prices by paying subsidies to growers was expected automatically to reduce fluctuations in income.

But the funds did little to promote stability from year to year. Over longer periods payments to cotton growers were smoothed but not payments to coffee growers, nor those to cotton and

[1] Hall, 'Aspects of Economic Development', loc. cit., p. 129; Agricultural Department Annual Report, 1948.

coffee growers in total.[1] The major effect introduced by the
Price Assistance Funds was in fact to transfer income from the
earlier periods to the last five years. The building up and running
down of government general reserve balance and development
funds (both heavily dependent on cotton and coffee export
taxes) followed the same pattern, so that personal income was
maintained in the last period, instead of declining as it would
otherwise have done. The stability obtained was not in the
incomes of growers but in the level of gross domestic product.

Another consequence of this putting aside of large funds was
that loss to the grower, and to the country, occurred through the
fall in value of the securities in which the Price Assistance and
general reserve funds were invested. Net depreciation of these
funds amounted to about £4 million. In addition to the funds'
decline in money terms there was a fall in their real purchasing
power. It had, as already mentioned, been confidently expected
on the basis of the inter-war experience that the opposite change
would occur. Speaking in 1952, Sir John Hall forecast that 'in
a few years' time the general reserves that the Uganda Government have built up . . . will be worth, in terms of goods and
services, much more than they are today.'[2] In fact, the general
import prices probably rose by more than 10 per cent from
1950 to 1960, and prices of machinery and manufactured goods
perhaps by as much as 50 per cent.

---

[1] If payments to growers are stabilized the fluctuations in that series will be less
than the fluctuations in the series of export proceeds. A comparison of the year-to-
year changes is as follows:

	Payments to growers	Export proceeds
Cotton	15·3	18·1
Coffee	28·2	23·4
Cotton and Coffee	15·5	16·8

These figures were obtained by taking the years in succeeding pairs, percentaging
the higher figure to the lower, and then averaging the percentages over the whole
period. The situation over longer periods is given by the following figures, taking the
middle period as a base = 100.

	Cotton		Coffee		Cotton and Coffee	
	Payments to growers	Export proceeds	Payments to growers	Export proceeds	Payments to growers	Export proceeds
1945/6–1949/50	40	48	16	24	30	39
1950/1–1954/5	100	100	100	100	100	100
1955/6–1959/60	106	76	155	132	126	97

[2] Hall, 'Aspects of Economic Development', loc. cit., p. 129.

The Marketing Boards were 'strong' and efficient sellers from the time they were given freedom of action, that is, from the cessation of bulk-buying agreements in 1952.[1] But in the earlier period prices accepted under the bulk-buying agreements were generally less than might have been obtained on the free market.[2] One function of the Marketing Boards was to bear risks which, in the absence of a market for hedging, it would have been difficult and expensive for the cotton ginner to bear.[3] Further, the boards, or some similar organization, were necessary to operate the minimum price system. Unfortunately, when the growing and processing of crops are carried out by different groups, the administrative result is a 'cost-plus' stage, and those operating this stage usually make easy profits. This was so with both cotton ginners and coffee curers. In addition to the normal difficulties of assessing actual costs fairly the percentage out-turn of clean coffee and the cotton lint they obtained from *kiboko* and seed cotton was underestimated. The processing industries were

---

[1] See *Report of the Commission on Inquiry into the Cotton Ginning Industry of Uganda* (Entebbe, 1962), pp. 41–2.

[2] For example prices and quantities for sales of cotton in 1947 and 1948 were as follows:

	Bulk sales to U.K.		Bulk sales to India		Sales on free market	
	'ooo bales	cents per lb.	'ooo bales	cents per lb.	'ooo bales	cents per lb.
1947	22	150	180	146	25	167
1948	56	192	64	216	48	265

Source: *Uganda Herald*, 3 August 1948.

The extent of the loss is difficult to gauge: partly because the bulk contracts were concluded earlier in the season than the free market sales, and thus in the rising market that existed there was bound to be some differential; and partly because of the impossibility of estimating what the overall average free price would have been by considering that obtained for marginal sales. It is also fair to recall that some part of the difference should be regarded as payment for the insurance against uncertainty that the bulk contracts were thought to provide at the time. Even so, a low price was sometimes deliberately accepted: thus in 1949 it was announced that the sale of all the 1948/9 cotton crop (less 7,000 bales) to the United Kingdom Raw Cotton Commission and the Government of India at 250 cents per lb. had been 'approved by the Board and the Protectorate Government, at the suggestion of Her Majesty's Government, as part of the Protectorate's contribution to the economic recovery of the sterling area'. (*Uganda Herald*, 8 Nov. 1948.) Except for the first years of bulk buying, the only season in which the arrangements were in fact to the advantage of Uganda was 1951/2, and then there were difficulties in getting payment. On 11 Aug. 1953 it was announced that £1·5 million was still outstanding on the Indian bulk purchase of the 1951/2 cotton crop, and the account was finally closed in 1955 with a loss of £33,000. (Leg Co *Debates*, 11 Aug. 1953.)

[3] Leg Co *Debates*, 26 Apr. 1955.

in effect given monopoly status, and profits in these industries were excessively high. Since the firms in them were at the beginning of the period entirely non-African and throughout the period substantially so, economic conflict was aggravated by racial feeling.

There were other grounds for the growers' feeling that processors were benefiting more than they should. The cotton-ginning industry in 1949 was sharply criticized by the chairman of the Empire Cotton Growing Association: '[the] buildings [are] out of date; the gins are in bad condition; the rollers are bad and not properly cared for and the knives are defective . . . many [owners] just do not care what happens because they are paid by weight.'[1] However government proposals in 1951 provided for the retention of ginners' pools and quotas with the minor exception of allowing the limited entry of African enterprises. The government agreed to buy up 35 'silent' ginneries to reduce redundant capacity. These purchases may have been, in the explanatory phrase used, 'in the interests of cotton industry *as a whole*':[2] but why should the growers have had to bear the burden of providing nearly £1 million for these purchases when processors were receiving such excessive profits?[3]

---

[1] Mr. J. Littlewood, in *Uganda Herald*, 4 Oct. 1949.

[2] Agricultural Department Annual Report (1951).

[3] Some idea of the 'feather-bedding' provided by the cost-plus system can be obtained from figures collected by the 1962 Ginning Commission. The profit allowed by the government formula was 6 cents per lb. lint cotton (excluding incentive bonus). More than half the private ginners shown were earning between 11 and 16 cents per lb. lint, and 6 out of 12 co-operative unions were earning more than 15 cents per lb. If one exceptional ginnery is excluded, profits—including incentive bonus—averaged about 9·5 cents per lb. lint and depreciation averaged about 2·5 cents. If the period of ten years is allowed for writing off existing assets, the profit ratio was nearly 40 per cent—and this for firms in a monopoly position with guaranteed sources of supply and a guaranteed market. Further, these figures related to 1959/61, after the out-turn percentage had been raised and after the concession of allowing ginners to keep some free cotton seed had been withdrawn; profits earlier were even higher. No wonder ginneries continued to change hands at what the Agricultural Department in 1953 blandly described as 'puzzlingly high prices' (Annual Report).

Similar figures for coffee are not available, but the mission sent in 1960 by the International Bank for Reconstruction and Development to report on the Uganda economy stated that 'the major item in the (cost-plus) formula is the allowance for the cost to the curing works of the weight of dried cherry (*kiboko*) required to produce one ton of clean coffee—there is considerable loss of weight in processing the *kiboko* and any formula that bases the out-turn of clean coffee per ton of *kiboko* at a lower figure than the actual out-turn would give the producers a windfall profit—this

African co-operative organizations were, however, introduced to the processing industries and, in so far as growers were members, they retrieved some of the cost-plus bonus. In 1960/1 co-operative unions collected 67,000 tons of seed cotton, or 31 per cent of the total crop. They were allowed to process 42,000 tons of it themselves in the 15 ginneries they then owned, but under the pool system they had to re-allocate or sell the remaining 25,000 tons to private ginners.¹ The coffee-processing monopolistic group had ceased with the ordinance of 1957 which allowed associations of coffee growers² to make their own arrangements for processing, and by 1961 the total Bugisu (*arabica*) coffee crop was handled by the Bugisu Co-operative Union and nearly three-quarters of the African-grown *robusta* coffee was processed by African concerns.

One argument used to support the controlled marketing system was that it would improve quality; but although the quality of Uganda cotton lint did improve, prices were not properly linked to economic aspects of quality. The differential between the export prices of the different types of cotton was scarcely passed on to the grower, and the differential between prices to grower for clean and dirty cotton was greater than it need have been. As between Uganda coffee and other coffee prices, the differential widened during the period and the International Bank mission which was invited to report on the economy in 1960 recommended a change in the system of marketing specifically to improve the quality of Uganda coffee.

To sum up: it appears natural that the government should have taken action to cream off some of the windfall gains by tax. There is force in the argument that regards the high prices of cotton and coffee in the earlier years as containing a large element of economic rent; and rent has generally been regarded as a source of income more appropriately taxed than other factor incomes. But government policy was too stringent. The upper limit to taxation provided by the test of political practicability

---

appears to have been generous and the processors have made substantial profits both in respect to the out-turn and to the curing allowance.' *Economic Development of Uganda*, p. 130.

¹ Cotton Ginning Industry *Report*, p. 24.

² 'Any regular co-operative all of whose members are African or any other group satisfying the Coffee Industry Board that it works co-operatively.' Ordinance No. 2 of 1957.

was exceeded. There were riots in Buganda in 1949 and the commission reporting on them found that 'the only one of the alleged grievances [with] any substance is the fact that a large sum of money derived from the sale of produce is retained by the government',[1] and recommended that in future prices should be more liberal. Some action to try to secure stabilization however, would appear to have been inevitable. As Professor Arthur Lewis said in 1956:

the fury with which some economists have attacked these measures is astonishing to me . . . any kind of stabilisation measure calls for political wisdom and administrative experience . . . Hence mistakes will be made, and it will take some time to learn how to operate such measures. But I do not see how the governments of these countries can avoid trying to stabilise their economies so long as international trade continues to be as erratic as it is.[2]

The price policy for cotton probably had a depressing effect on its cultivation. The relative taxation of cotton and coffee was badly adjusted. Cotton growers were, by a roundabout use of funds, forced to finance the elimination of surplus ginning capacity, and by the cost-plus pricing system the processors obtained excessive profits. But ginners might still have done so in an unadministered market by combining. It may be noted that in 1930–38—when entry to the ginning industry was prohibited and Cotton Buying Associations were supported by government, but there was no Lint Marketing Board—growers obtained about 60 per cent of the export proceeds of their crops. In 1945–60 they obtained about 55 per cent: and at the same time built up the Price Assistance Funds and provided the major source of finance for a growing range of services, from which they and other Ugandans benefited.

On the other hand, if the higher prices had been entirely passed on to the growers much of their resulting extra income, in the absence at that time of an unrestricted import of consumer goods, would have been lost in inflation. There was no way, except through government action, by which the money could have

---

[1] *Report of the Commission of Inquiry into the Disturbances in Uganda during April 1949* (Entebbe, 1950), p. 21.

[2] In *Stability and Progress in the World Economy*, edited by D. C. Hague (London, 1958), p. 238.

been turned quickly into the stream of medical and educational services which was being demanded by all sections of the community. African entry into the processing industries was finally helped; short-term (within the season) prices were generally more stable than they would have been, and the minimum price was known in advance of planting. A final advantage was the possibility of injecting money into the economy in the late 1950s by drawing on Price Assistance and Reserve Funds. This had a steadying effect at a crucial period in the transition to independence.

But the question still remains whether a faster transition to an exchange economy could have been achieved if the money (or more of it) had been left in the farmers' hands, and if the opportunity of moving away from district self-sufficiency had been welcomed and supported by appropriate measures to improve marketing and transport. Conjecture here must take into account the fact that the main scope for paying much higher prices occurred in the years up to 1952. The quantity of goods that could then be imported was severely restricted by phasing at the main port of entry: goods did not move freely through Mombasa until 1955 (the phasing scheme was not formally brought to an end until 1956). The production of local commodities and services could not be expanded rapidly. Existing prices for cotton were already reducing some other production for the market—for example because of the cotton prices they were receiving, cotton growers in cattle areas preferred to keep their animals and to buy more. There was extra demand from other areas and so cattle prices rose from 150 shillings to 240 shillings in Teso in 1951. It is clear therefore that there would have been considerable risks in attempting a rapid dismantling of the self-sufficiency policy at that particular time. The penalty of failure would have been heavy and it can be argued that the chance of success would not have been high enough to warrant the attempt.

Government development policies

It was relatively easy for the government to hold back large sums from the grower: it was more difficult to use them effectively to develop and diversify the economy. There was no lack of will: both Sir John Hall and Sir Andrew Cohen were exceptionally

energetic governors, and during their terms of office the underlying political situation and the administrative structure was
still such that their personalities counted.[1]

Government was originally more concerned with production
than with trade. In 1946 Sir John Hall said: 'First things must
come first and for the next few years our principal task will be to
win the race between population and wealth production'[2] and
in 1952, when his term of office was over, he summarized his view
of the problems and of his policy thus:

As the present population of 5,000,000 will ultimately need to
cultivate, in order to enjoy a decent standard of living, practically
the whole area of Uganda at present regarded as cultivable, how
will all of the next generation, numbering 10,000,000, be able to
support themselves? . . . The answer, and there would seem to be
only one answer, lies in industrialisation.[3]

In response to Sir John Hall's vision, a group of large-scale
industrial projects was accordingly prepared and put in hand,
although they were not completed until after he had left Uganda.
There was to be a hydro-electric installation on the Nile at Owen
Falls near Jinja. The cement for the dam was to come from a factory at nearby Tororo. The railway was to be extended to Kasese
to provide a railhead for copper ore which, mined at Kilembe,
would be transported for reduction by cheap electricity at Jinja.
Power would also be used in a textile factory at Jinja. These
proposals were of a much wider scope than the limited programmes of government capital spending which formed the
basis of most of the colonial development plans of the period.

Although none of these projects was an overall failure, their
results—especially in the early years—were less spectacular than
expected. The costs of development proved much heavier than
anticipated. The first project to be completed, the cement
factory, ran into trouble over production methods; and, while
in the long run it was to make good, when it was transferred to
the Uganda Development Corporation set up in 1952 (see
below), a substantial part of its cost had to be written off. The
textile mill was owned originally in partnership with a British

---

[1] See David Walker, in a study 'Balanced Social and Economic Development in
Uganda: a case study' for the UN.

[2] *Uganda Herald*, 26 July 1946.

[3] Hall, 'Aspects of Economic Development', loc. cit.

company, but this was subsequently bought out by the government and continued only as management agents. Operations were not successful and the accumulated loss by the end of 1958 was nearly £400,000. It was only when a heavy increase in duty rates in 1958 (imposed in the main for revenue and not protective purposes) reduced the competitiveness of imported cloth not only in Uganda but in Kenya and Tanganyika as well, that profits began to be made.

The copper mine was mainly a private venture, capital and direction being provided by a Canadian company. The deposits contained in addition to copper a small proportion of cobalt which, at the prices ruling when the mine was planned, could have been profitably extracted. This prospect was one of the main factors in the decision to go ahead with the mine. By the time it came into production in late 1957, however, the price of cobalt had fallen so far that it was no longer profitable to exploit the Kilembe cobalt ore.[1] This, together with copper prices much lower than had been anticipated at the time of the Korean war, meant that it was not until the 1960s that the concern became profitable. The reserves of copper also declined more quickly than forecast, but nevertheless the project made a substantial contribution to the economy.

Perhaps the greatest disappointment—at least in relation to the hopes placed upon it—was the failure of the Owen Falls power supply to initiate a rapid increase in industrialization. The situation in 1960 was summarized sympathetically and dispassionately in the International Bank mission's report:

When the Owen Falls Station was first conceived and after it went into commission, it was confidently expected that the availability of ample energy at a reasonable price would bring about an industrial revolution in Uganda. The township of Jinja . . . prepared for this by heavy expenditure on services of all kinds, but although several important industries have established themselves there, the early hopes have not been realised . . . maximum demand was still only 52·6 per cent of the installed capacity in 1960 . . . The natural result of the failure to attain expected sales has been that the undertaking has not yet become profitable.[2]

---

[1] IBRD, *Economic Development of Uganda*, pp. 211-2.
[2] Ibid., p. 269.

Expectations had been far too high: the most optimistic being that the dam would make Jinja 'the Detroit of Africa'. Much was made of the concentration of population around Lake Victoria, but its relatively low income and purchasing power and the lack of effective transport and distributive networks in the lakeside areas were overlooked. For only a few of the industries operating in Uganda were electricity charges a significant part of production costs; while for the textile mill and copper smelter—which were central to the overall scheme—it soon became apparent that even in Jinja the price which these could economically pay, and the price at which electricity could be profitably offered by the Uganda Electricity Board (UEB), were far apart.

For many industries proximity to the main market was a more decisive factor than the cost and availability of electricity. Within Uganda, Kampala rather than Jinja attracted much of the new industrial activity, especially small-scale enterprise. More serious was the fact that for East Africa as a whole Nairobi and Mombasa were often more attractive for the siting of industry, both on account of the greater purchasing power available and because of their easier access to imported raw materials. In fact Uganda could not compete even in terms of cheapness of electricity supply. In its bid for outlets for its surplus power capacity, the UEB in 1955 concluded a long-term bulk supply agreement with Kenya: but this simply had the effect of making electricity available as cheaply—if not more so—in Nairobi as in Kampala or Jinja.

By the late 1950s the UEB had given up the idea of large-scale new industrialization as the principal means of exploiting the expanded electricity supply. A new pattern was emerging, in which the board derived its revenue rather from connecting up existing potential industrial and domestic concentrations of demand than through pioneering the creation of new major industrial development. The emphasis shifted to the electrification of rural concerns such as cotton-ginning and coffee-processing, of trading centres, government offices, hotels, schools and domestic consumers. While the few big consumers and the Kenya bulk supply contract might account for the main volume of power supplied, their specially negotiated rates meant that they produced too little revenue to enable the UEB to meet its capital and running costs.

By 1962 the board was in serious financial trouble. While net capital expenditure on the scheme already amounted to nearly £30 million, revenue was running at only £2·4 million per annum against capital and running costs of £2·7 million per annum.[1] The World Bank mission had in the previous year recommended the ending of any attempt to make electricity play a pioneering role in industrial development, and the emphasis shifted to securing the financial viability of the UEB itself. The main priority in this was to be 'to set prices for all public utility services . . . at a level high enough to ensure, at a minimum, that each pays its way,' and this was made a mandatory condition of a £3 million World Bank loan.[2] Thus, at best, electricity supply during this period was to keep pace with Uganda's economic development rather than to accelerate it. It was not to be the decisive catalyst in an industrial 'take off' that had initially been hoped for.[3]

Government's interests in the other large-scale projects mentioned and in some smaller ventures were taken over and carried through by the Uganda Development Corporation, a para-statal body set up for this purpose in 1952. The UDC was also intended to act as government's main instrument in industrial development, and to attract investment, particularly by partnership ventures. But the initial undertakings retained great importance in the corporation's holdings and still comprised about half of its net assets at the end of 1960. The other half then consisted of agricultural investments (mainly in tea), a property company, a chain of hotels, and a number of smaller miscellaneous undertakings. There were no other industrial companies, and the two manufacturing projects in which UDC later took part came to grief. Attempts to promote small-scale industries by the UDC and by credit provision through the Credit and Savings Bank were also not very successful.

Although these projects were clearly of the utmost importance they were, because of the methods of financing and control finally used, not directly covered in the formal Development

---

[1] UEB Annual Report, 1962, pp. 18, 27, 33.

[2] IBRD, *Economic Development of Uganda*, p. 39. For conditions of International Bank Loan, see Ordinance No. 19 of 1961.

[3] See Gail Wilson, *Owen Falls: electricity in a developing country*, (Nairobi, 1967), pp. 102–5. The author is grateful to Mr. Garth Glentworth for supplementary information on this and the other Uganda projects in the light of his own more recent research.

Plans of Uganda, the most important of which was drawn up by
Dr. E. B. Worthington in 1946.[1] These were thereby reduced to
exercises in the standard fields of government expenditure.
However, within this framework two points should be remarked.
Sir John Hall was anxious that the provision for social services
made in Uganda's post-war Development Plan (prepared under
his predecessor, Sir Charles Dundas) should be reduced. Further,
with more foresight than many planners at that time, he was
determined that the recurrent implications of any programme
should be examined. He had told the Legislative Council that
he would be 'reluctant to launch the protectorate upon an extensive programme of capital expenditure without a reasonable
assurance that the resultant recurrent expenditure will not be
beyond our resources'.[2]

Worthington's plan accordingly showed the recurrent provision in 1946, items of capital expenditure for the ten years
1947–56 (together with the extra recurrent expenditure required
during this period as a result of these items), and the resulting
recurrent expenditure picture projected for 1957. The limit for
expenditure, obtained by assumptions about revenue, cotton
and coffee profits, and external assistance, was £16 million; and
Dr. Worthington estimated that as a result of his programme the
pattern of recurrent expenditure would have changed as follows:

	1946	*1957*
	%	%
1) Productive Services	10·7	14·8
2) Social Services	28·3	29·2
3) Administration, Law Defence & Police	26·3	21·4
4) Other Common Services	34·7	34·6

Source: Worthington, *Development Plan*, Table L.

This new pattern clearly fitted in with Sir John Hall's
priorities. But no sooner had the plan been approved than a
revision was required. It was carried out by Sir Douglas Harris,

[1] Sir John Hall included them in the Notes he wrote for Dr. Worthington. But
when the Worthington Plan came forward it had to qualify its suggestions by comments such as—on hydro-electricity—'This matter is under consideration and it is
premature to give more than an outline of the possibilities. No reference can be made
to the financial implications . . . and no provision is made.' E. B. Worthington,
A Development Plan for Uganda (Entebbe, 1946), para. 267.

[2] *Leg Co Debates*, June 1945. See *Uganda Herald*, 18 June 1945.

who had been appointed Development Commissioner, and included detailed budget estimates for each of the next ten years. The revised figures totalled more than twice those in the Worthington Plan, but even these revised estimates were also soon overtaken by events. External and internal prices rose: revenue receipts continually exceeded expectations, and expenditure followed in their wake.

Sir Andrew Cohen succeeded Sir John Hall in 1952, in the middle of this expansive period. His influence on development policies was not, of course, confined to any one aspect, but the change of emphasis he introduced can be indicated by a single comparison: under the Worthington Plan recurrent expenditure on education by 1957 was to be 13·8 per cent of the total: in the actual outcome it reached 21 per cent.

The rapid out-dating of the Worthington Plan and the Harris revision eased this change in emphasis and in the method of approach. The post of Development Commissioner was allowed to lapse and committees were set up to deal with specific problems. In his final speech to the Legislative Council Sir Andrew Cohen made special mention of 'four notable reports'. Two of these—the Agricultural Productivity Report and that on the Advancement of Africans in Trade—are dealt with elsewhere in this chapter. The others were the De Bunsen Committee's Report on African Education and the Frazer Committee's Report on Medical and Health Services. Action on the latter hung fire, but the recommendations of the De Bunsen Committee were enthusiastically implemented. By 1959, half the children of appropriate age were at primary school, and the number of children at secondary schools more than doubled between 1955 and 1960. As with most programmes for African education conceived at this time, the relative emphasis on secondary education should have been greater. The financial provision for technical education (arising from the report of a separate Technical Advisory Committee) was substantial; but the results of the expenditure were disappointing and only a few people were trained. This was a serious failure.

Other fields in which substantially increased programmes were adopted were African housing in towns, urban development in general, and community development. The African Housing Programme provided subsidized housing for a number of the better-off workers, but did little to touch the basic problem of creating satisfactory conditions for the much larger numbers of unskilled workers earning the minimum wage or a little over. The purpose of the community development programme was to stimulate 'self-help' in rural areas. Between 1952 and June 1957, the Community Development Department spent nearly £1·5 million, but was unable to create a series of self-sustaining activities. Thus its 1956 Annual Report lamented that 'few (councils) have really succeeded in putting across the idea of self-help to the ordinary man and woman. Not infrequently so-called community development projects have been manned by compulsory labour instead of genuine volunteers.' The more active role of government in the social field caused an unparalleled increase in government expenditure, which soon overtook revenue. One striking example was the substantial provision made for the housing of the growing number of officials. During the peak years 1954/5 to 1957/8 an average of over £700,000 a year was spent in this fashion. In 1951 revenue had been £15.8 million and expenditure £12·3 million; by 1955/6 expenditure had nearly doubled to £23·0 million, while revenue had increased by only about one-third to £21·6 million. Much of the additional expenditure was financed by the transfers—already noted—from the Cotton Price Assistance Funds to the African Development Fund set up in 1952. The amounts transferred and expended up to 1955/6 were:

	Transfers	Expenditure
	£m.	
1952	5·0	0·8
1953	9·5	1·9
Jan.–June 1954	1·5	1·1
1954/5	2·2	2·3
1955/6	—	2·4

Source: Uganda Government Accounts;
Lury, 'Cotton and Coffee Growers',
East African Economics Review,
loc. cit.

This fund was supplemented, and eventually absorbed, by a Capital Development Fund created with another £5 million from the Price Assistance Fund and £4·6 million from General Reserve. The projects on which most of these funds were spent were set out first in a five-year plan (1955–60) and then in three-year capital expenditure forecasts presented at budget time and revised annually. But a special feature of the African Development Fund was that money in it was used for both capital and recurrent expenditure. The idea was that some recurrent expenditure would be carried for a few years until, it was hoped, recurrent revenue caught up with the long-term demand on it. Although this procedure did not ignore the recurrent implications of capital expenditure, it was far removed from the watchful attitude expressed by Sir John Hall. And there can be little doubt that a general feeling of euphoria based on the large funds available led to a more rapid expansion of government expenditure than the country could really afford, leading by 1960/1 to a deficit of £4·6 million.

Thus, over the period, public expenditure in Uganda was out of step with revenue and receipts into the other funds controlled by government. In the early years revenue was buoyant but expenditure was held back—justifiably at first but finally too carefully. Then social programmes multiplied, expenditure expanded rapidly and built up recurrent costs and commitments which could not be adequately restrained within the likely long-term capacity of the country. In 1960/1 central and local government expenditure was £31 million when monetary gross domestic product was running at the rate of £110 million a year.

The other most striking feature of public finance in this period was that nearly all of the programmes with which government was associated were financed wholly or partly from internal sources. In 1945 the public debt had been £2,850,000: in 1960 'ordinary' public debt was only £850,000 (there was also £19 million re-loaned to the Uganda Electricity Board). Direct post-war assistance from the metropolitan government had amounted to only £4·5 million over the period to 30 June 1960, and this and the limited foreign participation in the Uganda Development Corporation are little in the balance against the increases of £33 million in the reserves in the development and price assistance funds.

This self-sufficiency in the public sector was matched in the private sector. Attention was attracted to this peculiarity of the Uganda situation by the large balance of visible trade with the world outside East Africa. For various reasons the figure for this gave an exaggerated picture of the situation; but even when the necessary corrections are made Uganda's trade surplus still averaged over £10 million a year during the period 1950–60:

> Uganda's international payments account in eight out of the last ten years showed a sizeable positive balance . . . official sources and private observers agree that a large part of it must represent private capital flows from Uganda.[1]

We are therefore presented with the paradoxical situation in which a country allegedly in need of assistance for development is busily presenting to the outside world a substantial part of its unaided command of resources. This indicates a serious failure of development planning. However, it is also clear that any attempt to channel these extra resources into the extension of its existing policies would have been of dubious value, since ordinary development expenditure was running ahead of the likely recurrent revenue and government plans to initiate industrial and commercial undertakings had had little success.

The private sector and employment

What then was the character of private enterprise? First, the part played by industry in the Uganda economy was relatively small during this period, the two headings of manufacture of food products and miscellaneous manufacturing amounting to only about 5 per cent of domestic product in the late 1950s.[2] The most important sections were devoted to the processing of materials, such as the cotton-ginning and coffee-milling already discussed. In addition saw-milling and oil-milling (with some associated manufacture of soap) were important recorded activities and there was widespread beer-brewing on a small scale besides the few large breweries.

Two other agricultural commodities processed were tea and sugar. Both these commodities were produced on estates mainly in private ownership, although some of the tea estates were owned by the Uganda Development Corporation. The production of sugar was organized by two Asian companies in Buganda

---

and Eastern Province. As with cotton- and coffee-processing, the pricing arrangements provided the sugar millers with a 'wholly unwarranted windfall'.[1]

The most important private enterprise activities—other than agriculture—were commerce, transport, and construction. A substantial part of African participation in these sectors was not fully recorded in the regular statistical series. Indeed the official estimates of the time explicitly excluded hut-building by farmers for their own occupation from the calculation of gross domestic product. Even so, African income from commerce and transport alone (that is, excluding the missing construction element) amounted by 1960 to nearly £8 million—nearly 15 per cent of all African cash income—and almost equalled the net output of non-African enterprises in these fields. Most of this activity was on a fairly small scale and, except in the supply of foodstuffs to towns, the larger-scale wholesale and retail establishments remained almost entirely in non-African hands.

It has been argued that an excessive 'paternalism' on the part of government prevented the development of a 'social environment congenial for economic activity.'[2] Paternalistic policies have been described as being based on two assumptions:

(a) that primitive peoples could not be exposed to the cold winds of individual competition and market forces, for which they were not ready, and

(b) that the Natives had, in any case, to be protected by the paternal hand of Government from European and other immigrants.[3]

Such policies would naturally be restrictive, particularly in matters of trade, and there is no doubt that there were considerable restrictions in Uganda. In addition to the cases given in the sources cited—the most important of which in Uganda was the prevention of effective participation by Africans in cotton trading, except in so far as they were acting for a co-operative—the following example from the Veterinary Department may be

[1] IBRD, *Economic Development of Uganda*, p. 140.

[2] C. Ehrlich, 'Some Social and Economic Implications of Paternalism in Uganda', *Journal of African History*, 4, 2 (1963). See also S. H. Frankel, 'The Tyranny of Economic Paternalism in Africa', Supplement to *Optima*, Dec. 1960, and of course several sections of the *East Africa Royal Commission Report, 1953–1955*, Cmd. 9475 (London, HMSO, 1955).

[3] S. Frankel, 'Tyranny of Economic Imperialism', loc. cit. p. 6.

quoted, since it also illustrates the point that these policies did not always obtain even their desired ends:

During 1945 more than 700 cattle traders were operating in Teso and Lango Districts, and were handling an export trade . . . which did not exceed 3,000 head of cattle per month. It was clear that a marked reduction in the number of exporters was essential if the trade was to continue to develop along rational lines. In the consuming areas demand always exceeded the supply and cut-throat competition between traders continued to force up the price of cattle . . . Under the terms of the Cattle Traders (Amendment) Rules . . . the number of traders or groups of traders exporting cattle was materially reduced . . . By limiting the number of exporters it was hoped that a stabilisation of selling prices of cattle would result in the producing areas. This has unfortunately not been the case.[1]

Key words here are 'developed along rational lines' and 'cut-throat competition'. They occur regularly in discussion of trade and the processing industries and echo the debate in more advanced countries, particularly in the Britain of the 1930s—a period which, as has already been suggested, considerably influenced colonial administrators' thinking. With the distrust of competition went fears of over-capacity and bankruptcy. No one would suggest of course that bankruptcies are to be regarded with complacency; but in any developing system of private enterprise there have always been a fair number of them and over-caution does not breed initiative. In addition an insistence on excessive building standards and the prohibition on trading within a certain radius of townships held back African participation in trade.[2]

This was also hindered by 'the fact that the bulk of the turnover in African trade was in "bread and butter" lines such as sugar, cigarettes and kerosene which carry only a small margin of profit.'[3] The existing trading firms, which were Asian family businesses, provided no channel for recruiting Africans and bringing out their latent commercial ability. Asian traders also, of course, had their network of contacts in Kenya and abroad which enabled them to dominate the profitable import side.

[1] Annual Report of the Veterinary Department for 1948, paras. 39–41.
[2] C. and R. Sofer, *Jinja Transformed* (East African Studies No. 4, Kampala, 1955); and IBRD, *Economic Development of Uganda*, p. 226.
[3] *The Advancement of Africans in Trade*, Report of a committee under the chairmanship of M. A. Maybury (Entebbe, 1955), p. 22.

TABLE V

AFRICAN PARTICIPATION IN COMMERCE: NET OUTPUT

	1954 £000	%	1959 £000	%	Per cent change
African	3,918	33·4	6,080	43·6	+55·2
Non-African	7,818	66·6	7,875	56·4	+ 0·7
	11,736	100·0	13,955	100.0	

SOURCE: *Gross Domestic Product of Uganda 1954–1959*, Table II and Appendix IV.

Nevertheless growth was rapid from 1954 on, even though profits were often not high. Table V shows that almost the entire increase between 1954 and 1959 occurred in African enterprises. Although the rate of increase in African activity might have been faster if there had been fewer restrictions, these figures do not seem to indicate that excessive paternalism by itself was such a brake as has been suggested, at least in the later years. The government's scheme of instruction and advice to individual traders, and its providing of loans, helped this advance, although consideration of the detailed net output figures shows that growth was also rapid amongst produce traders—who were often not likely to come within the scope of the official Trade Development Officers. One striking example of African trading organization was the supply of basic foodstuffs, particularly plantains, to Kampala. This trade involved operators at all levels, from the farmer turning his hand to collection and distribution in his spare time to the specialist trader owning several lorries. Plantains deteriorate rapidly once picked, and the speed and timing of collection and distribution reached a high state of efficiency.[1]

African participation in transport was exuberant. Table VI shows its rapid growth between 1954 and 1959. In 1957 Africans owned over a third of the private cars and over a fifth of the commercial vehicles and omnibuses. Many traders (of all races) ran a vehicle on a mixed commercial/private basis, but a widening of the market was providing the opportunity for greater specialization in the provision of transport services. A strict

[1] See A. B. Mukwaya, 'The Marketing of Staple Foodstuffs in Uganda', in P. Bohannan and G. Dalton, (edd.), *Markets in Africa* (Evanston, 1962).

TABLE VI

AFRICAN PARTICIPATION IN TRANSPORT: NET OUTPUT

	1954 £000	%	*1959* £000	%	*Per cent change*
African	584	42·4	1,166	61·7	+99·7
Non-African	794	57·6	724	38·3	−8·8
	1378	100	1890	100	

SOURCE: *Gross Domestic Product of Uganda 1954–1959*, Table II and Appendix IV.

licensing control on passenger services led to widespread evasion through the proliferation of 'pirate' taxis.[1]

The recorded construction industry accounted for about 4 per cent of total income. It was particularly important for employment, accounting for about one-fifth of the total number of employees in the early 1950s. At its peak it employed over 40,000 workers (of whom just under one-half were working for private builders). By 1960 employment was down to 13,000 in private industry and 18,000 in the public services.

This decline in construction activity was one of the main reasons why the total number of employees in Uganda increased by only a small amount. There had been about 215,000 in 1951 and the number had grown to only 245,000 in 1960. Nearly 100,000 of these were working in government or other public services. The level of skills within this force, particularly within the African part of it, rose considerably, the numbers of Africans with training and experience doubling from 35,000 to 70,000. Thus jobs for unskilled workers probably fell slightly from about 170,000 to 160,000.[2]

This failure of employment to expand was not mitigated by any substantial migration of Ugandans to other countries. On the other hand, there was extensive migration within Uganda and considerable immigration from other countries. About 15–20

[1] Road transport was studied in detail by E. K. Hawkins and his report to the government was subsequently published in an abridged form as *Roads and Road Transport in an Underdeveloped Country: a case study of Uganda* (Col. Research Study No. 32, London, HMSO, 1962).

[2] Employment figures from the reports of the annual *Enumeration of Employees* (East African Statistical Department, Entebbe), and Uganda *Statistical Abstracts*.

per cent of adult males from Ankole, Kigezi, and West Nile districts were working elsewhere in Uganda (mainly in Buganda). African cash incomes per head in these three districts were about £3—£4 per annum compared to nearly £20 in Buganda. Migration was frequently for short periods of a year or two, the purpose often being to obtain cash for capital expenditure. For example, the price of a cow in Kigezi was equivalent to a few months' wages of an unskilled worker in Kampala; the bride-price in some parts of West Nile (3 cows, 2 goats, and 6 shillings) required a year's wages. There were also over 100,000 short-term male migrants from surrounding countries in Uganda in 1959, and a number of more permanently settled families, but most of these were not employed in industry or commerce: they worked for Ganda farmers or cultivated land independently.

It was to be expected that such a mixed and migratory labour force would be difficult to incorporate into urban life and modern productive systems. Both government and employers made much—probably too much—of the problems, although it may be readily conceded that the character of the labour force acted as a check on expansion and affected the type of investment which, from a consideration of the changes in output and employment, seems to have been capital- rather than labour-intensive. Further, the higher standards and skills of the labour force in Kenya added to its geographical and other attractions, thus further reducing Uganda's chances of industrial development.[1]

The lack of growth in employment in the private enterprise sector cannot be ascribed to a shortage of investible funds. Although the exact amount is not known, there is no doubt that there was—as suggested earlier—a large and continuing flow of private capital from Uganda. These transfers were made mainly by non-Africans and although some of them in the later years were due to fears of expropriation or exchange control, a very important cause was the difficulty in finding profitable investment outlets in Uganda.

There were two problems, in addition to the question of the size of the local market: there were no satisfactory arrangements

---

[1] For a detailed discussion of labour problems, see W. Elkan, *Migrants and Proletarians* (London, 1960); and *An African Labour Force* (East African Studies No. 7, Kampala, 1956); and P. G. Powesland, *Economic Policy and Labour* (East African Studies No. 10, Kampala, 1957).

for bringing together African agriculture and non-African capital, and little prospect of any progress in this direction. Secondly, relative opportunities for investment and for business and industry were much better in Kenya. The World Bank mission summed the situation up thus:

The long distance of Uganda from the sea is a geographical fact that must always handicap the country in competing in world markets, and even in the East African common market. Apart from agriculture, natural resources of raw materials and trained manpower will not for a long time be sufficient to overcome this disadvantage.[1]

The emphasis on agriculture in this chapter reflects the importance of this geographical constraint which, although obvious and well-known, was often overlooked in the formulation of expectations about the possible returns to industrialization and general development. Recognition of the constraint also highlights the difficulties of achieving rapid change and thus underlies the tone in which policy has been discussed.

The period dealt with here is only an episode in a longer term perspective. The changes that occurred during its fifteen years were considerable; the economy expanded as a whole and, particularly in Buganda and Eastern Province, the network of economic interrelationships ramified and extended. The speed with which this happened might have been somewhat more rapid if a different mixture of government policies had been adopted, but it is doubtful whether it would have been very different. Any assessment of the rate of structural change must accept that in Uganda the size of the harvest and the level of world prices for cotton and coffee are likely to remain the most important factors for some time to come.

---

[1] IBRD, *Economic Development of Uganda*, p. 212.

VI

THE MANAGED ECONOMY: AGRICULTURAL CHANGE, DEVELOPMENT, AND FINANCE IN KENYA

MICHAEL MCWILLIAM

THE fifteen years that followed the Second World War in Kenya were a period of rapid growth. Agriculture became vastly more productive, industry more diversified, government services more wide-ranging and efficient, and a local capital market emerged. There was a buoyancy in the economy and there were confident expectations of continued rapid progress. But the 1960s had scarcely dawned when the drastic reappraisal of the constitutional timetable for independence dramatically changed the economic climate. In seeking an explanation for this abrupt change and for an understanding of the complex events of the post-war period, four general factors will be considered before we turn to a review of the main sectors of the economy.

The first of these, the predominance of the white settlers, is described in its political aspects elsewhere in this volume.[1] It rested on a solid economic basis. Their farms and plantations produced most of the country's exports and the greater part of its marketed food supplies, while they were prominent—perhaps dominant—in commerce, industry, and the professions. There is no doubt that this economic dominance, and the confident belief in the white right to leadership which went with it, were a powerful factor in attracting overseas capital and skills—to a far greater extent than could be justified simply on a cold assessment of the country's economic assets. The benefits of this influx were felt in many directions: more intensive development of the mixed farming areas of the Highlands; capital for the expansion of the plantation industries (particularly tea); the establishment of subsidiaries by British manufacturing companies; the development of the resources and facilities of Nairobi. The result of the

[1] See chap. ii above.

settlers' presence was that economic opportunities tended to be
exploited more quickly in Kenya than in many other small
African countries.

Inevitably the sector of the economy that benefited most
conspicuously from this inflow of capital and skills was the White
Highlands, particularly in the expansion of cereals, meat, and
dairy products. Kenya came to be seen as the food-producing
centre not only for East Africa but for other African countries
and parts of the Middle East as well. Yet it would be wrong to
suggest that the settlers were concerned exclusively with their
own economic interests. The African reserves had emerged from
the war in a state of apparent agrarian crisis, with overpopulation, damaging agricultural practices, and cramping
land tenure systems all aggravating soil erosion; and European
leaders played a notable part in alerting opinion to the gravity
of the situation. Cavendish-Bentinck in particular, appointed in
1945 to the newly created post of Member for Agriculture,
conceived his main challenge to be the African agrarian problem.
The settlers moreover displayed a lively interest in many
economic questions of national rather than merely sectional
importance and thereby helped to keep the colonial administration on its toes on a wider front than most other African
administrations had to face at that time.

The second factor in the Kenya economic situation was the
character of the colonial relationship as it affected this particular
administration. The key element in it in the post-war period was
a self-confident perfectionism. If Kenya was not quite a social
laboratory in the eyes of its administrators, it was a country
where technically ideal solutions were devised and tried out on a
wide range of problems. Thus in pursuit of an agrarian ideal of
one-family holdings of economic size under individual ownership, a revolution in land tenure was launched in 1955 which, in
the space of a few years, literally changed the face of the
countryside in the richer and more densely peopled areas. At the
same time the Agricultural Department evolved a policy for the
fertile areas of the country based on the controlled development
of scientific mixed farming. To implement this the government
greatly expanded its extension services and took elaborate
statutory powers to try to ensure that the new cash crops and
improved livestock were produced at a high level of technical

efficiency. In the field of labour policy, an attempt was made to break the traditional pattern of male migrant workers moving from their rural homes to the employment areas for limited periods; and to create in its stead a stabilized work-force, permanently divorced from the land. Following the Carpenter Report of 1954,[1] the government began to try to secure, through minimum wage legislation, an urban family wage-level which had no element of rural subsidy. The realities of economic life in fact prevented it from getting very far along this road before the end of the colonial era, and the far-reaching implications of the full Carpenter philosophy—on labour costs, industrial development, urban growth, old age security—were never really tested.

The ebullience of the colonial administration was reflected in a striking growth of the civil service machine, not only in the central departments but in the provincial administration and in local authority administrations. The financial consequences did not prove a restraining factor until the end of the 1950s, thanks to the substantial support from the United Kingdom during the crucial years of expansion—which were also the years of the Mau Mau Emergency. The realization—both in London and within the colonial administration—that the response to Mau Mau must have a social and economic as well as a military and administrative content released a flood of constructive energy through practically every branch of government which was directed particularly at speeding up African economic development. Indeed it is arguable that the preoccupation with implementing these policies was responsible in some measure for the government's difficult relations in the late 1950s with the burgeoning nationalist movement. While the impact of direct government intervention often caused popular resentment, the large technical and administrative problems of engineering fundamental social changes pointed to gradualist political development which would give time for the substantial completion of the programmes; and administrators felt that the mechanisms of economic transformation were too complex and delicate to be exposed to the buffetings of political debate. The final transfer of power after the 1960 Lancaster House Conference

---

[1] *Report of the Committee on African Wages*, Chairman F. W. Carpenter (Nairobi, Govt. Printer, 1954).

provided the bare minimum of time to put in train some of the fundamental changes required. In an impressive final demonstration of technical expertise, huge settlement schemes were initiated on European farms in the Highlands, elaborate crash programmes were organized in the civil service, the administrative structure of the government was recast to fit a regional model; and, by no means least, massive financial payments were coaxed out of the British Treasury.

The conjunction of European economic and political predominance with the tremendous last-minute effort to hasten African economic and social progress was linked with a third assumption which governed colonial thinking in this period—the vision of a workable multi-racial society. Apart from its impact on constitutional development and political organizations in the period, the multi-racial philosophy also had significant economic repercussions through its rational justification of a permanent leading political role for the racial minorities and because of its misunderstanding of the character of African nationalism. Even after this position was seriously eroded, the argument that the minorities' valuable economic functions would indefinitely continue to be essential to Kenya's progress was felt to be unchallengeable. The practical consequence of such a climate of opinion was a common belief that there was still a lot of time to adjust Kenya's dominant minorities to the reduction of racial barriers in sensitive areas such as education and to the removal of economic discrimination, particularly in the Highlands. In short, multi-racialism was a complacent doctrine in that it refused to acknowledge the possibility of the white and brown élites being either temporary or expendable, believing rather that they would become diluted over time as individual Africans broke through the social and economic barriers to join the establishment. Given the British policy that the multi-racial society should be brought into being by mutual consent of the races, the (to later eyes) slow pace of change becomes explicable. Although the civil service was declared non-racial in 1954, it was not until 1960 that steps were taken to accelerate African advancement in it. The opening of the Highlands to African farmers (urged by the Royal Commission in 1955)[1] was planned towards the end of the decade on similar lines of acceptance in

[1] See Appendix 1, pp. 550 sqq. below.

principle but with minimal practical change. Perhaps in political terms the multi-racial vision of the 1950s did provide the essential psychological transition for the European community on its difficult passage from a position of racial dominance to one of subordination. But it also meant temporizing with a number of issues of major importance to the continued economic health of the country.

Finally, the period came to be increasingly characterized by the expectation of continued economic progress. It is true that the ending of the war brought temporary misgivings—of the recurrence of the depression of the 1930s, the loss of wartime markets, the threatening condition of the eroded African reserves. In the event, however, there was strong demand abroad for Kenya's products and internal conditions were buoyant (partly owing to the influx of fresh capital and of settlement), so that by 1950 the tangible signs of development and of growing prosperity had led instead to strongly optimistic expectations about the country's economic prospects. This confident atmosphere—which persisted even through the Mau Mau Emergency—was undoubtedly of great importance in encouraging private investment in Kenya. In the public sector the rapid growth of revenue and expenditure, including a series of increasingly ambitious development programmes, came to be accepted as normal.

Looking back, it can be seen that the image of a burgeoning prosperity was in fact based upon conditions that were largely special and temporary. There was the boost given by special military factors: in the early post-war period the construction of the strategic stores base at Mombasa (later abandoned); then expenditure on the Mau Mau Emergency; followed by the building up of military and air force strategic bases and the stationing of troops in the country after the Suez crisis. Kenya was of course also a beneficiary while it lasted of the commodity boom generated by the Korean war. Besides this, there was the net inflow—although its magnitude is difficult to establish—of private capital for investment in mixed farming, plantations, industrial development, urban expansion. It was associated with a steady flow of skilled expatriates. Both enabled the government to borrow and to attract skilled staff from abroad more easily than most small developing countries.

A more durable factor in Kenya's prosperity was her rise during the 1950s to a position of economic dominance within the East African common market. Kenya's high-grade food surpluses, her favourable geographical position in relation to her neighbours, and the large and enterprising non-African community there, meant that East Africa's commercial and financial services came increasingly to be centred in Nairobi, and most secondary industry also came to be based in Kenya.

The conjunction of these favourable trends masked the meagreness of the country's real resources and in particular the low level of development of African agriculture and skills. The expansion that took place, particularly in the earlier part of the period, was primarily in the European farming areas and in the towns and was based essentially on non-African enterprise.

Nevertheless, over the eighteen years from 1945 to independence the foundations were laid for a considerable change in the basis of the country's economy. Three phases may be readily distinguished. During the first, up to the outbreak of the Emergency, the keynote of economic thinking was set by Sir Philip Mitchell, the first post-war governor and—among the local European community—by Sir Ferdinand Cavendish-Bentinck. Although deeply concerned with the underlying economic problems, especially that of land deterioration, the approach to these problems was essentially conservative and long-term. The Emergency gave scope to the economic and financial vision of two men—Sir Evelyn Baring and Ernest Vasey—to whom Kenya owed much of the economic stability and growth which prevailed even through the darkest days of violence and tension, and which lasted up to the Lancaster House Conference of January 1960. Finally, there were three years of stagnation and regression as the full impact of imminent British withdrawal made itself felt.

The crucial phase of the three was that of Baring and Vasey. At one level the Emergency was a bitter and damaging insurrection. But Baring also seized on the opportunities presented by a country on a war footing to foster a profound transformation of a traditional colonial administration into one that became interventionist, sponsoring change and reform, actively concerned with economic development. It was Kenya's fortune to have as governor a man with a real interest in and understanding of economic policy, whose life had been spent largely outside the colonial service, who yet had impeccable credentials when it came to establishing his gubernatorial leadership.

A remarkable partnership evolved between the patrician in Government House and Vasey, the actor's son from England who had made good as a local businessman and then gone on to make his mark in politics. Vasey already held the Finance portfolio at the time of Baring's appointment and retained it throughout his governorship. At a technical level Vasey's special contribution was his skill, including legendary aid negotiations with the British government, in mobilizing ever-increasing revenues for the country, while retaining wide freedom of action from the Colonial Office over expenditure. But his achievement was at a deeper level since he perceived so strongly that his job was not just to finance a civil war, but also to foster the broader development of the economy, including especially African economic advancement.

Agriculture

Agricultural production was the mainstay of the Kenya economy, and it was in the field of agriculture that the European politico-economic dominance was most strongly marked. By 1960 there had been created a substantial plantation sector of tropical export crops (sisal, coffee, and tea) covering more than 350,000 acres and, more remarkably, a mixed farming sector of cereals, livestock, and other crops in which over a million acres were brought under active cultivation together with more than two million acres of paddocked natural grazing. In 1960 this large-farm sector still employed almost half the African labour force and accounted for four-fifths of Kenya's overseas exports.

Although the foundations had been laid in the 1920s and 1930s, it was the war which seemed to indicate the true potential of the White Highlands. Substantial demand appeared for the whole range of produce; to meet it a powerful administrative and financial technique was evolved in order to promote the expansion of productive capacity. In shaping and administering this technique the farmers themselves, through local production committees and through their representation on the central Board of Agriculture, played an outstanding part, and in the post-war period the pattern of producer-dominated committees and boards determining agricultural policy and controlling its implementation became widespread. It was enshrined in the Agriculture Ordinance of 1955[1] and in many commodity ordinances. Such a system of agricultural self-government proved immensely efficient in expanding European agricultural productivity. Less satisfactory was the result that the viewpoint of the European producer acquired a disproportionate weight when other interests were at stake. In short, Kenya was over many matters in effect ruled by a 'farmers' government' during much of the post-war period. Perhaps the clearest examples are afforded by maize policy and by the difficulties of bringing about a balanced system of alternate husbandry.

Maize was of course the staple food of Kenya. The fact that it was a principal, often the principal, element in farm incomes in the Highlands for so many years had important repercussions on the economy as a whole. For it meant that the most powerful pressure-groups were from 1945 to 1958 able to keep maize prices—determined by the government—at a high level which became increasingly artificial. With attractively high export prices ruling at the beginning of this period, they secured from the government the principle of a guaranteed price which would automatically compensate them for rising costs, in order to keep the maize on the domestic market. The result was that until 1958 the maize farmers were largely insulated from inflation at the expense of the maize consumer and were under no pressure to cut costs. Since the maize consumer was the labour force of the country, there was a general upward pressure on labour costs and on the cost of living of urbanized Africans; this in turn brought about a flourishing black market in *posho*, due to the large margin between the price paid to the producer and the final controlled consumer price, and an increasing tendency on the part of employers to grow their own maize wherever they had access to agricultural land.

Paradoxically, rather more than half the maize sold to Maize Control was ordinarily provided by African, not European, farmers. African production was, of course, very much larger in

[1] 'An Ordinance to Promote and Maintain a Stable Agriculture, to Provide for the Conservation of the Soil and its Fertility, and to Stimulate the Development of Agricultural Land in accordance with the Accepted Practices of Good Land Management and Good Husbandry'. Kenya Government Ordinance No. 8 of 1955, p. 17.

total but most of it was consumed within the reserves; nevertheless it was a cash crop in many districts of Nyanza and Central Provinces. Yet official policy persisted in regarding African production as a fortuitous and unstable contribution to the total supply, and the European farmer as the mainstay of the industry. It was this that made it so difficult for the government to have a sensible maize policy. In the end the system had become patently absurd—when the high fixed prices called forth a large surplus which had to be exported at a loss which Maize Control then recouped by means of a cess, but producers still found it profitable to grow maize at a net price far below the original guaranteed price. Only then did the government take steps gradually to bring down the price.[1]

The desirability of a balanced system of mixed farming to replace substantial cereal monoculture was a constant theme of official exhortation as soon as the war was over. The pace of change was rather slow, however, since cereal farming was both simpler and for some time more profitable. Livestock meant heavy capital costs; the development of more advanced farming skills; the problems of disease; the time-lag in building up herds suitable to Kenya conditions; the difficulties of grassland improvement. Not until the mid-1950s did government action provide incentives and technical assistance to make the change reach an effective scale, and not until the latter half of the decade did the expansion of herds begin to put big pressure on marketing outlets.

It was on the marketing side that the short-sightedness and inequities of government policy became marked. The organizational pattern had been set soon after the war with the decision to establish a statutory meat-marketing monopoly, owning cold-storage and canning facilities, and able to exploit cattle by-products. This it was hoped would help farmers to plan on the basis of an offtake geared to their own seasonal interests rather than to market requirements, with the guarantee of known controlled prices and of full commercial value for their animals.

In the case of maize marketing there was no basic conflict of interest between European and African producers. With meat-

---

[1] See Sessional Paper No. 6 of 1957/8, *The Maize Industry* (Nairobi, Govt. Printer, 1958), which also reviews earlier enquiries.

marketing the situation was less happy. When the organization, the Kenya Meat Commission, which operated on a strictly commercial basis, applied a differential pricing policy—based on the greater costs of obtaining cattle from the African areas—on top of its large margins to cover capital and overhead costs, the prices for African cattle were reduced. This led to a severe fall in African supplies and, more serious, to a major loss of confidence. African cattle owners were in any case far from eager to market stock; it they did wish to sell, they could get better prices from other buyers. Although the KMC was legally a monopoly buyer, in practice it was in no position to cope with organizing the African meat trade outside the towns. And the impression was created that the KMC was an organization for European farmers first and African farmers a poor second. The government's belated solution was to set up a separate body to deal with the offtake of meat in the African areas which then sold mainly, but not necessarily or exclusively, to the KMC, its operations being a charge on the budget. But so far as fresh meat was concerned, the KMC did become an organization for marketing primarily European produce, with only marginal contributions from the African areas. Only its canning plant, which did not start operating until 1958, was really orientated towards African supplies.

An essential corollary to the more intensive development of the Highlands was an increase in European settlement. Such importance was attached to this that a settlement scheme was one of the first and largest projects included in the first ten-year Development Plan.[1] In 1945 £1·6 million (later augmented to £2 million) was provided for the purpose, and by 1952, 240 new farmers had been established by the European Agricultural Settlement Board, mostly as tenant farmers. But just as significant as this direct financing of new farmers was the board's general promotional work in England fostering new agricultural settlement. It was claimed by the government in Legislative Council in 1948[2] that the settlement scheme represented 'the greatest hope of an immediate increase in our national income', a line of thinking which reached its apotheosis in the report of the Troup

---

[1] *Report of Settlement Scheme Committee, 1944* (Nairobi, Govt. Printer, 1944); *Post-War Settlement in Kenya: proposed schemes* (Nairobi, Govt. Printer, 1945).
[2] Leg Co *Debates* (1948), vol. xxix, p. 70.

Commission, set up in 1952 to enquire into the general economy of farming in the Highlands.[1] An explicit comparison was made between the agricultural prospects in the African and European areas and the conclusion was reached that only in the latter could a rapid increase in production be looked for. The report went on to draw up a blueprint for bringing the mixed farming areas of the Highlands up to a 'full' state of development, by means of a Ten Year Programme costing £55 million. It reflected faithfully the informed opinion of the time that serious agricultural development such as would produce large marketable surpluses was mainly the province of European agriculture, whereas African agriculture was primarily concerned with the fundamental struggle for food self-sufficiency and soil fertility. Yet already by 1952 marked changes had occurred in the thinking of the Agricultural Department on the nature of the African agrarian problem and the action required to deal with it.

At the end of the war there was serious alarm at the agricultural condition of the African reserves.[2] Soil erosion was spreading in many districts and there appeared to be a general decline in soil fertility due to overcrowding and to the success of wartime exhortations for increased production of food for sale. The settlers were particularly concerned, as they were keenly aware of the explosive implications of 'reserves' inadequate to provide a livelihood for the main part of the African population and they were strongly critical of what they felt to be the government's failure in allowing such a situation to develop. Cavendish-Bentinck, appointed as the first Member for Agriculture under the newly introduced 'membership' system in 1946,[3] regarded African agriculture as his chief challenge and presided over a crucial period in the evolution of agricultural policy. Perhaps his most important contribution was in recognizing the need for a greatly expanded research programme in the African areas, and in this Kenya's great advantage of a unified agricultural service dealing with both European and African agriculture provided a

---

[1] *Report of the Inquiry into the General Economy of Farming in the Highlands, excluding . . . Sisal, Wattle, Tea and Coffee*, Chairman L. G. Troup (Nairobi, Govt. Printer, 1953).

[2] See e.g. N. Humphrey, *The Kikuyu Lands: the relation of population to the land in South Nyeri* (Nairobi, Govt. Printer, 1945); Sir Philip Mitchell, *General Aspects of the Agrarian Situation in Kenya*, Despatch No. 44 to the Secretary of State for the Colonies (Nairobi, Govt. Printer, 1946).

[3] See chap. ii above.

welcome flexibility. This became all-important when in the 1950s the government's attitude to African agriculture underwent a fundamental change of emphasis.

At first the solution to the condition of the reserves was seen largely in terms of soil engineering—terracing, contour-ploughing, and dam construction—linked with the concept of resettling 'surplus' populations in new areas, of which the Makuami settlement in Machakos District was the most famous example. But more intensive study of agricultural practices in the existing African areas was leading to a reappraisal of the whole concept of overcrowding. When examined in relation to intelligent land use as appropriate to the different ecological zones, it appeared that the carrying capacity of the land could in fact be greatly increased. In particular, application of the alternate husbandry ideas being tested in the Highlands suggested that in all but the semi-arid pastoral areas the cattle population was after all not too great. The principal villain was now identified as traditional land tenure customs.[1] A wiser objective was seen to be a consolidation of individual farmers' scattered holdings and the preparation of a scientific layout based on alternate husbandry principles and suitable to the district. In some lightly-populated areas such as Kipsigis country a simple enclosure process was all that was needed, and this proceeded with great speed in the late 1940s. An attempt to achieve a short cut in solving the fragmentation problem through group farming was made in Nyanza but proved unsuccessful.

The first two landmarks in crystallizing the new thinking of the Agricultural Department were a memorandum by Frank Swynnerton in 1951,[2] and a submission by the department to the East Africa Royal Commission early in 1953.[3] The first set out the objective of the creation of integrated family holdings whose minimum size in each ecological zone would enable the family to be self-sufficient in food while practising alternate husbandry, and which would allow the gradual build-up of a

[1] Notably by L. H. Brown, Assistant Director of Agriculture, 1954, Deputy Director, 1956, Chief Agriculturalist, 1959. For a fuller review of thinking at this time see M. McWilliam, 'Economic Policy and the Kenya Settlers', in K. E. Robinson and A. F. Madden (edd.), *Essays in Imperial Government* (Oxford, 1963).

[2] Kenya Department of Agriculture Memorandum 1951, 'Report on Agrarian Policy for dealing with Population Increase, Land Tenure and Fragmentation in Kenya'.

[3] Kenya Department of Agriculture Memorandum 1953, 'The Agricultural Problems and Potential of the African Lands in Kenya'.

cash income. It envisaged the establishment of individual title to consolidated holdings, but also the displacement of 170,000 families from Nyanza and Central Provinces (without allowing for population growth) in consequence of the creation of economic holdings. The submission to the Royal Commission showed a marked toughening in the department's attitude to land tenure obstacles and a note of impatience with the provincial administration's unwillingness to force the issue. It also reached the conclusion, as a result of more detailed studies, that—except in North and Central Nyanza—the reorganization of holdings into economic units would not after all entail substantial displacement of population; in other districts there was considerable absorptive capacity.

There was moreover a shift of emphasis detectable in the attitude to cash crops. Whereas earlier there was a tendency to regard them more in the nature of an incentive to better farming, now the concept of a target income of £100 had been firmly incorporated into the definition of an economic holding; in other words there had been a decisive move away from acceptance of the principle that the reserves should be partly dependent on wage-labour remittances. The exciting implications were more fully appreciated as the detailed district estimates were aggregated. This can be seen by comparing the estimates made of the potential African acreage of four major crops (after providing for substantial food surpluses) with the actual acreages in the European areas in 1952:[1]

	European Areas Actual	African Areas Potential
	(acres)	
Coffee	60,500	61,000
Tea	21,000	46,000
Sisal	248,900	317,000
Pyrethrum	22,900	59,000

Whether the government would have overcome its qualms in facing the land tenure issue or would have been able to raise the large sums of capital required, but for the trigger of the Mau Mau Emergency, will always be a matter for conjecture. Happily for Kenya, the rising tide of knowledge and self-confidence in the Agricultural Department was caught at its flood. As part of the larger strategy for combating Mau Mau, the British government

[1] From statistical material in the possession of the author.

agreed to provide substantial assistance to speed up African agricultural development; accordingly towards the end of 1953 the Kenya government decided to draw up a comprehensive five-year plan on the assumption of nearly doubling the rate of expenditure envisaged two years earlier.[1] The total came to nearly £7 million, of which the British government agreed to provide £5 million as a grant.

Swynnerton, who in the three years since he came to Kenya had been deeply involved in planning a new agrarian policy for the African areas, was given the responsibility of drawing together all the threads and for compiling the plan which thereafter bore his name.[2]

The Swynnerton Plan assumed that about twenty years would be needed to complete the consolidation process. In the event the Emergency conditions, and the enthusiastic backing of Baring as governor, led to a psychological break-through by the administration in the Central Province, and the whole operation went through with enormous speed, being virtually completed in six years. While this in itself produced problems, by mid-1962 nearly 300,000 farms had been consolidated and enclosed, covering some 2·4 million acres, and amounting to approximately 51 per cent of the high potential land in the African areas.[3] The revenue earned to producers from newly established African cash crops (tea, coffee, rice, pyrethrum) rose from virtually nothing in 1950 to over £4 million on the eve of independence.[4]

[1] For the earlier provision, see *Report of the Planning Committee* (Nairobi, Govt. Printer, 1951), para. 50.

[2] *A Plan to Intensify the Development of African Agriculture in Kenya*, by R. J. M. Swynnerton (Nairobi, Govt. Printer, 1954).

[3] International Bank for Reconstruction and Development, *The Economic Development of Kenya* (Baltimore, 1963), pp. 66–7.

[4] The figures for small and large farms respectively in 1962 for *all* the main cash crops were as follows:

	Rice	Coffee	Tea	Pyrethrum £000	Cotton	Tobacco	Maize
Small farms	314	3,295	54	533	460	66	1,131
Large farms	—	6,187	6,640	1,681	—	—	2,196
Total	314	9,482	6,694	2,214	460	66	3,327

Source: *Kenya Statistical Abstract 1963* (Nairobi, Govt. Printer, 1963), Table 82.

The agricultural transformation so set in motion was a real one. It may up to a point be interpreted as establishing Kenya, albeit at the eleventh hour, on the path of peasant cash-crop agriculture which had long been characteristic of West Africa and Uganda. In West Africa the policy had been largely a matter of giving continued play to a commercial economy already fairly established. In Uganda the creation of the peasant economy had initially been set in motion by the administration, but had quickly acquired its own momentum. In Kenya the transformation was achieved against the whole trend of the country's economic development over forty years, by a powerful administration that succeeded in carrying with it the basic co-operation of a European community which had previously staked its future on an economic pattern geared to its own hegemony.

But partly just because this was its character, the transform-ation stopped a good deal short of revolution.[1] A proportion of African farmers, through their own enterprise or by being politically well placed to take advantage of the situation, did well. But many of the holdings, although now held by absolute title, remained fragmented. The smallholding cash-crop econ-omy, while it expanded significantly, did not expand to the point at which it replaced the country's large-farm basis. For the most part its produce was fed into the domestic, not the export, market. Bureaucracy and the growing affluence of a compara-tively small sector of the farming population, albeit a sector enlarged and substantially Africanized, remained the order of the day. It is a moot point whether this result owed something also to the intensely individual character commonly ascribed to the Kenya African farmer. This individualism was in some measure held in check by the power of government action, which continued to operate through marketing and other controls; but both combined to inhibit anything like the grass-roots co-operative initiative which for instance substantially transformed the economy in parts of Tanganyika.

In the semi-arid pastoral regions the problems and objectives were different from those in the more fertile African areas. Here

---

[1] See especially M. P. K. Sorrenson, *Land Reform in the Kikuyu Country* (London, 1967). More recently the question of the real extent of the changes brought about by land consolidation and registration has been critically discussed by Colin Leys, 'Politics in Kenya: the development of peasant society', *Brit. J. of Pol. Science*, 1, 1 (1971).

no such revolutionary change in thinking was required. The root problem was the traditional attitudes of the pastoral tribes towards cattle ownership, where the values held seemed to be opposed at every point to the requirements of scientific stock management: quantity over quality, the assumption of limitless grazing, apparent indifference to the commercial value of live-stock. But the war, in this as in so many other matters, was a catalyst of change. The government, in the interests of the war effort, found the resolution to insist on regular stock disposal and the cattle-owners became used to the flow of income which this generated; afterwards demobilized African troops, accustomed to a superior wartime diet, engendered a greatly increased demand for meat among the African population. At the same time other developments greatly improved the technical prospects for the livestock industry: the elaboration of grazing schemes in different parts of the country to raise stock-carrying capacity and give eroded land a chance to regenerate, the expansion of water supplies, the construction of stock routes, progress in disease control and stock-breeding.[1] Only the failure to organize effective marketing arrangements prejudiced the results that should have flowed from such widespread progress. Apart from the damaging financial policies of the KMC already described, there were fluctuations in demand by the official marketing agencies during the early post-war period, and veterinary restrictions imposed from time to time in the interests of the valuable herds of exotic stock in the European areas. There was a failure to realize the crucial psychological import-ance of maintaining confidence in the marketing mechanism. There was also a failure to appreciate the importance of the rural market for meat in Nyanza and Central Provinces; distribution arrangements were poor, and little was done to mitigate the serious effects of the virtual closure of the Central Province market for several years during the Emergency. It was not until the end of the 1950s that steps belatedly taken to remedy these shortcomings restored the number of cattle coming forward to market to near the wartime levels of 15 years earlier. The great drought of 1960-1 enforced a ruthless natural culling of herds, far beyond any targets of official policy and, although it led also

---

[1] The progress of these measures can be traced in the Kenya annual Agricultural Department Reports.

to a breakdown of discipline on many grazing schemes, it had provided a basis for a new start in many areas, particularly as the ensuing prolonged floods led to a remarkable regeneration of pastures.

Even in the periods of greatest contrast between African and European agriculture in Kenya, there was still a unified technical service. This proved to be a factor of great importance during the post-war period as the emphasis of government effort shifted from European to African agricultural problems.

As we have already seen, in the European areas the farmers themselves played a major role in the formulation and implementation of government policy, with the technical officers acting very much in an advisory capacity. This became entrenched in the consolidating Agriculture Ordinance of 1955; a measure essentially drawn up for the White Highlands, and designed to strengthen the element of consultation and veto attributable to the European farmers. The idea was that when agriculture in the African areas had made sufficient progress these areas would adopt a similar structure of agricultural self-government and could thus become 'scheduled' so as to obtain the full benefits of the act. To this end an analogous system of sub-committees, etc., was created in the African areas, save that the members of these committees, instead of being local farmers, were members of the colonial administration (technical and administrative). The district and provincial committees thus became the spearhead of agricultural reform in the African areas. Towards the end of the decade they gradually acquired an African membership of leading farmers. At the top—again mirroring the Board of Agriculture—was a board, commonly known as the Aldev (African Land Development) Board. This was primarily a development agency for African agriculture, but in time became also its top policy board.[1]

In the European farming areas, although in the post-war period government extension services did play a valuable stimulatory and advisory role, the main requirement for the attainment of intensive mixed farming was capital expenditure—on piped water, fencing, improved herds, farm buildings and machinery. In the African areas the position was very different.

[1] See Kenya Ministry of Agriculture, *African Land Development in Kenya, 1946–62* (Nairobi, Govt. Printer, 1962).

Here for most of the post-war period government extension services were the dominant influence in developing agriculture, since the crucial step was to bring about new attitudes to land and stock management. Capital expenditure was mainly for communal purposes: dams and water supplies, erosion control for whole districts together. But as the agricultural revolution caught on, the focus of interest inevitably came down to the individual 'better farmer', his needs for his own water supply, improved cattle, and cash crops. In short, towards the end of the 1950s the need for greater capitalization of African farmers came more and more to the fore. Until individual security of title was available, neither the Land Bank nor the commercial banks would lend to African farmers. The commercial banks changed their policies as evidence of agricultural prosperity accumulated, but the Land Bank's policies were not revised until just before independence. As a result almost the whole burden of providing the capital needed fell on the government. At first the main source was Aldev, which between 1955 and 1962 made loans totalling £271,000 to over 3,800 farmers, but this was still woefully short of demand. Later the interest of the World Bank was enlisted and in 1960 the government was able to designate £1 million for this purpose from a loan made by the bank for African agricultural development. By then the government's problem was becoming that of setting up an effective banking organization to administer many thousands of small loans.[1]

With the growing evidence of successful commercial farming by Africans, and against the rapidly evolving political background, further prevention of African farming in the Highlands became more and more indefensible. Settler opinion had just been brought to accept the possibility of carefully selected African farming neighbours when the whirlwind struck in 1960, setting up a political imperative to bring African farmers into the Highlands at a much faster rate. Settlement schemes hurriedly drawn up in 1960 and 1961 secured the financial backing of the World Bank and the Commonwealth Development Corporation,[2] on the basis that they were to bring about an

[1] See M. McWilliam, 'Banking in Kenya, 1950–1960', *East African Economics Review*, 9, 1 (1962), 16–40.

[2] The Colonial Development Corporation was established in 1948 as part of the machinery for carrying into effect the Colonial Development and Welfare Acts. It was expanded into the Commonwealth Development Corporation in 1956.

intensification of high-grade agriculture in the Highlands and therefore enhance the productivity of the area. In the event an even more urgent political imperative supervened: to settle quickly a substantial number of African unemployed on farms bought from Europeans, at a time when there was some doubt whether there would long continue to be sufficient administrative authority to control the process. Here the most that could be hoped for was that productivity would at least be maintained.

In the early post-war period agricultural policy in the African areas had been primarily conceived as a survival exercise directed mainly towards areas of lower economic potential where land deterioration was most marked. In terms of land use it was the great achievement of the Swynnerton Plan that it brought the high potential areas on to the centre of the stage and drew dramatic attention to their possibilities. In terms of the social economy, the individualization of agricultural holdings provided the opportunity for a decisive breakthrough for many hundreds of 'better farmers' whose skill and commercial success was proved within only a few years. Compared with the substantial effects of consolidation and enclosure in the arable areas, reforms in grazing management and stock control in the semi-arid pastoral regions left no such enduring mark. There the opportunity for a similar emergence of prosperous individual farmers had, at the time of independence, not yet occurred.

Industrial production

'Industrial development' is perhaps too grandiloquent a term to be used of small agricultural countries in the early stages of diversifying their economies. It conjures up visions of heavy engineering and complex technologies when reality reveals only the processing of agricultural products, a construction industry and the manufacture of a few consumer goods. Nevertheless, these elementary industrial activities were by 1960 more intensively developed in Kenya than in any other part of tropical Africa except Southern Rhodesia. And in fact in 1955— although after that date some industrial activities temporarily declined or grew more slowly—the industrial contribution to the gross domestic product almost equalled that of commercial agriculture and paid a higher wage bill.[1]

[1] *Kenya Statistical Abstract 1955* (Nairobi, Govt. Printer, 1957), Tables 149 and 163.

The expansion of Kenya's industrial activity at this time was primarily to meet the needs of her domestic economy; in 1961, against sales in the domestic market to the value of £61 million, those to the other countries of the East African common market were £15 million, to overseas countries £7 million. The principal exports depended on the basic processing of fresh agricultural products—coffee berries, tea and sisal leaves, hides, and cotton lint. One important exception was the preparation of pyrethrum extract begun under government auspices during the war, carried on by a commercial firm during much of the post-war period, and then largely taken over by a statutory board. Other agricultural exports where the manufacture element was significant were canned meat, butter, and canned pineapples. The main mineral exports were sodium bicarbonate from the Lake Magadi deposits, and copper concentrates from the Nyanza mines run by the Commonwealth Development Corporation.

The most important group of manufacturing activities developed round the provision of food, drink, and tobacco products. Manufacture of most of these was begun in the inter-war years, and the rapid growth thereafter of urban populations and of the employed labour force provided favourable conditions for expansion. With meat processing, dairy produce, and grain milling, it was achieved mainly through statutory organizations with financial help from the government; with canning, bakery, confectionery, drink, and tobacco, it was through private enterprise, both local and international. Many of these products found important export outlets in Tanganyika and Uganda, whose food industries were much less developed.

The development of a country's local construction industry is a key factor in determining the rate of economic development which is possible. Constructional activity is labour-intensive and provides an important training ground in managerial skills and entrepreneurial ability; while the wide variety of material imports gives stimulus for a considerable range of ancillary trades.

In Kenya the demands of the military authorities during the war were very important in expanding the capacity of the industry and in providing the incentive to develop new products. Timber production was expanded to five times its pre-war level, while local firms were encouraged to produce roof tiles, asbestos cement tiles, and fibre board. The brick production was largely contributed by the Italian prisoners of war—whose most enduring monument was the superb highway up the Rift Valley escarpment between Naivasha and Nairobi. The import bottleneck persisted for several years after the war, and the problem of building materials for the post-war plan was one of the main preoccupations of the committee set up to advise on development in 1945.[1] With the government as one of the main spenders on building works, the role of the Public Works Department became a matter of importance; and, following a reorganization of the department, the government throughout the 1950s carried out an extensive programme of replacing and expanding the stock of government buildings. By 1960 it was rare to find a pre-war administrative building anywhere in the country. Facilities were established within the Ministry of Works to let and control contracts with private builders to supplement the work of the ministry. Transfer payments were made through local authorities—particularly for African housing—and a Central Housing Board was set up in 1953, with a fund of £2 million from a Colonial Development Corporation loan. There were extensive building programmes to house the organs of the East Africa High Commission, centred mainly in Kenya; and also military building programmes, particularly towards the end of the decade when Kenya was scheduled as a defence base by the UK defence planners.

Besides these official efforts, and indeed stimulated by them, there was a great wave of private building—more than half of it residential—which was only momentarily checked by the Mau Mau Emergency.

In the constructional field, landmarks included the building of a modern international airport in the mid-1950s, and the initiation in 1958 of a major highway programme followed up by a World Bank loan in 1960 for subsidiary roads in the African agricultural areas. In this as in other contexts, the Emergency made its own contribution to development. It is doubtful whether resources would otherwise have been found for the great Yatta irrigation canal, nearly 40 miles long, or when the irrigation system on the Mwea flats would have been constructed.

---

[1] *Report of the Development Committee*, Chairman J. F. G. Troughton (2 vols., Nairobi, Govt. Printer, 1945).

More piquant for future archaeologists were the fortified moats round Kikuyu villages later turned into banana terraces. Other land engineering works included terracing, fencing, damming, and draining, only the smaller part of which was ever directly costed in money payments.

The extent of Kenya's building boom attracted to the country several of the leading British firms of civil engineers, which established local organizations and tendered for the major contracts. Probably the bulk of the private building activity in the country was carried out by Asian firms, in which was concentrated most of the indigenous expertise in this field. But an important development towards the end of the decade was the appearance of a class of African builders working in brick and stone and sawn timber. This development was particularly associated with the improvement of African trading estates, with an upgrading of housing standards in the more prosperous areas, and with the extensive rebuilding that was needed in the post-Emergency phase in the Central Province.

There is a special importance in the emergence of firms working in metal and producing machinery, as these provide the chief nucleus of a country's engineering skills. The main stimulus to the engineering industry was the transport sector of the economy, and here Kenya profited by her geographical position within the East African common market. The principal workshops of the railway system were situated in Nairobi, while Mombasa was the main port for East Africa and ship-repairing facilities were developed there. The rapid increase in the motor vehicle population[1] provided opportunities for repair facilities around the country and substantial workshops in the main towns. Vehicle assembly during this period was mainly limited to body-building.

Despite intensive oil-prospecting, Kenya's indigenous resources of power were limited to fuel timber and hydro-electricity. By 1960 a single commercial firm, the East African Power and Lighting Company, was responsible for all electricity distribution. A substantial proportion of the country's electricity was imported, first on a small scale from Tanganyika for the

---

[1] It was not until 1950 that with the introduction of a Road Fund any regular count was made, but between 1953 and 1960 the motor vehicle population more than doubled from 44,000 to 90,000. *Kenya Statistical Abstract*, 1963, Table 65.

coastal area, subsequently from Uganda's Owen Falls station on the Nile. By 1960 the latter was supplying 40 per cent of the Kenya demand. Although there was a strong body of opinion in favour of a fully independent source of supply from the Seven Forks project on the Tana River, this was held back by financial and demand considerations until after independence.

While electricity distribution was in the hands of a private company, electricity prices to the public were subject to government approval. At the same time, the government had a substantial stake in the supply side: the transmission line from Uganda and the principal hydro stations were owned by a separate company in which the government (at nil cost) was a one-third shareholder; and all the assets of the company were due to revert to the government in 2004. Thus virtually the whole of the supply and distribution system for electricity—representing in 1961 an installed capacity of some 130 megawatts and a largely post-war investment of some £14 million—had been supplied by commercial investment at no public expense, while the public interest, as represented by the government, nevertheless remained in a very strong position in relation to the company.

There could be no greater contrast than that between the intensity of government intervention (with settler support) in agriculture and most other spheres, and the muted role of government in industrial development. During the war, indeed, £200,000 had been provided to start manufacture of a number of products under the administration of an official holding company, the East African Industrial Management Board. But at the end of hostilities the successful ventures were sold off to commercial interests and the board languished in obscurity.

It was not so much that the desirability of fostering industrial development was challenged, as that positive pressures to shape and direct it were lacking. The settlers' influence was mainly confined to creating an industrial counterpart to the agricultural machinery which they were already using to such good effect. The Development Committee in 1945, while it thought that an official finance corporation might be useful, found that capital was not at that time a limiting factor in industrial development.[1] The only important measure to reach the statute book was the

---

[1] *Report of the Development Committee*, i. 74, ii. 184.

1948 Industrial Licensing Ordinance,[1] under which new entrants to scheduled industries were granted statutory protection from competition.

In this as in other matters Ernest Vasey was outstanding amongst the unofficial members of the Legislative Council for his constructive and positive views; he was in favour of tariff protection, but he failed to carry his colleagues in the early years and underestimated the obstacles imposed by a common market structure. Nevertheless tariff policy did give some assistance, and was elaborated during the 1950s. On the one hand the overall tariff rate of 25 per cent provided considerable protection in practice; inter-territorial agreement was secured to a small group of protective tariffs; and the device of suspended duties had an effect similar to protective ones. On the other hand capital equipment and industrial raw materials were generally admitted duty-free, and customs drawbacks were allowed on otherwise dutiable raw materials.

On the whole, however, unofficial opinion tended to welcome industrial development not so much for its own sake, but as a palliative to absorb surplus rural populations. In 1954 the Industrial Management Board was turned into the Industrial Development Corporation, but with no permanent staff this signified little, and by 1960 it had disbursed less than £350,000. The truth was that during the period up to 1960 private capital for large-scale developments was generally forthcoming. There was no real need either for a special development agency supported by official funds, or for special industrial promotion policies beyond keeping the rate of company taxation moderate and giving generous tax treatment to capital expenditure. A more lively development corporation might indeed have found interesting opportunities: but its presence was not a precondition of industrial investment.

It has often been pointed out that the vigour of European and Asian business in Kenya inhibited the emergence of an African entrepreneurial class. Indeed, the major business success stories in the post-war period were of Indian merchants growing into substantial manufacturers, side by side with settler opportunists. But behind this first wave of Kenya tycoons a vigorous jostling could already be discerned amongst emergent African business-

[1] Kenya Government *Ordinances* 1948, p. 81.

men, in trade, transport, building. The government endeavoured to foster the process with loan schemes and advisers and the banks began to experiment gingerly with a new class of borrower. But essentially this was an area where the blight of the Emergency had to wear off before African—and especially Kikuyu—entrepreneurship could come into its own.[1]

Employment and labour

Although the Kenya economy rested squarely upon agriculture and upon agricultural exports, only a small fraction of the country's manpower was involved in agriculture as wage labour. At the beginning of this period the overwhelming majority of the two and a half million people of working age were still engaged primarily in subsistence farming. An increasing but still small number of African farmers were growing cash crops, but as yet employed few paid workers. Of those who did work for wages, a substantial proportion were indeed employed on European farms and plantations, but already by the end of the war there was as much wage labour employed out of agriculture as in it—in domestic service, in private commerce and industry, and above all in government service. Nevertheless, the Kenya problem was, at least up to 1939, still conceived in the classic settler terms of extracting labour from the subsistence economy and deflecting it from cash-farming to meet the demands of white farmers and planters; demands which had led to some famous controversies between the wars—over the extent of government encouragement to work, over tax policies, over the freedom of African farmers to grow export crops.[2] Underlying it was the implicit assumption of cross-subsidization between wage-earning and the economy of the reserves; the low incomes from smallholdings in the reserves needed wage remittances to pay taxes and to supply a minimum of consumer goods, while the low wages paid both on the white farms and in the towns presupposed the existence of holdings in the reserves to supplement them and to

[1] Aspects of this question are discussed in *African Businessmen*, by Peter Marris and Anthony Somerset (London, 1971) and *Who Controls Industry in Kenya?*, by the National Christian Council of Kenya Working Party (Nairobi, 1968).

[2] See chap. v in volume ii of this *History*. 'In East Africa there has hardly ever been a lack of work for an African genuinely seeking it.' G. St. J. Orde-Browne, *Labour Conditions in East Africa*, Col. 193 (London, HMSO, 1946), p. 5.

provide security in sickness and old age. If these wages failed to attract sufficient labour, government pressure in some form on the 'lazy African' was widely regarded by those holding political power as legitimate and appropriate. The growing problem of inadequate urban wages against rising living costs implicit in the Mombasa dock strike of 1939 and in labour unrest during the war went largely uncomprehended and unregarded.[1]

At the end of the period, by contrast, the classic post-colonial picture was beginning to emerge: a considerably enlarged peasant cash-cropping sector, a fairly highly-paid wage-earning élite; and massive urban unemployment and under-employment. Some of the unemployed and under-employed were supported by wage-earning relatives. Others continued to supplement their living from the subsistence sector. For there persisted the basic fact of a predominantly non-wage-earning population which helped to subsidize, though at a meagre level, both the unemployed town-dweller and the irregularities of cash-crop incomes. The percentage of the potential labour force in registered paid employment was actually lower in 1963 than it had been in 1955.[2]

Probably the most powerful factors in this development of the labour situation lay outside the field of deliberately pursued policies.

There was, in the first place, the flooding of the labour market after the ending of the war in 1945. During the war itself of course the problem continued to be the reverse one: at its height more than 90,000 were either in the armed forces or in some form of conscripted service; labour was sought after on farms and plantations struggling to meet increased demands for produce for military needs; and in the new industries which came into being to produce consumer goods unobtainable from overseas.[3] But with the cessation of hostilities much of this manpower was released on to the labour market, and the cities

[1] Margaret Kiloh, 'The Labour Movement in Kenya, 1929–1963' (unpublished typescript, University of Sussex, 1972).

[2] E. R. Rado, 'Manpower Planning in East Africa', *East African Economic Journal*, 3, 1 (June 1967), 24. The difficulties of giving statistical precision to the degree of unemployment or under-employment in an economy with a large subsistence sector are brought out by A. G. Dalgleish, *Survey of Unemployment* (Nairobi, Govt. Printer, 1960). See also *Unemployment*, S.P. 10 of 1959/60 (Nairobi, Govt. Printer, 1960).

[3] Orde-Browne, *Labour Conditions in East Africa*, p. 69.

and reserves were crowded with demobilized soldiers and ex-conscript labour.

Secondly, there was throughout the 1940s and 1950s a rapid expansion in the population. As against some 4·8 millions in 1945, there were 6·3 million in 1955, and over 8·5 millions by the time of independence in 1963.[1] The population increase was accompanied by the economic transformation which brought land consolidation and individual tenure over large areas of the Central Province; this involved the displacement of a number of those who had previously been landholders, although the degree to which such displacement added to the labour surplus is hard to ascertain.[2] At the same time, the developments of the war years had brought about profound changes in social habits and in the demand for goods and services which conformed with them. There was consequently a much increased demand for money incomes, leading in turn to a 'structural' increase in the number of those seeking paid employment. In particular the extension of education[3] meant an expanding number of young people leaving school for whom the conditions of unpaid labour as smallholders in the reserves no longer seemed adequate.

Within this overall picture of a growing demand for paid work, the distribution of wage labour as between the different sectors of the Kenya economy remained fairly stable. Rather less than half of it was employed in agriculture. Surprisingly, despite frequent claims in retrospect that one effect of the Emergency was to reduce the number of workers employed on European farms—with the further suggestion that this reduction proved permanent—the figure of agricultural employment continued to show an almost unbroken upward trend to 1957; there were 5,000 more agricultural workers in 1954 than in 1952, and 25,000 more in 1955 than in 1954.[4] Even after 1955, agriculture

---

[1] *Kenya Population Census, 1962* (Nairobi, Govt. Printer, 1965), vol. iii, reconstructed population trends from Table 10, p. 78.

[2] Sorrenson, *Land Reform*, pp. 218 sqq, and Leys, 'Politics in Kenya', loc. cit., suggest that the criteria for holdings were in practice rapidly abandoned, and that there was therefore little direct displacement.

[3] Rado, 'Manpower Planning', loc. cit., pp. 2–3.

[4] *Report of the Committee on African Wages*, p. 6; *Reported Employment and Wages in Kenya, 1958* (East African Statistical Department, Kenya Unit, 1959), Table 1. The 1955 figures were however somewhat inflated by the labour demands of an unusually heavy coffee crop. *Kenya Agricultural Census, 1955* (East African Statistical Office, 1957), p. 14.

was the last sphere in which the pressure of shrinking employment was felt. It was, not unnaturally, in government services that the pinch was felt soonest, for here the number of those working on government account was considerably inflated by the conditions of the Emergency. By 1956 employment was 7 per cent less than in the previous peak year. In the non-agricultural private sector the downward trend in employment set in in 1957.[1]

Nor was there any great change in the patterns of labour movement. The largest element in urban wage-labour continued to be from Nyanza and, despite some movement to replace Kikuyu labour on the farms, the Central Province continued to supply the great majority of farm workers.

It is perhaps ironic that the main effect of deliberate pressures, both governmental and non-governmental, during this last phase of the colonial period was to aggravate rather than remedy the imbalances of the labour and wage situation.

The attitude adopted by the government was heavily conditioned by the engineered revolution in agriculture and land tenure which was taking place at the same time. If the aim in agriculture was to establish viable units able to supply a minimum cash income, the corollary to this was that there should be an urban wage capable of supporting non-agricultural workers and their families as a settled town population, without subsidization from the reserves, and of permitting the 'emergence of an effective African labour force'. Statutory minimum wage-fixing machinery had in fact been in existence since 1932, but it was only applied for the first time in 1944 (excluding agriculture).[2] From 1952 Wages Councils were progressively introduced with the aim of opening out the wages concertina. But the really revolutionary document was the *Report on African Wages* of the Carpenter Committee of 1954—linked in timing and intention with the Swynnerton Plan for agriculture published in the same year. This aimed at the creation of a stabilized family urban labour force fully remunerated from wage earnings. In defining it the committee viewed with equanimity the prospect that employers would economize on their labour and that there would

---

[1] *Reported Employment and Wages*, Table 1.

[2] *Report of the Committee of Inquiry into Labour Unrest at Mombasa*, Chairman Arthur Phillips (Nairobi, Govt. Printer, 1945).

consequently be a check in the growth of paid employment. If this failed to happen at once on a conspicuous scale, it was principally because the immediate results were limited: there were some improvements in the costing formula for the minimum wage; official pressure on the wage level was increased, but remained well short of the target set by the committee; and although an 'adult' minimum wage replaced the 'bachelor' wage, this was far from the 'family' objective. Nevertheless the course was set in what proved to be the prevailing direction—the securing of relatively high urban wages at the cost of a static and even dwindling total labour force.

The same effect followed in the long run from the pressures of the trade unions, although first steps towards effective labour organization were halting and uncertain. It was characteristic of the climate of wartime and post-war thinking on the colonies in Westminster and Whitehall that, irrespective of the prevailing labour situation in any individual territory, trade unions should be given positive and practical encouragement. In 1940 the receipt of grants under the Colonial Development and Welfare Act was made conditional on the presence in the receiving territory of freely-operating trade unions.[1] And in Kenya as in other parts of colonial Africa—particularly those with settler minorities—trade unionism became closely interwoven with wider politics. There was constant friction over the Colonial Office requirements about unrestricted trade unions, and in the 1950s, under Tom Mboya's inspiration, trade unionism proved in Kenya one of the most effective means of circumventing the ban on African nationwide political parties. But it was inevitable that the same strength, once the main political battle had been won, should be used primarily to safeguard the position of the existing wage-earning class rather than to extend that class. As labour organization became more politically effective, the paternalistic low-wage attitude still widely characteristic during the early post-war years gave way to what has been called the 'new look of employers'. Much influenced by the Mau Mau emergency and its catastrophic possibilities, employers—

[1] *Statement of Policy on Colonial Development and Welfare*, Cmd. 6175 (London, HMSO, 1940), p. 8. See also *Labour Administration in the Colonial Territories 1944–1950*, Col. No. 275 (London, HMSO, 1951); and Orde-Browne, Col. No. 193, paras. 89–91, 289, 325, for trade union encouragement in East Africa.

particularly those in newly-established industries familiar with a European industrial background—formed themselves into associations and readily entered into negotiations based on relatively high living standards and mutual profitability.[1] At the same time, the presence of a substantial sector of European Kenya-born wage- and salary-earners (whose claims could not be met by the device of expatriate allowances) tended to push up still further the general rate of earnings.[2]

The overall effect of these trends and pressures—an increasing skilled or semi-skilled working population, growing landlessness, and rising expectations on the one hand, government and trade union action on the other to maintain wage levels, is to be traced in the relationship between wages, and employment over the period.

From 1944 to 1953 the numbers in paid employment did considerably increase, under the stimulus of post-war expansion particularly in agriculture. But urban wages appear to have remained static;[3] and, although the incomes of those African farmers able to take part in the booming export market rose, agricultural workers on the European farms failed to receive anything like a proportionate share of the rising incomes of their employers. These disparities were certainly a factor in the frustrations that culminated in the outbreak of violence in 1952.

After 1954, following the radical re-thinking engendered by the Emergency in agriculture and other fields, there was a steep rise in African wages. In the private sector (including domestic service) they increased by 40 per cent, in agriculture and government service by 50 per cent, between 1954 and 1958. At the same time the number of those employed—or at all events of those fully employed within the wage-earning sector—began to tail off. Kenya remained up to independence and beyond an only slightly modified peasant society.[4]

---

[1] Alice H. Amsden, *International Firms and Labour in Kenya: 1945–70* (London, 1971), chap. iv.

[2] See e.g. D. P. Ghai, 'Incomes Policy for Kenya: need, criteria and machinery' *East African Economics Review*, N. s. 4, 1 (1968), 19–34.

[3] Cp. the urban wages reported in the Carpenter *Report* (p. 26) and those given in the Phillips *Report* for Mombasa in 1944.

[4] *Reported Employment and Wages*, Tables 5 and 1; Leys, 'Politics in Kenya', loc. cit.

Finance and development

Kenya emerged from the Second World War in a strong budgetary position, and with a comfortable balance on general revenue account. With the experience of the First World War in mind, however, many people were apprehensive that this rising prosperity might within a few years give way to depression.[1] At the same time there was pressure for the abolition or reduction of income tax, which had been introduced for the first time in 1938, and in 1947 an official report by R. P. Plewman, a civil servant loaned by the South African government, recommended that it should be reduced.[2] For the most part the country had to continue to rely on indirect taxation.[3]

Nevertheless the experience of wartime planning, the obvious need to make good some of the ecological damage which the pressures of war production had aggravated, and the current trend of thinking in Whitehall on colonial economic questions, all combined to make the need for economic development a proposition generally accepted. In 1946 a fiscal expert, Sir Wilfred Woods, was appointed to make a preliminary review of financial prospects for the next five years and, despite the widespread misgivings, was broadly optimistic. He believed that the lesson of the need for closer international co-operation to prevent world depression had been learned, that revenue, including taxation revenue, could be maintained, and that it would be enough to furnish a substantial contribution to the development programme.[4]

His cautious optimism proved far short of the mark. With persisting high prices for Kenya's exports the budgetary position continued to strengthen. The general revenue balance, which in 1945 had stood at £1·9 million, had by 1952 reached £9·0 million, while from 1947 to 1952, notwithstanding steadily rising expenditure, there was a comfortable budget surplus each year.[5]

---

[1] Leg Co *Debates*, 11 Jan. 1946, vol. xxiii, pp. 678 sqq.

[2] *Report of the Taxation Enquiry Committee, Kenya*, Chairman R. P. Plewman (Nairobi, Govt. Printer, 1947).

[3] Kenya *Annual Reports*, 1946–62.

[4] *Report on a Fiscal Survey of Kenya, Uganda and Tanganyika*, by Sir Wilfred Woods (Nairobi, Govt. Printer, 1946), Part II.

[5] Kenya *Annual Reports*, 1946–53.

In connection with the proposed large expansion in aid allocations, reflected in the 1945 Colonial Development and Welfare Act, colonial territories were instructed to draw up ten-year development plans. This evoked a characteristic response in Kenya in that the Development Committee established in 1945 to draw up a plan was made up of both settlers and leading officials, and it considered submissions from the public as well as from departments before publishing a substantial report.[1]

The Development Committee recommended that the implementation of the ten-year plan should be entrusted to a special agency, the Development and Reconstruction Authority (DARA), rather than to the appropriate government departments. From the point of view of revenue, there was a desire to segregate the finance for the plan into a separate fund, so that it should be quite clear that the finance for development projects was quite independent of recurrent budgetary considerations. The surpluses which had been accumulated from the war, and which were seen as the main source of funds for the plan, lent plausibility to this view, as did the contemporary pessimism on the possibilities for revenue expansion in the post-war period. The desire for a separate executive agency stemmed also from the well-founded distrust of the European elected members in the ability of the government machine as it was in 1945 to implement expeditiously a capital expenditure programme.[2]

In the event the plan proved, once the bottlenecks of staff and construction capacity began to be overcome, to be an unrealistic straitjacket. With the revenue position buoyant, the original expenditure allocation of £17·5 million was increased progressively to over £40 million. £29 million had actually been spent by the time the plan was terminated at the end of 1953, after eight years. By then the impact of the Emergency was already transforming the financial situation.

The experience of these years had shown that development planning was not an occasional exercise that could be handed to an expert committee once a decade and then followed rigidly, but was a continuing process which was at the centre of govern-

---

[1] *Report of the Development Committee*, 1945 (Nairobi, Govt. Printer, 1946).

[2] These and other general observations in the paragraphs immediately following are based on the author's personal experience as an official in the Kenya Treasury during the last few years before independence.

ment policy and responsibility. Final decisions on priorities, revision, and new schemes could only be handled under the authority of the highest forum in the government, at that time the Planning Sub-Committee of Executive Council (which became the Development Committee of Council of Ministers from April 1954). The conditions of rapid economic change that Kenya was experiencing indicated that long-term expenditure forecasts were unrealistic, and this applied even more strongly to forecasts of development revenue. A pattern of three-year development programmes was therefore adopted up to the time of independence, as striking a reasonable balance between the requirements of flexibility and of disciplined finance.[1]

By 1953 the need for DARA as an executive agency with independent financial resources had disappeared. In the first place, the exhaustion of the bulk of the government's surplus funds, coupled with the removal of the prospect of substantial budget surpluses as a result of the Emergency, meant that DARA could no longer be insulated from the government's general financial position. Secondly, departmental executive capacities had been greatly improved, and in particular there had been a major reorganization of the public works department. The introduction of the membership system had also played a significant part. Thirdly, there was the increasing authority and expertise of the Treasury, especially after Vasey went there in 1951. Its right to vet departmental proposals before they were embodied in the budget was already established in 1949 under the arrangements for the conduct of the Standing Planning Committee. When the Development Committee of Council of Ministers was established in 1954, the Minister of Finance became chairman of the Committee, thus establishing the primacy of the Treasury in development matters at the ministerial as well as at the official level.[2]

The Emergency imposed an immense financial burden on the colony, but the remarkable thing was the extent to which it proved possible to mobilize resources sufficient to maintain and

---

[1] *Development Programme 1954–1957*, S.P. 51 of 1955; *Development Programme 1957–1960*, S.P. 77 of 1956/7 (Nairobi, Govt. Printer, 1957); *Development Programme 1960–1963*, S.P. 4 of 1959/60 (Nairobi, Govt. Printer, 1960).

[2] K. W. S. MacKenzie, 'The Development of the Kenya Treasury', *East African Economics Review*, 8, 2 (1961), 59–73.

expand government services concurrently with the special cost of the Emergency. In 1951 current expenditure totalled just under £15 million; five years later in 1956/7 it amounted to almost £35 million. Meanwhile the Emergency had by then cost £50 million, of which half had been paid by the British government. Thereafter Emergency spending tailed off rapidly and the British government assumed a progressively larger proportion of the total, so that by 1960 it met the full cost in that year amounting to £1·6 million. In contrast to the situation that occurred in the transition to independence, it is worth under-lining that the financing of the Emergency was so organized that Kenya did not become grant-aided by Britain on its ordinary budget, and retained responsibility for its finances, albeit in the closest consultation with London.

Similarly, the development effort during the Emergency was characterized not by a stunting but by a significant enlargement of programmes. In the 1954–7 plan the rate of disbursement rose from an annual figure of £5–6 million to nearly £10 million. Security and closer administration considerations were a notice-able priority; nevertheless agricultural expenditure actually increased during the plan period to account for 28 per cent, reflecting the progress of the Swynnerton Plan and the momen-tum established by the administration on land reform. A boom was under way by 1957, especially in the construction industry, so that in the following plan period to 1960 government deliber-ately opted for more modest public sector pressure on resources, with an annual expenditure of £8 million. However, agricultural spending was maintained and its proportionate share increased further to 39 per cent of the total.

Two phases can be distinguished in the financing of public sector development programmes in the period up to 1960. To begin with the government relied primarily on accumulated balances and on contributions to DARA from general tax revenues. Then—apart from a substantial subsidy from Britain to meet the main cost of the Swynnerton agricultural plan—came a period of public debt expansion through loans raised in the London market and the fostering of a capital market in Kenya. Finally, after 1960, as will be seen below, in the transition to independence there was to be a very heavy reliance on direct loans and grants from the British government.

Some 20 per cent of DARA's total resources was accounted for by special funds that had been built up during the war and were then transferred for development. These balances were largely used up by 1954; meanwhile the government was able to make important contributions from its current revenue surpluses, which in turn accounted for some 27 per cent of the programme. However, the advent of the Emergency quickly altered the pattern. It is true that one effect was to prompt the massive metropolitan aid of £5 million to development embodied in the Swynnerton Plan—the most ambitious contribution up to that date. At the same time the general revenue balance disappeared and a situation emerged whereby important recurrent services were in fact financed by development funds, especially in agriculture.

Between 1948 and 1960 Kenya raised nearly £45 million through long term public loans, which was a notable achievement. Up to 1950 only £6 million was raised, all in London. Then in the next five years £24 million was raised and the local capital market was tapped for the first time for £3·5 million of the total. There was a further change of emphasis in the five years to 1960 when, of the £14·5 million borrowed all but £1·7 million came from the local capital market. That such an expansion of the local capital market was achieved during a period of acute political strain and uncertainty is a striking tribute to the confidence which Kenya's financial administration inspired.

While the government's development initiative was of crucial importance in agriculture and in the establishment of the country's infrastructure, Kenya was distinctive insofar as it experienced a high level of development in private enterprise which many other colonies, without the energizing resources of an immigrant community, lacked. For example, between 1950 and 1958 capital investment in Kenya was estimated at over £300 million (excluding land improvement under the Swynnerton Plan), of which the private sector accounted for 62 per cent of the total. Unlike that of Uganda, the government of Kenya did not have to take the lead in initiating industrial development and, despite the Emergency, could be reasonably confident that the country's pivotal position in the East African common market, as well as its other attractions, would stimulate industrial and commercial development.

During the final phase before independence, however, neither private enterprise nor the initiative and expertise of the Kenya government were sufficient to see the country's finances through a period of stress and shaken confidence. In part this arose from the fact that the main revenue account had eventually to absorb continuing expenditure which during the Emergency had been partially disguised in development and defence programmes. At the same time, in the confidence crisis following the Lancaster House Conference of 1960 the government found itself unable to issue public loans in Kenya or London and had to rely exclusively on the British government for its general development borrowings. In 1959–60 Kenya began to borrow directly from Britain for general development purposes and this quickly became the main source of development finance.

One new and significant element entered into the picture during this final phase. The Kenya government was gaining experience of tapping sources of development finance outside the direct colonial relationship. Although this was not very substantial in quantitative terms at first, Kenya was able to initiate a considerable diversification of sources of finance which had the great merit that the United Nations agencies and a number of foreign governments (notably the United States and West Germany) got to know the country's economic situation well before independence.

Conclusion

The need to call upon both British and foreign external aid between 1960 and 1963 was one aspect of the more sombre mood in which, after the spectacular expansion of the 1960s, the Kenya economy entered the last phase before independence. The dominant factor in this was undoubtedly the uncertainty that followed on the rapid political re-orientation of 1959–60. By February 1960 the Nairobi share price index had dropped by more than a quarter from its 1955 level, a year later by more than half. Capital formation slowed to a halt, and capital exports reached serious proportions. Political uncertainty and financial stringency were reflected in some measure in every sector of the economy.[1]

[1] K. G. V. Krishna, 'Kenya's Economy in 1960', *East African Economics Review*, 8, 1 (1961), 24–34.

In agriculture it is true the effects were not immediate. Production continued on the whole to increase, only partially set back by the losses due to drought and floods.[1] But development on European farms virtually ceased, and since at this time the European sector was still responsible for some 80 per cent of gross production, the long-term outlook was discouraging. In industry there was considerable recession, reflected most seriously in the construction industry. The rapid contraction in building demand and the uncertain future outlook caused the loss of architects and other professionals concerned with the industry. Overseas civil engineering firms departed as contracts ran out, the Ministry of Works organization was curtailed; and firms in the building supply trade closed down.

In both industry and agriculture there was a drastic shrinkage in employment, the former particularly owing to the reduction of labour employed in building and construction, the latter to the falling off in farm employment as European landowners moved out, selling their farms where they could. At the same time the political pressure towards Africanization, especially in the government sector, contributed to the widening of the gulf between the highly-paid élite and the growing number of unemployed or under-employed. This picture of declining economic activity inevitably reacted in turn on the Kenya government's finances. A substantial fall in imports from the latter half of 1960 resulted in a shortfall of some £2·5 million on import duties, and there was also a decline in income tax yield.[2] At the same time the imminence of independence, apart from the crisis of confidence it engendered, had its own financial implications for the cost of government. The Kenya civil service (excluding unskilled subordinate posts) had grown from 16,200 in 1950 to some 40,000 in 1960, but it was only in that year that the process of Africanization, which had been theoretically going

---

[1] Production of main crops in the last four years before independence:

Yr.	Wheat	Maize	Coffee	Barley	Yr.	Tea	Pyrethrum	Sisal
		'000 tons					'000 tons	
1959/60	127·4	143–8	23·4	24·0	1959	12·4	4·8	55·2
1960/1	99·7	139·7	33·1	13·3	1960	13·6	8·5	62·6
1961/2	84·1	156·7	27·4	9·9	1961	12·4	10·2	62·3
1962/3	118·4	193·1	44·0	19·2	1962	16·2	10·0	55·7

Source: *Kenya Statistical Abstract 1963*, p. 50. Tables 77 (a) and (b).

[2] Krishna, 'Kenya Economy in 1960', p. 30.

on since racial salary scales were abolished in 1954, became dramatic in tempo. The result was a sudden exodus of expatriate officers who had to be not only compensated, but replaced at short notice by expensive temporary officials working on contract. This coincided with a substantial rise in civil service pay rates and with increased costs in financing the East Africa High Commission.[1] The situation was exacerbated by the consequences of drought, famine, and floods.

In the end, having just brought to an end the subventions to help meet the cost of the Emergency, Britain had to come to the rescue with fresh grants in aid to the extent of £9·2 million in the two years 1960–2.

Yet although the immediate economic prospect as independence approached was a weak one—a country without foreign exchange reserves, heavily dependent upon recurrent budget and capital aid, suffering from a flight of private capital, facing formidable problems of reorientation in its crucial agricultural sector—the transition was in fact effected with an aplomb that astonished contemporary observers. This is not the place to analyse that phase, but it does prompt a broader reflection. We have sought in this survey to explain something of the *élan* which the Kenya economy showed in this period, and to draw attention to some significant motivating concepts affecting the economic life of the country. In 1960 and for a short period thereafter these same influences seemed to account for some of the unreadiness of the economy for political independence; yet on a longer view it is more fruitful perhaps to look for those elements of strength which in fact helped the economy to emerge so strongly a few years later once the political maturity of the new government had become evident. Thus the extensive infrastructure of communications, hotels, and far-sighted wild life conservation policies laid the groundwork for a tourist industry which in the following years was to rival coffee as the country's main foreign exchange earner and to make Kenya by far the most visited tourist country in Africa. Again, the extensive commercial and industrial development of the 1960s was not really disrupted but only checked by the transition period, and this broad industrial base was of great importance when the post-independence boom

[1] M. McWilliam, 'Economic Viability and the Race Factor in Kenya', *Economic Development and Cultural Change*, 12, 1 (Oct. 1963).

eventually got under way, compounding Kenya's attractions as a regional centre for international companies in the East African common market. Finally, the financial expertise and professionalism of the administration was not so impaired during the transfer of power as many had feared and—partly by comparison with other developing countries—Kenya became something of a favoured recipient of assistance from the international agencies and individual foreign governments, demonstrating a much greater capacity than many other countries for effective aid procurement and disbursement. In the event, therefore, many of the expected financial pains of the transition were eased and much of the development impetus was after all maintained. Furthermore, although many of the assumptions of the racial minorities had turned out to be illusory, they did not become totally disillusioned, and a crucially high proportion found that they still had a worthwhile place in the economy during the transition phase and beyond. The diversification of Kenya's economy in the post-war period was not so insecurely based as many had feared.

VII

THE POOR COUNTRY:
THE TANGANYIKA ECONOMY FROM
1945 TO INDEPENDENCE

CYRIL EHRLICH

IN 1945 Tanganyika was desperately poor. To some extent, of course, this was due to the exigencies of war. But there were longer-term causes of poverty: a population ill-educated and ill-equipped to master its harsh environment; an infrastructure whose sparseness and inadequacy was remarkable even by the standards of tropical Africa; an administrative policy essentially negative in tone, particularly as regards economic policy; an international status which since 1918 had been of sufficient ambiguity further to discourage investment and entrepreneurial effort. During our period the losses of wartime were repaired, but the deep-rooted barriers to economic development proved more intractable. An appraisal of Tanganyika's economic achievement in the years before independence will hinge upon our assessment of the extent to which these barriers were ascertained and tackled. That they were not overcome is self-evident: Tanganyika entered the 1960s as one of the poorest and least developed of African countries.

This chapter is concerned with Tanganyika's economic growth, with the policies of its government, and with the living standards of its people. The general pattern of growth is illustrated by the statistics in Table 1 which provide a rough outline of quantitative change, and indicate some of the main events of this period, such as the Korean boom of 1951-2. But the reader should avoid too facile an interpretation of these statistics. It would be unwise, for example, to accept literally the view that 'the rate of growth of exports gives a fair indication of the rate of growth of the economy as a whole,'[1] or to assume that the figures tell us much about

[1] International Bank for Reconstruction and Development, *The Economic Development of Tanganyika*, (Baltimore, 1961) p. 25. On the dangers of naïve interpretations of growth see the correspondence between a 'special correspondent' and Professor Peacock and Mr. Dosser, in *Economist*, 5, and 12 Apr., 31 May, and 7 June 1958.

TABLE I

SOME STATISTICS OF ECONOMIC GROWTH IN TANGANYIKA

Year	Exports £m.	Imports £m.	Government revenue £m.	Government expenditure £m.	Gross Domestic Product Monetary economy £m.	Gross Domestic Product Subsistence economy £m.
1945	8·2	6·7	4·8	4·8		
1946	8·9	8·1	5·1	5·1	23	
1947	11·1	13·7	5·9	6·1	28	
1948	16·2	22·2	6·9	6·8	38	
1949	20·9	28·8	9·1	8·7	45	
1950	24·0	27·9	11·5	11·6	53	
1951	40·5	31·7	13·1	14·6	70	
1952	47·4	41·9	17·5	18·3	79	
1953	35·4	33·9	15·6	18·0	71	
1954	37·3	37·8			79	63
1955	37·9	49·1	20·0	19·8	82	65
1956	47·0	42·2	19·5	22·6	89	63
1957	41·4	47·0	19·4	23·1	93	69
1958	44·3	42·6	20·8	24·1	98	69
1959	47·9	42·6	21·8	24·7	106	71
1960	57·1	47·0	23·6	25·1	123	62
1961	53·8	54·6			121	56

Exports and imports include those to and from Kenya and Uganda. Government revenue and expenditure include both current and development items. The years 1945 to 1953 are calendar years; 1955 to 1960 are financial years; i.e. '1955' = 1954–5, etc. (Definitions differ slightly from those used in Appendix 3).

The GDP figures for 1946 to 1953 are estimates by H. W. Ord, and for 1954 to 1959 are official estimates; all are at factor cost and have been rounded to the nearest £m. Add the two columns together for an estimate of the total GDP.

SOURCES: *The Gross Domestic Product of Tanganyika, 1954–57* (Dar es Salaam, 1959), *The Budget Survey, 1961–2* (Dar es Salaam, 1962); Peacock and Dosser, *National Income of Tanganyika*, Annex VI; and H. W. Ord, 'The Growth of Money Incomes in East Africa', *East African Economics Review*, 9, 1 (June 1962).

human welfare. In 1954, for example, agricultural cash crops accounted for over 75 per cent of total exports but were estimated as contributing only 13 per cent of the country's gross domestic product in contrast to the 34 per cent attributed to non-marketed staple crops.[1] The relationship between exports and welfare was even more tenuous than these proportions suggest, for the leading

[1] A.T. Peacock and D.G. Dosser, *The National Income of Tanganyika, 1952-54* (London, HMSO, 1958), p. 51.

export (30 per cent of total export values) was sisal, an alien-owned plantation crop whose fortunes affected the incomes of a mere 130,000 Africans, less than 2 per cent of the population—and this only through their meagre wages as unskilled labourers. Coffee, by contrast, which was second on the export list, was grown mainly by African peasants whose cash incomes were directly affected by world trade. The belated expansion of cotton-growing, forty years after a similar drive in Uganda,[1] also directly affected the incomes of some 250,000 Africans by the end of our period. Yet the significance of even peasant-grown exports can be exaggerated. In 1954, the best year for coffee throughout this period, the value of the crop was not much higher than that of native beer[2] which, of course, was not exported. The production of native beer, a major component in African diet and welfare, depended primarily on weather conditions and was not much affected by foreign trade.

Considerations of this kind are irritating but necessary for the understanding of economic change in societies like Tanganyika, where cash failed to penetrate deeply into the lives of most people. In highly commercialized market economies, growth and welfare—at least as conventionally measured—can be quantified with relative ease. Even when the sophisticated data of modern social accounting are not available there are usually abundant statistics which can be processed and refined so as to illustrate changes in prosperity. It is a commonplace that in underdeveloped economies such figures are rarely abundant or reliable. Less obvious is the fact that some data of apparent significance may give the unwary reader a misleading impression of the trends which they purport to illustrate. In addition to the example already quoted an interesting case is that of the official East African estimates of gross capital formation. These omit such items as bicycles, sewing machines, and the hand tools used in subsistence agriculture—capital goods whose productivity is probably higher than that of many more spectacular and more readily calculable items of investment. All this is not to deny the influence of exports and investment upon growth and ultimately welfare, but to advise caution in the acceptance of too simplified

---

[1] See vol. ii of this *History*, chap. viii, 'The Uganda Economy 1903-1945', by C. Ehrlich.
[2] Peacock and Dosser, *National Income of Tanganyika*, p. 33.

a relationship. The growth of the *exchange* economy has been determined primarily by the value of exports which in turn has depended mainly on the level of world prices for a few primary products. Imports of consumer goods have affected African tastes significantly and have probably acted as an incentive to acquire higher cash incomes. Capital investment and government policy have also affected economic progress. But a final determinant of growth, both in the subsistence and exchange sectors, has simply been the weather, and the extent of its influence throughout our period offers some evidence of the persistence of economic backwardness.

An understanding of Tanganyika's economy must begin with the harsh geographical facts.[1] Its area was approximately 343,000 square miles, larger than France and the British Isles together, yet in 1945 its population was a mere 7 million. Moreover an average density of 20 people per square mile obscured enormous regional variations, as for example in the Northern Province, ranging from 2 per square mile in the Masai District to 138 in Moshi. Nearly two-thirds of the country was virtually uninhabited and people tended to settle on land where simple hand agriculture was possible. Thus the size and the distribution of the population resulted from an oppressive physical environment over which men exerted little control. A notable example of this was human subservience to the tsetse fly which, as a result rather than cause of underpopulation,[2] infested some 60 per cent of the land.

Rainfall exhibited all the vices—it was inadequate and irregular in its geographical distribution, capricious in its seasonal visitations. Prolonged periods of drought were common everywhere except in the vicinity of Lakes Victoria and Nyasa. The Central Province was particularly vulnerable; between 1941 and 1946 there was famine in at least one part of the province every year except 1944.[3] Since throughout the country the overwhelming majority of the people grew their own food the incidence and reliability of rainfall was therefore the principal immediate determinant of their welfare. An example from two

---

[1] For detailed geographical description see chap. i in the first volume of this *History*.

[2] C. Gillman, 'A Population Map of Tanganyika Territory', *Geographical Review*, 26 (1936), 354, quoted in P. Gourou, *The Tropical World* (London, 1953), p. 11.

[3] Central Province, Provincial Commissioner's Annual Report, 1947.

consecutive seasons will illustrate this argument. 1946 was a bad year with food shortages in every province; in some areas the government had to organize famine relief and distribute 'unpopular foods', such as cassava. The rice crop failed almost completely, and maize and even sorghum and millet, the most drought-resistant of grain crops, were grievously affected.[1] During the following year rainfall was heavy and well distributed —indeed in the highlands it was excessive, destroying crops through flood and disease. But generally harvests were the biggest since 1943 and 'a long back-log of tribal ceremonies' was celebrated.[2] As it is generally accepted that 30 inches is in East Africa the minimum reliable rainfall necessary for the satisfactory cultivation of grain,[3] the precariousness of existence can be illustrated by rainfall statistics for two representative areas. Iringa district, in the Southern Highlands, was the home of the Hehe tribe, whose staple crop was maize and who numbered approximately 192,000 in 1948. For three decades average rainfall there was 29 inches with wide fluctuations about this mean. Dodoma district, in the Central Province, had an average of only 22 inches, again with wide fluctuations.The majority of the district's population, some 270,000 Gogo, were predominantly a pastoral tribe, but 40 per cent of them had no cattle and were thus utterly dependent upon this exiguous rainfall. Settlement was therefore concentrated round the few areas with permanent water with inevitable consequences of overstocking and erosion. A 'development plan' for the area was too poorly financed and staffed to have much effect; 1953 and 1954 were years of severe famine.

Throughout our period Tanganyika was a simple agricultural society in which the production of non-marketed staple foodstuffs was by far the most important form of economic activity. We have already suggested that in 1954 subsistence agriculture accounted for approximately one-third of gross domestic product. Estimates for 1960 give a similar proportion.[4] No similar calculation exists for 1945 but the dominance of staple crops was

[1] Department of Agriculture Annual Report, 1946.
[2] Department of Agriculture Annual Report, 1947, p. 2.
[3] See *East Africa Royal Commission 1953–1955 Report*, Cmd. 9475 (London, HMSO, 1955) chap. xx.
[4] *The National Accounts of Tanganyika, 1960–62* (Central Statistical Bureau, Treasury, Dar es Salaam, 1964), Table 5.

certainly even greater. During the war there had been a marked tendency for rural Africans, who were the mass of the people, to move back from cash towards a subsistence way of life, providing 'a measure of protection from market forces which is absent in a more highly specialised economy based on more intensive division of labour'.[1] The scarcity and high prices of consumer goods discouraged peasants, who were already largely self-sufficient, from making much effort to obtain money. Transport facilities were even poorer than before the war, market outlets for their products were fewer and less remunerative, and the movement towards subsistence was reinforced by official enencouragement of agricultural self-sufficiency. By 1945 the emergence of a modern economy with exchange as a normal object of productive activity was even more remote from attainment than it had been in 1939.

The size of the African population was known only approximately. There had been no census since that of 1931 which, like its predecessors, was little more than an estimate.[2] This was typical of a general lack of fundamental data, due primarily to the absence of a government statistical department which had been sacrificed during the years of retrenchment before the war. Such figures as did exist were compiled by administrative officers as an additional burdensome chore. But paucity of statistical information also reflected the life of a society whose culture was non-literate and non-numerate, and whose people distrusted enumeration for its association with tax collection and labour service. The 1948 East Africa census was a landmark in the demography of tropical Africa.[3] In Tanganyika it was the first 'serious attempt to enumerate rather than merely estimate the African population'[4] and revealed the inaccuracy of existing figures. The last estimate, in 1947, had given the African population as 5,838,000. The 1948 census showed it to be 7,408,000. It is useless therefore to attempt to indicate the rate of population growth before 1948 but it is clear that birth and death rates were

[1] B. Yamey, 'The Study of Peasant Economic Systems', in B. Yamey and R. Firth, *Capital, Saving and Credit in Peasant Societies* (London, 1964), p. 378.

[2] J. G. C. Blacker, 'The Demographic Statistics of Tanganyika and Uganda', in T. E. Smith and J. G. C. Blacker, *Population Characteristics of the Commonwealth Countries of Tropical Africa* (London, 1963), p. 57.

[3] Blacker, 'Demographic Statistics', loc. cit., p. 58.

[4] United Nations, *The Population of Tanganyika* (New York, 1949), p. 14.

very high, the latter probably among the highest in the world.[1] This population was made up of 120 tribes which varied considerably in their mode and standard of living, from the Sukuma[2] and Chagga with comparatively high incomes, to the poor and unsophisticated Gogo.

Estimates of the European and Asian population were naturally far more accurate. In 1947 there were approximately 10,000 Europeans excluding the temporary presence of 7,000 Polish refugees. Asians[3] numbered about 60,000 predominantly Indians and Pakistanis, but including some 12,000 Arabs and 3,000 Goans. Tanganyika's Europeans were of notably diverse national origin, in marked contrast to those of Kenya and Uganda, reflecting earlier German influence and the mandate years. A census taken in 1952 showed that over 30 per cent were non-British, and a few years later a visitor to the European primary school in Arusha noted that sixteen different languages were spoken as the mother tongue.[4] The geographical distribution of non-Africans resulted from their specialized economic roles. A large proportion lived in towns in 1948—36,488 out of the total of 70,160. The Arabs were least urbanized, about 25 per cent, Goans the most—approximately 75 per cent; 31 per cent of Europeans and 64 per cent of Indians lived in townships. Outside the towns Europeans were mainly in plantation areas of the coastal hinterland and Southern Highlands. Indians dominated retail trade, as in the rest of East Africa, but a distinctive feature in Tanganyika was their role in plantation agriculture, again reflecting mandate obligations upon the administration to allow racial equality in immigration and settlement.

During the Second World War the size and structure of Tanganyika's foreign trade had changed in ways which were seriously to affect the country's development after 1945. Imports fell severely from a level which had already been low even by the standards of tropical Africa. A calculation of the value of imports per head of the population in 1937 listed Tanganyika seventh

[1] See C. J. Martin, 'The East African Population Census, 1948: planning and enumeration, *Population Studies, 3*, 3 (1949); J. E. Goldthorpe, The African Population of East Africa: a summary of its past and present trends', in Appendix VII to *East Africa Royal Commission Report.*

[2] By far the largest group, accounting for some 12 per cent of the total population.

[3] See J. S. Mangat, *A History of the Asians in East Africa* (London, 1969).

[4] Kathleen Stahl, *Tanganyika, Sail in the Wilderness* (The Hague, 1961), p. 39.

out of eight British African territories. Only Nyasaland spent
less on imported goods than Tanganyika's 13*s*. 10*d*. per head of
the population.[1] Between 1938 and 1946 this situation deteriorated. Unreliable population statistics preclude an exact comparison with the example just quoted, but some relevant figures
are set out in Table II.

TABLE II

FOREIGN TRADE AND GOVERNMENT FINANCE 1938–1946

	Exports		Imports		Public finance £m.	
	Value £m.	Quantity Index[1]	Value £m.	Quantity Index	Revenue	Expenditure
1938	3·7	106	3·1	97	2·1	2·2
1939	4·6	121	3·3	99	2·1	2·3
1940	5·7	121	3·5	70	2·3	2·2
1941	6·8	127	3·7	71	2·7	2·5
1942	7·6	141	3·7	52	3·1	3·1
1943	6·4	106	4·8	49	3·7	3·7
1944	7·8	114	5·8	61	4·2	4·2
1945	8·6	112	6·9	78	4·8	4·8
1946	9·3	105	8·1	100	5·1	5·1

Sources: Tanganyika *Statistical Abstracts*; Tanganyika *Annual Reports*; East African
Economic and Statistical Bulletins.
  [1] Monthly average quantities revalued at base prices and expressed as % of base
value (1935–8 = 100).

When allowance is made for steeply rising prices it is evident
that there was a considerable fall in the real value of imports. In
addition to the disincentive effect described already this decline
had several implications. In the first place it obviously indicated
a fall in the standard of living. A whole range of popular consumer
goods—cooking pots, enamelled ware, knives, lamps, bicycles,
and sewing machines—became virtually unobtainable. 'The
man was forced to return to the old native-made tools and
appliances, while his wife cooked in earthenware pots of local
manufacture in place of the aluminium saucepan to which she
had grown accustomed.' Cotton-piece goods 'expensive and

  [1] C. Leubuscher, *Tanganyika Territory* (London, 1944), p. 205.

shoddy, alone found a limited attraction'.[1] Even these were in
short supply, annual imports falling from an average of 41
million yards during the period 1934–9 to 32 million yards
between 1940 and 1945. Moreover aggregate statistics of this
kind conceal qualitative changes which seriously affected standards of living. During the 1930s the régime of non-discrimination
stipulated by the mandate had allowed the import of cheap
Czechoslovakian shoes and Japanese manufactured goods which
significantly helped to raise African standards of living.[2] The
wartime loss of such sources of supply was a serious blow to
African consumers.

Falling imports also led to depreciation of the country's
exiguous capital assets. Some indication of this is provided by the
statistics of cement imports, which declined from a pre-war average of 20,000 tons to 5,100 tons in 1943, and did not regain
former levels until 1947. There were similar falls in the import
of such materials as galvanized sheet iron. This depreciation
of physical capital cast long shadows into the next decade; as
late as 1954 the Member for Finance and Economics justly
remarked that much of 'what is called capital development is
unfortunately more truly described as deferred maintenance.'[3]
The value of exports grew rapidly (Table II) but quantitative
change was less spectacular. The output of sisal, by far the most
valuable export, actually declined during the first three years
of the war because of labour shortages and restricted government
purchases of the crop. In 1942 the Japanese invasion of Indonesia
and the Philippines created a shortage of hard fibres which
stimulated an increase in Tanganyikan production. Nevertheless
by 1945 output was only 112,000 tons as compared with the
103,000 tons of 1939. Coffee exports, second on the list, fell from
16,600 tons to 14,400 tons during the same period.

The potential significance of government activity in such an
economy can scarcely be exaggerated, but in 1945 the Tanganyikan administration was singularly ill-equipped to initiate and
guide development. Its income failed to keep pace with rising
prices, but government enterprise was not limited solely by

[1] G. St. J. Orde Browne, *Labour Conditions in East Africa*, Col. 193 (London, HMSO,
1946), p. 17.
[2] Leubuscher, *Tanganyika Territory*, p. 125.
[3] Tanganyika Leg Co *Debates*, 26 May 1954, p. 104.

finance. Lack of equipment, men, and ideas held up development even when money was available. Thus a small surplus of revenue over expenditure arose in 1945 because staff and supplies could not be procured for development or even 'arrears of maintenance'.[1] Nevertheless lack of finance was crucial; existing levels of revenue together with some £2 million reserves were inadequate to satisfy even pre-war requirements: the proposals of a 1939 committee for improvements in education facilities were thought in 1945 to be 'far beyond the capacity of the territory'.[2] Meanwhile Tanganyika like other economically backward countries was beginning to experience the first impact of what has since been dubbed the 'revolution of rising expectations'. Together with new standards of colonial development and welfare, this involved not merely a desire to raise levels of living but an assumption, by no means confined to colonial areas, that the government would be a principal agent of such progress.

A fiscal survey of East Africa offered little hope for these aspirations. In Tanganyika annual current expenditure on education, for example, was a derisory £330,000 and even this required a grant of £70,000 from Britain. Universal elementary education up to Standard III and a modest programme of higher education would have required recurrent expenditure of £1,500,000, yet taxable capacity was too small to 'provide sufficient funds for anything approaching this without drastically curtailing the prior claims of economic development'.[3] Moreover within the next decade such development could only be expected to increase taxable capacity 'to a minor degree', and the provision of recurrent finance for 'schemes after they have been completed is a bigger problem even than the provision of the capital required to carry them out.'[4] Such was an informed assessment of Tanganyika's economic position at the beginning of our period. Today its tone and approach to the problems of development appear remote and peculiarly negative, but to contemporaries its realism seemed unassailable.

[1] Financial Secretary in Leg Co Debates, 3 Dec. 1945, p. 2.
[2] Ibid., p. 5.
[3] Sir W. Woods, Report on a Fiscal Survey of Kenya, Uganda and Tanganyika (Nairobi, Govt. Printer, 1946), p. 7.
[4] Ibid., p. 145.

Foreign trade and growth: boom and recession, 1946–1960

It was a steady rise in the prices of primary products on world markets that gently shook Tanganyika's economy from its quiescence. Between 1946 and 1952 export values increased more than five times, and because of this the government's revenue multiplied threefold. Most products enjoyed buoyant markets, but the leading participant was sisal, which accounted for approximately half the value of all exports during the period, reaching a peak of 58 per cent in 1951.

Sisal is a hard fibre used mainly in the manufacture of ropes and agricultural twines. Before the war Tanganyika was already an important producer, sharing 70 per cent of the world's production with the East Indies. In 1942 the Japanese invasion of its rival left Tanganyika's industry in a dominant position which it retained until the mid-1950s. For several years, however, the industry was unable to gain full benefit from this situation. Between 1941 and 1948 the whole crop was sold under a bulk-purchase agreement to the British government at prices far below those obtainable elsewhere.[1] Sisal was particularly important to Britain, not only because of its intrinsic qualities, but also because the alternative fibre, manilla, had to be purchased from the Philippines with scarce dollars. In 1946 the Tanganyika price was at last substantially raised to £46 a ton, and subsequently increased until the end of the bulk-purchase agreement. It has been estimated that between 1940 and 1948 Tanganyikan producers lost £11 million by being forced to accept prices which were consistently below world levels. This loss to the industry and, by implication, to the Tanganyika government's revenue, appears to be a fairly clear example of 'exploitation' by the metropolitan power, and the erosion of its profits seriously weakened the industry's ability to replace and develop capacity.[2] Sisal takes from three to seven years to mature, and staff and equipment were scarce, but these unavoidable delays were aggravated by short-sighted government policy. The industry failed to increase production sufficiently in time to reap the full

---

[1] Producers in Portuguese Africa received almost twice as much from the American government. C. W. Guillebaud, *An Economic Survey of the Sisal Industry of Tanganyika* (Welwyn, 1958), p. 26. On the general problem of bulk purchase see C. Leubuscher, *Bulk Buying from the Colonies* (London, 1956).

[2] Cf. Guillebaud, *Sisal Industry*, pp. 33, 62 sqq.

harvest of the boom years when, after 1948, it enjoyed uniquely favourable markets. In the newly independent republic of Indonesia political conditions stopped producers from approaching pre-war levels of output and a world shortage of hard fibres was exacerbated by the United States government's stockpiling of raw materials. Then in September 1949 Britain's devaluation of the pound increased sterling receipts from hard currency buyers. Finally in June 1950 the outbreak of the Korean war gave an immense stimulus to raw material prices as manufacturers amassed stocks in anticipation of future shortages. All these factors enhanced the value, and more slowly the quantity, of sisal exports (Table III).

TABLE III

PRINCIPAL EXPORTS 1945–1962

	Sisal			Coffee			Cotton		
	'000 tons	£m.	% total expts.	'000 tons	£m.	% total expts.	'000 tons	£m.	% total expts.
1938	100	1·4	38	13	0·4	11	9	0·4	10
1945	110	3·1	37	14	0·9	11	7	0·7	9
1946	111	3·9	44	10	0·7	8	4	0·4	4
1947	96	5·5	49	14	0·9	9	7	0·8	7
1948	117	8·9	55	11	0·9	5	10	1·3	8
1949	132	11·1	55	12	1·5	7	11	2·0	10
1950	119	11·9	48	15	3·5	15	7	1·4	6
1951	142	23·7	58	17	4·5	11	8	2·8	7
1952	158	21·7	45	19	5·5	12	11	4·7	10
1953	171	12·8	37	15	5·8	17	15	4·8	14
1954	168	10·9	30	19	10·0	28	12	3·4	9
1955	174	9·9	27	18	6·9	19	20	5·5	15
1956	186	10·8	24	21	9·2	21	28	7·5	17
1957	182	9·5	24	18	7·1	18	27	6·6	17
1958	198	10·3	25	22	7·6	18	32	7·2	17
1959	209	13·1	29	20	5·7	13	31	6·7	15
1960	207	15·4	28	25	7·3	13	39	8·8	16
1961	201	14·0	24	25	6·8	13	30	6·8	13
1962	220	15·7	28	26	6·6	12	33	7·4	13

In Tanganyika sisal was grown almost entirely on alien-owned plantations, in contrast to Brazil, where it was a part-time peasant crop. Soon soaring prices encouraged the rapid development of an African peasant industry in the Lake Province where sisal was planted as boundary hedges and sold to 'non-native opportunists'.[1] Official reaction to this was wholly negative. The peasant crop, it was said, 'disrupted the normal economy of the area to the detriment of food and cotton production'[2] and its poor quality was allegedly damaging the reputation of plantation sisal in world markets. Restrictions were therefore imposed upon its sale. Nevertheless the peasant crop continued to flourish while prices were high; 6,000 tons were produced in 1950, putting about £700,000 into the poorly lined pockets of its growers. With the fall in prices after 1952 the crop reverted, to use another official phrase, 'to its rightful place as a useful reserve cash crop to which people can turn when they require money'.[3] The hazard, presumably moral, of unrequired cash now being removed, restrictions were abandoned in 1954.

Meanwhile the plantation industry flourished. Its entrepreneurs were all non-Africans of various nationalities. In 1947 out of 142 firms 52 were Indian, 40 Greek, 35 British, and the remainder under Swiss, Dutch, Lebanese, and Danish ownership. British estates produced 36 per cent of the total crop, Indians and Greeks accounted for 25 per cent and 22 per cent respectively. At a time when Uganda was making serious attempts to encourage African participation in cotton ginning, and later, retail trade and tea, Tanganyika did nothing to promote similar ends in her largest industry. The African's role was exclusively that of an unskilled labourer with no social ladder for him to climb. Only after independence was this question of African participation squarely faced, the government offering plantations more land if they needed it. 'But in return, they will be expected to help local farmers to participate, on a co-operative basis.'[4] After independence prospects for estate agriculture in general, and sisal in particular, deteriorated.[5] During the colonial period however, it was a dominant force. The sisal industry was second only to the government in its demand for wage labour,

---

[1] i.e. Indian traders. The phrase appears in J. F. R. Hill and J. P. Moffett, *Tanganyika: a review of its resources and their development* (Dar es Salaam, Govt. Printer, 1955), p. 442, and faithfully reflects official attitudes.

[2] Ibid.

[3] Department of Agriculture Annual Report, 1954, p. 7.

[4] Julius Nyerere, *Address on the Tanganyika Five Year Development Plan*, 12 May 1964 (Dar es Salaam Inform. Service, 1964), p.1.

[5] See A. R. Roe, 'The Future of the Company in Tanzanian Development', *J. Mod. Af. Studies*, 7, 1 (April 1969). Prospects worsened, not merely because of political change but as a result of growing competition from man-made fibres.

employing 120,000 workers which represented about one-third of the total number of Africans in paid employment. A large proportion of these men were temporary immigrants from Portuguese East Africa and Ruanda-Urundi,[1] where incomes and employment opportunities were even poorer than in Tanganyika. Most of them were unskilled, inefficient, and there-fore lowly paid. But wages, food, housing, and welfare benefits were, on the whole, better than in alternative employments and there was some improvement during the prosperous early 1950s. By the standards of tropical Africa industrial relations were good.[2] Considering its significance in the economy the industry's use of land was not extravagant, amounting to less than 0·5 per cent of the total land area. Even in the Tanga District where sisal was most concentrated, the 690 square miles of estates represented less than 5 per cent of total land, a significant fact for an alien plantation industry in an African country approaching indepen-dence and sensitive to land alienation. Moreover the drought-resistant nature of the crop and its modest soil requirements enabled inferior land to be utilized. The industry's capital needs, however, were considerable, by Tanganyika's standards if not by those of plantations elsewhere. The total capital invested in it was some £20 million, very little of which was raised on the open market because the dividend record of sisal companies was too poor to attract overseas investors.[3] Long-term investment was therefore dependent upon the ploughing back of profits by individual firms. This made them particularly sensitive to taxa-tion and they were extremely articulate in representing their views.

Apart from sisal the country's principal exports were coffee and cotton (Table III). It is noteworthy that before 1952 there was little significant increase in the production of either crop. Cotton did not yet attain the level of several pre-war seasons and coffee's peak output of 1952 only equalled the 1935 figure. Coffee was primarily an African peasant crop. Some 15 per cent was grown by 200 alien planters as part of their general farming, but the rest was produced by some 120,000 African farmers,

---

[1] In 1957 approximately 40 per cent were 'distance' labourers, but there were wide variations as between individual plantations.
[2] See Guillebaud, *Sisal Industry*, chap. iv.
[3] Ibid., p. 45.

typically on farms of less than one acre. In 1945 output was almost equally divided between hard (*robusta*) and mild (*arabica*) coffees. After several years of declining output caused at least in part by miserably low contract prices from the British Ministry of Food, production—particularly of *arabica*—began to expand steadily under the stimulus of higher prices. By 1960 approximately two-thirds of Tanganyika's coffee was of the more valuable *arabica* type. Its main centre of production was in the Northern Province where, on the lovely southern slopes of Kilimanjaro, flourished the largest[1] and best known co-operative society in East Africa. In 1946 the Kilimanjaro Native Co-operative Union had over 29,000 members who produced about two-thirds of the country's *arabica* coffee; by 1960 membership had increased to about 30,000. The visitor to Moshi could not fail to be impressed by the KNCU's elaborate establishment—curing works, offices, school of commerce, public library, hotel, and restaurant—and share Mrs. Stahl's enthusiasm: 'Chaggaland is a yardstick for other parts of Tanganyika. It represents the highest standard reached in economic prosperity, in local government, in social development.'[2] Later he might soberly reflect that all this activity had been financed by a people whose standard of living was still low and whose productivity poor. Despite its apparent progressiveness the KNCU did little to improve the husbandry of its members and thus develop the basis of their prosperity.[3] Yet during our period the Chagga coffee-growers were evidently one of the most prosperous groups of Africans in Tanganyika. Even while the price of their crop was restrained below world levels, average payment per grower increased from about £6 in 1964 to £34 in 1952.[4] In 1954 a record crop of 6,400 tons generated over £3 million of income

---

[1] In Sukumaland the Victorian Federation of Co-operative Unions was created in 1955 and could rival this claim. Cf. G. Andrew Maguire, *Toward 'Uhuru' in Tanzania* (London, 1969), particularly chap. iv, 'Traders, Cotton Co-operatives and Politics'.

[2] Stahl, *Sail in the Wilderness*, p. 35. Compare J. W. F. Rowe, *The World's Coffee* (London, 1963), p. 132. The burden of taxation was to be greatly increased after independence. See P. H. Gulliver (ed.), *Tradition and Transition in East Africa* (London, 1969), p. 221.

[3] For a valuable assessment of the general problems of co-operatives see *Report of the Presidential Special Committee of Inquiry into the Co-operative Movement and Marketing Boards* (Dar es Salaam, Govt. Printer, 1966).

[4] Hill and Moffett, *Tanganyika*, p. 772. See also R. J. Swynnerton and A. L. B. Bennett, *All About K.N.C.U. Coffee* (Moshi, 1948).

in the Moshi area. This relationship between coffee and the prosperity of the Chagga was well known. Less familiar, however, was the fact that their main source of cash was not coffee but bananas sold in local food markets.[1] An important implication of this was that Chagga prosperity, unlike that of most other African producers of cash crops, was not immediately dependent upon fluctuating world prices.

The main centre for the cultivation of *robusta* coffee was the Bukoba district of Lake Province where the Haya people practised inefficient methods which had changed little since the crop was first grown in the 1880s. But high prices stimulated considerable increases in production and Bukoba became one of the most highly commercialized parts of Tanganyika. The proceeds of the coffee boom were spent on stone houses with iron roofs, bicycles, piece goods, better food, education, and beer. Attempts by the Agricultural Department to improve husbandry were ineffective during the late 1950s when the political climate discouraged co-operation with alien tutors, but by 1960 the certainty of independence began to change this attitude and agricultural education was able to begin its long-delayed task of improvement.

The principal cotton-growing areas covered about 20,000 miles of the Lake Province, south of Lake Victoria. Annual production averaged only 40,000 bales, yet this was more than 80 per cent of the country's total crop. In 1952 a new peak of 71,000 bales was reached, thus belatedly introducing a trend which was to make the Lake Province, with its obvious transport advantages, a comparatively lively centre of economic growth. Over 100,000 bales were produced in 1955, and this figure was doubled by the early 1960s.[2]

Three other products are worthy of notice during this period. Hides and skins, a long-established typically 'primitive' export, were greatly improved under the relentless pressure of the Veterinary Department. By control and propaganda the traditional practice of extensive branding, ruinous to hides, was reduced and improved - methods of preparation were established. These improvements allied to a buoyant market resulted in greatly increased incomes. Despite a slow increase in the quantity,

---

[1] Makerere Coffee/Banana Survey (Unpublished), 1959.
[2] Maguire, *Toward 'Uhuru'*, p. 81.

marketed values increased eightfold between 1946 and 1952, contributing about 4 per cent of total exports. There was a similarly large increase in the export value of oilseeds. In this case export prices were high but internal prices of groundnuts and simsim were controlled at very low levels for the sake of local consumers. Since, contrary to the prevailing myth, 'economic men' did exist in Africa, the result of this policy was to divert activity towards the production of sunflower seed and castor seed for export at uncontrolled prices. Thus exports, which were negligible in 1947, had risen by 1952 to 30,000 tons valued at £1·3 million,[1] while the total value of all oilseeds and nuts was £2·5 million in that peak year. By 1960 it was over £5 million.

The most striking development among 'secondary' exports during this period was in the diamond industry, not least because a rapid increase in export values was the result of greater production rather than of a mere rise in prices. Mining, which had been moderately successful but irregular during the 1920s, almost collapsed in the 1930s. Then in 1940 Dr. J. T. Williamson, a Canadian geologist, made his spectacular discovery at Mwadui, near Shinyanga in the Lake Province. Despite wartime difficulties the output of both gem and industrial diamonds now began to increase rapidly and leaped forward in 1945, lifting the scale of production on to a completely new level which was maintained throughout the 1950s. Henceforth diamonds were fourth in the export lists, accounting for between 5 per cent and 10 per cent of total exports and contributing 15 per cent of their earnings to the government's revenue. Unfortunately output had to be limited by an agreement between the Diamond Corporation and the three Tanganyikan companies, which allowed the latter a quota of 10 per cent of the corporation's annual sales. The sudden fall in exports in 1950 and 1951 was the result of a price dispute between Dr. Williamson's firm and the corporation, but production was maintained during these years and in 1952 a record export of 332,000 carats was valued at over £4 million. By 1961 the quantity had doubled and its value increased to nearly £6 million.

The dire poverty of Tanganyika in 1945 suggests that one of the country's most urgent needs was a rapid increase in imports

[1] Department of Agriculture Annual Reports, 1950–2.

to replace depreciated capital and depleted stocks of goods, meet long-felt consumer demands, and encourage greater economic activity by providing incentives for the people to earn cash. Several years were to elapse before these desirable objectives began to be achieved. One reason for this was the world-wide shortage of manufactured goods. Further delays were imposed late in 1947 when Britain's balance of payments crisis forced[1] East African governments to classify all imports in categories evocative of that period: 'Suspended, Restricted, Programmed, and Essential'.[2] These austere restrictions lasted only a few months, but not until 1948 was there a comparatively free flow of imports, and there were much longer delays in the delivery of some supplies which were essential for development. As late as November 1953 a government spokesman answered complaints about inadequate railway services by revealing that rolling stock ordered in 1948 had not yet been delivered.[3]

The rapid increase in import values after 1947 (Table IV) cannot be accepted as an unequivocal index of increasing welfare. Allowance must be made for steeply rising prices and the poor quality of many, perhaps most, industrial products during the early post-war years. Even more serious was the distorting effect of the Groundnut Scheme. Between 1947 and 1950 the Overseas Food Corporation imported vast quantities of agricultural machinery and materials regardless of cost, which were 'mainly responsible for the adverse trade balance'.[4] Converted Sherman tanks, imported as 'agricultural machinery', but destined to rusty impotence, are scarcely to be counted among Tanganyika's reviving physical assets during the post-war decade. Although it is one of the most familiar events in Tanganyika's recent history, the Groundnut Scheme[5] was of limited relevance to the country's economic development except in this negative sense. Its conception was wholly metropolitan, untainted by Tanganyikan experience or needs. The claim has been made that it 'provided an impetus just at the right time to spark

---

[1] Leg Co Debates, 26 Aug. 1947, p. 2.
[2] Financial Secretary in Leg Co Debates, Dec. 1947, p. 21.
[3] Leg Co Debates, Nov. 1953, pp. 119–20.
[4] Hill and Moffett, Tanganyika, p. 734.
[5] The classic analysis is in S. H. Frankel, in The Economic Impact on Underdeveloped Societies (Oxford, 1953), Essay viii. See also A. Wood, The Groundnut Affair (London, 1950).

TABLE IV

FOREIGN TRADE 1945–1960

	Exports[1] £m.	Imports[2] £m.
1945	8·2	6·7
1946	8·9	8·1
1947	11·1	13·7
1948	16·2	22·2
1949	20·9	29·8
1950	24·1	27·9
1951	40·5	31·7
1952	47·4	41·9
1953	35·4	33·9
1954	37·3	37·8
1955	37·9	49·1
1956	46·9	42·2
1957	41·4	47·0
1958	44·3	42·6
1959	47·9	42·6
1960	57·1	47·0

[1] To all destinations, including Uganda and Kenya.
[2] Including imports from Uganda and Kenya.

off development and so shake Tanganyika from the quiescence to which it had been subdued for so long,'[1] but little evidence exists for this quixotic judgement. Its essential aim, from the viewpoint of British politics, was that groundnuts should be produced at the greatest possible speed. During the late 1940s Britain faced severe economic difficulties, particularly in her balance of payments. Among the various panaceas invoked was a belief that the alleged untapped wealth of Africa could provide abundant food and raw materials and could help both to save and earn scarce dollars.[2] Admittedly, the scheme was also intended to play an important role in the economic development of Tanganyika. Successive annual reports spoke of raising groundnuts to 'first place in the agricultural export list' and, as

[1] A. Kirby, 'Tanganyika Triumphant', *African Affairs*, 61, 243 (April 1962), 115.
[2] Colonial Development Corporation *Report* for 1949, p. 59. A similar brand of sentiment was popular thirty years previously, cf. W. K. Hancock, *Survey of British Commonwealth Affairs*, vol. ii, part i (London, 1942), 'Economics of Siege', pp. 94 sqq.

hopes of quick results were dampened, the scheme was even described as 'a long term development rather than a speedy way of easing a particular shortage'.[1] Profound social benefits were also invoked: 'Among the permanently employed labour an endeavour is being made to inculcate a corporate community spirit in which tribal laws are replaced by a more appropriate code of conduct.'[2] There was, at the outset, some popular appeal in England during this period of rather self-conscious idealism, in a project which promised the joint benefits of development for a poor country and more food at home, but in practice there can be little doubt that the latter aim was paramount. Hence the otherwise inexplicable decision to make the British Ministry of Food responsible for the scheme's administration, and the reckless quest for speed regardless of cost. Success, it was thought, could be achieved only by the injection of huge quantities of capital which would overcome all barriers, 'given the will'—an attitude of mind inherited from the simplicities of wartime planning, when costs and the logic of choice were perforce ignored. In all this the scheme was a child of its time, when 'winning the peace' was a popular sentiment with its implied failure to appreciate that peace-time economic problems are more complex than and demand a different approach from those of war.[3] A few years earlier John Strachey had confided to his diary, 'Thus far it has been possible to produce major collective efforts for the purpose of war alone. What could not be done if an expedition . . . could be fitted out . . . in order actually to develop Africa.'[4] Now a comparable naiveté pervaded the official report advocating the scheme: 'The same determination is called for in the execution of this project as was needed, and found, for the major operations of the war. Given this attitude, the chances of failure are remote.'[5]

The mission, headed by A. J. Wakefield, which made this report completed its investigations in nine weeks, despite the lack of adequate information on rainfall, soil, and other essential data. The fact that Kongwa, the main area of operation, was

---

[1] *Tanganyika Annual Report for 1949* (London, HMSO, 1950), p. 49.
[2] Ibid.
[3] Cf. Lord Robbins, *The Economic Problem in Peace and War* (London, 1948).
[4] Quoted in *Tropical Agriculture* (Dec. 1950).
[5] *A Plan for the Mechanized Production of Groundnuts in East and Central Africa* (Chairman, A. J. Wakefield), Cmd. 7030 (London, HMSO, 1947), p. 47.

sparsely inhabited was regarded as an advantage:[1] unhampered by the presence of men the machine would triumph. The absence of indigenous human skills and facilities for maintenance, or even of machines suitable for the work, was ignored. The keynotes of the mission's report were bigness and speed. In Tanganyika 80 units would be cultivated, each of 30,000 acres. Of course success on this scale would have required nothing less than an industrial and agrarian revolution. The failure of the early hurried investigations to appreciate this was unfortunate but explicable. It is easy, looking back, to see that the scheme courted disaster from the outset, but in the brave new world of the late 1940s there were many who welcomed its boldness. The *Economist* described it as 'the sort of economic planning that is needed to change the face of the colonial empire' and praised not only its 'vision' but 'the hard-headed practical thinking and costing which have gone into the immediate plan for producing ground-nuts'.[2] More puzzling was the later refusal of those in charge to face the facts revealed by failure, mounting costs, and belated scientific enquiry. The most likely explanation lies in the scheme's rather absurd involvement in British politics. 'Groundnuts' became a term of abuse, and the leading protagonists were so sensitive to constant political attack that all criticism was regarded as malicious and cautionary advice was difficult to accept. Grandiosity continued to be a distinctive feature. Thus a technical training centre opened in 1948 would give, it was claimed, 'technical education and training to some 10,000 Africans during the next few years'.[3] Compare this with the grand total of 240 students then receiving vocational training in all government training schools throughout the country.

When the Overseas Food Corporation's first report was published in November 1949 it was already evident that things were going badly wrong. The £23 million which the original White Paper had estimated as the scheme's total capital cost had already been spent. The auditors were 'unable to report that in our opinion proper books of accounts were kept and that we have obtained all the information and explanations which, to

[1] The local peoples, Loso and Kagutu, traditionally knew this area as '*Yisi Yanghwanu*', 'the country of perpetual dryness'.

[2] The *Economist*, 15 Mar. 1947.

[3] Overseas Food Corporation, *First Annual Report for period ended March 31st, 1949*, pp. 66–7.

the best of our knowledge and belief, were necessary for the purpose of our audit.'[1]

It had originally been intended to clear 3,210,000 acres of bush by 1953. Now the minister announced that 600,000 acres would be cleared by 1954. A year later the estimate was lowered to 250,000 acres, to be cleared by 1957 with hand labour substituted for much of the work originally planned for machines.[2] The project was not entirely abandoned, though £36 million was written off—a little less than the *total* expenditure of the Tanganyika government between 1946 and 1950. It now became 'a scheme of large scale experimental development to establish the economics of clearing and mechanised or partly mechanised agriculture under tropical conditions'.[3] £6 million was voted, and a seven-year programme was launched for this purpose and to run down the vast organization already established. The Colonial Office at last took over administration; Kongwa, which had grown from nothing into a small town, was handed back to the Tanganyika government and soon became nothing again. The 'experimental development' rapidly deteriorated and after one year the agricultural trading account presented 'a disturbing picture'.[4] Operations were again slowed down and the decision finally to abandon the mechanized production of groundnuts was taken in December 1953. The maximum export of groundnuts by the OFC in any year was 9,345 tons in 1952—over 26,000 tons had been produced in 1937 with virtually no capital investment.

The scheme's impact upon Tanganyika was almost wholly negative. It placed a great strain on transport facilities—not, of course, to ship out produce, but to import extravagant and useless materials and equipment. It distorted, as will be seen below, the pattern of communications development. It left people with a distrust of grandiose schemes which, although fundamentally sane in a poor community, was perhaps dampening to those who, in the halcyon days of 'development and welfare', might have favoured an intelligently planned 'big push' where it was clearly needed. It severely damaged Tanganyika's

[1] Ibid., pp. 66–7.
[2] *The Future of the Overseas Food Corporation*, Cmd. 8215 (London, HMSO, 1951).
[3] Ibid., p. 5.
[4] OFC *Report*, 1951–2.

already faded 'image' in the minds of potential investors. A few thousand Africans gained temporary employment: 28,000 in the peak year of 1949. A useless railway, port, and town were left as bleak reminders of the folly of this 'model failure'. Its best epitaph was the opinion of local Africans, who 'said it was like a war'.[1]

In 1953 the value of Tanganyika's exports fell abruptly by 25 per cent and they did not regain their 1952 level until 1959. The chief element in this slump was the collapse of sisal prices, which fell from the 1952 average of £137 per ton to £74 in the following year and, after further decline, remained depressed for the rest of our period. Despite the considerable increases in production shown in Table III, the value of sisal exports was for several years less than half that of the peak years, 1951 and 1952. This blow to the economy was cushioned to some extent by a rapid increase in the price of coffee, culminating in 1954. Further diversification of exports was provided by a great expansion of cotton production, mainly in the Lake Province, which increased more than threefold by the end of the decade. But Tanganyika's three main products remained vulnerable to fluctuations in world markets for primary produce, whose depressed state set severe limits to possibilities of economic growth after 1952.

What general conclusions can be reached about the growth of the economy during our period? No simple quantitative answer is acceptable since comparable estimates of national product are available only after 1954 and their interpretation is a hazardous and possibly dubious enterprise. One estimate[2] suggests that the economy grew by at least 5 per cent per annum between 1948 and 1958. A later official guess[3] is that the growth rate 'can hardly have been less' than 4·5 per cent between 1954 and 1960. Scepticism as to the value and meaning of such aggregates has already been expressed, but a few relevant figures are set out in Tables I and V. When growth rates are discussed it must be remembered that exports accounted for only about one quarter of productive activity and that, at least for the period before 1954, we know little of what was happening in the re-

[1] Leg Co *Debates*, 8 Feb. 1951, p. 163. For the later history of Kongwa, Urambo, and Nachingwea, see R. Chambers, *Settlement Schemes in Tropical Africa* (London, 1969).
[2] IBRD, *Economic Development of Tanganyika*, p. 25.
[3] *The National Accounts of Tanganyika 1960–2*, para. 231.

maining three-quarters of the economy, most of this being devoted to subsistence production, the valuation of which is arbitrary. The International Bank team guessed that it was growing at a rate of 2·5 per cent and thus reached their estimate of 5 per cent for the whole economy.

It is arguable that the economy's performance, judged even by the undemanding standards of the 1930s, was so poor up to 1948 that an annual growth rate of 5 per cent would not be particularly impressive even if it could be proved. In 1948 the export quantity index was lower than it had been in 1939 (Table v, *Series A*). Given the vastly improved world economic climate of the late 1940s and early 1950s little effort was needed thereafter to improve upon so modest a base. One of the saddest facts of the post-war period is that the response of exports to rapidly rising prices came so slowly (Table v, *Series B*), thus limiting Tanganyika's benefits from the Korean boom. Since cash income levels were particularly dependent upon export prices such inflexibility was very damaging. This was most evident in the case of sisal where, as has already been argued, market conditions were such that far more could have been sold

TABLE V

INDICES OF EXPORT GROWTH

Quantity index		Value index	Quantity index		Value index
(1935/8 = 100)			(1954 = 100)		
Series A			Series B		
1939	121	88	1948	51	37
1945	112	164	1949	67	52
1946	105	223	1950	67	65
1947	102	267	1951	73	108
1948	118	335	1952	96	127
			1953	91	93
			1954	100	100
			1955	115	100
			1956	136	124
			1957	124	109
			1958	142	115
			1959	147	125
			1960	171	151

SOURCE: East African *Quarterly Economic and Statistical Bulletin*, Dec. 1950 and June 1961.

without depressing the remarkably high prices (Table III). A significant contribution to economic growth during the later 1950s came from the great increase in cotton production, but this also was too late to benefit from high prices. Given that it was a peasant industry wholly dependent upon government initiative and encouragement, the significance of official policies is even clearer here than in the case of sisal. Perhaps a government with more drive and a firmer grasp of economic priorities would have realized the potentialities of cotton rather earlier; it had only to look to neighbouring Uganda for tutelage. Few visitors to East Africa during the 1950s could help noticing the contrast between the dynamism—or pretension—of Uganda, and the slackness—or modesty—of Tanganyika; 'nobody could believe that Dar es Salaam was the capital.'[1] Was the impression misleading?

The role of the government

Many factors contributed to the shaping of economic policy. Among the least important of these was the country's status as a United Nations Trust Territory. Except possibly on the issue of land alienation,[2] the Trusteeship Council's debates did little to influence government thinking and less to affect its actions. Education was a remarkable example of this; despite its repeated emphasis in United Nations discussions, little was done to build up an educational system which would prepare the country for independence. The number of Africans passing the School Certificate examination between 1945 and 1960 was approximately half that of Kenya and compared even less favourably with that of Uganda. Moreover half of this number were 'produced' during the last three years. Graduates were a mere handful.[3] Nor could this be excused simply in terms of inadequate resources, a reasonable defence during the 1930s,[4] for a very small proportion of the greatly increased expenditure of the 1950s was devoted to investment in man.[5] In 1960 Tanganyika had 560 doctors and 10,453 teachers for a population of over

---

[1] Mr. G. C. Kahama in Leg Co *Debates*, 11 June 1958, p. 843.

[2] See Kirilo Japhet and Earle Seaton, *The Meru Land Case* (EAPH Historical Studies, 2, Nairobi, 1967); Anton Nelson, *The Freemen of Meru* (Nairobi, 1967).

[3] Cf. G. Hunter, *Education for a Developing Region* (London, 1963), chap. i, particularly the table on p. 2.

[4] Cf. Leubuscher, *Tanganyika Territory*, pp. 82–9.

[5] See Table VII below.

9 million. But trusteeship status had one significant implication: it seemed to guarantee a measure of political stability at last. Paradoxically this was achieved only 15 years before the country's independence, but time appeared to be the one factor that was not scarce, and this belief persisted almost until the end.[1] In April 1957 the governor could say of universal suffrage, 'I can state bluntly that there is no intention whatever of introducing it, even considering it at an early date.'[2] Such attitudes profoundly influenced the government's conception of priorities, enabling it, for example, to ignore the need to educate the country's incipient masters. This lack of urgency was probably reinforced by the groundnut fiasco—'planning' and speed had apparently been discountenanced. It was further encouraged by comparative political quiescence; there was no Mau Mau crisis, no vociferous affluent articulate group like the Ganda. Above all the governor seems to have had less interest in economic than in administrative matters, and this was reflected in the balance between departments. In the absence of a Hall or Cohen, responsibility for economic policy fell chiefly upon the Treasury. Accountancy rather than economics or politics therefore tended to be paramount—'Heaven preserve us from imaginative government', said a senior civil servant to the present writer, not unaffected by happenings elsewhere in East Africa. His prayers did not go unanswered. To speak of government economic policy is therefore to imply something more positive than existed in Tanganyika during our period. But many official acts inevitably had some effect upon economic growth and welfare. Perhaps the most significant of these were the government's approach to problems of marketing and of public finance.

Reference has already been made to the damaging physical legacies of war. More serious, perhaps, was an intellectual inheritance which continued to pervade official attitudes towards agriculture and did much to impede its necessary development. This was the idea of self-sufficiency, a keystone of colonial paternalism. Attempts to control the movement, marketing, and prices of agricultural produce were not new, but during the war

---

[1] 'The feature of British colonial policy that stands out is the tranquil assumption of the long term character of colonial rule.' K. Robinson, *The Dilemmas of Trusteeship* (London, 1965), p. 7.
[2] Leg Co *Debates*, 30 Apr. 1957, p. 9.

years they were intensified and consolidated into a rigid system, the main elements of which were retained until 1953, and even in some cases until 1956. Self-sufficiency in food was regarded as 'a major objective of Government policy'[1] and was defined not merely in terms of the country, but of the province and even the district. No reliance was placed upon the market's ability to stimulate food production and adjust supplies to demand for, it was believed, 'no matter what the price [native] production will remain about the same.' Some added the dubious proposition that a higher price might even lead Africans to produce less.[2] Therefore as an insurance against famine, peasants were ordered to grow certain staple foods, such as cassava, despite their unattractiveness both as subsistence and cash crops. In practice, however, 'far from being handicapped by the absence of economic man . . . the agricultural authorities were embarrassed by his presence.'[3] They complained that the 'peasant has become increasingly money-conscious and has been developing the idea that if you have money you cannot be short of food.'[4] Instead of encouraging such market-consciousness and the enlargement of the exchange economy for which it was an essential prerequisite, the authorities reacted by restrictions on the movements of crops which 'fasten upon the producer the strait-jacket of subsistence production'.[5] He could rely upon the market neither to supply food when he wished to buy, nor to act as an outlet and stimulus for him to produce for sale. Far from preventing famine this policy added to the environmental difficulties which were responsible for its continuance. Fortunately, and rarely for Tanganyika, nature was kind. A series of good harvests temporarily removed the spectre of famine and, allied with the ineffectiveness of controls and with the Royal Commission's swingeing attack upon the basic philosophy,[6] led eventually to deviations from the government's policy. By the late 1950s some district commissioners, trying to operate in that climate of ambivalence

[1] Hill and Moffett, *Tanganyika*, p. 547.

[2] Leg Co *Debates*, 25 July 1946, p. 221. Economists will recognize the 'backward sloping curve of labour'. See E. J. Berg, 'Backward Sloping Labor Supply Functions in Dual Economies: the Africa case,' *Quarterly Journal of Economics*, 75, 3 (Aug. 1961).

[3] W. O. Jones, 'Economic Man in Africa', *Food Research Institute Studies*, 1, 2 (Stanford, May 1960).

[4] Department of Agriculture Annual Report, 1950, p. 155.

[5] East Africa Royal Commission *Report* (Cmd. 9475), p. 66.

[6] Ibid., particularly chaps. v and vii.

so typical of paternalist societies, were uncertain what was and was not permitted,[1] but in its essentials the government's marketing policy had been abandoned, after failing to give much technical benefit to agriculture and, almost certainly, hindering its commercialization.

The approach to public finance was similarly negative. This may seem a curious verdict when measured against the superficially impressive figures of revenue and expenditure in Tables VI and VII. But the shopping list, though eventually extensive, was ill-considered, and the smallness of the public purse was

TABLE VI

GOVERNMENT REVENUE

	Revenue† £m.	Import duties %	Income tax %	Native house and poll tax %	Export duties %	Development plan UK & foreign grants £m.
1938	2·1	34	—	32	—	—
1945	4·8	21	10	15	—	—
1946	5·1	25	13	15	—	—
1947	5·8	32	10	14	1	0·1
1948	6·7	40	10	13	1	0·3
1949	8·6	37	13	11	1	0·6
1950	10·4	29	18	9	7	1·1
1951	11·9	30	17	9	12	1·2
1952	16·4	26	24	9	8	1·0
1953	14·5	29	29	12	<1	1·1
1954 Jan/June	9·1	21	33	13	<1	0·4
1954/5	19·1	25	24	10	3	0·8
1955/6	18·3	30	25	8	<1	0·7
1956/7	17·5	29	23	7	<1	0·9
1957/8	18·8	28	22	7	<1	0·9
1958/9	19·4	34	18	7	<1	1·3
1959/60	22·1	35	17	6	<1	1·4
1960/1	21·4					
1961/2	21·9					

† Excluding transfers from reserves and grants for development from UK, etc.

[1] Ian Livingstone, 'The Marketing of Crops in Uganda and Tanganyika', in *African Primary Products and International Trade* (Edinburgh, 1965). This, and the article by Professor Jones quoted above, provide a close analysis of policies whose rationale and damaging effects are still inadequately understood.

accepted with a strange acquiescence. In contrast to those of several other countries[1] the Tanganyika government did little to swell its coffers and, for most of our period, its demands were modest. By 1954 revenue amounted to some 24 per cent of monetary gross domestic product, or 17 per cent of GDP (i.e. including subsistence production). By 1960 the proportion of monetary product was approximately the same, while that of GDP had *fallen* to roughly 14 per cent; a 'normal' for such an economy would be about 21 per cent.[2] Increasing government revenue was therefore essentially a mere concomitant of economic growth (Table VI). Despite the various curbs upon imports already described, duties upon them continued to be the principal source of funds, making up some 30 per cent of the total. In this respect there was little change from the pre-war structure of public finance. But inflation and fixed rates had led to a marked decline in the proportional contribution of direct taxes upon Africans which, before the war, had never accounted for less than 30 per cent of total revenue. But now they fell from 15 per cent to 9 per cent by 1952, in spite of attempts to adjust them to taxable capacity. Taxes were adapted to conjectural incomes by levying different rates upon districts according to their widely varying levels of development or wealth. Thus in 1949 the lowest annual rate was Sh. 7/50 in part of the Chunya district of the Southern Highlands: Sh 15/- was paid in Tanga, in parts of Bukoba and, curiously, in Masai, where wealth in cattle, rather than development, was the criterion. Clearly this method of graduation was crude[3] and as independence approached and African cash incomes slowly increased, the case for a thorough reform of the tax system became increasingly strong but, for administrative and political reasons, difficult to achieve.[4]

[1] Cf. U. K. Hicks, 'The Search for Revenue in Underdeveloped Countries', in *Revue de science et de legislation financière* (Paris, Mar. 1952).

[2] Our estimates are based on figures in Table V and VI. For the analysis on which this argument depends, see H. H. Hinrichs, 'Determinants of Government Revenue Shares among Less Developed Countries', *Economic Journal*, 65,299 (Sept. 1965); and G. K. Helleiner, 'Agricultural Export Pricing Strategy in Tanzania', *East African Journal of Rural Development*, 1, 1 (January 1968).

[3] The desirability of greater differentiation had been much discussed during the 1930s. See Leubuscher, *Tanganyika Territory*, p. 135.

[4] See J. F. Due, 'The Reform of East African Taxation', *East African Economics Review*, 6 (1964); D. P. Ghai, *Towards Tax Reform in East Africa*, EDRP No. 43 (Makerere University College, 1964); and E. Lee, *Local Taxation in Tanzania* (Institute of Public Administration, Dar es Salaam, 1965).

The most remarkable increase was in the revenue from income tax,[1] first introduced in 1940. Falling upon companies and the few individuals who enjoyed high incomes, this was almost entirely paid by non-Africans[2] and was inevitably opposed by its aggrieved and highly articulate subscribers.[3] Criticism took two forms: that the burden of taxation was unequally shared by the races, and that it deterred investment. The former argument is inconclusive. A small group of people did indeed pay a large proportion of direct tax revenue throughout our period: in 1958, according to the Minister of Finance, 124,000 non-Africans contributed more cash than 8·5 million Africans.[4] But it could be argued that this was an easy burden for so privileged an élite, while the mass of Africans contributed not primarily through direct taxation but indirectly as consumers of severely taxed imports. Well over half the revenue from import duties was paid on consumer necessities and only in 1949 was a 10 per cent surcharge removed which had affected cotton-piece goods, kerosene, and bicycles. A real weakness of the income tax system, from the standpoint of equity, was the fact that as incomes and profits rose during these years an increasing burden fell upon individuals rather than companies because the company rate was proportional and not progressive.[5] The role of taxation as a barrier to enterprise and investment was much argued and almost certainly exaggerated,[6] particularly in so far as it was alleged to affect public companies. More serious, perhaps, was the effect on small firms, by far the most prevalent form of business organization, which were liable to the heavier incidence of taxation as individuals rather than as companies.

Also new were the export taxes which were reluctantly[7] introduced in 1946. Initially these were imposed upon beeswax,

---

[1] Far more rapid than in Kenya and Uganda, because, among other reasons, collection was comparatively easy.

[2] African exemption from its incidence, however, was a result of poverty, not as in Uganda of political accident.

[3] In marked contrast to the much more heavily taxed but inarticulate African cash crop producers of Uganda.

[4] Leg Co Debates, 10 June 1958, pp. 781–2.

[5] Report of the East African Commission of Inquiry on Income Tax, 1956–1957 (Nairobi, East Africa High Commission, 1957), p. 17.

[6] These arguments are discussed ibid., pp. 15–22.

[7] 'Export duties are bad in principle', Revenue Committee Report, 28 Feb. 1946, para. 22.

Lake Province coffee, and hides and skins, all of which were enjoying steeply rising prices. Revenue was small but the taxes were by no means negligible to those who paid them; thus in 1947 approximately £78,000 was collected on exports worth a little over £1 million. In 1949 these taxes were extended to several coconut products with the intention not of raising revenue, but of maintaining controlled internal prices in the face of rising export prices. Only between 1950 and 1952 did export taxes, mainly on sisal and cotton, make a significant contribution to revenue, in marked contrast to their vital role in Uganda. For most of our period the taxation of agriculture was extremely modest: it has been argued that in 1960 'on balance there was probably a subsidy.' By the mid-1960s agriculture was to yield over £5 million in government revenue.[1]

It is commonly said that in most of British Africa the post-war decade of 'colonial development and welfare' was a period of transformation in the range and impact of government economic activity. But we should neither antedate nor exaggerate this change—a matter of some importance when considering so short a period. In Tanganyika public expenditure increased slowly for several years, gathered pace in 1949, and continued to grow after the end of the export and revenue boom in 1952 (Table 1). A 'development plan' for the period 1947–56 envisaged the expenditure of £18 million in addition to normal annual budgets. In 1950, after some £3 million had been spent, this target was raised to £24·5 million. Much of the capital was to come from overseas. About £6,250,000 was given by the United Kingdom government under the Colonial Development and Welfare Scheme, another half million came from the United States as Marshall Aid; and £9·5 million was borrowed. Some internal reserves were available, including a £2·5 million Agricultural Development Fund, amassed from wartime profits on cotton and coffee sales, and nearly £500,000 from an excess profits tax. The remainder was to be raised from current resources. Many difficulties arose from the government's failure to predict how long the boom in export prices and therefore in revenue would last. Seen with the facile wisdom of hindsight the first development plan and the budgets of the late 1940s look timid. Revenue was consistently underestimated and expendi-

[1] Helleiner, 'Export Pricing Strategy', loc. cit., pp. 4–5.

ture therefore curbed. In 1945 the Financial Secretary had every excuse for saying 'we are spending up to the hilt and must not, in common prudence, assume further recurrent commitments until new sources of revenue became available to us.'[1] But by November 1948 it was perhaps unduly Gladstonian for his successor to urge caution because of his 'belief that revenue is near its peak and that no marked increase should be anticipated in the near future.'[2] A year later he admitted error and forecast 'with modest confidence' that revenue in 1950 would amount to some £7·6 million[3]—nearly £3 million less than the ultimate figure. Similarly inadequate forecasting is of course common in advanced economies, particularly when world conditions are unstable. Given their inadequate statistical services and changing economic and fiscal structure, it would therefore be unfair to castigate the Tanganyikan authorities for delay in appreciating the need and opportunity for more adventurous budgeting. Nevertheless the results of such timidity cannot be ignored; indeed the World Bank Commission regarded them as a 'lesson of recent budgetary history': 'Underestimation of prospective finances may lead to unnecessary restriction of public activities, thus holding back the rate of development of the economy and hence the future increase of public revenues.'[4]

This argument has some force as a guide to the future, but as an interpretation of the past it overlooks a significant fact. Even if the continued rise in revenue could have been foreseen, expenditure would have been delayed for a few years by physical shortages of men and materials outside the government's control. In this sense therefore some delay in the expansion of public activities was probably inevitable.

But the available evidence does suggest that over the longer period the government was unduly and persistently negative in its approach to the economy. 'I want to stress this point,' said the Financial Secretary introducing his feeble 1948 budget, 'it is the prospective drop in imports and nothing else, that is responsible for this very uninspiring budget.'[5] By lack of inspiration he meant a mere inability to reduce taxation, rather than a

[1] Leg Co *Debates*, 3 Dec. 1945, p. 17.
[2] Leg Co *Debates*, 2 Nov. 1948, p. 12.
[3] Leg Co *Debates*, 23 Nov. 1949, p. 28.
[4] IBRD, *Economic Development of Tanganyika*, p. 47.
[5] Leg Co *Debates*, 1 Dec. 1947, p. 21,

failure to accept greater responsibility for promoting economic growth. Such timidity had strong historical roots. In 1932 a visiting commissioner had severely criticized the government for attempting to build up far too costly a system of administration and social services.[1] The impact of this report was inevitably great at a time of world-wide economic retrenchment. But as international markets improved, German colonial ambitions and British appeasement of Hitler had presented a serious threat to Tanganyika's political future.[2] Despite growing prosperity therefore economic policy had remained 'far more cautious than it had been between 1925 and 1930'.[3] Finally, any possible resurgence of optimism had been cut short by another financial crisis in 1938. By 1945 the austere habits of more than a decade were not to be lightly discarded.

Available statistics do not allow precision about the ultimate allocation of public expenditure. But it is clear that, at least until 1954, the government preferred 'economic' to 'social' projects which 'do not immediately show a productive return'.[4] An obvious effect of this policy was to delay progress in education and public health, despite mounting criticism in United Nations debates.[5] Here we must beware of anachronism. Emphasis upon 'investment in man' as an essential prerequisite for economic growth was not yet fashionable, and in neglecting social expenditure the authorities reflected the prevailing conventional wisdom. Later the wheel was to swing full circle.[6] Meanwhile a strategy of quick returns appeared sensible in a country where capital was scarce and costly. But the strange fact is that practice was at odds with alleged policy. By far the greatest emphasis was given to the improvement of communications which dominated the 'development plan' and made increasingly heavy demands upon current expenditure. (Table VII). For this type of investment the gestation period was inevitably long—in some cases infinite.

    [1] Sir Sydney Armitage Smith, *Report... on a Financial Mission to Tanganyika*, Cmd. 4182 (London, HMSO, 1932). See pp. 600–1 in the second volume of this *History*.
    [2] J. Listowel, *The Making of Tanganyika* (London, 1965), pp. 117–19.
    [3] Leubuscher, *Tanganyika Territory*, p. 132.
    [4] Tanyanyika *Annual Report* for 1950, p. 191.
    [5] See B. T. G. Chidzero, *Tanganyika and International Trusteeship* (London, 1961), particularly chap. vi.
    [6] A provocative but sensible guide to this changing field is to be found in Guy Hunter, *The Best of Both Worlds* (London, 1967), particularly chap. v.

TABLE VII

GOVERNMENT EXPENDITURE ('DEVELOPMENT' AND CURRENT) ON
CERTAIN ECONOMIC AND SOCIAL SECTORS

	Total expenditure £m.	Roads & bridges £m.	Agriculture & veterinary services £m.	Water dept. £m.	Medical & public health £m.	Education £m.
1947	5·7	0·2	0·3	0·1	0·4	0·3
1948	6·8	0·3	0·5	0·1	0·5	0·4
1949	8·7	0·4	0·7	0·2	0·6	0·9
1950	11·6	1·4	0·8	0·2	0·7	1·0
1951	14·6	1·5	0·9	0·2	1·0	1·2
1952	18·3	2·2	0·8	0·3	1·1	1·5
1953	18·0	2·1	0·9	0·3	1·2	2·0
Jan/June '54	9·1	0·9	0·5	0·2	0·6	1·0
1954/5	19·8	1·9	0·9	0·6	1·4	2·8
1955/6	22·6	1·9	1·0	0·8	1·9	3·3
1956/7	23·1	1·8	1·2	0·9	2·1	3·9
1957/8	24·1	1·8	1·2	0·9	2·0	4·3
1958/9	24·7	1·8	1·1	1·1	2·0	4·4

[See however cautionary note in Appendix 3, p. 598 below].

The problems of transport were almost overwhelming. In a vast backward region with scattered centres of population and economic activity the density of traffic was inevitably low. Such conditions had long impeded the development of the railway system. In 1932 it was argued that only a major gold discovery could justify further railway construction. Existing communications were obviously inadequate, but Tanganyika could not afford more railways and 'must rely for the future on motor transport to open up new areas'.[1] Later experience appeared to confirm the wisdom of this judgement. In 1934 a branch of the central line was opened between Manyoni and Kinyangiri. It was a hopeless failure and was abandoned after the war. By 1945 the railway system was not much better than in German days. It consisted of two quite separate parts. The Northern Line ran for 272 miles from Tanga to Moshi and Arusha, and the 1,104 miles of the Central Line connected Dar es Salaam with the lake ports of Mwanza and Kigoma. The system was little used; indeed few railways in the world had to operate on so meagre a

[1] Armitage Smith, *Financial Mission to Tanganyika* (Cmd. 4182), p. 85.

traffic.[1] The boom in exports after the war inevitably led to some improvement. On the Central Line goods traffic approximately doubled between 1945 and 1950 and had doubled again by 1956. On the Northern Line growth was less spectacular but still significant. Nevertheless there is little evidence in the economic history of Tanganyika of a successful interaction between railway construction and economic growth. Between 1947 and 1950 the track built in 1934 and later abandoned was used to construct a new branch of the Central Line from Kaluwa to Mpanda where lead was being mined. In itself it appeared to be a viable project, attracting a loan of over $1·5 million, but in due course it was discovered that the lead deposit was smaller than had been estimated and in 1960 the mine was closed. Meanwhile the railway ran for 131 miles through dense bush-country infested with tsetse fly, and its impact upon agriculture development was therefore confined to the immediate locality of Mpanda. By 1957 the line was still being run at a loss and once more its removal was canvassed.[2] In 1961 it was used to move out the mine's equipment thus completing an unhappy cycle of non-development.

Two railway projects were undertaken as part of the Groundnut Scheme. A short branch was built from the central line at Msagali to Kongwa in 1947 and later to Hogoro. The latter was abandoned in 1951, the former in 1956. A more expensive operation was the construction of the Southern Province Railway from the new port of Mtwara to Nachingwea. The inevitable risks and difficulties of railway construction were exacerbated by the importunate demands of the Overseas Food Corporation. With frantic haste under conditions of post-war scarcity, second-hand rolling stock of dubious quality and appropriateness was imported from India, Malaya, and the Middle East. A more inept approach to railway development could hardly be imagined. By the time the Southern Province Railway was completed the Groundnut Scheme had collapsed, but great results were still expected from improved transport: 'In economic potential the southern railway dominates every other project in Southern Province.'[3] 121,000 tons of freight were anticipated by

---

[1] J. R. Farquharson, *Tanganyika Transport: a review* (Dar es Salaam, Govt. Printer, 1945).

[2] Leg Co *Debates*, 1 May 1957, p. 43.

[3] *A Review of Development Plans in Southern Province, 1953* (Dar es Salaam, Govt. Printer, 1954), p. 41.

1956; 242,000 tons by 1960. In fact the figures fell steadily from 32,000 to 25,000 in those years and to 21,000 tons in 1961, when the line's revenue was £45,000 and expenditure £290,000. It was closed in June 1962.

The government's greatest effort was concentrated on roads, but again economic geography presented insuperable barriers. The need for an adequate road-system was hardly open to doubt; its desirability and potential benefits were later argued with some eloquence by the East Africa Royal Commission:

The present condition of the roads is . . . especially in the African areas, a main cause of the high cost of food, of the recurrence of famines, of the relatively slow rate of expansion in the volume of agricultural production, of the persistence of subsistence economies, and of unduly high cost of road transport due to excessive wear and tear on the vehicles in use. . . . The construction of a proper system of roads is, in a modern state, not merely a question of serving the convenience of the inhabitants but of providing the very arteries of economic expansion.[1]

But the provision of an adequate road system was a task beyond the resources of Tanganyika's government. In 1931 £400 a mile had been quoted as a reasonable estimate for 'good metalled roads'.[2] By 1946 standards and costs had risen and the estimate in the Development Plan of that year of £2,500 a mile for bitumenized roads was increased four-fold by 1950. Between 1950 and 1955 the government concentrated on building first-class roads whose cost per mile rose to an average of £18,000: 240 miles were built before standards and costs were lowered,[3] but the provision of main roads remained a primary concern. It was not until the end of our period that the government chose instead to encourage the improvement and expansion of feeder roads at much lower unit costs.[4]

Objective appraisal of this policy of road building is difficult. Soaring costs might imply some technical or administrative incompetence on the part of the authorities and their contractors,

---

[1] Cmd. 9475, pp. 133–4.
[2] Armitage Smith, *Report* (Cmd. 4182), p. 85.
[3] *Handbook of Tanganyika*, ed. J. P. Moffett (Dar es Salaam, 1958), p. 348.
[4] For estimates of road costs in the mid-1960s see Tanganyika *Five Year Plan for Economic and Social Development* (Dar es Salaam, Govt. Printer, 1964) vol. ii, Chap. vi.

but the technical problems of constructing anything more permanent than a gravel road were intractable and little explored.[1]
Local materials were often inadequate and imported substitutes
costly, not least because inland transport was so poor. Quality
standards were probably too ambitious, particularly during the
early 1950s, yet it could be argued that traffic densities did, on
the whole, justify the insistence upon bitumenized surfaces.[2]
Clearly by 1960, despite the establishment of main highways, a
satisfactory road *network* still did not exist. Measured in terms
of road miles per square mile of land, Tanganyika's system
remained one of the poorest in Africa, little more than half that
of Uganda.[3] In terms of potential economic effect the result was
even less impressive. Only an integrated system could have
helped to open up the economy, but feeder roads had been
neglected, and without them main highways could pass close to
settlements yet leave them uninfluenced by market forces,
particularly during the rainy season. Granted the immense
geographical difficulties, the government's policy would still
appear to have achieved a poor return for the expenditure set
out in Table VII. The World Bank Report took a more favourable view. Admitting that feeders were neglected, it believed
nevertheless, that

this was the right policy to start with. A feeder road could serve
little purpose until the main road could take up its traffic. The
alternative of providing a complete system of main and feeder roads,
area by area, would have prejudiced the economic development of
important areas of the territory, and would have severely hampered
administration.[4]

This argument appears to be based upon a 'balanced growth'
view of economic policy which is by no means universally upheld
but has far-reaching implications in a country as poor and large
as Tanganyika. It is a commonplace that planning in the public
sector should be related to resources and development in the

---

[1] Cf. E. K. Hawkins, *Roads and Road Transport in an Under-developed Country: a
case study of Uganda* (London, HMSO, 1962), chap. ix, 'The Economics of Roads'.

[2] Hawkins quotes a 'rule of thumb' that gravel roads become too difficult to
maintain when traffic exceeds 300 vehicles per day (ibid , p. 154). Most main roads
exceeded this figure by 1960.

[3] Ibid., Table 2, p. 23.

[4] IBRD, *Economic Development of Tanganyika*, p. 277.

private sector. Dealing with a large, backward, but hetero-geneous area, it might have been wise for the government to concentrate upon existing 'islands of economic activity'. By attempting to spread its limited resources over a vast territory the Tanganyika government, buying experience and knowledge at great cost, provided transport facilities which were under-utilized in backward areas yet inadequate for developing areas.

By 1960 the country found itself with an infrastructure im-proved yet incomplete and expensive to maintain. It was, perhaps, victim of the philosophy characterized by an American economist as 'belief in the propitiatory powers of social overhead capital'—a belief akin to the 'cargo cults' of New Guinea.[1] The mere creation of physical capital is no guarantee of economic growth; what matters is its relevance and use. Indeed Tan-ganyika had, in the Groundnut Scheme, ample and costly evidence that inappropriate investment could actually slow down the progress of the economy.[2] Such arguments may be regarded as tendentious. Perhaps the period is too recent and our understanding of economic growth too primitive for definitive analysis. But the World Bank's favourable view is not beyond dispute and different conclusions could have useful implications for future policy. Certainly the allotment of funds among various economic projects during the 1950s gave extraordinary emphasis to transport without much improvement to com-munications. Complaints continued, and in 1958 a harassed minister was moved to declare that 'even to bring our terri-torial grid up to a tolerable standard—that is far from tarmac all the way—would on our present allocation of money take something like 50 years.'[3]

Such results were achieved at great cost to alternative eco-nomic projects (Table VII) quite apart from their crippling effect in the broader field of social policy. Irrigation and flood control, both fundamental requirements, limped along until the last years of British rule, and were emphasised as future needs by the World Bank.[4] Expenditure on roads far exceeded total

[1] A. O. Hirschmann, *The Strategy of Economic Development* (New Haven, 1958), p. 94.
[2] A. K. Cairncross, *Factors in Economic Development* (London, 1962), p. 43.
[3] Leg Co *Debates*, 13 June 1958, p. 898.
[4] IBRD, *Economic Development of Tanganyika*, chap. viii.

expenditure on *all* agricultural and veterinary services, a distortion which is probably the most surprising aspect of these policies and is difficult to justify. One reason, perhaps, is that 'development' was assumed to entail only expenditure on physical capital, and never on services, an example of maladroit bookkeeping economics.[1] Another possible cause is that agricultural extension activities became increasingly difficult as independence approached. A violent controversy in 1957 over a cattle-dipping scheme in Iringa which ended in the closing of a TANU branch is one example of this.[2] The peasant's ingrained distrust of new attitudes, ideas, and techniques, strengthened by the inevitable polemics of nationalism, had now created in many areas an almost impossible environment for agricultural improvement.[3] But agricultural extension was assisted neither by adequate funds, nor always by sensible administration; a peculiar weakness of the system was that extension workers were expected to report those who disobeyed the rules, thus jeopardizing any friendly relationship between advisers and advised. By 1958 attempts to regulate land use and enforce good husbandry were meeting with so much opposition that many rules were actually repealed. Even in areas where some progress had been made, 'the people ceased for the time being to carry them out and exhibited a widespread reluctance, even in the absence of sanctions, to listen to any advice offered by the extension staff.'[4]

The general theme of this chapter has been that Tanganyika's economic achievement was not impressive, and that this was due not merely to a harsh environment but also to a fundamental lack of driving force. A developing economy requires powerful motors. These can be provided by an intelligent and fortunate

[1] Comprehensive development planning was not attempted until after independence. See P. G. Clark, *Development Planning in East Africa* (East African Studies No. 21, Nairobi, 1965); and P. Robson and D. Lury, *The Economies of Africa* (London, 1969), pp. 350–73.

[2] See Leg Co *Debates*, 11 Dec. 1957, pp. 280 sqq. Cf. an unpublished paper by Lionel Cliffe, 'Nationalism and the Reaction to Enforced Agricultural Improvement in Tanganyika during the Colonial Period', in *Socialism in Tanzania*, ed. L. Cliffe and J. Saul (Dar es Salaam, 1973).

[3] See P. H. Gulliver, *Land Tenure and Social Change among the Nyakyusa* (Kampala, 1958), particularly pp. 42–6.

[4] IBRD, *Economic Development of Tanganyika*, p. 107.

combination of market forces, capable entrepreneurs, and determined appropriate government policies. In Tanganyika no motor was sufficiently powerful or sustained. Foreign trade, after a long period of quiescence, began to exert some pressure as an engine of growth in the late 1940s. But Tanganyika, unlike Uganda, enjoyed only a short boom whose impact was muted both by the structure of agriculture, where plantations were still dominant, and by inept policies. Meanwhile the government motor started up, but despite considerable drive after Twining's arrival,[1] its meagre power was dissipated over too wide a geographical area and concentrated upon too narrow a range of economic activity. Moreover the authority of those in charge of its controls was being constantly eroded by political change without their successors yet taking command.

What of the people's welfare? If we ask whether their standard of living was higher in 1960 than in 1945, the answer is undoubtedly yes. But this says little, for in 1945 they were perhaps worse off than at any time since 1918. A delegation from the United Nations which visited Tanganyika in 1945 alleged that they saw 'a subsistence economy, not far removed for some hundreds of thousands, if not millions, of people from mere existence.'[2] This was unequivocally dismissed by Peacock and Dosser as 'rather absurd. To suggest that millions of Africans in Tanganyika are on a starvation diet is a travesty of the truth.'[3] But the sunny evocation by many Europeans of 'God's own country' was equally misleading.

Generalizations about a people's standard of living are notoriously unreliable, and attempts at its measurement often imply a precision which is spurious, particularly in poor countries where much subsistence activity persists. It is fashionable, for example, to group together 'developing economies' with low national income and imply that they offer similar living standards:[4] but few Tanganyikans would benefit by changing places with a Bengal peasant. Nevertheless, by any standards of

---

[1] Twining was the first governor of Tanganyika to visit every one of its districts.

[2] UN Trusteeship Council, *Report of the UN Visiting Mission to Trust Territories in East Africa, 1954, on Tanganyika*, p. 231.

[3] Peacock and Dosser, *National Income of Tanganyika*, p. 50.

[4] For a simple but sceptical approach to quantitative assessment see H. Myint, *The Economics of the Developing Countries* (London, 1964), particularly chap. i.

measurement available to us, Tanganyika remained at independence one of the poorest countries in tropical Africa. Estimated at £21 a year, its gross domestic product per head was one quarter of that of Ghana. Very few people were fully engaged in the money economy, and even they rarely earned more than £100 a year. For most other Tanganyikans cash incomes were probably in the range of £10 to £20 a year.[1] Mortality rates, in so far as they were known, were high even in the few areas of comparative prosperity: an infant mortality of perhaps 220 per thousand in the Western Province, as against 150 among the Chagga.[2] For most people diet was poorly balanced and remained ultimately dependent upon the 'niggardliness of nature'; seasonal local famines, an infallible indicator of economic backwardness, remained a threat. Regional disparities continued and were even probably increased during our period. The expansion of cash transactions, when and where it occurred, was both cause and effect of such improvements as took place. Thus during the coffee boom, the Haya of Bukoba 'put their profits into stone-built houses with corrugated iron roofs, bicycles and greater purchases of piece goods . . . larger purchases of meat, fish, sugar, etc. became customary, and bottled beer began to be imported. More money was also spent on education.'[3]

But such bouts of prosperity were short-lived and were enjoyed by a small proportion, almost certainly less than 10 per cent, of the population. For the rest life, whatever its quality, was certainly short, its expectancy being estimated at something between 35 and 40 years. Medical and educational facilities were minimal—one doctor per 16,000 people, 2 per cent of the school-age population at secondary school. Such achievements were poor, even by the standards of colonial Africa. With this inheritance a new leadership faced in 1961 the unenviable task of creating 'the basis of a healthy, educated, and prosperous people.'[4]

---

[1] Tanganyika Government Central Statistical Bureau, *Village Economic Surveys 1961/62* (Dar es Salaam, 1963).

[2] Smith and Blacker, *Population Characteristics of Tropical Africa*, p. 69.

[3] Rowe, *The World's Coffee*, p. 143.

[4] Nyerere, *Address on the Five Year Development Plan*, 12 May 1964.

VIII

ECONOMIC LINKS IN EAST AFRICA FROM 1945 TO INDEPENDENCE

WALTER ELKAN and LESLIE NULTY

GEOGRAPHICAL contiguity and the fact that all three East African territories were under British rule made close economic relations between Kenya, Uganda, and Tanganyika natural. This chapter begins by describing some of these links, and how they came into being, and then goes on to examine why Tanganyika and Uganda in particular became increasingly dissatisfied during the 1950s with the way in which the links were operating. Both Uganda and Tanganyika felt that the East African common market and the various East African institutions were operating more to the advantage of Kenya. Uganda was more concerned than Tanganyika because even though her economic links with Kenya were exactly analogous to Tanganyika's, it was Uganda which was land-locked by Kenya and therefore critically dependent upon Kenya's port and entrepôt position.

Background

At the end of the Second World War the three territories were associated with one another in a number of ways. In the first place they constituted a common market. There were no internal tariff barriers either on imported or locally produced goods, and there was free movement of capital and labour within East Africa. They also had a common external tariff, 'revenue-raising' rather than protective in intent. Some of the import duties were nevertheless protective in effect, and as early as the 1920s had been the subject of frequent disputes between the Kenyan and the other two governments, which felt they protected European-produced goods in Kenya, at the expense more particularly of African consumers, in all three of the territories.

Although the common market was perhaps the most important link between the three countries, it was largely the result of a pursuit of common policies and was not based on a treaty. There were, indeed, a series of agreements, but there was no institutional framework within which policies were agreed. Although each territory was free to fix or vary its own rates of import duty, as also of excise and income tax, there was in fact little divergence, if only because this would have at once led to attempts by businesses to rearrange their affairs so as to ensure that only the lowest rate was paid. Since these three forms of taxation constituted between them about three-quarters of the public revenue of East Africa as a whole, this policy of 'fiscal harmonization' constituted both an important element in the common market's structure and a serious limitation (albeit voluntarily imposed) on each territory's freedom of action. At no time did any one of the three territories alter its tax rates without first consulting the other two.[1] The foundations of the common market had been laid in 1917 when free trade between Uganda and Kenya had been established and at the same time the customs authorities of the two territories had been amalgamated. Tanganyika had become part of the common market by stages; a common external tariff had been adopted in 1922, free interchange of products with Kenya and Uganda was inaugurated in 1923, and free transfer of imported goods had followed in 1927.[2]

The second form of association was the common currency and the common participation in the East African Currency Board. The currency-board system was intended to provide absolute international acceptability to colonial currencies by making them freely convertible into sterling at par. Stability was to be maintained by having the currency backed pound for pound by sterling assets held in London. There were no restrictions whatever upon the movement of money and since, in addition, the commercial banks were all (with one exception) subsidiaries of British banks, the whole system could be viewed as in a sense part of the British banking system, with its apex in the Bank of England rather than in East Africa.

---

[1] See chapter by P. Robson and J. F. Due in Carl S. Shoup (ed.), *Fiscal Harmonization in Common Markets* (New York, 1967); also Peter Robson, *Economic Integration in Africa* (London, 1968), pp. 107 sqq.

[2] For a summary of this background, see *Report of the Economic and Fiscal Commission*, Chairman Sir Jeremy Raisman, Cmnd. 1279 (London, HMSO, 1961), p. 7.

Thirdly, the three territories shared a number of common services which came to be administered after the Second World War by the newly created East Africa High Commission.[1] Before the High Commission came into operation in 1948, policy decisions concerning common matters had been taken at a Conference of Governors of British East Africa which since 1926 had met formally about once a year but which was served by a small permanent secretariat. In 1947 it was decided to provide for the establishment or expansion of jointly financed and operated services and to give these common services a constitutional basis by a setting up of the East Africa High Commission which was to be responsible to another newly established body, the East African Central Legislative Assembly.[2] The High Commission was to be served by a permanent secretariat in Nairobi.

The services which it came to administer were often classified into two categories according to whether or not they were 'self-contained', that is, financed or not from their own revenue. Thus, the principal self-contained services after 1948 were the East African Railways and Harbours—which for the first time administered the Tanganyika system jointly with that of Kenya and Uganda—and the East African Posts and Telecommunications Administration. Later, East African Airways was added to the list, and although it was not officially classified as a self-contained service under the High Commission it was to be operated on similar lines: the High Commission was to be responsible for financing capital expenditure, or at any rate their permission was required to raise loans abroad, whilst all recurrent expenditure was to be covered by current revenue.

The 'non-self-contained' services administered the collection of customs and excise duties and income tax, and provided a number of agricultural, medical, and other research services, including meteorological research. The current cost of these

[1] *Inter-territorial organization in East Africa*, Sessional Paper, Col. 191 of 1945 (London, HMSO, 1945); *Revised Proposals*, Sessional Paper, Col. 210 of 1947 (London, HMSO, 1947). For the political background of these proposals, see chap. ii above.

[2] For a good description of the transition from the Governors' Conference to the formation of the East Africa High Commission see Jane Banfield, 'The Structure and Administration of the East African Common Services Organization', in C. Leys and P. Robson (edd.), *Federation in East Africa* (Nairobi, 1965).

services rose from about £1·6 million in 1948 to £4·75 million in 1960/1 and in the latter year constituted about 5 per cent of the combined recurrent expenditures of the three governments. One weakness of the High Commission was that it had no independent source of revenue. The greater part of its finance came to it in the form of allocations voted by each territory's Legislative Council, each service being subject to a separate vote. Thus the allocation of High Commission expenditure among all the services under its authority was largely determined in the territorial legislatures. Local dissatisfaction with any of the services could result in a cut in the territorial contribution to the general fund. This might cause the other territories to make proportionate cuts in their votes so as to maintain their relative shares, and the net outcome might be a fall in High Commission revenue even to the extent of three times the initial cut. The only revenue which was independent of local politics and rivalries was that derived in the form of grants in aid of recurrent expenditure from the UK government. These, however, formed a small and declining share of rapidly rising High Commission expenditure and by 1960/1 amounted to no more than about 12 per cent of the total. Long-range planning of the sort now common in development programmes, for instance to build up the statistical services or to concentrate on long-gestation projects such as agricultural research, was made very difficult as a result.

Unequal economic development

It is against this background of institutions that we must now view certain aspects of the economic development that is described in the three preceding chapters, since it was the divergence in the way they respectively developed which, towards the end of the 1950s, caused Tanganyika and Uganda to feel increasingly dissatisfied with the operation of the common market and the other institutions that linked them with Kenya.

Between 1945 and the early 1960s, Tanganyika almost certainly developed more slowly than the rest of East Africa. Virtually no industrial development took place there as it did in Kenya; and after the disaster of the Groundnut Scheme, there was no agricultural development comparable in scale to the expansion of coffee- and cotton-growing in Uganda. Sisal benefited less than cotton and coffee from the favourable conditions in world markets for primary products in the 1940s and 1950s. In any case it provided neither backward nor forward linkages to promote further development, and suffered from all the well-known disadvantages of an 'enclave' industry. Coffee-growing was confined to a few thousand farmers around Mount Kilimanjaro and in the Bukoba area, while cotton-growing was similarly limited to a small area adjacent to Lake Victoria where there happened to be a coincidence of favourable natural conditions and the availability of transport.

The view was commonly expressed that Uganda, too, was being left behind by Kenya but this is objectively less obvious. Much depends on what valuation one places on the relative importance of economic growth and of the distribution of its benefits. In terms of the growth of GNP it is probably the case that, over the period as a whole, Kenya's grew somewhat faster than Uganda's. Thus between 1950 and 1960 Kenya's national income appears to have risen from £63·7 million to £175·3 million, whilst Uganda's increased from £47·6 million to £110·8 million. But in Kenya the benefits of economic growth were largely confined to Europeans and Asians: for the majority of Africans the standard of living increased only slowly. In Uganda on the other hand the benefits of growth were much more widely distributed, so that even if Europeans and Asians benefited disproportionately, the incomes of very large numbers of small African farmers, especially in Buganda and Eastern Uganda, increased very substantially. It was precisely this wider distribution of the growth of income which gave rise to such industrial development as occurred in Uganda, and which, if more modest than Kenya's—and less ostentatious—has always been grossly under-estimated, more especially by the British administration in Uganda and Ugandans more generally. The one characteristic which distinguished Uganda's industrial development from Kenya's was that much of it—tobacco and textiles apart—required a market no larger than Uganda itself possessed.

Meanwhile, Kenya's position *vis-à-vis* East Africa as a whole came increasingly to display three salient characteristics. First, more and more businesses coming to East Africa, and intending to operate throughout the region, followed the precedent set by the large European and Asian export and import businesses and sited their head offices in Nairobi. Secondly, in its natural and processed form Kenya's agricultural produce found a growing market throughout East Africa; in milk and meat, for instance, and also in tinned peas, pineapples, and jams: the market may have been confined to a fairly small élite, but its quantitative importance was not to be ignored. Thirdly, Kenya was a preferred location for new manufacturing industries, especially if they were branches of overseas firms or if they were established by locally domiciled European businessmen. With the exception of a textile mill and an enamelware factory built in Uganda, virtually all those new industrial enterprises which hoped to serve the region as a whole came to be sited in Nairobi or elsewhere in Kenya. There were several reasons for this. First, Kenya had the advantage of the early start; there were external economies to be gained from a location in which others had already begun and where they were in close proximity to the headquarters of the principal import houses with their detailed knowledge of the East African market. Secondly, Nairobi and its environs with its large European and Asian population constituted the largest single concentration of purchasing power for manufactures in East Africa. Consequently, except in the case of goods for which demand was specifically African, such as textiles, enamelware, or bicycle tyres, and for which the region around Lake Victoria provided the greatest market concentration, Nairobi and some of the smaller towns of the White Highlands formed the area which minimized transport cost. Thirdly, Nairobi and its environs had more 'high level manpower'; this was, of course, mostly European and Asian, but among Africans Kikuyu and Kamba were regarded as displaying the greatest commercial and mechanical aptitudes in East Africa and they were close at hand as well. A fourth reason was that some of the industrialization took the form of the processing or canning of Kenyan dairy produce, vegetables, and fruit. Since these products lose their weight and bulk whilst being processed, and are more fragile in their unprocessed form, the location of processing was bound to be nearer the farm than the market *if* there was a conflict—and the farms were in Kenya. In practice Kenya initially provided the largest part of the market so the location was never in much doubt. It was in any event the Kenyan farmers who initiated these processing industries.

Criticisms and their basis

The unequal rate of development, and especially of industrial development, was however the major reason why in the late 1950s Uganda and Tanganyika felt increasingly dissatisfied with the arrangements by which they were linked economically to Kenya and the common market. The advantage of the common currency was not at first questioned. There was indeed criticism, as Britain lurched from one credit squeeze to another, of the arrangements whereby East African bank credit was regulated not by economic conditions in East Africa but by those in Britain. The objection to the currency and banking system was not that it might favour Kenya, but rather that it made variations in the supply of credit in East Africa depend upon economic conditions in Britain rather than in East Africa. It was argued that every time Britain had one of its periodic balance of payments crises, the East African branches of British banks were obliged to curtail credit and raise interest rates to borrowers so as to keep them in line with the British bank rate. An independent banking system, it was argued, would have been more responsive to the East Africans' need for variation in their money supply. It was also alleged that this 'dependence' precluded East African governments from pursuing active monetary policies aimed at promoting long-term economic development. Both grievances manifested themselves in a demand for an East African Central Bank.

The objection that the system restricted the supply of money unnecessarily docs not seem very well-founded when it is remembered that there had been provision for a fiduciary issue since 1955 and that this was never fully taken up. The second grievance arose from a belief that was commonly held at that time by a generation who had grown up, and were still living, in the intellectual atmosphere of the 1930s and the New Deal, and who thought that underdevelopment was the result of an insufficiency of aggregate demand. Development seemed to them to need a priming of the pump by running a budget deficit. A liberal supply of new bank-notes appeared to be all that was needed to cause the apparently intractable problems of underdevelopment to melt away like snow. In this extreme form the thesis is no longer tenable,[1] though it is possible that the pendulum has swung too much the other way and that not sufficient attention is now given to the effect on aggregate supply of a buoyancy of demand, as witness all the new enterprises and services which sprang up in Uganda following the post-Korean boom in cotton and coffee, her principal exports.

The currency board and banking systems of course also facilitated movements of capital out of East Africa and between the three East African countries. These movements are difficult to document. During the Mau Mau period capital appears to have moved out of Kenya, as it was to do again shortly before independence. Sometimes the movements were in both directions simultaneously; as for instance when the Uganda marketing boards transferred surpluses to London to be invested in securities which could be readily realized if need be, whilst at the same time British firms engaged in direct investment by setting up factories in Kenya. In this way an indirect transfer took place from Uganda to Kenya. It is however a mistake to infer from this that the currency board system in itself was responsible for these transfers. It in no way precluded the East African governments from applying exchange control had they so wished. If they did not exercise such control it was because they thought it might deter prospective foreign investors.

The major complaint, therefore, which both businesses and governments had against the monetary system was its close adherence to Bank of England policy, which was in turn dictated by economic circumstances in Britain and which often had the effect of aggravating the instability caused by fluctuations in export earnings instead of moderating it. The solution to this problem was thought by some to lie in the creation of an East African Central Bank; territorial independence of monetary policy was not at that time sought.

What was increasingly questioned was the benefit of the common market and of the High Commission. These may be considered in turn.

As early as the 1920s there had been controversy between the territories on issues arising out of the operation of the common

---

[1] For an exemplary refutation, see A. Hazlewood, (ed.), *African Integration and Disintegration* (London, 1967), pp. 111–12; and also F. Benham, *The Columbo Plan and Other Essays* (London, 1956), chap. ii.

market. Kenya had taken the initiative in pressing for protective duties above the general tariff, and in 1922 a number of such duties were imposed on imported agricultural products that competed with those grown by European farmers. There were strong and continuing protests from Uganda, and to a lesser extent from Tanganyika also. The protests abated in the 1930s after the revision of the tariff schedule and the introduction of freedom for each territory to impose or suspend duties on certain items; moreover the case for protection exerted a wider appeal in the years of depression than in the world trade expansion of the previous decade.[1]

During the war of 1939–45 East Africa could not in any case have imported food and her self-sufficiency in a wide range of agricultural products which had received protection before the war was viewed as a blessing; for several years after the war prices for these commodities were lower than those obtaining on the world market. Meanwhile the main agricultural exports were enjoying a boom which reached a climax in 1951 but continued into the middle of the decade. In these circumstances there was little ground for dissension on trade or fiscal questions and it was only in the later 1950s that there was a resurgence of conflict between the three territories over the question of protective tariffs.[2] It is perhaps no coincidence that this should have happened just when Uganda and Tanganyika found their proceeds from exports stagnating instead of rising, and Kenya accordingly seemed to benefit, relatively, from her greater and faster-growing volume of manufacturing industry as well as commercial and financial activity. At this time, with falling revenue from export taxes, which were much more important to Uganda than to the other two,[3] the policy of fiscal harmonization was seen in Uganda more as one of a 'fiscal strait-jacket', in that it prevented her from raising other tax rates.

It is not easy to determine what effect the common market had on the growth of GDP in the three territories. The common market clearly mattered least if the recorded growth was the result of a growth of export earnings overseas, rather than of

---

[1] Raisman *Report*, Cmnd. 1279, p. 8.
[2] Ibid., p. 8.
[3] Uganda's export tax yield fell from over £7 million in 1956/7 to £4·1 million in 1959/60. *The Economic Development of Uganda*, International Bank for Reconstruction and Development (Baltimore, 1962), p. 90.

trade with the partner states. In some years Tanganyika, for instance, experienced impressive rates of growth of GDP, but their source was the increase in earnings from the sale of crops overseas, and this would have occurred just the same if there had been no common market. In general, the effect of a common market on economic growth will be greater the more of each country's exports are destined to its partner states.

One indicator of the importance of the East African common market might therefore be the growth of trade between the three territories; and, judged by this standard, the effect differed considerably in each. Taking locally-produced exports to the rest of East Africa as a proportion of gross domestic product one finds that in the case of Tanganyika this never exceeded 2 per cent, except in 1957 when it was 2·7 per cent. In Uganda inter-territorial exports as a proportion of GDP fell from a peak of nearly 10 per cent in 1953 to an average of about 6 per cent in the years 1960–2. In Kenya, by contrast, the proportion of exports to GDP rose from an average of about 5 per cent in 1951–3 to about 8 per cent in 1960–2 and was to reach nearly 12 per cent in 1965.

Alternatively one may examine the relationship between the growth of inter-territorial and total exports. For Uganda and Tanganyika exports to the rest of East Africa were such a small proportion of the value of total exports that they are unlikely to have had any great influence upon the growth of their economies. Economic growth was for them much more determined by the growth of their exports outside East Africa. For Kenya the common market was much more important. The importance of inter-territorial trade to Kenya emerges even more clearly when one looks at exports to and imports from the rest of East Africa and compares these with their trade outside East Africa.

Table I shows that by 1957 Kenya's exports to the rest of East Africa far outweighed the inter-territorial exports of Uganda and Tanganyika and had come to be nearly a third of her total exports; whilst in the case of imports from the rest of East Africa Kenya's only accounted for 6 per cent of her total imports, in contrast to Uganda which imported 17 per cent from the rest of East Africa, and Tanganyika 16 per cent. These imports came, of course, mostly from Kenya. Kenya's exports to the rest of East Africa had expanded steadily over the years, and although in the

TABLE I

EAST AFRICA'S FOREIGN AND INTER-TERRITORIAL TRADE, 1957

A. *Exports*

	Exports to foreign countries £m.	Exports to rest of E. Africa £m.	Total £m.	Exports to rest of E. Africa as % of total
Kenya	26·4	11·4	37·6	31
Uganda	45·9	5·3	51·2	10
Tanganyika	39·5	2·0	41·5	5
TOTAL East Africa	111·7	18·8	130·5	14

B. *Imports*

	Imports from foreign countries £m.	Imports from rest of E. Africa £m.	Total £m.	Imports from rest of E. Africa as % of total
Kenya	72·0	4·5	73·5	6
Uganda	28·9	6·6	35·5	17
Tanganyika	39·3	7·7	47·0	16
TOTAL East Africa	140·2	18·8	160·0	12

Note: Owing to rounding, totals do not always correspond to the sum of the separate items. (Definitions used differ slightly from those used in Appendix 3.)

SOURCE: T. A. Kennedy, 'The East African Customs Union: some features of its history and operation', *Makerere Journal*, 3 (1959), 33.

late 1950s they still consisted mostly of foodstuffs, the statistics gloss over an important qualitative change. During the 1930s these foodstuff exports had been in unprocessed form. By the late 1950s, however, most of them were processed, packaged, and canned, and in addition, something of the order of one third of Kenya's exports to the rest of East Africa took the form of manufactured goods other than foodstuffs.[1] Throughout the post-war years Tanganyika and Uganda enjoyed persistent foreign trade surpluses but were in deficit on their balance of trade with Kenya. It was Kenya's trade surplus with the rest of East Africa which enabled her to finance imports from abroad far in excess of the value of her own exports outside East Africa. The common monetary and banking system then also had the

[1] Cf. Robson, *Economic Integration in Africa*, p. 122.

incidental effect of facilitating transfers of funds from Tanganyika and Uganda to Kenya.

Kenya's success was resented in Uganda and to a lesser extent in Tanganyika. It was argued that Kenya's development of industries that were a substitute for imports was depriving the other two of revenue from import duties and that their own industrial development was retarded by having to compete with Kenya without the advantage of tariff protection. There was also resentment over the fact that the Kenya marketing boards sold some commodities in East Africa at prices higher than those received on the world market, and at times refused to handle Ugandan maize—which was equivalent to restricting imports from Uganda.[1] The system of railway freight charges was thought moreover to give further advantage to Kenya. Freight charges were based on the principle of low rates for exports and local produce and high rates for imports.[2] This was felt to reinforce customs protection for Kenya's manufactures and help the competitive strength of her agricultural and dairy industries, especially in the Uganda market. At the same time there was resentment that African consumers should have to pay more for locally-produced goods than they would have cost on the world market, especially when the benefit appeared to accrue primarily to non-African farmers and industrialists. New industries would of course generate new employment and perhaps yield increased revenue from income tax, but again the benefits would go principally to the territory in which most of them were established, namely Kenya.

It is probable, however, that these allegedly adverse effects of the common market were exaggerated. No doubt Kenya had a more rapid rate of industrialization and derived advantages from being the commercial capital of East Africa. But it is by no means clear that in the absence of the customs union the course of events would have been very different. Kenya always had the very real advantage of a large, geographically concentrated, European and Asian population (about a quarter of a million) with high *per capita* incomes which constituted both a sizeable market and a supply of enterprise and skill. But the 1963 Kenya Census of Production shows moreover that even then no more

---

[1] See IBRD, *Economic Development of Uganda*, pp. 89 sqq.
[2] Arthur Hazlewood, *Rail and Road in East Africa* (Oxford, 1964), chap. iv.

than 20 per cent of her industrial output was sold to Tanganyika and Uganda.[1] It is of course very likely, as the Raisman Report said, that Kenya gained more from the common market than Uganda and Tanganyika: but, as Hazlewood has pointed out, this does not mean that the latter two were actually made worse off by it, as was commonly believed at the time.

Tanganyika and Uganda also felt that they had cause for dissatisfaction with the operation of the High Commission. First, it was argued that since its secretariat and many of the research institutes associated with it were located in and around Nairobi, Kenya gained disproportionately both from the employment opportunities which were thus generated and from the income and other taxes which were paid by those so employed. Secondly, it was felt that High Commission officials and research workers alike were more responsive to Kenya's needs than to those of the rest of East Africa. There was never any suggestion of deliberate favouritism. Rather it was regarded as natural that research workers, for example, should be more influenced by the problems facing the country in which they were located than by those of its neighbours. In practice, however, only four of the ten research centres were located in Kenya in 1960, although it was certainly true that other services administered by the High Commission were more preponderantly situated in Kenya.

Although the non-self-contained services could hardly be described as vital to the total East African economy, they often became the focal point for grievances with the common market in general. This was perhaps due in part to the fact that the Central Legislative Assembly offered a convenient platform for airing these grievances. The persistent complaint was that Kenya was receiving a disproportionate share of the benefits of the common market and common services while Uganda and Tanganyika bore a disproportionate share of the costs.

Whether or not these complaints are borne out by the statistics,[2] they remain important as a reflection of discontent

[1] Hazlewood, *African Integration and Disintegration*, pp. 111–12.

[2] One partial attempt to make such estimates for later years (1964/5) after major changes had been made in the operation of both the common market and the common services, can be found in Arthur D. Hazlewood, 'Territorial Incidence of the East African Common Services', *Bulletin of the Oxford Institute of Economics and Statistics*, 27, 13 (Aug. 1965), 161–76.

with the concentration of economic activity in Kenya and particularly in the Nairobi area. The precise balance of gain and loss is difficult to determine. It has been estimated however that in 1957 nearly 70 per cent of the total income directly generated by the High Commission was paid in Kenya but that Kenya contributed only just under one half of that part of the High Commission's revenue which came from the three territories' governments.[1]

Measures to remedy grievances

By the late 1950s both the common market and the High Commission had become the subject of heated controversy between the three territories. Uganda in particular felt that the cost to her of continuance exceeded the benefits. It was therefore decided to appoint an Economic and Fiscal Commission under the chairmanship of Sir Jeremy Raisman (a Governor of the Bank of England) and including also Professors R. C. Tress and A. J. Brown, to investigate the allegation and to make proposals for reform.

Before considering the Raisman Report it is perhaps pertinent to ask why Uganda's grievances should have been so fervently proclaimed at this time. To understand this, one must recall how much Ugandan politics were dominated throughout the colonial period by a fear of Kenya, the country of settler domination that lay between her and the coast. This fear was probably much more potent than any 'nicely calculated less or more'. So long as all three countries were under British hegemony, the fears and discontents could to some extent be contained. But as early as 1953 the crisis which led to the deportation of the Kabaka demonstrated the strength of feeling in Uganda against the possibility of any closer association with Kenya. The presence of large numbers of European workers engaged on the construction of the Owen Falls Dam had aroused the fear that Uganda, like Kenya, was to be dominated by white immigrants. In 1953 a Colonial Secretary's careless after-dinner speech interpreted (wrongly) by a local paper as indicating the British government's intention to foist political federation on

[1] H. W. Ord, 'Social Accounting and Inter-territorial Transactions in East Africa', *East African Economics Review*, 9, 2 (Dec. 1962), 139 sqq.

East Africa proved to be dynamite in the prevailing atmosphere of suspicion.[1] The Kabaka's stand, originally against federation, soon turned into opposition to industrial development in Uganda. Yet a few years later it came to be the allegation of Uganda's industrial backwardness which was hurled against Kenya. These grievances, it is suggested, make sense only if they are set in a political framework.

Kenya, far from being intransigent, was in fact prepared to make important concessions to help Uganda's industrial development. When the Nyanza Textile Factory was built, Kenya and Tanganyika not only agreed to give Uganda exclusive rights to manufacture but also eventually agreed to a rise in the tariff on imported textiles, to some very high specific duties, and even to quantitative restrictions on imports. The new factory charged lower prices in Kenya and Tanganyika than in Uganda in order to forestall criticisms, but even so the prices of clothes for African consumers undoubtedly rose in all three countries. Similar protection was given to Uganda's enamelware products. None of Kenya's industries appears ever to have obtained comparable protection—at least not since 1922.[2]

The Raisman Commission had no easy task and in fact studiously avoided saying anything in their report which might be interpreted as a judgement about the merits of any particular case. They concentrated instead upon making proposals which were likely to improve the operation of both the common market and the High Commission services. The impending independence of Tanganyika in any case called for new arrangements especially for the High Commission services.

The report strongly advised against the break-up of the common market and common services. It sought to demonstrate that no country was actually worse off as a result of the existing arrangements; but it implicitly conceded that the gains were unevenly distributed.

The main recommendation of the report was the replacement of the High Commission by an East African Common Services Organization (EACSO). This was implemented to coincide with

---

[1] See chap. i above.

[2] Dharam Ghai, 'Territorial Distribution of the Benefits and Costs of the East African Common Market', in Leys and Robson, *Federation in East Africa*, p. 74.

Tanganyika's independence. The details of the way it differed from the High Commission need not concern us here,[1] though it is pertinent to point out that since its headquarters were to remain in Nairobi, the new arrangement did nothing to allay the suspicion that its work would continue to be excessively oriented towards Kenya's interests. This old concern continued to rankle. The executive authority of EACSO was now to be vested in the chief ministers of the three countries and there were to be four 'triumvirates' of ministers from the territories, each responsible for a certain range of matters. But for the rest the basic structure of EACSO was not to be substantially different from that which had previously obtained.

At the same time the report suggested a number of steps to promote the 'equalization' of gains. The major economic and fiscal change it proposed was the institution of a 'Distributable Pool'. This was to have the dual object of fiscal redistribution between the three territories and of providing an independent source of revenue for the common services. Hitherto each of the non-self-contained services had been separately financed by the three territories by annual appropriations from their revenues. Instead the common services were now to be financed directly from the Distributable Pool. A fixed percentage of the receipts of income tax and customs and excise duties were to be paid into the Pool. Half its funds were then to be used to pay for the common services, thus giving them an independent source of revenue; while the other half was to be paid in equal shares to the three countries. The objects of this device were to make Kenya with its greater revenue pay a larger proportion of the cost of the common services, and also to bring about a direct fiscal transfer from Kenya to Uganda and Tanganyika. By 1963/4 Kenya was paying twice as much into the Distributable Pool as either of the other two countries, whilst the half that was redistributed accrued to the three of them in equal proportions.

The proposals of the Raisman Commission were accepted and implemented. For the moment it appeared that inter-territorial co-operation which had been on the brink of collapse was saved and given a new lease of life. Within less than three years all three territories were to be independent and, far from going their

[1] See Hazlewood, *African Integration and Disintegration*, pp. 72–3 for a summary.

separate ways, the three independent countries looked to be
moving nearer to the 'Closer Union', envisaged in the proposals
of 'Col. 191' of 1945, than ever before. The dream of East African
Federation proved in the event however to be short-lived.

IX

THE DEVELOPMENT OF THE EAST AFRICAN LEGAL SYSTEMS DURING THE COLONIAL PERIOD

ANTHONY ALLOTT

IN 1960 the then British territories of Kenya, Tanganyika, Uganda, and Zanzibar each possessed a typically colonial system of law and courts, organized—though with some striking variations—on basically similar lines. The key feature of these systems was that they were dualistic, that is, they embraced on the one hand courts and law of western patterns or origins, and on the other hand courts and law deriving from traditional, indigenous institutions. The western or 'general' territorial laws represented, in each of these territories, a mixture of English, Indian, and locally drafted statute and common law (with, for good measure, a dash of German law in Tanganyika); the laws of African origin comprised local customary laws varying more or less in detail from place to place, and those portions of Islamic personal law (varying according to the different schools or sects) which have survived to the present day.

Despite the basic similarities of the contemporary legal systems, the juridical status of the different territories, and the manner in which jurisdiction was first acquired and later extended, could hardly have been more various. Zanzibar, from being an independent state in which the British, along with the nationals of other European and American powers, claimed limited extra-territorial rights, became first of all a protected state, and later a British protectorate, though of a special kind. Kenya, which territorially developed from the East Africa Protectorate, originated in part as a protectorate superimposed upon the Sultan's dominions, and in part as a sphere of influence enlarged first into a protectorate and then into a colony[1]. Uganda,

[1] *Note on 'colony' and 'protectorate'.* A colony was a dependent territory of the Crown, acquired by settlement, by annexation, by conquest, or by cession (under a treaty or agreement). Its soil was considered British, and its inhabitants were British subjects.

A protected territory might be a protected state, a protectorate, or a mandated or trust territory. The jurisdiction of the Crown over it might have been acquired

although in name a single protectorate, in practice included both advanced kingdoms with which the British Crown was in treaty relations, and the territories of peoples whose political institutions were less complex and developed than those of the kingdoms. Tanganyika, finally, underwent a double colonization, first by the Germans and German law, and thereafter by the British and British law; but, once it had been constituted a mandated territory (and later a trust territory) under international supervision, it represented yet another distinct juridical category of dependent territory.

From the point of view of the international and the constitutional lawyer, these differences in the acquisition of jurisdiction by the British Crown and in the status of the territories under it are of extreme importance. Thus the Crown's powers of legislation are in principle quite distinct over colonies on the one hand, and over 'foreign' (i.e. protected) territory on the other; and the powers of the Crown, as administering authority under the mandate and later the trust territory system, were limited by the terms of the mandate and the supervisory powers of the international organs concerned.

Despite these constitutional differences between the East African territories, it is a remarkable fact that the colonially created or recognized judicial and legal régimes in each territory steadily grew more alike as time wore on. Nor does the variation in governmental policy towards the different territories— treating Kenya, for instance, as a colony of settlement, and Tanganyika as the object of an international trust—seem to have procured in the long term any striking differences in the legal systems. By the end of the period under review, for example, the courts systems of Tanganyika and Kenya were organized on highly comparable lines. In short, East Africa under British

by treaty, usage, or sufferance. Its soil was foreign, and its inhabitants British-protected only. Originally such British jurisdiction was limited both in kind (by the nature of the agreement if any with the local ruler) and as to persons (to British subjects, nationals of other 'civilized' powers by express agreement with them, and local inhabitants so far as expressly conceded by their rulers); but self-regarding constitutional doctrines introduced later in the twentieth century led to the abandonment of both these limitations (cf. the Uganda Order in Council, 1902), and British jurisdiction in protectorates became substantially as extensive as in colonies. What constitutued 'usage' or 'sufferance' under the Foreign Jurisdiction Acts was never satisfactorily defined. For a full discussion, see Sir K. Roberts-Wray, *Commonwealth and Colonial Law* (London, 1966), esp. pp. 98–116.

administration had become, despite the diverse history of its constituent portions, a largely integrated law area.

There were several factors which contributed to this growing together. They were, first and most obviously, the mere fact of a common British suzerainty; though this never, in the British colonial empire, implied the sort of legal uniformity imposed on the French African empire. Next, undoubtedly, one must mention economic factors: the development of an East African common market, tied together by an integrated communications and business system, stimulated moves towards the unification of East African laws, more particularly in the commercial field; from an early period the governors' conferences and the conferences of East African law officers[1] helped to promote uniformity in such fields as company law, contract, and the like. And finally, the existence of a common court of appeal,[2] the Court of Appeal for Eastern Africa, helped both to spotlight divergences in the territorial laws, and to provide a stimulus for their removal.

The beginnings of British jurisdiction

The first British jurisdiction established in East Africa was in the sultanate of Zanzibar, and any account of the growth of British legal and judicial institutions in East Africa, any explanation of the special character which they exhibit, must begin with the sultanate. As Tarring could say,[3] writing of the effect of the Zanzibar Order in Council, 1884: 'It is hardly too much to say that by it Zanzibar is made, so far as concerns the administration of justice to British subjects, a part of Her Majesty's Indian Empire.'[4] The most important legal fact about the East African territories was that they abutted on the Indian Ocean. The system of codified law introduced into British India, the criminal and civil courts and the procedure that they followed, were copied or applied in the British East African possessions; and it was through Zanzibar that this Indian influence came to the mainland territories.

---

[1] The first formal recorded meeting was in 1926.
[2] Established in 1902.
[3] C. J. Tarring, *British Consular Jurisdiction in the East* (London, 1887), p. 43.
[4] Made 29 Nov. 1884. Hertslet, *Commercial Treaties* (31 vols., London, 1827–1925), xvii. 1093.

Extra-territorial privileges had been granted to the citizens of various states (Great Britain, United States, France, the Hanseatic Republic, and others) resident in Zanzibar from an early date; but it was in 1869 that the jurisdiction exercised by the British consul over British subjects in Zanzibar was first regulated by Order in Council.[1] The High Court in Bombay acquired an original civil, and also an appellate, jurisdiction over suits arising in Zanzibar. Rules and regulations made by the consul in 1867[2] provided that 'the Indian Penal Code shall be considered the criminal law to which British subjects at Zanzibar are answerable. . . .' This is the earliest mention of Indian law in East Africa. The 1884 Order in Council[3] clarified the position, directing the British courts in Zanzibar to apply the statute law as applied by the courts in Bombay, and in default thereof then 'in accordance with the common and statute law of England in force at the commencement of this Order'.

British consular jurisdiction, as exercised over British subjects and later over other persons under British protection, was regularized and extended both by statute and practice. In 1890 a British protectorate had been established over Zanzibar; and thereafter the Sultan authorized the delegation of some part of his jurisdiction to the British representatives in the island. In 1897, yet another Order in Council constituted 'Her Britannic Majesty's Court for Zanzibar', the offices of Judge and Assistant Judge were created, subordinate courts were established, and the jurisdiction of the British courts was extended to foreigners whose governments had surrendered their jurisdiction in Zanzibar. The jurisdiction of the powers other than Britain gradually vanished as British power grew, and by 1907 had all disappeared by agreement with Britain.

The British courts established by these means were merely excrescences on the already existent Zanzibar judicial and legal systems established by the Sultan for his dominions. The Sultan's courts, which continued to exercise jurisdiction over the subjects of the Sultan and of other non-Christian powers, were completely reorganized by decree in 1899. In that year a Supreme Court was set up as a court of appeal, having under it a 'Court for

---

[1] Made 9 Aug. 1866. Hertslet, *Treaties*, xii. 973.
[2] Made 28 Feb. 1867. Ibid., p. 986.
[3] Article 8 (a).

Zanzibar and Pemba' consisting of two *kadhis* and a judge of the British court if called on. Subordinate courts were also constituted. Between 1908 and 1923 all magistrates received a double appointment from the Secretary of State and the Sultan; a unique form of dual jurisdiction had thus evolved through the delegation of jurisdiction by the Sultan, and the constitution of the Sultan's courts by British officers.

The duality of courts was exactly reflected in the duality of laws prevailing in Zanzibar. In the famous leading case of *Secretary of State* v. *Charlesworth, Pilling*[1] the Privy Council had to consider what law to apply in a case arising in Mombasa—on that part of the mainland, that is to say, where Zanzibar law applied. But what was the 'Zanzibar law' in these circumstances? By the Order in Council of 1884, Indian enactments applied. These enactments indicated that English law should govern the question; but English law said that the *lex situs*, in this case Zanzibar law (i.e. Islamic law) should apply. The land involved in this case had been compulsorily acquired by the British government and had been in the occupation of British subjects; and by the Article 16 of the treaty of 1886, the Sultan had conceded extra-territorial rights to British subjects and their property. Should, then, British law be applied after all? No, said their Lordships:

[Extra-territoriality means for a British subject] complete personal protection, assurance of satisfactory judicial tribunals, and such enjoyment of his property for himself and for those who claim under him as British law would afford him for British property. It is going a long way beyond that, and beyond the reason for these immunities, to say that the moment a plot of land is purchased by an Englishman it is stamped with the same character and is attended by the same incidents that would belong to it if it were actually transferred to England and surrounded by other English land.

The vice-consul at Mombasa had been right, said their Lordships, to hold that the local law should apply, but wrong in thinking that this was foreign law to him. He was acting in his capacity as a Zanzibar judge, and as such could take judicial notice of the Zanzibar law applicable to the case before him. No case could better illustrate the impossible complexity of the legal

[1] (1901) 1 *Zanzibar Law Reports*, 105, P.C.

system of Zanzibar at the turn of the century, the assortment of laws concurrently applied there, and the bizarre position of the judges who administered them. At the same time Lord Hobhouse's words, cited above, have an ominous ring when we turn to look at the legal situation as it developed in the East Africa Protectorate, in which the European settlers in effect claimed extra-territorial privileges for themselves and their property.

The Charter of the Imperial British East Africa Company, dated 3 September 1888, provided by Article 12 that:

in the administration of justice by the Company to the peoples of its territories or to any of the inhabitants thereof, careful regard shall always be had to the customs and laws of the class or tribe or nation to which the parties respectively belong, especially with respect to the holding, possession, transfer, and disposition of lands and goods, and testate or intestate succession thereto, and marriage, divorce, and legitimacy, and other rights of property and personal rights.

And Article 13 provided that the Court of Directors could make legislation in force in the territories of the company.

The Concession by the Sultan of Zanzibar to the British East African Association of 24 May 1887[1] had already granted the company power to 'pass laws for the government of the districts; to establish courts of justice,' etc.

The judges shall be appointed by the Company or their representatives, and the Sultan shall confirm all such appointments, but all 'Kathis' shall be nominated by his Highness. . . . In aboriginal tracts the law shall be administered by the Company or their officials.

There is little available evidence on the way in which these powers were actually exercised, especially in the hinterland; though McDermott indicates that one of the first acts of the company's representatives in the interior was to proscribe any form of slavery.[2] In the Sultan's dominions the company merely exercised a jurisdiction delegated by him, though this interpretation was contested. In 1890, the company had instituted a British court in Mombasa, presided over by a British barrister.[3] Jurisdiction in the protectorate generally was regulated by the

[1] For which see P. L. McDermott, *British East Africa or I.B.E.A.* (London, 1893), Appendix I.
[2] Ibid., p. 223.
[3] R. W. Hamilton, Introduction to vol. i of *East African Law Reports* (1906), pp. iii–iv.

Africa Order in Council, 1889.[1] Under this the British governor provided for the establishment of consular courts in its African possessions, regulated the law that they were to administer ('the substance of the law for the time being in force in and for England'—Article 13), and provided for a system of appeals. Instructions issued by the Secretary of State under the Order in 1890[2] constituted 'the territory outside Zanzibar which is under the authority of the British East Africa Company' a local jurisdiction for the purposes of the Order; and by Article 21 provided that appeals from this territory should lie to the Supreme Court of Natal. This last arrangement was speedily altered, however, by a further Instruction of 1891,[3] which provided that appeals from 'the British sphere on the East Coast of Africa, excluding the dominions of His Highness the Sultan of Zanzibar', should lie to the Supreme Court at Bombay, thus bringing the appeal system into line with that already established for Zanzibar itself.

By a further Order in Council of 1892 the Secretary of State was given power to apply Indian legislation in East Africa. In June 1895, the Imperial government took over from the company the administration of the protectorate; and on 31 August 1896 the British Foreign Office notified the establishment of an East Africa Protectorate. The post of 'Legal Vice-Consul' was established. In 1897 an East Africa Order in Council was made, which by Article 7 established 'Her Majesty's Court for East Africa', presided over by 'Her Majesty's Judicial Officer for the East Africa Protectorate'. Provision was also made for the constitution of provincial and native courts. By analogy with the situation in Zanzibar, the law of British India, more particularly as applied in Bombay, was made the fundamental law of the protectorate; and criminal and civil appeals henceforth lay under the order to the Court for Zanzibar, and not to the High Court in Bombay as heretofore. The civil jurisdiction of the British Protectorate Court was further regulated by an Order in Council of 7 October 1899.

By the Native Courts Regulations of 1897, 'Native Courts' (that is, 'courts for the administration of justice to or between

---

[1] Made 15 Oct. 1869. Hertslet, *Treaties,* xviii. 1.
[2] Issued 22 Feb. 1890. Ibid., p. 63.
[3] Issued 31 July 1891. Hertslet, *Treaties,* xix. 1.

natives') had been established; and there was also a system of subordinate courts. One of the more peculiar and fascinating types of the latter were the so-called 'Railway Courts'.[1] A slight digression concerning these unique courts may not be out of place here.

Some of the railway engineers had already been appointed magistrates, but this was 'very little help', because they were ignorant of 'the natives and their ways'.[2] In 1899 a set of Railway Courts Rules and Orders was issued, which formally established these courts as being constituted by railway personnel and having jurisdiction over 'natives' in the employ of the railway. Most of the persons appointed Railway Magistrates appear to have been recruited in India or to have had Indian service. The Railway Zone was administered by the Chief Engineer until 31 March 1902, when its administration was assumed by the protectorate government. An official notice in the Gazette of 15 May 1903 indicates that such magistrates were usually appointed to exercise jurisdiction within three miles of the station-master's office at a named station, and within one mile of the railway therefrom to the next station.

In Uganda the basis of British jurisdiction was laid by the treaty with Captain Lugard, the agent of the Imperial British East Africa Company, which was signed on 30 March 1892 by Mwanga, Kabaka of Buganda. This treaty acknowledged the suzerainty of the British company, and by Clause III agreed that 'the Resident, as Arbitrator, shall decide all disputes and all differences between Europeans in Uganda. . . . His decision in all matters connected with Europeans shall be final, and subject only to appeal to the higher authorities of the Company . . .'[3] The 1892 agreement was replaced by another provisional agreement concluded between Sir Gerald Portal and Mwanga on 29 May 1893,[4] the company having been replaced on 1 April 1893 as administering authority by the British government and a protectorate having been proclaimed. This second agreement

---

[1] I wish to express my deep gratitude to the management of East African Railways and Harbours in Nairobi, and more particularly to Mr. Harrop and his colleagues, for making available to me the railway archives on this matter.

[2] Letter, H.M. Sub-Commissioner to H.M. Consul-General, 16 Nov. 1898.

[3] The text of the 1892 treaty is printed in J. V. Wild, *The Story of the Uganda Agreement* (London, 1955), pp. 62–6.

[4] Hertslet, *Map of Africa by Treaty*, i. 393.

made more precise the jurisdiction claimed for the British authorities, and at the same time extended it:

5. I freely recognise that so far as I, the King, am concerned, the sole jurisdiction over Europeans and over all persons not born in my dominions, and the settlement of all cases in which any such persons may be a party or parties, lies exclusively in the hands of Her Majesty's Representative.
6. In civil cases between my subjects the Court of Her Majesty's Representative shall be a Supreme Court of Appeal, but it shall lie entirely within the discretion of the said Representative to refuse to hear such appeals.
7. In criminal cases where only natives are concerned, it is left to the discretion of Her Majesty's Representative to interfere, in the public interest and for the sake of justice, to the extent and in the manner which he may consider desirable.

The final treaty of 27 August 1894 between Mwanga and Colonel Colvile, as British representative, repeated these latter provisions.

These provisions can be usefully read in the light of a despatch from the British Foreign Secretary, Lord Salisbury, dated 22 March 1892, which laid down, *inter alia*:

The administration of justice, as regards Europeans and others, not natives of the country, will be exercised under the Order in Council of 15 October 1889. . . . The Order in Council does not apply to the Sultan's dominions, in which the administration of justice is governed by His Highness's Treaties. . . .

It will not be your duty, in the portion of your district outside the dominions of the Sultan of Zanzibar, to undertake judicial administration as regards natives. This should, for the present, remain in the hands of the Chiefs; but you should check abuses, and let the Chiefs understand that, under British influence, injustice will not be tolerated. In special cases, where no other remedy may appear adequate, you will be justified in obtaining the delegation to you of the Chief's powers, in order that you may undertake the direct administration of justice. Such cases should always be reported by you.[1]

The basis of British jurisdiction thus firmly rested upon agreement with local rulers as regards jurisdiction over non-natives,

---

[1] Hertslet, *Map of Africa by Treaty*, i. p. 337.

and delegated supervisory jurisdiction even in cases affecting those rulers' own subjects where apparent gross injustice had occurred, such jurisdiction being exercised under the Africa Order in Council, 1889, and the Foreign Jurisdiction Acts.

Instructions issued by the Foreign Secretary on 31 July 1891[1] had constituted the 'British sphere on the East Coast of Africa' a local jurisdiction under the Africa Order in Council; and the first commissions to hold consular courts in Uganda under the Africa Order in Council were issued in 1894 to Colonel H. Colvile and to F. J. Jackson, with appeal lying to Bombay. A major problem soon arose in regard to areas adjacent to the protectorate in which there had been no formal concession of jurisdiction by the local ruler. The kingdom of Bunyoro had been partly occupied by the British and placed under martial law; and two men, denizens of the portion of East Africa under German suzerainty, were convicted by the Commissioner and Consul-General (Mr. E. Berkeley), in his consular court at Kampala, of running gunpowder into Bunyoro. It was agreed that Bunyoro was not at this date in the protectorate, although it was under British influence; and the High Court at Bombay, to which this case came by way of revision in 1896, naturally wished to know on what basis the consular court had purported to exercise criminal jurisdiction outside the protectorate over persons who were not natives of the protectorate or British subjects. The answer was that 'the king and his judicial authorities had disappeared; we must necessarily assume, however temporarily, jurisdiction in their place.' But this view found no favour with the High Court (14 January 1897), and the convictions were quashed.[2]

There could be no better illustration of the uncertain character of the jurisdiction exercised by the British judicial authorities, which was ill-defined both in geographical extent and in subject-matter. Similar difficulties had for long been perplexing British authorities on the other side of Africa (notably in the hinterland of the Gold Coast), where British jurisdiction was being relentlessly pushed forward, at first by voluntary concession by the local rulers, and later by usurpation in the name of justice

---

[1] Hertslet, *Treaties*, xix. 1.
[2] *Imperatrix* v. *Juma bin Fakir and anor.* Bombay High Court, Crim. Reference No. 27 of 1896.

and morality. It is a commentary on the uncertainties of the situation that, in a case in 1959 in the Court of Appeal for Eastern Africa,[1] both judge and counsel should have been in doubt as to the system of appeals from the Uganda Court in 1899. Mr. Wilkinson argued that at that date appeals lay from the consular court in Uganda to the High Court in Mombasa and thence to the High Court in Zanzibar; whilst Forbes, J. A., felt that appeal probably lay direct to the High Court in Bombay, though it might have lain either to Zanzibar or Mombasa. The *Juma* case cited above conclusively demonstrates the position in 1896; but Sir Harry Johnston, writing in 1902 just after his retirement as Commissioner of the Uganda Protectorate (apparently before the coming into existence of the Court of Appeal for Eastern Africa), could write: 'At present appeals from the two Protectorates (East Africa and Uganda) are sent to Zanzibar, where the judicial officers appointed to try these appeals know little or nothing of native laws and customs and the general conditions of Inner Africa.'[2]

The East Africa Order in Council, 1897,[3] had, for the East Africa Protectorate, constituted 'Her Majesty's Court for East Africa', and had provided that appeals therefrom should lie to the Court for Zanzibar, and not to Bombay; but this order does not appear to have applied to Uganda. One assumes that Johnston, as supreme British executive in Uganda, was in the best position to know the judicial arrangements of the protectorate; but the legal doubt remains.

The early development of the judicial system

The year 1902 marked, for much of East Africa, the introduction of substantial alterations in the basis upon which judicial administration was carried on.

In Uganda, the Uganda Order in Council of 1902, itself founded upon the Buganda Agreement of 1900,[4] replaced the

---

[1] *Musa Mubira Luwala* v. *Collector for Western Uganda Railway Extension* 1959 E.A. 848.

[2] H. H. Johnston, *The Uganda Protectorate* (London, 1902), i. 70.

[3] Made 7 July 1897.

[4] 'Founded', in that (a) the authority for the making of the Order derived from the cession by the native rulers of jurisdiction to the Crown, under the Foreign Jurisdiction Acts, and (b) the judges in Uganda clearly held that the 1902 Order 'must be read as subject to the Agreement'; *per* CARTER, J., in *Masanairi Kibuka* v. *Bertie Smith* (1908) 1, *Uganda Law Reports*,4 1, p. 43. See also *Katosi* v. *Kahizi* (1907), 1,

Africa Order in Council as the basis of British executive, legislative and judicial institutions, and remained the foundation of the protectorate's government until recent times. By it a High Court was established and provision made for the establishment of courts subordinate thereto. The recognition accorded in Buganda to the Buganda legislature, courts, and law by the various treaties between British representatives and the Kabaka was quite out of the ordinary.[1]

From the beginning, Europeans were excluded from the jurisdiction of the native tribunals thus recognized, and jurisdiction over them was vested exclusively in the British courts. The contrary was not the case, as Article 17 of the Africa Order in Council, 1889, gave jurisdiction to the consular courts in cases affecting 'natives' (with the consent of such natives). Criminal jurisdiction over Africans was conceded to the British courts, and was later made statutory by the 1902 Order in Council and legislation thereunder. Under the 1900 Buganda Agreement, however, the jurisdiction of the Kabaka's courts in criminal cases, even those which were capital, was preserved; but no death sentence could be carried out without the sanction of Her Majesty's Representative. A right of appeal to the British courts in criminal cases, including cases where the sentence 'may seem to Her Majesty's Government disproportioned or inconsistent with humane principles', was also conceded by the Kabaka. The right of legislation vested in the Lukiko was however preserved.

Similar though less far-reaching agreements were made with the kingdoms of Toro (1900) and Ankole (1901); and the Unyoro Native Courts Ordinance of 1905 gave formal recognition to the system of native courts in Bunyoro. It was partly on this basis, and partly on the basis of the Orders in Council and Ordinances, that recognition was given to native courts and law in the Uganda Protectorate. It is worth remembering in this connexion that the Charter of the Imperial British East Africa Company in 1888

---

22 (*re* Ankole and Toro), in which the Secretary of State's concurrence in this view, by a despatch of 31 July 1907, is recorded on p. 24; and see H. F. Morris and J. S. Read, *Uganda; the development of its laws and constitution* (London, 1966), pp. 20 sqq. Later, however, a quite different view of the juridical effect of treaties with African rulers was taken, and it was frequently held by the Privy Council and courts in Africa that treaties ceding jurisdiction to the Crown should not bind the Crown in the exercise of that jurisdiction. Cf. *Shobhuza II* v. *Miller* 1926 A.C. 518.

1 For a fuller account of the development of the courts and law in Buganda, see E. S. Haydon, *Law and Justice in Buganda* (London, 1960).

had, by Article 12, required the company to pay 'careful regard . . . to the customs and laws' of persons to whom it administered justice; the Uganda Order in Council, 1902, made similar provision:

Article 12. (3) 'In making Ordinances, the Commissioner shall respect existing native laws and customs except so far as the same may be opposed to justice and morality.'
Article 20. 'In all cases, civil and criminal, to which natives are parties, every court (a) shall be guided by native law so far as it is applicable and is not repugnant to justice and morality. . . .'

Provisions of this pattern became the standard form in the legislation of the other East and Central African territories.

Judicial and legal matters in Buganda were more precisely regulated in a series of agreements and ordinances over the next few years: among them the Uganda Judicial Agreement, 1905, the Buganda Agreement (Native Laws), 1910, the Uganda Agreement (Clan Cases), 1924, the Native Courts Ordinance, 1905 (which provided for the constitution of 'British Native Courts' presided over by a Collector, and for the recognition by proclamation of native courts), and the Native Courts in Buganda Proclamation, 1909.

The general effect of these provisions was to recognize formally the existence of a well-defined set of courts—the 'native courts'—administering customary law and 'native laws' (i.e. legislation) to Africans only. Such courts were, however, placed under the supervisory jurisdiction of British courts and officers; and their jurisdiction was now concurrent with that of the British courts proper—the High Court and the subordinate or magistrates' courts. The native courts administered no law of western origin; but the British courts were competent to take account of and apply the native customary law where it was applicable, though many such cases would doubtless have been transferred to the appropriate native court. This pattern (though with the eventual deletion of the so-called 'British native courts') remained the standard one in Uganda, and to a lesser extent in other parts of East Africa, for many years. It was not so easily applied in an area with no clearly defined judicial and legislative authorities, as we shall see when we turn our attention to the East Africa Protectorate. Indeed, in those portions of Uganda outside the treaty kingdoms, the same sort of problem faced the early administrators; and here the tendency was to recognize native courts constituted, not by the pre-colonial indigenous authorities, but by the 'chiefs' officially appointed by government. The continuity of judicial administration in Uganda outside the kingdoms was thus not great.

So far we have been speaking of the recognition of indigenous laws and courts in Uganda; but it is time to turn our attention to the development of the general legal system.

The Africa Order in Council, 1889, provided for the application in the territories affected of the English law currently in force in England; but the Indian influence in Eastern Africa was too strong, and the power given by the Order in Council of 1892 to the Secretary of State to apply specified Indian Acts in East Africa was soon exercised,[1] so that a large number of Indian Acts had been applied to the Protectorate by the time of the making of the Uganda Order in Council, 1902. Under the Order of 1902 the basic law of the protectorate consisted of the same Indian legislation as had already been recognized in Zanzibar— the Civil and Criminal Procedure Codes, the Indian Penal Code, Evidence Act, etc. By an amending Order of 1911, it was provided that in so far as these codes did not apply, the courts were to apply the common law, doctrines of equity, and statutes of general application in force in England on 11 August 1902. But the local legislature (at first the Commissioner) was given power to amend or replace any of such introduced laws by local ordinances; and it is noteworthy that Uganda, in exercise of this power, replaced much of its Indian law rather more speedily than the other East African countries. The local ordinances of this kind (for instance the Succession Ordinance and the Evidence Ordinance) were however often merely re-enactments of the Indian legislation.

In 1896 the East Africa Protectorate had been formally established by the British government by official Notice,[2] the British company's rights having lapsed in the previous year. By

---

[1] For a list of Indian Acts applied in the period 1898–1902 see *Chronological Table of Enactments 1895 to 1964*, printed in *Laws of Uganda* (rev. edn., 1964), vol. i, pp. xxv–xxvi.

[2] Issued 31 Aug. 1896.

the 1897 East Africa Order in Council the British had, as already noted, established a Court for East Africa, also known as the 'Protectorate Court', and presided over by a 'Judicial Officer', whose title was changed in 1899 to that of 'Judge'.[1] The East Africa Order in Council, 1902,[2] by Article 15 constituted a 'High Court of East Africa', thus keeping in step with the other territories. This High Court was of course located in Mombasa, where it remained until the creation of Kenya Colony in 1920.

Both in the East Africa Protectorate and in Uganda at this time the legal structures were rudimentary in form. There were no British law officers in East Africa until 1902, when the office of Crown Advocate was created; up till then the law firm of Messrs. Mead and Wilson was retained at an annual fee to advise the Crown and to appear on its behalf in court.[3] A Crown Advocate was appointed in 1906. The position in Uganda was similar. Until 1906, when an Attorney-General was first appointed, the relevant duties were carried out in so far as they related to non-contentious business, at first by the Chief Judicial Officer, and Legal Adviser, and afterwards by the Judges of the High Court. In so far as contentious business was concerned, they were carried out by a private firm of solicitors in Mombasa.[4]

A Court of Appeal for Eastern Africa was also established in 1902,[5] appeal from which lay direct to the Judicial Committee of the Privy Council in London. The Court of Appeal was empowered to hear appeals from the High Courts in Uganda and the East Africa Protectorate (and also from Nyasaland); but appeals from Zanzibar continued to go to the High Court in Bombay until 1914.[6]

As far as the indigenous tribunals were concerned, the most important consideration in East Africa was that there were no powerful chiefs or kingdoms (except in the coastal region where the position was regulated by agreements with the Sultan of Zanzibar) with whom agreements could be reached or whose

---

[1] Order in Council of 7 Oct. 1899.
[2] Made 11 Aug. 1902.
[3] As stated in 'Contribution to Official Handbook on Kenya from Protectorate to 1923', in file L/1091/6, Attorney-General's Chambers, Nairobi.
[4] The 'Red' Book, 1919. The 'Standard' British East Africa and Uganda Handbook and Directory (Nairobi and Mombasa, 1919), p. 203.
[5] By the Eastern African Protectorates (Court of Appeal) Order in Council, 1902.
[6] This was brought to an end by the Zanzibar Order in Council, 1914.

jurisdictions could be recognized. The situation was thus fundamentally different from that of Uganda. A further source of divergence lay in the rapid growth of a settled European and Indian population, of whom the former at least demanded the application of a law with which they were familiar.

The East Africa Order in Council, 1897, had (in terms very similar to those applying in Zanzibar) applied the civil and criminal codes of British India in the protectorate.[1] The judicial and legal system was further regulated by the Native Courts Regulations of the same year, and made under the Order in Council. These regulations provided for the recognition of certain native courts constituted by a European officer, a native authority, or a 'Mussulman' religious authority; and such courts were to be 'guided by the native law or custom existing in their respective jurisdictions'. An informal administrative power of supervision over these native courts was given by Regulation 48, including a power to disallow their judgements, but only where they were 'essentially inhuman or unjust'. The jurisdiction of the collectors' courts was restricted to 15 miles from the *boma*, or further at the discretion of the Commissioner. As in Uganda, the power was one of recognition of native courts, not their establishment. The Courts Ordinance, 1907, conceded the power to the governor (by section 10) to recognize the jurisdiction of 'a Tribal Chief or Council of Elders or Village Headman' (the last being an official and non-traditional appointment); and such courts were further regulated by the Native Tribunal Rules of 1908 and of 1911; but the latter rules, as pointed out by Phillips, mark a re-orientation of official policy in the direction of recognition of existing customary institutions only,[2] as the rules were limited to 'councils of elders . . . constituted under and in accordance with native law and custom' (rule 2 (1)); but this change was speedily deleted by further rules of 1913.

By section 13 of the Courts Ordinance, 1907, subordinate courts (in effect the courts of administrative officers) were granted supervisory powers over the native tribunals; and as appeal lay from the decisions of the subordinate courts to the

---

[1] Thus carrying on the application of the 'Indian civil and criminal codes' by the Imperial British East Africa Company. Cf. the agreement between H. M. Agent at Zanzibar and Mackenzie regarding the administration of Witu. McDermott, *British East Africa*, p. 322.

[2] A. Phillips, *Report on Native Tribunals* (Nairobi, Govt. Printer, 1945).

highest tribunal, the indigenous courts were partially integrated into the general judicial system of the territory, as in Uganda. But this system was not to last, as we shall see.

Sir Charles Eliot, who was Commissioner for the East Africa Protectorate from January 1901 to June 1904, has given us a picture of life and administration in the protectorate during that period.[1] Despite the fact that he himself presided in at least one reported case in the Chief Native Court, he does not devote much of his attention to legal and judicial matters. 'In theory', he says, the chief duties of the collectors and sub-collectors placed at each administrative station 'are to collect revenue and administer justice'; but in practice the administrative officer found himself a cross between an emperor and a general servant. This partly resulted from understaffing. From the point of view of keeping the peace, an enlarged police force and civil administration were preferable to a large military force used for periodical expeditions.[2] The elimination of the fiction that the coastal regions were part of the Sultan of Zanzibar's territories and administered as such was also essential, he thought. One of the main disadvantages of this legal distinction between the coastal strip and the interior was that the status of slavery was recognized at the coast, but proscribed inland.[3] But the major disadvantage of the theory that the coastal strip was foreign territory was that

the British authorities, as representing the Sultan, have no jurisdiction over foreigners, including natives of German East Africa who may happen to cross the boundary, and the native servants of such Europeans as are not British subjects ... During my stay in East Africa the foreign representatives were most considerate in the use they made of those rights in Mombasa; but as long as they exist legislation is often hampered.[4]

Although steps were taken to improve the situation through the surrender by other European powers of their extra-territorial privileges,[5] the legal division between coast and interior remained, of course, to plague legislators until after independence.

---

[1] Sir Charles Eliot, *The East Africa Protectorate* (London, 1905).
[2] Ibid., pp. 186, 199 sqq.
[3] Ibid., pp. 182, 233 sqq.
[4] Ibid., p. 182.
[5] See p. 351 above.

One of the changes introduced in 1902 was the transfer of the Kisumu Province from Uganda to East Africa. This had a surprising legal consequence. A man had been sentenced to death by a native court (presided over by a European officer) in this area when under Uganda administration; but the execution had not taken place at the time when the territory was transferred. As this type of court was not then allowed in East Africa, Eliot tells us that the authorities in the East Africa Protectorate could not execute the sentence, and the Uganda authorities had lost their power to do so by the transfer of territory. 'To let him go free would have been a scandal to the natives; to go through the process of trying him again before another court hardly less scandalising and mysterious. It was the man himself who helped us out of the difficulty. In ignorance of his security he tried to escape, and was shot by a warder.'[1]

One cannot help feeling that if competent legal advice had been available to the governments at this time, this legal impasse would never have occurred. As it was, the solution of the problem was convenient but hardly commendable.[2]

Early policy regarding the native courts and customary law

So much, then, for the judicial framework in the earlier part of our period. Not much has been said as yet about the indigenous tribunals and the law that they were applying; but since the one was intimately linked with the other it is more convenient to discuss indigenous courts and indigenous law together.

At the time of the arrival and extension of the British presence at the coast and in the interior, legal and judicial systems were functioning throughout the area. That of the Sultan of Zanzibar in Zanzibar itself and on the mainland we have already referred to; but outside the Sultan's dominions equally such systems were in existence, even if their details were less clearly grasped at the time by the incoming alien administrators. The indigenous systems ranged in sophistication all the way from a centralized,

---

[1] Eliot, *East Africa Protectorate*, p. 198.

[2] One would have expected the British and local governments to have made transitional arrangements covering pending cases, sentences, etc. If there were none, this was a startling commentary on the rough-and-ready character of the administration. And why was the warder not dealt with for shooting a man who had a right to escape?

highly developed, judicial structure and precisely formulated law, as in Buganda, to the decentralized, mainly arbitral, adjudicatory institutions and more elastic legal systems of peoples such as the Kikuyu or the Kamba.

Some of the European visitors, administrators, and the like were so struck by the barbarity of the punishments, the arbitrary character of accusation and conviction, and the prevalence of slavery in some of the indigenous legal systems that they found it difficult to appreciate the merits and rationality of these systems generally. A general prejudice against the indigenous systems of law and in favour of 'civilized' law was the result. If the traditional courts and law were allowed to continue, it was not because of an understanding of their merits so much as from a want of the necessary power and administrative machinery to implement the replacement of such systems at that time. Another inhibiting factor for a while was the limited character of British claims and jurisdiction in the area; in so far as power was claimed only over 'non-natives' or by virtue of rights expressly conceded by treaty—as with Zanzibar and Buganda—a direct interference with native tribunals was out of the question.

But this appreciation of the limits of British authority was eroded by circumstance. The time-honoured phrase 'peace, order and good government', which the British administrations were charged with advancing under their Orders in Council, exactly indicated in its successive components the process by which claims to extended jurisdiction were asserted. Peace—the suppression of inter-tribal warfare and slave trade—was the first requirement, achieved mainly by military force and extra-legal means. Order—the imposition of a stable system of overrule or government—was procured through the establishment of administrative stations throughout the interior; but their establishment did not imply at this period any more than minimal interference with indigenous institutions except where it was believed by the British that some manifest injustice or abuse was involved. Good government—the leading of the inhabitants to a new and better way of life—implied the insinuation of modes of conduct borrowed from another, and presumed superior, culture; in the legal sphere, it connoted the forced evolution, or even replacement, of customary laws in the direction of the imported British (English and Indian) laws.

But the view that 'native law' was inescapably inferior to western 'civilized' law and that it must in the long run disappear or be replaced, even if in the short term it was convenient or unavoidable to retain it, was by no means the only view on the place of customary law in the newly constituted judicial systems of eastern Africa. An enlightened individual like Sir Charles Eliot could write in 1905 that 'it often seems unreasonable to apply civilized law to simple savage life.'[1] His view was echoed much later in 1926 (by which time, of course, the recognition of 'native law and custom' and of the indigenous courts had become one of the main planks in the policy of indirect rule) by Sir Donald Cameron, then governor of Tanganyika: 'It was not the intention and is not the policy to impose upon the tribes a judicial system devised for them by ourselves and founded upon our idea of law and law courts, but to legalise and regulate the activities of whatever judicial machinery existed in the customs of the people.'[2]

If, however, recognition was accorded to indigenous courts and law at the beginning of the twentieth century, one feels that this was often a question of *faute de mieux*. The contrary point of view to that expressed by Sir Charles Eliot can also be illustrated by a quotation from a much later period, which nevertheless seems to echo the common opinion of earlier times. The Report of the Bushe Commission on the administration of justice in East Africa (published in 1933) averred, in speaking of customary law and its ideas of punishment, that 'clearly a system of substantive law which proceeded on such principles as these could not be tolerated in any part of the British Empire. It is the duty of the Government to civilize and to maintain peace and good order, and this can only be done by the introduction of British concepts of wrong doing.'[3]

Although titles to land by English law, or a variant thereof, had early been recognized in the East Africa Protectorate and the basis of a dual legal system had already been laid, nevertheless in theory at any rate Europeans and Africans were equal

---

[1] Eliot, *East Africa Protectorate*, p. 197.

[2] D. Cameron, *Native Administration Memoranda, No. II, Native Courts* (Dar es Salaam, 1926), p. 1.

[3] *Report of the Commission of Inquiry into the Administration of Justice in Kenya, Uganda and the Tanganyika Territory in Criminal Matters, May, 1933, and Correspondence arising out of the Report*, Cmd. 4623 (London, HMSO, 1934), p. 57.

under the general law. In practice, this ideal picture did not correspond with the facts. For a start, the lawlessness was not all on the part of the indigenous population: in 1903 three Europeans were tried on a charge of dacoity,[1] and the introduction of the jury system for Europeans only, which involved the trial of Europeans by Europeans, led to several evident miscarriages of justice. One of the most striking occurred in 1918, when two Europeans were tried for murder for beating an alleged thief, an African, to death. The jury of nine Europeans found the accused guilty of 'simple hurt'. This verdict led the *East African Standard* to comment in an editorial that 'there must be no suspicion of the existence of one penalty for crimes of this nature for the white man and another for the black. If the white man expects the black man to respect the law, he must respect it himself.'[2] But such suspicion existed, and it was well founded, so long as jury trial for Europeans only continued.

The old scheme of separate law and separate courts for Africans and non-Africans took its origin in two contradictory ideas, the one contemptuous, the other patronizing. On the one hand, it was thought by some Europeans, the Africans were not yet ready or fit for the wholesale application to them of 'civilized' law, but it was the Europeans' role to make them ready as soon as possible. On the other hand, argued others, uneducated people living a tribal way of life must be protected from the harmful consequences of total exposure to western ways and institutions. The history of the courts and law in East Africa over the succeeding decades was in large measure the history of the struggle between these two ideas. The two quotations from Cameron and Bushe already cited aptly summarize these points of view at a later era. The remainder of the legal history of East Africa will be an examination of the outcome of this struggle; but first we must look at an additional dimension that was added as the result of the First World War. This was the appearance of Tanganyika as a British territory, governed under the League of Nations mandate system which put the interests of the native inhabitants as the primary test of good government. The combination of this system and of the man chosen to put it into effective action in Tanganyika, Sir Donald Cameron,

[1] Cf. W. McGregor Ross, *Kenya from Within* (London, 1927), pp. 60–1.
[2] *East African Standard*, 7 Sept. 1918.

re-aligned the course of East African legal history for a generation.

Tanganyika and the early period of British administration

Nothing has been said as yet about the position of German East Africa while it was still under German administration. An instructive comparison could doubtless be made between the legal philosophy and practice of the Germans and the British in their neighbouring spheres; but materials for a detailed comparison are not available as yet on either side. But it seems probable that a comparison of this kind would disclose that the divergences in practice were by no means as great as appearances might suggest.

The Germans had established, once imperial rule had been introduced, a system of courts, supreme and subordinate, not dissimilar to that of the British in East Africa. If there was a contrast, it was in the different use that the two powers made of indigenous tribal authorities, and the varying respect which they paid to indigenous law. To a large extent the Germans were heirs to the Zanzibar system of administration through *liwalis*, *akidas*, and *jumbes*, at least on the coast and in the main centres up-country. These officials generally had little or no traditional (that is, tribal) claim to rule or administer justice. Elsewhere, so far as one can tell, an attempt was beginning to be made to discover and use the indigenous authorities (chiefs in council) for judicial purposes, notably in the Residencies in the north-west. This attempt was terminated by the outbreak of the First World War and the military struggle which supervened.

The Allied Powers were able, despite vigorous German resistance, to occupy a considerable part of the territory, and on 12 March 1916 martial law was proclaimed in the areas under British occupation, and on 1 April regulations were issued under martial law. British political officers were quickly introduced to assist with the administration of the area, and their powers were prescribed by further proclamations of 9 October 1916 and 12 June 1917. German law and the punishments prescribed thereunder were retained in force;[1] and the military

---

[1] As later Regulations, 22 Feb. 1919, made clear: 'The German Ordinances, Rules and Circulars which were in force on the 4th day of August 1914 are hereby declared to be in force and any contravention or breach thereof shall be deemed to be an offence and shall be punishable as therein stated.'

administration arranged for the publication of extracts from German laws for the benefit of the British political officers.

Apparently the courts established in the British-administered areas must have been applying Indian laws, as the Application of Laws Ordinance, No. 7 of 1920 (which came into effect on 4 December 1920), provided for the retrospective application, from 1 April 1919, of certain Indian Acts (notably the Penal Code and Criminal Procedure Code) and regularized anything done under such Acts between that date and the date of the Ordinance.[1]

By an Order in Council of 22 July 1920 Tanganyika Territory was constituted, under the government of a governor. A High Court was established under the presidency of a Chief Justice. The basic Indian character of the general law was maintained by the Order in Council, but the 'common law, doctrines of equity and the statutes of general application in force in England' on 22 July 1920 were introduced as the residual law of the territory. This date is thus critical for the establishment of both the judicial and legal systems of Tanganyika.

An amusing picture of legal life and the work of the High Court during this period has been given by Gilchrist Alexander,[2] who was one of the newly appointed judges of the High Court. The first governor, Sir Horace Byatt, formerly the civil Administrator of the Territory under martial law, having been 'bred in the lawyer-free atmosphere of Somaliland' did not look with favour on lawyers; he accepted judges as an 'unhappy necessity', 'but of lawyers he would have kept the territory free. As it was, he succeeded in preventing lawyers having audience at all in native courts.'[3] This hostility to professional legal men on the part of the administration was a recurrent feature of British colonial rule in Africa, and helps to explain such a striking characteristic of the colonial and legal judicial systems as the creation of a parallel system of native

[1] Note also the Regulations under Martial Law (Civil Area) of 5 Oct. 1918, issued by the Civil Administrator, which made mention of 'theft under the Indian Penal Code'. Proclamation No. 4 of 1920, regulating the jurisdiction and constitution of the courts, provided by s.21 that the Indian Penal Code 'shall henceforward be regarded as the standard of criminal law throughout the . . . territory'; but preserved the German civil law, by s.25.

[2] G. Alexander, *Tanganyika Memories: a judge in the red kanzu* (London and Glasgow, 1936).

[3] Ibid., p. 17.

courts insulated from the judiciary and the advocates and under the sole charge of administrative officers.

The judges had a heavy task to fulfil: the arrears of civil work were dealt with by a specially constituted court, the Special Tribunal; but in addition the judiciary had, by exercise of their revisionary powers, to educate the magistrates, many of them administrative officers, in how to exercise their criminal jurisdictions. 'At the beginning some of the errors made were quaint and almost grotesque', says Alexander;[1] but the standard rapidly improved.

The High Court had been established in what had formerly been military headquarters, and before that a German court.[2] But the judges also went on circuit, the Chief Justice travelling on occasion in a special coach on the Central Railway which was attached to any convenient train, and which could be detached at any station where cases were for trial. The coach in a siding then functioned as the judge's temporary lodgings. The first visit of this judicial coach, bearing a judge clothed in all the majesty of the law—scarlet robe, lace ruffles, silk stockings, silver buckles and full-bottomed wig—was an awe-inspiring sight to the waiting people, be they assessors, accused, witnesses, or bystanders, clad in their own traditional and sometimes just as picturesque garb.[3]

The advocates were a very mixed body, including barristers and solicitors from England, Ireland, Scotland, South Africa, and India. The bench was equally cosmopolitan.

The importance of Tanganyika in the legal development of East Africa has been considerable; this was almost entirely due to the arrival of Sir Donald Cameron as governor from Nigeria in 1925. Imbued with the theory and practice of indirect administration, he proceeded to put these into effect on his arrival in the territory. Expediency and the terms of the mandate under which Tanganyika was governed were put forward by Cameron as the two main justifications of this policy.[4] Not surprisingly, the policy found its main expression in the reorganization of the native courts, and the importance that was

---

[1] Ibid., p. 25.
[2] Ibid., p. 13.
[3] Ibid., pp. 27, 36 sqq., 59.
[4] D. Cameron, *My Tanganyika Service and some Nigeria* (London, 1939), p. 84.

attached to the preservation of indigenous legal institutions. Handling of native law and custom must be very gentle in the early days of administration; if an act under customary law is 'so flagrantly and dreadfully barbarous, so contrary to the accepted standard of modern civilization', then it must be stopped; 'if, however, it is merely something which we should not do ourselves in our own society, but is in accordance with native law and custom without gravely offending against the standards of modern civilization, let it alone for the present.'[1] There were special problems in applying this philosophy where witchcraft and sorcery were involved, or where the defence of property was an overriding necessity.[2]

The first recognition had been given to native courts under the Courts Ordinance, 1920, by which they were supervised by administrative officers in their capacity as magistrates and subjected to the overall supervision of the High Court. The system was much altered by the passing of the Native Courts Ordinance, 1929; the native courts were linked with the newly devised system of native authorities, and responsibility for the courts was placed fully and solely in the hands of the administration (not without protests from the judiciary).[3] A completely parallel system of courts was thus created of which one half primarily administered the general territorial law and from which appeal lay to the High Court, and the other half administered local customary laws and from which appeal lay through district officers and provincial commissioners to the governor.

The objects of these reforms, and the ways in which administrative officers should implement them, were set out by Cameron in a series of *Native Administration Memoranda*, of which the first, relating to native courts, was issued on 31 December 1926. 'The adoption of the policy of Indirect Rule implies *a priori* the recognition of Native Law and Custom' (p. 1); the judicial systems of each tribe must be carefully studied (p. 2); 'Native Courts are set up . . . to administer Native Law' (p. 5); there is a great danger of unhealthy development of native law, through

---

[1] D. Cameron, *My Tanganyika Service and some Nigeria* (London, 1939), p. 195.
[2] Ibid., pp. 195–9.
[3] Cf. the debate in the Legislative Council on the Bill. Tanganyika Leg Co *Debates*, 1028–9, Part ii.

the tendency of native courts to mimic the procedure, evidence, etc., of the British courts (pp. 6–7); an administrative officer must from time to time set aside native law 'as being repugnant to European ideas of justice and morality' (p. 8); it is not possible to specify exactly when and how this should be done, but a sense of proportion is required, and 'that which is different is not necessarily repugnant' (pp. 8–9); there can be changes in native law, which can be adapted to changing conditions, but such changes should be express and deliberate, achieved through the act of the native authority (p. 10).

The later development of the native courts systems and of the territorial courts

The subsequent history of the judicial systems in East Africa is the history of the reversal of Cameron's policies. The policy of maintaining separate judicial institutions for Africans alone was at first eroded and later abandoned, although the development of parallel courts was imitated in Kenya, as we shall see. The idea that these special 'native' or 'African' courts should be protected from the allegedly baleful hand of the higher judiciary and should be under the exclusive charge of administrative officers was also rejected in the post-1945 period, with the progressive elimination of the administrative officer as such from control of these courts, and the handing over of responsibility for the work of the native courts to the professional judiciary and magistracy. The notion that these native courts were an essential feature or prerogative of the traditional 'native authorities' also disappeared, with the constitution of statutory courts whose composition did not reflect traditional prerogatives of adjudication, and indeed with the disappearance of the native authorities themselves as significant elements in the structure of local administration. Equally the idea that African customary laws should be permitted to mark time, or to evolve in their own slow way, was increasingly rejected, for various reasons and by various means. Where a branch of the law, such as that relating to the tenure of land, had not evolved, or had evolved in an unsatisfactory way, the tendency was to replace it entirely by a statutory system owing nothing to customary law (as with the land consolidation programme in Kenya).

The reasons for these changes are not far to seek. The first is the development of political consciousness, which—often allied with or inspired by educational advance—led to a rejection of the traditional and tribal institutions in favour of the modern and western. The native authorities were superseded, and their going destroyed the basis on which the traditional native courts, as they had been 'recognized' by the British, had continued to survive. The second reason was the commitment to raising the standards of the native courts, both through judicial supervision and through informal or formal education outside the court. Demands for higher standards in the maintenance of court records, and the need to equip court members to administer statutory laws (such as minor Penal Code offences or local by-laws), were among the factors which made it imperative that the courts should be staffed by persons who could read and write and who could have some appreciation of the methods, objectives, and contents of the western-type laws of the territory. More rigorous selection of judges or the exclusion of the manifestly unsuitable, special training schemes for judges and court clerks, and the establishment of judicial work as a full-time job and not merely as a part-time ancillary public service, contributed to the evolution of the native courts (or African or local courts, as they came increasingly to be called) away from the traditional institutions. Let us now trace the processes by which the traditional tribunals evolved into modern statutory courts in greater detail in each of the territories.

The earlier history of native tribunals in Kenya has already been traced. In Kenya the native tribunals had not been mere appurtenances of the native authorities, and the policy of indirect rule was never adopted as the guide in this matter. In the 1920s a general concern developed on the part of administrative officers about the corruption and inefficiency of the native tribunals; this concern led to the passing of the Native Tribunals Ordinance, 1930. There was increasing dissatisfaction with the system whereby appeals lay from the native courts to subordinate courts and thence to the Supreme Court. This was felt to be harmful because it added greatly to the cost of litigation; because it encouraged the activities of lawyers' touts, who fomented litigation in the reserves; and because it led to technical decisions based on an alien law which worked injustice in the eyes of the African population.

The major effects of the 1930 Ordinance were to debar advocates from appearing in native tribunals or in proceedings on appeal therefrom; and to create a new channel of appeal through administrative officers, and not to the Supreme Court as previously. A parallel system closely comparable to that of Tanganyika at the same period was thus established.

In 1951 the system again came under review, largely as a result of an exhaustive investigation which had been made by Mr. Arthur Phillips[1] in 1944. Under the new African Courts Ordinance, 1951, the last link of the African courts (as they were now called) with the Supreme Court was broken, through the abolition of the case stated to the Supreme Court, and the creation of a new Central Court of Review as the final court of appeal in cases from African courts. This system remained in force, with modifications, up to the end of the colonial period.[2]

Similar reforms were introduced in Tanganyika in 1951. The old ordinance was repealed, and the previous native courts were reconstituted as 'local courts' under a new Local Courts Ordinance. The local courts were still largely customary in origin and jurisdiction, at least in rural areas; but in the urban areas and in courts of appeal another policy was now actively pursued;[3] this was to eliminate, if it had existed, the idea of courts as composed of benches of traditionally qualified elders, and to develop new types of courts with a specialized bench and in some instances constituted by a single magistrate or 'stipendiary' who, although lacking professional legal qualifications, would have a better educational and professional background than the ordinary local court president. This line of development foreshadows the contemporary evolution of the local or African courts systems in Tanzania, and indeed in the other East African countries.

[1] Later appointed Judicial Adviser.
[2] A completely new system of courts was introduced by the Judicature Act, 1967, which suppressed the African courts and replaced them by a system of District Magistrates' courts, from which appeal lies to the High Court.
[3] Cf. the clear statement of policy by the then Local Courts Adviser, Mr. J. P. Moffett, in the memorandum which he issued with the authority of government, *Local Government Memoranda No. 2* (Dar es Salaam, 1953), pp. 18–19.

Another striking change introduced by the 1951 Ordinance, which again was full of significance for the future, was the constitution of a new 'Central Court of Appeal' to hear appeals from the local courts. This court was in substitution for the previous appeals to provincial commissioners and the governor. The court consisted of a president who was a judge of the High Court, and two other administrative members. The link between the local courts system and the High Court was thus partially re-established, and the first step had been taken towards the complete integration of the local courts system with the other components of the judicial system in the territory.[1]

In Uganda judicial development, at least at the native court level, consistently proceeded along separate, though often comparable, lines in Buganda and the rest of the protectorate respectively.

A number of events of great significance for the Uganda courts systems occurred just about the beginning of the 1939–45 war. The first of these was the appointment of a 'Judicial Adviser' for Buganda. The idea for this appointment originated with the then governor, Sir Philip Mitchell; and he subsequently summarized its purpose as follows:

It seemed to me therefore that it was of great importance to devise a link between the two systems (the British and the Buganda), capable of interpreting them to each other, and of gradually bringing the native system into closer accord with the British and with the basic principles of judicial practice and procedure upon which the supreme judicial authority must in the last resort insist.[2]

The Judicial Adviser, the first such appointment in the British African territories since the Judicial Assessors of nineteenth-century Gold Coast, was both an adviser, helping to mould Buganda law and improve the Buganda courts, and an inter-mediate court of appeal between the Lukiko Court and the Uganda High Court. Later, the other East African territories appointed similar advisers, though without appellate powers. The first Judicial Adviser for Buganda was Mr. Charles (later Sir Charles) Mathew.

[1] The integration was completed by the Magistrates' Courts Act, 1963, which replaced the local courts with 'Primary Courts', which are staffed by career magistrates, and from which appeal lies through the ordinary judicial hierarchy.
[2] Sir Philip Mitchell, *African Afterthoughts* (London, 1954), p. 171.

One of the first tasks of the new Judicial Adviser was to draft a new ordinance to regulate Buganda courts, and this ordinance was duly enacted in 1940. In 1941 the Lukiko Court was restyled 'The Principal Court of His Highness the Kabaka'. The subordinate courts were re-organized under the ordinance, and a number of further changes were made in the Buganda courts in subsequent years, notably in the period 1954–7. The effect of these changes was to set up a full-time Buganda judiciary, and the number of lay, part-time, and executive magistrates or judges was progressively reduced.

Parallel legislation was introduced in 1940, by a Native Courts Ordinance, for the rest of Uganda outside Buganda. By this time the separate legislation which had existed at an early period for Bunyoro had been repealed, and courts in the other kingdoms were all regulated by the same ordinance as applied elsewhere, even if the membership and sophistication of the courts varied from place to place. Until the 1940s the composition of these courts had tended to be entirely official (i.e. chiefly) in character; but from the 1950s the tendency was for the chiefs to be replaced in their judicial functions by full-time specialist 'judges'. Nevertheless the then Attorney-General could claim, somewhat dubiously, in an official memorandum published at the time of the new ordinance, that the native courts and their membership were but a continuation and embodiment of the traditional institutions which had existed in pre-British times.[1]

In 1957 a new African Courts Ordinance was passed, which carried the process of integration with the non-customary courts a stage further.[2]

No such sweeping changes took place in the other half of the judicial system: that comprising the subordinate or magistrates' courts, the High or Supreme Courts, and the Court of Appeal. The history here was a simple one of the expansion in the numbers of the judges—reflecting the growth of judicial business—and the progressive replacement of administrative officer magistrates by full-time, professional, resident magistrates.

---

[1] H. R. Hone, comp., *Handbook on Native Courts for the Guidance of Administrative Officers* (Entebbe, Govt. Printer, 1941), pp. 1, 4.

[2] No. 1 of 1957. The Magistrates' Courts Act, 1964, completed the process of suppression of the African courts outside Buganda, and was in 1966 extended to Buganda also.

In Uganda the subordinate courts were the subject of amending legislation in 1911, 1919, and 1950. In Zanzibar the main change was that, as from 1914, appeal lay from the High Court to the Court of Appeal for Eastern Africa. This development was symptomatic of the extent to which the Zanzibar legal system, despite the uniqueness of its origin and the peculiarity of its dual system of courts with largely identical jurisdiction and personnel, kept in step with the systems of mainland East Africa.

In Kenya the most noteworthy event was the abolition of the High Court of the East Africa Protectorate, and the constitution in 1921 of a new Supreme Court, consequent on the redesignation of the territory as the Colony and Protectorate of Kenya. At the same time the seat of the court was moved from Mombasa to Nairobi. A system of subordinate courts, comprising courts of resident magistrates, administrative officers, and Muslim courts at the coast, was established under the Courts Ordinance of 1931. In Tanganyika, courts subordinate to the High Court had been established by the Courts Ordinance, 1920, and these courts had at first included the *liwalis'* courts (the courts of Muslim *liwalis* or *kadhis* at the coast); appeals from such courts lay ultimately to the High Court. But in 1941 the *liwalis'* courts were, for reasons of policy, re-established as native courts under the Native Courts Ordinance; in other words, they were removed from the jurisdiction of the High Court and equated with the courts of a more traditional African type.

The constitution of the Court of Appeal for Eastern Africa in 1902[1] was of special interest on two counts: first, it demonstrated the legal cohesion of the then British East African territories; and secondly, the court became from the time of its establishment one of the most important means by which this cohesion could be preserved. As such it had a permanent influence on the shape of East African legal systems.

The first Court of Appeal, as established in 1902, sat in Zanzibar, staffed by judges of Zanzibar and the protectorates.[2]

---

[1] Eastern African Protectorates (Court of Appeal) Order in Council, 1902. I am grateful to the staff of the Court of Appeal, and to the Librarian of the Supreme Court Library in Nairobi, for assistance with the procurement of information on the history of the court.

[2] The Zanzibar judges were the most prominent members of the court, and the court sat at Zanzibar, but appeals from H.B.M.'s Court for Zanzibar lay not to the Court of Appeal, but to Bombay, a truly bizarre arrangement.

Its jurisdiction covered the Protectorates of East Africa, Uganda, and British Central Africa. In 1909 a new Order in Council[1] established His Majesty's Court of Appeal for Eastern Africa; the court sat at Mombasa and was staffed by judges of the protectorates. Zanzibar came under the court in 1914, thus breaking the long-established link between the island and the High Court of Bombay. In 1921 the court was again reconstituted.[2] The members were still not full-time, being the Chief Justice of Kenya, Tanganyika, and Uganda, assisted by the Chief Justice of Zanzibar and the puisne judges of the territories. But in 1950 a new and permanent court, having its own full-time personnel (a President, a Vice-President, and one or more Justices of Appeal) was constituted.[3] The superior court judges continued to be entitled to sit when required, however. At the same time the court, which had formerly been itinerant between the East African territories, acquired a permanent seat in Nairobi. The territorial jurisdiction of the court was continually enlarged, and at one time included the Somaliland Protectorate (withdrawn with the independence of Somalia), Aden, Seychelles, and St. Helena. Alternative arrangements had been made for appeals from Nyasaland in 1947.

Conclusion

What have the East African countries done with the legacy of western and indigenous laws which accrued to them as a result of the piecemeal and gradualist extension of British jurisdiction over them? How far, by the end of the period, had the features which were characteristic of the original legal systems survived?

The first of these characteristics was, as we have briefly noted, the Indian character of the East African laws. Alexander, coming to this law as one previously experienced in English law, found it not very different from the English law with which he was familiar; but he felt that for the guidance of 'amateur lawyers' (by which he meant the administrative officer magistrates) 'the very elaborateness of the Indian codes tended to direct attention too much to the technicalities of the law.'[4] This comment is

---

[1] Eastern African Protectorates (Court of Appeal) Order in Council, 1909.
[2] Eastern African Court of Appeal Order in Council, 1921.
[3] Eastern African Court of Appeal Order in Council, 1950.
[4] Alexander, *Tanganyika Memories*, p. 24.

unexpected, since the original purpose of the codes had been to rationalize and simplify the English laws, and one might have felt—with those responsible for the introduction of the Indian codes into East Africa—that they were eminently suitable for application by inexperienced magistrates who found themselves far from any law library.

Be that as it may, in more recent times a strenuous effort was made to remove, or at least diminish, the Indian element in East African law.[1] Here Uganda was in the van. Some of the Indian laws were replaced by identical local ordinances; in other cases (for instance with the law of crimes and criminal procedure), new codes based more closely on the law of England were introduced.

However, the repeal of the Indian Penal Code in the East African territories in 1930 did not meet with the universal approval of the bench and the practising profession. Disquiet about the administration of criminal justice in East Africa led to the appointment of a Commission of Inquiry, under the chairmanship of the Legal Adviser to the Colonial Office, Mr. H. G. Bushe, which reported in 1933.[2] The commission bluntly stated that 'the machinery for the administration of justice as apparently set up by law in those territories does not work, and, as at present constituted, cannot work.'[3] The reasons for this extremely grave and damaging assessment were to be found in the giving of excessive jurisdiction to administrative officer magistrates, and the absence or shortage of sufficient professionally qualified judges and magistrates. The result was delay in the High Courts and remoteness of the courts from the people. Administrative officers, the commission said, found it difficult to put administrative considerations out of their minds when sitting as judges. According to the commission the 'native' was generally speaking 'unable to appreciate the British conception of a crime as an anti-social act and an offence against the state rather than

---

[1] Thus the Indian Contract Act has been replaced in Uganda and Kenya by English law (Contract Act, 1962, of Uganda; and Law of Contract Ordinance, 1960, of Kenya), and in Tanganyika by a local re-enactment of the Indian Contract Act (Law of Contract Ordinance, 1961). At the time of writing, no Indian statute law applies in Uganda, and only a relatively limited amount in Kenya and Tanzania.

[2] *Report of the Commission of Inquiry into the Administration of Justice in Kenya, Uganda and the Tanganyika Territory in Criminal Matters*, Cmd. 4623 (London, HMSO, 1934).

[3] Cmd. 4623, p. 8.

a personal wrong to the person injured thereby'.[1] If this conclusion was justified, then it could be said that a similar misunderstanding prevailed in respect of other branches of the English law which had been applied *volens nolens* to the African population.

Although the territorial governments angrily rejected the commission's criticisms, both particular and general, much was done in subsequent years to meet them, both by expanding the numbers of professional judges and magistrates and by cutting down the judicial powers of administrative officers. The basic complaint, that the British system of law and justice was unintelligible to Africans, remained undealt with.

But something was being done about this problem, though by more indirect means. As Hone put it in 1941:

There can be little doubt that the development of native law and custom has to a very considerable extent been achieved by the adoption by the courts [i.e. native courts] themselves of advice and guidance given to them in the past by administrative officers—advice which, consciously or unconsciously, the courts have incorporated as part of their native system of jurisprudence.[2]

And, quite apart from such guidance, the educational and economic evolution of the African populations led to the adoption of western ways of doing things, including western legal ways, in such matters as marriage or the tenure of property.

By the end of the period this trend was being reinforced by legislation (such as that concerning land in Kenya). As a result of these pressures, the customary laws became progressively emancipated from their traditional form and background, and at the same time their rules—and the language in which they were expressed—approached ever more closely those of the general English-type law. In this way the second of the major features of the original colonial legal systems, that they preserved the ancient African laws for the African section of the population, receded in importance. A considerable dualism remained, however, to the end of the colonial period.

The task which faced the independent East African governments was to complete the processes already at work and described above: to unify the legal systems, both in the sense

---

[1] Ibid., p. 63.
[2] Hone, *Handbook on Native Courts*, p. 10.

that no one should find himself living at one and the same time under two kinds of law, English and African, and in the sense that persons of different communities or races should not find themselves, by reason only of their origin, placed under different legal systems; to revindicate the African heritage of law, submerged for so long under alien laws and conceptions; and to evolve a new and integrated legal system, adapted to the needs of the day, and free from archaisms whether of western or indigenous origin.

X

THE IMPACT OF CHRISTIANITY ON EAST AFRICA

F. B. WELBOURN

B Y an interesting piece of linguistic juggling, the Catholic missionary and historian J. Gorju[1] was able to identify Buganda with the Christian empire of Magdasor, which in 1304 is said to have sought the help of missionaries from Peking; and he found residual Christian influences in the sign of the Cross, made from right to left in the orthodox manner, by priests of the Ganda god Muwanga. Certainly the Christian Portuguese were on the coast of East Africa from the early sixteenth century; and in 1630 Yusufu bin Hasan, educated in Goa and known to the Portuguese as Dom Jeronimo Chingulia, was installed as the first Christian king of Mombasa. The following year, he expelled his Portuguese masters; and all Christian converts were either forcibly reconverted to Islam or killed.

Not till 1844 was any further attempt made to plant Christianity in East Africa. In this year Ludwig Krapf, a German Lutheran employed by the English Church Missionary Society, arrived at Mombasa, to be joined two years later at his mission

---

General bibliographical note: The basic historical facts are in C. P. Groves, The Planting of Christianity in Africa, 4 vols. (London, 1948–58). Fundamental to this chapter are D. A. Low, Religion and Society in Buganda, 1875–1900 (London and Kampala, 1957); R. Oliver, The Missionary Factor in East Africa (London, 1952); J. V. Taylor, The Growth of the Church in Buganda (London, 1958). I have drawn so freely on them that individual references are not given in the text. I have treated in the same way my own East African Rebels (London, 1961)—about independent churches in Buganda and Kikuyu; 'Some aspects of Kiganda Religion', Uganda Journal, 26 (Sept. 1962); Religion and Politics in Uganda, 1952—1962 (Nairobi, 1965); and (with B. A. Ogot) A Place to Feel at Home (London, 1966)—about the African Israel Church and the Church of Christ in Africa. I have treated the subject-matter of this chapter at greater length for sixth forms, in East African Christian (London, 1965). The impact of Christianity on the non-élite is delightfully described in E. H. Winter, Beyond the Mountains of the Moon (London, 1959), esp. pp. 262–5. Monica Wilson, Communal Rituals of the Nyakyusa (London, 1959), chaps. xii–xiv, is an intimate account of its impact, and adaptation, in a small area of south-east Tanzania.

[1] J. Gorju, Entre le Victoria, l'Albert et l'Edouard (Paris, 1920), chap. x.

station at Ribe by his fellow-countryman Johann Rebmann. If they had little immediate success in spreading the Gospel, their explorations stirred the imagination of British geographers and paved the way for those more ambitious journeys which in 1875 brought H. M. Stanley, and in 1877 CMS[1] missionaries, to the court of Mutesa I of Buganda. In the meantime, a party of three secular priests from the island of Réunion, assisted by three nuns of the Daughters of Mary, a mechanic, a blacksmith, a joiner, and three others, landed at Zanzibar in December 1860.[2] Their work was taken over in 1863 by the Holy Ghost Fathers. In the same year the British Methodists succeeded to the work of Krapf and Rebmann at Ribe; in 1864 the Universities' Mission to Central Africa transferred its headquarters from the Shire Highlands of Malawi to Zanzibar; and in 1868 both they and the Holy Ghost Fathers opened stations on the mainland. In 1875 the CMS founded its settlement for freed slaves at Freretown near Mombasa.[3]

Most of the early work on the coast was, in fact, among freed slaves; and the effective entry of Christian missions into East Africa must be dated from the arrival of the CMS in Buganda, to be followed two years later by the White Fathers, the Catholic missionary order founded by Cardinal Lavigerie in the 1860s. In less than seven years there were martyrs; and in thirteen Christianity had become the established religion of the country. From this kingdom, Christianity spread outwards through Uganda and into the Bantu and Nilotic areas of what is now western Kenya. Christianity in Buganda presents, in highly dramatic form, all the major problems with which the Church throughout East Africa was to be faced; and it is inevitable that frequent reference to it should be made in the narrative which follows.

According to the census of 1959, Buganda had 1,834,000 inhabitants, of whom 49 per cent were Roman Catholic, 25 per

[1] The following abbreviations are used throughout: AIC—Africa Inland Church formed by AIM—African Inland Mission; BCMS—Bible Churchmen's Missionary Society; CMS—Church Missionary Society; PCEA—Presbyterian Church of East Africa; UMCA—Universities' Mission to Central Africa.

[2] I am grateful to Mr. J. A. Kieran, for allowing me to read a draft of his work on 'The Holy Ghost Fathers in East Africa'. The term 'Black Fathers', which has been applied to this party, was used by the Germans to describe the Holy Ghost Fathers.

[3] A. J. Temu, *British Protestant Missions* (London, 1972), ch. iv, describes the contribution of 'Bombay Africans' to CMS work at the coast.

cent Protestant, and 8 per cent Muslim. In so far as it is possible to rely on the census of 1911, growth had taken place, over 58 years, by factors of 4·8, 3·3 and 2·4, compared with a factor of 2·6 in the population as a whole. These figures ought to dispose effectively of the belief that Islam in East Africa was growing at the expense of the Christian Church. Trimingham thinks that there had been no significant expansion since 1930. Islam was a force sufficiently large to enter into the calculations of politicians. But, as a competing missionary community, it is unlikely that it affected the growth of the Christian Church.[1]

Certain major issues seem to need special discussion. In the first place, missionary intentions may be variously defined: to establish Christ's Church in Africa, to ensure that in Africa also God is worshipped in Christ, or to bring salvation to individuals through the power of Christ. However they saw their chief end missionaries pursued it with eagerness, often enough with self-giving to the point of death; and there is ample evidence in individual African lives that they sometimes achieved it. What—

[1] *Uganda Census 1911*, Uganda Government (1911); *Uganda Census 1959*, Uganda Government (1963); J. S. Trimingham, *Islam in East Africa* (London, 1964). The only reliable religious statistics available in East Africa are those for the Uganda Census of 1959, which are based on a 5% sample area survey. In Uganda as a whole the proportions of Catholics, Protestants, and Muslims were 33%, 25% and 5·2%. The probability is that in Kenya and Tanganyika the percentages of pagans were higher, while in the Madi District of Uganda the estimate of Muslims was 37%, and on the coast of Kenya and Tanganyika and in Zanzibar the percentage of Muslims was also much higher. According to T. W. Gee, 'A century of Muhammedan influence in Buganda 1852–1951', *Uganda Journal*, 22 (Sept. 1958), Catholics in Buganda increased by a factor of 3·9 between 1911 and 1954, Protestants by 3·7 and Muslims by 5. If this were true, Muslims increased at twice the rate of the general population. It might be accounted for by the fact that Muslims may have four official wives and that, not going to school, they married relatively younger than Catholics and Protestants. No Ganda Muslim imagined that it would be due to conversions. But Gee's figures are based on chiefs' returns which must be regarded with the gravest reserve. Roman Catholic and Protestant sources both agree closely with the official estimate of Protestants. The former shows however 42% Catholics and 11% Muslims in 1959. More recently L. W. Swantz, (*Church, mission, and state relations in pre- and post-independent Tanzania* (Maxwell Graduate School of Citizenship and Public Affairs, Programme of East African Studies, Occasional Paper No. 19, May 1965) has used Christian sources to show that 25% of the population of Tanzania were Christian in 1964, compared with 10% in 1938, while 38% of those interviewed in an independent survey claimed to be Christian. Swantz also reports an annual increase of 8–10% in the membership of all churches since independence. His figures for the Lutheran Church of Northern Tanzania show 55,557 adults and 50,090 children in 1955, while 2,943 adults and 5,140 children were baptised in 1954. This is sufficient evidence of the tendency for the Church adherents to be recruited from the second generation and through the schools.

in the short view—is more significant, and what is far too often ignored in telling the missionary story, is that they achieved, for themselves and for their converts, something which they did not intend and which they would almost certainly have rejected had they seen its full implications. They became involved in the power structure of the colonial situation. The denominationalism which, inevitably, was imported from the west caused not only social but political division; and, as nationalism developed and the God of the Church became identified with the God of the Europeans, it began to be asked whether Christianity was in fact the religion for Africa, or whether it was no more than the religious edge of the imperialist policy of 'divide and rule'. An indigenous Church, against this background, is in an unenviable position when it tries to proclaim the universal Gospel to a nationalist society.

Secondly, and closely related to the former point, missionaries were earthen vessels, who found it extremely difficult (even if the question ever occurred to them) to distinguish between the Christian gospel and the western culture in terms of which they had learned to express it. For Africans, this was at first no great disadvantage. They saw the Church—as they would expect to see it in terms of their own culture—as concerned as much for agriculture, education, and medicine as for the salvation of souls. Christianity for them was integral to the superior culture; and nationalism arose at least in part as a demand for that human dignity which Christianity seemed to preach but its white representatives to deny. It was all very well to say that the affirmation came from the religion, the denial from the rest of the western culture. This was to make precisely the division between religion and life which is wholly foreign to Africa but has for centuries been accepted in the west.

It is possible to assert that 'religion should have nothing to do with politics' simply because nationalism has long ago taken the place of Christianity as the clue to the identity of western man. To be a Christian means no longer to be a member of what the African theologian Tertullian called 'a third race of men'. It means—to most people—simply to be a better Englishman or Frenchman rather than to claim a heavenly citizenship. 'It is unfortunate,' writes Apter, 'that in an age of secularism, Western observers have difficulty in grasping the proportions of pure belief. . . . a stubborn quality.'[1] Europe failed, this seems to say, to understand Hitler because it regarded him as a political, instead of a religious, leader. So not only Europeans, but Africans themselves, failed to understand the truth of African nationalism. It was a movement towards political independence only in so far as that independence was the political expression of a much more fundamental discovery, at the religious level, of a new identity as Africans. Christian beliefs and customs might claim observance as the 'religious' aspect of a society which 'politically' was nationalist. But they appeared irrelevant because, whether it is recognized or not, nationalism is itself the religious dimension of nationalist society.[2] In so far as Christians undertake 'as aliens and exiles' to 'honour the king', they are suspect and court elimination, because the nationalist 'king' demands more than honour.

Against this theoretical background, an attempt will be made to describe five fairly clear-cut areas in which missionaries worked: involvement in the colonial situation, the building of an indigenous ecclesiastical structure, the teaching of Christian morals, the development of medical services, and a vast pioneering work in the field of education. Finally, there will be discussion of the extent to which Christianity can rightly be said to have given rise to nationalism, and of the connections between Christianity, nationalism, and tribalism.

Throughout the chapter mention will be found both of independent churches and of the Revival. The former, under African leadership, frequently sought to dress Christianity in African clothes. They sprang out of, and continued alongside, the churches of missionary origin. The latter started in 1935 in the Rwanda Mission of the CMS and spread widely—though primarily in CMS and Presbyterian areas—throughout East Africa and in the Southern Sudan.[3] Both appear to have been attempts to find a new identity at a time when tribal solidarity

[1] D. E. Apter, *The Political Kingdom in Uganda* (London and Princeton, 1961), p. 460.

[2] Cf. A. MacIntyre and P. Ricoeur, *The Religious Significance of Atheism* (New York and London, 1969), p. 22: 'Thus religious formulas tend increasingly to be used in modern society for purposes other than that of expressing the theological statements for which they were originally framed.'

[3] M. A. C. Warren, *Revival* (London, 1954); J. E. Church, *Awake Uganda* (Kampala, 1957).

was failing and nationalism had scarcely yet emerged; and in fact it seems that the independent churches may be important guardians, in the African states of today, of the Christian tradition. The Revival, except in so far as it was able to express and meet the needs of Africans in Africa, was of much the same character as Revival elsewhere, and its English-speaking leaders found ready acceptance in Europe, in India, and in Brazil. Its strength lay in the very genuine moral renewal of its converts; the creation of a fellowship which gave not only spiritual guidance but detailed assistance in material crises; the development of an unpaid lay leadership; and a thorough crossing of the racial barriers such as was not always achieved in the Church at large. Its weakness was the weakness of all fanaticisms—a certain spiritual pride and relentless persecution of those whom it desired to save—while its insistent separation between individual salvation and the social and political problems of society rendered it unable to make any serious contribution to the issues which are the primary concern of this chapter. There is nevertheless the possibility that, in a nationalist society which has no room for competitors in the spiritual realm, Christian awareness in the social and political fields will have no permitted place. In that case the faith may reach the future only through those who ignore its secular implications.

Secular involvement and its complications

Within eight years of the arrival of the first missionaries in Buganda, there were African martyrs.[1] Within twelve, the Christians ruled the country and applicants for baptism were soon more than could be properly prepared. The Christian chiefs not only tried to destroy the old religion and made themselves responsible for furthering the new. By 1893 they were freeing their slaves and giving greater freedom to their womenfolk. When, in 1897, the majority of them sided with the British against the dissident Kabaka Mwanga,[2] and in 1900 alienated to their own advantage both clan and temple land, they seemed

---

[1] J. F. Faupel, *African Holocaust* (London, 1962).
[2] Mwanga succeeded his father, Mutesa I, as Kabaka of Buganda in 1884. His attempted *coup* in 1897 was directed as much against control by his own chiefs as against the British.

to have established a position from which they could not ignore tradition but could go forward to build a new Buganda. Some of them used on their notepaper a clan symbol surrounded by the motto, '*simudda nnyuma*', 'there's no turning back'. The blood of the martyrs seemed to have been not only the seed of the Church, but the sap of the political kingdom.

But events were to prove them wrong. The fatal division between Catholic and Protestant, here complicated by Islam, was to spread out from Buganda and create throughout Uganda indigenous religio-political institutions. The one God seemed to be divided against himself and could not act as a symbol of national unity. Moreover, when populist discontent arose in the 1930s against the chiefs who were heirs to the Christian rebellion, it could be thought that their Christianity was part and parcel of their loyalty to British government. Christianity became irrelevant to the struggle for self-determination; and this was confirmed by the deportation of Kabaka Mutesa II in 1953.[1] For the vast majority of Ganda the only adequate symbol, for both unity and integrity, became the kabakaship. The new God was accused of betraying Buganda. The old gods were recalled to restore the balance. By 1961 a new and more serious threat had arisen. Buganda was in danger of absorption into an independent Uganda ruled by African commoners. *Kabaka Yekka*[2] was formed as an all-Buganda party to fight the national elections in Buganda and won a resounding victory. While remaining Catholic and Protestant in name, Ganda demonstrated that they were, first of all, Kabaka's men. The Kabaka had achieved two positions unknown to any of his predecessors. On paper, since his return from exile in 1955, he had been a constitutional monarch. In practice, he was the focal point of Ganda religion.[3] The consequences of his election, in October 1963, as President of Uganda underlined the impossibility of being both at the same time.

---

[1] D. A. Low and R. C. Pratt, *Buganda and British Overrule* (London and New York, 1960), pp. 315–19.

[2] 'Kabaka only'. It was claimed that this organization was not a political party, but formed precisely to defend the Buganda state *against* the parties. It nevertheless fought the elections like any other party and formed a coalition with the Uganda Peoples' Congress in the central government. See I. R. Hancock, 'Patriotism and Neo Traditionalism in Buganda: the Kabaka Yekka movement, 1961–62,' *J. Af. History*, 11, 3 (1970), 419–34.

[3] The question 'Was Mutesa I a god?' is discussed by H. P. Gale, *Uganda and the Mill Hill Fathers* (London, 1959), chap. i.

Only in Uganda, owing to the circumstances of Buganda's conversion, were the churches as institutions to become involved in national politics. But, if Buganda was a special case, it is nevertheless a clue to what happened elsewhere. Missionaries aimed at converting men who would be servants of God and, *pari passu*, servants of their fellows. The schools they established were intended to produce not only instructed Christians but men who would serve with intelligence the new order in both Church and State. But at every point they were involved in power. Education led to paid employment, with its enlargement of material standards, of social status and of opportunity to influence the new rulers. In many cases, it led eventually to chieftainships. The clergy, in so far as they received stipends in cash, were better off than their contemporaries who remained peasants. Education—and in almost every case education meant passing through a mission school and acquiring baptism in the process—was the key to the white man's magic of reading and writing, and therefore to the white man's power. Below the all-powerful European, Christians formed the first power-structure of the new Africa.[1]

It was also a denominational power-structure. In Uganda, the dominance of Protestants in local government can, to some extent, be accounted for as a product of Lugard's settlement in 1892, when the Protestant minority was given the predominant place in the administration of Buganda. But partly also, Protestant missionaries were largely British, had good relations with British government officers, and assumed that education meant education for leadership. In contrast, Catholic missionaries were frequently French or Italian, were unsympathetic to British government as such, and regarded obedience to authority as the most admirable quality. Everywhere there was a tendency to Protestant dominance in society. Always Christianity tended to divide rather than to unite. Kikuyu students from neighbouring Catholic and Protestant villages, spending Christmas in Kampala at the height of Mau Mau, found that neither knew how the other would celebrate it; in Kilimanjaro, a chief of a

[1] J. M. Lonsdale, 'Political Associations in Western Kenya', in *Protest and Power in Black Africa*, ed. R. I. Rotberg and A. Mazrui (New York, 1970); M. G. Whisson, *Change and Challenge: a study of the social and economic changes among the Kenya Luo* (Nairobi, 1964).

denomination different from that of his people found it impossible to rule; among the Nyakyusa of southern Tanzania, where the Moravians established an almost tribal church linked closely with the vernacular and claiming all but a very few of the new élites, Catholics, Lutherans, and Pentecostalists could be regarded as only marginal Nyakyusa.[1]

Moreover, the missionaries had seemed to preach the white man's God. That this interpretation was often ill-founded is demonstrated by many instances to the contrary: by the way in which, in 1900, Tucker and Walker of the CMS argued the case for the Ganda chiefs:[2] by the fight of the Presbyterian John Arthur and others against the Kenya Labour Circular of 1919; and, later, by the identification with the Tanganyika African National Union of Miss Barbara Johansson of the Swedish mission in Buhaya. But appearances had often been different. When the committee headed by (the then) Archdeacon Beecher published its recommendations on African education in Kenya,[3] these were known to go much further than the administration had originally intended towards the provision of a comprehensive system of education. Yet they were condemned by Africans as wholly inadequate and seen as a serious reflection on the sincerity of the Anglican church. When the Kabaka of Buganda was deported in 1953, both Anglican and Catholic bishops were popularly supposed to have been consulted before the governor took action. There was a considerable falling-off in church attendance; and even some Revivalists defected.

In the 1920s it was discovered that the African Orthodox Church in South Africa was 'a church (of the Africans, governed by the Africans, and for the Africans) to make daily supplications to Almighty God led by priests who have the welfare of Africans at heart'. It was welcomed avidly both by Reuben Spartas in Buganda and by the Kikuyu independents.

Later, both the Tanganyika African Church in the Anglican territory around Dodoma and the Moravian parts of Tabora, and the Church of Christ in Africa, which split off from the Anglican church among the Luo in 1957, were founded in dis-

---

[1] Monica Wilson, *Communal Rituals*, does not notice this very strong sense among the Nyakyusa élites.

[2] Low and Pratt, *Buganda and British Overrule*, pp. 38 sqq.

[3] *African Education in Kenya*, Chairman L. J. Beecher (Nairobi, Govt. Printer, 1949).

satisfaction with the apparent dominance of the Revival in churches of the CMS tradition. They expressed their dissatisfaction by insisting that they were African. In Tanganyika, the course of relationships ran more smoothly; and an Australian bishop wisely allowed an African archdeacon to reconcile the CMS and the dissidents. In Kenya by contrast, where politics were still largely anti-European, schism flourished. Luo Christians exploited the traditional feeling against a Luhya bishop; the politician Oginga Odinga saw the advantage of support from a church among his own tribesmen which, while Christian in rather more than name, was not controlled by white missionaries;[1] and a European archdeacon thought that he could apply to dissident Luo methods which had been successful with communists in east London. In these circumstances there was no reconciliation.

The immigrant churches had come to stay; and they had a story of great excitement to tell.[2] They looked forward to attaining autonomy under a fully African leadership. But that leadership was as conservative as any; it had been trained to assume the superiority of western forms of church government, of doctrinal expression, of morals, and of liturgy; and the laity were imbued with the inertia of western Christendom, which tended to assume that all change must be initiated by the clergy. It was a serious question whether churches of this type were able to meet the challenge of Africanism implicit in the nationalist movements: or whether such Christian leadership as remained in society would pass to churches of more independent origin. Already the African Israel Church[3] counted among its leaders skilled artisans. One of its great strengths was that it had from the start a wholly African leadership. It had, therefore, never been able to assume a European leadership on which to lean, or funds from outside its own membership. In an independent Africa that might be no small advantage.

There is a Kikuyu saying, '*Gutiri mubia na muthungu*'—'there is no difference between a missionary and a settler'—which has to be taken into account at all points of the missionary impact on

---

[1] Odinga was later deserted by the church.

[2] e.g. Faupel, *African Holocaust*; E. M. Matheson, *An Enterprise so Perilous* (London, 1962).

[3] Mainly active among Luo and Luhya in Kenya.

East Africa. Its original implication was that a missionary was as likely as a settler to take Kikuyu land. It was applied later on to a missionary who admitted that she would drink alcohol in the company of Europeans, but never with Africans. In general, it applied to the impossibility, for any man, of distinguishing clearly between his faith in Christ and the culture of the society in which he had learnt it. Missionaries not only had the dominant personalities of their age and class.[1] They believed that 'civilization' was superior to 'barbarism'; and the more Protestant they were, the more they tended to denigrate everything African. Tribal beliefs were not only (in accord with the current scientific mood) nonsense: they were wicked.[2] Tribal songs and dances were of the devil. Tribal customs had to be destroyed without considering the possibility that they might have to be replaced.

More seriously, missionaries were seen—they themselves would have said, wrongly—as the pioneers of foreign government. An agent of government or commerce, on entering an area, paid his respects first to the missionary and only later, if at all, to the African chief. Missionaries were asked to explain official policy to their converts. Any white man was liable to break off a conversation with an African if another white man approached. In some areas, missionaries received Africans only at the back door. By African standards, all Europeans lived at a level of material culture which was inconceivable.

By the same standards, in the early days, a missionary was the greatest known farmer, carpenter, smith, doctor, dentist, linguist, and story-teller. By the very nature of his life in an undeveloped community, he had to be a jack-of-all-trades, not only for his own comfort but to meet the demands of charity towards those whom he had come to serve. In some cases, he became the civil magistrate of the new Christian settlements. Some missions developed plantations as the economic basis of self-supporting communities. The Moravians established their own trading stations; and a CMS missionary stimulated the formation of the Uganda Company, an independent trading venture counting

---

[1] O. Mannoni, *Prospero and Caliban* (London, 1956). Originally published in French as *Psychologie de la colonisation* (Paris, 1950).

[2] The same accusation against the teaching of Catholic missionaries is made by Fr. C. Haule, *Bantu 'Witchcraft' and Christian Morality* (Schöneck-Beckenried, 1969).

among its directors members of the CMS London committee.[1] But even the building of mission houses and churches involved the training of African masons and carpenters; and these initial training courses developed into technical schools, preparing artisans for independent employment in society at large.

Africans thus saw the Church—as it was rarely seen in the west—as an institution concerned not only in theory but in daily and detailed practice, with every aspect of man's life. For men in whose culture religion is not one institution among many possible choices of allegiance, but an essential dimension of living,[2] it followed that to accept a new God entailed the acceptance of the culture of his agents; to enter their culture and to acquire their techniques meant to worship their God. Behind the invitation from Mutesa I to missionaries to enter Buganda lay his desire to have European guns.

This experience was to have a profound effect upon the form of African-led independent churches at a later date. It makes it extremely difficult, in African society at large, to disentangle the effects of the Church from those of western culture as a whole. Like the early missionaries, Africans also saw the Church as integral to a superior culture. In the 1940s, converts to the African Israel Church were choosing Christianity as part of the western order which seemed to contrast so strongly with the disintegrating tribal life around them. Reuben Spartas' first experiment in independency was to found a school; and the Kikuyu independents insisted on English rather than Swahili as the medium of instruction. Baptism became identified with literacy; and the two together were the gateway into the new society.

It was to be discovered later that to work for Europeans, or even to worship with them, was not the same as being socially accepted by them; and this discovery was to act as a powerful stimulus in the formation of independent churches and the growth of nationalism. It was worse still when missionaries were seen to be condemned by their own standards. 'Two of them came from the Congo and introduced Congo-type treatment of Africans. When I came late to church one Sunday, while prayers were

[1] C. Ehrlich, *The Uganda Company Limited: the first fifty years* (Kampala, 1953).
[2] G. and M. Wilson, *The Analysis of Social Change* (Cambridge, 1945), diagram on p. 82.

being said, I found one of them cutting his nails.'[1] Remarks such as these did not find their way into the missionary magazines. But the evil that men do lives after them. There were too many memories of this sort even among Africans who became deeply Christian. Among the population at large, they tended to form the lasting image of the church. It was no easy task—and for reasons often not suspected—to be a Christian missionary. The archives of the African Israel Church are an eloquent commentary on missionaries who invited themselves to preach and then abused the hospitality offered by attempting to proselytize. But far more serious was the discovery that not all Europeans even pretended to be Christian. There was not even lip-service to the ideal of human brotherhood. There was economic exploitation, and legal as well as social discrimination. There was open drunkenness and sexual promiscuity. It was no longer possible to see the new culture as an integral whole. There was, it appeared, political and economic power; and there was religion; and, even if the preachers of the one were honest in their intentions, they were simply exploited by those who wielded the other. One white man got you on your knees in prayer while the other stole your land. Moreover, while they stopped tribal wars, they made war among themselves, expected Africans to join in the shooting, and appointed clergy to sanctify it.[2]

Thus it became possible to make a conscious distinction between 'religion' and 'culture'. The church not only came to be seen as standing over against, and criticizing, African culture. It appeared as an institution which, unlike 'African religion' in its own *milieu*, was not essential to the material aspects of western culture. Pagans—men who, in western eyes, clearly practised traditional 'religion'—were described in more than one vernacular as 'those who have no religion'; and, in the 1962 elections in Buganda, the kabakaship was claimed as an affair not of religion but of 'essential nature'. Catholicism, Protestantism, and Islam could be regarded as three denominations of spiritual merchandise which—like different brands of motor-car—were offered by aliens to Africans. They were a matter not of fundamental truth but of individual choice. And, like motor-cars, their purchase by

---

[1] Recorded, from Marakwet, by Dr. B. E. Kipkorir.
[2] See e.g. Elspeth Huxley, *White Man's Country* (London, 1953), vol. ii, p. 54.

Africans yielded profit to those who introduced them. It might be better, in the long run, to arrange for their local manufacture.

Nations and denominations

A crucial example of the involvement of Christianity in the secular was the multiplicity of missionary societies, often representing different European nationalities, through which it was offered to East Africa. To start with, in Buganda, Catholics and Protestants were known as 'French' and 'English'—agents not so much of different theological traditions as of competing western powers. By 1892 their Ganda followers had become indigenous political institutions. Seventy years later, the denominational associations of the main political parties had become blurred by other issues. But it was still possible to refer to the Uganda Peoples' Congress as 'United Protestants of Canterbury' and to the Democratic Party as '*Dini ya Papa*'—'Religion of the Pope'. In 1895 the entry of the British Roman Catholic Mill Hill Mission was deliberately planned to demonstrate the possibility of being at the same time both English and Roman Catholic. But it was to introduce a rivalry between the two leading Roman Catholic schools[1] which by no means led to social stability. The presence in Northern Uganda of the Italian Verona Fathers did not simplify the scene. But at least all Roman Catholic missions were 'RCM'; and, whatever the tensions at the local level, the figure of the Pope remained a unifying factor.

For Protestants in Uganda the issue was, at first, greatly simplified by the presence of the Anglican Church Missionary Society alone. The Bible Churchmen's Missionary Society, arriving late on the scene in Karamoja, was itself Anglican and worked under the Anglican bishop. The interdenominational Africa Inland Mission, at work in West Nile, had a natural institutional link with the Africa Inland Church, established by fellow-missionaries in the Congo, in Kenya and in Tanganyika. But it made the considerable sacrifice of sending only Anglican clergy to Uganda, so that their converts also might become part of the Anglican church. It was only later on that the Protestant scene was complicated by the entry of Seventh-day Adventists,

---

[1] Namilyango College in the Mill Hill area and St. Mary's College, Kisubi, in the White Fathers' area.

the Salvation Army, Baptists, two groups of Pentecostalists, and immigrant Luyia Friends.

Elsewhere, the Protestant picture was more complex. In Kenya Anglican work was shared by CMS and BCMS. But the vast diocese of Central Tanganyika—eventually split into two— was staffed by the Australian CMS and was bounded to south and east by dioceses served by the Universities' Mission to Central Africa. There were considerable liturgical differences, and divergent attitudes to co-operation with other non-Roman Christians. These sometimes made it difficult for adherents of the two missions to recognize that they were bound together at least by common allegiance to Canterbury. In Kenya, Scottish Presbyterians, Methodists, AIM (both British and American) and American Friends were early in the field. In Nyanza there were also the American Church of God, Canadian Pentecostalists, Seventh-day Adventists and, later, a small group of the Free Church of Sweden. In addition a number of American groups, refused permission to register officially as missions, bought farms from which their work could be extended.

In Tanganyika, work begun by the CMS in Kilimanjaro and Buhaya was taken over by German Lutherans as a natural consequence of political arrangements between the great powers. The inevitable displacement of German missionaries during two wars eventually placed their work, respectively, in the hands of the American Lutheran Augustana Mission and the Church of Sweden.[1] The former was not only opposed to the concept of an episcopate in the apostolic tradition. In 1961 it gave the title of bishop to one who was not consecrated within that tradition. The Church of Sweden, on the other hand, not only took pride in its own possession of the historic episcopate, but found itself working with an African church which had long and friendly relations with the episcopal Anglican Church of Uganda. Moravians were at work around Tabora and Tukuyu; the AIM had stations scattered round the east and south of Lake Victoria; American Mennonites and Seventh-day Adventists were to the east of the lake; American Baptists entered the south-west highlands around Mbeya, inaugurated urban work in Dar es Salaam and established a bible school at Arusha; the Salvation Army and

---

[1] Lutheran work in the Southern Highlands was adopted jointly by Finns, Danes, and Swedes.

Brethren founded scattered urban stations; and Pentecostals roamed the country at will. Zanzibar was the headquarters of a diocese served by the UMCA, though the greater part of its work lay on the mainland of Tanganyika. The American Friends had an industrial mission on the island of Pemba.

Within the denominational confusion, there was a double problem. It was necessary to establish an image of the Church as universal, rather than as a series of separate institutions in the hands of competing groups of immigrants. And Africans had to be trained to become its chief agents in their own land. Whatever the primary emphasis of their coming, all missionaries were concerned for the conversion of individuals. All believed that the regular corporate worship of God was central to the Christian life. All recognized that that life required the support of a community with at least a minimum of organization and, usually, the development of a professional ministry. In one form or another, 'mission' evolved into 'church'. This was a development which some African Christians found difficult to accept. There was a tendency to think of themselves as 'mission adherents'—as still dependents of an expatriate organization—rather than as 'the Church' in Africa; and perhaps some fundamentalist missionaries encouraged this view. But the norm of teaching was that the Church entered Africa as soon as the missionaries arrived. They and African Christians together became the local community which represented the universal Church. Then— whether by deliberate policy or by force of political circumstances—it was recognized that the Church in Africa had become the responsibility of Africans, while missionaries took on the guise of 'technical co-operation' provided by the Church at large.

For Roman Catholics the image of the Church presented no difficulty in theory. They were under a unified command and had no problems of conscience in declaring themselves to be the one Church. In practice, the fact that they worked through missions with a vast number of differing names offered an image of disunity; and, whatever their teaching, the very presence of Protestantism gave the impression to Africans that Roman Catholics represented no more than one of the competing groups of European Christianity.

For Protestants the problem was much greater. In the first place, their institutional diversity readily suggested that

Christianity was, in principle, organized into a number of separate, if not actually hostile, groups.[1] There was the further impression that these groups were concerned more with denominational allegiance on a world scale than with the unity of the Church in Africa. Anglicans and Lutherans alike could be accused of a primary allegiance not so much to other African Christians as to the Lambeth Conference or the Lutheran World Federation. When the All African Church Conference, affiliated to the World Council of Churches, met at Kampala in 1963, a solution in the minds of many delegates was the formation of a United Church of Africa which ignored the divisions of Protestantism in the wider world. Partly to avert this trend, the organization was renamed the All Africa Conference of Churches.

Meanwhile, however, an approach to the problem was made along the lines of Christian Councils, in which different Protestant churches co-operated to apportion territory and to co-ordinate such activities as medical, educational, and urban work. The Christian Council of Kenya had its beginning in a much earlier movement towards organic union between Anglicans, Presbyterians, Methodists, and the AIM.[2] As early as 1907 Willis of the CMS in Nyanza[3] held conversations with Scott of the Church of Scotland Mission. Negotiations were stopped partly by the vigorous objection by Frank Weston, the Bishop of Zanzibar, to the administration of Holy Communion to all members of a conference at Kikuyu in 1913: partly by the recognition of the AIM that co-operation with Anglicans meant also co-operation with the high church party. But in 1918 the four missions in Kenya formed the Alliance of Protestant Missionary Societies; and in 1924 the Kenya Missionary Council was able to include also the Seventh-day Adventists and the Friends. In 1942 the two bodies merged in the Christian Council of Kenya. The Alliance High School at Kikuyu, which in 1961 began teaching for Higher School Certificate, was primarily Anglican and Presbyterian in origin but admitted boys of all

---

[1] In Kenya, where general social discontent gave rise to fissiparous tendencies, this impression made it easy enough to justify the formation of independent Christian groups under African leadership.

[2] M. Capon, *Towards Unity in Kenya* (Nairobi, 1961). In order to preempt the claims of a group of independent churches the Christian Council of Kenya became in 1966 the National Christian Council of Kenya.

[3] Willis was later to become Bishop of Uganda.

denominations.[1] The theological college at Limuru was run jointly by Anglicans, Methodists, and Presbyterians.

The Christian Council not only attracted able officers from overseas. Especially against the background of Mau Mau, it received a considerable amount of overseas funds. It undertook responsibility for a monthly newspaper, for the development of urban work, work camps, famine aid, and a busy conference centre. In addition, it made the daring experiment of admitting to membership some of the independent churches. It thus associated them at the national level with those mission churches from which they had separated. But, owing to the suspicion of modernism inherent in the AIM, the Council was unable to affiliate formally to the World Council of Churches. On the other hand the Tanganyika Christian Council, formed for similar purposes in 1948,[2] was suspected by the UMCA of tendencies towards pan-Protestantism.

In 1960 the Anglicans of Kenya, Tanganyika, and Zanzibar resolved some of their own internal tensions by forming the Province of East Africa under its own archbishop. They thus acquired, in relation to the Church of England, a status analogous to that of newly-independent countries of the British Commonwealth in relation to the United Kingdom. A similar province was inaugurated in 1961 with the formation of the Church of Uganda, Rwanda, and Burundi.[3] These were steps in the direction of demonstrating that the Church was not only universal but indigenous; and Anglicans in East Africa take some pride in the fact that their autonomous provinces pre-dated the granting of political independence. Similar steps were taken by the Presbyterians when, in 1943, the Church of Scotland Mission became the Presbyterian Church of East Africa. Europeans were at first organized separately into an overseas presbytery of the Church of Scotland but united fully with the local church in 1956. In 1955 the AIM formed the Africa Inland Church in Kenya and

---

[1] Its story is told by L. B. Greaves, *Carey Francis of Kenya* (London, 1969). A more thorough investigation is by B. E. Kipkorir, 'The Alliance High School and the Origin of the Kenya African Elite' (unpublished Ph.D. thesis, Cambridge, 1969). For the dynamics of education in the Central Province, see John Anderson, *The Struggle for the School* (London, 1970).

[2] The Tanganyika Missionary Conference began in 1936.

[3] The Anglican Rwanda Mission worked in close association with the CMS. The Province of Uganda also included work at Mboga in Zaire (then the Congo).

Tanganyika; and in 1963 Lutherans, despite their differences over church government, established the Evangelical Lutheran Church of Tanganyika, the head of the church, be he bishop or president in his own tradition, being known by the Swahili name *Mkuu*.

But, while the granting of political independence meant that —subject to the pressure of world events—political power was put unambiguously in the hands of Africans, it is doubtful whether the churches were equally successful. An obvious weakness of the mission churches was that at all critical points European leadership could still be assumed and that, as political independence advanced, so increasing foreign funds were available for every appearance of the Church's advance. Perhaps the Church, with no established roots in society, was less able than the State to avoid the economic imperialism which is so often said to follow in the wake of political independence. One important motive for not, in the first place, integrating expatriate Presbyterians with their African fellows was the fear that the latter would be dominated by the former. There could be no healthy church, it was felt, unless it were manifestly under local leadership. There was a strong feeling, in sections of the AIC, that its formation was no more than a form and that real power still lay with the missionaries. Even in the Church of Uganda it was said that an essential condition of growth was the departure of the older missionaries with their tradition of paternalism.

By 1963 the Moderator of the PCEA and the Bishop of the Lutheran Church of North-East Tanganyika were Africans. The Anglican Church in East Africa had ten African bishops; but both archbishops and six bishops were still expatriate; at a time when it was assumed that permanent secretaries of government ministries should all be African, it was still difficult to find African clergy competent to fill the position of archdeacon or its equivalent in other Protestant denominations; and expatriate administrators—whether as archdeacons or as school supervisors —continued to exercise considerable influence in the Church. The impression was too easily given that, despite its theoretical autonomy, the Church was still the spiritual extension of the imperialist urge.

At first sight, Roman Catholics had done better. Two archbishops, a cardinal, and seven bishops were African; and there

was a growing African priesthood as highly trained as its expatriate counterpart. Some had doctorates from Rome. But
there was a common impression that missionaries still wielded
a vast influence and that, institutionally linked to Rome and (as
was all too readily supposed) committed to a Catholic plot for
world domination, they represented a much more serious threat
to genuine political independence.[1]

There were difficulties, however, over the issue of material
resources. From Apolo Kivebulaya,[2] the Ganda who in 1896
embarked on a mission to Mboga and thence, in 1921, to the
Congo pygmies, through the Ganda chiefs who took responsibility
for the teaching of Christianity to their own people, to the countless humble catechists who taught the faith as they cultivated
their own livelihood, the missions had been deeply dependent
on their African agents. Without them there could have been no
hope that, within 82 years of the coming of the first missionaries,
58 per cent of the population of Uganda would be professing
Christians.[3] In the early days, African Protestant clergy at
least were materially better off than their flocks. Indeed, as late
as 1928 this was one of the criticisms of Mabel Ensor, the CMS
missionary who resigned at that time to found a 'Mengo Gospel
Church'. They may not all, as at first in Buganda, have belonged
to the same social group as the chiefs. But they shared with others
—who became clerks and interpreters—the prestige of schooling
and of entrée into western culture. The finances of the Church—
relative at least to those of secular society—began to lag; that
society began to offer increasing opportunities of status without
the moral implications of clerical office; and so the attractive-
ness of the ministry decreased. The people, on the whole, were
not prepared to pay for a professional ministry; there were no

---

[1] A significant commentary, after less than seven years, was the enthusiasm with
which even politicians greeted the Pope's visit to Kampala in 1969. He was reported
by an African observer as having 'become Honorary President of UPC and of
Uganda'.

[2] Anne Luck, *African Saint* (London, 1963).

[3] *Uganda Census, 1959*, Uganda Government (1963). There is fascinating material
in M. M. L. Pirouet, 'The expansion of the Church of Uganda (N.A.C.) from
Buganda into northern and western Uganda between 1891 and 1941, with special
reference to the work of African teachers and evangelists'. Thesis accepted for the
degree of Ph.D. by the University of East Africa (1968). For the Roman Catholic
story in East Africa as a whole, see A. Shorter and E. Kataza, *Missionaries to Yourselves*
(London, 1972).

officials, as of government, empowered to compel the payment of Church dues; missionaries were so keen to spread their message that they were—quite erroneously—supposed to have as much cash at their disposal as their fellow-Europeans in government employment; and the services of the Church seemed to be available whether they were paid for or not.

Roman Catholics faced the same reluctance on the part of African Christians to give money. They had, however, at their disposal greater international resources both of money and of missionary personnel; they were not embarrassed by the need to support a married clergy; and they provided not only better buildings for churches and schools, but also African clergy better educated and better able to support the material needs of educated men.

Partly, however, the difference lay in attitudes towards the education of the clergy. Roman Catholic clergy were not necessarily highly educated; but they had all been through a long process of instruction; and it was assumed from the start that African priests should be prepared, in every case, as rigorously as expatriates. This was not to question the value of catechists. It was to assert that they were not enough; that there must be African priests; and that the priesthood implied a certain level of intellectual as well as moral achievement. The process entailed considerable wastage—sometimes to the gain of secular society; the seminaries produced not only archbishops but Semakula Mulumba, the representative in London of the Buganda Bataka Party.[1] But it was possible, for instance, to man the Masaka diocese wholly with African priests and to send others to take the Diploma in Education at Makerere College.

In contrast, Protestants until much later on set no great store by an educated ministry. Some ordinands with sufficient command of English were sent, after a period in the ministry, to British theological colleges; and, towards the end of the period, a few obtained American degrees. But the Anglican Church of the Province of East Africa had at the outset of independence no African graduate clergy; and the one British graduate among

[1] For the Bataka Party, see chap. i above. There was also Francis Walugembe, who played an important part in the campaign for the Buganda elections of 1962, in persuading Catholics to vote for *Kabaka Yekka*. He became Minister of Natural Resources in the Kabaka's government. For a positive Roman Catholic evaluation of catechists, see Shorter and Kataza, *Missionaries to Yourselves*.

the African clergy of the Church of Uganda could obtain sufficient for his needs only by employment in a grant-aided school.[1] Only in 1961 did teaching begin, in two theological colleges, towards a post-School Certificate diploma in theology, in 1962 the united theological college at Limuru advertised a course leading to an external BD of the University of London; and in 1963 Makerere College began teaching Religious Studies within the BA course of the University of East Africa. The department was established as a result of effort, extending over fifteen years, by Christians within the College (including a past Roman Catholic chaplain); it was made possible, in part, by a grant from the Theological Education Fund of the World Council of Churches; and it had a positive theological intention. But it regarded the teaching of African traditional religions, in their social context, as fundamental to the course; and in 1963 it had one Roman Catholic and one Muslim, in addition to twelve Protestants, among its students.

While the Roman Catholic priesthood provided an ecclesiastical status free of serious financial worry, the Protestant ministry in East Africa was uncertain of its place in society and lived always on the brink of poverty. It was hardly surprising if the best minds among young Christians saw in government service the real growing-point of society. Nor, in view of the general failure of the laity either to support the clergy or to take any initiative without them, was it surprising that Christian graduates found in the new nationalist society a greater challenge than in the Church. No doubt this failure was due in part both to the clericalism and to the paternalism imported by the missionaries. But it was due also to that other importation of western Christendom:

Only that which is on the files in the central office is recognized as part of the Church; only those activities which are initiated and supported from that office are regarded as the Church's work. So it is not easy for Christians (in secular employment) to feel that they also are fellow workers in a single Christian enterprise.[2]

---

[1] Only in 1968 did the Anglican Province of Uganda become aware that it could not indefinitely (owing to government employment policy) staff its theological college with expatriates. It then sent two Uganda clergy to read for a theological degree at Bristol. A recent Uganda visitor said, 'They will be able to serve the new Uganda. But they will be separated from the great majority of Ugandans.'

[2] J. V. Taylor, *Christianity and Politics in Africa* (London, 1957), p. 12.

It was not, perhaps, until African laity had laid hold on the Church and made it their own—until they had freed it not only of foreign dominance but of reliance on their own clergy—that it could hope to be the Church in East Africa. Apart from the Revival and some of the independent churches, there were still at the moment of independence few signs of such development.

Morals, African, Western, and Christian

The second line of development was in the field of morals; and here the tendency to puritanism—the tendency to denigrate everything African irrespective of its social function—had been least among Roman Catholics at one end of the theological spectrum, and greatest among fundamentalists at the other. It would be wholly improper to say of the former, with one AIM Christian in Marakwet, 'The ten commandments were recited all day and broken all night.'[1] It would be perfectly correct to say, with the district commissioner in 1940:

Owing to the broadminded attitude adopted by the Mill Hill mission towards pagan customs, some progress is being made and its schools are fairly well attended. . . . The anti-circumcision attitude of the AIM negatives any respect they may command.[2]

The first missionaries found a world in which many African societies were riddled with the slave trade. Africans themselves were making large profits out of selling their fellows to the Arabs. Polygamy was an accepted institution. Bride-wealth was an important aid both to social security and to the stability of marriage. The status of women was generally low, even if they did not—as in Buganda—do almost all the work while their husbands devoted themselves to hunting and to war. Drunkenness was rife. Dances were not only integral to social well-being but frequently an occasion of considerable licentiousness. In some tribes male circumcision, with all its accompaniments of pagan ritual, was an essential *rite de passage* into adult membership of the tribe; and the often brutal practice of clitoridectomy might be equally important for girls.

[1] Reported by Dr. B. E. Kipkorir, Marakwet.
[2] Kapsowar, *Annual Report 1941* (recorded by Dr. Kipkorir).

Over the slave trade there could be no two opinions; and, with the powerful support of the evangelically-inspired anti-slavery movement in England, there was no difficulty in persuading governments to stamp it out. It is an interesting reflection on the influence of Christianity that the Uganda Railway, which the British public was persuaded to finance in the interests of this campaign,[1] should have become the main economic highway for Kenya and Uganda.

Over polygamy, likewise, there was no doubt. For Christians monogamy was a law, to be enforced if necessary by exclusion from the sacraments; and it is an interesting comment on this policy that, in 1956, children of 87 per cent of families in one Anglican parish in Buganda were refused baptism for this reason. There is no reason to suppose that other churches, in other places, had any greater success. What was in doubt was the status of wives previously married by customary law. For some missions this was no marriage; and the man might be free of them all. For some, he must keep the first; for others, one only, of his choice. Nobody asked what was to become of those rejected.[2]

The only real alternative to polygamy was to be found through the education of girls so that they might find in employment—at first as teachers and nurses, later as doctors and members of parliament—a status not dependent on marriage; and, when the opportunity came, it was the missions which led the way. The development of a cash economy was another disincentive, for then wives, expecting manufactured clothes and other retail goods, became an economic liability instead of being unpaid producers of food. But even this did not prevent concubinage and the adoption of temporary unions in series as an alternative to the stability of the old system.[3] Meanwhile, many Africans asked whether monogamy was not a purely western, rather than a specifically Christian, custom. The Bamalaki in Uganda frankly permitted four wives. The African Israel Church Nineveh allowed a man to keep such wives as he had on conversion, but otherwise insisted on monogamy. Perhaps the worst

---

[1] The best existing authority on the building of the railway is still M. F. Hill. *Permanent Way* (Nairobi, 1950).

[2] There is a thorough discussion in A. Phillips (ed.), *Survey of African Marriage and Family Life* (London, 1953). For Buganda see Taylor, *Church in Buganda*, p. 243.

[3] See e.g. A. Southall and P. W. Gutkind, *Townsmen in the Making* (London, 1956).

confusion arose when British marriage law, inspired by the churches, conflicted with tribal custom. John married Mary, having completed the customary dues, in church. Tiring of her, he divorced her by custom and, by the same custom, married Margaret. Now he had intercourse again with Mary, thus committing adultery by custom but being still on the right side of the law.[1]

Bride-wealth was another source of doubt. To many it seemed to be no better than buying a wife. Indeed, at a later stage, although educated fathers tended to forego it, others found in their educated daughters an unexpected source of income. Young couples who sought to avoid the expense of customary dues found that their marriage was not recognized by tribal custom, and its stability thus threatened. For this reason, some churches refused to solemnize matrimony before the full customary formalities were complete. An absurdity of this situation was illustrated by the young man who, making his lover pregnant, was refused marriage by her father. Despite the majority of both partners, they were therefore refused marriage also by their church, but encouraged by a missionary to live together and rear a family. After two years of obviously successful and stable union, the father had still, by tribal custom, full power over his daughter; and the couple had to resort to civil marriage in order to establish their rights. Against the tribal background, the claims of the families of both man and wife remained stronger on them than those of one another. In these circumstances the building of monogamous families according to the western Christian ideal was of the greatest difficulty. Nevertheless, the ideal was present; and there were men and women, both of the older and of the younger generations, who succeeded in realizing it in practice. But the success was not always due to Christian causes. Christian marriage is a complex of ideals of relationship, with an economic and social structure enhancing the status of women, which cannot develop from preaching or from private resolve alone.

The whole question of the relationship between the sexes still awaited satisfactory solution. Some missions prohibited any private meeting between unmarried men and women. But this attitude did not prevent a degree of promiscuity wholly unknown

[1] H. F. Morris, 'Marriage and Divorce in Uganda', *Uganda Journal*, 24 (Sept. 1960).

in pre-Christian days. According to some members of the younger generation, it actually encouraged promiscuity by removing the old tribal sanctions and giving it all the zest of secret sin.

Drunkenness was another problem. Although it may not have been as universal as it was to become, it not only offended Christian consciences but, where crops such as maize and millet were used in the brewing of beer, might seriously deplete stocks of food. The situation was made no easier by drunken Europeans. Attitudes varied from that of Roman Catholics who, disliking drunkenness, nevertheless saw no religious reason for interfering with tribal custom at this point; through Weston of the UMCA, who thought in terms of prohibiting the brewing of native liquor and providing a locally-made European-type beer for sale to Africans and Europeans alike,[1] to the more Protestant bodies for whom to drink alcohol at all was to risk excommunication.[2] As with the attempt to control meetings between young men and women, this last attitude created difficulties in the relationship between the churches and their younger, educated members. Precisely because they were educated—rather than because they were Christian—they had come to value the temperate consumption of alcohol.

Similar problems arose over tribal customs such as dances, mourning, ceremonies concerning twins, circumcision. All were deeply involved in the whole tribal structure and religious outlook. Again, the Roman Catholic outlook was on the whole one of non-interference. It was thought that education, rather than law, would work the necessary change. Protestants tended towards complete prohibition. Lucas of the UMCA in Masasi successfully integrated tribal with Christian initiation;[3] but his work became irrelevant to those who, by living in towns, had lost all interest in the tribal rite. In parts of Kikuyu, where

---

[1] For this and other references to Weston, see F. M. Smith, *Frank, Bishop of Zanzibar* (London, 1926).

[2] Christians of Kigezi distinguished clearly between *obushera* and *amarwa*. The former is millet gruel, cooked overnight and by morning more than distinctly alcoholic. It is prepared as food and therefore regarded as harmless. The latter, in which honey is added to the gruel and deliberately fermented, is made for the purpose of getting drunk, and therefore forbidden.

[3] M. V. Lucas, 'The Christian Approach to Non-Christian Customs', *Essays Catholic and Missionary* (London, 1928). Reprinted in *Christianity and Native Rites* (London, 1950). For a recent assessment, see T. O. Ranger and I. Kimambo, *The Historical Study of African Religion* (London, 1972), pp. 221 sqq.

teaching against clitoridectomy began in 1906, it was estimated
that 99 per cent of the women were still circumcised in 1960—
some of them after return from boarding school, far later than
the traditional age. In Kilimanjaro, on the other hand, where
Lutherans insisted on the preservation of tribal custom, both
clitoridectomy and drunkenness among Christians became an
embarrassment to younger members of the Church and provided
an entry-point for Pentecostal evangelists. Unless Christianity
was prepared—like Islam—to be little more than a veneer on top
of traditional culture, what was needed was a radical change in
social structure making the old ways irrelevant. Through medicine and education a beginning had been made. But in the long
run there was little hope of making an impression without the
support of the State. So long as the State remained colonialist,
that support was necessarily suspect. Now that it was independent, national development might well appear a more important
faith.

The Church had become, in fact, involved in a breakdown of
tribal culture for which it was necesssarily—though by no means
wholly—responsible. Except in the very limited field of those who
were deeply convinced Christians, it had been unable to create
a new society providing the necessary stability for the practice
of individual morality. Nor, in this field, should it be expected
to have had any greater success in East Africa than in Europe.[1]
The problem which, perhaps more than any other, it had to face
was that of providing a fully integrated faith for the younger,
educated generation, which found it difficult to see in Catholicism any more than a set of rituals, and in Protestantism increasingly meaningless prohibitions.

Medicine and education

The third development was in medicine. When Dr. (later Sir
Albert) Cook reached Buganda in 1897, he had great difficulty
in persuading the local mission committee that his primary voca-
tion was as a doctor rather than as an evangelist. Nevertheless in

[1] According to *The Registrar General's Statistical Review of England and Wales for the year 1971* (London, 1973), pp. 7, 144, 6% of marriages were divorced and 8·4% of live births were illegitimate. The author spoke with a Presbyterian missionary of one of his Kikuyu flock who was marrying the girl he had made pregnant. 'Well', was the comment 'I think that's very noble of him. In the part of Scotland that I come from they don't usually marry till the second child is on the way.'

1902 he reported a journey of 510 miles in nine weeks, during the course of which he and his assistants saw 5,618 patients and performed 50 operations. He identified the first case of sleeping sickness to be reported in Uganda; while writing an MD thesis on malaria, he discovered the spirillum of tick fever; and he showed that one form of anaemia is caused by hookworm.[1] Betweenwhiles, he compiled a manuscript vocabulary of Dinka and Nubi words.[2]

The fundamental contribution of missions to the development of medicine in East Africa is symbolized by the fact that Cook opened the CMS hospital at Mengo in 1897 and started to train medical assistants in 1917. The first government medical centre in Uganda was opened only in 1912 and was concerned largely with the treatment of venereal diseases. The same story could be repeated from all parts of East Africa; and the changes which, again everywhere, had taken place in fifty years, are symbolized by the contrast in 1963. Mengo Hospital employed its doctors and expatriate nursing staff at 'mission' rates, and struggled to pay its way. Mulago Hospital, built for £2,300,000, housed the medical school, where men and women from the whole of East Africa received medical qualifications recognized by the British General Medical Council; and served as the specialist hospital for all Uganda. Medicine had entered an age when it could no longer be financed from private charity; and the future of the Church medical services was necessarily in the balance.[3]

The Christian effort in medical service had not been confined to the more obvious fields of curative medicine. Much of the highly specialized and sacrificial work required in the treatment of lepers in settlements had been undertaken by the Church. African wives had been brought with their husbands to theological colleges, and there had been taught standards of hygiene, nutrition, and child-care, so that a clergyman's house might be an example to the rest of his parish. In general, schools of all sorts had been training grounds for higher standards of health,

---

[1] A. R. Cook, *Uganda Memories* (Kampala, 1945), pp. 46, 161, 181 sqq.

[2] Now in the library of Makerere University.

[3] In the 1970s a reassessment is necessary. So inadequate are government resources for the fight against disease that mission-sponsored services have, if anything, increased, and receive positive encouragement. The Lutheran-supported Kilimanjaro Christian Medical Centre at Moshi in Tanzania supplements medical training provided by the University of Dar es Salaam.

learnt perhaps more by example than by formal teaching. A further development, as detribalization reduced clan responsibility for the care of orphans, was the growth of orphanages, sometimes associated with the training of nursery nurses, and the formation of welfare societies. In emergencies, such as the Kenya floods and famine of 1961, and the care of refugees from Rwanda and Burundi, Christian personnel and funds from the Church overseas played an important part.

In one particular part of the medical field the Church perhaps had an opportunity which during this period it largely missed. The implicit rationalism of the early missionaries—scarcely less noticeable among the Roman Catholics—made them unable to take seriously beliefs in witchcraft and spirit-possession. Weston in the UMCA was almost alone in being prepared to practise exorcism. But the resurgence of traditional modes of therapy[1] which was taking place in some areas—the evidence that a large proportion of the children admitted to Mulago Hospital first reported as part of the treatment prescribed by a diviner—raises a fundamental question. In a culture which still believed in occult forces, were they not a necessary therapeutic hypothesis? It raised the further question whether Christians, against the aetiology of disease accepted by the New Testament writers, were ever wise to rule out of court its African equivalent. It is possible that a willingness to work with, and to study, traditional diviners might have yielded therapeutic conclusions of great importance. It might be that at this point Christians, no longer involved in the support of expensive medical institutions, could have made a new and exciting contribution in the field of medicine and of thought.

It is in any case important not to imagine that, through education alone, traditional beliefs and attitudes were necessarily done away. There was evidence not only that African university students believed themselves bewitched but that, returning to full participation in their own society after the relative seclusion of school and college, they began to be haunted—however reluctantly—by the whole gamut of the occult.

[1] Outside East Africa, there is an excellent description in M. J. Field, *Search for Security* (London, 1960). For similar developments in independent churches, see H. W. Turner, *An Independent Church*, (Oxford 1967), ii, 141 sqq.; C. G. Baëta, *Prophetism in Ghana* (London, 1962); and B. G. M. Sundkler, *Bantu Prophets in South Africa* (London, 3rd ed. 1961).

But it was in the field of language and literary education that missionaries made their most important contribution outside the strictly religious field. Local languages had to be learnt and reduced to writing, as a means not only of everyday communication, but of putting at least the Bible and the Catechism into the hands of applicants for baptism. The latter had to be taught to read and, in due course, to write. The baptism class, lasting normally for six months or more, became the first experiment in adult education in East Africa. New missionaries could learn the language more readily if they had both grammar and dictionary to hand. So these were prepared—along with, in due course, a wider variety of Christian literature; and before long Africans were trained to print them on local presses. Mission bookshops were started for their distribution and gradually achieved a wider function. The CMS Bookshop in Kenya became an important general bookshop and was eventually taken over by a commercial firm. The Uganda Bookshop, while remaining under the control of the Church, was able to contribute out of its profits to Church finances. There was wide circulation of periodicals edited from Church offices.[1]

For the greater part of the period under review, the churches themselves played the central part in educating the public, who read not only these papers but the far larger number of purely secular periodicals in both English and the vernaculars. From the elementary reading and writing taught to catechumens developed more advanced classes for catechists and, later, for ordinands. They required not only to understand the faith, but to learn to teach it to others: the ability to read and write letters; the elements of music if they were to lead services; and such arithmetic as would enable them to keep simple accounts. All missions were to find that the most fruitful source of converts was in the boarding schools and that they had an obligation to train not only professional church-workers but an educated generation to take the lead in social and economic development. Boarding schools became the order of the day, partly because the long distances to be travelled by pupils put secondary day-

---

[1] Such periodicals were *Munno*, a Roman Catholic bi-weekly in Luganda; *Leadership*, a Roman Catholic monthly in English, published from Gulu; *New Day*, an Anglican monthly published in English from Kampala; and *Rock*, a monthly published in English from Nairobi.

schools out of the question; partly because only in separated communities did it seem possible to teach the Christian life in its fullness. That such secluded education was a questionable preparation for life in a world which remained predominantly pagan, is a conclusion which, even in 1963, found unwilling acceptance. Day schools remained in the villages, as the extension of the catechism classes, till they developed into the 'full primary schools' of modern Africa. It was only towards the end of the period that either church or government were able to conceive of secondary education except in terms of boarding schools.

When the missionary-sponsored Phelps-Stokes Fund published in 1924 its report on education in East Africa,[1] the governments of Kenya, Uganda, and Tanganyika were spending on education respectively 4 per cent, 2 per cent, and 1 per cent of their annual revenue. Uganda had no Director of Education till 1924. The general educational picture in Kenya was difficult to assess. The CMS had started night-schools in Nairobi, particularly important in a growing urban situation. The Alliance High School was shortly to be opened. Official enterprise in African education was limited to schools at Machakos founded in 1915, Waa founded in 1921 and the Masai Native School financed by the Masai Trust Fund. In Uganda, Makerere College had been opened in 1921, under the headship of H. O. Savile, a CMS missionary, to provide technical education at a higher level than that available in mission schools. Incorporating the Nyanjaradde Normal School, it was in due course to develop into the first university college in East Africa and, with the Royal College at Nairobi (now the University of Nairobi) and the University College, Dar es Salaam (now the University of Dar es Salaam)—both much later foundations—to create in 1963 the University of East Africa. King's College, Budo, had been founded by the CMS in 1906, four years after the Mill Hill Fathers' school at Namilyango. Both of them were designed primarily to educate the sons of chiefs. Mengo Hospital, in addition to the training of medical assistants (started in 1917 and transferred in 1923 to Makerere College) began to train mid-

---

[1] *Education in East Africa* (New York and London, 1924). For a recent discussion of the Phelps-Stokes Commissions and their impact on education in East Africa see Kenneth King, *Pan-Africanism and Education* (Oxford, 1971).

wives in 1920 and later developed—as did all mission hospitals —a full training course for locally-registered nurses. The various missions had about 2,000 village schools with a few central schools and teacher-training schools. In Tanganyika there was a considerable way to go before the level reached by the Germans in 1914 could be re-established. But there were 65 government elementary schools, with central schools at Dar es Salaam, Tanga, and Bukoba. The 'attractive buildings' which the Commission noted at Tabora were not yet in use, since no suitable master could be found. There were 2,200 mission schools with a total expatriate staff of 157.

Throughout East Africa there was a predominance of mission-ary education over against provision by governments. But it was conceived in terms of missionary needs and financed largely from voluntary sources. Only gradually was this predominance reversed.

Ever since 1921, J. H. Oldham, of the International Mission-ary Council in London, had been pressing on the Colonial Office a more active participation in African education; and in 1923 there had been set up a permanent Advisory Committee on Native Education in Tropical Africa, with distinguished rep-resentation from the Colonial Office, Catholic and Protestant missions, and English educationalists. A policy was devised by which governments agreed to give heavy subsidies to mission schools, while the latter agreed to submit to inspection, expert advice and some degree of rationalization. By 1949 government contributions had risen, in Kenya from £14,000 per annum to £300,000; in Uganda from £10,000 to £400,000; and in Tanganyika from nothing to £285,000. Oldham made himself responsible for ensuring that all Protestant missionary societies at work in Africa should understand the wholly new opportunity with which they were thus presented of bearing witness at the centre of the new forces which were shaping the life of Africa. In 1927 Mgr. Hinsley undertook the same work among Roman Catholics. 'Who owns the schools will own Africa', wrote Dubois.[1] Although the results of missionary education, after thirty years, did not altogether justify this forecast, it is not surprising if, on the same reasoning, the nationalists of the day

[1] H. Dubois, Le Répertoire africain (Rome, 1932), p. 133. Quoted in Oliver, The Missionary Factor, p. 276.

wished to take the place in the schools so far held largely by the missionaries.[1]

In Tanganyika the emphasis had always been towards the development of a government rather than a missionary system of education. Elsewhere, missionary resources had been inadequate to meet the demands for education not only of Africans but of governments. Government money was, in any case, required for the purpose; and everywhere there was a tendency, from 1946 onwards, for new schools to be built by governments themselves. But this did not mean the elimination of religious influence. Even at Tabora, which from the first was a government school, Muslims had turned Christian simply because the implicit content of English education was itself Christian in origin. In Kenya and Uganda there was insistence on school prayers and the teaching of 'religious knowledge'; and it was common to find a clergyman on the staff of government boarding schools.

It was, indeed, by now a question facing all churches whether their schools—almost wholly financed by government and therefore obliged to follow a syllabus imposed by government—did not involve a very great deal of missionary labour for the sake of providing a secular education with no more than a religious coat of paint. There is no evidence to suggest that the products of mission schools were any more firmly Christian than those of government schools. It was Protestants, by and large, who profited from the Christian influence of government schools, because it was they who were prepared to take the risk. But Roman Catholicism first entered Marakwet through natives of the district who had come under the influence of a convinced Catholic layman teaching at the Government School, Tambach;[2] and more than one priest, pastorally responsible for those who had passed through Catholic secondary schools, wondered whether they would have been any worse Catholics had they been exposed to the same risks as their Protestant fellows.

Roman Catholics, as elsewhere, were fighting to keep their schools; and one motive behind the formation of the Democratic Party in Uganda was the fear that the Uganda National

---

[1] And perhaps it will have no greater success, for the education which is needed in a dynamic society necessarily produces critics of society.

[2] Information from Dr. B. E. Kipkorir.

Congress[1] favoured complete nationalization. Among some leading Anglicans developed the suggestion that Christian schools should be wholly independent of government grants. They would then be free to experiment in an education which was Christian not only in 'atmosphere' and in Religious Knowledge periods, but at every point of the curriculum, whether in language, history or science. Lack of finance was likely, for many years to come, to prevent these ideas from taking institutional form; and the Uganda government at least was soon to prevent the encouragement of sectional schools by foreign money by insisting that all such aid should be channelled through itself. If it was the Christian missions which first taught to colonial governments their responsibility for education, the new nations not only accepted the responsibility but inherited the missionary zeal.

Christianity, tribalism, and nationalism

To the early missionary educators it did not occur that they were training the future politicians; and they might well, at that point, have been distressed by the suggestion. But that in fact is what happened. Not only the African administrators under colonial government, but all the leading nationalist politicians of Kenya and Uganda, passed through the mission schools. What was perhaps of greater importance was that, with the exception of Mboya (who went to a Catholic school and joined the trade union movement before spending a year at Ruskin College, Oxford), they were either Protestant or had some form of secular education after leaving school.[2] In Tanganyika, the Catholic and Muslim ministers either passed through Tabora or some other government school, or were further educated either at Makerere or overseas; whilst the nationalist politicians of Zanzibar were Muslims.

The belief that Christian education bred nationalism would perhaps be nearer the mark—at least in East Africa—if 'British'

---

[1] At that time the only other effective political party in Uganda. Through a series of adventures most of its members became the Uganda Peoples Congress. See chap. i above.

[2] Apter, *Political Kingdom*, pp. 313, 317, shows that the first genuinely nationalist organization in Uganda, the Uganda National Congress, held its first public meeting at the old boys' club of the leading Protestant school and had a central committee consisting of 75% Protestants. See also chap. i above.

were substituted for 'Christian'. For the headmasters of Protestant and government schools alike laid stress on responsibility and initiative, while continental Roman Catholics and American fundamentalists were concerned with obedience and orthodoxy. It is therefore necessary to examine in greater detail the relation between Christianity and the growth of nationalism.

In the past Christianity had often been the focus of national movements: Monophysites in Egypt, Donatists in North Africa, the churches of Armenia and Georgia all played a central part in national resistance against an oppressive empire. The Reformation in Europe was as much a nationalist as a theological movement. Much more recently, the Church had been central to the Greek resistance to the Turks and the Cypriot revolt against the British. But in every case the Church was rooted in the vernacular. In Buganda, at the end of the nineteenth century, it looked as if a similar phenomenon had occurred. But there, more than anywhere else save in Kikuyu, there was to be pagan reaction; and elsewhere, for all but the few, Christianity remained a 'foreign' religion. It played its part—along with secular forces—in breaking down the old society. It was able to do very little towards creating a new society to give stability to individual lives.

Moreover, with its emphasis on the vernacular as the proper medium for the religious life, it tended to be organized on a largely tribal basis. In Tanganyika, where Swahili became the national language at least of the men, it was possible for denominational societies to subordinate tribal differences. But congregations in Nairobi still tended to be vernacular—and therefore tribal—in composition. Immigrant Luhya in Kampala found a religious centre in the Friends' Meeting conducted in their own language; Nilotic visitors had to choose between worshipping in Ganda or in English; and there could be little effective contact between Lugbara workers on sugar plantations and the Ganda and Soga peasants among whom they lived. Short of fluency in English, the only religious society which genuinely passed tribal boundaries was the Revival—and then largely because the Ganda hymn *Tukutendereza* ,'we praise thee' became its common currency. Out of such material it might be possible to revitalize a tribe; there was little hope of building a nation out of many tribes.

It was at the level of boarding schools that the process started —when pupils of many tribes were brought together in a common experience, and began to think of themselves as Africans rather than as members of a particular tribe.[1] It was perhaps not till this point had been reached that Christian teaching, about both the value of individuals and their membership of a 'third race of men', could provide effective symbols for expressing the new experience of life in common, the recognition that there is a community wider than the tribe—wider, perhaps, than the nation. It was indeed at this point that a thoughtful Christian conviction might become a hindrance, rather than a spur, to nationalism. For the Revivalist privately saved within an accepted social order, there was no fundamental problem. God and the King were foci of the same faith. But for the man who knew that Christianity had consequences in obligation to mankind as a whole, tribalism was in conflict with his deepest convictions. So also was any kind of nationalism which had mythological pretensions beyond the political needs of the moment.

Such convictions were themselves seriously strained by experience of life in the Church. The missions as a whole had taken the initiative in training African leadership; and at least some of the Protestant churches had attempted, before the State, the creation of democratically-governed indigenous institutions. They had taught the equality of man and the importance of individuals. But, as a general rule, other Europeans had refused equality even to Africans better educated than themselves;[2] and too often they had given the impression that Africans had no value except as hewers of wood and drawers of water. Missionaries not infrequently managed to give the same impression; and nationalism developed, at least in part, as a rebellion against the failure of the Christian west to practise what it preached.

It is a serious question whether this rebellion would not have taken place in any case. Mannoni and Carothers[3] developed, in slightly different terminologies, the theme that the impact of

---

[1] But even at Makerere College it was noticed that tribal associations were more lasting than others.

[2] On the eve of independence in Uganda, the swimming club at Entebbe was still 'for Europeans only'. The same struggle was, in 1963, being waged over 'the club' at Kakamega in Kenya.

[3] Mannoni, *Prospero and Caliban, passim;* J. C. Carothers, *The Psychology of Mau Mau* (Nairobi, Govt. Printer, 1954).

the 'dominant' personality of the west on 'dependent' tribal society yielded, after an initial period of resistance, a high degree of acceptance of the one by the other: until, in time, the dependants came to feel that their needs were no longer met, or that they had even been deserted, by the dominant partner. At that point they rebelled. Driven to extremes, they might revolt. Another slightly variant analysis speaks of individuals who had been separated from tribal society by the impact of the west, but had never wholly been accepted into any other. They looked for security either in reversion to the imagined golden age of their tribal past or by rebellion against the expatriate leaders of the present. Mau Mau[1]—and to a lesser extent *Kabaka Yekka*—were examples of the former response; political nationalism of the latter.

Christianity, as it came to East Africa, was involved in the dominance of the west. It played its part in the destruction of tribal society. Perhaps both were needed if nationalism were to develop and East Africa to take its place in the technological society of the future. It is not at all clear, however, that Christianity as such was necessary to the process. What is much more likely is that, having contributed to that process, it would offer —if not to the whole of the new African society, at least to individuals of importance within it—an image of personal character and social aims which might modify the national societies of the future.

However this may be, the first overt signs of the rejection of the west were accompanied, in Uganda, by religious symbols. Mwanga's revolt in 1897 was, among other things, an attempt to restore the old paganism. Against the Christian parties of the time it was abortive. But Mugema, of the break-away Bamalaki group, in 1914 was able to symbolize his rejection of the west by his refusal of medicine and to give it respectability through overtly Christian forms.[2] In 1921 he had 91,000 followers in Buganda alone. Spartas attempted the African Progressive Association and the Christian Army for the Salvation of Africa before he formed the African Orthodox Church—'a church for

---

[1] *The Origins and Growth of Mau Mau* by F. D. Corfield ('Corfield Report'), Cmd. 1030 (London, HMSO, 1960), and Kenya Sessional Paper No. 5 1959/60; F. B. Welbourn, 'Comment on Corfield', *Race*, 2 (May 1961), 7–27.

[2] See F. B. Welbourn, *East African Rebels*.

all right-thinking Africans, who do not wish to be known as "boys" in their own house.' In Kikuyu, although the early stirrings were much more clearly political, the first oath of the Kikuyu Central Association involved the holding of earth in one hand and a Bible in the other; and, prior to the 1950s, the most successful Kikuyu organizations were the independent churches and schools. African Israel was widely supposed to desire freedom from European control 'in the same way as the Church of England sought freedom from Rome', although participation in politics was forbidden. Moreover the personal links, in both Buganda and Kikuyu, between leaders of the independent churches and the political parties were very striking.

What is important is that—in contrast with the overtly pagan movements of revolt[1]—the independent churches wished also to be catholic. Even Mugema declared that his was a faith for the salvation of all nations. Spartas and the Kikuyu independents sought apostolic orders. African Israel applied for membership of the Christian Council of Kenya. The Church of Christ in Africa, separating from the local Anglican bishop, approached the Archbishop of Canterbury to consecrate their own. There is in all this a suggestion that, when Christianity was grasped as the heart of the new society, it might suffer local schism but still present the ideal of a wider fellowship. It might not only transcend tribalism but help the new nations to see themselves more clearly as part of a large whole. On the other hand, with the partial exception of those in Buganda, the political parties were largely independent of overt religion, however deeply convinced some of their individual members might be.[2] It was by no means certain that their leaders felt the need for such religion, except in so far as it satisfied their private moments of mystical awareness and was necessary to gain the political support of its convinced adherents. There was indeed a growing tendency on the part of politicians to tell religion, in no uncertain terms, to keep out of politics. There was the implication that they were unable to think of religion except in institutional terms. In East Africa—except for a few sophisticated individuals—to be

---

[1] e.g. Mau Mau, *Dini ya Misambwa* in North Nyanza and Bugisu, the resurgence of traditional cults in Buganda after 1953.

[2] The Democratic Party in Uganda was at first largely Roman Catholic in inspiration. From 1958 its leaders strove—not very successfully—to erase its denominational image.

Christian implied institutional reference; 'the impact of Christianity' still meant 'the impact of an ecclesiastical institution'.

Out of the solidarity of tribal society—of which remnants were still to be found, for instance, in Karamoja or Masai—there emerged a society which might be called 'Christian-western'. It bred—even when they remained professing Muslims—most of the leaders of the new Africa. Some of them became deeply acculturated. But there remained the vast majority who, whether through education or simply through the impact of colonial administration, were uprooted and found no alternative soil. For them a new synthesis was necessary. At one end of the spectrum was a resurgence of tribalism with a return to the old gods. At the other was Revival. It offered a deeply emotional conviction of salvation, the satisfaction of close fellowship with others of the same experience, and very considerable fruits in moral reform. But, apart from a remarkable development among the pastoral Hima of Ankole,[1] and a contribution to the growth in maturity of some who passed through it to positions of responsibility in society at large,[2] it had little relevance to the problems of a society in rapid change.

Another possibility was the independent churches. They were not necessarily tribal in character, but attempted to rediscover in Christ the unity of the sacred and the secular which was characteristic of the old way of life. It seemed unlikely that they would ever promote a national movement. But, as centres of loyalty with a more than local vision, they might be of profound importance in the building of a new social stability. Alongside them remained the churches of missionary origin, still held in loyal affection by many of their older members. They tended to alienate the young. But there were those whose higher education had led, from a Christian upbringing, to a conviction that they could not be truly African unless they entered fully into the heritage both of the west and of the universal Church. To these the older churches were still the most profound challenge to a genuine catholicity. They were few; and it remained a question whether they could lead their churches out of institutional

[1] D. J. Stenning, 'Salvation in Ankole', in M. Fortes and G. Dieterlen (edd.), *African Systems of Thought* (London, 1964).
[2] Welbourn and Ogot, *A Place to Feel at Home*, p. 35.

dependence on the west into fundamental participation in the life of the new nations.

For by far the most important synthesis was the new nationalism which desired to be both African and technological at the same time, and had at least the suspicion that Christianity was an enemy of both. If the effective entry of Christianity into East Africa is dated with the arrival of the CMS in Buganda in 1877, 86 years of unceasing, and often sacrificial labour had produced extraordinarily little in the way of permanent results. The Church could claim—and perhaps claim with some pride—that it had ameliorated the impact of the west and provided an image which might go far to moderate the impact of nationalism. At many points it had established bridgeheads, which might in the future become growing points for a new African Christianity. But this depended on how deeply it had already affected the national leaders. If nationalism was itself a demand for human respect, how far did its leaders accord to those whom they ruled the respect which they themselves demanded from colonialist rulers? Already it was being said by thoughful Africans that political independence had meant no more than the transfer of power from a white to a black élite. Africa had neither the ascetic tradition of India nor the aristocratic tradition of England. Without some fundamental resource of moral self-criticism, it was difficult to see how nationalist rulers could avoid dictatorship or the churches a new erastianism.

At the moment of independence there seemed to be reasons —reasons which had little to do either with the inadequacies of colonial rule or with anything inherently undemocratic in Africa society—for supposing that independent Africa was heading for a period of illiberal government. It was possible that its leaders had learnt enough from Christianity not only to tolerate criticism but to seek it. It was more likely that they would feel all criticism as incipient treachery; and Christians, who had learnt to be socially aware, had then either to suppress their awareness or run the risk of being reckoned as traitors.

XI

THE IMMIGRANT COMMUNITIES (1): THE EUROPEANS

ALISON SMITH

The British East African territories up to 1918

IN 1895, when the British government first accepted responsibility for the great expanse of territory until then administered by the Imperial British East Africa Company, the Europeans scattered over its 320,000 square miles and amongst its several million inhabitants numbered something less than 500 souls. Some 150 were missionaries, a hundred more—most of them at the coast—employees of the Company; besides these there was a handful of railway engineers and military officers, the rest agents of trading firms, hunters, unemployed seamen, and the like.[1] It was intended that the whole area should be united under a single administration. Yet in the event the Uganda and the East Africa protectorates remained separate, and in the nineteen years between the take-over and the outbreak of the First World War there had developed in them two European communities which, small though they still were—less than 6,500 in all, already showed a marked contrast in their relations with the indigenous African societies, in their interpretation of the European role in East Africa. That the role was to be a

Most of the references given here, in what is necessarily an impressionistic sketch, are to published sources. They could be readily amplified from manuscript materials, notably the extensive files of the Colonial Records Project housed in Rhodes House Library at Oxford; but it is felt that a guide to the accessible literature is more likely to be useful to the general reader.

[1] For the staff strength of the Imperial British East Africa Company see P. L. McDermott, *British East Africa or IBEA* (London, 1895), pp. 440–5; for missionaries and others, C. 8683 (1898) *Report of Sir A. Hardinge . . . on the East Africa Protectorate . .*, *to 1897*, pp. 8, 26–7; A. R. Tucker, *Eighteen Years in Uganda and East Africa* (2 vols.. London, 1908), i, p. 310.

substantial one was common ground. But the contrast, which both conditioned and reflected their relative size, was not the least of the many factors which during the later colonial period stood in the way of subsequent union, and which after it helped to shape the different characters of the respective successor states.

Two decisions taken in 1901/2 played a critical part in accentuating the political and social divergence: the very much *ad hoc* one to promote white settlement in the cool highlands that flank the Rift Valley; and the decision after all not to set up a unified administration, while at the same time a frontier shift brought the whole of the area most suitable for temperate zone farming within what is now Kenya and was then the East Africa Protectorate. Yet these decisions themselves flowed in some measure from the differing patterns of relationship already established in the east and west of the region. As for instance in South America or in Eastern Europe, the representatives of the colonial power were not merely a projection of their parent societies, but also a part, even while they dominated and modified them, of the total societies within which they settled and worked.

In Uganda the important features of early European influence were, first, that it was missionary, intent from the outset upon the permeation and transformation of African societies, and not merely upon limited relations to further other purposes; and secondly, that both this and the political penetration that followed sought to work through and not against the dominant established order. The first secular Europeans arrived to find the interlacustrine state of Buganda which formed the nucleus of the protectorate already intensively influenced by both Protestant and Catholic missions. Representatives of both factions played a strenuous, often contentious, part in the internal and external disputes and negotiations of the kingdom. The members of the Protestant Church Missionary Society, far into the era of civil administration, were accorded a quite exceptional pre-eminence; at ceremonial banquets, for instance, the presence of the British Commissioner on the right hand of the young Kabaka was matched by that of the Anglican bishop on his left. As late as 1908 the 350-odd missionary members of the European community still exceeded in numbers all the rest put together and still often preceded the European agents of secular government in the spread of western administration.[1]

The building up of an administrative service which clearly broke away from the militaristic—and occasionally disreputable—character of that inherited from the East Africa Company owed much to the first Commissioner, Sir Harry Johnston.[2] He discouraged local recruitment, and lost no time in taking steps to turn the service over from a predominantly military to a civilian basis, believing this to be essential both to its internal solidarity and to the establishment of friendly local relations. And in fact the whole administration, civilian and military alike, continued in these early years to depend heavily on the social and political links with the Ganda forged during the original period of missionary contact. The first government posts were mostly set up on the sites of mission stations. Luganda was learnt from mission textbooks turned out on a mission printing press. More than 60,000 such books had been sold before the turn of the century. It was a missionary initiative which, combined with the accessibility to innovation of the Ganda political system, first set Buganda on the prosperous path of cotton cultivation.

The co-operation established with the Ganda, moreover, extended to a quite remarkable degree through the three professional groups concerned in dealing with them—the administration, the armed forces, and the missionaries. During the early years of the century, famine, fire, rinderpest, and sleeping sickness in turn caused major emergencies which drew together the whole European community and the Ganda ruling

---

[1] Uganda *Blue Book* 1908/9, Table Q 1; Sir Hesketh Bell, *Glimpses of a Governor's Life* (London, 1946), p. 194; A. R. Cook, *Uganda Memories* (Kampala, 1945), pp. 189, 207.

	1904/5	*1908/9*
Missionaries	197	c. 350
Officials	146	c. ⎫ 240
Others	43	⎭
Total	386	c. 590

[2] R. Oliver, *Sir Harry Johnston and the Scramble for Africa* (London, 1957), pp. 309–12. Sir Hesketh Bell, who arrived from the West Indies as governor in 1906, thought highly of the calibre of the administrative officials. Bell, *Governor's Life*, pp. 118–9, 159. For their previous reputation, see e.g. Cook, *Uganda Memories*, p. 187.

class in a series of impressive common efforts. In the sleeping sickness campaign, for instance, the missions established centres for the sick, their doctors worked alongside others seconded from the Indian army to investigate the disease, while the administration undertook—again with the co-operation of both missions and Ganda authorities—the wholesale evacuation of populations from the affected areas. When Namirembe Cathedral was destroyed by fire, two-thirds of the £30,000 needed for its replacement was raised within the territory itself; while there was massive Ganda support for the missionary foundation of King's School, Budo, on the English public school model. There was even, within the limited contexts of ceremony and recreation, a measure of social intercourse—such as for instance the football matches between Europeans and enthusiastic Ganda teams.[1]

Yet in 1914, on the eve of the First World War, an observer might with some reason have doubted whether this would be the pattern of the future. The boundary shift of 1902 had, it is true, removed from Uganda to the neighbouring protectorate the one region which even Johnston had envisaged as suitable for large-scale white settlement. Moreover, the Uganda Agreement of 1900 had secured Ganda landowners against involuntary dispossession. Nevertheless, a number of European planters had secured or applied for substantial estates, and the first crops of coffee and rubber were fetching high prices. From the departmental official reports of the period it would have been a reasonable prediction that Uganda was destined in substantial degree to become a 'planter's country'.[2]

Meanwhile, on the other side of the frontier dividing the two protectorates—a frontier pushed in 1902 some 150 miles west-

[1] Tucker, Eighteen Years, ii, passim, esp. pp. 342–3; H. R. Bateman, 'Research and Reminiscences: Uganda 1908–10', Uganda Journal, 15 (1951), 26–40; Bell, Governor's Life, p. 146; Cook, Uganda Memories, passim, esp. p. 397, J. R. P. Postlethwaite, I Look Back (London, 1947), pp. 83–4.

[2] See especially Reports of Lands and Survey Department. A similar conclusion could be drawn from the first report of a committee set up in 1911 to make recommendations on a land settlement in Busoga, Bunyoro, Toro, and Ankole; Cf. C. Wrigley, Crops and Wealth in Uganda (Kampala, 1959), pp. 25–30. For Sir Harry Johnston's views, see Cd. 671 (1901) Report ... on Uganda, p. 14, The Uganda Protectorate (London, 1902), ii, 296–7. Sir Hesketh Bell was opposed to European plantations, Governor's Life, pp. 159–60, and his successor, Sir Frederick Jackson, was exceedingly wary.

ward—Sir Charles Eliot, who arrived as the first Commissioner of British East Africa at the end of 1901, had launched that territory decisively on the half-century endeavour to build a 'white man's country'. Assurances of the British government's support for white settlement, given in January 1902 to a score of enthusiastic pioneers gathered at the railway depot at Nairobi, were followed in 1903 by a campaign to publicize in South Africa the attractions of the East African highlands.[1] In the same year Lord Delamere refused a post in the administration to take up a large tract of land in the Rift Valley. Yet here too the course of development owed something to the pattern of relationships established during the critical years that preceded Eliot's coming.

In the very early days the bulk of the few hundred European residents lived on the coast, where most of the East Africa Company's local staff had been concentrated. The cosmopolitan European colony of Mombasa, the principal port, was in some ways reminiscent of the older and larger one of Zanzibar, and retained into a much later period something of its old-world character, including ceremonious and leisured relations with the Arab authorities and reasonable harmony with the leading Asian merchants.[2] But soon the centre of gravity of the young protectorate shifted inland. Here two themes had been dominant in shaping early relationships: the nineteenth-century concept of the chain of fortified refreshment stations as a means of opening up the African interior—what might be called the 'enclave' pattern; and the technological, self-contained, and strongly Indian-influenced element introduced by the construction of the Uganda Railway.

In the early projections of the East Africa Company, the interior of Kenya had presented itself pre-eminently as an expanse of wastes inhabited by potentially hostile tribes on either side of the trade route to Uganda; and the penetration of the African hinterland by means of a series of fortified enclaves

---

[1] The main reason for the change was argued to be the desirability of having the whole of the railway system—which then ended at Kisumu—under a single administration. See K. Ingham, A. Matson, G. Bennett, various articles in the *Uganda Journal*: 20, 1 (1957), 41–6; 22, 1 (1958), 42–53; 23, 1 (1959), 69–72.

[2] Described by, e.g., W. R. Foran, *A Cuckoo in Kenya* (London, 1936), chaps. xix–xxii; and C. W. Hobley, *Kenya from Chartered Company to Crown Colony* (London, 1929), pp. 147 sqq.

protecting such routes was a concept familiar to European developers of the late nineteenth-century. Even the most competent of the young officers appointed to man these posts found the task of peaceful coexistence in the conditions of the Kenya highlands almost impossible. There were few effective and no traditional authorities through whom the constant frictions over pilfered crops, over women, and over cattle-raiding, could be abated; in consequence, the expedient of enlisting the help of one group as 'friendlies' against others was often resorted to; for years each post maintained its herd of cattle and goats, replenished from time to time by fines or simply by raiding. In short, rather as the first Europeans in Buganda were drawn into the vortex of Ganda politics, so those in highland Kenya were assimilated into the pattern of barter and small-scale predation, of cattle-lifting and woman-stealing, that was the established idiom of the region.[1] It was an idiom which, along with the chances for game-hunting, was not unfamiliar or unattractive to adventurous young Europeans of the period.[2]

The building of the Uganda Railway, begun in 1896 and pushed inland to Lake Victoria in less than six years, had introduced to the protectorate a new manifestation of the European presence: a world of manual labourers, technicians, engineers; of alcoholism and prostitution, of the tensions and enthusiasms evoked by an ambitious construction project. It had done nothing to mitigate the total lack of *rapport* between the peoples of the hinterland and the bearers of the external cultures and economic pressures which it thrust into their midst.[3] Since the labour employed was almost wholly Asian, there was little relationship (save at the level of prostitution) with the African peoples amongst whom it passed—regarded primarily as just one more impediment to the challenging job of getting the tracks laid.

[1] A revealing letter from a young official to an intending pioneer settler is among the Stuart-Watt papers at Rhodes House, Oxford. Hall to Stuart-Watt, 13 Dec. 1893, MSS Afr. S. 391. See also R. Meinertzhagen, *Kenya Diary, 1902–1906* (Edinburgh, 1957), *passim*.

[2] Meinertzhagen, *Kenya Diary*, p. 157: 'I like the African and I like the game, and I wish to preserve both'.

[3] M. R. Hill, *Permanent Way*, vol. i. *The Story of the Kenya and Uganda Railway*, esp. pp. 179 sqq. Oliver, *Sir Harry Johnston*, p. 293, quoting Johnston to Salisbury, 11 Nov. 1899, FO/2/204.

The missionary element, so powerful a mediating and constructive force in Buganda, had not been present to cushion these impacts. With no obvious authorities or stable centres to which missions could be easily accredited, and with practical difficulties in assuring a means of subsistence, the Kenya hinterland had until the coming of the railway been left alone by the major missionary societies. Along the coast the various missions at work had made little headway, and a number of ventures failed altogether.[1] None succeeded in allying and identifying itself with the positive elements in the African societies in which it worked.

This was the scene upon which, from 1902, the first wave of European settlement irrupted. It combined with certain other factors to give white settlement in the Kenya highlands a highly individual character.

In the first place, it was in no sense a response to the economic pressures which had driven millions of comparatively poor emigrants to seek their fortunes overseas during the nineteenth-century. It was tiny in scale, and was based on the premises of, on the one hand, considerable resources for investment[2] and, on the other, the availability of local labour to support living standards acceptable to people endowed with such resources. Secondly, it differed from the settlement that was taking place at the same time in south-central Africa in the important respect that the government was there first; it was government which, in however rudimentary a sense, had been responsible for the physical occupation and pacification of the country, and which acknowledged at least in principle a parallel obligation to the native African inhabitants. An important section of these inhabitants were themselves agriculturalists, farming in close proximity to the areas designated for settlement. Thirdly, the relationship between settlers, officials, and indigenous Africans was complicated by the presence in East Africa, intensified by the commercial opportunities offered by the railway, of another immigrant group—the Asians; a group which had, moreover, an arguable claim to priority in time.

[1] Hobley, *Kenya*, pp. 38–9. Almost half of the mission stations established in the coastal region before the turn of the century had been given up by 1914. Hardinge's *Report on the East Africa Protectorate*, C.8683 (1898), p. 40; *Blue Book* for 1913/14, T1–3.
[2] C. Eliot, *The East Africa Protectorate* (London, 1905), pp. 173–5; M. P. K. Sorrenson, *Origins of European Settlement in Kenya* (Nairobi, 1968), chap. iv.

To meet this unusual combination of conditions and challenges came a colourful assortment of founder settlers. Some were junior officers like Robert Foran who had fought in the South African war, ready to turn their hand indifferently to fighting, farming, or administering. Among those who migrated to East Africa from farming in other British overseas territories, the most notable contingent came from South Africa, described by Foran as 'an exceptional stamp of colonist, accustomed to giving and taking hard knocks in life; even better still, had mostly farmed in southern Africa and fully understood the handling of native African peoples'.[1] But, if it was the South Africans who early crystallized the direction of political and economic relations with the Africans, the class chiefly responsible for creating the distinctive flavour of Kenya settlerdom was that of the English landowning gentry. Partly under the original stimulus of Lord Delamere, and drawn by the lure of the country's magnificent game resources, young men came out to try to re-create in the Kenya highlands a slightly exotic version of the picture—already fading at home—of the life of the English gentry.[2] Lord Cranworth—himself an early landholder—thus exhorted the English public schoolboy to try his fortunes there:

one might almost go so far as to say that those very qualities which render him superfluous to our Canadian and Australian cousins are the very ones which cause him and this Protectorate to be almost ideally suited to each other. . . . For 300 years or more the whole aim of a public school education has been to fit a boy, not for work, but for the overseeing of work. . . . We have here a great stretch of splendidly healthy country. There is thereon a large and rapidly increasing native population, who always have done and always will do the actual manual labour connected with a farm. Most of these natives are moderately lazy, barely moderately honest, and decidedly intelligent. With a good master they form distinctly good servants; and I think that undoubtedly the best master, and the one whom they prefer is the old public school boy.[3]

[1] Foran, *Cuckoo in Kenya*, p. 96. Others were less impressed by the attributes of the South Africans. Tucker, *Eighteen Years*, ii, pp. 293–5, described them as 'bounders', and Bell, *Governor's Life*, p. 166, as 'stirring up complaints in Nairobi'. Foran too admits elsewhere (pp. 109 sqq.) that they could be a law and order problem. Most of the settlers who arrived in 1903 came from South Africa.

[2] Some of the most vivid, and most happy, descriptions of this Kenya variant are to be found in Karen Blixen's *Out of Africa* (London, 1937).

[3] Lord Cranworth, *A Colony in the Making: British East Africa* (London, 1912), pp. 182–6.

Young men of this class, accustomed at home to dominate rather than to respect local government, were no more likely than 'colonials' from South Africa or other white dominions to take kindly to the leading strings of a colonial administration.

Between 1906 and 1908 the population was also augmented by some 700 Boer 'irreconcilables', men, women, and children, and by 1911 a further 100 or so trekkers had joined them. Some of these trekked with their oxen up to the Uasin Gishu plateau and were allocated land there; some came by sea and settled on the Athi plains. Between the wars a further Boer offshoot from the original groups was consolidated in the neighbourhood of Thomson's Falls. Their members were bound together in a close-knit linguistic and religious group. Most came virtually destitute—in violation of the intention, and on the whole the early practice, that settlers should be men of some substance. Yet, thanks to their toughness and solidarity, a number of them made good. They determinedly remained, however, a community apart, and entered into the country's political and social development far less than their early numerical strength, or the extent of their landholdings, might have seemed to promise.[1]

Distrust of the whole principle of white settlement persisted, at least at senior official levels, and was reflected in friction over a wide range of issues; over red tape in the land-granting process and in the alleged inadequacy of public services, and particularly over the availability of African labour. Yet by the end of the period relations between settlers and officials had already begun to lose much of their personal bitterness. The Agricultural Department, established in 1903 under a South African Director, was from the start far more ready to promote European than African agriculture. A number of the junior and specialist officials also came from a South African background, and some of these were more willing than the old-timers to co-operate in a liberal interpretation of the revaluation and development conditions of European settler leases. In Nairobi the district

[1] R. A. Remole, 'White Settlers; the foundation of European agricultural settlement in Kenya' (Harvard Ph.D. dissertation, 1959), pp. 222 sqq.; Gerrit Groen, 'Education as a Means of Preserving Afrikaner Nationalism in Kenya', in *Politics and Nationalism in Colonial Kenya*, ed. B. Ogot (Nairobi, 1972). For comments on the Boers, see Meinertzhagen, *Kenya Diary*, pp. 185–7, Foran, *Cuckoo in Kenya*, p. 149, Cranworth, *Colony in the Making*, pp. 82–3. Eventually more than 1,000 square miles were held by Boer farmers.

officer successfully instituted a biennial series of sporting events between settlers and officials.[1]

In Uganda the early sporting fixtures had been between Europeans and Africans, and had been initiated by the Christian missions; here the missionary sector was held in little regard by settlers and with mixed feelings by the administration. While the number of missions had proliferated—by 1914 there were a dozen of them at work—their total strength was still limited, and the rate of conversion unimpressive.[2] A notable feature of the major early missionary establishments in the interior—the Consolata Fathers' mission at Nyeri, for example, or the Church of Scotland missions at Kibwezi and later at Kikuyu and Tumutumu—was the degree to which they embodied the 'enclave' conception of European penetration. In early days they were seen as refreshment stations for administrators and caravans, and sometimes missionaries were directly employed to implement government policies and even collect taxes; later several establishments were developed as large-scale estates run on plantation lines. Even the administration became critical of the missionaries' avidity for land, while to Africans this avidity and the imposition of labour–tenant relationships which went with it seemed indistinguishable from the practice of the settlers.[3] Only marginally were the missionaries regarded as mediators, and the whole underlying pattern of European–African relations continued to be one of distance, compartmentation, and distrust. As early as 1905 fears were expressed of 'the pioneers being slaughtered by the natives', to guard against which there should be a burgher militia of the Rhodesian stamp.[4]

Already the protectorate was developing something very like a caste society. Near the foot of its social scale were the agri-

---

[1] G. Mungeam, *British Rule in Kenya 1895–1912* (Oxford, 1966), esp. chaps. ix and x. Sorrenson, *European Settlement*, chap. vi. For a personal view of settler–official relations, see Foran, *Cuckoo in Kenya*, pp. 120–2, 268–73.

[2] *Annual Report* for East Africa Protectorate, 1911/12. No new missions were registered in the two following years.

[3] A. J. Temu, *British Protestant Missions* (London, 1972), chaps. v and vi.

[4] H. L. No. 158 (1907), *Papers relating to British East Africa*, pp. 34–5. It is fair to record that the petition to this effect was the work of only perhaps one-third of the Kenya settlers, mostly South African. But the 1905 Volunteer Reserve Ordinance permitted the settlers to set up both mounted and infantry reserve formations, while the practice of promoting Africans to officer rank in the King's African Rifles was quietly dropped. Remole, 'White Settlers', p. 295.

cultural peoples and more especially the Kikuyu, who disobligingly resented the role of agricultural labourers for which the settlers cast them. More estimable were the several pastoral tribes—the Masai, for instance, with their reputation for valour and their freedom from mission influence, and the trading Muslim Somalis from the north-east. The growing Asian population, itself split into tightly exclusive communities, was feared as an economic threat and accordingly castigated as socially and politically disreputable. The caste attitude extended markedly, moreover, into the European sector of society, epitomized by the gulf between the 'Hill' and the 'Plain' in Nairobi. The Club on the 'Hill', originally the preserve of the officer class, was gradually extended to admit the more aristocratic of the settler community—'settler-sportsmen'—as temporary members, and some handpicked members from the professions and commerce. The rest of the Nairobi world foregathered in the Railway Institute on the 'Plain'—the flat area where the bungalows of the railway subordinate staff and the less well-to-do were situated.[1]

Politically, the power of the ruling élite of this European community was centred in the Convention of Associations, the body consolidated in 1910 to protect and advance the farming interest;[2] and in the Legislative Council established in 1907, where the strident voice of the two unofficial members was only partially moderated by the six-strong official side. A material factor here, and in government generally, was the close *rapport* that existed between the most vocal part of the settler lobby and the majority of the territory's governors, who were often closer in background and sympathy to the leading settlers than to their own officials.[3]

Although settler influence was already proving effective in securing favourable land-holding terms and in resisting the acquisition by Asians of land in the highlands, the more fundamental question of the conflict in land rights between Europeans

---

[1] These generalizations can be readily substantiated from the memoir literature of both officials and settlers of the period. See e.g. Foran, Meinertzhagen, Cranworth.

[2] It combined the original Colonists' Association with the Pastoralists' Association formed by R. A. B. Chamberlain to contest Lord Delamere's dominant landholding interest. See vol. ii of this *History*, pp. 282–3.

[3] See particularly Girouard's 1910 report to the Colonial Office, Girouard to Crewe 26 May 1910, CO 533/74, quoted in Sorrenson, *European Settlement*, pp. 118–20.

and the indigenous agricultural African peoples had not yet come to the fore. Nevertheless, by 1914 some 7,000 square miles of the 12,000 square miles which was eventually to be designated as the 'White Highlands' had already been alienated, mostly in very large estates.[1] It was already clear that the bulk of the white farming community would be a cluster of geographically compact groups—in contrast, for instance, to that in the neighbouring protectorate of German East Africa.

Of the 6,500 Europeans in British East Africa on the outbreak of the First World War, more than four-fifths were in the East Africa Protectorate. In both territories the sex ratio had begun to even out,[2] but whereas in Uganda this represented mainly the strength of the female missionary contribution, in the East Africa Protectorate it embodied the beginnings of a genuinely settled community.

There were contrasts: but there were also similarities. It has been noted that even in Uganda it was not then certain that white plantations would not become the dominant factor in the country's economy. And, despite political and administrative jealousies, there was at a more elementary level much in common between the few thousands of Europeans—traders, administrators, soldiers, missionaries, and even settlers—scattered over the region. They were bound together by their fewness in a strange land, and by their common subjection to the discomforts and hazards of tropical Africa. They were bound together also by their participation in a common enterprise, the furtherance of economic development and European civilization (between which little distinction was then widely admitted) in a 'primitive' continent. Despite some criticism of extravagant settler claims in the Kenya highlands, the metropolitan society of which they were the representatives still regarded them on balance with pride and trust. Two quotations may serve to capture something of this mood and relationship. The first

---

[1] A summary of land alienations between 1903 and 1914 is given in the East Africa Protectorate *Blue Book* for 1915, Table BB.

[2]   *European Population 1914*

	M	F	Total
East Africa Protectorate	3,644	1,794	5,438
Uganda	761	256	1,017

Source: Blue Books for 1913/14.

comes from the report drawn up by the Economic Commission set up to consider the future of the East Africa Protectorate (soon to become Kenya Colony) towards the end of the First World War: 'The function of Europeans in Middle Africa is to act as a yeast leavening the inert dough of Africa's indigenous peoples. Where one white immigrant into Canada represents merely one additional participant in Canada's development, one white immigrant into East Africa may galvanize a thousand economically speaking 'dead' Africans into active participation in Imperial Trade'.[1] The second is the remark made to the governor over dinner by a young officer newly recruited to the Uganda service: 'Well, sir, if it is delightful to lay out a garden, how glorious it must be to lay out a protectorate'.[2]

The First World War and the Tanganyika mandate

The war and its aftermath shattered, along with much else, the simplicity of such visions. Before it there had been a real sense in which an essentially undivided European culture was claimed to stand for the pacification of warring black tribes of inferior culture. Now peaceful black Africans had been enlisted to help their white rulers in large-scale operations against other white-ruled territories. In the German East Africa campaign mission stations and Christian converts were roughly handled by both sides.[3] Mrs. Huxley recalls the shocked horror on the news of the first deaths in action of Kenya volunteers. Largely unperceived at the time, but probably even more damaging in the long run to the European role, was the sense of injury engendered by the enormously heavy losses, chiefly from hardship and disease, incurred by the African carrier corps and other ancillary units.[4] At the same time the social class from which not only settlers, but all those concerned with East African

[1] East Africa Protectorate, Economic Commission, *Final Report*, part i (Nairobi, 1919), p. 3.
[2] Bell, *Governor's Life*, p. 124.
[3] C. H. Wilson, *The History of the Universities Mission to Central Africa* (London, 1936), pp. 156–7. For the sense of unease at the idea of hostilities in East Africa, see K. Ingham, *The Making of Modern Uganda* (London, 1958), p. 133, and contemporary newspapers, e.g. *East African Standard*, 22 Aug. 1914.
[4] D. C. Savage and J. Forbes Munro, 'Carrier Corps Recruitment in the British East Africa Protectorate, 1914–1918', *Journal of African History*, 7, 2 (1966), 313–42.

pioneering, had been largely drawn had been that which suffered most dramatically in the carnage of the European battlefronts.

More subtly, the attempt to reassert a European consensus which was one aspect of the peace-making had been accompanied by a mood of self-questioning which sharpened scrutiny and analysis in Europe of the principles of colonial rule. This was represented by the establishment and working of the mandates system, and also by a more vocal criticism of settler attitudes and objectives.

These erosions of earlier assumptions, however, were not immediately obvious. Wartime conditions, including the loss of European manpower on farms and in administration alike, had politically strengthened the white position both in Kenya (as the East Africa Protectorate soon became) and in Uganda. In the latter territory a committee representing largely the planter interest produced a series of reports proposing that most of the land in the protectorate be freed for potential alienation. In the former the enlistment of picturesque irregular military units—successors to the earlier activities of such para-military bodies as the Boy Scouts and the 'Legion of Frontiersmen'—had also been a conscious echo of those burgher forces of southern and central Africa which the settlers had to their chagrin hitherto lacked.[1] At home the air was full of schemes for building new lives for the surviving heroes.

Viewed in this perspective, the granting to Britain of the Tanganyika mandate seemed not so much a test of the fragile concept of international trusteeship as a welcome chance to consolidate the core of white influence in Africa down the highland belt from Kenya to the Rhodesias and beyond. At this point it is necessary to go back a little and review the development of the third area of European settlement and exploitation in East Africa.[2]

---

[1] Huxley, *White Man's Country*, ii, pp. 3–12; A. Davis and H. J. Robertson, *Chronicles of Kenya* (London, 1928), pp. 97–110. The latter is a collection of fictitious satirical sketches of Kenya life during this period.

[2] The section that follows is so heavily indebted to John Iliffe's *Tanganyika under German Rule, 1905–1912* (Cambridge, 1969) and to his Cambridge doctoral thesis, 'The German Administration in Tanganyika 1906–1911: the governorship of Freiherr von Rechenberg' (1965), that detailed references to these would be invidious, and only the most general have been given.

In the early period of contact in German East Africa there is no such single strong theme as that of missionary–Ganda relations in the lacustrine region, or of mutual predation in the Kenya highlands. Half a century of trading contact and economic development had already created at the coast and along the trade routes a fluid society quite unlike those of the northern interior, and, by the time that in 1897 the German administration intervened to check the process, extensive land alienation on the coast had already taken place. Most of this land was in large plantations, financed by German-based companies. These were represented locally by managers and overseers rather than by settlers, and the leading part played by sisal plantations in particular ensured that this should remain a characteristic of the region's European community. Another feature of European society in the German protectorate was that it was more cosmopolitan, more diverse both in nationality and in social and economic status, than in the British territories. On the eve of the First World War, more than a quarter of the European population of five and a half thousand were listed as non-German.[1] Apart from the longer phase of pre-colonial contact, probably the most important cause of this was the less abundant reservoir of Asian skills and industry to draw upon in technical and artisan capacities. In 1913 these categories accounted for 15 per cent of the white community. Notably the building of the Central Railway, the main stretch of which was completed between 1905 and 1914, was carried out by Greek contractors employing Greek artisans, many of whom stayed on both as traders and as planters;[2] by buying up forfeited German estates at the end of each of the two wars, they later became a substantial element among the landholders. In any event, East Africa held little attraction for German emigrants at this time as against America on the one hand, and the eastern territories on the other; nor did Germany have anything quite corresponding either to the British South Africans or to the high-spirited and footloose country gentlemen who gave to Kenya settlerdom its initial colour.

[1] *Die Deutschen Schutzgebiete in Afrika und der Sudsee, 1912–13*, Population tables.
[2] Hill, *Permanent Way*, vol. ii: *The Story of the Tanganyika Railways* (Nairobi, 1958), part ii.

The development of Germany's new tropical dependencies was the subject of much theoretical and political discussion at home, and one expedient perseveringly tried out was the planting of successive *Kleinsiedlung* projects involving peasant communities from outside Germany. These were established on smallholdings in the neighbourhood of Mount Meru: first Boer 'irreconcilables' following the end of the South African war; then German Russians from the Caucasus, the descendants of pioneers who had settled there a century earlier; and finally the members of a German community in Palestine. Only the last showed some promise of success—to be cut short by the war—but a number of the Boers at least stayed on, mostly as hunters or carriers, to add to the varied character of the post-1918 European community.[1]

Another factor that made for variety was the widely scattered geographical distribution of European holdings in the German colony, representing a corresponding diversity of interests: the coffee and rubber estates of the Usambaras and the northern highlands; the sisal plantations on the coast and, together with cotton and rubber estates, stretching far along the Central Railway. To a much greater extent than in Kenya there were sectional lobbies among the landholders at work on both the local administration and the metropolitan government, with rivalries which inevitably centred on the siting of the colony's transport system. A more general divergence of interest on some issues separated the producers, with their demand for cheap labour, from the traders who were anxious to expand African consumption and purchasing power.

As with the character of the European community generally, so with its missionary component, generalization is difficult. Early penetration by British-based missions along the trade routes had been followed by German and Swiss groups in the wake of the establishment of the German sphere of influence. The missions were geographically isolated; and apart from the cultural and other differences between the several societies, there was immense variety in the political contexts within which they worked: from the heavily islamized social background of

---

[1] In Moshi District there were still 282 Afrikaners in 1913, as compared with 364 at the beginning of the scheme. *Jahresberichte uber die Entwicklung der deutschen Schutzgebiete*, 1905/6–1913.

the coast and the trade routes, to the more politically oriented relationship experienced in the north-west and the Southern Highlands, and among the Chagga of Kilimanjaro.[1]

Nevertheless, within this composite picture, it is possible to make some general points about the nature of the European role as it was worked out during the period of German rule.

It was, in the first place, more authoritarian and military in character than in the British territories, reflecting the then prevailing ethos within metropolitan Germany. Not only did direct military rule persist over much of the territory for a full decade, but military officers continued to figure prominently among the administrators, and the settlers themselves were encouraged to take seriously their role as a militia, against the threat both of external aggression by rival European powers and of African opposition.

The authoritarian element did not of course generally work towards the consolidation of settler interests. The most outstanding of the German governors, Freiherr von Rechenberg, was an unswerving advocate of a primarily African peasant economy—albeit an economy run on severely paternalistic lines. He tightened up the conditions for the acquisition and development of land by immigrants. When a dispute arose over the school for European children established in Dar es Salaam, he had it shut down; similarly, though less successfully, he did his best to suppress the publication of views hostile to himself in the conspicuously outspoken local press.[2] Thus the relationship between governor and settlers, so generally friendly and intimate in the East Africa Protectorate, was for much of the period one of bitter hostility. Moreover the local armed forces, in any German territory a force to be reckoned with, were also on bad terms with the governor, while the administration in the field, itself with a considerable military element, was divided in its sympathies.

---

[1] See e.g. Marcia Wright, *German Missions in Tanganyika, 1891–1914* (Oxford, 1971), chaps. iii and iv; R. Austen, *Northwest Tanzania under German and British Rule* (New Haven, 1968), pp. 22–3, 135; S. von Sicard, *The Lutheran Church on the Coast of Tanzania* (Uppsala, 1970).

[2] The Dar es Salaam press had been a powerful factor on the local scene even in the time of von Rechenberg's predecessors, von Goetzen and Liebert. Iliffe, 'German Administration', chap. xii.

Yet by 1914, despite the strenuous policies of von Rechenberg and the authoritarian tradition within which he worked, and despite its own internal divisions, it was by and large the settler element—then one-quarter of the white working population—which held the upper hand within the German protectorate. Partly this was due to the configuration of German domestic politics, in which settler interests and the proponents of a railway policy favourable to them had a strong voice. Partly it derived from the forces of the world market, which, here as in Uganda, prospered the European sisal and coffee plantations in the four or five pre-war years. In 1910 Dr. Bernard Dernburg was succeeded as Colonial Secretary by Friedrich von Lindequist, a sometime governor of South West Africa and a staunch champion of white settlement, while in the following year von Rechenberg himself was followed at the expiry of his term of office by Heinrich Schnee, committed to a sharp reversal of policy. But it seems that the real, and surprising, strength of the settlers' position was rooted in local factors: in the alliance arrived at and made effective by their geographical proximity, between commercial and trading and planter/farmer interests; and more importantly, in the long and sturdy tradition of *Selbstverwaltung* (self-administration) imported from German provincial life. This, which was based on a substantial measure of local financial autonomy, had taken firm root even in the earliest days of the colony.[1] It had survived the efforts of Rechenberg both to undermine the local councils' powers and to extend their membership to non-Europeans. It expounded its views in a press that was at least as vocal as that of the British East Africa Protectorate. Under Schnee it was ready to form a flourishing basis for a move towards effective influence over the central advisory body—on which the new governor gave the representatives of the settlers a majority of twelve to four.

The fields in which this influence was expressed were chiefly, as elsewhere, those of land and labour. In parts of the Northern Province there was considerable African dispossession, and in other areas the pressure for labour recruitment caused depopulation and hardship. Even so, it is hard to reconstruct a

---

[1] The Dar es Salaam press had been a powerful factor on the local scene even in the time of von Rechenberg's predecessors. von Goetzen and Liebert. Iliffe, 'German Administration', chap. xiii. As early as 1901 nine 'communes' were established.

picture, such as is vivid for Uganda and discernible in British East Africa, of the dominant European minority in its relation to the total society. Among other things, the basically harsher and more explicitly racial domination of the Germans, settlers and government alike, did not make for articulation of attitudes on the African side. Perhaps the main reason for the lacuna, however, is the comparative silence of the missionary voice, which in Buganda at least made for a highly vocal African reaction, and which even in the East Africa Protectorate was audible in mediation and potentially revolutionary in education.[1]

Between the wars

To those who looked towards an indefinitely expanding future for European settlement and European enterprise in East Africa, the time of the peace settlement, 1919–20, must have seemed one of great promise. In the German territory newly acquired under mandate hundreds of estates lay derelict, an invitation to the new British settlers who would complete the chain of British influence from Kenya to the Union of South Africa. In Kenya their wartime participation in government had confirmed the settlers in their confidence of ultimate political control, and a great augmentation was looked for in the farming population. Even in Uganda the political and economic ascendancy of the few planters, encouraged by the new governor, Sir Robert Coryndon, temporarily smiled upon in Whitehall, and embodied in their representation on the newly established Legislative Council, seemed to augur the opening of a fresh chapter in local European influence.

But in fact the period between the wars witnessed no such smooth extension of European settler dominance. Fluctuations in the world economy exposed the vulnerability of the tropical economies, particularly as exploited by immigrant enterprise. In Tanganyika in particular, other interpretations of the European role, including the insistence that it should not be an exclusively British one, challenged the assumption of British farmer/planter hegemony. And there were sporadic signs—as yet little observed—that the European role as a whole was beginning to be questioned by some of the subject African peoples. The crucial fact was that the resident white population

[1] Cf. Austen, *Northwest Tanzania*, p. 70.

of East Africa did not grow large or powerful enough—unlike that between the Limpopo and the Zambezi—to substitute its own more repressive version of the colonialist mission. In 1939 the European population of the whole vast region was still less than 33,000, and 3,800 agricultural holdings occupied 14,000 square miles of land. In Rhodesia at the same date the number of holdings (3,500) was about the same: but they occupied more than 50,000 square miles, in a country one quarter the size of East Africa, and with a European population of 60,000.[1]

In Uganda, the prospects of a substantial planter interest were short-lived. Whether despite the administration's encouragement they could ever have matured in the fact of the articulate and broadly based opposition which would certainly have developed is doubtful; they were in the event effectually killed by the post-war currency crisis, by the depression which toppled coffee and rubber prices, and by the veto from London on anything in the nature of forced labour provoked by the 'Northey circulars' in Kenya. By 1930, apart from the largely Asian-owned sugar estates, few productive plantations remained.[2]

Yet even after the collapse of the planting interest, the scale of the European community in Uganda, and the role to which it aspired in the country's development, continued to be much greater than in, for instance, the British West African territories. This was due on the one hand to the absence of a developed indigenous trading system, together with the presence of Asian entrepreneurs; and, on the other, to a carry-over of the basically paternalistic relationship of the pre-1914 period into the changed circumstances of the 1920s and 1930s. It was perhaps most significantly characterized by the persistence of the 'missionary factor'. As late as the eve of the Second World War, the 570 Europeans directly attached to missions accounted for no less than a quarter of the white community,[3] and it was their leaders

[1]

	Mainland East Africa	Southern Rhodesia
		_1938_
No. of holdings	3,800	3,500
Area alienated (sq. miles)	14,000	51,000
Total land area (sq. miles)	693,000	150,000

[2] In 1931 there were 222 European estates recorded, comprising 104,313 acres. Less than a quarter of this land was cultivated. The only fresh development in the 1920s was some coffee plating in Toro.

[3] Uganda _Blue Book_ for 1938, pp. 124–7.

who supplied the element of continuity and permanence which in Kenya came from the early settlers. They were, moreover, closely involved with the administration, pre-eminently in education. Until the foundation of Makerere College, they were responsible for all the major secondary schools in the country. In some measure their influence even extended into the world of commercial development. The Uganda Company, for instance, was pioneered by the CMS lay missionary Kristen Borup, and for long continued to insist on an explicit affirmation of Christian principles by members of its staff.[1]

Despite occasions of difference between the official and missionary circles—they clashed for instance on several major issues of educational policy[2]—the relationship between them continued in the main to be one of consensus; a consensus, moreover, which extended to include both the commercial and the small surviving planter interests. Representatives of these were described in a senior official's reminiscences as constructive and co-operative, a verdict that might seem to be borne out by the singular dullness of the recorded proceedings of the Uganda Legislative Council—wherein the leading immigrant interests, both European and Asian, were the only unofficial representatives.[3] There was more to the consensus than apathy, however. While the sessions of the main Legislative Council were generally uncontroversial, the real influence of the leading commercial interests was exercised through informal channels. These included for instance membership of official and semi-official committees and boards, and the practice of referring draft legislation to the Uganda Chamber of Commerce; it was possible by these means to affect significantly such issues as the development of the country's rail and road infrastructure and the all-important question of the marketing of export crops. Because the partnership between administration and commerce worked harmoniously enough, the one issue on which Uganda unofficials did become vocal in debate was hostility to any

---

[1] C. Ehrlich, *The Uganda Company* (Kampala, 1953), pp. 47–9.
[2] See chap. ix in vol. ii of this *History*.
[3] See generally G. F. Engholm, 'Immigrant Influences upon the Development of Policy in Uganda, 1902–1952' (Ph.D. thesis, London University, 1968). Over the twenty-two years from 1930 to 1952 the Council spent on average only seven days a year in session. For the official regard for the planters etc., see e.g. Postlethwaite, *I Look Back*, pp. 78, 97.

proposal of closer union between the three East African territories which might expose them both to Kenyan exploitation
and to the frictions generated by that country's settler-dominated
politics. Less conspicuously but equally persistently they
opposed pressures, such as those from small Asian traders and
also from African sources, to introduce more competition and
flexibility into Uganda's economy.[1]

Thus within the European sector comparative harmony
continued to prevail. But the composition and the inertia of the
Legislative Council was also symptomatic of the falling apart of
that other fragile consensus, as between Europeans and Africans,
between rulers and some of the ruled. The participation of the
Ganda in government was with their own consent largely
confined to the proceedings of the Lukiko. Observers noted
sadly that European-sponsored welfare projects, such as the
building of the CMS Women's Hospital at Mukono, no longer
commanded an enthusiastic Ganda response.[2] Buganda refused
to accept a European expert as an agricultural adviser. More
importantly, the one serious attempt made by a group of Ganda
to buy themselves into the oligopolic processing and marketing
system ended in failure, recrimination, and a lawsuit.[3] It was
characteristic of the good intentions that still permeated Uganda
relationships that the attempt was made, and in part its collapse
was due to the economic crisis of 1930–1; it was characteristic of
the essentially immigrant-dominated nature of the export
system that it broke down and was not repeated.

It is possible that but for the presence of the intermediate
Asian community the *rapport* between an immigrant ruling
minority—even a community of some size—and an indigenous
ruling class might have continued longer. But the role of the
Asians, and particularly of the small Asian traders, in opening
up the possibilities and advantages of a freer market economy,
was among pressures which were already challenging the
position of the Ganda ruling class. Such a challenge added
powerfully to its tendency to resent the essentially paternalistic
friendliness of the representatives of the colonial power.

[1] Engholm, 'Immigrant Influences', *passim*.

[2] E. Dauncey Tongue, 'The Contact of Races in Uganda', *British Journal of Psychology*, 25 (1934–5), 356–64; Cook, *Uganda Memories*, pp. 362–3.

[3] C. Ehrlich, 'The Marketing of Cotton in Uganda, 1900–1950' (Ph.D. thesis, London University, 1957), pp. 260–2; *Uganda Company*, pp. 36–7.

Even so, the atmosphere in Uganda and the relations within the Uganda European community, by 1939 some 2,200 strong, remained conspicuously different from those of Kenya. Entebbe, with its government bungalows and planned lay-out, remained visibly set apart from the metropolis of Kampala. In Kampala the political capital of the kingdom of Buganda jostled with European and Asian immigrant commercial interests, with the headquarters of a dozen intensely active religious groups, with the country's principal educational institutions, and with a thriving busy populace of Ganda and immigrant Africans from the protectorate and beyond. Neither centre resembled the settler capital of Nairobi.

The European population of Tanganyika did grow substantially between the wars, from something under 2,500 to more than 9,000. By 1938 there were about 1,500 European agricultural holdings. But neither the community as a whole nor the farming part of it ever came near to fulfilling the hopes of the Kenya settlers for a massive southward extension of Kenya settlerdom. The failure to do so owed something to the legacy of the German past; but much more to the limitations on the whole concept of British exploitation in East Africa embodied in the mandate system and to the tenacity with which the local colonial administration enforced them.[1]

It is true that a considerable European contribution to agricultural production was assumed. The most profitable export crop was sisal, and the organization of the sisal industry, with its heavy capitalization, ruled out the possibility of handing these plantations over for immediate African exploitation. There remained, moreover, a fair number of non-German pre-war settlers, augmented by Kenya and South African farmers who had moved in after service in the East African campaign. Nevertheless the first post-war governor, Sir Horace Byatt, favoured an economy based wholly on African cultivation, and one of the early measures of the administration was to restore a limited area of alienated land to African occupation to relieve

[1] The most useful general sources for the European role in Tanganyika during the inter-war period are: Charlotte Leubuscher, *Tanganyika Territory* (London, 1944); Donald Cameron, *My Tanganyika Service and some Nigeria* (London, 1939); and Kenneth Ingham, chaps. x and xi in vol. ii of this *History*.

congestion on the crowded slopes of Mounts Meru and Kilimanjaro. It was not until 1923 that a Land Ordinance was passed
which cleared up doubts as to the conditions of tenure, and,
under the terms of the League of Nations mandate, these
ensured that no incoming alien landholders should for the future
enjoy wholly unrestricted rights of occupation. Henceforward
only leasehold titles were available, occasionally for 99 but more
generally limited to 33 years, and these provided for a government share in any enhanced land values. Only between Africans
could land transfers take place without government permission.
Sir Donald Cameron, indeed, who succeeded Byatt as governor
in 1926, was by no means opposed to increased European
investment and agricultural development, and opened up
extensive new areas to alienation in the Southern Highlands.
But he was insistent that those wishing to take up concessions
should have the large capital resources needed to exploit land
unprofitable for African peasant farming, a requirement which
further ruled out anything on the lines of the smallholder
settlements of the German period, or the soldier-settlement
scheme of post-war Kenya. Railway extensions were designed
to serve primarily areas of African, not immigrant, production.

If stringent limitations were thus placed upon the emergence
in Tanganyika of a European community securely settled on the
land, the requirements of the mandate militated equally against
the consolidation of a community with strong national or cultural
bonds. The varied origin of the minority of Europeans remaining
from the pre-war period has already been noted; now it was laid
down that no distinction must be made in allowing entry as
between nationals of any of the member states of the League of
Nations. The first non-British nationalities to profit by this
non-discriminatory provision were the Greeks and the Swiss,
but already in 1926 the territory was reopened to German
immigrants. Within four years these had acquired more than 20
per cent of the total alienated agricultural land, while in the
same year less than 40 per cent was held by British farmers and
planters. It was of crucial importance also that no restriction
could be placed on the acquisition of land rights by Asians. By
1930 these were in fact—with 17 per cent of the total acreage—
the third largest group of immigrant landholders. Their presence
alone ruled out the possibility of anything in the nature of

racially defined reserves comparable to Kenya's White Highlands.

To the fact of cultural variety must be added the already existing factors of geographical dispersion and of diversity of economic interest. Thus the picture of the European settlers of Tanganyika is of a group not only small but tremendously fragmented. A handful of Boer farmers and South African veterans from the East African campaign held large cattle ranches in the neighbourhood of Kilimanjaro and Meru; the sisal plantations, a number of them held by Greeks, were scattered along the coast and inland along the line of rail to Korogwe; the biggest estates, belonging to British and German landholders, were in the Southern Highlands in the neighbourhood of Iringa, producing tobacco, pyrethrum, and some livestock as well as tea and coffee. By 1939 all the alienated land together amounted to less than $2\frac{1}{2}$ per cent of the territory's habitable land.[1]

The nearest approach to a concerted settler lobby was to be found in the Northern Province, in the Usambaras and around the slopes of Kilimanjaro and Meru, where mixed farming was combined mainly with coffee-growing.[2] Here communications with Kenya had been made close by the Arusha–Voi rail link, and the Northern Province farmers were consistently anxious to strengthen ties with the neighbouring territory. But with so heterogeneous a settler body, and with the administrative and political cards stacked so heavily against it, the growth of any formidable bid for European settler control was out of the question. A Legislative Council was established by Cameron in 1926 with four nominated members (increased to six in 1929) but it was not until 1939 that they were represented on the Executive Council. Moreover, there was here another divisive factor—this time not due to, but in spite of, the terms of the mandate. Membership of the Legislative Council required an oath of loyalty to the crown which effectively ruled out German and Greek—though not Asian—participation.

[1] There is a useful account of the extending pattern of white settlement in Tanganyika by C. Gillman, 'White Colonization in East Africa with Special Regard to Tanganyika Territory', *Geographical Review*, 32, 4 (1942), 585–97.

[2] This and the following paragraphs draw upon an unpublished MS. by Professor Margaret L. Bates, of Sarasota College, 'Europeans in Tanganyika', which the author kindly put at my disposal.

There were indeed from the beginning vociferous representations, in the *Dar es Salaam Times* and elsewhere, on the part of
the settlers for a more effective voice, notably for a political
participation which was more fully representative than that of
the nominated members on the Legislative Council. Yet it may
be questioned whether in its operation (within the limits set for
overall policy) the system as it actually evolved did not suit a
number of the more influential of them rather better. For
nomination, particularly as used by Cameron, in effect meant
the representation of regional and sectional interest groups,
which were in practice regularly consulted by the government—
much as in Uganda—on matters of policy.

Probably the strongest argument for an indirect form of
influence such as this was the presence from 1926 onwards of a
growing German element. From the first the interests of this
group on some major issues ran counter to those of the British
settlers, most prominently on the question of closer union which
dominated the political scene in the early 1930s. With the rise of
the Nazi Party and Hitler's increasingly imperious demands for
the return of Germany's colonies, the German group presented
an acutely felt threat to the whole basis of British rule in the
territory.

The threat was echoed, although in less forthright tones, by a
number of the German missionaries. These too had been
excluded for the most part during the early years of the mandate,
and some returned genuinely committed to the cause of restoring
the colony to Germany. In at least one mission centre a picture
of the Führer hung above the altar. And, even apart from this
extremist handful, there was considerable German political and
financial pressure within the missionary field.[1] Moreover, the
missionary picture as a whole was intensely complicated. In
religious as in other matters, the mandate decreed that there
should be no discrimination against either nationality or
denomination, and the holding of the ring as between the
different and frequently competitive Christian missions became
one of the quite considerable preoccupations of those in the
administration concerned with health and education. The total
number of those working in some capacity in the mission sector
showed a substantial growth: at the beginning of the First

[1] Wright, *German Missions*, pp. 186 sqq., 215.

World War it had numbered perhaps 700; by the end of the second there were over 1,600 missionaries, representing no less than eighteen nationalities.[1]

It would not be over-imaginative to see in the Tanganyika administration, charged with the reconciling of so wide a range of interests and obligations, the development of a distinctive ethos. In the early years the keynote was one of improvisation and amateurishness while war damage was made good and the government was established on a more regular footing. This was followed by the period in which Cameron sought to instil into his subordinates his own enthusiasm for all that was involved in his personal interpretation of indirect rule. Throughout there was the need to take account of both smaller settler interests and of those responsible for major foreign investment and the earning of export revenue; of Greeks, Germans, and Swiss, as well as members of the British community; of Catholic and Protestant, Anglican, Lutheran, Moravian, and Seventh Day Adventist; and, not least, of the representations emanating from the Mandates Commission of the League of Nations enjoining the administration to take heed of all these things. Independence, patience, a sense of humour—these were perhaps more essential to the Tanganyika secretariat or district officer than to most colonial administrators.

They did not, however, readily tune with qualities which might have made for a more dynamic development of the economy. There can be little doubt that one sector which—for better or worse—tended to be atrophied by the overall atmosphere of cautious paternalism was that of commerce. The European 'interests' which the administration consulted on matters of policy were in general the producers, especially producers of sisal and diamonds. In so far as commerce was represented, it was by the big Asian houses. There was no Dar es Salaam parallel to either the European business community of Kampala or the more complex commercial and financial world of Nairobi. And Tanganyika remained a poor country.

---

[1] *Die deutschen Schutzgebiete*, 1912–13, population tables; Tanganyika Annual Report for 1947, p. 293. The main nationalities represented in 1947 were: German, 381; Dutch, 236; British, 230; Swiss, 205; Italian, 188. Comparison with 1913 can only be approximate, owing to the subsequent loss of Ruanda/Urundi.

In 1939 there were 23,000 Europeans in Kenya: more than twice as many as in Tanganyika, nine or ten times the number in Uganda, and nearly four times as many as in 1919. Tanganyika and Uganda had patently failed to fulfil the aspirations of those who had hoped for a consolidated belt of white dominion from the Sahara to the Cape. Yet in the event the limits set during these two decades on the concept of the white man's country within Kenya itself were not less critical.

The post-1918 rush of settlement did not match expectations, but was still substantial. Within five years the colony's white population had doubled, and the farming sector had attained a relative preponderance which was never to be regained thereafter.[1] This was a time at which high hopes—somewhat reminiscent of the German schemes before the war—were placed on the 'small man', and particularly on the ex-soldier. Of the 1,310 estates alienated under the Ex-Soldiers' Settlement Scheme, 257 were of less than 200 acres. Another small-farm project was that of providing farms for disabled officers in the Lumbwa District to the west of the Rift Valley.[2]

The schemes for smallholders in general fared badly; many of these farms were amongst those that fell victim to the depression and currency difficulties of 1921-2.[3] But for the farmers who survived, the years between 1926 and 1931 were perhaps the most prosperous and sanguine of the colony's history. There was a renewed drive for settlers in 1929-30, but this was cut short by the effects of the depression, and it was not until the eve of the Second World War that the economic outlook again seemed promising enough to attract immigrants.

Although the net increase in the number of farmers was thus moderate, and although farms on the average became somewhat smaller, there was still an extension in the area of the white

---

[1] The following table shows the numbers and percentages of the European population employed in agriculture at the various census dates:

	1921	1926	1931	1948
Numbers employed in agriculture	1893	2199	2522	3411
% of total European population	19·6	17·6	15·0	11·5
% of gainfully employed European population	37·2	34·3	28·6	24·4

Source: Census data for these years.

[2] M. Salvadori, La Colonisation européenne au Kenya (Paris, 1938), pp. 95-7; E. A. Brett, Colonialism and Underdevelopment in East Africa (London, 1973), pp. 177-8.

[3] Ibid. and chap. v in vol. ii of this History, pp. 234-5.

settlement in the highlands. West of the Rift Valley land was appropriated from the Kipsigis to provide disabled officers' farms; railway extensions opened up in turn the area north-east of Thomson's Falls in the Aberdares and around Solai in the Rift Valley, and the whole Trans-Nzoia region stretching up to Mount Elgon in the north-west. In contrast to those of Tanganyika, these railway extensions were expressly planned to serve European producer interests. The consolidation of the settler-occupied area as a virtually continuous stretch of country, dominating the territory's capital town and yet separated from the coast, thus continued.

There is an abundance of material for the depicting of Kenya's settler life during this inter-war period. Settlers and their wives described their experience with pride, humour, or disillusion-ment: locusts, droughts, the struggle with diseases of stock or crops, the overdrafts; and, always, the unfathomable and unpardonable ways of government on the one hand and of 'native labour' on the other.[1] The same themes recur, more prosaically and often more acrimoniously, in the records of the local District Associations; bodies which perhaps more faithfully than anything else reflect the parochial yet intensely political attitude of the farmers in the early post-war years. In 1937, about their peak year, there were some thirty of these associations, representing on the average less than 100 farmers each, and forming a colourful mosaic of variegated interests and jealousies. The greater part of their funds was spent on maintaining the Convention of Associations, which for some time represented them in relations with the government—but with which the local bodies frequently quarrelled, as they did with one another.[2]

---

[1] Among many may be cited (women authors predominate) Karen Blixen, *Out of Africa*, Alice and Maud Brodhurst-Hill, *So This is Kenya* (London, 1936), M. A. Buxton, *Kenya Days* (London, 1927), V. A. Carnegie, *A Kenya Farm Diary* (Edinburgh, 1930), Evelyn Cobbold, *Kenya, the Land of Illusion* (London, 1935), J. G. Le Breton, *Kenya Sketches* (London, 1935), Alyse Simpson, *The Land that Never Was* (London, 1937). Another revealing, if limited, glimpse comes from the pamphlets encouraging immigration. 'There are preparatory schools for boys, of exactly the same type as their counterparts in England, and the Government schools give a sound and practical education for very small fees. . . . There is no need to fear that if you should have an accident, an illness or a toothache in Kenya you would lack the most skilful attention and treatment. . . . And, above all things, there is in Kenya an endless variety of occupations and amusements. . . .' *New Homes, New Hopes in Kenya Colony* (Kenya Association, London, c.1932).

[2] The papers of the Convention of Associations have been deposited in Rhodes

The Convention itself had a decidedly military and 'gentry' character, and for some years had a close direct influence on the colonial administration; after 1927, however, the governor ceased to attend its meetings and the strong constitutional influence which the farmers continued to exercise flowed rather through the Unofficial Members of the Legislative Council.[1]

Politically the farming interest remained the spearhead of the claims for European political advance[2] and, given the discouragement of African production, it was indeed the European-grown crops and the resources brought into the country by those who grew them that formed the basis of such slender viability as the economy enjoyed. But numerically other sections of the white population were growing a good deal faster. Employment in commerce more than doubled in the decade from 1921, while that in industry was up by nearly 80 per cent (though this may have owed something to the brief effects of the Kakamega gold rush). During the same period the number employed in agriculture rose by only one-third.[3]

The non-agricultural population was overwhelmingly concentrated in Nairobi. By the end of the Second World War the capital had, with nearly 12,000 white inhabitants, about half of the European population of the colony, while the other three main centres—Mombasa, Kisumu, and Nakuru—had some 2,500 between them. By this time a number of the bigger international trading firms were moving in: Mitchell Cotts Dalgety's, Leslie & Anderson. Nairobi was becoming a financial centre for the whole East African economy. The railway system was reorganized and expanded.

The quality of European life in inter-war Nairobi is harder to recapture than that of the farms. It lent itself less readily to

House, Oxford, but are not yet open to general access. The accessible records of some of the constituent associations, however (also in Rhodes House), may be taken as representative of their proceedings. A light-hearted caricature is in Davis and Robertson, *Chronicles of Kenya*, pp. 37–44. For the Convention of Associations see also Huxley, *White Man's Country*, ii, *passim*.

[1] Their influence is corroborated, and welcomed, in a confidential memorandum written by Governor Sir James Grigg for the 1927 Conference of East African Governors in London. Quoted by Brett, *Colonialism and Underdevelopment*, p. 183.

[2] More detailed research indicates considerable divisions within the farming interest, notably between the larger, often overseas-based, concerns and the smaller settler-run farms, which cannot be elaborated here.

[3] Census data, 1921, 1926, 1931.

colourful and affectionate description, and the urban population was more transient. Probably the most authentic picture is that to be gleaned from the columns of the *East African Standard* and the *Mombasa Times*. One of the features that distinguished the urban white community from that of the farmers was its more direct contact, and competition, with the Asian community, a community expanding far more rapidly than itself. Nevertheless, the interests of a considerable section of the European town-dwellers of Nairobi (Mombasa views always remained distinctive) were closely intertwined with those of the farmers. There was much social mobility between the two, and where there were differences they were in general not sufficient to breach the broad harmony of the European socio-political front.[1]

It was a front which, in proportion to the tiny community that it stood for, wielded a quite out of the ordinary influence. This was not only by reason of the intimate and personal connection of leading Europeans with the local legislature, but also through their many and various contacts with both houses of parliament at Westminster. The most cursory following through in the pages of Hansard's volumes of any of the major issues of East African policy (notably that of Closer Union) demonstrates these contacts at work.

Yet, set against the hopes of the pioneers, the whole white Kenya community, and the farming sector which was its base, remained hopelessly small, hopelessly inadequate to the political and economic aspirations which had been built around it. In some part this can be attributed to impersonal factors beyond the reach of either metropolitan or local forces: the 1914–18 casualty rate, the impact of depression, the absence of substantial mineral resources which might have tided over the lean years and laid the basis for future expansion. But at the root of many of Kenya's troubles as a settler colony was the fact that, at a time when Britain's colonial role was undergoing searching re-evaluation at home, this particular territory lay torn between two interpretations.

[1] There are indications during the early 1920s, according to Brett, that business interests concerned with Kenya might well have welcomed policies directed more towards the promotion of peasant agriculture. *Colonialism and Underdevelopment*, pp. 178–9.

A sense of commitment to white settlers and to the form of development they stood for did persist, and was to be invoked until well after the Second World War. It was held to be vindicated by the economic contribution made by white farmers to the economy; it was strengthened by the strategic arguments for an effective British presence on the shores of the Indian Ocean. On the other hand there were the mounting political and economic arguments for indigenous peasant economies as against immigrant plantation ones. These were supported by expanding conceptions of trusteeship as enunciated in the mandates and forcefully put forward in demands for self-government by other non-white units of the British Empire.[1]

It was in fact the question of Asian, not African, rights which first set off the argument in Kenya, leading to the controversy which culminated in the 1923 White Paper asserting the paramountcy of African interests over those of all immigrants. The sequel was at the metropolitan end a vacillation which alternately exasperated and heartened Kenya Europeans for another thirty years. Settlement was encouraged, but the area to be settled was in the event closely circumscribed. They were invited to share in the 'trusteeship' for the African peoples, and on most specific issues the administration in practice responded to their pressures, but the way to an unimpeded local white control over the economy and the country remained firmly barred.

One consequence of this dualism was to endow Kenya with an exceptional number of European officials. In the attempt to hold the ring, to satisfy white demands for technical services and yet avoid conspicuous neglect of African development, the colony acquired relatively the largest and most expensive administration

[1] The high-water mark in political receptiveness in London for the settler viewpoint is generally taken to be the 1925 *Report of the East Africa Commission* (Cmd. 2387), a three-man all-party commission headed by Charles Ormsby-Gore. But Cf. the following passage from *East Africa: a new Dominion* (London, 1927), the work in which Major A. G. Church, the Labour member of that commission, reflected on their tour:

'Our modern barons of East Africa . . . might do well to consider that the system they would defend is one which was condemned and scrapped a century ago in the country where most of them were born. A privileged community has no survival value. . . . The white must develop an entirely different mentality as regards the native, and cease to cant about the advantages accruing to the natives if forced or officially "encouraged" to work for wages' (p. 226).

of any British African colonial territory. Thus in the early 1930s, whereas official salaries and pensions cost Tanganyika about £0.15s. per head of the population, and Uganda, £0.17s., in Kenya the figure was £0.29s. per head. The great bulk of this money was spent on paying European officials.[1]

Before the Second World War, there is no doubt that on balance the sympathies of the senior administrators were with the protection of African interests rather than with settler claims, which they castigated as 'South African' in tendency.[2] And between the wars, in so far as they were the official mediators of metropolitan distrust of settler ambitions, they continued as a body to attract censure—for instance on the withdrawal of administrative pressure to secure labour for white farms. There were complaints of their number and expense, particularly when farming and commercial incomes were harder hit than theirs by depression; and of the frequency with which they were moved from district to district.[3] Yet there is evidence—in a picture that is necessarily full of contradictions and exceptions—that at a social level the interests of this official element were drawing together with those of the group at large. Only a very few of the officials could now claim a longer experience than the older settlers; it was the latter who were the old hands. Then there was at least some tendency for Kenya to attract as administrative recruits those cadets who were attracted to the ideals of a 'white man's country'. Thirdly, a growing proportion of officials were locally recruited within Kenya itself.

Moreover, on its own small scale the country was developing its own self-sufficiency, its own compactness. In its temperate climate leave could be spent comfortably, children brought up and sent to the same schools as those of the permanent residents. Soon after the war this growing convergence of interest was given expression in the relaxing of the veto on land purchase by

---

[1] Based on salary and pension figures for 1935, set against more recent estimates of East African populations at that period (see Appendix Table 1). For 1931 the approximate ratios of European officials to over-all population are

Uganda	1 : 7,900 inhabitants
Tanganyika	1 : 5,300 inhabitants
Kenya	1 : 2,800 inhabitants

[2] Sorrenson, *European Settlement, passim*, esp. chaps. vi and xv.

[3] This is based in part on the records of the various farmers' associations, see note 2, p. 451, above. See also Davis and Robertson, *Chronicles of Kenya*, pp. 175–95.

members of the civil service.[1] Thus by 1939 the once fairly sharp distinction in outlook between settler and official was becoming blurred. When in the 1950s the deep fissures in Kenya's total society were revealed in open violence, the rank and file of the administration were for the most part ill equipped to comprehend them.[2]

The missionary element, now a dwindling proportion of the white community, was less assimilated. It remained on the whole outside the clubs and other social centres, and the settlers continued to regard the missions and their converts with suspicion. Yet several of their leading spokesmen, notably John Arthur of the Church of Scotland Mission, did play a not inconsiderable political role (for instance attending as observers the meetings of the settler Convention of Associations); and on the most burning source of African resentment, that of labour, these in the main accepted the central settler contention that it was right to put some pressure on Africans to leave the reserves and work for wages. It is true that missionary lobbying in Britain played a significant part in generating a more critical attitude to white settlement and its demands generally; and also that within Kenya the influence of the missionaries was exerted to prevent the worst abuses of the system. But by and large their commitment to the basic concept of white settlement was too deep to give them credibility as mediators and counsellors.[3] Although considerable efforts were made to channel and contain early African political mobilization,[4] only the CMS missions among the Luo of Nyanza Province succeeded in establishing a genuinely sympathetic and dynamic relationship with the African societies around them.[5]

---

[1] This change was made by Governor Sir Edward Northey, who also allowed official members a free vote in the Legislative Council. Volume ii of this *History*, p. 296. The free vote was ended by Churchill as Colonial Secretary in 1922.

[2] There were of course exceptions. One of the first attempts to analyse the socio-economic composition of the Mau Mau and anti-Mau Mau forces was made by a district officer in charge of the Githunguri Kikuyu Home Guard. M. P. K. Sorrenson, *Land Reform in the Kikuyu Country* (London, 1967), pp. 107–9.

[3] Temu, *British Protestant Missions*, chap. 6. Temu does less than justice, however, to the achievements of the CMS in Nyanza Province.

[4] Ibid., pp. 129–31. Cf. *Harry Thuku, Autobiography*, assisted and edited by Kenneth King (Nairobi, 1970), pp. 20 sqq.

[5] J. M. Lonsdale, *A Political History of Nyanza, 1883–1945* (in press), 'European Attitudes and African Pressures: missions and government between the wars', *Race* 10, 2 (1968), 141–51.

It could be contended that in the most crucial area, the Highlands, their half-success was more tragic in its consequence than complete failure. The restructuring of social behaviour demanded by the leading Protestant missions was so drastic—including monogamy and abstinence from liquor and dancing—that is was likely to cost their adherents a complete break with their own economic and social order.[1] Thus there was substance in the settler complaint of mission Africans as 'trouble makers'; among them there were necessarily many who were in the forefront of the process of growing acquisitiveness and mobility which made them more apt as students of western political techniques than of the technical skills useful to a European employer. What was not perceived was that those who had apparently made the break with tradition peacefully and successfully, the Kikuyu pastors and teachers and enterprising farmers who had identified with the new order and made some profit by it, would be the victims, in the Mau Mau rising, of the country's first episode of violent and more or less caste-based conflict.[2]

Meanwhile, the gulf between the European and African societies was still absolute. There was virtually no African middle class. The middle ranges of the economy, which in West Africa and even in Uganda were to a significant degree manned by Africans, were here filled at the upper end by Europeans, further down in the scale by Asians. The Kenya European community was not merely a privileged class: it was a caste, a world, apart.

The final phase

The eventual political eclipse of the European communities in East Africa in retrospect seems a foregone conclusion: their continued relatively minor role in Uganda, the rapid whisk through multi-racialism to majority African rule in Tanganyika, the only less swift and much more dramatic reversal and extinction of the partnership formula in Kenya. Yet this political evolution was by no means obvious at the time. In Kenya and

[1] Temu, *Protestant Missions*, pp. 106–14.
[2] See e.g. C. G. Rosberg and J. Nottingham, *The Myth of Mau Mau* (Stanford, 1966), esp. chap. 9; Sorrenson, *Land Reform in the Kikuyu Country* pp. 100–8.

Tanganyika land was still being taken up for settlement—in the latter territory alienations during this last period more than trebled the extent of alienated land as it stood in 1946,[1] and in heavily populated districts caused intense concern. In Kenya right up to the end of the 1950s a highly articulate section of the white community still regarded white local dominance as entrenched. And from the point of view of the African majority, the jugglings with the 'symbolic formulae' of representation[2] seemed to bear out the self-evident fact that the white element throughout all three territories was not decreasing, or even stable; it was growing at an unprecedented rate. In Tanganyika the European population in 1960 was half as big again as in 1945; in Kenya it was nearly three times as big; in Uganda— where admittedly its scale remained small notwithstanding—it multiplied more than fourfold. In 1960 the number of European children in school in Kenya reached a peak figure of almost 13,000.[3] Perhaps Africans were not altogether wrong in failing to imagine that such a ubiquitously expanding presence of the colonialists could really be a prelude to decolonization.[4] Algeria spelt one lesson of the late 1950s, but Rhodesia quite another.

A temporary, but locally very conspicuous, feature of the wartime and immediate post-war period was the presence of large numbers of non-British Europeans, including some thousands of Italian prisoners of war and more than 11,000 Polish refugees. In Tanganyika between 5,000 and 6,000 Poles were accommodated in camps, while in Uganda these refugees greatly outnumbered the whole regular European population.[5] Little has been recorded of the social impact of the refugee and prisoner-of-war camps, but it is perhaps significant that in Bunyoro they gave rise to a spirit medium cult in which

[1] Figures of land alienation are given in the statistical appendices to the Annual Reports on Tanganyika to the UN. Much of this was in the name of the Overseas Food Corporation and was in fact subsequently used by African farmers.

[2] See Introduction, pp. 55–6 above.

[3] Population figures from *East African Economic and Statistical Review*; education data from annual reports of Kenya Education Department.

[4] Some account of African fears during the 1950s in Uganda is given by P. C. W. Gutkind in 'Some African Attitudes to Multi-Racialism from Uganda', *Ethnic and Cultural Pluralism in Intertropical Communities*, INCIDI Report (Brussels, 1957), pp. 338–55.

[5] The principal Tanganyika camp was at Tengera, near Arusha, and there were others at Kondoa, and near Njombe in the Southern Highlands. The two Uganda camps were near Masindi, and at Koha in Buganda.

'Mpolandi'—the 'spirit of Polishness'—had to be come to terms with.[1] For two or three years after the war the net immigration rates were masked by the process of repatriating to Europe these Italians and Poles. In some ways their sojourn in East Africa formed a precedent for the various large contingents of European skilled manual workers who came out on contract to work on a variety of large-scale projects over the years that followed.

After the Second World War as after the first, farming figured prominently among the attractions held out to intending immigrants, and in Kenya more than 200 farmers of the soldier/settler type received direct government assistance through the Agricultural Settlement Board. The prosperous immediate post-war years, with rising productivity and high commodity prices, in fact made this a period of considerable expansion in white farming. Something like a million acres of fresh land was put under cultivation, and by 1952 4,000 Europeans in Kenya were engaged in agriculture as against 3,000 ten years earlier.[2] In Tanganyika, although there was no increase in white agricultural employment, the number of European landholdings continued to increase until well into the 1950s.[3]

But even in Kenya, the influx of immigrants arriving explicitly to take up farming tailed off after 1950, and overall, those directly involved in agriculture were a steadily diminishing proportion of the European community.[4] The resources derived from a thriving agricultural base went to nourish a whole range of commercial and ancillary activities in which they took part. There was also the effect of what has been described elsewhere in this volume as 'the second colonial occupation'—the intensification at all levels of the administrative and technical impact of Europe on East Africa. Again, this was most marked in Kenya, where the first post-war development schemes were soon swallowed up in the much more ambitious ones prompted by the Emergency: but the Tanganyika groundnut project and the Owen Falls hydro-electric scheme in Uganda were likewise

[1] J. H. M. Beattie, 'Group Aspects of a Nyoro Spirit Mediumship Cult', *Rhodes–Livingstone Journal*, 30 (1961), 30.

[2] Kenya *Annual Reports*, 1946–50; R. S. Odingo, *The Kenya Highlands* (Nairobi, 1971), chap. 2.

[3] See Annual Reports of Tanganyika Lands and Mines Department.

[4] Kenya, *Reports on Migration*, 1946–53, and see footnote 1, p. 450 above.

conceived on a scale previously unknown. If there was a characteristic type of European resident in East Africa, it was no longer 'the settler' or 'the administrator'; it was the technician or young professional in his thirties, whether working for government, for some massive semi-governmental enterprise, for a big business firm, or even a large-scale farmer: the engineer, accountant, locust research officer, statistician. Often (save in the lowest income groups) he brought his family. The social and economic consequences of the war included a wholly new level of facilities and assumptions for those working overseas. Refrigeration and improved health standards made living conditions not merely tolerable, but often more comfortable than at home; domestic servants could be taken for granted, leave was generous, air fares were paid. And, to minister to his other needs, yet other Europeans came out to man the upper ranges of the service industries: shops, hotels, hairdressers, offices. They also came out to provide the buildings demanded by an expanding economy; in Tanganyika the number employed in the construction industries nearly trebled in the four years between 1948 and 1952.

The missionary element declined, but less than might have been expected. In 1948 'religion' still accounted for 9 per cent of the whole working white community on the East African mainland; in Uganda for nearly one working European in four.[1]

With expansion in numbers there developed considerable changes in the structure and outlook of the white community. It was more variegated both in nationality and in class. Tanganyika was still, as in earlier years, the most cosmopolitan of the three countries. In 1948 35 per cent of its white population was of non-British origin, nearly one half of these being Greeks or Germans. But in Uganda too the foreign proportion was as much as 20 per cent, and even in Kenya it was more than 10 per cent. Many of the non-British were skilled manual workers employed on the various large-scale development projects, and the personnel engaged on these also illustrate another feature of post-war white society—its far greater range of social class and outlook. The consequences of this (in perhaps their more extreme form) have been well described in a social survey of

[1] Data in this and following paragraphs from 1948 and subsequent census returns.

Jinja in Uganda in the 1950s.[1] One distinctive feature of this description is the presence of a substantial body of white manual workers, often non-British, without families, and living a semi-communal life in some kind of barracks or compound. Such groups could not be assimilated into previous European social patterns, based as these were on the European club, and on the premiss of comfortable suburban houses, domestic staff, children and gardens.

Demographically, probably the most outstanding characteristic of these post-war Europeans was transience. Kenya was the most stable of the three communities, yet by 1952 64 per cent of the Europeans had been in the country for less than five years. In Uganda the figure in the same year of 9 per cent of the Europeans as local-born must be read together with the fact that 10 per cent consisted of children under 5 years old. There was a high concentration of young adults in the central 25–40 working age-group, and only a very small percentage—about 2 per cent overall—of those over the age of retirement. The sex ratio was more even than it had been before, and in the towns it was common for married women to go out to work.

And the towns were more than ever the place where most Europeans lived. In Kenya, 60 per cent of the whites in 1948 were town-dwellers, in Uganda and Tanganyika considerably more. Year by year the white suburbs of Nairobi and Nakuru, of Kampala and Dar es Salaam, spread outwards. While segregation was never legally mandatory, in practice there was little residential overlap between any of the three main racial groups and, except for the presence of domestic servants, virtually none between Europeans and Africans.

This national and social variegation, this degree of mobility within the region and of transience in East Africa generally, necessarily eroded much of what remained of the conventional solidarities within the white population. Even in small remote administrative communities in the bush tensions multiplied.[2] In the towns and amongst those engaged in large teams on development projects, modes of life changed much more brusquely. The

---

[1] C. and R. Sofer, 'Some Characteristics of an East African European Population', *British Journal of Sociology*, 2, 4 (1951), pp. 315–31; and *Jinja Transformed* (Kampala, 1955).

[2] R. E. S. Tanner, 'Conflict within Small European Communities in Tanganyika', *Human Organization*, 23, 4 (1964).

changes and uncertainties were all reflected in the vicissitudes of European clubs, those most sensitive barometers of white social harmony. Eligibility for membership was no longer general, while for the many who were 'unclubbable' there was no real social substitute to afford recreation and easy communication.[1] Yet there were still certain areas where the casual observer might have hardly noted change: among the long-established farmers of the Kenya Highlands; on some up-country mission and administrative stations where continuity—and sometimes complacency—was strong.

It is correspondingly difficult to generalize about relations between Europeans and Africans during this period, the more so in that these were set against a political background now in swift transformation. On many Kenya estates the old *baaskap* relationship was sustained by farmers—often well respected in their own profession—whose visions of eventual advancement by Africans were bounded by the need for them first to respond to the 'character-forming' leadership of their white employers.[2] At the other end of the scale, lower-paid white manual workers, excluded from European club society and exposed even marginally to the fear of non-white competition, reacted with predictable racial arrogance. In Jinja there were some complaints when Africans attended 'European' church services.[3] Between these there were all degrees of friction, respect, and sometimes friendship. It is likely that the extent to which Europeans from the other territories sent their children to school in Kenya resulted in some dissemination of 'Kenya' attitudes. But from early in the post-1945 period, it was becoming difficult, even in Kenya, to defend explicitly discriminatory measures in public debate. A prolonged controversy over the proposal to insist on finger-prints for the African *kipande* ended in its withdrawal. In a government White Paper on the financing of non-African education it was felt necessary to pay at least lip-service to the objective of a unified education system.[4] In the 1950s serious and

---

[1] Sofer, 'Some Characteristics of a [n] . . . European Population', loc. cit.

[2] Reflected for instance in the various works of J. F. Lipscomb, who until 1954 was Chairman of the European Agricultural Settlement Board; or in E. Whittall's *Dimbilil: the story of a Kenya farm* (London, 1956).

[3] Sofer, *Jinja Transformed*, p. 110. Also, the same author's 'The Working Groups in a Plural Society', *Industrial and Labour Relations Review*, 8 (1954), 70.

[4] *Report of the Committee on European and Asian Educational Expenditure* (Nairobi, 1952).

persevering attempts were made to create inter-racial social as well as political institutions.[1] Also indicative of the crumbling of old assumptions is the fact that there were now available for the first time analytical and critical accounts of East African society and the East African economy as a whole: reports such as that made by the East Africa Royal Commission, and studies by sociologists and economists at Makerere, spelt out and discussed the extent of European and Asian privilege in terms of status and resources.[2] What could thus be stated could more readily and widely be questioned.

Within itself, it may be that the white community had become more heterogeneous and divided: overall the Europeans in all three territories, outside as well as through government, continued to wield a preponderant political and economic influence. They held virtually all the senior posts in administration, and most of those in commerce, industry, and the professions; in Kenya and Tanganyika they formed the great majority of large landholders, and the products of their farms earned the bulk of these countries' export incomes. While there are no widely based surveys of income distribution before independence, it is noteworthy that in Jinja, where there was a substantial number of comparatively low white wage-earners, three-quarters of the Europeans received more than £500, and all near that figure; which was practically out of reach of any African.[3] A Kenya survey four years after independence still showed 84 per cent of Europeans as earning more than £1,200 per annum, while 88 per cent of Africans earned less than £360.[4]

Thus entrenched on the commanding heights of the economy, the European community—unofficial as well as official—

---

[1] Susan Wood's short work, *Kenya: the tensions of progress*, published by the London Institute of Race Relations in 1960, embodies one optimistic view of the possibilities in that country for inter-racial co-operation. She gives a more personal account in *A Fly in Amber* (London, 1964). A forthcoming work by Richard Frost makes a fuller study of the various efforts made to achieve co-operation. Some of the measures taken by the Tanganyika administration during the 1950s reflect a similar optimism.

[2] e.g. J. E. Goldthorpe, *Outlines of East African Society* (Kampala, 1958), and works by Gutkind, the Sofers, and Aidan Southall.

[3] Sofer, *Jinja Transformed*, pp. 46, 54.

[4] D. Rothchild, 'Ethnic Inequalities in Kenya', *Journal of Modern African Studies*, 7, 4 (1969), 694.

continued to be able to exert a strong influence on affairs. In Kenya up to at least the middle of the 1950s some of this influence was open and explicit. An articulate sector of white opinion still looked towards a 'Rhodesian' outcome; there was also brief support for some form of partition, possibly within a federal framework. But in Uganda and Tanganyika, and at a more unobtrusive level in Kenya also, the real aims were more limited. They were increasingly concerned with the safeguarding of minority rights within states which were destined (although it was supposed in a fairly distant future) to become African-controlled.

In Kenya and Tanganyika the traditional forms of white pressure-group continued to be active, and the European press continued to inveigh against both government shortcomings and African nationalism. But in all three territories a feature of this final period was the degree of working collusion between government and the non-governmental leadership of the white communities. This had happened indeed after the First World War, but now, with the increased scope for government action together with a larger but less stable white population, it took on a somewhat different character. In the key fields of finance, agriculture and trade in particular, European unofficials, their hands strengthened by wartime experience of participation, sat on every official and semi-official board and committee, and played a leading part in the direction of the economies. The Europeans who exercised this power formed a tiny handful—not more than two score perhaps over the whole East African region—and it was a group which transcended the territorial boundaries; in Nairobi, Kampala, Dar es Salaam, this small élite kept in close contact and read the overall political portents. It was with these men, and for the most part outside the political limelight, that in the last two or three years much of pre-independence bargaining took place. Only in Kenya, where the administrative structure was strong and already in close contact with institutions in the western world, was it successful in securing the continuance of a European role which involved no complete break with the colonialist past.

How did the Europeans themselves see their role in this concluding act of the drama that had begun seventy years earlier? In what sense did they represent, as they certainly had at the beginning, some of the aims and aspirations of European colonialism?

Already by 1945 the old visions of pioneering white settlement had ceased to command any popular backing at home. Those who emigrated to take up farming in Kenya did not expect to be applauded as the bearers and disseminators of a superior culture, but went with a shrewd appraisal of its risks and prospects and with a wary eye on the guarantees offered by the imperial government. Equally, missionary enterprise, in its various pre-1914 or even its inter-war interpretation, was a thing of the past. In Uganda although the missionary workers were numerous they were hardly a power in the land; in Kenya the voice of political protest ceased to be led or moderated by missionary counsels. Everywhere much of the educational, and some of the medical, role of the missions was being taken over by the state. Nor was there any longer in Britain the widespread trust that the modernizing and Christianizing roles of the missions were synonymous and self-evident. In administration likewise the principles of the 'dual mandate' no longer carried the authority of the inter-war years.

Yet, despite the withering of old aspirations, despite the fact that now as in the past individuals and groups did pursue or defend their own interests, it would be misleading to depict European aims as they appeared to those involved in them in starkly materialist or sectional terms. In 1948 as much as 9 per cent of the whole white working community was classified under the heading 'religion'—though the activities comprehended within that classification were many and various. The 'second colonial occupation' of the 1940s and 1950s was, to many of those who took part in it, a creative enterprise in which 'development and welfare', and the shift of emphasis from indirect rule to local government and thence to 'self-government', held not a little of the inspiration of the past. This was true not only of those working directly for the territorial governments, but also of the young professionals and technicians who took part, for instance, in the ill-conceived Tanganyika groundnut scheme, or the Colonial Development Corporation. Pre-eminently, perhaps, it was characteristic of the handful of those who, inside or outside government service, threw themselves into the tasks of promoting community development and of helping to build up African co-operatives.

How history will assess the role of these, or of all the other Europeans who lived and worked in East Africa over a quarter of a century, is another matter.

XII

THE IMMIGRANT COMMUNITIES (2): THE ASIANS

J. S. MANGAT

THE origins of the modern Asian population of East Africa can be traced back to roughly the middle of the nineteenth century—although there has existed a historical commercial connection between the East African coast and the western seaboard of India since about the second century A.D. Two factors in particular contributed to a major revival of Indian trade with East Africa during the nineteenth century. First, the consolidation of Omani rule in Zanzibar and along the coast, and the relatively enlightened commercial policy of Seyyid Said (1806–56), ensured freedom of enterprise for the Indian traders.[1] In fact from 1835 to 1886 the prestigious posts of customs collector and of principal financial adviser to the Zanzibar sultans were held by Indian firms—notably those of Jairam Sewji and Tarya Topan.[2] Secondly, a more important factor, the growth of British political support for the British Indian merchants—which became particularly marked after the establishment of a British consulate in Zanzibar in 1841—greatly facilitated the task of the Indian merchants.[3] In fact for most of the nineteenth century there was a close interrelationship between the growth of Indian enterprise in Zanzibar and that of the British diplomatic influence, first under the direction of the Bombay government which controlled the Zanzibar Agency

---

This chapter was originally completed before the publication of the author's study *Asians in East Africa* (Oxford, 1969). He is grateful to the Clarendon Press for permission to adapt and incorporate some of the material used in that work.

[1] In this chapter the words 'Asian' and 'Indian' are freely used to describe the people originating from India and Pakistan.

[2] See Kirk's report on Zanzibar 1870–1 in Foreign Office Confidential Print (FOCP) No. 1936, pp. 17–18; Frere to Granville, 7 May 1873 enclosed memorandum on the Indians, FO 84/139; Stanley, *Through the Dark Continent* (London, 1878), ii. 63, and Cameron, *Across Africa* (London, 1877), i. 23–4.

[3] See vol. ii, chaps. iv and v, of this *History*.

from 1841 to 1873, and subsequently the Government of India from 1873 to 1883.[1] It was not until the 1880s, when the rising momentum of the 'scramble' for Africa rendered the existing political arrangements untenable, that the prolonged control and patronage of the Zanzibar Agency by the Government of India finally passed into the hands of the Imperial government.[2] This was a significant development, representing as it did the decline of the 'British Indian factor' in East Africa and its replacement by the 'imperial factor'—which was to become more marked later with the transfer of the administration of the East African territories to the Colonial Office, the settlement of Europeans in the Kenya highlands, and the growth of Indian nationalism. For the moment, however, the commercial revival of the nineteenth century had led to a sizeable settlement of Indian traders from the north-western ports—especially from the Indian west coast state of Kutch—along the East African coast. By the 1870s their number was estimated to be over 4,000; and, together with the European firms, they played an important part in the import-export trade of Zanzibar, while virtually controlling the distributive trade. A number of reports —by General Rigby in 1860, by Sir Bartle Frere in 1873 and by Frederic Holmwood in 1875,[3] as well as the accounts of various contemporary explorers—attest to the extensive growth of the Indian role in Zanzibar at this time. Such developments were to form the background for the various proposals after the partition of East Africa in 1886 to associate British Indians with the imperial effort to 'open up' the interior. While the old-established Indian traders were able to penetrate the interior in search of trade under the protection ensured by European rule, in the British sphere the reliance on British Indian precedents and manpower paved the way for officially-sponsored immigration of Indians into Kenya and Uganda.

[1] This interrelationship is fully discussed in J. S. Mangat, *History of the Asians in East Africa* (Oxford, 1969). See also Bombay Archives, Political Dept., vol. 43 of 1842, compilation no. 350; Indian Archives, Foreign Dept., Jan. 1873, secret proceedings 226–31 and Kirk's evidence in the *Report of the Committee on Emigration from India to the Crown Colonies and Protectorates*, Cd. 5192 (1910), p. 92.

[2] India Office (IO) to Govt. of India, 20 and 31 July 1883, and FO to Kirk, 19 July 1883, Indian Archives, Foreign Dept. May 1884, proceedings 29–71, A Pol. E.

[3] See note 2, p. 467 above; Rigby, *Report on the Zanzibar Dominions* (Bombay, 1861); and Holmwood's report of Jan. 1875 in India Office Records, Political Dept., Letters from Zanzibar 1875–83, i. 73.

This policy received its first and rather tentative expression under the Imperial British East Africa Company, 1888–95.[1] But it was later more fully implemented—especially after the decision to construct the Uganda Railway 'upon the Indian methods and chiefly by means of Indian coolies (indentured labourers)' was taken in 1895.[2] The Railway Committee appointed by the Foreign Office arrived at the conclusion, as a later report in 1897 indicated, that 'it would be hopeless to expect that the railway could be constructed at any reasonable cost and speed unless they were allowed to recruit Indian labour freely.'[3] Accordingly, negotiations were opened with the India Office in October 1895 with a view to an amendment of the Indian Emigration Act of 1883 to legalize the recruitment of labour for the Uganda Railway. A subsequent Notification by the Government of India in May 1896 provided for approved three-year contract terms—involving on an average an overall expenditure of roughly £2 per month per coolie—under which such labour could be hired.[4] After this date, therefore, recruitment and shipment of Indian indentured workers for the Uganda Railway began in earnest, and was to continue on a substantial scale until 1902. In 1897 an Agency was established in Karachi to deal with the railway's growing demands for men and materials; and a branch office was opened in Lahore in order to exploit fully the resources of the 'coolie recruiting grounds of the Upper Punjab'.[5] By 1902 nearly 32,000 labourers and artisans, and another 5,000 subordinate employees, had been recruited in India[6] and this 'alien army', working under the direction of

[1] Especially in attempts to recruit Indian staff and police and in proposals for Indian agricultural settlement. See P. L. McDermott, *British East Africa or IBEA* (London, 1893), pp. 210–11, 217–18; *Reports Relating to the Administration of the EAP*, Cd. 2740 (1905), p. 2; IO to FO, 24 Jan, 1890, FO 2/117, and IO to FO, 23 Oct. 1895, FO 2/671.

[2] *Final Report on the Uganda Railway*, Cd. 2164 (1904), p. 7.

[3] FO to IO, 30 Jan. 1897, FOCP No. 7040, p. 10; and Bombay Archives, General Dept. vol. 142 C of 1897, compilation 671 part I: Emigration to of Coolies to Africa.

[4] India Office Records, Emigration Dept. July 1896, proceedings 9–17, file 38, pp. 783–8; and proceedings 18–55, file 2, pp. 789–853.

[5] IO Emigration Dept. Oct. 1897, proceedings 6–9, file 10, pp. 1097–9; Jan. 1898, proceedings 35–43, file 10, pp. 559–66; FO to IO, 17 Dec. 1897.

[6] Cd. 2164 (1904), pp. 12–13; IO, Emigration Dept. Apr. 1899, proceedings 3–8, file 24, p. 667; and *Report on the Uganda Railway by Sir Guildford Molesworth*, C. 9331 (1899), pp. 13–14.

British experts and officials, undertook the construction of the railway. Of the total number of workers recruited during this period, only 6,724 opted to remain in East Africa after the expiry of their contracts,[1] so that only a small proportion of the later Asian population of East Africa can be regarded as the descendants of the indentured railway workers. The real significance of this shortlived influx of Indian workers, in fact, lay in the impetus that their officially-sponsored immigration, and the Indian presence in the interior initiated by it, provided for future Indian immigration to East Africa. As Sir Harry Johnston remarked in 1899:

I wonder if in England the importance of one aspect of this Railway construction has been realized? It means the driving of a wedge of India two miles broad right across East Africa from Mombasa to Victoria Nyanza. Fifteen thousand coolies, some hundreds of Indian clerks, draughtsmen, mechanics, surveyors and policemen, are . . . carrying the Indian penal code, the Indian postal system, Indian coinage, Indian clothing, right across these wastes, deserts, forests and swamps . . . .[2]

This process was accelerated by the employment of British Indian troops and subordinate staff for the establishment and extension of British administration. In 1895 a special Indian contingent consisting of 300 troops was raised for service along the coast and the Uganda Railway.[3] Later in 1898 a similar contingent was raised for Uganda following the mutiny of the Sudanese troops there in 1897.[4] Both these contingents were subsequently disbanded—the former at the turn of the century when the King's African Rifles were organized, and the latter in 1913. Meanwhile, additional military reinforcements were sought from India from time to time, especially during the 1890s, for the purposes of the 'pacification' of the East African territories.[5]

[1] Cd. 2164 (1904), pp. 12–13.

[2] Johnston to Salisbury, 13 Oct. 1899, FO 2/204.

[3] IO to FO, 23 Aug. 1895 and 25 Mar. 1896, FO 2/117; and Hardinge to Salisbury, 24 Sept. 1898 enclosure, FO 2/171.

[4] Viceroy to IO, 6 Oct. 1898 and Hardinge to Salisbury, 23 Oct. 1898, FO 2/171; and IO to FO, 31 Jan. 1899 enclosure Govt. of India to IO 27 Oct. 1898, FO 2/256.

[5] Notably for the suppression of the Mazrui revolt 1895–6, the Sudanese Mutiny, 1897, and revolt of Kabaka Mwanga; for operations against the Ogaden Somali and finally, during the First World War, when two Indian expeditionary forces were employed in the campaign against German East Africa. The following Foreign

The practice of employing Indian administrative staff in East Africa was as old as the British Agency in Zanzibar; and the East African administrations later made frequent demands for Indian personnel. A private firm at first acted as agent in Bombay from 1896 to recruit the required staff. Later in 1898 a government official was appointed to act in this capacity;[1] and subsequently in 1901, after Foreign Office urging, the government of India further amended the Indian Emigration Act in order to legalize the employment of Indian administrative staff in East Africa.[2] Following the completion of the Uganda Railway, and the resulting decline in the functions of its agency at Karachi, the Bombay Agency became the principal centre in India for the recruitment and shipment of a wide variety of personnel for service with the East African administrations—until 1912 when its functions once again reverted to a private firm.[3]

The Imperial government viewed the growing British Indian role in East Africa with considerable favour—indeed in May 1900 the Foreign Office commented that 'in the present condition of the African Protectorates they are likely to be benefited by Indian immigration.'[4] Various early officials— ranging from Captain (later Lord) Lugard in 1893 to Sir Harry Johnston during 1899–1901, and including the authorities in German East Africa—similarly gave enthusiastic support to the idea of encouraging Indian immigration and agricultural settlement in the East African territories with a view to their speedy development.[5] Indeed a series of proposals were formulated by the East African governments at various times in the course of the early colonial period in order to facilitate Indian

Office volumes deal directly with the employment of Indian troops in the early colonial period: FO 2/117, 2/143, 2/170, 2/171, 2/256 and 2/429.

[1] FO 2/431, 2/552 deal directly with the Agency in India; and see IO to FO, 27 Jan. 1899 and Govt. of India to Bombay Govt., 26 Apr. 1899, IO Emigration Dept. Apr. 1899, proceedings 9–14, file 27, part A.

[2] FO 2/671 deals directly with the Agency in India; and see IO to FO, 5 Mar. 1901, IO Emigration Dept. May 1901, proceeding 12, file 41, part A.

[3] IO Emigration Dept. Nov. 1902, proceeding 1, file 20, p. 1425; FO to IO, 30 Sept. 1902 and Feb. 1913, proceedings 25–7, file 11, part B.

[4] FO to IO, 16 May 1900, FO 2/671. See also minute by Clement Hill on Eliot to Lansdowne, 5 Jan. 1902, FO 2/569: 'We are rather looking to India for our East African system and development.'

[5] F. D. Lugard, *The Rise of Our East African Empire* (London, 1893), i. 488–9; and for similar views, Hardinge to Salisbury, 24 Aug. 1900, and Johnston to Salisbury, 26 Oct. 1900, FO 2/671, and Eliot's report on the East Africa Protectorate, FOCP

Immigration. But, apart from the small settlement of Indian agriculturists at Kibos, near Kisumu, after 1903, most of these proposals came to nothing.¹ The whole question of state-aided Indian immigration into East Africa was eventually placed before a committee appointed by the Colonial Office in 1909 for detailed consideration. The Sanderson Committee, as it was called after its chairman, concluded in favour of continued voluntary Indian immigration into East Africa—in view of its role in the development of the area—but the committee was opposed to any schemes for officially-sponsored or indentured Indian immigration.²

Meanwhile, however, the officially-sponsored immigration of the 1890s had introduced East Africa to people from certain parts of India, notably Punjab and central Gujerat, who, unlike the old-established traders, had no previous contact with that region. Moreover, their role as artisans, administrative employees, and traders—at a time when no other equally competitive local agency was available to perform these functions— laid the foundations upon which new Indian immigration could build. Indeed the distinguishing characteristic of much of the subsequent Indian immigration into East Africa—by contrast with the indentured immigration that largely accounts for the present-day Asian populations of South Africa, the West Indies, and Mauritius, for example—was that it was overwhelmingly voluntary.³ And the 'free' or 'passenger' immigrants, as they

No. 7867, p. 7. For German East Africa, see British Ambassador Berlin to FO, 21 Nov. 1900 and Govt. of India to IO, 21 Mar. 1901, IO Emigration Dept. Mar. 1901, proceedings 16–17, file 19, pp. 249–57; FO to IO, 23 Mar. 1901 and IO to FO, 30 Apr. 1902, proceedings 5–8, file 19, pp. 445–73 and report on German East Africa, 1901, by Hollis, in FOCP No. 7690, p. 65.

¹ See, inter alia, IO to FO, 5 Mar. 1901, FO 2/671; Eliot to Lansdowne, 5 Jan. 1902, FO 2/569; FO to IO, 6 Aug. 1901 and enclosure, IO Emigration Dept. Sept. 1901, proceeding 12, file 41, 617; report of committee on Indian immigration 1905, Feb. 1904, proceeding 11, file 19, pp. 97–113; Aug. 1906, proceedings 13–16, file 73, pp. 499–501; Report of the Committee on Emigration from India . . ., part III, Cd. 5194 (1910), pp. 43, 49, 95, 152; Jackson to Crewe, 21 May 1909, CO 533/59; Girouard to Crewe, 23 Sept. 1909, and CO 533/62.

² Report of the Committee on Emigration from India . . ., part I, Cd. 5192 (1910), p. 92.

³ For the beginnings of voluntary emigration, see IO Emigration Dept. Oct. 1896, proceedings 15–16, file 66, p. 1103; Aug. 1897, proceedings 4–6, file 37 part B; July 1897, proceedings 9–32, file 5, pp. 761–7; and Protector of Emigrants to Bombay Govt. 11 July 1896, Bombay Archives, General Dept. vol. 120 C of 1896, compilation 671 part III; Govt. of India to Bombay Govt. 11 May 1897, vol. 142 C of 1897, compilation 671 part I.

were called, who came to East Africa took to employment largely on the middle rung of the economic ladder—as artisans, skilled and semi-skilled staff, and as traders. A majority of them, aided by the old-established commercial connections between East Africa and the west coast of India, sought to explore the more familiar avenues of commercial enterprise—but both the administrations and the railway continued to depend heavily on Indian administrative staff. As Sir Percy Girouard pointed out in his report of 1909: 'His [the Indian's] presence, in our existing financial conditions, makes government possible in that he provides the subordinate staff of nearly every department.'[1]

Indian commercial penetration of the interior coincided largely with the extension of European rule, although a few of the old-established coastal traders had preceded 'the flag' in some areas. A series of reports indicate how petty Indian merchants established stores, or *dukas*, during the 1890s along the advancing railways, at the newly-established administrative posts and sometimes in the 'outback'—and helped to create trade 'first in a small way and then in a large way in areas where none had existed previously.'[2] In German East Africa, Indian commercial expansion into the interior from the coastal settlements at Tanga, Bagamoyo and Dar es Salaam occurred at first along the old caravan routes—with Tabora, Ujiji, and Mwanza emerging as the major centres of Indian trade in the interior by the turn of the century.[3] These posts, and to a lesser extent the caravan route through the East Africa Protectorate from Mombasa to Mumias, were also used by the Indian traders to penetrate Uganda. Between 1899 and 1901, as Sir Harry Johnston later remarked, the Indian traders had spread into various parts of

[1] Girouard to Crewe 13, Nov. 1909, enclosed interim report on the EAP and Uganda, CO 533/63. The various Blue Books for Kenya and Uganda up to about 1914 provide full details of the variety of subordinate posts held by Indian recruits on the railway and in the administration.

[2] See, *inter alia*, H. H. Johnston, *The Uganda Protectorate* (London, 1902), i. 294; *Reports by Sir A. Hardinge on the BEA Protectorate* . . . C. 8683 (1897), ppl 43, 47–48, C. 9125 (1999), p. 17, C. 9331 (1899), p. 2; Cd. 2740 (1905), pp. 18–19; report of chief engineer Uganda Railway, June 1902, FOCP No. 7922, p. 200; Stewart to Lyttelton, 9 Aug. 1905, enclosed memo. on trade by Ainsworth and Marsden, CO 533/3; W. M. Ross, *Kenya from Within* (London, 1927), p. 298; and C. W. Hobley, *Kenya from Chartered Company to Crown Colony* (London, 1929), p. 242.

[3] Hollis's report on German East Africa, 1901, FOCP No. 7690, pp. 65, 80–7.

Uganda—ranging 'from Kampala (Mengo) to Toro and all the posts at which European or native soldiers were established in the Nile Province [and to] . . . all the stations in the eastern half of the Protectorate'.[1] Similarly in the East Africa Protectorate, important Indian trading centres in the interior had been established at Voi, Machakos, and Nairobi by the turn of the century. Perhaps the entire phenomenon of Indian commercial expansion during the early colonial period can be understood best in terms of the career of Allidina Visram (1863 1916), a career which in many ways symbolizes the role of the other lesser Indian traders.

Visram began his career in East Africa in 1877 when he established himself at Bagamoyo as an agent of an old-established Zanzibar firm. At first he undertook business largely as a supplier of porters and provisions for the European explorers going inland. But later, as the political and commercial importance of the interior increased following the partition in 1886, Visram began to engage directly in the trade with the interior. By the early 1890s, he had established a small business network based on Bagamoyo with branches spreading along the caravan route to Tabora and Ujiji. The posts in the interior were supplied with a variety of imported goods by Visram's caravans—and in exchange they obtained local produce, principally ivory in the early days. Subsequently, from 1898 onwards, Visram's caravans began penetrating northwards from Mwanza into Uganda and he opened *dukas* at Kampala, Jinja, Kisumu, and other posts well before the Uganda Railway was completed. In 1899, he opened another branch of his firm at Mombasa and later built a chain of *dukas* in the East Africa Protectorate on a pattern similar to the one adopted by him in Uganda. The completion of the Uganda Railway in 1901 greatly facilitated Visram's task— obviating the need to supply Uganda from the caravan routes through German East Africa—and Mombasa soon came to replace Bagamoyo as his principal base for commercial operations in East Africa. A number of other petty Asian traders were also moving inland in a similar fashion at this time, but Allidina Visram was one of the most enterprising and successful of them—

---

[1] Johnston, *Uganda Protectorate*, i. 294; *Report by H. M. Special Commissioner on . . . Uganda*, Cd. 671 (1901), p. 7, and *Report of the Committee on Emigration from India . . .*, part II, Cd. 5193 (1910), p. 238.

blazing fresh trails of trade in areas where others were later to follow in his wake.

The pattern of commerce adopted in the interior by Visram and the other Asian traders revolved largely around the exchange of an increasing variety of imported goods—such as cloth, wire, glassware, and lamps—for local produce of every description. At first, for example, Allidina Visram's chief export from Uganda was ivory—as one contemporary account pointed out: 'One recollects many huge safaris of tusks wending their serpentine way through Uganda forests and swamps to Allidina Visram's store.'[1] But later he purchased an increasing variety of other produce: hides and skins, groundnuts, chillies, sesame, and cotton. Sir Frederick Jackson reported from Uganda in 1902:

Our present difficulty lies in the circulation of specie, but I am doing all I can to induce the people through their chiefs, to cultivate sugar cane and simsim (sesame). An Indian trader, named Alidina Visram, is already prepared to buy up as much as the natives would like to cultivate of each . . . and this should materially assist in the circulation of . . . rupees and pice . . . .[2]

A later minute from the Chief Secretary's office in Entebbe similarly explained Allidina Visram's role in this respect:

He was always ready to help the encouragement of local industries by buying native crops which no one else would touch . . . I remember myself that when natives on Elgon were encouraged in 1909 to make beeswax, and made it in large quantities, no buyer could be found except Allidina . . . The same thing happened in the early days of the cotton industry in the Eastern Province.[3]

The role of the Asian traders generally in exploiting the commercial potential of the interior is perhaps revealed in the following comment of Dr. Heinrich Schnee, Governor of German East Africa, 1912–14:

With the gradual pacification of the country . . . the Indians moved towards the interior and settled in all commercial centres of the Protectorate . . . Their export and import trade accounts for the German East Africa line running a special service to Bombay and

---

[1] *Leader of British East Africa* (Nairobi), 15 July 1916.
[2] FOCP No. 7946, p. 197.
[3] Memo. of 9 June 1925, Entebbe Archives, file no. 4832.

other Indian ports. The Indians now buy in the interior products of every sort—rubber, wax, hides, skins, cotton, grain and foodstuffs, ivory, copra, copal, and supply natives with cotton cloth, beads and earthen ware, glass and simple household furniture . . . . For the present the Indians are indispensable as middlemen between the larger European firms and the natives.[1]

A number of other reports similarly reveal the growing Asian role in produce trade in the East Africa Protectorate and Uganda—in the latter territory, Indian participation in the marketing, ginning, and export of cotton was to become particularly marked.[2]

Meanwhile, the various *dukas* established in the interior by traders such as Allidina Visram were also able to provide a variety of services for the administration in the early years. This is well described in a minute from the Chief Secretary's office in Entebbe in 1925:

Allidina Visram, . . . was one of the pioneer traders in Uganda: I think he was one of the first Indians to take up trading in the Protectorate; certainly the first who did so on a large scale, about 30 years ago. He opened a store at nearly every Government station, and in the early days was of the greatest assistance to Government in many ways such as transport, purchase of local produce, etc. Officers in out-stations were dependent, in those days, upon Allidina's agencies for the necessaries of life . . .[3]

A number of other reports similarly speak of the contribution of the early Indian traders to the establishment of cart or wagon transport in different districts and in the circulation of currency.[4] John Ainsworth, for example, reported in 1905 from the East Africa Protectorate that 'previous to 1898, the Government kept stores of trade goods, and trade goods formed the entire medium of exchange with the natives' but 'by degrees the Indian traders created local centres of trade' and 'with the opening of Indian

[1] Article by Schnee in *Deutsches Kolonial-Lexikon* (Berlin, 1920), vol. ii.

[2] Confidential report on Uganda cotton industry by S. Simpson, 31 July 1912, CO 536/79; *Report of the Commission of Inquiry into the Cotton Industry of Uganda* (Entebbe, 1929), pp. 3–4 and Buganda Annual Reports for 1915–16, 1917–18, Entebbe Archives. See also chap. viii in vol. ii of this *History*.

[3] Minute of 9 June 1925, Entebbe Archives, file no. 4832.

[4] Eastern Province Annual Reports for 1909–10, 1911–12 and Buganda Monthly Reports, 1914, Entebbe Archives.

bazaars, the Government began to close down their stores, and payment began to be made in rupees and pice . . .'[1]

From their small beginnings as petty traders, a number of Asian merchants were gradually able to extend their commercial operations into a variety of new fields. In fact within the first two decades of this century, Asian capital and business enterprise came to represent an important expatriate factor in the economic life of East Africa.[2] The process of growth and diversification can again be seen in the career of Allidina Visram, who built an extensive *duka*-based business network at this time. His operations spread from Bombay through Mombasa and Bagamoyo to over thirty major branches in various parts of East Africa.[3] Moreover in 1909 he was reported to have seventeen agents operating in the Congo, exchanging trade goods for ivory.[4] In the same year, he obtained special permission from the government to send out caravans in the northern Uganda district of Karamoja. Further to the north, Allidina's activities spread to Juba and Addis Ababa—from the latter place he was reported in 1909 to be importing firearms into Uganda.[5] Meanwhile, he had diversified his business interests to include oil mills at Kisumu and the coast, obtaining oil from sesame and copra; a soap factory at Mombasa in 1907; soda factories and furniture shops at Kampala and Entebbe; two small cotton ginneries at Mombasa and Entebbe, and sawmills in Uganda and near Nyeri.[6] Later, between 1912 and 1914, Visram built a substantial cotton ginnery in Kampala which, together with another ginnery established by a Bombay firm in the latter year, was to provide the foundations for the subsequent Asian role in the cotton industry of Uganda.[7] There

[1] Cd. 2740 (1905), pp. 18–19.

[2] A mass of evidence bears this out. See e.g. Cd. 5192 (1910), p. 91; W. S. Churchill, *My African Journey* (London, 1908), pp. 52, 59; T. Sleith, *Report of Trade Conditions in British East Africa, Uganda and Zanzibar* (Cape Town, 1919), pp. 13, 49, 63; Jackson to Lyttelton, 11 Nov. 1905 enclosed minutes, CO 533/5; and Sadler to Crewe, 10 May 1908, IO Emigration Dept. Sept. 1908, proceedings 5–6, file 79, pp. 589–95.

[3] Entebbe Archives, files 4832 and 5677, *passim;* S. Playne and F. H. Gale, *East Africa (British)* (London, 1908–9), pp. 120–2; *Handbook for East Africa, Uganda and Zanzibar* (Govt. Printer, Mombasa, 1904).

[4] Entebbe Archives, files 72 (1909) and 57 (1910).

[5] Entebbe Archives, files 1323 (1909) and 1330 (1910).

[6] Kenya Archives, file Msa 103/7 for soap factory; Entebbe Archives, files 131 (1910) for ginnery at Entebbe, 806 (1907) for leather tannery at Entebbe; 569 (1908), 146, 409, 483 (1909) for timber interests; and Payne and Gale, *East Africa*.

[7] *Leader of British East Africa*, 8 July 1916. See also Cd. 5193 (1910), pp. 318–19.

were a number of other Asian traders in East Africa who made similar progress in their business operations—although not on the same scale as Allidina Visram—during the early colonial period, notably A. M. Jeevanjee.[1] But an overwhelming majority of the Asians were small-scale traders.

The extension of the commercial enterprise of the Asians in the interior, coupled as it was with the growth of their role as skilled and semi-skilled staff, contributed to a steady expansion of the Asian population in East Africa. By 1911, Kenya had 12,000 Asians, rising to 23,000 by 1921; Uganda had 2,216 in 1911 and 5,000 in 1921; Zanzibar's Asian population rose from 8,500 in 1910 to 13,500 in 1921; while German East Africa had nearly 10,000 Asians on the eve of the First World War and also in 1921. Meanwhile, however, there had been a parallel growth of the European population and enterprise in the East African territories. The numbers of Europeans were relatively small—Kenya had 3,175 in 1911 rising to about 10,000 in 1921, while German East Africa had 5,000 in 1914—but both their power and influence greatly increased during this period under the impact of policies that sought to assert European paramountcy in the territories. In the event political developments in East Africa came increasingly to be influenced by the often conflicting interests and aspirations of the two immigrant communities.[2] The growing economic rivalry between them especially aroused increasing racial friction—which reached a high point in the controversy surrounding the Indian question in East Africa in the immediate post-war years.

Much has been written about this controversy—and it is perhaps sufficient to underline some of its principal features. Firstly, it was mainly in Kenya that racial tensions precipitated a major breach between the European and Asian populations—

[1] Kenya Archives, file ARC (GH)—77, and *Leader of British East Africa*, 7 May, 17 Sept., and 1 Oct. 1910.

[2] For the racial conflict in Kenya before the First World War see e.g. Eliot to Lansdowne, 21 Jan. 1902 enclosed petition of European settlers committee, FO 2/805; Jackson to Lyttelton, 18 Oct. 1905 enclosed petition of Colonists' Association, CO 533/4; *Correspondence relating to the tenure of land in the EAP*, Cd. 4117 (1908), p. 25; A. M. Jeevanjee, *An Appeal on behalf of Indians in East Africa* (Bombay, 1912); IO Emigration Dept. May 1911, proceedings 1–2 file 48, part A; August 1914, proceedings 22, file 34, part A and Indian Archives, Emigration Dept. Sept. 1925, proceedings, 1–92, part A, memo. by Ewbank. The issue is also traced in chap. vi and Appendix I in vol. ii of this *History*.

although inevitably the neighbouring countries were influenced. Secondly, and more important, broken down to its essentials— from the mass of the often conflicting racial polemics that surround it—the controversy in Kenya revolved around the Europeans' 'irreducible minimum' demands: for unofficial majorities in the legislative and municipal councils, the reservation of the Kenya 'White Highlands' and the enforcement of residential segregation, the restriction of Indian immigration and generally the paramountcy of European interests in the country. The Indian position, on the other hand, centred largely upon the demands for a common system of franchise, based on property and education qualifications; for the abandonment of land reservation and segregation, and generally for equal treatment with the Europeans in the eyes of the law. The controversy was precipitated by a suggestion of Sir Theodore Morison after the war, that Tanganyika should be mandated to British India in recognition of her services to the war effort; this prompted an anti-Indian campaign in Kenya under the leadership of Lord Delamere and Colonel Grogan, which was to reach a high point in the report of the strongly settler-influenced Economic Commission published in 1919. The Indians in turn, already restive over the series of measures that had imposed racial disabilities upon them—notably the Crown Lands Ordinance of 1915, the Segregation Rules of 1918, and the grant of elective representation to the Europeans in 1919—were spurred into political action by the East African Indian National Congress, founded in 1914 and reorganized under new leadership five years later. The Congress had the support of the parent body in India; while the Government of India, conscious of the repercussions Indian disabilities in a crown colony would have on politically turbulent India, also intervened in support of the Indian demands. What had begun as a purely local controversy was, in the circumstances, catapulted into a major imperial issue involving India as well as the European settlers of Southern Africa. The Devonshire Declaration of 1923, which asserted as against both European and Indian claims the ultimate paramountcy of African interests in Kenya, did not thereby settle the 'Indian question'. In fact neither of the protagonists were satisfied with the White Paper of 1923: the Europeans, because it denied them the right of self-government; and the Indians, because it denied them the ideal of equality. Moreover, for all practical purposes the existing racial disabilities against them persisted.

In the event the political controversy in Kenya was to continue; and Indian political agitation was to acquire fresh intensity as the European pressures for constitutional advancement increased and as Kenya—and to a lesser extent the rest of East Africa—evolved a three-tier system of development.[1] The continuation of imperial control and the support of the India Office ensured that the Indian view would at least be heard, but the occasions on which it could affect the final implementation of policy steadily decreased after 1923. Indeed by the end of the Second World War, many of the issues that had formed the 'Indian question' in East Africa had been resolved largely to the advantage of the Europeans—and Indian opposition had proved of little avail.[2]

The emergence of the modern Asian population of East Africa can therefore be seen largely within the context of the three-tier system that was adopted in the territories during the later colonial period. Within this system the Asian community was to make important social and economic progress in East Africa, while at the same time the community was increasingly isolated from the other races.

The progress in establishing a modern system of Asian education in East Africa, modelled on the English pattern, contributed significantly to the socio-economic improvement of the community. From the 1920s onwards, the question of government support for the various schools privately established by the community became a major political grievance of the Asians in view of the support to European education.[3] A policy of extending government control and supervision over the Asian schools was subsequently initiated in the various East African territories in the late 1920s. An Indian education tax was levied and government grants-in-aid were made available to the various schools. In addition provision was made for government capital expenditure

---

[1] Mangat, *Asians in East Africa*, chap. v, 'The Crucial Decades'.

[2] Among these issues were those of a common electoral roll, marketing legislation, land tenure, and immigration. See ibid., pp. 146–67.

[3] See, for example, Kenya, *Report of the Select Committee on Indian Education* (Nairobi, Govt. Printer, 1949), note by A. B. Patel, p. 27; and the minority report by Chanan Singh in *Report of Committee on Educational Expenditure* (European and Asian) (Nairobi, Govt. Printer, 1948), p. 28.

on the basis of a 50 per cent contribution by the Asian community to undertake the construction of modern schools in the various towns. Attempts were also made to improve the standard of education in the Asian schools through the recruitment of trained staff and the introduction of Cambridge School Certificate and London Matriculation syllabuses. By 1941 Kenya had made enough progress in this respect for compulsory primary education to be introduced for Asian children in Nairobi, Mombasa, and Kisumu. It was however only after the Second World War that the various problems of Asian education— poor standards, overcrowding, insufficient expenditure—were effectively tackled by the East African governments, following a number of enquiries and reports on these matters.[1] A series of development plans extending over the rest of the colonial period were formulated in the various territories with a view to developing secondary education and to establishing teacher training colleges to train staff. The Indian education tax was increased, and government grants-in-aid as well as capital expenditure on Asian education were correspondingly raised. The resulting improvements in the facilities for education, especially in the standards of secondary schools—although not quite comparable to the progress made in African and European education at this time[2]—helped to create a comprehensive modern system of Asian education in East Africa. This had far-reaching importance for the socio-economic progress of the Asian community: apart from enabling the younger generation to acquire greater fluency in the English language and familiarity with British institutions, it enabled an increasing number of candidates to obtain the required qualifications for further training overseas, especially in England, in professional and technical fields—and generally enhanced the economic usefulness and mobility of the generation of Asians born and educated in East Africa. In this respect it can be regarded as a relatively advanced group comparable to the urban élites of their homelands.

The economic role of the Asians meanwhile continued to expand along the channels for middle-grade employment and commercial enterprise laid open at the beginning of the colonial period.

---

[1] See reports cited in preceding note, and *Report on Asian and European Education in Kenya* (Nairobi, Govt. Printer, 1958).

[2] Ibid., pp. 3, 23.

Within the first two decades of this century, the Asian traders had established a variety of business interests in the urban and rural areas of East Africa; while Asian subordinate staff were extensively employed by the various public and private organizations. And in these and related capacities the Asian economic role was to continue to grow during the rest of the colonial period. The process of expansion and diversification was aided by a number of factors. The opportunities created by an advancing economy, especially after the Second World War, the general competitiveness of the Asians, their business skills and economic resilience, were particularly important in this respect. The family-based Asian enterprises were able to extend their operations with the steady accumulation of capital and the acquisition of new professional and technical skills into secondary manufacturing industry or sugar, sisal, and cotton-ginning interests; while others were able to operate as building contractors, saw-millers, or motor transporters.[1] The nature of Asian economic activity in East Africa generally was also influenced by the government policies adopted. In Kenya, for example, in contrast to Uganda and Tanzania, there was little Asian participation in the agricultural industry. Similarly, the racial ban on the Asian advancement to senior administrative posts encouraged the community to concentrate its energies on commerce or to seek opportunities in the professional and technical fields. Moreover the growth of competition from Africans as petty traders and artisans, coupled as it was with the marketing legislation of the 1930s (which largely deprived the community of the dominant role it had played in the rural trade since the early colonial period), paradoxically provided an impetus for diversification of Asian business activity in East Africa.

The later colonial period also witnessed a transition from small-scale to larger Asian enterprises, and the development of these on an inter-territorial basis. This process was aided by the common factor of British rule in the East African countries. A few examples will help to illustrate this phenomenon. The Nanji Kalidas Mehta family, for example, had earlier acquired interests in the Uganda cotton industry. During the 1920s Mehta branched out into the sugar industry, opening a factory at Lugazi in 1924. At the same time his family acquired additional

[1] Kenya *Statistical Abstracts*, 1955 and 1962; Uganda *Statistical Abstract*, 1958.

cotton-ginning interests in Tanganyika as well as sisal estates. Such interests, coupled with the extension of his business operations to Kenya and Bombay, were to form the basis for the extensive Mehta enterprises in East Africa. Another Uganda group—that of Muljibhai Madhvani and the related Hindocha families—which had earlier acquired cotton interests in that territory, made similar progress. In 1929, Madhvani built the second sugar factory in Uganda at Kakira. Later the family branched out into sugar and cotton enterprise in Kenya and Tanganyika; and its later industrial and business network in East Africa traced its origins to the diverse inter-territorial interests acquired by the family during the interwar years. Equally significant was the expansion of the activities of the old-established Karimjee Jivanjee family, which held considerable commercial interests in Zanzibar and along the coast. Its operations based on Zanzibar, Dar es Salaam, and Mombasa were substantially diversified during the colonial period, following the family's acquisition of sisal, coffee, and cotton interests in Tanganyika, and its expansion into secondary industry. Both Tyabali Karimjee and Yusufali Jivanjee, who were later knighted, were leading traders in East Africa during much of the colonial period; while the career of the latter's successor, A. Y. A. Karimjee, as a subsequent mayor of Dar es Salaam and as a prominent politician, provides an interesting parallel with that of A. N. (later Sir Amar) Maini in Uganda, who similarly succeeded to the business and cotton interests acquired by his family in Kenya and Uganda and later, from 1950 to 1955, became the first Asian mayor of Kampala. A number of other Asian families with substantial financial, business, or professional interests in East Africa can similarly be mentioned. But the overall picture of the Asian economic role in East Africa during the colonial period continued to be one of a majority of the community being engaged in small-scale enterprises or employed as subordinate staff.

There was however a steady increase of the Asian population in the East African territories—both because of a free flow of immigrants until restrictions were placed on Indian immigration in 1944, and because of natural increase estimated at 2 to 3 per cent per annum. By 1948 Kenya had a population of 87,000 Asians, Uganda 35,000, Tanganyika 46,000, and Zanzibar

16,000. By the end of the colonial period the Asian population stood at well over 350,000 in an East African population of about 25 million. The 1948 census reports revealed that a majority of the Asian working population (roughly 80 per cent) were engaged in private industry, commerce, finance, building and contracting —about half of this percentage being involved in wholesale and retail trade; while the balance were employed in public transport and the civil service. This picture did not change noticeably in the various territories for the rest of the colonial period—except that the post-war period witnessed a rapid rise in incomes generally. But the rate of their earnings also reflected upon the essentially middle position of the Asians within the three-tier system. For example, the civil service salaries introduced in 1935 provided for an Asian maximum of £502 as against the European £2,117, and this officially-sanctioned disparity in incomes was not finally abandoned until 1955. Figures available for Asian earnings in 1948 show however that the economic condition of the community had steadily improved. In Kenya roughly a quarter of the Asian working population had an income of up to £15 per month, about 60 per cent earned between £15 and £30 and the balance up to £50 per month. During the 1950s the rise in incomes became more marked: the average Asian earnings in Uganda in 1957 stood at £400–£500 per annum, while a majority of the Asians in Kenya earned between £180 and £550. Figures available for Kenya in 1961 reveal further progress in this respect—which can be taken as indicative of the pattern generally in the rest of East Africa: about a quarter of the working Asians earned between £540 and £719, while nearly another quarter earned over £720. The overall economic position of the Asians in East Africa on the eve of independence, was therefore, one of a community with substantial financial, capital, and business resources, providing crucial services in a wide variety of fields: as wholesalers and retailers, property owners and building contractors, manufacturers and industrialists, mechanics and technicians, and administrative and professional staff.

The gradual educational and economic improvement of the Asian community during the colonial period contributed to a process of social change within their society, especially among the younger generation. Exposed to a highly urbanized environment (for the nature of Asian economic activity coupled with the racial restrictions against them had led to their settlement largely in the urban areas), to a system of education based on the English pattern, and to the higher standard of living in East Africa, this generation developed marked changes in food habits, mode of dress and language—the last being influenced by their greater fluency in both English and Swahili. Moreover, they developed a greater consciousness of their countries of adoption and in the process lost much of the sympathies of their parents for their places of origin in India and Pakistan. This process was aided also by the general act of settling down on the part of the immigrants—who became progressively less temporary visitors with roots in India and more 'settlers' with an increasing stake in the East African territories. Such developments, when viewed in terms of the socio-economic backwardness of the early immigrants originating from Indian villages, can be regarded as representing a major transformation of the Asian society in East Africa in the course of the colonial period.

The process of social change among the Asians was, however, partly checked by their growing isolation as a distinct racial and cultural minority in East Africa. This isolation owed its origins to two factors: firstly to the religious and communal traditions of the Asians themselves, so that their society represented an aggregation of close-knit communities; but more particularly to what the East Africa Royal Commission described in 1955 as the historical process in East Africa—which had been 'one of communities for the most part living separately and not one of partnership in development'.[1] The stratification of East African society on racial lines, the socio-economic discrimination inherent in the three-tier system and the political vulnerability, presented a marked contrast to the progress made by them and helped further to underline their separateness. Such conditions were hardly conducive to the social mobility of the community—indeed they aroused European and African hostility towards the Asians, rendering them an ideal target as scapegoat. The resulting vicious circle reinforced the general isolation of the Asians as a minority community in East Africa

[1] *East Africa Royal Commission 1953–1955 Report*, Chairman Sir Hugh Dow, Cmd. 9475 (London, HMSO, 1955), p. 380.

which was constantly under critical scrutiny by the other races.

The political vulnerability of the Asians was intensified by developments in the post-war period. The growth of African nationalism during this period contributed to a decline of the racial politics that had characterized much of the political activity in East Africa during the colonial period—and led in the process to an end of the Asian role as a political pressure-group in the territories. Moreover, Asian political activity after the war tended to become increasingly subservient to African nationalism in so far as the under-privileged status of both Africans and Asians vis-à-vis the Europeans seemed to provide a common cause for the two races.

Some measure of political collaboration between the Asians and Africans had occurred as early as the 1920s, when the Indian Congress established connections with the various emerging African political organizations.[1] Similarly, Asians gave assistance in printing articles and pamphlets for Harry Thuku, and later the newspaper Muigwithania—which was edited by Johnstone (later Jomo) Kenyatta.[2] A few Asian leaders—notably Isher Dass who accompanied Kenyatta to London in 1929, and the trade unionist Makhan Singh—were later to be more closely associated with African politics. As a member of the Legislative Council between 1933 and 1942, Dass sought frequently to speak on behalf of the Africans;[3] and during 1938-9 he was particularly active in publicising the representations made by the Kikuyu Central Association and the Kavirondo Taxpayers' Welfare Association to the Imperial government, and by the Kamba tribe over the government's destocking policy.[4] Meanwhile, Makhan Singh helped to organize the trade union movement in Kenya during the 1930s, when he founded the Labour Trade Union of East Africa. This union, together with the Young Kikuyu

[1] See e.g. H. Thuku, Harry Thuku: an autobiography (Nairobi, 1970), pp. 17–24; George Bennett, 'The Development of Political Organizations in Kenya', Political Studies, 5, 2 (June 1957).

[2] See Felice Carter, 'The Asian Press in Kenya', East Africa Journal, 6, 10 (Oct. 1969).

[3] Kenya Legislative Council Debates, 25 Apr. 1934, p. 97; 28 June 1935, pp. 69, 73; 12 Nov. 1936, pp. 548, 559, and 17 Nov. 1937, p. 406. See also Kenya, Land Commission, Evidence (Nairobi, Govt. Printer, 1934), iii, 2887–8.

[4] Leg Co Debates, 9 Aug. 1938, pp. 67–72; 10 Aug. 1938, pp. 113–23; 17 Aug. 1938, pp. 226–41; and 21 Apr. 1939, pp. 284–9, 322.

Association, was later responsible for organizing the Mombasa dockworkers' strike in 1939.[1]

It was however after the war that a more concerted effort was made towards Asian–African political co-operation. The immediate impetus for this was provided by Indian independence in 1947, and the arrival in Nairobi in 1948 of the Indian Commissioner Apa Pant—who was to pursue an active pro-African policy. The resulting political situation in Kenya can be explained in the words of Elspeth Huxley: 'African newspapers are printed on terms of easy credit on Indian presses; Indians give money to such bodies as the K.A.U.; African political leaders are made welcome in Indian houses; one of the K.A.U. officials . . . is now touring India as a guest. The latest move, which has aroused great African enthusiasm, is the award of five scholarships to take Kenya Africans to Indian universities.'[2] Moreover, Makhan Singh and the Indian Congress Secretary, P. G. Pinto, took an active anti-government stand during the worsening post-war political situation. The former was arrested in 1950 and spent over ten years in jail, while the latter was imprisoned for five years in 1954. Other Indian leaders meanwhile took up a campaign for the release of the various African leaders, who were placed in restriction after the Kapenguria trial. Moreover, at the trial itself a number of Asian lawyers participated in the defence.[3]

Such political co-operation between the Africans and the Asians was, however, soon overshadowed by the rising intensity of African nationalism during the 1950s, and the growing African resentment of the Asian position as a middle, and therefore relatively privileged, group within the three-tier system. Indeed some of the pro-nationalist Asian political organizations established towards the end of the decade—notably the Uganda Action Group and the Kenya Freedom Party—found it difficult to win the acceptance of the African nationalist parties. The Asian role as a pressure group had ended, and the political initiative lay elsewhere; but the community continued, largely as an act of

[1] Evidence of Mombasa Labour Commission of Enquiry, Kenya Archives, file Msa 106/58, p. 3; Makhan Singh, *History of Trade Unions in Kenya* (London, 1969).
[2] E. Huxley, *The Sorcerer's Apprentice* (London, 1951), pp. 57–8.
[3] M. Blundell, *So Rough a Wind* (London, 1964), pp. 95, 112–13, and F. D. Corfield, *The Origins and Growth of Mau Mau* (Nairobi, Govt. Printer, 1960), pp. 56, 223, 266.

faith, to support the demands for independence.[1] At the same time, the Asians were faced with a growing dilemma as to their future prospects in the territories, in view of the rising intensity of anti-Asian feeling which threatened to obscure the more positive contributions they had made to the evolution of modern East Africa.

[1] See T. J. Mboya's comment in *Freedom and After* (London, 1963), pp. 112–13, and R. Cox, *Pan-Africanism in Practice* (London, 1964), p. 29.

XIII

THE IMMIGRANT COMMUNITIES (3): THE ARABS OF THE EAST AFRICAN COAST

JOHN MIDDLETON

The Arabs and Coastal society

THE principal historical data about the Arabs of East Africa have been outlined in the earlier volumes of this *History*.[1] In this chapter an attempt will be made to present the historical and the sociological significance of the Arabs in the total social system of eastern Africa over the past millennium. There are two points to be made immediately. The first is that they were the first invaders of the region from overseas who had any marked economic, social, and political effects on the indigenous peoples—or at least any effects that we can still trace. They entered the area many centuries before the Indians or Europeans (and possibly before many of the 'African' groups also). Their early history has been described in volume i of this *History*, but certain aspects of it are still significant for an understanding of their role in the colonial period and since its ending: their consciousness of their own antiquity was part of their role and a partial cause of the views held about them by members of other groups. They themselves were the first colonial rulers in East Africa and were later to find themselves colonized by the Europeans. The Sultanate of Zanzibar, the centre of Arab power, became a subject state in its latter days, although given the face-saving title of 'protectorate'. The second point is that,

[1] See vol. i, chap. iv, 'The East African Coast until the Coming of the Portuguese', by Gervase Mathew; chap. v, 'The Coast: 1498–1840', by G. S. P. Freeman-Grenville; chap. vii, 'Zanzibar and the Coastal Belt, 1840–84', by Sir John Gray; and chap. viii, 'The Southern Section of the Interior', by Alison Smith; also chap. xiii in vol. ii, 'Zanzibar, 1890–1950', by J. E. Flint.

This chapter does not include discussion of the Arabs of Uganda. Their social and historical importance has been slight compared to that of the Coastal Arabs; locally their impact was significant mainly as perpetrators of the Sudanese slave trade and as ancestors of the present-day Nubi population of Uganda.

representing essentially a pre-industrial or mercantile form of colonialism, they were the first of the major invaders to lose their power. Unfortunately, the available information about the Arabs has been very inadequate, being both superficial and undetailed; it has also been affected by emotionalism—whether nostalgia for a supposed noble past or indignation about the former organizers and controllers of the Indian Ocean slave trade.

A perennial difficulty in discussing the Arabs of the East African coast has been that of definition: just who have been and are 'Arabs'?[1] The Arab communities in East Africa have always been physically and ethnically mixed and have come to belong to a culture different from those of southern Arabia, Egypt, or elsewhere in the Arab world. In addition, the ethnic and social composition of the Arab communities has changed at various times and in various parts of the coast and the interior; and this internal composition has affected and been affected by the other elements in coastal society. Arabs have been part of the general coast culture of the Swahili peoples, who have a similar geographical distribution. Not that Arab and Swahili cultures are the same; but they have always been so intimately linked that neither is fully intelligible without reference to the other. The role of the Arabs before, during, and since the colonial period has been tied to those of the other communities of the coast; it is not possible to separate them. There have been many attempts to define the various ethnic terms used for the so-called 'communities' of the coast.[2] These communities include Arabs, Swahili, Africans, and others, most of them having meanings that have changed both in time and in space.

Perhaps the pre-eminent factor in the migration of the Arabs to eastern Africa and their settlement there was that their principal motive was always trade. The degree of movement between Arabia and Africa was considerable, mainly in the direction from Arabia to Africa. Their position as an essentially

[1] This section is based on several works, in particular A. H. J. Prins, *The Swahili-speaking Peoples of Zanzibar and the East African Coast* (London, 1961); J. S. Trimingham, *Islam in East Africa* (Oxford, 1964); C. S. Nicholls, *The Swahili Coast* (London, 1971); and the older works by Coupland, Pearce, and Ingrams.

[2] Perhaps the term 'groupings' or even 'social categories' would be as accurate as 'communities', if not more meaningful, but 'communities' is at least supported by custom and will be used here.

mercantile group, as with many other colonial and mercantile communities elsewhere, necessitated some form of political protection and stability, with control of communications, customs, and coinage; some form of banking and credit facilities; a subservient population to be exploited; and means for links to be maintained with that population that were not totally (nor even to any marked extent) based on force unless that force was easy to administer. Such a list of functional prerequisites is somewhat simplistic but none the less true; and the nature of the Arab communities in East Africa can correctly be analysed only within this frame of reference.

The Africans proper, the indigenous peoples of the region, have always been a numerical majority. They were the subjects—the porters, the soldiers, the ivory-collectors, and the slaves. Ultimately therefore they also provided the wealth that was transferred across the Indian Ocean for over a thousand years. And consisting as they did of many small and relatively weak ethnic groups they were generally unable to put up much of a resistance to outside overlordship, although there were of course exceptions to this statement. The 'Indians' or 'Asians' supplied the credit for the Arab-controlled trades; until a few centuries ago they seem mainly to have been seasonal visitors. The Europeans essentially played the same roles as had the Arabs whom they superseded by virtue of superior military and economic power; and as mercantile colonialists they also required the same kind of total social system in the early part of their overrule. Finally there were the Swahili, the people of the coast proper (who although classed as 'African' have always held an intermediary position and so merit being distinguished as a separate community); they provided the link with the local country and were thus a force for additional stability over the generations.

The Arabs of the coast immigrated at various times over the past millennium from southern Arabia, particularly from Oman and Muscat (Omani Arabs) and from the Hadramaut and its coastal towns (Hadrami Arabs). The Hadrami were the earliest settlers but continued to immigrate until the 1960s. They were usually known as Shihiri and were divided among themselves according to the tribes and clans of the Hadramaut. The early coastal ruling houses such as the Nabhani of Pate originated in the Hadramaut, and the Hadrami were represented in East Africa mainly along the coast, the Omani Arabs being concentrated to a greater extent in the islands. The Omani migrated principally from the early part of the nineteenth century when their ruling dynasty assumed control of the coast and ruled it from Zanzibar. Among the Omani there has always been a marked social distinction between those from the Arabian coast and those from its hinterland; the latter, who always recognized indigenous Arabian groupings, often despised the former, who in general did not. The hinterland Omani are divided into two main groupings, the Ghafiria and the Hinawia, each of which comprises several hundred tribes and sub-tribes. All (or virtually all—the information is lacking) were represented in East Africa, and each seems always to have recognized the internal authority of a *sheikh* who was both the representative of a senior descent line within the tribe in East Africa and also a representative of the principal tribal *sheikh* in Oman. There were certain other tribes independent of this dual division; they were notably the el-Busaidi and the el-Yoorbi (from which tribes came the royal families of Muscat), and the coastal groups known as Besa, who occupied an inferior and often semi-servile status to the tribal groups. The complex networks of marriages and alliances, although recognized in East Africa and highly significant in the internal organization and history of intrigues and feuds of the Arab community, are too detailed to be included here.[1]

The Swahili were essentially a population of mixed Arab and African ancestry which evolved its own culture on the coast whether its members in any particular place were historically more African than Arab or more Arab than African. By now it has been in existence for enough centuries to have evolved a fairly stable and clearly defined culture, although there are still great variations both in that culture and in its language. The Swahili are difficult to define clearly other than geographically— the name is from the Arabic *Sawahila* and means simply 'coast-dwellers'. Nevertheless certain main groupings may be distinguished, all closely associated with 'Arabs'. Few of these ever referred to themselves as 'Swahili' but used more inclusive names.

---

[1] This section owes much to an unpublished paper by K. T. Clarke and D. C. Yalden-Thomson, 'A Paper on the Oman Arabs in Zanzibar Protectorate' (Zanzibar, 1942), generously made available by the authors.

They included the Shirazi, who derived from the original ruling groups of the medieval settlements and used the name to reflect a legendary Persian origin and so to mark themselves off as distinct from and earlier than the Arabs who succeeded them as rulers; the inhabitants of Zanzibar and Pemba in particular (the Hadimu, Tumbatu, and Pemba) used this term to distinguish themselves from later Omani immigrants. Many Shirazi, especially in the northern areas, claimed Arab ancestry also, to strengthen their class position by membership in the politically dominant community; they included the twelve clans of Mombasa, divided into the Three Tribes and the Nine Tribes. The term 'Afro-Arab' has often been used by outside writers for a second category, those who trace patrilineal descent from an Arab ancestor but 'whose appearance shows that they are the sons of their mothers'. Among these were included the ancient families of the Nabhani of Pate and the Ma'awi of Lamu. Later 'Afro-Arabs' included the powerful Mazrui clan whose members, migrating from Oman in the early eighteenth century, long controlled Mombasa and Pemba. Also in this category should be included the Shurafa (generally known as Sharifu on the coast), descendants of the Prophet, who seem first to have settled in this region in the sixteenth century and who were held in esteem for their spiritual qualities although they lacked political power. All these 'Afro-Arab' groups were frequently indistinguishable in appearance or ways of living from the other Swahili and might use both Swahili and Arabic in everyday intercourse. Other categories of Swahili both showed and claimed less Arab ancestry: those of slave descent were the most important. Finally there were often included, as Swahili, various people who adopted Swahili culture and Islam but who remained on the periphery of Swahili 'society': the Bajun of Somalia and Kenya, the Segeju of Tanzania, the Comorians, and others who need not be considered here.

The history of the Arabs of the coast is basically that of their relations with these various Swahili groups. Even if at times the Swahili resented and fought Omani intrusion into what they claimed historically to be their own country, they acted as allies of the Arabs in the exploitation of non-Swahili coastal and hinterland peoples. It was a history of continually changing alliances among the several elements of coastal society, and the

Arabs played an integral and usually politically superior part despite their demographic minority.

Within a wider context, the history of the Arabs—their relationship with other parts of East Africa, as well as with Arabia and other countries of the Indian Ocean—falls into several phases: from the beginnings through the coming of the Portuguese at the end of the fifteenth century, and including two and a half centuries of Portuguese domination; the period during which the Omani Arabs consolidated their hegemony and expanded into the interior, from the early eighteenth until the end of the nineteenth century; and the period of the decline of Arab power as a consequence of British overlordship, culminating in its final eclipse in the Zanzibar revolution of 1964.

It should be stressed that the data for most of these periods are both historically and sociologically very inadequate. We know a good deal about such matters as the quarrels of the Zanzibar sultans with their British advisers, but almost nothing of the internal Arab intrigues that may largely have determined the sultans' policies; and we know virtually nothing about details of the everyday relations between Portuguese settlers (whose ruined farmhouses can still be seen across the Zanzibar landscape) and their Swahili neighbours, of the lives of ordinary Swahili farmers or fishermen, of Arab plantation organization, slavery rolls, and the like.

The development of Arab society on the coast up to the eighteenth century

The outlines of the early economic and political development of the Arab communities of the coast have been given in the first volume of this *History*.[1] The centres of Arab settlement and power were first in the north, within easy sailing distance of Arabia itself and the countries immediately beyond it; later the emphasis switched to Kilwa in the south, the main entrepôt for the wealth in gold and ivory from Monomatapa, which were sent up from the port of Sofala. The basic pattern of settlement for the Arabs was the city-state, and in later periods the coastal Arabs were almost all urban dwellers. Mogadishu and Pate were the most important of these states by about the thirteenth century; Kilwa dominated during the fifteenth century; by the time of the Portuguese arrival at the end of that century

[1] See also Sir J. M. Gray, *A History of Zanzibar* (London, 1962).

Mombasa had gained the senior position, as it was almost impregnable militarily and controlled the monsoon traffic across the Indian Ocean.

By the fifteenth century there were some thirteen large coastal towns, many built of stone, and the more powerful of their rulers were minting their own coinages. The people of these states were literate; they spoke forms of Swahili and used Arabic script. The earliest rulers were Shirazi, although they regarded themselves as being closely allied with the Arabs and, being Muslims, as distinct from the mass of neighbouring peoples; some of the later rulers were probably more Arab than Shirazi. Arab and Shirazi merchants provided the wealth on which these states were based, as their military power cannot have been very great. These city-states exploited at least their immediate hinterlands and traded with communities across the Indian Ocean, exporting ivory, gold, slaves, and many other commodities in Arab-manned vessels. There was a marked increase in this trade during the fifteenth century (presumably a cause of the building of more large stone buildings at this time), because of new demands in India for slaves and the growing European interest in spices. We know a certain amount about these cities, mainly from the various Swahili 'chronicles', but the accounts are set in a curious kind of vacuum, in which immigrant merchants live luxurious and scholarly lives surrounded by lesser intermediaries between overseas markets and indigenous tribes. We do not know much of what lay behind the luxury.

During this period the pattern of evolution of the Arab communities may have been true also of the other immigrant groups such as the Debuli and others, who established the little-excavated coastal towns of Zanzibar, Pemba, and elsewhere. Their history is outside the scope of this chapter and in any case cannot be reconstructed without much archaeological research. But presumably the Arab-controlled towns, continually reinforced by fresh immigration from Arabia and well supported by Arab trade routes across the Indian Ocean, proved strong enough slowly to absorb them. At the same time Arabs appear continually to have been absorbed into the Swahili population, presumably in general from the 'lower' strata of the Arab community. But the influx of new immigrants provided continuity in the Arab upper class (using this term very loosely) and also maintained an adequate level of education, religious enthusiasm, mercantile and sailing skills, and what has been in those confused centuries a continual renovation of a sense of purpose. It is important that it was only from Arabia that there was continual immigration. It was the Arabs who forged and maintained links with the outside world, and as traders they retained the urge to control, and to expand their influence and power over, the more stagnant world of the Swahili and what must have seemed the turbulent wilderness of the hinterland from which sprang the traders' wealth. However, reports of this trade, at its height in the fifteenth century, reached the newly burgeoning societies of Europe; the Portuguese decided to establish a foothold on the western shores of the Indian Ocean.

Economically the Portuguese intrusion weakened and in some areas virtually destroyed the Arab-controlled communities and the trade on which they depended. This was so particularly in the gold-exporting areas of the south based on Monomatapa and Sofala, but would seem to have been true throughout the region. The Portuguese took the production of trade goods and their export into their own hands but in fact found themselves unable to control or to expand them. We know little of the impact on local society of the Portuguese, although they left a few traces in local Swahili culture. Politically they weakened the semi-autonomous powers of the city-states and the equilibrium between them; and by taking Mombasa as the centre for their control of the coast they continued to aid the long decline of the outlying regions to the north and south. One consequence was the growth of a measure of unity among the city-states, which led them at length to request the help of Oman in expelling the European invaders. However, the removal of the Portuguese did not lead to a new independence but to a series of confrontations and conquests by the Omani Arabs, who in their turn were to prepare the way for later European annexations.

The essential features of these early periods of coastal history were two. The first was the establishment under Arab control of Indian Ocean trade based on the monsoons; the trade routes included eastern Africa although the trade was focused on Arabia and India. The second was the growth of mercantile depots and towns along the African coast, which supplied the northern and eastern lands with certain African products. These communities were on the periphery of a wide network of trade routes and their impact on the African hinterland was only enough to ensure its immediate exploitation by Arab and Swahili traders who recognized no responsibility towards its inhabitants. The power of these little states—despite their evident wealth at certain periods—rose and declined relative to one another in their competition to control the external trade, and was devoted essentially to a defensive role *vis-à-vis* the hinterland proper.

Although the local actors throughout this early period were mainly the various Swahili groups, the region and its trade were controlled by outsiders whose principal role was precisely to provide and control trade and political links with the overseas markets. These 'outsiders' were so only in terms of their origins; they settled, intermarried with Swahili and others and became part of the total Swahili population, and were continually replenished by further immigration. As far as the Arabs were concerned the consequence was the continuing segmentation of the Arab population: those of recent Arabian provenance as against those longer-settled and more intimately part of the local Swahili population; Omani as against Hadrami; one Arabian tribe as against another; rich and powerful as against poorer and weaker. Yet the Arabs also brought with them certain unifying institutions which helped to form the Arab and Swahili segments into a single society, and which also enabled non-Swahili Africans to become Swahili by accepting them. The most important of these was Islam. Another was the Arabic language which, even if not spoken by Swahili nor indeed by most of the long-settled Arabs, provided both a form of writing for Swahili and many loan-words and concepts. In addition, Arab influence on architecture and everyday living patterns was significant for the same reasons.

The eighteenth and nineteenth centuries

The essential features of East African Arab history during the later eighteenth and the nineteenth centuries were the rise of Omani power at the expense of those local Arabs who were already settled along the coast, and the extension of Arab influence into the interior. Before Seyyid Said ibn Sultan took over Zanzibar as his political base in East Africa in 1832, the hinterland of the coast had been only very slightly affected by Arab-Swahili society. But after the advent of Sultan Said the coast and its hinterland were transformed from a string of small Swahili city-states, each with its local sphere of influence, into a single mercantile state based on Zanzibar city and ruled by its Omani dynasty. It is important to stress that this state had as its purpose trade: Said and his successors were not interested in territorial expansion as such. The establishment of this economic system required both political actions, to clear the way for economic growth, and others that were more purely economic in character. The former involved both conflicts between Omani and local Arab families, with Swahili allies on each side, and also efforts by the victorious Omani to expand their influence into the interior, making and using fresh allies as they did so. The consolidation of Zanzibar hegemony over the other Arab and Swahili communities of the coast took a good half-century; it began with the conflicts between Sultan Said and the Mazrui between about 1822 and 1837 and continued until the destruction of the threat of the so-called 'Northern Arabs' about 1860, the death of the last Hadimu ruler in Zanzibar in 1865 and the defeat of Mbarak ibn Rashid of Gazi in 1882. The general consequence was the supremacy of the Omani dynasty and of their followers, who migrated in ever-increasing numbers from Oman to Zanzibar during the middle decades of the century.

The Omani sultans took great care also to develop the coast economically, with striking success. The first main step was the development of export crops, particularly in Zanzibar and Pemba. Cloves were introduced early in the nineteenth century, and the export of cloves and coconut products produced great wealth for the islands; there was established a plantation system with faithful Omani Arabs as landlords granted their lands by decree of the sultans. The indigenous Swahili peoples were increasingly confined to those areas unsuitable for clove-growing and so cut off from the acquisition of wealth.[1] The three important aspects of this economic development were the growth of a plantation-owning class of Arabs; the ever-increasing need for labour, for which slaves from the interior provided the answer; and the growth of the Indian credit-providing community, whose wealth and influence increased throughout the century.

[1] See J. Middleton, *Land Tenure in Zanzibar* (London, 1961).

Although these developments took place along the entire coast, the centre of wealth and power remained firmly anchored in Zanzibar and Pemba.

From the middle of the nineteenth century two other factors contributed towards the growth of an expanding coastal economy: the demand for slaves in the French islands of the Indian Ocean (as well as the constant demand for slaves from Arabia and India), and the increasing European market for spices, ivory, oils, and gums. The response was the greatly increased exploitation of the interior.

Even in the eighteenth and early nineteenth centuries there had been a few Arabs and Swahili engaged in trade in the interior. But they were in general ancillary to, and closely dependent on, those African societies and their rulers who had pioneered and controlled the overland trade routes. And they had been coastal, not Omani, Arabs who typically settled and married in the interior. They were followed towards the middle of the century by richer and more powerful caravan traders from Zanzibar, supported by the sultans. Between 1840 and 1850 Omani colonies were established at Tabora in Unyanyembe and at Ujiji and Urua by Lake Tanganyika, while Zanzibari Arabs had reached the court of Buganda by 1844. There was considerable competition between Omani and pre-Omani Arab traders, each trying to set up their own spheres of influence and alliances with local African rulers. The interior settlements were often large and permanent, with Arabs and Swahili controlling farms and stores of ivory, copper, and other goods for barter. On the coast were the entrepôts under the more immediate control of Zanzibar; each typically had its governor, its customs official, some Baluchi soldiers, the Arab-Swahili traders, and the Indian financiers who supplied the credit for the long and arduous—but highly profitable—caravan expeditions.

But the phase of Arab expansion and settlement in the interior was a brief one. With the rapid spread of firearms after 1850, indigenous African rulers found themselves able to be more independent of Arab support and to control more of the trade for their own benefit. By the 1880s the situation was so out of hand that Sultan Barghash made a last-minute attempt to establish formal Zanzibari authority over a wider area of the interior, but was forestalled by the partition of the continent by the European powers. After the Berlin Conference of 1884 the political influence of Zanzibar beyond the coast quickly evaporated, and Arabs remained in the interior only as individuals profiting on their own plantations by the cheap slave labour made available by the general unrest. Arab political and economic influence in Zanzibar and on the coast likewise declined, first with the abolition of the export trade in slaves across the Indian Ocean, and then with the establishment of European overlordship and the abolition of slavery itself within Zanzibar and its dependencies.

The Arabs of East Africa were carrying out four main developments during the nineteenth century. First, they consolidated and increased their economic, political, and religious hegemony along the coast, based on Zanzibar; this involved the rise to supremacy of the more recent Omani immigrants and the corresponding decline of the local coastal Arabs. Secondly, they extended their influence across the Indian Ocean, especially to Madagascar and the smaller French islands, through the export of slaves. Thirdly, they extended their region of economic exploitation from the coast into the hinterland, and increasingly controlled the profitable trades in ivory, slaves, and other commodities for themselves, rather than acting merely as local shippers. Finally, they set up nuclei of political power throughout the interior, based on their possession of firearms. They acted as political catalysts throughout this region, whose individual tribes were beginning to face a common new and external power; although in the long run power in this region was to be held by Europeans and not by Arabs, it did not look like that at the time to the African peoples themselves.

The final decline

Details of events in the final phase of the history of the East African Arabs need little telling. The abolition of slavery and the steady decline in trade in other goods that had formerly passed through Arab hands, the increasing indebtedness of Arab plantation owners (see below), and the competition by British and German colonial companies and their successor governments, all contributed to the economic decline of the Arabs. The diminution of the sultans' dominions on the mainland, and the increased influence and control by the European powers, contributed to their political decline also. So did their changing relationship to the African majority in the population. Whereas the position of the Arabs weakened during the European colonial period, those of the Europeans, to a less extent of the Asians, and of the Africans, all grew stronger until the period of the gaining of independence, after the Second World War. The Arabs' relationship to the mass of the African population was therefore very different from those of the other immigrant communities: their nostalgia for their past and resentment and fear about their present and their future set them—all but a few of the most politically alert—far apart from the aims and plans for social and political development that became of increasing importance during the last years of the colonial period. Colonial government reports from the beginning of the century continually mention that the Arabs were 'proud', 'idle', 'decadent', and so forth, all terms referring to the fact that the Arabs resented the power of their new colonial rulers and wished to have as little to do with them as they could. The subject African population, however, considered that the Arabs were allied to the colonial power, especially in Zanzibar, where the British guided and supported the sultans' position. At the end of the period Arab political leaders, especially in Zanzibar, took great pains to appear to lead opposition to the British and thereby obtained some African support. However, they were unable to play this role for long and found that the independence of Zanzibar of 1963, which they tried to lead, gave way almost immediately to the Zanzibar revolution of 1964, which marked the end of Arab power in East Africa.[1]

Conclusion: the Arab community and its part in the history of East Africa

It remains to summarize the role played by the Arabs in East Africa, in particular during the period between the rise of the Omani sultanate in Zanzibar and the end of the British protectorate and the granting of independence to the East African territories.

Essentially we have been describing the growth and decline of a pre-industrial colonial system, the power of whose rulers was

[1] See chap. xiii in vol. ii of this *History*, and chap. ix above; J. Middleton and J. Campbell, *Zanzibar, its Society and its Politics* (London, 1965); M. Lofchie, *Zanzibar: background to revolution* (Princeton, 1967).

based on trade and their control of the ocean shipping that made it possible to export locally produced commodities. The Arabs came from southern Arabia, settled on the African coast, and amalgamated the previous congeries of small competing city-states; they then built up a wealthy and powerful empire based on the production and export of agricultural, animal, and human commodities and on its control of the trade between the African interior and the countries of the Indian Ocean. When their control over these factors was no longer possible, the entire system fell apart. The Arabs' inability to muster effective military force against other would-be exploiters of the region was a crucial factor in their decline, since they had to accept and rely upon the support of European colonial powers that ultimately swallowed them. The crucial reliance upon slave labour and the slave trade, although highly profitable, led to collapse once slaves were no longer available. Also the tensions in the social system of the coast made it unstable and in the end unviable once the profitability of economic exploitation of the hinterland had ceased. As has been mentioned, a continual problem that faced the Arabs in East Africa was their relationship with the Swahili. The largely urban Arab minority had both to retain its own identity and yet also to merge its interests with those of the Swahili majority, since it lacked any other means of keeping its superior position. In the later years (until the 1950s) immigration from Arabia continued at an ever-increasing rate, enabling the more 'pure' Arab group to retain its numbers to compensate for the continual process of absorption into the Swahili population. But as a result the Arabs antagonized the Swahili, who came more and more to regard the Omani as alien masters and to resent the favoured position of the lower-class Arab immigrants.

Clearly, an important factor in the position of the Arabs was always their numerical minority despite their superior political and economic power. Information on this point is slight and unreliable, due both to the difficulty of defining 'Arab' and to the fact that in the years immediately before independence the Arabs took pains to conceal their numbers for political reasons. However, a few figures are available, all from government censuses. In the Zanzibar Protectorate figures for Arabs have generally been given separately, and show that in 1907 the Arabs were 4 per cent of the population of the islands; in 1924 the proportion was 9 per cent, in 1931 it was 14 per cent, in 1948 it was 17 per cent, and in 1958 an estimated 16 per cent. Even if none of these figures are wholly reliable, they do show an acceptedly steady increase until the very end of the colonial period, when immigration from Arabia was being sharply curtailed. The long-term increase was due both to immigration and (to a probably less but unknown extent) to the increasing self-definition and acceptance as 'Arab' of some of the less 'pure' categories mentioned earlier in this chapter. But in any event the Arabs were always in a numerical minority. Figures for the coastal strip proper are even less satisfactory, but again they show that Arabs were always a small minority, and proportionally more numerous in the small coastal towns than outside them in the surrounding rural areas.

The Arabs came to East Africa as traders, but they also became landowners. Those more favoured by the sultans became landed proprietors, the less favoured became small farmers, especially in Pemba, or worked as local traders, labourers, and in other menial occupations.[1] The wealthier landowners were attached in various ways to the court; they were expected to spend a good deal of their time in their town houses in Zanzibar city and to attend court functions as supporters of the ruler and as representatives of their own tribes and clans. To play this role needed wealth, senior and respected genealogical position, the profession of Islamic piety, a knowledge and use of Arabic rather than Swahili, and a sense of ethnic pride in Arabic custom and origin. The ownership of land gave a secure basis of wealth and a regular supply of food, and many writers mentioned the very high standard of living of the wealthier Arab families. The Arab landowner left the everyday running of his plantations to Arab overseers, often his junior kinsmen. But he would normally spend regular periods in his country home where he would be the adviser of his labourers, clients, and often slaves, who would pay him respect as a quasi-father rather than as a landlord; the

[1] Figures for the 1948 census of Zanzibar, which distinguished Arabs from other ethnic categories, showed the occupations of Arabs as including 7,500 cultivators and agricultural workers (of whom 6,500 were in Pemba), 2,800 shopkeepers, 1,100 various 'sellers', 'makers of goods', and tailors, 650 labourers and servants, 400 fishermen and fish-sellers, 300 'landlords'. 250 hotel-keepers, and 1,100 in other occupations.

personal content of this relationship was very important to both parties. Outside Zanzibar Island the situation was similar although the sophisticated court life was lacking; however, the sultans appointed their personal representatives (*liwali*) in other areas and paid regular visits themselves.

We know little of the actual plantations despite their central importance in the system. Treatment was frequently extremely harsh for field slaves, although domestic slaves and concubines seem to have been treated with some trust and kindliness. The former seem not to have become Muslims, but the latter were encouraged to do so and were often manumitted on the death of their owner. The plantation owners depended on slavery for their wealth and position, and the abolition of slavery was disastrous for them. Slaves were legally freed but in many, perhaps most, cases merely remained where they were as 'squatters'. Squatters were allocated plots for their own use and were expected to provide labour for clove and coconut harvesting and processing, but they had freedom to move and were an inefficient form of labour. The institution continued until independence, although in later years the depersonalization of landlord–squatter relations greatly weakened it. Landowners came to depend rather on the seasonal importation of mainland labourers during harvest seasons, some of whom remained each year as squatters on the islands (in 1948 mainlanders were 26 per cent of the population of Zanzibar and Pemba). Not all of these mainlanders were Muslims and even those who were had few cultural links with the Arabs, who despised them. In the turbulent period after the Second World War they were to lead anti-Arab agitation and finally to take power in the 1964 revolution.

The economic position of the Arabs was also always closely linked to that of the Indians, who provided capital, loans, and mortgages. By the 1890s over half the Arab landowners were reported in debt, with many plantations mortgaged to Indians, and by the mid-1930s at least a third and more probably a half of the Arab plantations were mortgaged to Indian financiers. The various government reports on this problem of the period[1]

---

[1] See especially C. F. Strickland, *Report on co-operation and certain aspects of the economic condition of agriculture in Zanzibar* (London, 1932); C. A. Bartlett and J. S. Last, *Report on the indebtedness of the agricultural classes* (Zanzibar, Govt. Printer, 1934);

point out that the abolition of slavery had weakened the basis of both plantation and urban life, and had destroyed much of the pleasant social position of the landowners, who had been moving into the towns where the amenities were better. Such remarks imply that the traditional Arab culture remained significant. It was not easy for colonial overlords to adapt themselves to a less than superior position, and the reports are filled with phrases saying that the Arabs were 'indolent' and suffered a 'lack of business capacity and self-dependence'. The lack of cheap credit for short-term loans to clove-growers (cloves being a notoriously uncertain crop) was certainly a serious factor, and interest rates were always extremely high. The same situation occurred along the coast itself, with a decline of rural landlordism among the Arabs and their movement into the small coastal towns. In brief, the Arab role during this century changed from one of an upper segment of society controlling trade and agriculture to that of an impoverished former aristocracy living on the memory of its glorious past. This is an over-simplification, as many younger Arabs continued in trade and in government, but it is not an untrue picture.

Something should be said here about the influences left by the Arab occupation of the East African coast and parts of its hinterland. The main influence has been that of Islam, although its significance is not easy to estimate.[1] The coast has been Muslim for a thousand years, in the formal sense that the Swahili peoples accepted the basic Islamic institutions and in the main the principles of Islamic law, although many aspects of pre-Islamic faith have been retained throughout the region. However, despite the unifying role of Islam, the division between the Ibadhi minority and the Shafi'i majority tended to divide the total society.[2] The Ibadhi school was linked to the ruling house of Zanzibar and the urban aristocracy, the Shafi'i to the ordinary

E. M. Dowson, *A note on agricultural indebtedness in the Zanzibar Protectorate* (Zanzibar, Govt. Printer, 1936).

[1] See J. S. Trimingham, *Islam in East Africa* (Oxford, 1964); J. N. D. Anderson, *Islamic Law in Africa* (London, 1954); A. Abel, *Les Musulmans noirs du Maniema* (Brussels, 1960).

[2] The Shafi'i, with the Hanafi, Maliki, and Hanbali, is one of the four 'orthodox' schools of Islamic law; the Ibadhi is a sect regarded by the ('orthodox') Sunni as heterodox, and its members are the only surviving representatives today of the Khariji seceders of early Islam. See J. N. D. Anderson, *Islamic Law in Africa* (London, 1954).

people (although many wealthy Arab families were also Shafi'i). But the importance of this distinction should not be exaggerated; differences of wealth, occupation, and tribal origin were certainly equally important.

The concomitant social and political aspects of Islam have also been significant in East Africa. Besides a formal individual affirmation of a religious belief, the acceptance of the faith has involved affiliation to a particular social network. To be an Arab or a Swahili (whatever the actual ethnic identity of an individual) has meant to have a particular kind of tie with Zanzibar and even with Oman. This tie has meant a consciousness of sharing a highly valued and literate culture and language, an acceptance of the *shari'a*,[1] a formal disapproval of non-Islamic beliefs and practices, and other criteria of the kind adopted by colonial rulers anywhere else in Africa or beyond, whether Muslim or not. Not unnaturally non-Arabs wished to enter this culture, both for its prestige and for more material advantages. To become a Muslim was to ally oneself with the powerful ruler both on the coast and, in the nineteenth century, in the interior. In more recent times it involved the loosening of tribal ties and an attachment instead to the wider world of law and trade; a Muslim could usually step outside tribal legal and social obligations, be called before Muslim rather than tribal courts, send his children to special schools, often be taxed differently, and be free of various governmental regulations and tributes. To be a Muslim was often a prerequisite for being able to indulge in trade of any sort, since Arabs and Swahili in many places controlled the wholesale distribution of commodities and services. Islam was a passport to a wider, pan-tribal world, one controlled by the coastal Arabs. Yet even though the controllers may have wished to keep their Islamic purity and identity, they were caught in the dilemma that they could not do so if they wished to retain effective economic and political superiority. The decline of Arab pre-industrial colonialism and the rise of its Western and Christian industrial counterpart meant that in the long run the social importance of Islam also

[1] The acceptance of the Shari'a has been particularly significant in matters of inheritance, by which a son inherits two shares of property to one held by a daughter; this inheritance leads to the wide dispersal and fragmentation of land, and so is closely involved with the observance of cross-cousin marriage. See J. Middleton, *Land Tenure in Zanzibar.*

diminished, a part of the eclipse of the purely social position of the Arab community.

In the long-term view the Arab occupancy of the coast has left little beyond the actual presence of the few remaining members of the once powerful community,[1] their religious faith, some influences in the vocabulary of the coast language, in architecture, clothing, and forms of poetry, and a memory (whether nostalgic or resentful) of an indolent and arbitrary aristocracy whose attitude to the mass of the population veered from a slave-owning arrogance to a gentle paternalism. The East African coast in this respect resembled many other parts of the Indian Ocean littoral, such as the coastlands of south-eastern Asia: it endured for centuries being nominally subject to, and affected culturally by, an external trading aristocracy of different ethnic origin, language, and religion. Yet viewed from the hinterland, where lay and still lies the majority of the population of the region, an Arab presence may have brought the wider world within reach but in other ways was peripheral and even in many respects irrelevant to that population's long-term historical development.

---

[1] The great majority of the Arab population of Zanzibar was killed or deported in the 1964 revolution in Zanzibar; Arabs still live in the small towns of the coastal strip proper.

XIV

CHANGES IN EAST AFRICAN SOCIETY

CHRISTOPHER WRIGLEY

In the political sphere the period of East African history covered in this book was obviously a revolutionary one. It begins with the British colonial structure, shaken indeed by the war, by new ideological currents in Britain itself, and by the profound changes which had taken place in the international balance of power, but still deeply entrenched and confident of a long future —more assured and forward-looking, in fact, than it had been for a long time. It begins with a steady influx of young Englishmen, many of them expecting to spend their working lives at least in East Africa, as farmers, in business, in the professions or as paternal administrators; with a society whose structure of racial caste was only slightly chipped at the edges; with a political system which was still a bureaucracy, tempered only by some concessions to the demand for representation of the immigrant communities. It ends with three sovereign states in which the leading roles were occupied by black men, with a society structured, in idea at least, on the non-racial principle, with a political system organized by universal suffrage. The question naturally poses itself: whether there were changes of corresponding magnitude outside the political sphere; and whether a causal relationship may be established between such changes and the political movement for which nationalism is the accepted shorthand. And, politics apart, in so far as history is the record of past human life, we naturally want to know what was happening to the African 98 per cent of the lives that were being lived in the region.

By the outbreak of the Second World War colonial East Africa had reached a kind of stability. To say this is not to subscribe to the myth that the middle period of colonial rule was one of total docility, and that the subsequent revolt was a product of the war and of the exposure of a new élite to European radical philosophy. But it is perhaps necessary to be even more wary of the opposite mythology, which projects the ideas and programmes of the 1950s far back into the past, accords the title of proto-nationalism to the specific protests and sporadic disturbances of the inter-war years, sees every neo-pagan cult not only as the anti-authority movement that it undoubtedly was but also as a primitive expression of the modernizing urge, and assumes a general and impassioned, though as yet imperfectly focused resentment of the British presence. That the African peoples never wholly acquiesced in the colonial situation can legitimately be inferred from the prevalence of myths such as those of the serpent which would one day arise to drive the strangers from the land. But probably more typical of the period were the obsequious rationalizations which told of a fault committed against God by the primal black man.

Independent tribal life was by now, for both good and evil, a fading memory of the old people. The great majority of living Africans had grown up into ways of life which were already acquiring the sanction of custom and normality, and into an ordered world which had all the appearance of permanence. There was, everyone knew, an entity called 'government', manifested in people with white (or rather, red) faces and peculiar manners, an entity which it was necessary to treat with caution but usually possible to propitiate. Government demanded taxes, in the form of counters called shillings, which could be acquired only by tedious exertion or by disposing of livestock which people would have much preferred to keep. It also bore heavily on those who behaved in some of the ways in which their fathers had behaved. One did not now, except in some of the remotest areas, go out on cattle raids. One did not immolate people on the death of chiefs, or cut off the hands of thieves, whom government preferred to keep confined for long periods like stall-fed cattle. It was considerably more dangerous than before to take a spear to one's neighbour in anger, for instead of the risk of being speared in one's turn by his kinsmen, who could usually be bought off, there was the probability of being put to death by government after a terrifying ritual. For the rest, government did not impinge very much on the lives of people. Above all, it seemed to be willing to leave the people with land to live on. Even for the Kikuyu, the only people (apart from the Masai) on whom land alienation had made a serious impact, this proposition still held good. For the amount of land actually available to the Kikuyu had greatly increased in the first quarter of the century, as they flowed into the Rift Valley and the Uasin Gishu to 'squat' on European estates. This tide had begun to turn before the end of the 1930s, but the full implications of its turning were not yet apparent.

There were also the new priests: the priests of Christ, who were white men and connected with government, though also separate from it in some way that to most people was not entirely clear; and the emissaries of Muhammad, who were usually black and not connected with government at all. These *dini* carried with them new rituals and taboos, of which those of Muhammad were on the whole less mysterious and exacting. Only the religion of Christ, however, offered people the chance to apprentice their sons to the white men and so to gain access to some part of the sources of their power. (That the strangers would not disclose *all* their secrets was obvious, and only a few had begun to resent this fact.) In many places the village school, with its football field and its throng of boys in neat shorts, was the most imposing edifice for miles around and the most evident symbol of the new order. In a few areas, notably in Buganda, not only had literacy become widespread, but the new religion had become the religion of the society; and here the weekly and yearly rituals provided a frame for social life in the same way and in the same degree as they had long done in Europe. Elsewhere, Christianity, like Islam, was still a minority cult, and on the whole a cult for the more opportunist members of African societies, though everywhere there were people for whom it provided a new insight into the human condition and a light to live by.

Then there were the new goods. Some of these were of genuine utility. Steel hoes and matchets from Sheffield or Charleroi were obviously more effective than tools made from local iron. If the culture already required people to be clad, cotton cloth was an obvious improvement on skins or barkcloth. Bicycles (but these were common only in parts of Uganda) had a value which no one could doubt. Motor lorries, apart from their strictly economic functions, improved the quality of life by enabling people to travel more and to keep in touch with distant relatives and friends. Many of the new consumer goods, however, were merely new means of purchasing esteem and wives, and as both these desirable things were available in fixed quantity, the real gain in well-being from the growth of trade and of money incomes was probably small. More important were the services, meagre though they still were, provided by government and by the missions. Education, however, was regarded by most people as a capital investment rather than as a good in itself; and the health services so far provided had hardly yet compensated the people for the biological disasters of the period from 1890 to 1920, when smallpox, sleeping sickness, and influenza had wrought unprecedented havoc, and venereal disease had made deep inroads into the vitality of the people.

To obtain the new goods, as well as to pay taxes, it was necessary to have shillings, which could, broadly speaking, be acquired in one of two ways: by clearing an additional half-acre or so of land, and planting it with certain kinds of food crop or with the new crops such as cotton and coffee for which the strangers had an apparently insatiable demand; or by going out to work for a month, for six months, or more under the orders of the government or of the other strangers who had set themselves up as chiefs in parts of the land. Now that flogging had become exceptional, the balance of advantage between these alternatives was a narrow one, varying from place to place. Except for those who were very favourably placed, with good coffee land (and permission to use it), the return for effort was probably somewhat higher in paid employment, which also offered a change of scene and a chance to see the world—advantages which were not less real for having been sometimes overstated. Against this, there was the humiliation of being ordered around and the tiresomeness of working for set hours. Neither method, of course, yielded anything that could be called wealth, but the meagreness of the reward was less resented than its variation over time, and its tendency to decline in money and even in real terms. The slump of the early 1930s had left a deep imprint on the public consciousness. Since the conquest, it was the most serious general blow to the people's confidence in the good faith of their overlords.

In more formal terms, the peoples of Africa had travelled some way along the road that leads from tribal society to peasant society or to proletarian status. Neither destination had been arrived at by more than a minute fraction of the population. In the villages, men spent more time in digging and less time in fighting, guarding, and conferring, but none were yet true peasants, confined to the function of primary production.[1] (Women, except for those who had found freedom, at a price, in the towns, did what they had always done.) Outside the villages, even those men who were most thoroughly integrated into the modern sectors of the economy—the Mombasa dockers, the long-service railwaymen, the domestic servants, the growing population of clerks—had rarely severed completely their social links with the village or abandoned the intention, and the right, to return to the family land. No one yet felt himself to be permanently dependent on what he could earn in the labour market. The East African territories thus occupied an anomalous position, for which the usual schemes of social typology do not provide a ready set of labels. They were caste societies, whose boundaries were only slightly blurred by the measure of respect accorded, in Uganda and to a lesser extent in Tanganyika, to the more senior African chiefs and clerics. Yet the African communities which formed the lowest stratum were nevertheless still whole societies, not fundamentally transformed by the superstructure which had been erected over them. They were exchange economies in which the vast majority of households still provided themselves with the necessities of life. In retrospect, it may already be easy to see that this was a transitional situation, which was bound to evolve in the directions in which it has evolved, but in the late 1930s this was far from being apparent. On the contrary, the pace of social change, very rapid in the first decades of colonial rule, had clearly slowed down in the past two decades, partly because of the unfavourable external economic conditions, but partly also for the fundamental reason that adjustment to the new economic environment created by the revolution in transport was more or less complete; and a kind of equilibrium seemed to have been reached, in which many elements of tribal life were combined with some elements of capitalism and, in Kenya, of feudalism as well.

It is also clear that very few Africans yet wished this equilibrium to be disturbed, for the situation which existed was preferable to any which they could realistically envisage. The system

---

[1] Cf. L. A. Fallers, 'Are African Cultivators to be called "Peasants"?' *Current Anthropology* 2 (1961) 108–10.

provided them with a material standard of living that was definitely though not dramatically superior to that of the past. It
secured them against warfare, and latterly against famine and
pestilence as well. And so long as they had land they were secure
also against the incalculable dangers of a full exchange economy
and against the loss of the way of life to which they were accustomed. They were, of course, a subject people and knew themselves to be so. But a caste system is subjectively intolerable only
when it has been called in question, and before 1929 there were
very few who had begun to question it in any fundamental way.
For the able and ambitious the posture of deference required by
the system was undoubtedly galling, but even they—especially
they—sought to enlarge their place within the system rather
than to overthrow it. For within the African caste the development of commerce and education, however modest in scale, had
given rise to a greater measure of social and economic differentiation than had been known in the pre-colonial period, and the
opportunities open to Africans for exercising power over their
fellow-men were more, not less, numerous than before; and
those who enjoyed or hoped to enjoy these opportunities, as
government-backed chiefs and headmen, as schoolmasters,
interpreters, agricultural assistants, did not yet look much
further.

Perhaps the greatest malaise that resulted from the loss of
independence was simply ennui. When the village and the chiefdom ceased to be self-defending units, much of the virtue went
out of them. Though most of the rituals which gave shape to the
lives of the people were still performed, there was a certain sense
of going through motions which had lost their meaning. What,
after all, was the point of initiating boys into the warrior grade
when it was known that they would never have to fight? What
was the fun of politicking over the selection of a chief whose
appointment would only be valid if the district commissioner
approved it, or of keeping up the elaborate ceremonial at the
court of a king who in the last resort must heed the governor's
advice? How convenient to be able to buy salt at the *duka* down
the road with the money one has made from the cotton plot, but
how much more exciting to go on a dry-season expedition to the
distant lake as one's fathers had done! Hence, of course, the
'apathy' of the people, which worried the administration much

more than their potential disaffection, and which was the system's greatest condemnation.

Even in the 1930s there were numerous signs that the equilibrium was not truly stable, but it was mainly members of the governing class who discerned them. It was they, not the people, who saw the threat to the security of the land implicit in the growth of population and the spread of cash crops. It was they who listened to the 'warning from the West Indies',[1] and who felt the stirrings not only of anxiety but of discontent. Was it enough to have preserved what was best in native institutions and to have protected their wards from sinking either into a shanty-town proletariat or into a debt-enslaved peasantry of Asian type? Tanganyika, its officials were saying in a self-critical inquest on twenty years of British rule conducted in 1939, might be a model of native administration, but was it not also a rural slum?[2] Even the complacency of Uganda was not immune to the reproach of the term 'happy valley';[3] administrative and educational reform was in the air here before the war. In Kenya, the most urbanized, the most locally overpopulated, and most obviously eroded of the territories, the signs of strain were more evident, and there were many in government who knew that the 'final' demarcation of the dual economy on the map was not the final solution either of the racial or of the economic problems.[4] Even without the war, East Africa would clearly have undergone a period of more rapid change, initiated from above.

The war delayed the onset of change but also made it in the end far more drastic than it would otherwise have been. For the people, the later years of the war and its immediate aftermath were profoundly disturbing. They had remained loyal, even

[1] The title of an influential book by W. M. Macmillan (London, 1936), in which the dangers of inadequate growth were stressed. Cf. W. K. Hancock, *Survey of British Commonwealth Affairs*, vol. ii, part 2 (London, 1942), p. 199.

[2] Tanganyika, *Report of the Central Development Committee*, (G. R. Sandford), (Dar es Salaam, Govt. Printer, 1940).

[3] Applied to it by a distinguished visitor from the Sudan, Sir Douglas Newbold, in 1944 and quoted from his biography, K. D. D. Henderson, *The Making of the Modern Sudan* (London, 1953), p. 380, in D. A. Low, *The Mind of Buganda* (London, 1971), p. xi.

[4] 'Finality' was the aim of the Kenya Land Commission headed by Sir Morris Carter in the 1930s. *Kenya Land Commission Report*, Cmd. 4556, (London, HMSO, 1934). For a critique of its assumptions see the *Report of the Royal Commission on East Africa, 1953–55*, Chairman Sir H. Dow, Cmd. 9475 (London, HMSO, 1955,) pp. 53–62.

actively loyal, to the imperial cause, but at the end they knew, or were half aware, that the permanence of the empire had been called in question, not only by its military reverses but also by the half-promises of eventual self-liquidation which it had felt obliged to make. And if this awareness stimulated hope, it also stimulated fear. If the king departed, who would take his place? Also, the period was one of serious economic retrogression. East Africa's terms of trade deteriorated even below the low levels of the 1930s,[1] and the real incomes of farmers and labourers declined with them. Thus between 1943 and 1950 there was growing and well-grounded economic resentment. At the same time the war had given a sharp stimulus to the growth of towns, which was taking place in highly unfavourable circumstances, with wholly inadequate funds for the concurrent formation of social overhead capital in the form of housing, sanitation, police, and education, and at a time of deepening though still largely unfocussed discontent. One of the most obvious phenomena of this period was the rapid increase in crime and violence which disturbed the citizens of Nairobi and other towns.

But the greatest source of disturbance in these years was undoubtedly London, which for a variety of reasons, including Britain's economic difficulties, the ideology of the Labour Party, and the need to establish economics which could support the costly superstructures of self-government, was now abruptly willing to sacrifice stability to progress, and was interested as it had never been before in the development of the region. The immediately visible consequence was that 'government' began to exert far more pressure than before on the lives of the people, who were lectured and legislated into doing a great many things which were all unfamiliar, mostly onerous, and rarely of any immediate benefit to themselves: to terrace or contour-bund their hillsides, to cultivate unwanted plots of cassava, to sell their produce at fixed prices, to observe grazing restrictions and sell off their 'surplus' male livestock. Worse, there were signs that government was preparing to tamper with the existing systems of land tenure, the pillar on which the previous equilibrium

---

[1] In 1946 the net barter terms of trade for Kenya, taking the average of the years 1935–8 as 100, had fallen to 62, while the figures for Tanganyika and Uganda were 90 and 79. Thereafter the terms began to improve, but it was not until 1949 that the pre-war levels were surpassed. (Calculations from data in the *Statistical Bulletins* published by the East Africa High Commission.)

rested, whether by the compulsory acquisition of *mailo* land in Buganda or by the schemes for individual consolidated holdings which the Kenya authorities were already mooting. Though few could know that some of their rulers had written off 'the ignorant man and his wife with a hoe' as a possible instrument of progress, many obscurely sensed that government was about to break the implied concordat of the middle colonial period: namely, that the people would acknowledge its authority, pay taxes to it and grow cash crops or go out to work for it, provided that in essential matters they were left alone. Already in the inter-war period much the most serious disturbance had been occasioned by the quarrel over female circumcision among the Kikuyu,[1] a practice which lay on the disputed borderland between that which cultural relativism must sanction and that which was repugnant to humanity. During the war much the greatest causes of disturbance among the Ganda had been the remarriage of the widowed queen-mother with the sanction of the Church, and the compulsory purchase of Makerere hill.[2] Later, a much-discussed grievance would be the construction of a railway line within sight of the Kabaka's palace. Yet by general consent the Kikuyu and the Ganda, in their very different ways, were among the most receptive of all East African peoples to the call of modernity. The attitude of more conservative peoples may be illustrated by the response of the elders of a Kenya pastoral tribe to the solicitude of the Royal Commission in 1953. 'We have three things to say, sir. One, thank you for coming to see us. Two, we do not want anything. Three, please go away and leave us alone.'[3] But the new self-confidence of the governing class and its growing impatience with African tradition made it certain that neither they nor anyone else would be left alone.

Even those who had responded with hope to the talk of self-government were more perturbed than encouraged by what was actually happening. Independence, after all, should mean the departure of the strangers, but the plain and obvious fact was that there were more of them around than ever before. Already in the war there had been the locally alarming influx of Italian

---

[1] See e.g. C. G. Rosberg and J. Nottingham, *The Myth of 'Mau Mau': nationalism in Kenya* (New York, 1966), pp. 105–25.

[2] See Low, *Mind of Buganda*, pp. 119–31, 145–6.

[3] Oral communication from a member of the Commission, 1953.

prisoners and Polish refugees.[1] Now there were the tractor-drivers and typists of the Tanganyika Groundnut Scheme and the polyglot construction-teams of the Uganda's Jinja dam—Europeans of a new kind, more human but worse-mannered.[2] Young English settlers arrived in Kenya by every boat, and with them came many who were not cast in the feudal mould: bank clerks and shop assistants and technicians, pressing closer than their predecessors on the ceiling of current African aspirations. There were more businessmen and schoolmasters and soon there would be the new breed of university lecturers. And there were far more officials, mostly of the unwelcome kind who interfered in the daily lives of the people much more than the district commissioner had ever done. And though it was said that most of the newcomers had been brought in for the people's benefit, it could hardly fail to be noted that many of them lived in much greater affluence than the old type of missionary or colonial official or struggling settler.

Again, self-government should surely mean the resumption of independence by those who had formerly enjoyed it. The authorities however did not speak now of Buganda or Kikuyu or Shambaa but of 'Uganda,' 'Kenya', and 'Tanganyika', which were names of local manifestations of the imperial power. To speak of independence for these entities seemed to be either a contradiction in terms or something more sinister, a device for depriving the people of the measure of independence and security which they had hitherto possessed.[3] And as though to confirm this inference it was made clear that the king's governors would indeed hand power to assemblies in which not less than half the votes would be held by the aliens who were known to the people as their landowners, employers, and trading partners. It is not surprising, therefore, that the prevalent emotion during the first part of our period should have been fear, not hope; or that the agents of progress in the colonial administrations should have found themselves confronted nearly everywhere, if not by active

---

[1] The refugees gave rise to a new and fierce divinity in Bunyoro, called *Mpolandi* or the 'spirit of Polishness'. See J. H. M. Beattie, 'Group Aspects of the Nyoro Spirit Mediumship Cult', *Rhodes–Livingstone Journal*, 30 (1961), 30.

[2] See chap. xi above.

[3] The rejection of 'Uganda' by the Ganda is discussed by D. A. Low in *Buganda in Modern History* (London, 1971), chaps. iv and vii. But their attitude was only the extreme case of fears which were general in the early 1950s.

hostility, by a wary distrust; or that the effective symbols of opposition to the ruling power should have been so often those which evoked the pre-colonial past—Mumbi the earth-mother of the Kikuyu, the spirits of grove and rock that were appealed to in the *Dini ya Misambwa*, the totemic clans of Buganda, and *Kibuuka*, its ancient hero-god.[1] In a time when all landmarks were shifting and the earth itself seemed no longer firm, it was natural to look for reassurance to the powers which had been strong before the strangers came. The intensity of fear varied, from the desperation that exploded in Kikuyuland in 1952 to the low-temperature unease which was a far more widespread condition. Small incidents revealed that most of the people half-believed, or quarter-believed, that their rulers intended to kill them, or more probably to deprive them of posterity, by poisoning their springs with insecticides or by lethal injections of their cattle, or by dosing the sugar which was marketed to the people under government controls. These fears and suspicions were probably not new; they arose in part from the inherent insecurity of a conquered people; but they had acquired a new edge of urgency from the real evidence that surrounded them of impending change, which was more likely to be for the worse than for the better.

Even if 'London' had not been actively impelling it, radical change would still have confronted East Africa, for reasons both external and internal, from causes which were truly novel and from others which had been silently at work for a generation or more. Perhaps the most obvious, as well as the most inexorable, of the disturbing forces was the growth of population; and one of the few assertions that can be made with real confidence about East Africans in our period is that there were many more of them at the end of it than there had been at the beginning. Two efficiently conducted sets of population censuses enable it to be said that, give or take a decimal or two, the region, excluding Zanzibar, contained 17·8 million Africans in 1948 and 24·8 million in 1962.[2] The analysts of the 1962 census in Kenya

---

[1] For Mumbi see Rosberg and Nottingham, *The myth of 'Mau Mau'*, p. 259. For the revival of the Kibuuka cult see F. B. Welbourn, 'Kibuka Goes Home', *Transition*, 5 (1962). Cf. the same author's *Religion and Politics in Uganda* (Nairobi, 1965), p. 42.

[2] For the 1948 census, see East African Statistical Department. *African Population of Kenya Colony and Protectorate; African Population of Tanganyika Territory;* and

reckoned from converging lines of evidence that the African population had been growing on average at the rate of 2·8 per cent per annum, probably rising to 3 per cent by the end of the period. Uganda produced a figure of 2·3 per cent per annum between 1948 and 1959, and Tanganyika, rather less assuredly, one of 1·8 per cent per annum between 1948 and 1957. All this, of course, is rapid growth, and Kenya's could hardly fail to be described as an explosion. Here is a phenomenon which is significant equally as an indicator of change in being, and as the motive force of change to come.

It would be pleasant to infer from the rapidly increasing numbers of the East Africans an equally spectacular improvement in their health and general well being, but the evidence would hardly support such an optimistic view. The health services did, of course, have much more money to spend than in previous decades, and they also had at their disposal many new and powerful weapons, especially from the armoury of chemotherapy. Variations in coverage and classification make it difficult to give a precise account of the expansion of medical services for Africans during the period, but it seems that the number of hospital beds available to them in Kenya rose from about 3,000 to more than 10,000 and that the advances made in the other territories were not much less.[1] Much more emphasis was placed on the development of the peripheral services, particularly on the training of the medical assistants and orderlies who ran the increasingly comprehensive network of dispensaries and aid posts. For most of the period something like 2 million cases were treated annually in each of the territories, and it may reasonably be said that medical attention of some sort was accessible to the bulk of the population. The profession was well aware, however, that its services were very thinly spread, and that it was still attacking little more than the outer fringes of the vast domain of African

African Population of the Uganda Protectorate (Nairobi, 1950). For the later censuses, see East African Statistical Department, Tanganyika Population Census 1957, General African Census (Nairobi, 1958); Uganda Population Census 1959, General African Census (Nairobi, 1960); and Kenya Government, Kenya Population Census, 1962, vol. iii (Nairobi, 1966). The total figure given in the text for 1962 includes rough projections for Tanganyika and Uganda. For a summary of population figures in 1948 and 1963 see Appendix 3, Table 1.

[1] Annual Reports of the Department/Ministry of Health for each territory; A. Beck, A History of the British Medical Administration of East Africa, 1900–1950 (Boston, 1970).

sickness. It knew too, in principle, that a shilling spent on prevention was worth more than a pound spent on cure. This was
a position which it was hard to maintain in face of the pressures
of popular demand; for the people's earlier scepticism had been
replaced by exaggerated faith in the potency of European
medicine, and they were hard to convince that an injection
might do them less good than a lecture on latrine construction.
Nevertheless, some headway was made on this front too, and by
1962 Kenya had over 100 rural health centres which earned the
special commendation of the World Health Organization.[1]

The enemy, as ever, was protean. During the 1950s DDT
virtually eradicated the *simulium* fly and with it the disease
onchocerchiasis, a major source of blindness, stunted growth,
and sterility in all the riverine lands. But against that, malaria
became endemic in some of the highland areas which had
hitherto been almost free from it. Victory over yaws and marked
success in the struggle against venereal disease were partly offset
by stalemate at best in the conflict with tuberculosis and by the
advent of new killers such as tetanus (apparently a consequence
of intensive cultivation) and sandfly fever. All the same, the
proportion of hospital deaths that were attributable to 'infectious
and parasitic diseases' was reduced from about one-third of the
total in the early 1950s to little more than one-fifth a decade
later; and so far as it goes this is evidence of real advance toward
the elimination of the more readily avoidable causes of mortality—as, in its perverse way, is the threefold rise in the number of
people dying in hospital from cancer.

But the medical and sanitary advances achieved during our
period were hardly sufficient in themselves to explain the
dramatic expansion of the population. Nor can this plausibly
be attributed to the current improvement, real though it was,
in general living standards, for there were few radical changes
in the mode of daily living that could have had much effect on
health. The coffee boom of the early 1950s found the cottages of
rural Buganda mostly thatched and left them mostly roofed
with metal, thus reducing the scope for vermin as well as the
risk of death by fire. Cash-crop farmers and others whose money
incomes rose at this time gave high priority to the consumption
of meat and fish and so obtained the balanced diet that in the

[1] Kenya, Annual Report of the Ministry of Health for 1962.

days of subsistence economy had often eluded them. But these were marginal gains. There is little reason to think that the normal diet of most East African peoples in the 1950s was significantly better (or worse) than it had been twenty or a hundred years before. The most important material change in the colonial period was probably the substitution of washable cloth for garments of skin or bark, and that had been substantially completed well before the Second World War.

Tentative though they are, the statistics of mortality suggest that improvement during our period was useful rather than revolutionary. The censuses taken towards the end of it indicated an annual death rate of 20 per thousand or a little more and an average expectation of life of 40 years or a little less. The figures from the 1948 census suggest that the death rate in the immediately preceding years had been over rather than under 25 per thousand, but not much over. Even the later figures, of course, left East Africans far ahead of the people of developed countries in mortality, but even the earlier ones are much better than would be expected in countries untouched by modern improvements. So the really decisive break with the past would seem to have occurred at an earlier time.

The birthrate was very high and in Kenya exceedingly so: nearly 50 per thousand, in fact, compared with about 42 per thousand in Uganda and a little under 40 in Tanganyika. Possibly it had risen somewhat in recent years, for while the age of female marriage (18·4 years in Kenya in 1962) is unlikely to have fallen, the decline in polygyny (there were only 1·1 wives for each household head in Kenya) and the new opportunities open to young men to acquire wealth and to support a family at an early age may well have been conducive to increased fertility. But the change was probably not large enough to account for any significant part of the population explosion. It would be tempting but almost certainly erroneous to correlate the high fertility and rapid growth of Kenya with its status as the most modernized of the territories. For the lower rates registered in Uganda are entirely due to the notoriously low natural increase experienced by the peoples of the interlacustrine kingdoms. Buganda in particular, one of the most fertile and prosperous areas in East Africa or indeed in all Africa, showed a very moderate density of 114 to the square mile in 1959, despite the massive influx of war captives in the nineteenth and of immigrant labourers in the twentieth century. (Compare the 252 to the square mile of the Bukedi District, not to mention the 506 of the Central Nyanza district of Kenya.) The reason for this and other patches of low fertility (there was a similar one in the northern coastlands of Tanganyika) remain obscure—for venereal disease, even if it were established as the main proximate cause, would itself need explanation.[1] The ultimate causes presumably lie deep in the family structure, perhaps even in the political structure of the societies concerned. Conversely the very high densities and rapid growth rates characteristic of the Central and Nyanza Provinces of Kenya seem to reflect an acceleration of trends which were not of recent origin.

The fundamental cause of the explosive growth witnessed by the post-war censuses was clearly not to be sought in any drastic current change either in the true birthrate or in the true rate of 'normal' deaths. All historical experience would suggest that the initial upsurge of population was due to a sharp reduction in the number of abnormal or cataclysmic deaths, to a weakening of the malthusian triad: famine, pestilence, and war. And the demographic turning-point can be located with great precision to the years immediately after the First World War. Thereafter, the mortality from organized violence became and remained almost negligible. The famine of 1919 was reckoned to have cost as many as 150,000 lives in Kenya alone,[2] but it was the last such disaster; there would be severe shortages of food from time to time, as in 1943 and in 1953, but no true famine. And from almost the same point in time came the last of the real outbreaks of epidemic disease on the grand scale. The great killers, plague, smallpox, and sleeping sickness, smouldered on in the background and broke into fitful flame, but the health authorities had won that battle, to all intents and purposes, by the early 1920s, and by the beginning of our period deaths from these scourges had become no more than sporadic. The inference is

---

[1] See A. I. Richards and P. Reining, 'Report on Fertility Surveys in Buganda and Buhaya, 1952', in F. Lorimer (ed.) *Culture and Human Fertility* (Paris, 1954), pp. 353–403; D. F. Roberts and R. E. S. Tanner, 'A Demographic Study in an Area of Low Fertility in North-east Tanganyika,' *Population Studies*, 13 (1959), 61–80.

[2] F. Goldsmith, *John Ainsworth, Pioneer Kenya Administrator, 1864–1946* (London, 1955).

clear, that although health continued to improve slowly in the 1940s and 1950s the demographic upsurge of that time was mainly the cumulative result of processes which had had their beginning a generation earlier. The decisive decade was that of the 1920s, when epidemics and famines were first restrained and modern medicine first came within the reach of a large part of the people. Once these conditions have been established, it is well known that a people needs to be only very slightly above the barest subsistence level to multiply at a very rapid rate, and the large excess of births over deaths in East Africa at the close of the colonial period cannot, unfortunately, be taken as an index of any large increment of well-being.

This cautious conclusion should not cause it to be forgotten that the defeat of plague and famine was a mighty victory, and that even the lesser advances that were made afterwards in the war against the less spectacular agents of death and misery were abundantly worth the effort. It is fortunate that the doctors of the colonial era did their professional and human duty without regard for the sophisticated calculation which would insist that the peoples of the Third World must practise contraception before they can be allowed to survive. For not only was the great burden of suffering and grief lightened but the countries of East Africa were provided with what, from all historical precedent, would seem to be the most fundamental prior condition of economic growth: an expanding population. That this is not a sufficient condition of economic growth must, of course, be conceded; and the people undoubtedly sensed the truth of which their rulers were perhaps excessively aware: when men multiplied so fast it was not possible that other things should remain as they were. The point would soon be reached when there would not be land for all, to use as they were accustomed to use it. That point was slow to arrive, because East Africa undoubtedly began its modern economic history with a large reserve of usable land, which the disasters of the past had prevented the people from bringing into use, and an even larger reserve which could be made usable by relatively small investments in wells and fertilizers. The crisis was further deferred by the circumstances that the area of most rapid growth and most acute congestion lay on the edge of the main white colony. The distribution of this land to the thronging population of the

Kikuyu heartland might be no more than a palliative, but it was a palliative which was humanly bound to be applied before the more drastic remedies of structural change.

The nature of the impending crisis perhaps needs to be more closely defined. It was not the strictly malthusian apocalypse, for East Africa was a very long way from exhausting its capacity to produce food; the techniques for increasing output were known and available; and the economic mechanisms, though clumsy, were sufficient to ensure that the techniques would be used when they were really called for. The problem was rather that the necessary agricultural changes required units of control which were larger than the traditional ones. How much larger, was a subject of intense debate throughout the period. The initial presumption in favour of very big units (of which the Groundnut Scheme was the grotesque extreme) tended to give way to more modest schemes of reform, featuring the 'yeoman farm' and the smallholding. But even the smallholding, as the agronomists conceived it, would be at least twice as large as the area at the disposal of a nuclear household in most of the traditional systems. Moreover, the new methods of farming, though primarily intended to economize land, tended to economize labour as well. Thus the population would be fed by the labour of a part of it, and in default of massive industrial development the other part would become surplus to requirements. This process was just beginning to get under way in the final colonial years. On the confines of Nairobi in particular and to a lesser extent of the other main towns there was emerging that peculiar feature of developing countries, the marginal population, neither rural nor industrial, which lives, literally and structurally, on the fringes of society.[1] These populations do not starve; in East Africa they do not even go particularly ill-fed. One way or another, the productive sectors of the economy contrive to sustain them, and their perplexity is not the lack of food but the lack of a secure role. The full emergence of this problem lies beyond our period, but already in the 1950s in Kenya, though hardly yet in the other territories, it was plain to see that the nature of the economic system was undergoing a fundamental change; no longer 'labour shortage' but 'unem-

[1] The first comprehensive account of this population is in an unpublished study by the Rev. A. Hake.

ployment' would be the dominant theme of debate and anxious prescription.

Second only to the growth of numbers as a disturbing force was the growth of knowledge, and indeed the expansion of education after the Second World War does almost deserve to be described as a revolution. Before the war the numbers of children enrolled in schools was already quite impressive, but the great majority were in 'bush' schools or would drop out after the first or the second year, having acquired nothing more than a hazy acquaintance with Christianity. Literacy, in any meaningful sense, was achieved only by a minority, and education beyond the primary school was the privilege of a few—outside Uganda, a very rare privilege indeed. By the time of independence, Kenya was approaching universal education for boys, though not yet for girls: Uganda was not far behind, and even Tanganyika was giving at least a bare literacy to about 40 per cent of the male age group. In the next generation, it was clear that the ability to read and write would be the East African norm and no longer the exception.[1]

The growth of mass education, if it did not exactly go against the grain of administrative inclination, was nevertheless viewed with some official misgiving. A common European view in the 1940s, in Kenya especially, was that the primary schools (and not only the much-distrusted 'Independent' ones) 'inculcated wholly wrong attitudes,'[2] particularly towards the land, and moreover that their products were of virtually no economic value. Six years' schooling, mostly in a foreign language, naturally did not equip boys for clerical employment, and there were few other evident uses for their rudimentary literary skills. Later, such reservations would be echoed by commentators who were less conservative by temperament and interest, and in the 1960s it would become the conventional wisdom, throughout Africa, that the expansion of education, particularly at the primary level, had been greatly excessive in the last colonial decade, not only

[1] According to D. Berg-Schlosser, 'minimal literacy' in 1962 had already reached 51 per cent among the Kikuyu and was above 30 per cent for most of the other main tribes. *The Distribution of Income and Education in Kenya* (Munich, 1970), p. 40.

[2] The opinion of most district commissioners, as reported by the Committee headed by Archdeacon Beecher in 1949. *African Education in Kenya* (Nairobi, Govt. Printer, 1949).

because it absorbed a disproportionate share of the nations' resources but because it aroused expectations which the economy would be unable to fulfil.[1] It is undeniable that the popular hunger of education in the 1950s was partly the outcome of a misconception, which attributed intrinsic value to an asset whose yield was high only because it was scarce. Yet here again the instinct of the people, and that of their rulers, was basically sound. Knowledge, like health, could not be an undesirable thing and could not be withheld, nor, in the long run, could an illiterate people hope for any other kind of 'development'. Moreover, East African experience went far to contradict the dogma which asserted that a few years' exposure to the art of writing necessarily rendered people unfit for village life. The main reason no doubt was that for most of this period agriculture was a genuinely rewarding activity, and particularly so in the most educated areas. At the height of the coffee boom it was not only normal for the recent graduates of primary schools to be plying the hoe with apparent contentment, but there was also a significant reflux of more highly educated men from skilled employment in what is sometimes arbitrarily called the 'modern sector' of the economy. The balance of economic advantage, given the much higher urban cost of living, was often heavily in favour of the countryside; and the ghettos of Nairobi, the slum quarters of Kampala and Dar es Salaam, had little non-pecuniary allure. The urban unemployment that began to cast a shadow over Kenya in the 1950s was, it seems, a genuine economic phenomenon and not, as in some other parts of Africa, a by-product of educational expansion. The youths who were trying to pick up a living on the fringes of Nairobi were doing so not because they had refused to live on the land but because the land could not sustain them.

Nevertheless there were sound reasons for the official view that secondary and technical education would be more productive than the wider spreading of a veneer of literacy over the villages of East Africa, and that the right answer to the incompetence of the primary school leavers was to give as many as possible of them more education, not less. Despite the pressures of popular demand, which forced more funds into village schools than the

[1] See especially G. Hunter, *Manpower, Employment and Education in the Rural Economy of Tanzania* (Paris, 1966: UNESCO African Research Monographs No. 9).

governments would really have chosen to allot, the growth of secondary education was even more rapid. In 1945 there was only one school in Tanganyika that took boys to School Certificate level and there were less than a thousand children in the entire secondary system. Kenya Africans were then not much better off, and only in Uganda, where the ceiling of the African compartment of society had always been higher, could secondary education really be called a going concern. Here there were in 1945 some 4,000 children in the post-primary classes and nearly 100 in the twelfth, or 'Cambridge' year of schooling. By 1960 there were almost 1,000 Ugandans in the twelfth class (which was no longer the final one) but Kenya had caught up, and even Tanganyika, with over 400 such students, was rapidly gaining ground.[1] By this time, of course, the grammar school had ceased to be a frontier zone, and a growing army of young East Africans was pressing on into the new territories of higher education that lay beyond it.

Education being a long-term investment, all this development could have little effect on the adult life of East Africa before independence, and leadership in our period had still to come from the small number of Africans who had acquired the keys of modern learning before the war. It is arguable, moreover, that in this field too the changes of the 1940s and 1950s were the working out of decisions which had been taken some time before. J. W. Tyler is surely right to insist that the truly epoch-making event in the colonial history of East Africa occurred in 1935, when six young Ugandans sat (five of them successfully) for the Cambridge Overseas School Certificate.[2] For, once even a handful of Africans had secured a qualification of extra-colonial validity, the education of their fellows could not be confined to the narrowly utilitarian ends to which many members of the ruling class had wished to confine it. With 'Cambridge', Africans were free to enter universities and professions,

---

[1] Annual Report of the Department/Ministry of Education in each territory. The most significant quantitative index is perhaps the number of African passes in the Cambridge Overseas School Certificate. In 1946 and 1947 these averaged 72 for the whole region, almost equally divided between Kenya and Uganda. In 1960 and 1961 they averaged 1,935 (Kenya 800, Uganda 715, Tanganyika 420.) See G. Hunter, *Education for a Developing Region* (London, 1963), p. 11.

[2] J. W. Tyler, 'Education and National Identity', in P. H. Gulliver (ed.) *Tradition and Transition in East Africa* (London, 1907), p. 171.

and could not therefore be made to acquiesce for ever in sub-ordinate roles. For some time yet the attempt would be made to ration the more advanced kinds of education to precisely such types and numbers of student as the colonial social system could absorb without transformation, but after 1935 the attempt was necessarily vain in Uganda—and in this field as in others what held good for Uganda could not long be denied for any part of East Africa.

There is another landmark, however, which does fall within our period, and that is the point at which it became profitable to produce print for people to read. Despite the efforts of the East African Literature Bureau the number of books, other than of a strictly utilitarian kind, that were produced specifically for the African market remained very small, but a momentous development of the period was the emergence of the vernacular press. Newspapers were not a new thing, but the widely read and highly political journals that proliferated in the 1950s were the sign of the formation of a literate *class*, which could no longer be fed only with the ideas and information that the authorities of church and state wished it to receive. Print, more-over, was only one of the means by which the scale of African consciousness was being enlarged. The transistor revolution was only just beginning at the time of independence, but already radio and cinema were supplementing the written word as channels through which the world presented itself to communit-ies whose intellectual isolation had been perhaps their greatest disability. Still more important was the greater physical mobility of their members. Though there were Ganda in Mombasa and Kikuyu in Nairobi in the early 1900s, and though Kamba, Nyamwezi, and Yao had been travelling to the coast for a century before that, it cannot be doubted that by the 1950s the pro-portions of the African population who were living or had lived outside their native village and their tribal area were much greater than they had ever been before. They had observed the ways of Europeans at close quarters, and they had talked, or tried to talk, to Africans whose social customs, manners, and values were not their own. From this variegation of experience, this multiplication of human contacts, there came a liberating ferment, and from the countless personal odysseys of the period the villages were enriched by the new wisdom of those who had seen the cities of men. It is a commonplace that the intermingling of Africans from many areas made them aware, as never before, of common interests and a common identity as black men and members of a subject race, and to some extent also as citizens of a quasi-state. But the effects of contact were not only integrative; they were also divisive. Or rather, they disrupted other things besides the colonial system, and integrated other units besides the 'new nation'. For people now became aware, as never before, that there were Africans who did not speak the same language as themselves, and so, while in one sense meetings made for better understanding, they also produced a new consciousness of not being understood. For many, English provided a bridge, and in Tanganyika especially there was also Swahili; and travellers could often get along in the local tongue. But in the deeper sense communication was not established by these means. The nuances of understanding were lost, and the man who did not share the same mother tongue remained a foreigner.

Hence the phenomenon, which seemed so paradoxical, of urban tribalism, and more generally of the new vigour of allegiances which had been thought to be obsolescent. The paradox in fact arises from a verbal confusion: between 'tribal society', a qualitative term connoting small-scale, primitive techniques and conservative habits of thought; 'tribe' in the sense customary among British social anthropologists, denoting the maximal political groupings of pre-colonial Africa; and 'tribe' in the usage which has become conventional in the description of modern Africa, denoting a unit which is defined by the possession of a shared cultural inheritance, which is to say a common language. Failure to distinguish these meanings has often led to a serious misunderstanding of the nation-building process.[1] It is not only that Africans are confronted by the enormous problems of adjustment which may be summed up as the transition from village to state, from relations based on kinship, neighbourhood, or patronage, to the impersonal nexus of modern large-scale society, from particularistic to universalistic values. Simultaneously they have to attempt what highly

---

[1] The misunderstanding, which perhaps stems from C. Geertz, *Old Societies and New States* (New York, 1963), is not entirely avoided by Gulliver, *Tradition and Transition*, or by most of his contributors. A useful corrective is administered by A. I. Richards, *The Multi-cultural States of East Africa* (Montreal, 1970).

modernized peoples do not find easy, namely, to operate multi-lingual states. Occasionally, the boundaries of language unit and pre-colonial polity might coincide, as most notably in Buganda, so that 'tribalism' might appear to be a single instead of a double phenomenon. More often, the former was considerably larger, so that the transition from the old to the new form of 'tribalism' —that is, the emergence of language as the principal definition of identity—was, as was emphasized in the first chapter, part of the general enlargement of scale that we have seen to be the dominant mode of change in our period. The transition to the cultural 'tribe' was not yet as complete as it had become in some other parts of Africa. Historical criteria, for instance, preserved the separate identity of Nyoro, Toro, and Ankole, of Alur, Acholi, and Luo, of Nyamwezi, and Sukuma, even though the linguistic differences within these groupings were at most dialectal. But the consolidation of cultural units was proceeding rapidly, as was shown by the birth of completely new 'tribes' such as Luhya, Kalenjin, and Mijikenda, and the sharper edge given to hitherto somewhat nebulous concepts such as 'Chagga' or 'Kikuyu'; and the trend, to judge from experience elsewhere, was an inexorable one. Outside Africa, it has long been well known that the importance of cultural community (linguistic as in nineteenth-century Europe, or religious as in twentieth-century India or Ireland) increases with modernization, and for two main reasons: the growth of mobility heightens the awareness of cultural difference, and the growth of state activity makes it seem more vital to the citizen that the levers of power should be in the hands of those whom he can trust. It was entirely natural that new-comers to the African cities should foregather by preference with those who spoke their own language, even if, as members of a different clan or chiefdom, they would have been strangers or even enemies in the traditional context. For such people were predictable, and thus reliable, in a way that others were not. And the new feeling of identity generated in the 'modern' areas was transmitted back to the villages, where it led to the revival or reinvigoration of those 'tribal' institutions, such as kingship or circumcision rites, that could serve to reinforce the sense of cultural unity.[1] Thus the old tribalism interacted with the new,

[1] See especially J. S. La Fontaine, 'Tribalism among the Gisu', in Gulliver, *Tradition and Transition*, pp. 177–92.

in ways which helped to obscure the fundamental difference between these manifestations.

It is not to be supposed, of course, that people of different linguistic nationality were unable to live together in friendly neighbourhood, or that community of professional interest or of economic class might not be in some contexts more operative than community of culture.[1] But the linguistic divisions provided ready-dug lines of cleavage along which other conflicts, whatever their actual source, were likely to flow. Moreover the growing activity of the state was ensuring that all such conflicts would be politicized, as it became more and more important to ordinary people that the levers of social action should be in 'friendly' hands. At the same time, as was shown in the Introduction to this volume, the trend away from laissez-faire was accelerating the transformation of the territorial units, into which British East Africa had been accidentally divided, from mere administrative compartments into nascent states, a tendency which was in progress independently of the transfer of power to African politicians. In the early 1950s the Uganda government was withholding from the producers a large part of the proceeds from the sale of their coffee. The government of Tanganyika was not doing this to the same extent, and so a wide gap opened between the purchase prices of robusta coffee in the Masaka District of Uganda and the adjoining Bukoba District. Not surprisingly (though the Uganda officials seem to have been surprised as well as pained) lorries began to trundle nightly southwards from Masaka; and the Uganda authorities decided that, in order to protect their rightful revenue, the latitude 1° S. must become a real frontier, policed by day and by night.[2] Though a suggestion that this innocent border would, within twenty years, be the scene of military confrontations would have seemed a wild fantasy, there is a real sense in which 'Uganda' and 'Tanganyika' (or 'Tanzania') came into existence at that moment. The exigencies of the new forms of central economic management were creating countries which had not previously been thought of. As metaphysical entities, the territories hardly existed outside the minds of Europeans (especially civil servants,

[1] D. J. Parkin, 'Tribe as Fact and Fiction in an East African City', ibid., pp. 273–96.

[2] Uganda, Masaka District Office Files, 1951.

for whom they formed a strong corporate identity) until about half-way through our period—except perhaps when 'Kenya' confronted 'Uganda' on the football field. But the very fact that football matches were arranged on this basis indicated that the territories were being institutionalized and that new identities were being forged, with a sharp double edge. For almost all our period Luo were no more and no less foreign in Kampala than their cultural kinsmen the Acholi. At the end of it Acholi would no longer accept the status of aliens in the capital of Uganda but Luo would be aliens there in a sense that had never been thought of before. In celebrating the birth of new and larger allegiances, we must also mourn the miscarriage of the still greater one that had been prayed for by many in the 1950s: East Africa. Political fears during most of the colonial period, and in the last years economic disparities, stood in the way of forming a larger polity.

'Tribalism', as we have said, began in towns; and one of the most obvious changes was that by the time of independence many more Africans were living in towns than at the end of the war. Between the 1948 and the 1962 censuses the African population of Nairobi increased by about two and a half times and most of the main towns of East Africa had registered comparable increases, while some of the smaller centres had grown at an even faster rate.[1] The absolute dimensions of urbanism, however, remained small. In 1962 Africans living in towns were only 5·3 per cent of the population of Kenya; in Uganda, a little earlier, the figure was 2·3 per cent and in Tanganyika 3·2 per cent. The definition of a town is inevitably arbitrary to some extent, but these figures do not err on the side of restrictiveness, for they include agglomerations of as few as 2,000 people and allow a fairly generous reckoning of the outer boundaries of Nairobi and Kampala. In another sense, however, the figures are an understatement, for the number of people living in towns at the point of time selected for the census was of course much less than the number who had at one time lived there and whose life-styles and thought-patterns had been in some degree altered by the experience. Here again one must insist on the fluidity of East African society in the final colonial years. From one point of view the cities of East Africa were enclaves of an extremely novel and

[1] Population censuses. See note 4 above.

alien way of life. Except for the old Muslim trading centres on the coast and the capitals of one or two of the most powerful kings, the region had known nothing that could be called a town before the twentieth century. Moreover one of its most distinctive features was that its peoples, by long-established preference, did not live in villages even, but in networks of dispersed hamlets and homesteads. The stockaded settlements which had grown up in response to the greater nineteenth-century anarchy disintegrated as soon as the British peace permitted. But the new cities were not walled, nor were they 'extra-customary centres' like those created by the Belgians in the Congo. They merged almost imperceptibly into the countryside, so that between the full-blown townsman, living by wage-labour or commerce alone, and the genuine countryman, there was, spatially as well as functionally, a large intermediate zone occupied by market-gardeners, beer-brewers, thieves, and casual labourers as well as by clerks and traders whose wives could still grow part or most of their basic food. Even from the deep 'tribal' countryside, movement to the towns was unimpeded and frequent, and the reverse movement hardly less so. These transitions were perhaps easiest for the Ganda, whose culture had always been urbane, less so for such peoples as the Kikuyu or the Luo, who had no such tradition. But everywhere the institutional structures were such as to preclude the formation among Africans of a 'burgher' society clearly separate from the rural population.

There were, moreover, many sorts of town.[1] Nairobi by the late 1950s was well on the way to becoming an East African variety of international Neopolis, with a total population of nearly half a million and a growing complex of tall buildings in the new cosmopolitan manner, as well as extensive high-class suburbs and vast dismal compounds, surrounded for much of the decade by barbed-wire fences. Nairobi, of course, was a new

[1] The only comprehensive survey of East African urbanism seems to be A. W. Southall, 'The Growth of Urban Society' in S. Diamond and F. G. Burke, *The Transformation of East Africa* (New York, 1966), pp. 464–93. For particular studies see especially A. W. Southall and P. C. Gutkind, *Townsmen in the Making* (Kampala 1956: East African Studies No. 9); P. C. Gutkind, *The Royal Capital of Buganda* (The Hague, 1963); J. A. K. Leslie, *A Survey of Dar es Salaam* (London, 1963); R. and C. Sofer, *Jinja Transformed* (Kampala, 1955: East African Studies No. 4); and, more recently, David Parkin, *Neighbours and Nationals in an African City Ward* [Kampala] (London, 1969).

town in the fullest sense, created wholly by the colonial impetus, a town where everyone was almost equally a stranger. The port towns, Mombasa and Dar es Salaam, had a more complex structure and subtler social atmosphere, compounded of Arabia and India (and in Dar of pre-industrial Germany) as well as of Africa and the modern west. But the older forms of culture were rapidly giving way. Since 1939 the Mombasa docks had been the scene of the most open confrontation of capital and organized labour in all East Africa; and the tranquil grace that delighted the tourist in Zanzibar would soon be revealed as a dangerous illusion. Dotted along the coast were the many remnant ports which the railways had ignored and so destroyed, and these at least slept on—unless disturbed by tourism or the Groundnut Scheme—as markets for local fishermen and farmers. Kampala was a different blend again, in part a tropical parody of a quiet English county town, with its cathedral closes and its high school, now growing into a university; in larger part an Indian commercial centre; but still also the royal capital of Buganda. Here too the impact of modernity was felt by the time of independence, with new hotels and office blocks, and on the periphery the small factories and the neat little housing estates which had sprung up to meet the needs of the growing community of African clerks and artisans. But the three original components were neither overwhelmed by the new elements nor drawn into effective contact with one another. It was fifty miles away, at Jinja, with its new turbines, that the hopes and fears of revolutionary modernization had been concentrated in the early post-war years; but reality had fallen short of expectation. By 1962 there were some new factories at Jinja, and the town had grown fast, but the scale remained small.

So the great process of the making of townsmen had only just begun in East Africa at the end of our period. But at least it had begun. Before the Second World War practically all the Africans who were found in towns were regarded and regarded themselves as visitors. Twenty years later some had committed themselves economically and socially to urban life. Hardly any had severed their links with the rural community of their youth, but some had crossed the imperceptible frontier between temporary exile and effective residence. The land of their fathers was a place for a holiday, a dream of retirement, but home was in the city. This change was both reflected and accelerated by the crucial decision, taken by the authorities in principle by the mid-1950s, that a bachelor wage was no longer enough and that an urban worker's dwelling must be something better than a bivouac.[1] It remains true, none the less, that even in the early 1960s the population of East Africa was still overwhelmingly rural.

It was also still overwhelmingly self-employed. Even in Kenya in 1961 the total number of African registered male employees was only 433,000, less than 23 per cent of the total male population. In Uganda the corresponding figure was 220,000 and in Tanganyika it was 195,000.[2] Moreover, if any faith at all can be placed in the official statistics the movement towards formal employment in the previous decade had been far from spectacular. We have to conclude that no truly structural change had taken place in the East African economy in this period. In essentials, the pattern which had been established in the first quarter of the twentieth century still held good. Most Africans were still farmers and nearly all farmers still grew most of their own food, and also cultivated a small area of cash crops, from which they paid their tax and acquired a narrow range of consumer goods. There had always been individual Africans, most numerous in Kenya, who took themselves out of the agrarian system for longer or shorter periods to work for European employers or for the government, or who engaged in local trade or the practice of a craft. There had always been clerks and teachers, whose separation from the village economy was one step greater. By 1960 there were more such people, but not so many more as would amount to a basic change in the nature of the economic system, comparable with that which had occurred at the beginning of the century. East Africa still remained in an intermediate condition, neither tribal nor capitalist. Its cultivators were still not quite peasants, and its wage-earners were not quite proletarians.

Yet clearly there is a sense in which fundamental change did occur in these years in the social system. In the high colonial period East Africa was a caste society, based on the essentially

---

[1] *Report of the Committee on African Wages*, Chairman F. W. Carpenter (Nairobi, Govt. Printer, 1954).

[2] Annual Reports of the Ministry of Labour for each territory.

military distinction between officers and other ranks. The distinction itself reflected the traditional structure of British society, but with the crucial difference that the lines of class, being reinforced by colour, were transformed into lines of caste. Within the African caste the authorities confirmed differences of status where they already existed and created them where, as among the Kikuyu, they did not. But the superior status of chiefs and headmen remained that of NCOs only. (Sir Apolo Kagwa had fallen because he would not accept that even a subaltern could command deference from even the most senior and lavishly decorated of sergeant-majors.)[1] There were rare exceptions; their Highnesses the Sultan of Zanzibar and the Kabaka of Buganda were perhaps honorary officers. And the structure was complicated by the presence of Asians, who straddled the major social divide. But these were relatively minor flaws in the system. Leaving aside the NCOs, the African population was treated as an undifferentiated mass, the *watu*, 'the chaps'—still more revealingly referred to in the singular collective: the African, the Mkamba.

But after the Second World War there were many Europeans in East Africa whose claim to officer status was clearly somewhat hollow, and others who wished to make no such claim. Such people were a sign that the basic principle of colonial society had been rejected in the metropolitan country and so could hardly survive for long in Africa. By 1945 the authorities were committed in principle to its modification. Before the war the training of Assistant Medical Officers, Assistant Agricultural Officers, and so on was already in hand, but after it the vital word 'assistant' was quietly dropped. By 1953 the first graduates of Makerere were moving in ones and twos into the bungalows of the district stations. A year earlier the Tanganyika Education Department had noted with evident satisfaction the names of the first two Africans to return from Britain with the status of graduate teachers: Mr. Matthew Ramadhani and Mr. Julius Nyerere.[2] The official assumption of the time was that the intake would gradually increase and the new entrants would move up the ladder at the normal rate: in ten years' time, if he applied

---

[1] See D. A. Low and R. C. Pratt, *Buganda and British Overrule* (London 1960) pp. 213–19.

[2] Tanganyika, Annual Report of the Department of Education for 1952.

himself to his work, Mr. Nyerere would no doubt be eligible for the headship of a training college. In this way, by the gradual admission of Africans to the uppermost stratum it would be transformed from a caste into a class, and so the structure would be preserved in its essential form. In the event, as we know, the chariot of Africanization escaped from the control of the colonial drivers, and its career was much more headlong than they had intended. We have seen too how in the political sphere the various 'Whig' programmes for the controlled admission of Africans to a defined share of power were defeated, and how the composition of the governing class was not modified but almost totally transformed.[1] This change, however, was not paralleled in the economic sphere. Despite the large sums of money made by some individual African farmers and traders, despite the new role of African co-operatives in the processing and marketing of produce, despite the African names that began to appear on boards of directors, the upper ranks of industry and commerce were still filled almost exclusively by Europeans and Asians, and the controls were held by organizations based outside East Africa.

The penetration of Africans into the middle strata of the economy, however, proceeded rapidly and brought with it a far-reaching differentiation of the African mass. To begin with the great upsurge in commodity prices at the beginning of the 1950s yielded incomes hitherto unheard of to those farmers who could take full advantage of it. The opportunities, however, were distributed very unevenly in a geographical sense, the real gains being limited to the occupants of the islands of high fertility, and especially to those with coffee land and trees already planted. But even in the favoured areas not everyone was able to make the decisive advance away from the modified subsistence economy of the middle colonial period. In Buganda, for example, everything might seem to have fallen into the lap of the land-holding farmer. The land was good, the market beckoned, an external proletariat stood ready to be exploited, a wide gap opened between the average value of his product and its average cost. But to get more than half an acre of coffee into bearing, the farmer needed initiative and application, and just a little capital. These assets being unequally shared, very marked variations began to appear

[1] See chaps. i–iv above.

in the living standards of Ganda farmers, variations which supplemented and even cut across the old distinction between chief and peasant. Prosperous employing farmers moved on from bicycle to car; the uniform scattering of thatched roofs was varied by roofs of corrugated metal, and when these became common the brick-built house began to set a new standard of aspiration. At the other end of the scale there began to separate out a class of people, the sick, the feckless, the recent immigrants, who lived in more than traditional wretchedness.[1]

These differences were probably more pronounced in Buganda than anywhere else, and even in Buganda they were far from hardening into a system of clearly marked economic classes. But in all the more fertile and commercialized areas the entrepreneurial farmer, distinctly more prosperous and more professional than his fellow-villagers, was coming to the fore. In Kenya he was even institutionalized as a 'better farmer', one of the minority on whom the agronomists of the government decided to concentrate their help and guidance. For there was now a marked shift away from the old paternalism, which sought slowly to raise the level of efficiency and income of the general mass of African peasants, towards a new doctrine of the deliberate encouragement of African capitalism. One powerful stimulus in this direction was the growing awareness that demographic change, if nothing else, would soon make the old form of rural society untenable. Landlessness in the full sense of the term was a threat rather than an actuality, except in parts of Kenya, where the effects of exceptionally rapid population growth were aggravated by the racial demarcation of the land. But the Kikuyu Land Unit, where the subdivision of holdings was bringing many of them close to zero, and where latent legal distinctions between landholder and tenant were acquiring a harsh reality, was a portent which the rest of East Africa could not afford to ignore. That structural change was inevitable was generally accepted in governmental circles. That the weight of the administration should be used to assist and accelerate such change became orthodoxy in the early 1950s.[2] But there was no clear agreement

---

[1] Cf. C. C. Wrigley in L. A. Fallers (ed.), *The King's Men* (London, 1964), p. 53.
[2] On these matters see M. P. K. Sorrenson, *Land Reform in the Kikuyu Country* (Nairobi, 1967) and H. Ruthenberg, *African Agricultural Production Development Policy in Kenya, 1952–65* (Berlin, 1966).

on the pattern of society that was either desirable or likely to take shape. A socialist pattern was not excluded, and indeed the idea that co-operative organization might make it possible to secure the benefits of large-scale and of technical modernization without sacrificing the fraternity of traditional village society attracted British administrators long before it was translated into Swahili as *ujamaa*, though little was done to give it practical effect. Even within a broadly capitalist framework several very different possibilities were open. There might develop a small minority of fully modernized and highly capitalized farmers, coexisting with a mass of poor peasants whose destiny would be to become a proletariat. There was the 'yeoman' solution, clearly favoured by many in the Kenya administration, whereby a more broadly-based minority of more modestly prosperous farmers would disengage itself, more definitely than at present, from the peasant mass. Or there was the solution, adopted in post-revolutionary France, which would cleave rural society more or less down the middle, allowing half or rather more of the cultivators to establish themselves as land-holding peasants while the unfortunate remainder drifted into proletarian status. The choice would depend partly on technical factors, such as the pace of mechanization and the size and cost of the machinery that would prove best fitted for local conditions, and partly on political development, adult suffrage being naturally an impediment to any very inegalitarian distribution of the land. But in our period the changes were incipient only and the future by no means foreclosed, even in Kenya, where the pressures were greatest and where internal cleavages between landed and landless Africans had already added the dimension of class conflict to a colonial uprising.[1]

Nevertheless the rudiments of an agrarian bourgeoisie were discernible in many areas by the time of independence. Meanwhile Africans were painfully feeling their way into the commercial sector of the economy and just beginning to form a bourgeoisie *stricto sensu*. Perhaps it would be truer to say that they were re-entering the commercial sector, for there is little doubt that the restrictive policies adopted by the governments on

---

[1] For a recent discussion of these issues, see Colin Leys, 'Politics in Kenya: the development of peasant society', *British J. Political Science*, 1 (1971), 307–37.

produce marketing in the 1930s,[1] together with the economic depression and the Asian ascendancy, had reduced the relative share of the trade and industry of the region that had been in African hands in the early colonial period. After the war, the scales were tilted back towards the African entrepreneur, though, as the boycott of Asian shops was to show in Uganda, not as far as he himself would have liked. The various measures taken to provide Africans with commercial education, the transfer of cotton ginneries to African cooperatives on easy terms, above all perhaps the restriction of non-African business to gazetted townships, all helped to break down what had been almost a *de facto* caste barrier; but more important were the general economic expansion of the period, the inflationary bias that made profit-making easy and the growing self-assurance of large numbers of young Africans. The results were not immediately impressive. By the early 1960s there were in the four main towns a very small number of African businessmen properly so-called, whose operations were comparable with those of a middle-rank Asian merchant. Between these people and the villagers who opened a kiosk for a few hours in the middle of the day for the sale of soap and cigarettes there were a growing number of small shopkeepers and artisans in the fringes of the cities, in the still predominantly Asian trading centres and in the even smaller clusters that were springing up at cross-roads in the depths of the countryside. Here, it may be noted, was a change in the spatial configuration of society that was in its way hardly less important than the expansion of the towns. Most of the East African tribal areas were remarkable to English eyes for the absence of clustered villages. The exigencies of traditional agriculture required, or at any rate permitted, life to be lived in hamlets or in an apparently random scatter of individual homesteads. The result was a society without nodes, for the district headquarters and mission stations and trading centres were alien enclaves which stood outside the African society that they served. Now there were little knots of shops and beer-gardens which were potential foci for new kinds of social interaction. Certainly they were reputed nests of sedition through which the administrative chief drove hurriedly for fear of insult.

[1] See C. Ehrlich, 'The Uganda Economy, 1903–1945', in vol. ii of this *History*.

Besides commercial agriculture and trade the main forces making for social diversity were the related ones of education and bureaucratic expansion. Unlike the farmer or even the trader the clerk was a new kind of man, using a skill which had no parallel in the traditional economy. He had to live in or near a town; during working hours he had to talk and think mainly in English; he was likely to be in closer contact with Europeans than most Africans were and to model his life-style to some extent on theirs. And now above the clerks there was forming the new African professional class: the entrants to the upper ranks of the civil service, a handful of lawyers and doctors, the most highly qualified schoolmasters, the new breed of journalists. In all, a group so small that in each territory most of its members were personally known to one another. Here, of course, is that much discussed phenomenon, the African élite. The word is unsatisfactory, but there is no real substitute. The people concerned certainly did not constitute a class, for they had no common economic base and no common and distinctive interest, except for the destruction of the racial privileges from which they alone directly suffered. And yet they did constitute an observable entity, marked out from the rest of society by their fuller mastery of the discourse of the governing class. The division was sharper in Kenya than elsewhere because the difficulties placed in their path had been greater; the Africans who were admitted to liberal drawing rooms in the 1950s were indeed a select group. But even in Kenya their separateness must not be exaggerated, and in the other territories there was an even clearer continuum linking them to the main more or less unmodernized masses. The most modern member of the new élite differed only slightly in education, life-style, or function from the more senior of the administrative 'chiefs'; and there were many other linking groups, such as the clerks and the many gradations of school-teacher, who shared some of the *mores* and the aspirations of the graduate professionals. Much of the fascination of East African society in this period, in fact, lies in its fluidity, in the absence of clearly defined classes, in the sense that all options lay open, and that the structure of social relations could still be moulded in many different ways.

In this chapter it has seemed proper to insist that no fundamental change in society accompanied the transformation of the political system. It is to be hoped, however, that we have not lost sight of the powerful forces that, even before independence, were loosening and modifying the rigid fabric of colonial society, making it more various, more flexible, more capable of change. And since we stressed that the period began in fear, we must not omit to say that it continued in hope. In 1950 the economic tide turned. In the next few years most people became somewhat better off and a number of people, including some Africans, became dramatically better off. At the same time there was suddenly much more money to spend on public services. The arid prose of departmental reports hardly conceals the exhilaration of officials who saw that the long years of fiddling with shoestrings were over and that things could at last really be done; and something of this delight communicated itself to the people, who for all their deeply-rooted suspicions, could not fail to see the changes of a kind that they did passionately want—schools and roads and dispensaries—were beginning to appear. The experience of progress bred a belief in its possibility, and many began to look forward rather than back. In the economic sphere the momentum of progress was not in fact sustained, and by the end of the decade the chill voices of Economy Committees were to be heard in the land once more. But by then the pace of political change had quickened, and it was borne in upon the people that their rulers really were about to depart.

And it was the political change, after all, that mattered. To the old rebel Warui, in James Ngugi's tale, the Independence Day celebrations might seem a sad anticlimax, like warm water in the mouth of a thirsty man.[1] Besides the inevitable disillusion that accompanies any triumph that has been wished for too eagerly and too long, we may perhaps read into his mood the knowledge that small, poverty-stricken states faced an uncertain future in a cold world, that the spoils of victory were being very unequally divided, that almost everything was still to do. But it would have been right to say to him, 'One thing at a time'; and the young could surely be permitted at least a moment of exuberance as the sheltering but constricting framework of colonial rule was dismantled. About this time a cheerful band of TANU youths congregated in a little hotel on the slopes of

---

[1] J. Ngugi, *A Grain of Wheat* (London, 1967), p. 273.

Kilimanjaro, having come down from the summit of the mountain, where no African had climbed before except as a servant. Duly refreshed, they gave three cheers for the Irish woman who kept the hotel, and went singing down the hill.[1]

---

[1] Desmond Brice-Bennett, personal communication.

APPENDIX 1

THE EAST AFRICA ROYAL COMMISSION
1953-1955

HUGH MACMILLAN

The report of the East Africa Royal Commission, published in 1955, is a document unique in the history of British colonial administration in Africa. Unlike most government commissions, it was not appointed to give answers to specific political questions, although rising tensions in Kenya gave to its initial appointment some political significance. And although chiefly prompted by economic conditions in Kenya, its survey and recommendations covered all three of the mainland British territories, and it therefore does not easily fit into the territorial chapters in this volume. Yet it does have a real significance in the history of metropolitan thinking on colonial development in general, and on East African development in particular.

Sir Philip Mitchell, governor of Kenya from 1944 to 1952, was primarily responsible for the timing and terms of reference of the commission, which was originally intended to enquire into matters concerning land and population in East Africa. Although Mitchell stressed that East Africa was an economic region which should be treated as a whole, and that in his request for a Royal Commission he had the support of the governors of Tanganyika and Uganda, it is clear that he was mainly concerned with the problems of Kenya.[1] Mitchell had a long-standing interest in agricultural questions, and inherited a concern over Kenya's apparently imperilled national resources which had been voiced as early as the 1930s. He was alarmed by reports that indicated that the population was increasing at an annual rate of over 2 per cent in areas which were already overstocked and over-cultivated.[2] He was particularly concerned with the problems of development in a multi-racial society. He was already familiar with the multi-racial states of New Zealand and Fiji, and he

---

[1] *Land and Population in East Africa, Exchange of Correspondence between the Secretary of State for the Colonies and the Governor of Kenya on the Appointment of the Royal Commission*, Col. No. 290 (London, HMSO, 1952). Mitchell's despatch of 16 Nov. 1951, p. 24.

[2] N. Humphrey, *The Kikuyu Lands: the relation of population to the land in South Nyeri* (Nairobi, Govt. Printer, 1945); *The Liguru and the Land: sociological aspects of some agricultural problems of North Kavirondo* (Nairobi, 1947).

was acutely conscious of the lessons which could be learned from the history of African reserves in South Africa. In a series of despatches, and in a pamphlet, *The Agrarian Problem in Kenya*, published in 1947, he examined the land situation, and possible remedies.[1] He was, of course, acutely aware of the amount of emotional capital that the European settlers had invested in the White Highlands, and of the degree of bitterness felt by the Kikuyu in particular at what they regarded as the theft of their land. He believed however that the handing over of areas under European ownership to the African population, without bringing about any improvement in land use, would not solve the problem of overcrowding, but would merely extend the area available for erosion following over-cultivation and overstocking.[2]

Mitchell argued that East Africa was undergoing 'an agrarian, social, and economic revolution' and that this process should not be allowed to pass 'unregulated and undirected', as it had been in Great Britain.[3] It was essential to hasten the transformation from subsistence to 'economic' agriculture, to allow for changes in the system of land tenure which would facilitate this, while at the same time making provision for the stabilization in towns of the population which would be forced off the land as an inevitable consequence of more efficient land use. He did not expect that a Royal Commission would be able to produce 'cut-and-dried recommendations which will immediately solve the complex and recalcitrant problems' which confronted the region, but he did hope that it would not only 'point the way to the solution of our problems, but bring a clearer understanding of these to those who at present advocate facile solutions divorced from reality'.[4] In other words he hoped that the commission would support his own analysis of the situation, and would dismiss as irrelevant any suggestion that the whole, or part, of the White Highlands should be handed over for African settlement. He also hoped that the commission's report would help to educate the critics of Kenya's policies in Britain and Africa and, by making clear the magnitude of the development work to be done in East Africa, encourage the supply of funds from the British government.

Oliver Lyttelton, the Colonial Secretary, informed Mitchell of the decision to appoint a Royal Commission in July 1952, but the decision was not made public until October of that year, and the

---

[1] *General Aspects of the Agrarian Situation in Kenya*, Despatch No. 44, 17 Apr. 1946 (Nairobi, Govt. Printer, 1946); *The Agrarian Problem in Kenya* (Nairobi, 1947). See also *Report of the Kenya Land Commission*, Cmd. 4556 (London, HMSO, 1934).

[2] *Land and Population in East Africa*, pp. 1–8.

[3] Ibid., p. 20.

[4] Ibid., p. 23.

Royal Warrant was not sealed until January 1953.[1] Since the writing of Mitchell's despatch in November 1951, there had been several developments which served to highlight the problems with which the commission had to deal. Most important of these was the declaration of a state of emergency in Kenya in October 1952. The latter occurred within days of the arrival of Mitchell's successor, Sir Evelyn Baring.[2] There was by this time moreover a renewed fear throughout East Africa about land expropriation, following the determination of the new Conservative government to go ahead with the Central African Federation in spite of vociferous protests from the people of Northern Rhodesia and Nyasaland.

The chairman appointed for the commission was Sir Hugh Dow, who had wide administrative experience in India, and had more recently been concerned with Israeli–Arab relations in Jerusalem. Of the other members the two most influential were Professor S. H. Frankel, Professor of Colonial Economics at Oxford University, who had special interests in investment, mining, and transport; and Arthur Gaitskell, manager of the Gezira scheme in the Sudan from 1950–2, and an expert on agriculture and irrigation. Besides these there were R. S. K. Hudson, a member of the Northern Rhodesian civil service and an authority on administration; the economist Daniel Jack, an expert on industrial relations with African experience; Chief Kidaha Makwaia, a member of the Tanganyika Legislative Assembly, from Sukumuland; Sir Frederick Seaford, chairman of Booker Brothers' McConnell Ltd.; and Frank Sykes, an agriculturalist and farmer with interests in sisal estates in Tanganyika.[3] Audrey Richards, the social anthropologist, was invited to be a member of the commission but declined. It is significant that only one of the members, Professor Frankel, had made any notable contribution to the study of colonial development economics as such. The era of the development economist was yet to come.

The commission's terms of reference followed closely on those recommended by Sir Philip Mitchell. They were instructed

to examine measures necessary to be taken to achieve an improved standard of living, including the introduction of capital to enable peasant farming to develop and expand production; and (to) frame recommendations thereon with particular reference to

　　1) the economic development of the land already in occupation by introduction of better farming methods;

---

[1] *Land and Population in East Africa*, p. 31; *East Africa Royal Commission, 1953–1955, Report*, Cmd. 9475 (London, HMSO, 1955), p. ix.
[2] See chap. ii above.
[3] *East Africa Royal Commission Report*, pp. ix–x; *Who's Who* (London, 1952, 1960).

2) the adaptations or modifications in traditional tribal systems of tenure necessary for the full development of the land;

3) the opening for cultivation and settlement of land at present not fully used;

4) the development and siting of industrial activities;

5) conditions of employment in industry, commerce, mining and plantation agriculture with special reference to social conditions and the growth of large urban populations;

6) the social problems which arise from the growth of permanent urban and industrial populations.

They were also to enquire into matters concerning health and education where these were relevant, and to consider 'probable trends of population in East Africa and make such recommendations as they consider appropriate on this subject in relation to the other problems involved'.[1] The commission was initially referred to under the title of 'Land and Population', but the final report was published simply as the *East Africa Commission 1953–1955 Report*.

The terms of reference, though very general, were clear except on one crucially important point. The commission was enjoined

to take account of existing obligations incurred by treaty, agreement or formal declaration of policy in relation to the security of land reserved for different races and groups in various parts of the Territories concerned.[2]

Mitchell had definitely intended that the land settlement should be regarded as sacrosanct, and that the commission should not be in a position to question the existence of the White Highlands reserve.[3] It must therefore be surmised that the drafting of this clause was deliberately obscure, and reflected radically opposing views on the functions of the commission. The Kenya African Union, for instance, had demanded in their manifesto of October 1952 'that the terms of reference of the Royal Commission be widened to include a survey of all lands in Kenya.'[4] The European Kenya Electors' Union, on the other hand, attempted to use this clause to preclude any consideration of the possibility of change in the land settlement which had followed the Morris Carter Commission of 1932.[5] The members of the

---

[1] *East Africa Commission Report*, p. xi.

[2] Ibid.

[3] Sir Philip Mitchell, 'An East African Enquiry', articles in *The Times*, London, 24 and 25 Sept. 1952.

[4] Copy in Creech Jones papers, Rhodes House, Oxford, MSS Brit. Emp., s. 332/21/3.

[5] M. Blundell to Sir H. Dow, 11 Mar. 1953, and Dow to Blundell, 31 Mar. 1953. European Elected Members' Organisation papers, Rhodes House, Oxford, MSS Afr. s. 596/123/1.

commission tended towards the former interpretation, and emphasized that many of those who had given evidence would have regarded
their work as useless if they had not examined land questions bearing
in mind 'the negative aspect of these reservations, which in some
instances has kept land for the future use of those who do not at
present need it, as against others who feel circumscribed and
clamorous for new outlets'.[1]

Owing to the wide-ranging nature of their enquiry the commission
relied very largely on research that was done for them by the relevant
territorial departments, and it is in this sense among others that the
survey became in part a retrospective commentary on the years of the
territorial development plans that had preceded it. They made two
visits to East Africa between February 1953 and February 1954,
staying for about three months in Kenya, and dividing the rest of
their time equally between Uganda and Tanganyika. Zanzibar was
not included in the scope of their enquiry. They considered over a
thousand items of evidence, both oral and submitted memoranda,
from individuals, associations, and groups. Their report was not
finally published until June 1955.

As a background to their assessment of the situation in East Africa,
and their recommendations for the solution of the problems that they
diagnosed, it seems necessary to give some indication of the underlying assumptions of the report, some of which reflected their terms
of reference, and some the collective philosophy of the members of
the commission. In the first place they were certain that East Africa
should be treated as a whole, and that any solutions proposed should
be applicable in all three territories. They carefully refrained from
using the then very emotive word 'federation', but underlying the
report there was a strong feeling that the barriers between the
territories should be broken down, that rivalries retarded development, and that closer co-operation, possibly even 'closer union', was
desirable. Secondly there was an assumption that 'development'
could best be measured in terms of an increase in the gross domestic
product, or income. They stated that their 'whole approach to the
question of the future economic development of East Africa is
governed by the assumption that the African population . . . will
respond to new opportunities to acquire income. . . .'[2] Thirdly, they
were unanimous that development must consist primarily in the
transition from a subsistence to a modern exchange economy, the
prerequisite of which was the overcoming of 'the many obstacles to
the economic mobility of the factors of production'.[3]

[1] *East Africa Commission Report*, p. 4.
[2] Ibid., p. 80.
[3] Ibid., p. 34.

Among these obstacles they included not only the complicated structure of marketing controls then in operation, but the exclusive claims to security in land made by tribal and sectional interests. Whilst attacking the restrictions and controls on production and distribution imposed by over-protective governments, they pointed out that 'the security which rests on tribal exclusiveness . . . is the illusory security of the subsistence economy within which no economic advancement is possible'.[1] They felt that the Europeans in the White Highlands were as guilty as any of tribalism, and that the rigid preservation of their position was incompatible with the full development of the East African economy.[2]

They were sceptical of the value of the development plans which had been drawn up by the three territories in 1946 in connection with the implementation of the Colonial Development and Welfare Acts of 1940 and 1945:

> the most important economic expansion of East Africa occurred independently of these plans and owes nothing to them. What is important is not that there should be development plans, but that there should be capital resources available to promote expansion. Some of these resources may come through the ordinary channels of trade and industry; others may come through agencies to which only the governments of the territories have access.

But to describe the result of the use of funds from the latter source, they said, as 'development' was unjustified.[3]

Although the report of the commission was unanimous, it shows signs of debate and of compromise between the *laissez-faire* economic theories of Frankel on the one hand, and the more interventionist approach of Gaitskell on the other. It is noticeable that the agricultural sections of the report place more emphasis on the need for central direction and planning than do those on commerce and industry. The emphasis in the latter on the removal of restrictions, and on the free working of the market, may have contributed to the very common misunderstanding of the report as advocating *laissez-faire* policies without sufficient protection for the economically weak. The *Economist* entitled its leading article on the report: 'Adam Smith in East Africa', and this interpretation was widely held.[4] The basic

---

[1] Ibid., p. 49.
[2] Ibid., p. 385.
[3] Ibid., p. 95. See also *Report of the Development Committee* (Nairobi, 1946) 2 vols.; *A Ten Year Development and Welfare Plan for Tanganyika Territory, Report by the Development Commission* (Dar es Salaam, 1946); E. B. Worthington, *A Development Plan for Uganda* (Entebbe, 1947).
[4] The *Economist*, 18 June 1955. See also A. Creech Jones in *Venture*, Aug. 1955; M. Perham in *The Listener*, 18 Aug. 1955; and in *New Commonwealth*, 5 Sept. 1955; and a series of articles in *The East African Economics Review*, Jan. 1956.

premises of the report were, in fact, *laissez-faire* rather than interventionist. Critics who complained of a lack of safeguards, however,
were unjust. Many readers seem to have overlooked a crucial passage
which stated

a) that economic efficiency can not be the only criteria of change but its
social effects must be taken into effect; and b) adverse social effects cannot
be compensated merely by the increased individual incomes which greater
economic efficiency may bring about.[1]

Land and agriculture

In their assessment of the situation on the ground the commission
dealt first with the question which had aroused Sir Philip Mitchell's
main concern—the pressure of population on the land. They
concluded that the rate of increase had been exaggerated, and that
it probably came closer to 1 per cent per annum than to the 2 per
cent that Mitchell feared.[2] In any event, even if the increase was over
2 per cent this need not be cause for alarm. They argued that there
was no optimum rate of increase; that East Africa as a whole was
more restricted by lack of population than by surplus; that the
standard of living could well be higher in places of high fertility and
population than in areas of scattered population; and that high
densities encouraged the division of labour, and so led to a less direct
dependence on the land for a livelihood. The problem was not one of
overpopulation as such, but of undue restriction on movement, and
of the retention and jealous guarding of land by communities which
had no immediate use for it.[3]

The key to development lay in the modernization of agricultural
techniques, and of systems of land-holding. Agricultural development
was bedevilled by 'the dilemma of security'—the fact that many more
people relied on the land than it could adequately support, but that
there could be no alternative security until productivity could be
sufficiently increased to stimulate secondary industries and the
exchange economy.[4] This dilemma led to 'the Maginot line mentality', the rigid preservation of sectional land claims at the expense of
the community at large.[5] The commissioners argued that 'the test of

---

[1] *East Africa Commission Report*, p. 197.

[2] Ibid., pp. 31–2, and Appendix vii, 'The African Population of East Africa: a
summary of its past and present trends', by J. E. Goldthorpe, pp. 462–73. See also
R. R. Kuczynski, *Demographic Survey of the British Colonial Empire*, vol. ii (London,
1949). Cp. p. 519 above.

[3] *East Africa Commission Report*, pp. 32–8.

[4] Ibid., pp. 48–53.

[5] The phrase is that of Arthur Gaitskell, in an informal talk to the Fabian Colonial
Bureau, 6 Oct. 1955. Rhodes House, Oxford, MSS Brit. Emp. s. 365/112/3.

land needs must be replaced by a test of *land use*', and 'that no tribe can now afford to pursue that self-sufficient isolation which constituted its traditional heritage'.[1]

They undertook a detailed survey of the agricultural potential of the region, and made a series of recommendations affecting all sectors. Stock control should be encouraged among the pastoral peoples, and new wants stimulated among them which would provide more incentive for the commercial management of their herds. They considered irrigation schemes on the pattern of the Gezira, and the possibility of encouraging co-operative farming ventures, which seemed to provide the only scope for the economic use of mechanical methods. They were anxious to encourage crop specialization, and the abolition of restrictions on African production of cash crops, such as tea, sisal and sugar. They proposed the setting up of Land Development Boards which would plan development on the basis of detailed territorial surveys.[2]

But the most important recommendations in this field concerned land tenure. They were certain that efficient mixed farming was impossible under the customary systems, and they argued that properly demarcated smallholdings should be set up which would allow 'the progressive individual' to improve his stock, rotate his crops, and use his land as security for loans. In considering individual, as against collective or co-operative tenure, they maintained that

policy concerning the tenure and disposition of land should aim at the individualization of land ownership, and at a degree of mobility in the transfer and disposition of land which, without ignoring existing property rights, will enable access to land for its economic use.[3]

It was realized that the rationalization of land-holding would lead to some displacement. This should partly be relieved, however, by the stimulation of the economy which would follow from greater productivity, and which would provide more jobs in the towns. They also felt that if the barriers of tribal and sectional exclusiveness could be broken down, there was much scope for the reallocation of unused land. In particular they believed that the pressure on the reserves of the Kamba and Kikuyu could be relieved by the leasing of land (though they did not recommend its sale) in the White Highlands.[4] This was the most crucial of all their recommendations, and politically the most controversial.

---

[1] *East Africa Commission Report*, pp. 49–50.
[2] Ibid., p. 339.
[3] Ibid., p. 346.
[4] Ibid., pp. 197, 358. They acknowledged that fears about land were so widespread that outright sales between the races might cause insecurity.

While improvements in agricultural techniques, and the rationalization of land-holding, were essential for the expansion of the economy, it was recommended that these should be accompanied by the removal of the complex structure of regulations which they believed had inhibited the economic advancement of the East African territories. The commission was critical of the attempts which had been made to assure self-sufficiency in food in all districts, and of the controls on production and distribution which had been imposed during the war and had survived into the post-war world. They were also critical of the retail and wholesale licensing regulations which hindered the enterprise of Indian traders in African areas, and made it difficult for African traders to raise capital. They did not, however, propose 'the complete and sudden removal of all existing marketing controls but rather the adoption of a policy which will increase economic flexibility in order to yield the greatest increase in income'.[1]

Non-agricultural development

Throughout their report the commissioners viewed the economy of East Africa as a whole; not merely in a territorial sense, but in terms of the interaction between the agricultural and the non-agricultural sectors. They were interested in the stimulation of industry, and in the provision of employment opportunities in the towns, but they were sceptical of the possibilities of large-scale development. They pointed out that mining development was the most significant form of industrial development in tropical Africa, and suggested that there should be more intensive mineral prospecting, and that this could be facilitated by the adoption of a regional mining policy, and the setting up of an East African Prospecting and Mining Leases Board.[2] The growth of secondary industry would be dependent on the expansion of the agricultural sector, and would be limited by the small size of the market. They were doubtful of the capacity of local savings to finance industrial development, and were certain that the region would have to depend on external investment and skill for the foreseeable future. They were critical of those who opposed foreign investment for 'political as distinct from economic reasons',[3] but they were not in favour of the granting of inducements such as protective tariffs or tax concessions. Governments were not justified, in view of their scarce financial resources, in making industrial investments themselves, but they could play a part in the siting of industries, and in the provision of basic services. They

[1] *East Africa Commission Report*, pp. 75–6.
[2] Ibid., pp. 113–16.
[3] Ibid., p. 79.

concluded that 'new industrial development should not be thought of in the language of relief works, which are not as a rule economic, and which . . . do not generally afford employment to any large number of persons.'[1] Transport was another factor which appeared to restrict industrial growth, and the report was critical of the 'cheap' transport policies of the East African Harbours and Railways Board which, it said, had led to the quoting of uneconomic rates, and had diverted profit which might have been used for improving the services into the hands of some producers. It called for the establishment of a Colonial Transport Development Fund, and recommended the reduction of political influence on the working of the railways by the replacement of the Railways Board by a Corporation.[2]

The problems of the towns could not be considered in isolation from the rural background. The commission were not in favour of controls on the flow of people to the towns, and felt that the only way to reduce this flow was to increase rural incomes. At the same time the stabilization of workers in the towns, and the reduction of migrant labour, which they considered desirable in the interests of efficiency, and the alleviation of pressure on the land, could be brought about only by improved urban security and welfare. While they favoured an increase in the minimum rate of wages they believed that the real cure for low wages lay not in legislation, but in the reduction of the supply of labour by a raising of the rural standard of living. There should be more African participation in the running of the towns, which had come to be thought of as non-African enclaves, and whose municipalities were on occasion guilty of arbitrary evictions and compulsory land acquisition without adequate compensation.[3] They were anxious to improve the standard of African housing, but felt that this could best be done by a more flexible approach to housing regulations, and by the encouragement of 'self-help' improvement schemes. 'Only the members of a society themselves can create a community.' The government could assist in the organic growth of towns, but much depended 'on the emergence of a responsible African middle class who can meet members of other races on equal terms'. In pursuit of the latter objective they made various recommendations on the provision of primary education, on reducing the school drop-out rate, and on the encouragement of apprenticeship schemes and technical education.[4]

The commission concluded with the hope that the policies for the breaking-down of barriers that they had proposed would lead to the

[1] Ibid., p. 105. See also pp. 86–9, 105–11.
[2] Ibid., pp. 127–9.
[3] Ibid., pp. 146–73, 200–50.
[4] Ibid., pp. 214, 177–82.

replacement of 'mutual fear by mutual hope'. They emphasized the need for long-term planning for the economy of the region, in which every effort should be made to ensure the fullest African participation. Finally they stressed the importance of seeing the problems of East Africa in the context of the wider world, and of the fundamental difficulty of 'finding a bridge between the under-developed poverty-stricken territories and those countries with technical knowledge and capital'.[1]

Reactions to the report

Official reaction to the report can only be described as negative. That it should be so was inevitable against the background of changes in both the political and economic rate of developments in East Africa which made its specific findings not so much unacceptable as irrelevant.

The major recommendations on agricultural, tenurial, and urban problems were addressed most directly to Kenya, but Sir Evelyn Baring, in a long analysis, rejected most of them. It is true that many of his criticisms looked backward rather than forward: on the fundamental issue of land transfers between the races he argued 'that the time is not yet ripe for the removal of those safeguards which have been developed over the last half-century';[2] he had reservations on marketing controls, on the minimum wage, and on the reform of squatting in the White Highlands and in the Forest Reserves; and he denied that conditions in the towns, or the extent of real malnutrition, were as bad as the report had suggested.[3] On the other hand he could point, in accepting the recommendations on land consolidation, to the considerable progress already made and the radical and detailed proposals for development contained in the Swynnerton Plan.[4] He might have added that for Kenya the massive input of development funds, and the re-structuring of the country's whole finances, brought about during the Mau Mau emergency and his own governorship, had by-passed many of the issues with which the commission had been concerned.

In Uganda also the report quickly acquired a dated look. The governor, Sir Andrew Cohen, was unsympathetic to the *laissez-faire*

---

[1] *East Africa Commission Report*, p. 387.

[2] *Despatches from the Governors of Kenya, Uganda and Tanganyika, and from the Administrator of the East African High Commission concerning the East African Royal Commission 1953–55 Report*, Cmd. 9801 (London, HMSO, 1956), p. 2.

[3] Ibid., p. 23. See also pp. 40, 54, 67.

[4] Ibid., pp. 86–97. See R. J. Swynnerton, *A Plan to Intensify the Development of African Agriculture in Kenya* (Nairobi, Govt. Printer, 1954).

philosophy as applied to colonial economies,[1] which was the dominant theme of the report in relation to Uganda. The worst abuses of the forced saving system imposed through the cotton and coffee stabilization funds had, he pointed out, already been reformed.[2] But in any case he himself had inspired a number of new policies on subjects which the report discussed (e.g. on agricultural productivity) even before the commission had considered them; indeed the only previously unconsidered matter so far as Uganda was concerned with which the commission dealt—urban development—was generally thought to have been primarily inspired by its Uganda secretary.

Sir Edward Twining in Tanganyika was the least responsive of the three, presumably because, whereas the other two territories had during the middle 1950s been following their own paths of economic advance, Tanganyika remained too poor to be in much of a position to put the recommendations into effect anyway. Twining's strongest opinion was against the adoption of a regional approach to development planning.[3]

In fact, all three governors were opposed to the commission's recommendations on closer regional co-operation. All three rejected the proposed Railways and Harbours Corporation. Cohen could imagine 'nothing which would be more likely to turn African opinion against mining development' than the proposed East African Mining and Leases Board, and he felt that the development of the Lake Victoria basin on a regional basis 'was not necessary or practical'.[4] The attitude of Cohen and Twining reflected the fear common to officials and people, in Uganda and Tanganyika, of domination by Kenya's white settlers, while Baring's attitude reflected Kenya's fear of too close association with the other two territories.

The Colonial Secretary, Alan Lennox-Boyd, while congratulating the commission on stimulating 'a vigorous reappraisal of the economic and agrarian policies of the Governments', accepted the governors' reservations.[5] He agreed that the status of the White Highlands must be left unaltered until 'public opinion' was ready for change. Calculations indicated that the three territories would need about

---

[1] It is reported that Sir Andrew, invited to attend a seminar at Makerere to discuss the report, placed it on the floor, put his foot on it, and announced, 'Gentlemen, *that* is what I think of the report'. Personnal communication, Cyril Ehrlich.

[2] *Despatches from Governors*, Cmd. 9801, pp. 108–23.

[3] Ibid., p. 160.

[4] Ibid., pp. 125, 148.

[5] *Commentary on the Despatches of the Governors of Kenya, Uganda and Tanganyika etc.*, by the Secretary of State for the Colonies, Cmd. 9804 (London, HMSO, 1956), p. 1.

£250 millions to spend between 1955 and 1960 in support of developments recommended by the Royal Commission, and accepted by the governors as desirable; this gave some measure of the gap between what was practicable and what was desirable if sufficient outside capital was to be available to 'match the needs and opportunities described by the East African Governors'.[1] That calculation was one way in which the metropolitan government signified its view that the report lay outside the sphere of working politics. Another was its steadfast refusal to allow time for a debate on the report in the House of Commons. The report's wide range made it difficult to debate, but the government's reluctance was undoubtedly also political, due to its unwillingness to commit itself on the White Highlands. It was not until May 1957 that there was a debate on a private member's motion.[2] The report was never debated in the territorial Legislative Assemblies, and even in Kenya it seems to have provoked no very pronounced political response.

While the immediate impact of the report was not great, its recommendations were not totally without influence. Many of the most restrictive regulations concerning production and marketing were relaxed. The specific recommendations on tenurial reform led to the calling of a conference on the subject at Arusha in February 1956, and it was in this sphere that the report had the most tangible results. It may have led to the speeding up of the process of land registration which was already under way in Kenya's Central Province and in some other areas where land was a scarce and saleable commodity, and which has continued since independence.[3] It helped to pave the way towards the final abandonment of the White Highlands reserve in 1960.

The report might have had more impact had its scope been narrower. Its specific recommendations tended to be buried in the great mass of material that it presented. Its great bulk may have contributed to misunderstandings of its tone. Superficial readers accused it of bias towards the unfashionable *laissez-faire* school of economic theory at a time when state intervention and centralized planning were coming into favour. Perhaps predictably it pleased neither side, being accused by paternalists on the right, and by socialists on the left, of encouraging the unrestrained working of

[1] *Commentary on the Despatches of the Governors of Kenya, Uganda and Tanganyika etc.*, by the Secretary of State for the Colonies, Cmd. 9804 (London, HMSO, 1956), p. 6.

[2] *Hansard*, vol. 571, 31 May 1957, cc. 765–859.

[3] e.g. *Report of the Mission on Land Consolidation and Registration in Kenya, 1965–6* (Nairobi, Govt. Printer, 1966); and F. D. Homans and R. Sands, 'Land Tenure Reform and Agricultural Development in the African Lands of Kenya', 1960, Rhodes House, Oxford, MSS Afr. 1267.

market forces. Few seem to have remarked upon the intricate pattern of checks and balances. The report was commissioned at a time when it was still apparently possible to take a long-term view of development within the colonial framework. It was written at a time when no dates had been fixed for independence in East Africa, and when the colonial order was expected to last for several decades at least. While the individual members of the commission must have been conscious of the quickening pace of change, the report itself shows no sign of awareness of the impending crisis.

It stands now as a noteworthy period piece, the first officially-sponsored intellectual appraisal of the socio-economic development of British colonial Africa in its last phase before independence. In economic analysis its successors were to be the dogmatic blueprints of the planning experts imported on independence, and the cautious and arid evaluations of the World Bank reports. Politically, it was in some ways the precursor of the debates on East African socialism which gathered momentum in the 1960s. In perceptiveness and balance it had much to teach to both.

THE FORMULAE OF REPRESENTATION
CHANGES IN REPRESENTATION IN LEGISLATIVE AND EXECUTIVE COUNCILS AND IN THE BUGANDA LUKIKO 1920–1963

1. KENYA *Composition of Legislati*

					LEGISLATIVE COUNCIL			
	Unofficial side							
	(i) Nominated				(ii) Elected			
Year	*European*	*Asian*	*Arab*	*African*	*European*	*Asian*	*Arab*	*African*
1920[1]	—	—[2]	1	—	11	2[2]	—	—
1924	1 (rep. Afr. inter- ests)	—[2]	—	—	11	5[2]	1	—
1934	2 (rep. Afr. interests)	—	—	—	11	5	1	—
1944	1 (rep. Afr. interests)	—	—	1	11	5	1	—
1947	—	—	—	2	11	5	1	—
1948 (1st un- official majority)	—	—	1	4[5]	11	5	1	—
1952 (Griffiths changes of 1952)	—	—	1	6[7]	14	6	1	—
1954[9] (Lyttel- ton Con- stitution)	—	—	1	6	14	6	1	—

[1] The Executive Council and Legislative Council were set up in 1907, but 1920 was the first year in ⸱ any elected representatives sat in the Legislative Council.
[2] The Asian community was granted two separately elected representatives in 1920, increased to five 1923 White Paper (Cmd. 1922). The community as a whole, however, refused to elect to these seats until In the meantime, a varying number of Asian representatives did sit in the Legislative Council, chosen by v compromises between election and nomination.
[3] Including from this date one Arab official, the Liwali for the Coast.
[4] Generally being adopted in British African territories at this time. Groups of departments were ma specific responsibility of individual members of the Executive Council.
[5] Those nominated were selected from short lists submitted through the Local Native Councils. The thus an element of elective representation.

nd Executive Councils 1920–1963

(iii) Ratio [Eur]opean: non-[E]uropean	Total	Official side	Executive Council
			EXECUTIVE COUNCIL
11:3	14	Governor, plus— 15 { 10 *ex officio* / 5 nominated officials }	Governor, plus— 7 { 5 *ex officio* / 2 nominated unofficials }
12:6	18	20 { 10 *ex officio* / 10 officials[3] }	8 { 5 *ex officio* / 3 European nominated unofficials }
13:6	19	20 { 11 *ex officio* / 9 officials }	12 { 8 *ex officio* / 3 European nominated / 1 Asian unofficials }
2:7	19	20 as above	['membership' system introduced 1947][4]
1:8	19	Speaker, plus—	
:11	22	16 { 7 *ex officio*[6] / 9 nominated officials }	11 { 7 *ex officio* / 3 European nominated / 1 Asian unofficials }
:14	28	26 { 8 *ex officio* / 7 European / 1 Arab / 2 African nominated officials / 8 nominated unofficials[8] }	12 { 8 *ex officio* / 2 European / 1 Asian / 1 African nominated unofficials }
			COUNCIL OF MINISTERS[11]
:14	28 [−8][10]	26 as above[10] [+8]	14 { 6 *ex officio* / 2 nominated officials / 3 European nominated / 2 Asian Leg Co / 1 African unofficials }

[i]n order to create an unofficial majority, the five officials seconded to the East African inter-territorial [struct]ure in 1948 were not replaced.
[f]or the further elaboration of the elective element in selecting African 'nominated' representatives between [a]nd 1957, see G. F. Engholm, 'African Elections in Kenya, March 1957', in *Five Elections in Africa*, edited [by] J. M. Mackenzie and Kenneth Robinson (Oxford, 1960), pp. 394–6.
[fr]om this time until the 1963 elections, sufficient nominated members from outside the public service were [added] to the official side to ensure that the government retained its over-all majority on the Legislative Council.
[se]e Cmd. 9103, Cmnd. 369.
[e]ight of the Elected Members, as Ministers, in effect should here be counted on the 'Official Side' of the [Execu]tive Council. See similarly below.
[W]hile the Executive Council did not immediately cease to exist, it was largely superseded by the Council [of Mini]sters.

1. KENYA *Composition of Legislativ*

	LEGISLATIVE COUNCIL							
	Unofficial side							
	(i) Nominated				*(ii) Elected*			
Year	*European*	*Asian*	*Arab*	*African*	*European*	*Asian*	*Arab*	*African*
1957 (following African elections of March 1957)	2 corporate[12]	—	1	—	14	6	1	8[13]
	Specially elected/'national' seats[14]							
1958 (Lennox-Boyd Constitution)	4	3	1	4	14	6	2	14[15]
After 1961 elections (following 1960 Lancaster Hse. Conference)[16]	4	3	1	4	33 open seats, plus—			
					10 reserved	8 reserved	2 reserved	

After 1963 elections (following 1962 constitutional conference)

12 'national' members
7 Africans ⎤
3 Europeans ⎬ actually elected
2 Asians ⎦

117 single member constituencies[17]
No European candidates elected
1 Asian ⎤
111 Africans ⎬ elected
5 elections boycotted

[12] The creation of two extra seats to represent corporate interests was part of the general policy of streng‍ing the non-government side of the Council. They were to be filled by nomination, and in practice were a‍ bound to go to Europeans: they were not subject to the government whip, however, and are thus listed he the 'unofficial' side.

[13] The first elections for 8 African seats, on a limited franchise, were held following the Report of the C Commission of 1956.

[14] These seats were filled by the elected members voting as an electoral college, until 1963 in the presc racial proportions. At the 1963 elections the voting was not thus regulated, but the procedure was nevert‍ used to secure the return of a few non-African ministers.

[15] Elections for the 6 additional African seats were held in March 1958.

[16] In the 1961 elections there were 33 open seats—the first common roll elections—plus 20 reserved se the proportions indicated. Only one unreserved seat was won by a non-African (a European). The 'espe elected seats' were filled by 'national members' elected as previously by the elected members sitting electoral college.

[17] No reserved seats. Universal adult suffrage.

ınd Executive Councils 1920–1963—continued

		Official side	EXECUTIVE COUNCIL
(iii) *Ratio* *European:* *non-European*	*Total*		
16:16	23 [−6]	26 as above [+6]	14 as above
18:30	48 [−9]	38 { 8 *ex officio* / 30 other nominated members [+9 { 4 European / 3 Asian/Arab / 2 African } Ministers from Leg Co]	16 { 6 *ex officio* / 5 European / 2 Asian / 1 Arab / 2 African } nominated unofficials
15:50		KADU minority government in office with necessary official side reinforcement	21 { 12 Ministers / 9 parliamentary secretaries = 8 Europeans / 8 Asians/Arabs / 11 Africans
			CABINET
:126		Full responsible government under majority party Prime Minister	32 { 17 Ministers / 15 parliamentary secretaries = 3 Europeans / 2 Asians/Arabs / 27 Africans

s:
ıual *Reports* for Kenya Colony.
ıya, *Proposals for a Reconstruction of the Government*, Cmd. 9103 (Lyttelton Constitution).
ıya; *Proposals for New Constitutional Arrangements*, Cmnd. 309 (Lennox-Boyd Constitution).
ıya; *Despatch on the New Constitutional Arrangements*, Cmnd. 369 (Lennox-Boyd Constitution).
ort *of the Kenya Constitutional Conference held in London in January and February 1960*, Cmnd. 960 (First ıster House Conference).
ort *of the Kenya Constitutional Conference, 1962*, Cmnd. 1700 (Second Lancaster House Conference).
ırge Bennett, *Kenya, a Political History: the colonial period* (London, 1963).
F. Engholm, 'African Elections in Kenya, March 1957', in *Five Elections in Africa*, edited by W. J. M. enzie and Kenneth Robinson (Oxford, 1960).
Bennett and C. G. Rosberg, *The Kenyatta Election: Kenya 1960–1961* (London, 1961).

2. UGANDA *Composition of Legislative an*

	LEGISLATIVE COUNCIL							
	Unofficial side							
	(i) *Nominated*			(ii) *Representative/Elected*[1]			(iii) Ratio non-African : African	
Year	*European*	*Asian*	*African*	*European*	*Asian*	*African*		*Tota*
1921[2]	2	(1)[3]	—	—	—	—	3:0	3
1934	2	2[5]	—	—	—	—	4:0	4
1945/6[6]	3	3	3	—	—	—	6:3	9
1949	3	3	4	—	—	—	6:4	1
1951[8]	4	4	8[9]	—	—	—	8:8	
1952/3[10] (following arrival of Cohen)	4	4	8	—	—	—	8:8	

[1] In Uganda, as will be seen from the footnotes below, the transition from nominated, via 'represent to full elected membership of the Legislative Council was more gradual and complicated than in the oth African territories. It has seemed best, however, to maintain the same broad division as in the other ch

[2] The Executive Council and the Legislative Council were both set up in 1921 under Royal Instr implementing the Uganda Order in Council 1920.

[3] In Uganda as in Kenya the Asian community opposed separate racial nomination, demanding a cc roll. It was only in 1926 that the first Asian representative took his seat on the Council.

[4] The Lukiko, or traditional assembly of Buganda, was given formal recognition by the Buganda Agr of 1900. Its membership was then fixed at 89 as shown. It comprised besides the 20 *saza* (county) chi their deputies—3 other chiefs from each *saza* appointed by the Kabaka, and thus was virtually an asser landowners.

[5] While it was officially denied that any formal ratio was maintained, in fact the 2:1 Europear proportion remained unchanged until Asian pressure secured a second representative in 1933. The European/Asian parity was maintained until the 1960s.

Executive Councils and of the Lukiko 1921–1962

Official side Governor, plus—	Over-all ratio non-African : African	EXECUTIVE COUNCIL Governor, plus—	LUKIKO Kabaka, plus—
ex officio	7:0	4 ex officio	89 { 3 Ministers[4] / 6 members nominated personally by Kabaka / 80 *Saza, gombolola* and *miruka* chiefs appointed by Kabaka
ex officio	10:0	7 { 6 ex officio / 1 official (Provincial Commissioner Buganda)	89 as above
6 ex officio / 3 officials	15:3	8 { 6 ex officio / 1 official / 1 nominated unofficial	89 { 3 Ministers / 6 Kabaka nominees / 49 chiefs appointed by Kabaka / 31 indirectly elected through electoral colleges etc.
6 ex officio / 4 officials	16:4	9 { 6 ex officio / 1 official / 2 nominated unofficials	89 { 3 Ministers / 6 Kabaka nominees / 44 appointed chiefs / 36 indirectly elected as above[7]
6 ex officio / 10 officials	24:8	9 { 6 ex officio / 1 official / 1 European } nominated / 1 Asian } unofficials	89 { 3 Ministers / 6 Kabaka nominees / 40 appointed chiefs / 20 indirectly elected through electoral colleges / 20 indirectly elected by County Councils
as above	24:8	15 { 6 ex officio / 3 officials / 2 European } nominated / 2 Asian } unofficials / 2 African	89 { 3 Ministers / 6 Kabaka nominees / 20 appointed chiefs / 40 elected through electoral colleges / 20 elected by County Councils

Steps taken to broaden the basis of consultation at the end of the Second World War. All three of the new ican members, added in 1945, were officials: one Buganda Minister, one of the Katikiros to represent the stern, and one Secretary General to represent the Eastern Province. An official representative of the newly blished Northern Province was added in 1947. The additional European and Asian members, and the first fficial member of the Executive Council, were appointed in 1946. In the same year indirect election to a portion of Lukiko seats was introduced.

The elected element in the Lukiko was extended in 1947.

The expansion of the Legislative Council here shown was approved late in 1949.

2 African officials to be chosen by each Provincial Council. The Buganda representatives should have been ninated by the Lukiko, but when that body refused to do so they were nominated by the Kabaka.

The first stage of the reforms inaugurated by Sir Andrew Cohen after his arrival as Governor in 1952, ging Africans for the first time into the Executive Council. The elected majority in the Lukiko was oduced in 1953.

2.   UGANDA *Composition of Legislative and*

	LEGISLATIVE COUNCIL							
	Unofficial side							
	(i) Nominated			(ii) Representative/Elected[1]			(iii) Ratio non-African: African	Total
Year	European	Asian	African	European	Asian	African		
1954 (main Cohen reform of Leg Co)[11]	7	7	—	—	—	14[12]	14:14	28
1955[13]	6	6	—	—	—	18	12:18	30
1958 (following 1958 elections)[14]	6	6	—	—	13 { 10 elected[15] / 3 representative (5 elections boycotted)		12:18	30
1961[16]	—	—	—	91 { 82 directly elected members / 9 specially elected members[17]			7:84	9
1962[19]	NATIONAL ASSEMBLY							

[11] See *Correspondence relating to the Composition of the Legislative Council in Uganda* (Entebbe, 1953). The Europea[n] and Asians would be nominated by the Governor after consultation with the respective communities; of the Africans one would be elected by each of the 11 District Councils outside Buganda and 3 by the Lukiko. T[he] cross-bench members were free to vote against the government save on motions of confidence.

[12] The Lukiko again refused to nominate the 3 Buganda members; representatives were once more nominat[ed] by the Kabaka.

[13] These changes followed the achievement of broad agreement on the Buganda crisis at the end of 195[ ] which led eventually to the new Buganda Agreement of October 1955. Of the additional African members t[wo] came from Buganda, one from Busoga and one from Ankole. With the settlement of the crisis the Gan[da] representatives rejoined the Legislative Council: but when two of these resigned at the end of 1957 the Bugan[da] government did not replace them.

[14] The 1958 elections were originally proposed for Buganda only, with country-wide elections to follow 1961. They were advanced through pressure from the non-Ganda African members of Leg Co. Voting was a qualified franchise.

[15] The Buganda government boycotted the elections; one member for Bugisu was nominated, and two Ankole were returned by indirect election. There was no representative for Karamoja.

[16] Based on recommendations of the Wild Committee, *Report of the Constitutional Committee* (Entebbe, 195[ ] chairman J. V. Wild. Virtually universal adult suffrage. Although the elections were again largely boycot[ted] in Buganda, they did in fact take place for all 82 seats.

Executive Councils and of the Lukiko 1921–1962—continued

Official side	Over-all ratio non-African: African	EXECUTIVE COUNCIL	LUKIKO
28 { 9 *ex officio* 8 officials } nominated 4 European } crossbench 1 Asian } unofficials 6 African }	36:20	15 { 8 *ex officio* 1 European } officials 1 African } 2 European } nominated 2 Asian } unofficials 1 African }	89 as above
30 { 7 European } Ministers 1 Asian } = Parliamentary Secretaries 5 African } 4 officials (European) 4 European } backbenchers 2 Asian } 7 African } Speaker, plus—	30:30	13 { 3 *exofficio* } European ministers 4 official } 1 Asian minister 3 African ministers 2 nominated European officials	92 { 6 Ministers 6 Kabaka nominees 20 County chiefs 60 indirectly elected (as above)
42 { 10 European } Officials and Ministers 1 Asian } 6 African } 4 European } backbenchers 1 Asian } 10 African }	26:34	12 { 3 *ex officio* } European ministers 4 official } 1 Asian minister 3 African ministers Resident Bugandan (nominated)	92 as above
		COUNCIL OF MINISTERS Governor, Deputy Governor, plus—	
0 { 3 *ex officio* } Ministers 10 other } 7 parliamentary secretaries + about 40 elected members]	approx 10:90	13 { Chief minister 3 *ex officio* } ministers 9 elected }	*c.* 100 { 6 Ministers 6 Kabaka nominees 20 County chiefs (up to) 68 directly elected members[18]

CABINET
Headed by Prime Minister

[17] These seats to be filled by the 82 elected (including 24 from Buganda) and 3 *ex officio* members sitting as n electoral college (up to 5 candidates might be proposed by the Governor).
[18] See *Report of the Uganda Relationships Commission 1961*, Chairman Lord Munster (Entebbe, 1961), pp. 55–6; and Uganda, *Report of the Uganda Constitutional Conference, 1961*, Cmnd. 1539 (London, HMSO, 1961), 63.
[19] The only substantial difference in the pattern of the 1962 National Assembly was that 21 of the Buganda presentatives were to be elected by the Lukiko, the remaining 3 being directly elected in Kampala.

urces:

Uganda *Annual Reports*.
Correspondence relating to the Composition of Legislative Council in Uganda (Entebbe, 1953).
Uganda Protectorate: Buganda, Cmd. 9320 (London, HMSO, 1954).
Tamukedde, W. 'Changes in the Great Lukiko' (EAISR mimeograph, 1954).
Report of the Constitutional Committee 1959, Chairman J. V. Wild (Entebbe, 1959).
Supplementary Report of the Constitutional Committee (Entebbe, 1960).
Low, D. A. and Pratt, R. C., *Buganda and British Overrule* (London, 1960).
Uganda, *Report of the Uganda Constitutional Conference, 1961*, Cmnd. 1523 (London, HMSO, 1961).
Uganda: the making of a nation (London, COI, 1962).

3. TANGANYIKA *Composition of Legislative*

	LEGISLATIVE COUNCIL							
	Unofficial side							
	(i) Nominated			(ii) Elected			(iii) Ratio Europeans : non-Europeans	
Year	European	Asian	African	European	Asian	African		Total
1927[1]	5	2	—	—	—	—	5:2	7
1938	7	3	—	—	—	—	7:3	10
1946	7[2]	3	2[3]	—	—	—	7:5	12
1949	7	3	4	—	—	—	7:7	14
1951 Mathew Committee proposals[6]		7	7	—	—	—	7:14	21
1952	7	3	4	—	—	—	7:7	14
1954	7	3	4	—	—	—	7:7	14
1955 (following report of Mackenzie Commission)[8]	10	10	10	—	—	—	10:20	30
1957	11[9]	11	11	—	—	—	11:22	33

[1] The Executive Council was set up in 1920, Legislative Council in 1926. In the early years the proporti[on] of European and Asian members were not formally prescribed but were at the Governor's discretion.

[2] Including one European representing African interests. This however does not seem to have persisted a[s] the number of African members was increased.

[3] Provision was made in 1945 for 4 African representatives, but two of these were appointed only in 1[947] and 1948 respectively. Three were chiefs, the fourth a Dar es Salaam schoolmaster.

[4] This was the system generally being adopted in British African territories at this time, whereby group[s of] departments were made the responsibility of individual members of the Executive Council, who were respons[ible] for them directly to the Governor, instead of through the Chief Secretary.

[5] In 1949 it was decided that the distribution as between *ex officio* and other official members should be m[ore] flexible.

and Executive Councils 1927–1961

Official side	Over-all ratio Europeans : non-Europeans	EXECUTIVE COUNCIL
Governor, plus—		Governor, plus—
3 *ex officio* and officials	18:2	6 *ex officio*
3 *ex officio*	20:3	6 *ex officio*
5 { 8 *ex officio* / 7 nominated officials	22:5	10 { 6 *ex officio*/officials / 3 European ⎫ nominated / 1 Asian ⎭ unofficials ('membership' system introduced 1948)[4]
5 as above[5]	22:7	12 { 8 *ex officio*/officials / 3 Europeans ⎫ nominated / 1 Asian ⎭ unofficials
2		
5 as above	22:7	14 { 8 *ex officio*/officials / 4 European ⎫ / 1 Asian ⎬ nominated / 1 African ⎭ unofficials
Speaker,[7] plus—		
{ 8 *ex officio* / 7 nominated unofficials	22:7	14 { 8 *ex officio* / 2 European ⎫ / 2 Asian ⎬ nominated / 2 African ⎭ unofficials
{ 8 *ex officio* / 6 unofficial members of Ex Co / 17 nominated officials & unofficials	31:30	14 { 3 *ex officio* / 5 officials / 2 European ⎫ / 2 Asian ⎬ nominated / 2 African ⎭ unofficials
{ 21 Europeans / 6 Asians / 4 Africans		[Ministerial system introduced 1957]
{ 9 *ex officio* / 7 unofficial members of Ex Co / 18 nominated officials and unofficials	31:36	13 { 7 *ex officio*/officials / 1 European ⎫ / 3 Asian ⎬ nominated / 2 African ⎭ unofficials
{ 20 Europeans / 3 Asians / 11 Africans		

[*] In 1949 a Committee under the chairmanship of Charles Mathew, Member for Law and Order, was set to report on constitutional development. Its proposals, though published in 1951, recommended that no ~ion should be taken on those parts dealing with the central government for a further five years. They were ~s superseded by the recommendations of the Mackenzie Commission (see below).

[†] In 1953 it was enacted that, in the place of the Governor, the Legislative Council should be presided over a Speaker who should not be a Member of the Council and who would have no vote.

[‡] The report of the Special Commissioner, Professor J. W. M. Mackenzie, appointed in 1952 to consider ~resentation on the Legislative Council, was published in 1953, but no effective change was made until 1955. May 1954 the Governor announced that there would be 9 three-member constituencies, each with one ~mber from each race, but this was not put into effect, being amended in 1955 to provide also for the ~nination of a tenth non-constituency member of each race.

10 three-member constituencies, plus 3 non-constituency members.

3. TANGANYIKA *Composition of Legislative*

	LEGISLATIVE COUNCIL							
	Unofficial side							
	(i) Nominated			(ii) Elected			(iii) Ratio Europeans: non-Europeans	
Year	European	Asian	African	European	Asian	African		Total
1959[10]	[1]	[1]	[1]	10	10	10	10:20	30[−5][11]
1960	—	—	reserved[13] unre-served	10 —	11 —	— 50	10:61	71
1961	NATIONAL ASSEMBLY							

[10] In 1958/9 elections on a limited franchise were held in two parts, 15 seats being contested on each occasion. Each elector was required to vote for one candidate of each race. The further provision for three candidates to be nominated by the Governor was not in fact made use of.

[11] Five of the elected members, as Ministers, in effect should here be counted on the 'official side' of the Legislative Council. Cp. chart for Kenya.

[12] The Council of Ministers, set up in 1959, largely superseded the Executive Council, though the latter continued to exercise limited functions.

[13] 10 seats were reserved for European, 11 seats for Asian candidates. All the 50 open seats were won by African candidates.

and Executive Councils 1927–1961—continued

	Official side	Over-all ratio Europeans: non-Europeans	EXECUTIVE COUNCIL
			COUNCIL OF MINISTERS[12]
			Governor, plus—
23 { 7 *ex officio*, 16 nominated, [+ 5 Leg Co Ministers][11] = 13 Europeans, 5 Asians, 10 Africans, 28 in all		23:35	12 { 3 *ex officio*, 1 European ⎫ Ministers, 1 Asian ⎬ from Leg Co, 3 African ⎭
			Governor, Deputy Governor, plus—
11 { 2 *ex officio*, 4 Europeans ⎫ nominated, 2 Asian ⎬ members, 3 African ⎭		16:66	13 { 2 *ex officio*, 2 European ⎫ Ministers, 1 Asian ⎬ from Leg Co, 7 African ⎭, 1 nominated official
			CABINET

Sources:
Tanganyika *Annual Reports.*
Report of the Committee on Constitutional Development (Dar es Salaam, 1951).
Report of the Special Commissioner (W. J. M. *Mackenzie) Appointed to Examine Matters arising out of the Report of the Committee on Constitutional Development* (Dar es Salaam, 1953).
United Nations, *Report of Visiting Mission on Tanganyika 1954* (New York, U.N., 1955).
Tanganyika (Legislative Council) (Amendment) Order in Council, 1959.
Tanganyika: the making of a nation (London, COI, 1961).
Report of the Tanganyika Constitutional Conference, 1961, Cmnd. 1360 (London, HMSO, 1961).
Taylor, J. Clagett, *The Political Development of Tanganyika* (London, 1963).

4. ZANZIBAR
Composition of Legislative and Executive Councils

	LEGISLATIVE COUNCIL								EXECUTIVE COUNCIL
	Unofficial side¹							Official side	
	(i) Nominated Members					(ii) Elected Members	Total		
Year	European	Arab	Asian	African	Total				
1926²	1	3	2	—	6	—	6	Resident, plus— 8 {3 ex officio, 5 officials}	Sultan and Resident, plus— 6 {3 ex officio, 3 other officials³}
1942⁴	1	3	2	—	6	—	6	8 {4 ex officio, 4 officials}	8 {4 ex officio, 3 officials, Seyyid Abdulla as heir apparent}
1946	1	3	2	1	7	—	7	8 as above	8 as above
1947	1	3	2	2	8	—	8	8 as above	8 as above
1955 proposals⁵	1	4	3	4	12	(common roll from outset)	12	13 {4 ex officio, 9 officials}	Resident, plus— 10 {4 ex officio, 3 officials, 3 appointed representative members, probably one from each main racial group} ⁶
	Representative Members								
after 1957 elections (following Coutts Report)⁷	6⁸ [4 Arabs, 2 Asians] in fact appointed								
1959⁹	[4]					[8]	[12]	13 as above	12 {4 ex officio, 3 officials, 5 appointed representative members, including 2 from elected members of Leg Co}

			Speaker, plus—	Resident, plus—
1960 (following Blood Constitution)[10]	22[11]	22	8 { 3 ex officio / 5 appointed / up to members	8 { 3 ex officio / 5 ministerial members of legislature, one as Chief Minister[12]
1963[13] (following 1962 Constitutional Conference)	31	31	No agreement reached	Deputy Resident (ex-Chief Secretary), plus COUNCIL OF MINISTERS 8 Ministers (also 2 Assistant Ministers)

[1] The racial distribution of nominated membership was a matter of practice, not of law.

[2] In 1925 a Protectorate Council was established as an advisory body with the Sultan as President and the British Resident as Vice-President. This was superseded by Decree No. 1 of 1926 setting up an Executive and a Legislative Council.

[3] No limit but usually 3 appointed.

[4] Decrees Nos. 14 and 18 of 1942.

[5] These proposals were announced by the Resident, Sir Henry Potter, in 1955 (see Sessional Paper No. 9 of 1955), and approved by the Legislative Council (which was, however, largely boycotted by its Arab members). In the event they were partially superseded following the Coutts Report on elections (Zanzibar, 1956).

[6] The proposals also provided for the setting up of a Privy Council, over which the Sultan would preside, while ceasing to preside over the Executive Council. The Privy Council was established in 1956. See council Decree No. 1 of 1956.

[7] Councils Decree No. 1 of 1956, and Legislative Council Elections Decree No. 4 of 1957, implementing the recommendations of the Coutts Commission (see Sources below).

[8] Representatives were nominated from lists submitted by the various racial group associations. While no racial proportions were prescribed, the intention was that the procedure should be used to bring about, in conjunction with the election results, a balanced over-all racial representation.

[9] Decree No. 22 of 1959. In fact this was not put into effect, being superseded by the recommendations of Sir Hilary Blood in the following year.

[10] Report of the Constitutional Commissioner, (Zanzibar, 1960).

[11] Thus establishing an unofficial majority. Sir Hilary Blood in fact recommended 21 constituencies, but it was subsequently decided to divide Stone Town into two constituencies. As the result of deadlock in the 1960 elections, the number was subsequently raised to 23.

[12] Provision was also made for Assistant Ministers, but not as Members of the Executive Council.

[13] See Cmnd. 1699. No agreement was reached at the 1962 Conference on either the number of constituencies or the total strength of the Legislative Council. The 1963 elections were held on the basis of 31 constituencies recommended by the 1963 Delimitation Commission.

Sources:

Zanzibar Annual Reports.
Sessional Paper No. 9 of 1955 (Zanzibar, 1955).
Methods of Choosing Unofficial Members of the Legislative Council, Commissioner W. H. Coutts (Zanzibar, 1956).
Report of the Constitutional Commissioner, Zanzibar 1960, Sir Hilary Blood (Zanzibar, 1960). A summary of earlier constitutional changes is given on p. 57.
Report of the Zanzibar Constitutional Conference 1962, Cmnd. 1699 (London, HMSO, 1962).
Zanzibar (London, COI, 1963).
Ayany, S. G., A History of Zanzibar: a study in constitutional development, 1934–1964 (Nairobi, 1970).

APPENDIX 3

STATISTICAL TABLES[1]

A. POPULATION

B. TRADE

[1] The editors are grateful to Arthur Hazlewood for much valuable help in the compilation of these statistics.

A. POPULATION

In 1948 a general census was taken, under the direction of the East
African Statistical Department, of the whole population of the four
East African countries. The data collected in that year, and the
analyses of it, form the central and indispensable basis for all work on
East African population trends before and since. No subsequent
census has covered the whole region in a single year, but a number of
separate counts were taken for individual countries: in 1957 for
Tanganyika, 1958 for Zanzibar, 1959 for Uganda, and 1962 for
Kenya. The over-all demographic picture from 1948 onwards is thus
reasonably clear.

For the period before 1948, as R. R. Kuczynski demonstrated in
the East African section of his monumental *Demographic Survey of the*

British Colonial Empire (London, 1949), fairly accurate information is available only for the European and Asian communities, and in lesser and varying degree for the urban centres and the islands of the Zanzibar Protectorate. Although censuses were taken—the most extensive in 1911, 1921, and 1931—the estimates made in these for the African population are now generally regarded as being virtually worthless. The most valid estimates now available are those based on backward projections of the 1948 data, as indicated in the footnotes to the tables that follow.

TABLE I

POPULATION OF EAST AFRICAN TERRITORIES, SHOWING MAIN RACIAL GROUPS, SELECTED YEARS 1921–1963

	Kenya		Uganda		Tanganyika		Zanzibar		Total
	'000	%	'000	%	'000	%	'000	%	millions
1921									
Africans and Arabs[1]	3,800·0	99·1	3,400·0	99·8	5,900·0	99·8	217·0	94·2	13·3
Asians	25·3	0·7	5·0		10·2	0·2	13·1	5·7	0·1
Europeans	9·7	0·2	1·3	0·2	2·4		0·3	0·1	
Est. Total (millions)	3·8	100·0	3·4	100·0	5·9	100·0	0·2	100·0	13·4
1931									
Africans and Arabs	4,100·0	98·6	3,600·0	99·5	6,000·0	99·5	220·0	93·4	13·9
Asians	43·6	1·0	14·2	0·4	25·1	0·4	15·2	6·5	0·1
Europeans	16·8	0·4	2·0	0·1	8·2	0·1	0·3	0·1	
Est. Total (millions)	4·1	100·0	3·6	100·0	6·0	100·0	0·2	100·0	14·0
1939									
Africans and Arabs	4,800·0	98·1	4,200·0	99·5	6,500·0	99·4	232·0	93·6	15·7
Asians	66·2	1·4	18·7	0·4	32·9	0·5	15·5	6·3	0·2
Europeans	22·8	0·5	2·2	0·1	7·9	0·1	0·3	0·1	
Est. Total (millions)	4·9	100·0	4·2	100·0	6·5	100·0	0·2	100·0	15·9

1948	No.	%	No.	%	No.	%	No.	%	Total (millions)
Africans and Arabs	5,300·0	97·6	4,900·0	99·2	7,400·0	99·3	248·0	93·9	17·9
Asians	97·7	1·8	35·2	0·7	46·3	0·6	16·5	6·1	0·2
Europeans	29·7	0·6	3·4	0·1	10·6	0·1			
Est. Total (millions)	5·4	100·0	4·9	100·0	7·5	100·0	0·3	100·0	18·1
1963									
Africans and Arabs	8,600·0	97·4	7,100·0	98·6	9,700·0	98·9	299·0	93·5	25·7
Asians	180·0	2·0	82·0	1·2	90·0	0·9	20·0	6·5	0·5
Europeans	53·0	0·6	10·0	0·2	21·0	0·2			
Est. Total (millions)	8·83	100·0	7·2	100·0	9·8	100·0	0·3	100·0	26·2

[1] The small Arab population of the East African mainland—some 37,000 in 1948—is deemed to be included in the totals for the African population as estimated for earlier years (see note on Sources below.) In Zanzibar the proportion of Arabs was of course much higher, being given as 17 per cent in 1948: but since political factors entered into the classification at different times, the two communities are here grouped together.

Note on Sources: All figures for 1948, and those for all except mainland Africans for 1921 and 1931, are taken directly from the censuses for those years. Figures for 1963 are from the East African *Economic and Statistical Review*, No. 13 (1964), and from the mid-year estimates, based on censuses held in 1957 (Tanganyika), 1958 (Zanzibar), 1959 (Uganda), and 1962 (Kenya). No census figures for the African population of the mainland territories before 1948 can be regarded as reliable, and those used here are based on the article by D. A. Lury in the *Economic and Statistical Review*, No. 16 (1965), pp. viii–xii, which seeks to extrapolate the 1948 material back to 1921 on broadly defined premisses. 1939 figures for Europeans and Asians, and for Zanzibar, are approximations only, and are based on the data compiled by R. R. Kuczynski, *Demographic Survey of the British Colonial Empire*, Vol. II, pp. 146–51, 250–1, 352–4, 654–5.

Table 2

East African Asian and European Immigrant Communities, Selected Years 1911–1953 and 1956–1963

Year	Asians ('000)					Europeans ('000)				
	Kenya	Tanganyika	Uganda	Zanzibar	Total	Kenya	Tanganyika	Uganda	Zanzibar	Total
1911	**11·9**	**7·6**[1]	**2·0**	**8·8**[2]	30·3	**3·2**	**4·3**[1]	**0·6**	**0·2**[2]	8·3
1921	**25·3**	**10·2**	**5·0**	**13·8**	**54·3**	**9·7**	**2·4**	**1·3**	**0·3**	**13·7**
1931	**43·6**	**25·1**	**14·2**	**15·2**	**98·1**	**16·8**	**8·2**	**2·0**	**0·3**	**27·3**
1948(a)	**97·7**	**46·3**	**35·2**	**15·9**	**195·1**	**29·7**	**10·6**	**3·4**	**0·3**	**44·0**
(b)	100·0	47·5	36·3	16·0	199·8	30·8	11·3	3·7	0·3	46·1
1953[3]	131·1	64·5	47·4	17·2	260·2	42·2	20·3	6·6	0·4	69·5
1956	149·0	74·3	62·9	17·9	304·1	54·0	20·2	9·0	0·5	83·7
1957	158·0	77·6	66·2	18·1	319·9	58·0	20·7	9·7	0·5	88·9
1958	161·0	80·9	69·6	18·4	329·9	59·0	21·2	10·4	0·5	91·1
1959	165·0	84·1	72·9	18·7	340·7	60·0	21·8	11·0	0·5	93·3
1960	169·0	87·3	75·1	18·9	350·3	61·0	22·3	11·4	0·6	95·3
1961	173·0	88·0	77·4	19·2	357·6	59·6	22·7	11·6	0·6	93·9
1962	176·0	88·7	79·9	19·5	364·1	56·0	22·0	11·2	0·6	89·8
1963	180·0	90·2	82·1	19·7	372·0	53·0	21·1	9·3	0·7	84·6

Notes and Sources:

Figures in bold type are census returns. Except where otherwise indicated, all other figures are mid-year estimates based on the latest available census returns. After the 1948 census, which covered all four territories, censuses were taken in 1957 in Tanganyika, 1958 in Zanzibar, 1959 in Uganda, and 1962 in Kenya.

[1] Slightly adjusted from the returns of the 1913 census carried out by the German administration, viz. 9,400 Asians, 5,300 Europeans.

[2] 1910 Zanzibar census.

[3] Estimates given in Appendix IV of the *East Africa Royal Commission Report, 1953–1955*, Cmd. 9475. p. 457, with additional estimate for Zanzibar.

TABLE 3

MAINLAND EAST AFRICA, MAIN TRIBAL
GROUPS 1948 AND SUBSEQUENT CENSUS DATES

(1) *Kenya*

	1948		1962[1]	
	'000	%	'000	%
Kikuyu	1,026	19·5	1,642	19·6
Luo	757	14·4	1,148	13·7
Luhya	654	12·5	1,086	12·9
Kamba	612	11·7	933	11·1
Meru/Tharaka[2]	325	6·2	478	5·7
Nyika	296	5·6	...	4·9
Mijikenda	...		415[3]	5·0
Kisii	255	4·9	538	6·4
Embu	204	3·9	Not comparable[4]	
Kipsigis	160	3·0	342	4·1
Others	963	18·3	1,821	21·3
Total	5,251	100·0	8,366	100·0

[1] The 1962 Kenya census was carried out on a more strictly linguistic basis than that of 1948. A number of people, especially in the Rift Valley, classified themselves as 'Kalenjin'-speakers.

[2] The Tharaka in 1948 were included in the Meru figure, but in 1962 were separately enumerated.

[3] The Mijikenda include Digo, Duruma, Chonyi, Giriama, Rabai, Ribe, Jibana, Kauma, Kambe; that is, rather more groups than the Nyika of the 1948 classification.

[4] The figure given for Embu-speakers in 1962 is only 95,647.

TABLE 3—continued

(2) Uganda

	1948		1959	
	'000	%	'000	%
Baganda	836	17·0	1,049	16·3
Basoga/Banyole	484	9·9	595	9·2
Iteso	463	9·4	525	8·1
Banyankole	388	7·9	519	8·1
Bakiga/Bahororo	316	6·4	460[5]	7·1
Banyaruanda	289	5·9	379	5·9
Lango	265	5·4	364	5·6
Bagisu	244	5·0	329	5·1
Acholi	209	4·2	285	4·4
Lugbara	183	3·7	236	3·7
Banyoro[6]	181	3·7	183	2·9
Batoro	163	3·3	208	3·2
Others	898	18·2	1,313	20·4
Total	4,918	100·0	6,450	100·0

(3) Tanganyika

	1948		1957	
	'000	%	'000	%
Sukuma	889	12·0	1,094	12·6
Nyamwezi	363	4·9	363	4·2
Ha	286	3·9	290	3·3
Makonde (including Matambwe)	301[7]	4·0	340	3·9
Gogo	279	3·8	299	3·5
Haya	276	3·7	326	3·8
Chagga	239	3·2	318	3·7
Hehe	192	2·6	252	2·9
Nyakyusa	193	2·6	220	2·5
Others	4,393	59·28	5,164	59·6
Total	7,410	100·0	8,665	100·0

[5] It seems likely that some of those enumerated as Banyaruanda in 1948 reclassified themselves as Bakiga in 1959.

[6] Some irregularities reported in 1948 census, which may have resulted in an over-count.

[7] The Matambwe were counted separately in the 1948 census, when the number returned was 19,665.

Sources:
Kenya: *Geographical and Tribal Studies; Kenya 1948, African Population, Kenya Population Census, 1962*, Vol. III (Nairobi, 1966), pp. 34–6.
Uganda: *Uganda Census, 1959, African Population* (Entebbe, 1962), pp. 18–19.
Tanganyika: *African Census Report, 1957* (Dar es Salaam, 1963), p. 42.

TABLE 4

EAST AFRICAN URBAN GROWTH

(a) *Main East African Urban Centres, 1948 and subsequent
census dates*

	1948	1962
KENYA		
Nairobi	118,976	266,795
Mombasa	84,746	179,575
Nakuru	17,625	38,181
Kisumu	10,899	23,526
Eldoret	8,193	19,605
Thika	n.a.	13,952
Nanyuki	4,090	10,448[1]
		1957
TANGANYIKA		
Dar es Salaam	69,277	128,742
Tanga	20,619	38,053
Mwanza	11,296	19,877
Tabora	12,768	15,361
Morogoro	8,173	14,507
Moshi	8,048	13,726
Dodoma	9,414	13,453
Mtwara	8,577	10,459
Lindi	n.a.	10,315
Arusha	5,320	10,038
		1959
UGANDA		
Kampala	22,094	46,735
Jinja	8,410	29,741
Mbale	n.a.	13,569
Entebbe	7,942	10,941
		1958
ZANZIBAR		
Zanzibar Township	45,284	57,923

[1] As given in the *Kenya Population Census, 1962,* Vol. I, p. 24. In subsequent statistical abstracts etc. the figure given is 11,154.

Source: Census data for years given.

TABLE 4—*continued*

(*b*) *Growth of principal East African cities 1894–1960*

Year	Nairobi	Mombasa	Dar es Salaam	Zanzibar	Kampala
1894/95	—	25,000	10,000		
1911/12	17,000		21,000	36,000	15,000
1921			24,600		
1926	29,000	40,000		40,000	
1931	47,900	57,300	34,300	45,300	
1937/38	65,000	60,000			
1948	119,000	84,700	69,300	45,300	22,100
1960	260,000	175,000	130,000	60,000	50,000

Note on Sources: Except for the general East African census year 1948, the above figures give no more than the roughest order of magnitude. For Kampala in particular, the presence of two or three closely adjoining centres of population raises problems of definition which make any comparisons virtually impossible. For general guidance on the sources of the figures given (apart from the 1931 and subsequent censuses) see: *Nairobi, Master Plan for a Colonial Capital*, by L. W. Thornton White, L. Silberman, and P. R. Anderson (London, HMSO, 1948); 'Dar es Salaam, City, Port and Region', *Tanzania Notes and Records* No. 71, edited by J. E. G. Sutton (Dar es Salaam, 1970); *The Royal Capital of Buganda*, by P. Gutkind (The Hague, 1963), pp. 14–15, and the Zanzibar Censuses of 1910, 1924, and 1931. The 1895 estimate for Mombasa is taken from Sir Arthur Hardinge's *Report* for 1897, C. 8683 (HMSO, 1898), that for 1926 from the 1926 census and that for 1937/38 from the 1939 *Report on a Malaria Survey*, quoted by Kuczynski, *Demographic Survey*, p. 151.

TABLE 5

RACIAL PROPORTIONS OF MAIN EAST AFRICAN URBAN CENTRES 1948

City	Group	Number	%
NAIROBI	African	64,397	54·1
	Asian/Arab	42,436	35·7
	European	10,830	9·1
	Total	118,976	100·0
MOMBASA	African	42,853	50·6
	Asian/Arab	39,065	46·1
	European	2,027	2·4
	Total	84,746	100·0
NAKURU	African	12,845	72·9
	Asian/Arab	3,420	19·4
	European	1,159	6·6
	Total	17,625	100·0
DAR ES SALAAM	African	50,765	73·3
	Asian/Arab	16,270	23·5
	European	1,726	2·5
	Total	69,227	100·0
TANGA	African	14,973	71·3
	Asian/Arab	5,214	25·3
	European	355	2·0
	Total	20,619	100·0
KAMPALA	African	11,905	53·8
	Asian/Arab	9,102	41·2
	European	1,039	4·7
	Total	22,094	100·0
JINJA	African	4,445	52·8
	Asian/Arab	3,756	44·6
	European	194	2·3
	Total	8,410	100·0
ZANZIBAR (Town)	African	22,125	48·8
	Arab	7,288	16·1
	Asian	12,945	28·6
	European	240	0·5
	Other	169	0·4
	Total	45,284	100·0

Source: 1948 Census data. Other miscellaneous racial groups account for the small differences between the main components and the totals.

B. TRADE

Study of the development of the East African economies during the colonial period has in the past been hampered by the absence of reliable and comparable trade statistics for the whole area. Trade statistics always present considerable problems of definition—such as the inclusion or omission of bullion and specie—which were often dealt with in different ways by individual colonial adminstrations. In East Africa these problems are compounded by the large volume of inter-territorial and transit trade, and by the fact that before 1949 there was no uniformity of practice in the way in which such trade was shown in the returns. For the period before 1923, indeed, it is impossible to distinguish between the trade of Kenya and of Uganda.

During recent years much progress has been made towards producing trade statistics which are firm and comparable for the whole of at least mainland East Africa. Figures on a fully comparable basis for the three mainland territories are available from 1949, when the separate customs departments of Tanganyika and of Kenya and Uganda were amalgamated. Recent work on the earlier statistics has made it possible to present in the following tables some comparable figures for the three territories for the period before 1949. References to the statistical research from which the tables are derived is given in the footnotes. To fill out the picture, data are also given, so far as possible on similar lines, for Zanzibar.

For the above reasons, figures in these tables often differ from those given in the text of the volume.

TABLE 6
MAINLAND EAST AFRICA, IMPORTS, EXPORTS, AND BALANCE OF TRADE, 1923–1944

Year	KENYA				UGANDA				KENYA–UGANDA				TANGANYIKA			
	Net imports £m	Domestic exports £m	Re-exports £m	Balance £m	Net imports £m	Domestic exports £m	Re-exports £m	Balance £m	Net imports £m	Domestic exports £m	Re-exports £m	Balance £m	Net imports £m	Domestic exports £m	Re-exports £m	Balance £m
1923	n.a.	1·6	n.a.	n.a.	n.a.	2·4	n.a.	n.a.	4·4	4·0	0·2	−0·2	n.a.	1·6	n.a.	n.a.
1924	n.a.	2·3	n.a.	n.a.	n.a.	3·9	n.a.	n.a.	6·2	6·2	0·2	0·2	1·4	2·4	n.a.	n.a.
1925	n.a.	2·7	n.a.	n.a.	n.a.	5·1	n.a.	n.a.	8·5	7·8	0·2	−0·5	1·4	2·8	0·1	0·2
1926	n.a.	2·3	n.a.	b.a.	n.a.	3·6	n.a.	n.a.	7·1	5·9	0·2	−1·0	2·7	2·8	0·1	0·1
1927	n.a.	3·0	n.a.	n.a.	n.a.	2·3	n.a.	n.a.	7·4	5·3	0·3	−1·8	3·0	3·1	0·1	−0·1
1928	6·5	3·1	0·3	−3·1	2·0	3·4	—	1·4	8·6	6·5	0·3	−1·8	3·4	3·6	0·1	0·2
1929	6·4	2·6	0·3	−3·5	2·2	4·2	—	2·1	8·7	6·8	0·4	−1·5	3·5	3·8	0·2	0·2
1930	5·2	3·3	0·3	−1·6	1·6	2·0	—	0·4	6·8	5·3	0·3	−1·2	4·0	2·6	0·1	0·0
1931	3·6	2·2	0·3	−1·1	1·3	1·9	—	0·6	4·9	4·1	0·3	−0·5	3·7	1·7	0·1	−1·0
1932	2·6	2·1	0·3	−0·1	1·2	2·2	—	1·0	3·8	4·3	0·3	0·8	2·2	2·1	0·1	−0·4
1933	2·5	2·1	0·4	—	1·2	3·4	—	2·2	3·8	5·5	0·4	2·1	2·7	2·4	0·1	−0·5
1934	2·8	1·7	0·4	−0·7	1·5	3·7	—	2·2	4·3	5·4	0·6	1·5	1·7	2·4	0·1	0·8
1935	3·5	2·8	0·6	−0·1	1·6	3·5	0·1	1·9	5·1	6·3	0·6	1·8	2·0	3·4	0·2	0·5
1936	3·9	3·7	0·5	0·3	1·9	4·4	0·1	2·6	5·8	8·1	0·6	2·9	2·6	4·5	0·2	1·0
1937	5·6	3·8	0·6	−1·2	2·7	4·6	0·1	3·0	8·3	9·3	0·7	1·7	3·0	4·9	0·2	1·7
1938	4·9	3·6	0·5	−0·8	2·4	3·9	0·1	2·3	7·3	8·2	0·7	1·6	3·4	3·7	0·2	1·7
1939	5·1	3·9	0·6	−0·6	1·9	5·1	—	3·2	7·0	7·8	0·6	1·4	2·9	4·2	0·2	1·0
1940	7·1	3·9	0·8	−2·4	2·3	5·6	—	3·3	9·0	8·9	0·9	0·8	2·5	5·0	0·1	1·9
1941	9·4	4·5	1·6	−3·3	1·7	4·6	—	2·9	11·7	10·1	1·6	0·0	2·3	5·1	0·3	2·8
1942	9·0	4·6	2·0	−2·4	2·5	5·2	0·2	2·9	10·6	9·2	2·1	0·7	3·0	6·1	0·3	2·4
1943	9·0	4·0	1·6	−3·4	2·7	5·2	—	2·9	11·5	9·2	1·8	−0·5	3·8	5·3	0·3	3·5
1944	9·7	4·5	1·3	−3·9	2·8	7·0	0·2	4·3	12·5	11·6	1·3	0·4	4·6	6·8	0·1	2·3

Inter-territorial trade, and specie, are excluded throughout. See note on sources below. Slight discrepancies in the columns showing balance of trade are due to the rounding of figures in the preceding columns.

Net imports: goods entered at the time of importation for consumption or for warehousing in Kenya, Uganda, or Tanganyika, including in both cases goods subsequently re-exported; to which have been added or from which have been deducted goods transferred inter-territorially.

Sources: Kenya and Uganda *Trade Reports*, Tanganyika *Trade Reports*, 1923–1944. Before 1949 the Kenya–Uganda and Tanganyika customs departments were separate administrations, and trade between Kenya–Uganda on the one hand, and Tanganyika on the other, was treated as foreign trade by both administrations. After the amalgamation of the two customs departments at the beginning of 1949 this trade was excluded from the statistics of external trade and was separately listed as inter-territorial trade. The figures in the above table have been adjusted to make them comparable with the post-amalgamation statistics, in that trade with Tanganyika has been excluded from the Kenya–Uganda figures, and trade with Kenya–Uganda from the Tanganyika figures. The procedures used to obtain the adjusted figures are explained in 'Constituent Trade Statistics of Kenya, Uganda and Tanganyika for 1950 and earlier years', by Arthur Hazlewood, *Economic and Statistical Review*, No. 49 (Dec. 1973).

TABLE 7

MAINLAND EAST AFRICA, IMPORTS, EXPORTS, AND BALANCE OF TRADE (EXTERNAL AND INTER-TERRITORIAL TRADE), 1945–1964

(I) Kenya

Year	Total net imports from outside E. Africa £m.	Domestic exports to outside E. Africa £m.	Re-exports £m	Balance of trade from outside E. Africa £m	Inter-territorial		Balance of inter-territorial trade £m	Total imports £m	Total exports (including re-exports) £m	Overall balance of trade £m
					Imports £m	Exports £m				
1945	8·0	5·2	1·0	−1·8	1·4	1·1	−0·4	9·5	7·3	−2·2
1946	14·0	6·2	1·3	−6·5	1·6	1·5	−0·1	15·6	9·0	−6·6
1947	20·4	8·8	1·6	−10·0	1·8	1·6	−0·3	22·2	11·9	−10·3
1948	29·4	10·2	2·2	−17·0	2·2	1·8	−0·4	31·7	14·3	−17·4
1949	37·3	11·0	2·3	−24·0	2·1	3·1	1·1	39·4	16·4	−23·0
1950	31·7	17·2	2·5	−12·0	2·3	3·6	1·3	34·0	23·3	−10·7
1951	53·9	24·1	3·3	−26·5	2·4	3·7	1·3	56·3	31·1	−25·2
1952	59·2	25·8	3·9	−29·5	3·1	4·2	1·1	62·3	33·9	−28·4
1953	51·5	19·5	3·4	−28·6	3·4	5·1	1·7	54·9	28·0	−27·0
1954	60·3	20·3	2·4	−37·6	4·0	5·5	1·5	64·3	28·2	−36·1
1955	71·4	25·7	2·3	−43·4	4·3	5·7	1·4	75·7	35·7	−42·0
1956	69·7	29·0	3·9	−36·7	3·2	7·4	4·2	72·9	40·3	−32·6
1957	71·9	26·4		−40·7	4·1	9·3	5·2	76·0	40·5	−35·5
1958	60·7	29·3	3·8	−27·6	4·9	10·8	5·9	65·6	43·9	−21·7
1959	61·5	33·3	5·0	−23·1	5·5	12·3	6·8	66·9	50·7	−16·3
1960	70·0	35·2	4·9	−29·9	7·0	13·8	6·8	77·0	53·9	−23·1
1961	68·9	35·3	6·3	−27·3	7·0	15·9	9·0	75·9	57·6	−18·3
1962	69·4	37·9	7·1	−24·4	7·3	17·3	10·0	76·8	62·3	−14·4
1963	73·6	43·8	7·1	−22·7	9·2	19·8	10·6	82·8	70·8	−12·0
										−8·3

(2) Uganda

Year	Total net imports from outside E. Africa £m	Domestic exports to outside E. Africa £m	Re-exports £m	Balance of trade from outside E. Africa £m	Inter-territorial Imports £m	Inter-territorial Exports £m	Balance of inter-territorial trade £m	Total imports £m	Total exports (including re-exports) £m	Overall balance of trade £m
1945	3·2	9·3	—	6·1	0·6	1·2	0·6	3·8	10·5	6·7
1946	5·2	8·9	0·2	3·8	0·8	1·6	0·8	6·0	10·6	4·7
1947	6·8	10·7	0·3	4·1	0·8	1·8	1·0	7·7	12·8	5·1
1948	9·5	13·5	0·4	4·4	0·9	2·2	1·3	10·4	16·1	5·7
1949	12·3	23·4	0·1	11·2	1·2	1·9	0·7	13·6	25·5	11·9
1950	15·4	28·7	0·2	13·5	1·4	2·4	1·0	16·8	31·3	14·5
1951	22·1	47·2	0·2	25·3	2·0	2·4	0·5	24·1	49·9	25·8
1952	24·2	47·2	0·5	23·5	2·2	3·6	1·4	26·4	51·3	24·9
1953	25·6	33·4	0·2	8·0	3·1	4·6	1·5	28·7	38·2	9·5
1954	25·2	40·6	0·4	15·8	3·1	5·1	2·0	28·3	46·1	17·8
1955	33·9	41·9	0·4	8·4	3·8	4·8	1·0	37·8	47·0	9·3
1956	28·1	40·4	0·8	13·2	4·3	2·7	1·6	32·3	43·9	11·6
1957	28·9	45·9	0·9	17·9	5·3	4·0	−1·3	34·2	50·8	16·6
1958	27·0	45·4	1·0	19·4	6·2	4·8	−1·4	33·1	51·2	18·1
1959	25·4	42·1	1·1	17·8	6·5	5·2	−1·3	31·9	48·5	16·5
1960	26·0	41·6	1·2	16·8	6·6	6·7	0·1	32·6	49·5	16·8
1961	26·5	39·2	2·0	14·7	7·4	6·9	−0·6	34·0	48·1	14·1
1962	26·2	37·6	3·3	14·8	7·7	7·1	−0·7	33·9	48·0	14·1
1963	30·9	51·5	3·0	23·6	9·9	8·2	−1·7	40·8	62·8	21·9
1964	32·7	64·4	2·0	33·7	13·6	9·6	−4·0	46·3	76·1	29·8

TABLE 7—continued
(3) Tanganyika

Year	Total net imports from outside E. Africa £m	Domestic exports to outside E. Africa £m	Re-exports £m	Balance of trade from outside E. Africa £m	Inter-territorial Imports £m	Inter-territorial Exports £m	Balance of inter-territorial trade £m	Total imports £m	Total exports (including re-exports) £m	Overall balance of trade £m
1945	5·4	7·7	0·2	2·6	0·9	0·7	−0·2	6·3	8·6	2·3
1946	6·3	8·5	0·2	2·5	1·3	0·5	−0·8	7·6	9·2	1·7
1947	12·0	10·8	0·2	−0·9	1·2	0·5	−0·7	13·3	11·6	−1·6
1948	20·1	16·1	0·3	−3·7	1·7	0·8	−0·9	21·8	17·3	−4·6
1949	25·5	19·9	0·5	−5·1	2·7	0·9	−1·8	28·2	21·3	−6·9
1950	24·2	24·4	1·2	1·4	3·2	0·9	−2·3	27·4	26·5	−0·9
1951	28·1	39·3	1·0	12·2	2·9	1·1	−1·7	31·0	41·5	10·5
1952	37·4	46·5	1·0	10·0	3·4	0·9	−2·5	40·9	48·3	7·5
1953	28·3	34·2	1·3	7·2	4·4	1·2	−3·1	32·7	36·8	4·1
1954	31·9	36·2	1·5	5·8	4·6	1·0	−3·6	36·5	38·8	2·2
1955	43·5	36·2	1·2	−6·1	4·0	1·7	−2·3	47·5	39·0	−8·4
1956	35·9	44·9	1·3	10·4	4·7	2·1	−2·6	40·5	48·3	7·8
1957	39·2	39·4	1·6	1·8	5·9	2·0	−3·9	45·1	43·1	−2·1
1958	33·5	41·7	2·1	10·3	7·1	2·6	−4·5	40·6	46·4	5·8
1959	34·4	45·3	1·9	12·7	8·1	2·6	−5·5	42·5	49·7	7·2
1960	36·8	54·8	1·7	19·8	9·2	2·3	−6·9	46·0	58·9	12·9
1961	39·6	48·7	1·9	10·9	10·6	2·2	−8·4	50·2	52·8	2·5
1962	39·8	51·2	2·2	13·7	11·7	2·4	−9·3	51·5	55·9	4·4
1963	40·4	63·6	1·6	24·7	12·4	3·4	−8·9	52·8	68·6	15·8
1964	43·8	70·1	1·3	27·6	15·7	5·1	−10·6	59·5	76·5	17·0

Specie excluded throughout. Minor discrepancies in the columns showing totals and balance of trade are due to the rounding of figures in the preceding columns.

Sources: Figures throughout are derived from Kenya, Uganda, and Tanganyika Annual *Trade Reports*, but these have been summarized [...] *Trade Statistics of the Countries of East Africa, 1945–1964*' in the *Economic and Statistical Review*,

TABLE 8

ZANZIBAR, IMPORTS, EXPORTS, AND BALANCE OF TRADE
1928–1963

Year	Total imports of goods £m	Domestic exports £m	Re-exports £m	Total exports £m	Balance of trade £m
1928	1·5	1·0	0·6	1·6	0·1
1929	1·6	1·2	0·6	1·7	0·1
1930	1·4	1·0	0·5	1·5	—
1931	1·1	0·9	0·3	1·2	0·1
1932	0·9	0·7	0·2	0·9	—
1933	0·8	0·6	0·2	0·8	—
1934	0·7	0·6	0·1	0·7	—
1935	0·9	0·6	0·2	0·8	−0·1
1936	0·8	0·8	0·2	1·0	0·2
1937	1·0	0·7	0·2	0·8	−0·2
1938	0·9	0·7	0·1	0·8	−0·1
1939	0·8	1·0	0·1	1·1	0·3
1940	0·8	0·9	0·2	1·1	0·2
1941	1·0	1·3	0·2	1·5	0·5
1942	1·0	1·2	0·1	1·3	0·3
1943	1·1	0·9	0·2	1·1	—
1944	1·2	0·9	0·3	1·1	0·1
1945	1·2	1·0	0·3	1·3	0·1
1946	1·9	1·7	0·4	2·1	0·2
1947	1·9	1·1	0·3	1·4	−0·5
1948	2·6	1·4	0·6	2·0	−0·6
1949	2·8	2·1	0·6	2·7	−0·1
1950	3·7	4·3	0·6	4·9	1·2
1951	5·1	5·3	0·8	6·1	0·8
1952	5·0	4·0	0·7	4·7	−0·4
1953	5·8	7·2	0·7	7·9	2·0
1954	5·4	5·2	0·8	5·9	0·6
1955	5·7	5·0	0·9	5·8	0·1
1956	6·1	4·9	0·9	5·9	−0·2
1957	6·4	4·7	1·1	5·9	−0·6
1958	5·2	4·0	1·1	5·1	−0·1
1959	5·4	3·8	0·8	4·6	−0·7
1960	5·2	4·8	0·8	5·6	0·4
1961	5·5	3·6	0·8	4·4	−1·1
1962	5·4	3·2	1·3	4·5	−0·9
1963	5·4	4·3	0·8	5·1	−0·2

Bullion and specie excluded throughout, but trade with British mainland East Africa included. Slight discrepancies in the columns showing total exports and balance of trade are due to the rounding of figures in the preceding columns.

Source: Zanzibar *Trade Reports,* 1928–1960. Figures for 1961–3 are added from the East African *Economic and Statistical Review.*

TABLE 9
MAINLAND EAST AFRICA, TERMS OF TRADE
(1) 1938–1953
(1938 = 100)

Year	Kenya	Uganda	Tanganyika	East Africa
1939	112	88	122	109
1940	85	92	107	91
1941	83	84	93	86
1942	67	52	90	68
1943	43	44	60	49
1944	48	59	74	61
1945	59	80	88	75
1946	67	74	93	75
1947	83	77	102	86
1948	81	85	131	98
1949	84	143	157	129
1950	123	164	172	154
1951	139	218	236	198
1952	139	203	264	201
1953	116	157	214	161

Export value index as percentage of import price index.
Source: East Africa Royal Commission 1953–1955 Report, Appendix X. p. 482, col 4.

(2) 1954–1963
(1954 = 100)

Year	Kenya	Uganda	Tanganyika	East Africa
1955	100	89	101	94
1956	88	83	93	86
1957	84	86	92	84
1958	80	80	85	80
1959	82	70	90	78
1960	80	61	90	74
1961	84	63	91	77
1962	79	66	97	78
1963	77	60	101	77

Export price index as a percentage of import price index.
Source: East African *Economic and Statistical Review*, No. 13 (Dec. 1964), p. 29. Figure for 1955 calculated from data in No. 2 (Mar. 1962) issue of the *Review*, p. 31.

EAST AFRICA, PRINCIPAL EXPORT COMMODITIES, SELECTED YEARS 1928–1948, AND 1952–1963

Year	(1) Kenya									(2) Uganda			
	Total value domestic exports £m	Sisal %	Maize %	Coffee %	Tea %	Wattle-bark and extract %	Hides and skins %	Pyrethrum %	Sodium carb. %	Total value domestic exports £m	Cotton %	Coffee %	Hides and skins %
1928	3·1	16	10	36	—	—	11	—	13	3·4	73	5	8
1931	2·2	10	18	44	—	—	5	—	9	1·9	78	8	—
1938	3·6	12	6	21	13	—	5	5	—	4·6	75	7	—
1946	6·2	14	—	15	8	5	6	18	7	8·9	63	20	—
1948	10·2	23	—	20	6	7	8	—	9	13·5	55	24	—
1952	25·8	17	9	28	5	7	—	—	—	47·2	63	26	—
1953	19·5	13	—	34	—	8	8	6	—	33·4	50	35	—
1954	20·3	10	5	28	10	8	7	—	6	40·6	52	33	—
1955	25·7	8	7	35	11	9	5	—	6	41·9	39	48	—
1956	29·0	7	—	47	9	10	—	—	5	40·4	48	39	—
1957	26·4	8	—	41	11	6	6	—	5	45·9	38	47	—
1958	29·3	8	6	36	11	6	—	6	—	45·4	40	46	—
									Meat products				*Copper*
1959	33·3	10	—	32	11	—	—	7	6	42·1	37	44	7
1960	35·2	13	—	29	13	—	5	9	5	41·6	36	41	9
1961	35·3	12	—	30	11	—	—	9	7	39·2	43	36	8
1962	37·9	11	—	28	14	—	—	8	7	37·6	22	54	10
1963	43·8	17	—	25	13	—	—	7	6	51·5	28	53	7

Percentages are given only where the proportion is 5% or more of the total.

Sources: Kenya and Uganda Annual *Trade Reports*, 1928–1963. For the five selected years before 1952, the figures for total domestic exports have been adjusted as for Table 6, and thus exclude inter-territorial exports. For the years 1952–1959 the percentages are reproduced in the *Quarterly Economic and Statistical Bulletin* of the East African Statistical Department.

TABLE 10—continued

	(3) Tanganyika						(4) Zanzibar			
Year	Total value domestic exports £m	Sisal %	Coffee %	Cotton %	Diamonds %	Hides and skins / Oil-seeds %	Total value domestic exports £m	Cloves and clove oil %	Copra %	Coconut oil %
1928	3·6	31	20	14	—	10	1·0	72	24	—
1931	1·7	42	15	7	—	5	0·9	82	16	—
1938	3·7	37	10	10	—	6	0·7	78	15	—
1946	8·5	46	8	—	12	—	1·7	73	12	—
1948	16·1	55	6	8	6	—	1·4	75	—	12
1952	46·5	47	12	10	9	5	4·0	78	—	12
1953	34·2	37	17	14	5	—	7·2	85	6	7
1954	36·2	30	28	9	9	—	5·2	81	8	8
1955	36·2	28	19	15	9	7	5·0	81	7	7
1956	44·9	24	21	17	6	9	4·9	81	8	7
1957	39·4	24	18	17	8	7	4·7	83	—	9
1958	41·7	25	18	17	11	6	4·0	68	15	9
1959	45·3	29	15	13	10	6	3·8	72	15	5
1960	54·8	28	13	16	9	—	4·8	77	7	6
1961	48·7	29	28	14	12	—	3·6	71	11	6
1962	51·2	31	30	14	11	—				
1963	63·6	36	25	17	8	—	n.a.	n.a.	n.a.	n.a.

Percentages are given only where the proportion is 5% or more of the total.

... For Tanganyika the figures of total domestic exports for the

TABLE II

EAST AFRICA, DIRECTION OF TRADE

(1) *Kenya–Uganda, 1930–1948*

Year	Total imports £m	Source of imports					Total domestic exports £m	Destination of exports		
		From UK %	From India %	From Tanganyika %	From Japan %	From other sources %		To UK %	To India %	To other destinations %
1923	5·4	51	13	9	6	21	4·0	47	31	22
1930	8·1	44	8	7	6	35	5·5	43	26	31
1931	5·7	45	8	7	9	31	4·3	37	33	30
1932	4·9	39	7	12	11	31	4·5	39	33	28
1933	4·9	38	6	13	13	30	5·7	36	32	32
1934	5·7	38	5	15	15	27	5·7	22	37	41
1935	6·6	37	6	13	15	29	6·6	25	41	34
1936	7·4	38	5	10	15	32	8·4	29	21	50
1937	10·8	41	4	9	15	31	9·7	27	32	41
1938	9·7	45	4	9	11	31	8·5	33	35	32
1939	9·0	40	6	12	10	32	8·1	34	21	45
1940	11·1	31	11	11	6	41	9·2	30	22	48
1941	14·6	29	24	9	—	38	10·5	14	40	46
1942	13·9	20	22	12	—	46	9·7	26	19	55
1943	14·6	18	26	10	—	46	9·9	31	22	47
1944	15·7	23	25	10	—	42	12·4	17	41	42
1945	14·5	29	16	11	—	44	15·7	22	37	41
1946	22·7	39	16	6	1	39	16·8	29	25	46
1947	31·4	40	10	7	1	42	21·1	23	34	43
1948	45·3	52	7	6		34	25·8	30	22	48

TABLE II—*continued*

(2) *Tanganyika, 1930–1948*

Year	Total imports £m	Source of imports					Total exports and re-exports £m	Destination of exports			
		From UK %	From India %	From Kenya/ Uganda %	From Japan %	From other sources %		To UK %	To Kenya/ Uganda %	To British India %	To other destinations %
1923	2·2	38	13	24	—	25	1·7	22	29	3	46
1930	4·1	44	10	4	7	35	2·7	15	21	3	61
1931	2·5	38	10	7	10	35	1·7	18	23	3	56
1932	2·0	35	9	8	15	33	2·3	34	25	4	37
1933	2·1	34	7	10	20	29	2·7	32	23	6	39
1934	2·5	33	5	11	21	30	2·9	35	28	6	31
1935	3·3	35	4	9	20	32	3·8	38	21	8	33
1936	3·7	34	5	8	21	32	5·0	38	15	5	42
1937	4·2	29	5	9	22	35	5·5	35	14	8	43
1938	3·5	29	5	11	17	38	4·3	41	17	6	36
1939	3·3	31	6	12	20	31	5·2	38	16	4	42
1940	3·5	42	11	11	13	23	6·4	45	19	5	31
1941	3·7	23	41	11	4	21	6·9	21	23	9	47
1942	3·7	18	45	16	1	20	7·9	11	23	7	59
1943	4·8	19	46	16	—	19	6·6	21	28	7	44
1944	5·8	19	34	16	—	31	7·9	26	24	10	40
1945	7·0	23	25	18	—	34	8·6	33	21	9	37
1946	8·2	32	20	20	—	28	9·3	46	16	5	33
1947	13·9	33	12	11	1	43	11·6	42	19	7	32
1948	22·6	47	8	9	1	35	16·2	52	16	5	27

Bullion and specie included throughout.

... and Tanganyika Annual *Trade Reports*, 1930–1948. The figures of total imports and exports differ

(3) Zanzibar, 1935–1961

Year	Total imports £m		Source of imports				Total exports and re-exports £m		Destination of exports					
		From UK %	From India/Burma/Pakistan %	From Kenya/Uganda/Tanganyika %	From Japan £m	From other sources %		To UK %	To India/Pakistan %	To Kenya/Uganda/Tanganyika %	To Netherlands E. Indies/Indonesia %	To Straits Settlements %	To Other destinations %
1923	[Rs 2, 91, 45]	21	25	24	4	26	[Rs 3, 42, 06]	24	18	22	—	—	36
1935	1·0	21	7	10	13	49	0·9	5	31	10	23	—	31
1936	0·9	21	17	11	14	37	1·0	4	26	9	29	—	32
1937	1·2	23	20	12	14	31	0·9	8	10	11	23	—	32
1938	1·0	15	20	12	12	41	0·8	5	15	13	37	—	30
1939	0·8	10	21	14	10	45	1·2	9	24	9	33	—	25
1940	0·9	13	20	22	12	33	1·2	7	14	19	37	1	22
1941	1·0	12	40	17	6	25	1·6	8	23	15	27	1	26
1942	1·0	8	29	31	—	32	1·4	11	32	9	—	—	48
1943	1·2	10	25	30	—	35	1·1	10	23	18	—	—	49
1944	1·2	12	16	30	—	42	1·2	8	30	19	—	—	43
1945	1·2	13	17	36	—	34	1·4	10	31	15	—	11	44
1946	2·0	17	10	29	1	44	2·2	6	37	12	—	11	24
1947	2·0	23	9	29	2	38	1·5	7	32	22	—	5	34
1948	2·7	22	6	28	6	42	2·1	5	36	25	1	11	22
1949	3·0	25	8	21	7	40	2·8	33	14	20	—	7	26
1950	3·9	26	10	23	7	44	5·1	15	20	12	4	31	18
1951	5·3	21	16	16	10	37	6·2	10	28	16	8	27	11

TABLE II—*continued*

(3) *Zanzibar, 1935–1961—continued*

		Source of imports						Destination of exports					
Year	Total imports £m	From UK %	From India/ Burma/ Pakistan %	From Kenya/ Uganda/ Tangan-yika %	From Japan £m	From other sources %	Total exports and re-exports £m	To UK %	To India/ Pakistan %	To Kenya/ Uganda/ Tangan-yika %	To Nether-lands E. Indies/ Indonesia %	To Straits Settle-ments %	To Other destina-tions %
1952	5·2	28	17	18	6	31	4·8	16	1	14	2	42	25
1953	5·9	35	22	17	1	25	8·0	6	18	8	30	8	30
1954	5·9	28	29	15	1	27	6·4	6	21	19	31	1	22
1955	6·7	28	23	11	4	34	6·8	4	18	26	35	1	16
1956	6·4	37	14	13	4	32	6·2	3	24	15	43	—	15
1957	6·5	24	16	14	9	47	5·9	2	26	17	35	3	17
1958	5·3	28	11	15	6	40	5·2	3	19	19	29	5	25
1959	5·5	21	16	18	7	38	4·8	3	19	10	31	2	34
1960	5·4	19	14	17	7	43	5·7	4	15	10	37	1	32
1961	6·3	23	14	14	6	43	5·2	5	16	13	22	5	39

Source: Zanzibar *Trade Accounts*, 1923 and 1935–1961. Bullion and specie are included. The export percentages as given in the accounts include re-exports, which constituted a substantial part of Zanzibar export trade. For instance, re-exports to British mainland East Africa —mostly to Tanganyika—generally accounted for from 10% to 15% of the total. This somewhat obscures the dominant part played by clove exports to Asia.

TABLE 12

MAINLAND EAST AFRICA METROPOLITAN
SHARE OF TRADE 1949–1963

Year	Imports		Total exports and re-exports	
	Total £m.	% U.K.	Total £m.	% U.K.
1949	75.2	53·0	57·2	33·1
1950	71·3	54·7	72·9	33·7
1951	104·1	43·7	115·2	33·0
1952	121·1	47·6	124·8	31·7
1953	105·8	51·2	92·2	31·6
1954	117·5	44·3	101·6	30·0
1955	149·0	43·7	107·7	27·6
1956	133·8	43·8	120·8	26·2
1957	140·1	38·2	119·1	24·4
1958	121·4	37·1	123·4	25·8
1959	121·5	37·6	128·8	30·6
1960	133·9	34·2	139·7	24·3
1961	135·2	35·5	133·6	25·0
1962	135·5	33·8	139·7	27·1
1963	145·0	32·4	170·6	25·1

Sources: East African *Quarterly Economic and Statistical Bulletin*, Nos. 30 (Dec. 1955) and 37/38 (Sept./Dec. 1957), and *Economic and Statistical Review*, Nos. 1 (Dec. 1961), 5 (Dec. 1962), and 13 (Dec. 1964).

C. PUBLIC FINANCE

With the passing of the era when the balancing of a colony's budget was regarded as a primary objective of its administration, statistics of government revenue and expenditure must be regarded as being of limited value. Nevertheless, in a period before the elaboration of national accounting techniques, they do—together with trade returns—give some idea of the relative scale of the economies of the countries concerned.

Revenue and expenditure figures in East Africa as elsewhere, are among the few that go back, in some detail, to almost the beginning of the colonial period. But their function—that of determining how far, in strictly financial terms, each territory was 'paying its way'— did not require any rigidly consistent definition of which accounts were to fall within the system. Thus throughout the 1920s and 1930s the Kenya and Uganda railway administration was excluded from government finance, but the finances of the Tanganyika railway were often (though not always) included in the financial accounts of that territory's administration. From the beginning of the Second World War, however, there was a growing convergence in accounting procedures; the year 1938 therefore has been taken as the base line for the tables in this section. The tables also show the point at which each territory began to distinguish its development and capital account from that of general revenue and expenditure.

They provide moreover the starting-point at least for a comparative functional analysis of government revenue and expenditure. Although figures are sometimes quoted that claim to compare for either different countries or different periods the percentage of government expenditure devoted to say 'education' or 'health', these generally prove on investigation to be largely meaningless. Genuinely comparable analysis is possible, but it requires a rigorous and detailed breakdown of each expenditure head, as well as a broadly consistent series of overall revenue/expenditure figures. The only attempt made here at a rudimentary analysis of this kind is that represented by Table 14, which gives an indication of the sources of tax revenue, in selected years, of the four East African territories.

It should be noted that the figures of the central budget are far from constituting the total governmental revenues of each territory. In all of them local government authorities collected and disposed of considerable revenues of their own. The budget of the Kingdom of Buganda, for instance, was in the 1950s some 5% of the size of the overall Uganda Protectorate budget.

TABLE 13

EAST AFRICA, GOVERNMENT REVENUE AND EXPENDITURE

(1) *Kenya 1938–1962/63*

Year	Revenue £'000	Expenditure £'000	Year	Revenue £'000	Expenditure £'000
1938	3,776	3,649	1942	5,595	5,341
1939	3,812	3,808	1943	6,802	6,782
1940	4,111	4,064	1944	7,734	7,629
1941	5,349	4,511	1945	8,034	7,816

	Colony		Development Fund	
Year	Revenue £'000	Expenditure £'000	Revenue £'000	Expenditure £'000
1946	9,057	8,795	3,221	984
1947	9,877	9,024	2,196	1,588
1948	11,412	10,967	1,735	2,655
1949	13,031	10,762	1,307	4,223
1950	13,244	12,504	2,772	4,055
1951	17,468	16,437	7,485	4,095
1952	20,548	18,859	8,964	5,352
1953	21,352	22,853	8,263	6,163
[1954 (half-year)	15,081	18,700]	[679	2,752]
1954/55	36,722	39,055	2,345	7,160
1955/56	45,336	40,280	9,344	7,383
1956/57[1]	32,793	34,682	5,241	8,182
1957/58	33,429	33,290	6,782	7,864
1958/59	33,468	32,760	6,794	9,194
1959/60	32,997	31,671	8,087	9,695
1960/61	34,249	34,262	8,762	9,151
1961/62	34,978	33,287	8,923	9,320
1962/63	36,094	35,575	11,071	11,111

Sources: Kenya Annual *Financial Reports* and *Appropriation Accounts* for years 1938–1955/56; East African *Economic and Statistical Review* for years 1956/57–1962/63.

[1] A substantial change in the categorization was made for the years 1956/57 onwards: minor changes may have been made at other points.

TABLE 13—*continued*

(2) *Uganda 1938–1962/63*

Year	Revenue £'000	Expenditure £'000	Year	Revenue £'000	Expenditure £'000
1938	1,864	2,020	1947	5,331	4,474
1939	1,718	2,260	1948	6,405	6,530
1940	1,871	2,057	1949	8,094	6,687
1941	2,178	1,865	1950	11,037	8,000
1942	2,190	1,889	1951	15,826	12,346
1943	2,429	2,136	1952	17,289	15,951
1944	2,658	2,598	1953	17,735	17,432
1945	3,366	3,199	[1954 (half-year)	10,349	8,628]
1946	4,053	3,574			

Year	Revenue Budget Revenue £'000	Revenue Budget Expenditure £'000	Capital Budget Revenue £'000	Capital Budget Expenditure £'000
1954/55	19,476	18,967	4,649	5,243
1955/56	18,927	17,460	3,570	6,437
1956/57	19,047	18,261	5,543	6,647
1957/58	18,788	19,228	3,653	6,290
1958/59	20,248	20,286	3,857	5,398
1959/60	20,642	19,612	1,295	5,284
1960/61	20,587	21,812	1,756	5,128
1961/62	17,642	20,344	1,562	4,824
1962/63	21,949	21,457	3,126	4,787

Sources: Uganda *Reports on Accounts*, 1938–1960/61; *Economic and Statistical Review* for 1961/62–1962/63 figures.

TABLE 13—*continued*

(3) *Tanganyika 1938–1962/63*

Year	Revenue £'ooo	Expenditure £'ooo	Year	Revenue £'ooo	Expenditure £'ooo
1938	2,113	2,224	1943	3,730	3,725
1939	2,133	2,389	1944	4,209	4,181
1940	2,308	2,256	1945	4,768	4,756
1941	2,675	2,550	1946	5,147	5,140
1942	3,147	3,132			

	Territorial Budget		Development Budget	
Year	Revenue £'ooo	Expenditure £'ooo	Revenue £'ooo	Expenditure £'ooo
1947	5,777	5,665	236	424
1948	6,965	6,382	923	996
1949	5,856	7,772	1,742	1,687
1950	10,397	10,123	2,927	3,439
1951	11,931	12,305	4,348	3,830
1952	16,430	15,878	4,896	4,989
1953	14,728	14,724	3,518	3,726
[1954 (half-year)	9,133	9,005	1,588	1,601]
1954/55	19,277	17,700	3,688	3,711
1955/56	18,680	19,532	4,214	4,084
1956/57	17,492	18,157	5,282	5,282
1957/58	18,834	18,697	5,454	5,454
1958/59	19,412	19,527	5,159	3,939
1959/60	22,066	21,154	3,939	5,613
1960/61	21,355	21,267	5,672	7,341
1961/62	21,885	24,710	3,448	5,674
1962/63	25,028	31,082	6,054	7,263

Sources: Tanganyika *Treasurer's Reports* and *Accounts*, 1938–1960/61. Figures for 1961/62–1962/63 from *Economic and Statistical Review.*

TABLE 13—continued

(4) Zanzibar 1938–1961

Year	Revenue Total £'000	C.D.W. grants included in total £'000	Expenditure £'000	Year	Revenue Total £'000	C.D.W. grants included in total £'000	Expenditure £'000
1938	465	(1·0)	464	1943	535	(1·4)	499
1939	499	(1·5)	452	1944	639	(2·2)	566
1940	466	(0·3)	524	1945	629	(14·2)	648
1941	565	(0·4)	481	1946	795	(25·6)	750
1942	549	(0·7)	484	1947	746	(56·4)	878

Year	Revenue Excluding Development £'000	Revenue Including Development £'000	Expenditure Excluding Development £'000	Expenditure Including Development £'000
1948	809	901	850	938
1949	1,025	1,118	1,083	1,209
1950	1,470	1,703	1,028	1,242
1951	1,565	1,802	1,178	1,387
1952	1,381	1,644	1,433	1,664
1953	2,654	2,748	1,658	1,754
1954	2,652	2,763	2,391	2,425
1955	2,414	2,573	2,265	2,104
1956	2,431	2,605	2,395	2,553
1957	2,550	2,681	2,743	2,709
1958	2,382	2,496	2,531	2,712
1959	2,255	2,338	3,674	3,924
1960	2,573	2,604	2,525	2,677
[1961 (half-year)	1,398		1,563]	

Sources: Zanzibar *Annual Estimates* (*ex*cluding development finance); and *Annual Reports* from 1948 (*in*cluding development finance.)

TABLE 14

EAST AFRICA, SOURCES OF TAX REVENUE, SELECTED YEARS 1928–1957/58

Year	Country	Total revenue £'000	Tax revenue £'000	Components of tax revenue			
				(a) Indirect		(b) Direct	
				Customs/ excise[1] %	Licences and other %	Non-African income and other personal tax[2] %	African hut and poll tax %
1928	Kenya	3,021	1,823	50	16	2	31
	Uganda[3] (av. 1927–30)	1,477	1,200	44	9	11	45
	Tanganyika	1,973	1,617	44	8	1	46
	Zanzibar	472	278	92			—
1933	Kenya	3,121	1,541	47	16	9	28
	Uganda	1,350	1,014	30	16	1	52
	Tanganyika	1,563	1,214	34	10	6	50
	Zanzibar	475	285	90	10		—
1938	Kenya	3,776	1,877	47	16	9	28
	Uganda	1,864	1,371	44	12	3	42
	Tanganyika	2,113	1,558	44	12	3	41
	Zanzibar	465	254	91	9		—

1 Including crop taxes levied on quantities exported.
2 Including (a) non-African poll tax (b) estate duty, but excluding fines and forfeitures (these are, however, very small).
3 Rough estimate, based on data in *Majority Report of First Report of Finance Committee 1931* (Entebbe, 1931).

TABLE 14—continued

| Year | Country | Total revenue £'000 | Tax revenue £'000 | Components of tax revenue | | | |
| | | | | (a) Indirect | | (b) Direct | |
				Customs/ exise[1] %	Licenses and other %	Non-African income and other personal tax[2] %	African hut and poll tax %
1948	Kenya	11,412	8,122	62	13	18	7
	Uganda	6,405	4,820	73	4	10	14
	Tanganyika	6,965	5,487	59	11	14	16
	Zanzibar	809	551	87	6	7[4]	
1953	Kenya	21,352	16,256	46	9	39	7
	Uganda	17,735	11,106	75	3	17	5
	Tanganyika	14,728	11,521	38	8	38	16
	Zanzibar	2,654	2,183	93	3	4	
1957/58	Kenya	43,512	27,655	40	10	50[5]	
	Uganda	18,788	16,565	74	4	20	2
	Tanganyika	18,834	14,665	51	8	32	10
	Zanzibar (1958)	2,382	1,819	85	3	12	

[4] No separate racial taxes were levied in Zanzibar.
[5] African and non-African tax no longer distinguished in Kenya.

Sources: As for preceding tables, except for Uganda 1927–30 (for which see note 3 above). Although figures for total revenue are given in this table, the bases on which these were compiled, especially before 1938, varied so much that to try to express tax revenue as a percentage

TABLE 15

EAST AFRICA HIGH COMMISSION, REVENUE AND EXPENDITURE
1948–1962/63

Year	Revenue	Expenditure	Year	Revenue	Expenditure
1948	1,519	1,629	1955/56	4,348	3,971
1949	1,163	1,096	1956/57	3,993	4,274
1950	1,855	1,817	1957/58	4,971	4,611
1951	2,909	3,027	1958/59	4,608	4,455
1952	3,234	3,242	1959/60	3,850	4,646
1953	3,652	3,589	1960/61	4,858	5,094
[1954 (half-year)	1,986	1,947]	1961/62	6,467	5,726
1954/55	4,803	4,371	1962/63	6,154	5,584

Sources: For 1948–1957/58, the East African *Quarterly Economic and Statistical Bulletin*, Nos. 27 (Mar. 1955) and 45 (Sept. 1959). For 1957/58–1962/63, *Economic and Statistical Review*, Nos. 5 (Dec. 1962) and 19 (June 1966). The figures given in these abstracts sometimes differ slightly from the original accounts in the *Financial Reports and Statements* of the East Africa High Commisisson.

TABLE 16

EAST AFRICA HIGH COMMISSION, SOURCES OF REVENUE
1950 AND 1960/61

	1950		1960/61	
	£'000	%	£'000	%
(1) UK Government				
Direct Exchequer Grant	26	1·4	304	6·3
C.D.W. and Overseas Aid Programmes	520	28·0	583	12·0
Total	546	29·4	887	18·3
(2) East African Governments				
Kenya	540	29·1	1,571	32·3
Uganda	295	15·9	781	16·1
Tanganyika	355	19·1	1,071	22·0
Zanzibar	8	0·4	42	0·9
Total	1,198	64·6	3,465	71·3
(3) Other	111	6·0	506	10·4
Total	1,855	100·0	4,858	100·0

Sources: As for Table 15 above.

D. EXPORT CROPS

The following tables showing exports of the principal East African cash crops are given in the absence of any sufficiently firm and comparable data on the actual production of such crops. While production figures of sorts for all of these crops do exist for each country, the bases on which these were compiled vary so widely as to make them of little use for the purposes of comparison, either over time or as between one territory and another. The tables below do at least provide a broad overall picture of the relative contributions of the three mainland countries to the main export crops, and, taken in conjunction with the trade figures in Section B above, enable those interested to trace the broad relation between price and quantities exported.

TABLE 17

EAST AFRICA, SISAL EXPORTS 1923–1962
'000 tons

Year	Kenya	Uganda	Tanganyika	Total	Year	Kenya	Uganda	Tanganyika	Total
1923	9	—	13	22	1943	26	1	97	124
1924	11	—	18	29	1944	27	1	112	140
1925	14	—	18	32	1945	29	1	111	141
1926	15	—	25	40	1946	25	1	112	138
1927	16	—	33	49	1947	24	1	96	121
1928	17	—	36	53	1948	31	1	117	149
1929	16	—	46	62	1949	33	1	132	166
1930	16	—	50	66	1950	36	1	119	156
1931	16	—	56	72	1951	39	1	142	182
1932	15	—	61	76	1952	35	1	158	194
1933	20	—	70	90	1953	35	1	171	207
1934	24	—	73	97	1954	32	1	168	201
1935	32	1	83	116	1955	33	1	174	208
1936	35	1	81	117	1956	35	1	186	222
1937	31	1	91	123	1957	40	—	182	222
1938	28	2	101	131	1958	42	—	198	240
1939	29	2	93	124	1959	51	1	209	261
1940	25	3	79	107	1960	57	1	207	265
1941	22	1	76	99	1961	58	1	201	260
1942	32	2	136	170	1962	56	—	220	276

Sources: Kenya, Uganda, Tanganyika *Trade Reports*, 1923–1960. The figures for 1961 and 1962 have been added from the *Statistical Abstracts* for each territory for these years.

TABLE 18

EAST AFRICA, COTTON EXPORTS 1923–1962
'ooo centals (of 100 lbs) raw cotton

Year	Kenya	Uganda	Tanganyika	Total	Year	Kenya	Uganda	Tanganyika	Total
1923	1	382	33	416	1943	26	491	157	674
1924	1	514	57	572	1944	23	758	133	914
1925	2	784	101	887	1945	16	1,058	161	1,235
1926	1	723	109	833	1946	7	877	89	973
1927	—	527	88	615	1947	15	1,012	158	1,185
1928	2	554	110	666	1948	9	697	222	928
1929	1	816	111	928	1949	22	1,561	242	1,825
1930	5	516	82	603	1950	19	1,390	157	1,566
1931	3	756	54	813	1951	39	1,385	186	1,610
1932	5	829	72	906	1952	61	1,512	249	1,822
1933	11	1,179	114	1,304	1953	42	1,337	330	1,709
1934	12	1,143	126	1,281	1954	61	1,573	271	1,905
1935	28	1,013	224	1,265	1955	52	1,225	456	1,733
1936	58	1,285	253	1,596	1956	69	1,506	625	2,200
1937	71	1,354	258	1,683	1957	31	1,347	610	1,988
1938	49	1,609	199	1,857	1958	49	1,550	718	2,317
1939	60	1,319	261	1,640	1959	71	1,493	688	2,252
1940	38	1,214	238	1,490	1960	78	1,320	871	2,269
1941	42	1,464	294	1,800	1961	55	1,393	665	2,113
1942	34	944	179	1,157	1962	41	722	730	1,493

Sources: Kenya, Uganda, Tanganyika *Trade Reports,* 1923–1960. The figures for 1961 and 1962 have been added from the *Statistical Abstracts* for each territory for those years.

TABLE 19

EAST AFRICA, COFFEE EXPORTS 1923–1962
'000 cwt. raw coffee

Year	Kenya	Uganda	Tanganyika	Total	Year	Kenya	Uganda	Tanganyika	Total
1923	139	45	81	265	1943	156	403	218	777
1924	158	41	105	304	1944	149	383	311	843
1925	147	30	120	297	1945	149	405	289	843
1926	141	33	131	305	1946	192	628	200	1,020
1927	210	44	132	386	1947	212	421	277	910
1928	212	40	209	461	1948	286	756	225	1,267
1929	133	41	177	351	1949	156	478	241	875
1930	310	49	232	591	1950	205	637	300	1,142
1931	246	70	185	501	1951	198	872	331	1,401
1932	276	87	227	590	1952	338	788	373	1,499
1933	257	100	254	611	1953	296	714	305	1,315
1934	187	154	295	636	1954	214	690	386	1,290
1935	358	126	372	856	1955	386	1,485	368	2,239
1936	409	229	443	1,081	1956	531	1,229	431	2,191
1937	274	258	272	804	1957	443	1,674	368	2,485
1938	342	280	275	897	1958	498	1,568	443	2,509
1939	338	343	332	1,013	1959	515	1,762	391	2,668
1940	172	359	313	844	1960	556	2,329	501	3,386
1941	248	406	273	927	1961	643	2,064	492	3,199
1942	247	344	297	888	1962	609	2,619	512	3,741

Sources: Kenya, Uganda, Tanganyika *Trade Reports,* 1923–1960. The figures for 1961 and 1962 have been added from the *Statistical Abstracts* for each territory for those years.

TABLE 20

EAST AFRICA, TEA EXPORTS 1930–1962
'000 cwt.

Year	Kenya	Uganda	Tanganyika	Total	Year	Kenya	Uganda	Tanganyika	Total
1930	1	—	—	1	1947	86	22	9	117
1931	3	—	—	3	1948	53	21	9	83
1932	6	—	—	6	1949	53	21	9	83
1933	17	—	—	17	1950	83	19	10	112
1934	22	—	—	22	1951	82	17	16	115
1935	45	—	—	45	1952	86	19	20	125
1936	67	1	1	69	1953	60	25	22	107
1937	82	1	2	85	1954	96	44	31	171
1938	84	1	3	88	1955	115	45	34	194
1939	89	2	4	95	1956	139	48	39	226
1940	88	4	6	98	1957	143	54	44	241
1941	93	8	7	108	1958	162	53	46	261
1942	103	13	10	136	1959	188	66	53	307
1943	85	10	10	105	1960	213	77	63	353
1944	82	13	7	102	1961	195	76	63	354
1945	85	18	8	111	1962	265	104	78	447
1946	80	12	13	105					

Sources: Kenya, Uganda, Tanganyika *Trade Reports,* 1930–62. Tea was not exported before 1930. The figures for 1961 and 1962 have been added from the *Statistical Abstracts* for each territory for those years.

TABLE 21

ZANZIBAR, CLOVE EXPORTS 1925–1960
'000 cwt.

Year		Year		Year	
1913	159	1936	207	1949	152
		1937	121	1950	354
1925	219	1938	157	1951	232
1926	158	1939	264	1952	88
1927	259	1940	218	1953	162
1928	158	1941	330	1954	193
1929	175	1942	218	1955	225
1930	146	1943	140	1956	241
1931	217	1944	129	1957	236
1932	162	1945	164	1958	182
1933	215	1946	310	1959	185
1934	218	1947	151	1960	247
1935	190	1948	258		

Source: Zanzibar *Trade Reports,* 1913 and 1924–1960.

E. NATIONAL INCOME

Owing to variations in coverage and calculation, it is not possible
to present a single series of national income estimates even for the
mainland territories. For Kenya estimates of geographical income
and of *net* product were published from 1947 onward. For Uganda
there were estimates of geographical income only, beginning in 1950.
From 1954 all three mainland territories produced figures for *gross*
domestic product. Estimates on the old basis continued to be published for Kenya and Uganda until 1958, but the differences between
the two series are too large for linking to be practicable. It is therefore
necessary to present two overlapping tables: one showing the annual
estimates of geographical income for Kenya and Uganda up to 1958,
the second showing the gross domestic product of the three territories
in 1954, 1958, and 1962.

It will be appreciated that the estimates, being given in current
prices, cannot be used to calculate the rate of real economic growth.
They do, however, provide some information on the structure of the
territorial economies.

For a useful guide to the national accounts of the period, see 'On
the Calculation and Interpretation of National Accounting Material
in East Africa', by T. A. Kennedy, H. W. Ord, and D. Walker, in
African Studies in Income and Wealth, ed. L. H. Samuels (London, 1963).

TABLE 22

MAINLAND EAST AFRICA

ESTIMATES OF GEOGRAPHICAL INCOME 1947–1958

(1) *Kenya*

	1947 £m	1948 £m	1949 £m	1950 £m	1951 £m	1952 £m	1953 £m	1954 £m	1955 £m	1956 £m	1957 £m	1958 £m
Profits, Interest, and Rent	15·8	18·4	23·8	29·3	40·8	39·2	36·2	40·0	53·9	54·1	55·9	56·1
Surpluses of Public Enterprises	1·1	1·3	1·7	2·1	2·9	3·0	1·6	3·2	3·3	2·6	2·8	3·3
Wages and Salaries	18·2	21·9	24·7	28·1	32·4	37·4	42·9	49·9	66·0	65·7	73·9	74·8
African Marketed Produce	2·5	2·8	3·6	4·2	4·7	4·0	4·5	6·7	6·5	6·0	6·8	7·0
African Subsistence Income[1]	15·4	16·5	17·2	19·0	22·1	23·4	24·2	26·8	29·6	31·0	32·1	33·7
Total	53·0	60·9	71·0	82·7	102·9	107·6	109·4	126·6	159·3	159·4	171·5	174·9

[1] These are 'imputed' figures and should be treated with considerable reserve.

TABLE 22—*continued*

(2) *Uganda*

	1950 £m	1951 £m	1952 £m	1953 £m	1954 £m	1955 £m	1956 £m	1957 £m	1958 £m
Profits, Interest, and Rent	8·1	9·7	10·6	8·6	10·3	11·3	9·6	9·3	8·6
Surpluses of Marketing Boards[2]	12·9	25·2	21·9	6·2	7·9	2·7	6·2	8·2	4·8
Surpluses of other Public Enterprise	0·6	0·8	0·7	0·5	0·5	0·5	0·3	0·4	0·6
Wages and Salaries	11·4	14·2	18·8	21·9	23·2	27·3	29·1	31·0	32·5
African Marketed Produce	18·8	25·5	29·2	32·3	36·7	45·5	41·6	43·2	42·3
African Subsistence Income[1]	19·8	20·5	26·0	29·0	30·0	30·2	30·3	30·1	30·8
Total	71·6	95·9	107·2	98·5	110·4	118·0	117·1	122·2	119·6

[1] Includes export taxes and grants to local governments.

Sources: East Africa High Commission, *Quarterly Economic and Statistics Bulletins*, Nos. 22 (p. 76), 36 (p. 103), and 45 (pp. 70–1). For details and methods of computation see East African Statistical Department, *The Geographical Income and Net Product of Kenya, 1947–52* and *The Geographical Income of Uganda, 1950–52*.

(3) *Tanganyika*

No regular estimates of national income were made for Tanganyika before 1954. A 'very rough estimate' of net geographical product was, however, prepared in 1952 for the East Africa Royal Commission (see *Report*, Cmd. 9475, 1955, p. 479). It showed a total of £102 m, including £40 m from 'African subsistence activities'.

TABLE 23

MAINLAND EAST AFRICA

ESTIMATES OF THE GROSS DOMESTIC PRODUCT AT FACTOR COST, 1954, 1958 AND 1962

	Kenya			Uganda			Tanganyika		
	1954 £m	1958 £m	1962 £m	1954 £m	1958 £m	1962 £m	1954 £m	1958 £m	1962 £m
Agriculture (monetary output)[1]	28·4	34·6	39·9	52·7	53·0	46·4	35·1	39·1	48·4
Mining and Manufacturing	15·0	21·7	23·9	10·0	11·9	12·5	8·3	12·9	15·3
Construction	6·3	8·4	6·8	3·9	4·2	3·9	6·2	6·1	8·0
Other Services[2]	48·8	70·3	82·3	23·1	31·4	37·9	21·8	28·3	34·1
Government	13·9	20·5	28·1	3·3	5·6	7·3	7·7	11·3	17·3
Subsistence Agriculture	45·6	52·6	63·2	37·6	40·5	48·7	53·0	59·0	69·3
Total £m	158·0	208·1	244·1	130·6	146·4	156·7	132·1	156·7	192·4
Craft Industry[3] (non-monetary output)							(5·2)	5·7	6·1
Construction (non-monetary output)[3]							(4·3)	4·4	4·7
Total population (mid-year estimate) millions	6·0	7·7	8·6	5·4	6·4	7·0	8·2	8·9	9·6
Output per capita (£)	26·6	27·2	28·4	24·1	23·0	22·3	16·1	17·6	20·0

[1] Includes livestock husbandry, forestry, hunting, and fishing.

[2] Trade, transport, property, public utilities, and miscellaneous services.

[3] These figures were estimated only for Tanganyika, and are omitted from the totals in order to preserve comparability.

Sources: The *Statistical Abstracts* for each territory, 1957 to 1964. For further information see *East African Statistical Department, Domestic Income and Product in Kenya, 1954–58, The Gross Domestic Product of Uganda, 1954–59, and The Gross Domestic Product of Tanganyika, 1954–57.*

SELECT BIBLIOGRAPHY*

A. UNPUBLISHED SOURCES: BIBLIOGRAPHIES AND GUIDES

B. OFFICIAL PUBLICATIONS, REPORTS, ETC.
(excluding those classed as Periodicals below)
  (i) UK Government publications
  (ii) Kenya Government publications
  (iii) Uganda Government publications
  (iv) Tanganyika Government publications
  (v) Zanzibar Government publications
  (vi) Publications of the East Africa High Commission/Common Services Organization/Statistical Department, etc.
  (vii) United Nations publications

C. NEWSPAPERS AND PERIODICALS
(excluding official reports and statistics)
  (i) Published outside East Africa
  (ii) Published in Kenya
  (iii) Published in Uganda
  (iv) Published in Tanganyika
  (v) Published in Zanzibar

D. OTHER WORKS
(including a selection of unpublished theses, mimeographed papers, etc.)
I POLITICAL AND SOCIAL DEVELOPMENT, 1945 TO INDEPENDENCE
(broadly relevant to Introduction and Chapters I–IV)
  (i) General
  (ii) Kenya
  (iii) Uganda
  (iv) Tanganyika
  (v) Zanzibar

II EAST AFRICAN CO-OPERATION AND INTEGRATION (POLITICAL AND ECONOMIC), 1939–1963

III ECONOMIC DEVELOPMENT AND DEMOGRAPHY, 1945 TO INDEPENDENCE
(broadly relevant to Chapters V–VIII)
  (i) The East African economy generally
  (ii) Kenya
  (iii) Uganda
  (iv) Tanganyika

* This bibliography is based in the first instance on material supplied by the contributors to the volume. But owing to the length of time over which their contributions were made, much has been published since the earlier ones were written; and with the aim of making the bibliography as full as space permits, many items have been included which were not necessarily available to the authors when they wrote. Amongst the many who have given help and advice in its compilation, special thanks are due to Arthur Hazlewood, to Mrs. Pat Simmons, and to the Librarian of the Oxford Institute of Commonwealth Studies, R. J. Townsend.

IV RETROSPECT ON THE ALIEN IMPACT ON EAST AFRICA: THE IMMIGRANT
COMMUNITIES, THE INFLUENCE OF WESTERN LAW AND RELIGION
(broadly relevant to Chapters IX–XIII)
    (i) General
    (ii) Kenya
    (iii) Uganda
    (iv) Tanganyika
    (v) Zanzibar

A. UNPUBLISHED SOURCES: BIBLIOGRAPHIES AND GUIDES

Since the publication of the second volume of this *History*, many bibliographical guides to the primary documentary sources on African history have become available, covering the colonial as well as the pre-colonial period. Accordingly no attempt is made here to classify such source material, and the sections that follow are designed rather to give fairly full suggestions for further reading, on the topics discussed in the volume, of works likely to be accessible to the general reader. For fuller bibliographical guidance, reference should be made to the following:

DUIGNAN, P., ed.: *Guide to Research and Reference Works on Sub-Saharan Africa* (Stanford, 1972).

—— and GANN, L.: *Colonialism in Africa, 1870–1960*, Vol. 5; *A Bibliographical Guide to Colonialism in Sub-Saharan Africa* (Cambridge, 1973).

KING, K., and SALIM, A.: *Kenya Historical Biographies* (Nairobi, 1971).

LIBRARY OF CONGRESS: *Official Publications of British East Africa*, 4 parts (Washington, 1960–3).

MATTHEWS, N., and WAINWRIGHT, DOREEN, compilers, and PEARSON, J. D., ed.: *A Guide to Manuscripts and Documents in the British Isles relating to Africa* (London, 1971).

MOLNOS, ANGELA: *Die sozialwissenschaftliche Erforschung Ostafrikas, 1954–1963* (Berlin, Springer-Verlag, 1965).

—— ed.: *Development in Africa, Planning and Implementation: a bibliography (1946–1969) and outline, with some emphasis on Kenya, Tanzania, and Uganda* (Nairobi, East African Research Information Centre, 1970).

—— compiler: *Sources for the Study of East African Cultures and Development* Nairobi, East African Research Information Centre, 1968).

PECKHAM, R., et al.: *A Bibliography of Anthropology and Sociology in Uganda* (New York, 1966).

SEGAL, RONALD: *Political Africa* (London, 1961) [a contemporary handbook on political personalities and parties of the 1950s].

WEBSTER, J. B. et al., compilers: *A Bibliography on Kenya* (Syracuse, 1967).

Reference to recently published works on Uganda and Tanganyika/Tanzania respectively appear in the *Uganda Journal*, from 1963 (B. W. Langlands), and in *Tanzania Notes and Records* (B. W. Langlands, A. Roberts), from 1966.

Since 1960 a number of postgraduate theses on relevant subjects have been completed at the University of East Africa (up to 1970), and subsequently at the Universities of Makerere, Nairobi, and Dar es Salaam. A great deal of valuable material is also to be found in the mimeograph files of the East African Institute of Social Research at Makerere, and of the Institutes of Administration at Nairobi and Dar es Salaam. Copies of these mimeograph papers, particularly of the longer-established EAISR, are available in a number of African studies centres outside East Africa. Only a very few of the most directly significant of these papers are listed in this bibliography.

B. OFFICIAL PUBLICATIONS, REPORTS, ETC.

The period following the Second World War saw a vast proliferation of official publications and reports from both the UK and the colonial governments. Only a small selection from these are listed below. In making the selection emphasis has been given, first, to documents which proved to be significant in political and/or economic development, and, second, to works which represent substantial social science research in their own right. Mimeographed material is included only where it is believed to be widely accessible. A few pre-1939 documents especially relevant to the retrospective chapters are included.

Statistical material, including census returns, even where at some time published by the territorial government concerned, is in general listed under the East Africa High Commission/Statistical Department, below. Official periodicals appear in the Newspapers and Periodicals section.

(*i*) UK GOVERNMENT PUBLICATIONS
(Published in London unless otherwise indicated.)

(*a*) *General*

1929 Cmd. 3234   *Report of the Commission on Closer Union of the Dependencies in Eastern and Central Africa* (Chairman Sir E. Hilton-Young).

1934 Cmd. 4623   *Report of the Commission of Inquiry into the Administration of Justice in Kenya, Uganda and the Tanganyika Territory in Criminal Matters, 1933* (Chairman H. G. Bushe), *and Correspondence arising out of the Report.*

1946 Col. 191   *Inter-Territorial Organization in East Africa.*

1946 Col. 193   *Labour Conditions in East Africa* (G. St. J. Orde Browne).

1947 Col. 210   *Inter-Territorial Organization in East Africa: Revised Proposals.*

1948 Col. 223   *Report of the Commission on the Civil Services of Kenya, Tanganyika, Uganda, and Zanzibar, 1947–48* (Chairman Sir Maurice Holmes).

1950 Cmd. 7987   *The British Territories in East and Central Africa, 1945–1950.*

1951 Col. 275   *Labour Administration in the Colonial Territories, 1944–1950.*

1952–4 Col. 281–2   *An Economic Survey of the Colonial Territories, 1951:* Vol. 2. *The East African Territories.*

1952 Col. 290   *Land and Population in East Africa: exchange of correspondence between the Secretary of State for the Colonies and the Governor of Kenya on the appointment of the Royal Commission.*

1954   *Report of the Commission on the Civil Services of the East African Territories and the East Africa High Commission* (Chairman D. J. Lidbury).

1955 Cmd. 9475   *East Africa Royal Commission, 1953–55: Report* (Chairman Sir Hugh Dow).

1956   *Report of the Conference on African Land Tenure in East and Central Africa* (Special Supplement to *Journal of African Administration,* October 1956).

1956 Cmd. 9801   *Despatches from the Governors of Kenya, Uganda and Tanganyika, and from the Administrator, East Africa High Commission, commenting on the East Africa Royal Commission 1953-1955 Report.*

1956 Cmd. 9804   *Commentary on the Despatches from the Governors . . .* [as above]

1957 Cmnd. 281   *Correspondence between the Secretary of State for the Colonies and the Governors of Kenya, Tanganyika and Uganda, concerning the Financial Arrangements Applicable on the Transfer of the Local East African Forces from the Control of the War Office to that of the East African Territories.*

1961 Cmnd. 1279   *East Africa: Report of the Economic and Fiscal Commission, 1961* (Chairman Sir J. Raisman).

1961 Cmnd. 1433   *The Future of the East Africa High Commission Services: report of the London discussions.*

(b) *Kenya*

Annual Reports on the Colony and Protectorate of Kenya.

1923 Cmd. 1922   *Indians in Kenya: memorandum.*

1934 Cmd. 4556   *Report of the Kenya Land Commission* (Chairman Sir Morris Carter).

1954 Cmd. 9081   *Report to the Secretary of State for the Colonies by the Parliamentary Delegation to Kenya, 1954.*

1954 Cmd. 9103   *Kenya: Proposals for a Reconstruction of the Government* (Lyttelton Constitution).

1957 Cmnd. 309   *Kenya: Proposals for New Constitutional Arrangements* (Lennox-Boyd Constitution).

1958 Cmnd. 369   *Kenya: Despatch on the New Constitutional Arrangements.*

1959 Cmnd. 778   *Documents relating to the Deaths of Eleven Mau Mau Detainees at Hola Camp in Kenya.*

1959 Cmnd. 795   *Record of Proceedings and Evidence in the Inquiry into the Deaths of Eleven Mau Mau Detainees at Hola Camp in Kenya.*

1959 Cmnd. 816   *Further Documents relating to the Deaths of Eleven Mau Mau Detainees at Hola Camp in Kenya.*
1960 Cmnd. 960   *Report of the Kenya Constitutional Conference held in London in January and February, 1960.*
1960 Cmnd. 1030   *Historical Survey of the Origins and Growth of Mau Mau* (F. D. Corfield).
1961 Cmnd. 1459   *Despatch from the Governor of Kenya to the Secretary of State for the Colonies on the Release of Jomo Kenyatta.*
1962 Cmnd. 1700   *Report of the Kenya Constitutional Conference, 1962.*
1962 Cmnd. 1899   *Kenya: Report of the Regional Boundaries Commission. Detailed Descriptions of Boundaries.*
1963 Cmnd. 1900   *Kenya: Report of the Northern Frontier District Commission.*
1963 Cmnd. 1921   *Kenya: Report of the Constituencies Delimitation Commission* (S. Foster-Sutton).
1963 Cmnd. 1970   *Kenya Constitution: Summary of the proposed constitution for internal self-government.*
1963 Cmnd. 2082   *Kenya—preparations for independence.*
1963 Cmnd. 2156   *Kenya Independence Conference, 1963.*

[For Kenya Coastal Strip see under Zanzibar]

(c) Uganda
Annual Reports on the Uganda Protectorate.
1953   *The Development of Economic Agriculture in Uganda: a general survey.* (Colonial Office 1953, mimeo.)
1953 Cmd. 9028   *Uganda Protectorate: Withdrawal of Recognition from Kabaka Mutesa II of Buganda.*
1954 Cmd. 9320   *Uganda Protectorate, Buganda.*
1961 Cmnd. 1523 *Report of the Uganda Constitutional Conference, 1961, and Text of the Agreed Draft of a New Buganda Agreement Initialled in London on 9th October, 1961.*
1962 Cmnd. 1717 *Report of a Commission of Privy Counsellors on a Dispute between Buganda and Bunyoro* (Chairman Lord Molson).
1962 Cmnd. 1778 *Report of the Uganda Independence Conference, 1962.*

(d) Tanganyika
Annual Reports of HM Government to the General Assembly of the UN on Tanganyika under UK Administration (also numbered in the Col. Series).
1946 Cmd. 7030   *Report on a Plan for the Mechanised Production of Groundnuts in East and Central Africa.*
1947 Cmd. 7314   *Review of Progress on the East African Groundnuts Scheme to the End of November, 1947.*
1951 Col. 277   *Development of African Local Government in Tanganyika.*
1951 Cmd. 8125   *The Future of the Overseas Food Corporation.*
1954 Cmd. 9158, *The Future of the Overseas Food Corporation.*
     9198   „   „   „
1961 Cmnd. 1360 *Report of the Tanganyika Constitutional Conference, 1961, held in Dar es Salaam, March 1961.*

(e) *Zanzibar*

Annual Reports on Zanzibar Protectorate

1961 Col. 353	Report of a Commission of Inquiry into Disturbances in Zanzibar during June, 1961.
1961 Cmnd. 1585	The Kenya Coastal Strip: Report of the Commissioner (Sir James Robertson).
1962 Cmnd. 1699	Report of the Zanzibar Constitutional Conference, 1962.
1962 Cmnd. 1701	Report of the Kenya Coastal Strip Conference, 1962.
1963 Cmnd. 1971	Kenya Coastal Strip: Joint Statement by the Secretary of State for the Colonies and the Chief Minister of Zanzibar.
1963 Cmnd. 2157	Zanzibar Independence Conference, 1963.
1963 Cmnd. 2161	Kenya Coastal Strip: Agreement between the Government of the United Kingdom, His Highness the Sultan of Zanzibar, the Government of Kenya, and the Government of Zanzibar, 8th October, 1963.
1963 Cmnd. 2218	Exchange of Letters between His Highness the Sultan of Zanzibar and the British Resident Terminating the 1890 Agreement as respects the Dominions of the Sultan not Comprised in the Kenya Protectorate.

(ii) *Kenya Government publications*

(Published in Nairobi unless otherwise indicated.)

Kenya Legislative Council *Debates* and Sessional Papers.

Kenya *Official Gazette.*

The Laws of Kenya, revised edition, 8 vols. (Nairobi, 1948), and annual volumes 1948–.

Colony Estimates, Development Estimates, Financial Statements, and Appropriation Accounts.

Trade Reports (Kenya and Uganda to 1948, separately thereafter).

Reports of the Commissioner for Local Government.

Departmental Annual Reports, especially for:

African Affairs, Agriculture, Community Development (under various titles from 1949), Education, Labour, Immigration (from 1950), Police (from 1945, not published for distribution 1939–44).

Other periodical reports, including:

ALDEV (African Land Development Organization); African Land Utilization and Settlement Board; DARA (Development and Reconstruction Authority); Special Crops Development Authority; Land Tenure and Control outside the Native Lands; Notes on Commerce and Industry in Kenya; Progress Reports on Development Plans.

1941	Report on the Housing of Africans in Nairobi.
1943	Report of the Sub-Committee on Post-War Employment of Africans.
1945	The Kikuyu Lands: the relation of population to the land in South Nyeri (N. Humphrey); and Memorandum on Land Tenure in the Native Lands (H. E. Lambert and P. Wyn Harris).
1945	Post-War Settlement in Kenya: proposed schemes.

1945   *Report on Native Tribunals* (A. Phillips).
1945   *Report of the Committee of Inquiry into Labour Unrest in Mombasa* (Chairman Arthur Phillips).
1945   (S.P. No. 3) *Proposals for the Reorganization of the Administration in Kenya*
1946   *Report of the Development Committee*, 2 vols. (Chairman J. F. G. Troughton).
1946   *General Aspects of the Agrarian Situation in Kenya*, Despatch No. 44 (17 April 1946) from the Governor, Sir Philip Mitchell.
1947   *The Agrarian Problem in Kenya* (Note by Sir Philip Mitchell).
1947   *Report of the Taxation Enquiry Committee, Kenya, 1947* (Chairman R. P. Plewman).
1947   *The Liguru and the Land: sociological aspects of some agricultural problems of North Kavirondo* (N. Humphrey).
1948   *Nairobi, Master Plan for a Colonial Capital*, by L. W. T. White, L. Silberman, and P. R. Anderson (London, 1948).
1948   *An Inquiry into Indian Education in East Africa* (A. A. Kazimi); *and Report of Committee on Educational Expenditure.*
1948   *A Ten Year Plan for the Development of African Education.*
1949   *Report of the Select Committee on Indian Education.*
1949   *African Education in Kenya: Report of a Committee Appointed to Inquire into the Scope, Content, and Methods of African Education, its Administration and Finance, and to Make Recommendations* (Chairman L. J. Beecher).
1950   *Report of Committee on Agricultural Credit for Africans.*
1950   *Report of the Commission of Inquiry into the Affray at Kolloa, Baringo.*
1950   *Report of a Commission of Inquiry Appointed to Review the Registration of Persons Ordinance 1947* (Chairman B. J. Glancy).
1951   *Report of the Planning Committee.*
1951   *Agricultural Policy in African Areas.*
1951   *African Education: a statement of policy.*
1953   *Report of the Inquiry into the General Economy of Farming in the Highlands* (L. G. Troup).
1954   *The Psychology of Mau Mau* (J. C. Carothers).
1954   *Report of the Committee on African Wages* (Chairman F. W. Carpenter).
1954   *A Plan to Intensify the Development of African Agriculture in Kenya* (R. J. M. Swynnerton).
1955   (S.P. No. 51) *The Development Programme 1954–57.*
1956   (S.P. No. 39 of 1955/6) *Report of the Commissioner Appointed to Enquire into Methods for the Selection of African Representatives to the Legislative Council* (W. F. Coutts); *and Statement of Government Policy on the Coutts Report.*
1956   *Report on the General Administration of Prisons and Detention Camps in Kenya.*
1956   *Report of Enquiry into the Kenya Meat Industry* (C. Nevile).
1956   *Immigration Policy, 1956.*
1957   (S.P. No. 77) *The Development Programme 1957–60.*

1958   (S.P. No. 6 of 1957/8) *The Maize Industry.*
1959   *Report of the Committee on Emergency Detention Camps.*
1959   *Administrative Enquiry into Allegations of Ill-treatment against Detainees at Mayin Detention Camp, and Fort Hall* (A. P. Jack).
1958   *Report of Working Party on African Land Tenure 1957–1958.*
1958   *Report on Asian and European Education in Kenya.*
1959   *Report of the Working Party on Higher Education in East Africa.*
1959   *Reports of the Working Party Set up to Consider the Establishment of an Authority to Promote the Development of Cash Crops for Small-holders, and of the Working Party Set up to Consider the Financial Implications.*
1960   (S.P. No. 4 of 1959/60) *Development Programme 1960–1963.*
1960   (S.P. No. 10 of 1959/60) *Survey of Unemployment* (A. G. Dalgleish); *and Comments thereon.*
1960   (S.P. No. 7 of 1959/60) *Report of the Working Party Appointed to Consider Elections under the Lancaster House Agreement.*
1960   *Report of the Committee on the Organization of Agriculture* (D. Macgillivray, A. Lawrie and H. White).
1961   *A History of the Loyalists: a tribute to the tribal police, African guards, and all loyalists of the Kikuyu, Embu, and Meru tribes who resisted the Mau Mau revolt.*
1961/62 *Famine and Floods in Kenya: report on famine relief in Kenya.*
1962   *Report of the Economy Commission* (Chairman S. S. Meneer).
1963   *Report on the Kenya Maize Industry* (V. G. Matthews).

(iii) *Uganda Government publications*

(Published in Entebbe unless otherwise indicated.)

Uganda Legislative Council, *Proceedings* and Sessional Papers.

Uganda *Official Gazette.*

The Laws of the Uganda Protectorate in Force . . . 1951, revised edition, 9 vols. (London, 1951).

Estimates, Reports on the Accounts.

Trade Reports (with Kenya to 1948, separately thereafter).

Annual Reports on the Eastern, Western, and Northern Provinces and the Kingdom of Buganda.

Departmental Annual Reports, especially for:
Agriculture, Co-operatives (from 1946), Education, Labour (Inspectorate became Department 1943).

Other periodical reports, including:
Uganda Development Corporation, Uganda Electricity Board, Development Report 1946–7.

1945   *Report of the Commission of Inquiry into the Disturbances which occurred in Uganda during January, 1945* (Chairman W. H. P. Whiteley).
1947   *A Development Plan for Uganda* (E. B. Worthington).
1950   *Commission of Inquiry into Civil Disturbances in Buganda in April and May 1949* (Sir D. Kingdon); *and Memorandum by the Uganda Government.*

1952   *The Way to the West—Being an Economic and Railway Survey of Certain Areas of Western Uganda, together with Recommendations Based thereon* (F. J. Lattin *et al.*).

1953   *Report of an Inquiry into African Local Government in the Protectorate of Uganda* (C. A. G. Wallis); *with Government Memorandum on the same.*

1953   *African Education in Uganda* (B. De Bunsen); *and Memorandum by the Protectorate Government on the Report.*

1953   *Correspondence Relating to the Composition of Legislative Council in Uganda.*

1953   *Memorandum on Constitutional Development and Reform in Buganda.*

1954   *H.E. the Governor's Statement on Constitutional Development in Uganda.*

1954   *The Report of the Sub-Committee of the Lukiko which was set up to examine the recommendations made by the Hancock Committee* ('Kintu Report').

1954   *Mechanization of African Farming in Uganda.*

1954   *Agreed Recommendations of the Namirembe Conference; and Explanatory Memorandum issued by the Conference.*

1954   *Outline Scheme of Development of African Education, 1944–1954.*

1954   *A Five Year Capital Development Plan, 1955–60* (Chairman C. H. Thornley). First Revision, 1957.

1954   *Report of the Agricultural Productivity Committee.*

1955   *Report of a Committee on the Advancement of Africans in Trade* (Chairman M. A. Maybury).

1955   *The Buganda Agreement, 1955.*

1955   *Final Report of the Standing Committee on the Recruitment, Training and Promotion of Africans for Admission to the Higher Posts in the Civil Service* (Chairman J. V. Wild).

1955   *The Bunyoro Agreement, 1955.*

1956   *Northern Communications, a Report on Rail and Road Communications in the North and North West of the Protectorate.*

1956   *Report by Representatives of the Protectorate and Kabaka's Government on Discussions on the Introduction of Direct Elections to the Legislative Council in Buganda, 1957.*

1956   *His Excellency the Governor's Speech to Legislative Council on 24 April 1956* (Statement on Elections).

1956   (S.P. No. 4 of 1956/7) *Despatch from the Governor of Uganda . . . on the Report of the East Africa High Commission.*

1957   *A Bibliography of Land Tenure.*

1957   (S.P. No. 4 of 1957/8) *Elections to the Legislative Council.*

1958   (S.P. No. 14) *Report of the Commission of Inquiry into the Affairs of the Bugisu Co-operative Union Limited* (Chairman R. H. Gretton).

1958   (S.P. No. 19) *Memorandum by Government on the Future Organization of the Bugisu Coffee Industry.*

1958   *Correspondence Relating to Certain Changes in the Executive Council of the Legislative Council of the Uganda Protectorate.*

1958   *Report of the Commission of Inquiry into the Management of the Teso District Council* (Chairman R. L. E. Dreschfield).

1959   *Report of the Constitutional Committee, 1959* (Chairman J. V. Wild).

1959   *A Report on the First Direct Elections to the Legislative Council of the Uganda Protectorate* (C. P. S. Allen).

1960   *Report of the Commission of Inquiry into Disturbances in the Eastern Province, 1960* (K. G. Bennett and A. J. Loveridge).

1960   *Report of the Commission of Inquiry into the Affairs of the Bugisu District Council* (R. L. E. Dreschfield).

1960   (S.P. No. 5 of 1960/61) *Report of the Economy Commission, 1960* (Chairman R. O. Ramage).

1960   *Symposium on Mechanical Cultivation in Uganda*, ed. J. L. Joy (Kampala, 1960).

1960   *Despatch No. 1261 of 14th September 1960, from the Secretary of State for the Colonies in connection with the Report of the Constitutional Committee, 1959.*

1960   *Supplementary Report of the Constitutional Committee.*

1961   (S.P. No. 2 of 1961) *Future Development in the Public Service of Uganda.*

1961   *Report of the Uganda Relationships Committee, 1961* (Chairman Lord Munster).

1961   *Report on the General Election to the Legislative Council of the Uganda Protectorate held in March 1961* (R. C. Peagram).

1962   *Exchange of Despatches . . . concerning the Creation of Sebei District.*

1962   *Report of the Commission to Review the Boundary Between the Districts of Bugisu and Bukedi* (Chairman K. K. O'Connor).

1962   *Report of the Commission of Enquiry into the Recent Disturbances Amongst the Baamba and Bakonjo People of Toro* (Chairman F. C. Ssembeguya).

1962   *Report of the Commission of Inquiry into the Cotton-ginning Industry of Uganda.*

(iv) *Tanganyika Government publications*

(Published in Dar es Salaam unless otherwise indicated.)

Tanganyika Legislative Council, *Proceedings* and Sessional Papers.

Tanganyika *Official Gazette.*

The Laws of Tanganyika, 1947–1950, 10 vols. (London, 1951).

Estimates, Treasurer's Reports, and Accounts.

Trade Reports.

Reports of the Provincial Commissioners.

Departmental Annual Reports, especially for:

     Agriculture, Co-operative Development, Education, Labour (Department re-established 1940), Social Development (became Department 1949).

Other periodical reports, including:

     The Development of African Local Government; Notes on Commerce and Industry; Development Organization; Reports and Development Plans.

1940   *Report of the Central Development Committee* (Chairman G. R. Sandford).

1944   *An Outline of the Post-War Development Proposals.*

1944   *The Welfare of the African Labourer in Tanganyika* (K. C. Charron).

1945   *Tanganyika Transport: a review* (J. R. Farquharson).

1946   *A Ten Year Development and Welfare Plan for Tanganyika Territory: Report by the Development Commission.*

1947   *Report of the Arusha-Moshi Lands Commission* (Chairman J. M. Wilson).

1947   *A Ten-year Plan for the Development of African Education.*

1948   *The Land Bank of Tanganyika* (Arusha, 1948).

1950   *Revised Development and Welfare Plan for Tanganyika, 1950–1956.*

1951   *Report of the Committee on Constitutional Development, and Despatches Thereon.*

1951   *Report of the Committee on Manpower* (Chairman R. de Z. Hall).

1952   *Legislative Council Paper on the Meru Land Problem.*

1953   *Report of the Special Commissioner Appointed to Examine Matters arising out of the Report of the Committee on Constitutional Development* (W. J. M. Mackenzie).

1953   *The Cotton Industry, 1939–53.*

1953   *Land Utilization and the Allocation of Individual Rights over Land.*

1954   *A Review of Development Plans in the Southern Province, 1953.*

1955   *Development Plan, 1955–60, Capital and Works Programme.*

1956   *The County Council in Tanganyika 1951–1956.*

1956   *A Draft Five-year Plan for African Education 1957–1961.*

1957   *Detribalization: a study of the areas of Tanganyika where detribalized persons are living, with recommendations as to the administrative and other measures required to meet the problems arising therein* (M. J. B. Molohan).

1957   *Second Interim Report on the County Council in Tanganyika, 1956–1957.*

1957   *Some Comments on Mr. Nyerere's Speech at the Fourth Committee of the United Nations.*

1958   *Appointments at the Senior Levels in the Civil Service.*

1959   *Report of the Post-Elections Committee, 1959.*

1959   *Report of the Committee on the Integration of Education* (Chairman W. W. Lewis Jones).

1959   *Report on the First Election of Members to the Legislative Council of Tanganyika* (mimeo).

1961   *Development Plan for Tanganyika, 1961/62–1963/64.*

1966   *Report of the Presidential Special Committee of Inquiry into the Co-operative Movement and Marketing Boards.*

(v) *Zanzibar Government publications*

(Published in Zanzibar unless otherwise indicated.)

Zanzibar Legislative Council *Debates* and Sessional Papers.

Zanzibar *Official Gazette.*

The Laws of Zanzibar in Force . . . 1959, 5 vols. (London, 1961).

Estimates, Accounts.

Trade Reports.

Reports of the Provincial Administration.

Departmental Annual Reports, especially:

  Agriculture, Education, Labour (part of Provincial Administration), Police, Social Welfare.

Other periodical reports, including Progress Reports on Development/ Welfare Programmes.

1945   *Review of the Systems of Land Tenure in the Islands of Zanzibar and Pemba.*

1946   *Programme of Social and Economic Development in the Zanzibar Protectorate, 1946–1955.*

1947   *Statement on Administrative Policy and Local Government.*

1952   *Report on the Civil Disturbances in Zanzibar on July 30, 1957* (Sir John Gray).

1954   *Report* (by E. A. Vasey) *on Local Government Advancement in Zanzibar Township* (Nairobi).

1955   (S.P. No. 9) *Constitutional Development Zanzibar: Exchange of Despatches between the British Resident, Zanzibar and the Secretary of State for the Colonies.*

1956   *Programme of Social and Economic Development in the Zanzibar Protectorate, 1955–1959.*

1956   *Methods of Choosing Unofficial Members of the Legislative Council* (Commissioner W. F. Coutts).

?1957   *Selection of Appointed Representative Members of the Legislative Council.*

1958   *Report of the Arbitrator* (Sir John Gray) *to Enquire into a Trade Dispute at the Wharf Area at Zanzibar.*

1958   *The Report of the Supervisor of Elections on the Elections in Zanzibar, 1957* (J. C. Penney).

1958   (S.P. No. 3 of 1957/58) *Report of Select Committee of the Legislative Council Appointed on 16th February, 1957, to Consider the Legislative Council (Elections) Bill, 1957.*

1959   *Report and Recommendations on the Present Position and Future Prospects of Agriculture in the Zanzibar Protectorate* (A. G. Briant).

1959   *Report of the Committee on the Extension of the Franchise to Women.*

1959   *Report of the Zanzibar Clove Mission to India.*

1959   *Zanzibar Clove Industry: Statement of Government Policy and Report* (by R. A. Crofts).

1959   *Report of an Inquiry into Labour Conditions in the Port of Zanzibar* (Sir Ian Parkin).

1959   *Report of the Committee on Education, 1959* (Chairman P. A. P. Robertson).

1960   *Report of the Committee on Immigration, 1959.*

1960   *Report of the Constitutional Commissioner, Zanzibar, 1960* (Sir Hilary Blood).

1960   (S.P. No. 7 of 1959/60) *Report of the Select Committee Appointed to Enquire into the Public Order Bill.*

1961   (S.P. No. 14 of 1960/61) *Constitutional Reforms 1960.*

1961   *Report of the Supervisors of Elections on the Registration of Voters and the Elections held in January, 1961* (T. G. Moore).

1961   *Proceedings of the Commission of Inquiry into the Civil Disturbances of June, 1961* (Chairman S. Foster Sutton).

1961   *Report of the Supervisor of Elections, June 1961* (T. G. Moore).

1961   *The Kenya Coastal Strip, Report of the Commissioner* (Sir James Robertson) (Nairobi, 1961).

1962   *Report of the Delimitation Commissioner, Zanzibar, 1962* (Sir Robert Arundell).

1962   *General Statement of the Aims and Policies of His Highness's Government, 1961.*

1962   *Report on the Economic Development of the Zanzibar Protectorate* (P. Selwyn and T. Y. Watson).

(vi) *Publications of East Africa High Commission/Common Services Organization/ Statistical Department, etc. (and other statistical returns).*

(1) *East Africa High Commission/Common Services Organization, etc.*

1946   *Report* (by Sir W. Woods) *on a Fiscal Survey of Kenya, Uganda and Tanganyika* (Conference of East African Governors, Nairobi, 1946).

1957   *Report of the East African Commission of Inquiry on Income Tax, 1956–1957* (Nairobi, 1957).

1961   *Report* (by Sir R. Ramage) *on the Localization of the Civil Service of the Non-self-contained Services of the East Africa High Commission and in the East African Posts and Telecommunications Administration* (Nairobi).

1961   *East African Common Services Organization Agreement, signed December, 1961.*

Annual Reports from 1948 (numbered until 1954 in the Col. series).

Annual Trade Reports

Gazette, from 1948.

Proceedings of the East African Legislative Council, from 1948.

Revised *Laws*, 1951.

(2) *East African Statistical Department (and other statistical returns)*

(a) GENERAL

1958–60   *The Balance of Payments of East Africa, cumulative,* 1956, 1956/7, 1956/7/8.

1948–   Annual Reports.

1948–60   *Quarterly Economic and Statistical Bulletin.*
quarterly

1961–   *Economic and Statistical Review.*
quarterly

1963   *East African Trade Indices 1954–1961.*

(b) KENYA (all published Nairobi)

1946–   *Report on the Census of Non-native Employees in Kenya,* 1946, 1947, and 1948, 1949 and 1952.

1947–   *Report on Migration,* 1946, 1947, 1948, 1949–53.

1949–   *Estimates of Geographical Income and Net Product, cumulative,* 1947 -8, 1947–9, 1947–50, 1947–51.

1950   *African Population of Kenya Colony and Protectorate: geographical and tribal studies* [1948 census].

1950   *Report on the Census of the Non-native Population of Kenya, 1948.*
1950–   *Report on African Labour Census, 1947, 1948* (Labour Dept.), *African Labour Census, 1949.*
1951   *The Pattern of Income, Expenditure and Consumption of Africans in Nairobi, Oct.–Nov. 1950.*
[?1954] *Report on the Analysis of the Sample Census of African Agriculture in Kenya, 1950/51.*
1954–   *Survey of Industrial Production, 1954, 1956, 1957.*
1954–   *Reported Employment and Wages in Kenya, 1954, 1955/6, 1957, 1958, 1959, 1961, 1962.*
1955–   *Statistical Abstracts 1955, 1956/7, 1958–* annually.
1956–   *Agricultural Censuses, non-African:* 1954 and 1955 (Highlands and Asian Settled Area), 1957 (Scheduled Areas), 1958 (non-African, (a) summary of results (b) economic analysis), 1959 (non-African, summary of results).
1959   *Domestic Income and Product in Kenya: a description of sources and methods with revised calculations from 1954 to 1958.*
1959   *The Pattern of Income, Expenditure and Consumption of Africans in Nairobi, 1957–8.*
1960–   *Economic Survey, 1960, 1962, 1964.*
1960   *A Survey of Capital Assets held in Kenya, 1958.*
1960   *Capital Formation in Kenya, 1954–60.*
1962   *Kenya African Agricultural Sample Census, 1960/61, parts 1 and 2.*
1963   *The Growth of the Economy, 1954–1962.*
1963   *Kenya Census of Manufacturing, 1961.*
1964–66 *Kenya Population Census, 1962, vols. I–IV.*

(c) UGANDA (published Entebbe unless otherwise stated)
1949–   *Enumeration of Employees* [title varied slightly 1949–52], annually 1949–52 inclusive, 1955–.
1950   *African Population of Uganda: geographical and tribal studies* [1948 census] (Nairobi).
1950–   *The Pattern of Income, Expenditure and Consumption of African Unskilled Labourers in Kampala,* 1950–53 inclusive, 1957 (Nairobi). Some similar statistics also for Jinja, Mbale, Fort Portal.
1952–   *National Income: Preliminary Estimates of the Geographical Income and Net Product for the years 1950 and 1951* (Nairobi); *Estimates of the Geographical Income for the Years 1950–1952* (Entebbe); *the Geographical Income of Uganda, 1950–56, 1957* (Entebbe).
1953   *Report on the Census of the Non-native Population in Uganda Protectorate, 25th February, 1948* (Nairobi).
1957   *Index of Retail Prices in African Markets, Kampala.*
1957–   *Statistical Abstract,* 1957, 58, 59, 1961, 1963, 1965.
1960   *General African Census 1959,* 2 vols. (Nairobi).
1960   *Non-African Population Census, 1959.*
1961   *The Gross Domestic Product of Uganda, 1954–1959.*
1962   *The External Trade of Uganda, 1950–60.*
1964   *Real Growth of the Uganda Economy, 1954–62.*

(d) TANGANYIKA (published Dar es Salaam unless otherwise stated)

1938–   *Statistical Abstract*, 1938–51, 1938–52, 1954– annually (Dar es Salaam).

1949   *African Labour Census, 1949* (Supplement to *Quarterly Bulletin of Statistics*, No. 8, Nairobi).

1950   *African Population of Tanganyika Territory: geographical and tribal studies* [1948 census] (Nairobi).

1951   *The Pattern of Income, Expenditure and Consumption of African Labourers in Dar es Salaam, August 1950* (Nairobi);—*in Tanga, Feb. 1958* (Dar es Salaam).

1953   *Report on the Analysis of the Sample Census of African Agriculture, 1950* (Nairobi).

1953   *Report on the Census of the Non-native Population of Tanganyika, 1948* (Nairobi).

1953   *Report on the Enumeration of African Employees, July 1952* (Nairobi).

1954   *Report on the Census of the non-African Population, 1952.*

1958   *General African Census, August 1957, Tanganyika Population Census, 1957.*

1958   *Report of the Census of the Non-African Population, 1957* (Dar es Salaam).

1959   *Survey of Industrial Production, 1958.*

1959   *Tanganyika Agricultural Census, 1958* (in effect confined to non-African agriculture).

1959   *The Gross Domestic Product of Tanganyika, 1954–1957* (Dar es Salaam).

1959   *Public Finance of Tanganyika: an analysis* (Dar es Salaam).

1961–   *Census of Large-Scale Commercial Farming*, 1960, 1962.

1962   *Employment and Earnings in Tanganyika, 1961.*

(e) ZANZIBAR

1953   *Notes on the Census of the Zanzibar Protectorate, 1948.*

1959   *Summary Digest of Useful Statistics.*

1960   *Report on the Census of the Population of Zanzibar Protectorate, 1958.*

1963   *The Pattern of Income, Expenditure and Consumption of Unskilled Workers in Zanzibar, 1962* (Nairobi).

1963   *The Gross Domestic Product of the Protectorate of Zanzibar, 1957–1961* (Nairobi).

(vii) *United Nations publications*

1947   *Trusteeship Agreement for the Territory of Tanganyika, as approved by the General Assembly on 13 December, 1946* (General Assembly Document T/A/2).

1949   *Reports on the Population of Trust Territories, 2: the population of Tanganyika* (Department of Social Affairs, Population Div.).

1950   *Visiting Mission to Trust Territories in East Africa: Report on Tanganyika, 1948 and related documents* (Trusteeship Council Docs. T/218; T/218/Add.1; T/333; T/376).

1951   *Trust Territories: First Report of the Standing Committee on Administrative Unions: Tanganyika* (Trusteeship Council Doc. T/915).

1952   *U.N. Visiting Mission to Trust Territories in East Africa 1951: Report on Tanganyika together with related documents* (Trusteeship Council Doc. T/1032).

1955   *U.N. Visiting Mission to Trust Territories in East Africa 1954: Report on Tanganyika* (Trusteeship Council Doc. T/1169). *Observations thereon* (Doc. T/1162).

1957   *U.N. Visiting Mission to Trust Territories in East Africa 1957: Report on Tanganyika* (Trusteeship Council Doc. T/1345).

1959   *Economic Survey of Africa since 1950* (Department of Economic and Social Affairs, E/CN.14/28).

1960   *U.N. Visiting Mission to Trust Territories in East Africa 1960: Report on Tanganyika, together with related documents* (Trusteeship Council Doc. T/1550).

The *Official Records* of the Trusteeship Council, First (1947) to Twenty-sixth (1960) Sessions. (The Reports of Visiting Missions to Trust Territories are printed as supplements to these records.)

Petitions submitted to the Trusteeship Council in respect of Trust Territories. Those concerning Tanganyika are in the T/Pet/2 series.

C. NEWSPAPERS AND PERIODICALS

Official reports are excluded, and only the more long-lived, or politically important, of daily and weekly publications are listed. (For these the giving of 1963 as a closing date does not necessarily mean that they ceased in that year.)

(i) *Published outside East Africa*

Africa (London), 1928– (journal of the International African Institute).

Africa Digest (African Bureau, London) 1954– (formerly *Information Digest*).

Africa (Special) Report (Washington), 1956–.

African Affairs (London), 1944– (formerly *Journal of the Royal African Society*).

East Africa and Rhodesia (London), weekly, 1924–.

Empire Cotton-Growing Review (London), 1924–66 (thereafter *Cotton-Growing Review*).

International Review of Missions (*Mission* from 1970) (London), 1912–.

Journal of African Administration (HMSO, London), 1949–61 (thereafter *Journal of Local Administration Overseas*).

Journal of African History (Cambridge), 1960–.

Journal of Commonwealth Political Studies (Leicester), 1961–.

Journal of Modern African Studies (Cambridge), 1963–.

Tropical Agriculture (London), 1924– (journal of the Imperial College of Tropical Agriculture).

Venture (Fabian Colonial Bureau, London), 1949–1972 (thereafter *Third World*).

World Crops (London), 1949–.

(ii) *Published in Kenya* (Nairobi unless otherwise stated)

Baraza (Swahili), weekly, 1939–.
Colonial Times (Indian owned and edited, English and Gujarati), weekly, 1933–63.
Daily Chronicle (Indian owned and edited), 1947–54.
Daily Nation (and *Sunday Nation*) 1960–.
East Africa Journal, 10 issues p.a., 1964–.
East African Agricultural Journal, 1935–.
East African Economics Review, semi-annual, 1954–.
East African Standard, daily and weekly editions, 1905–.
Kenya Daily Mail (Mombasa) (Indian owned and edited, English and Gujerati), 1927–63.
Kenya Weekly News (Nakuru), 1928–69.
Mombasa Times (Mombasa), daily, 1910–.
Muigwithania (monthly journal of the Kikuyu Central Association), 1928–40.
Quarterly Economic and Statistical Bulletin (East African Statistical Department, Nairobi), 1949-60 (thereafter *Economic and Statistical Review*).
Reporter, fortnightly, 1961–.
Samachar (Gujarati), weekly, 1954–.
Sauti ya Mwafrika (organ of the KAU), 1945–54.
Sunday Post, 1936–.
Taifa Leo (Swahili), daily, 1960–.
Other Kenya African newspapers included the following: *Agikuyu, Mumenyereri, Muralimu, Muthamaki, Nyanza Times, Radio-posta, Ramogi, Uhuru.*

(iii) *Published in Uganda* (all in Kampala)

East African Geographical Review, annual, 1963–.
Makerere Journal, 1958–61 (thereafter *Transition*).
Proceedings of the East African Institute of Social Research (Makerere).
Transition (formerly *Makerere Journal*), irregular, 1961–.
Uganda Argus (English), 1955–63.
Uganda Eyogera (Luganda), daily, 1953–63.
Uganda Herald, twice weekly, 1912–63.
Uganda Journal (journal of the Uganda Society), 1934–.

(iv) *Published in Tanganyika* (all in Dar es Salaam)

Mamba Leo—1962 (main Swahili publication of the Public Relations Department).
Nationalist (Dar es Salaam).
Spearhead.
Tanganyika (*Tanzania* from 1967) *Notes and Records*, 1936–.
Tanganyika Standard, daily and weekly editions, 1930 -.

(v) *Published in Zanzibar*

Afrika Kwetu (ASP), 1947–63.
Al Falaq (Arab Association), 1929–63.

Mwongozi, 1942–63 (Independent but affiliated with Arab Association and from 1956 with ZNP).
Samachar (Independent, Gujarati), 1902–63.
Zanzibar Voice (Independent), 1922–63.

D. OTHER WORKS

These have been very roughly divided up into subject headings, but since precise classification is often impossible, the reader seeking works on such topics as, for instance, 'urbanization' should consult both the 'political' and the 'economic' sections. Unpublished theses are included only where their substance is not known to have been published, mimeograph material where it is believed to be widely accessible.

I. POLITICAL AND SOCIAL DEVELOPMENT, 1945 TO INDEPENDENCE
Works broadly relevant to the Introduction and to Chapters I–IV. See also many minor articles in the *Journal of African Administration*, only the more substantial being listed here.

(i) *General*

BECK, ANNE: 'Colonial Policy and Education in British East Africa 1900–1950', *Journal of British Studies*, 5, 2 (1966) pp. 115–38.
—— *A History of the British Medical Administration of East Africa 1900–1950* (Boston, 1970).
BRETT, E. A., and BELSHAW, D. G. R.: *Public Policy and Land Development in East Africa* (Nairobi, 1974).
BROCKWAY, A. FENNER: *African Journeys* (London, 1955).
BRUNS, L.: 'Trade Unions: function, structure, and style in East Africa' (Syracuse University, Program of East African Studies, Occasional Paper No. 8).
CHIDZERO, B. T. G.: 'African Nationalism in East and Central Africa', *International Affairs*, 36, 4 (October 1960) pp. 464–75.
COHEN, SIR A.: *British Policy in Changing Africa* (Evanston, 1959).
COLEMAN, J. S.: 'Nationalism in Tropical Africa', *American Political Science Review*, 48, 2 (June 1954) pp. 404–26.
—— 'The Politics of Sub-Saharan Africa', in *The Politics of the Developing Areas*, ed. Almond and Coleman (Princeton, 1960).
COLONIAL OFFICE, AFRICAN STUDIES BRANCH: 'The Member System in British African Territories', *Journal of African Administration*, 1, 2 (April 1949) pp. 51–9.
CREECH JONES, A., ed.: *New Fabian Colonial Essays* (London, 1959).
CURTIN, P. D.: 'Nationalism in Africa, 1945–1965', *Revue Politique et Parlementaire* (April 1966) pp. 143–53.
DIAMOND, S., and BURKE, F. G., eds.: *The Transformation of East Africa* (New York, 1966).
DUNDAS, SIR CHARLES: *African Crossroads* (London, 1955).

FARSON, N.: *Last Chance in Africa* (London, 1949).

GANN, L. H., and DUIGNAN, P., eds.: *Colonialism in Africa* (Stanford, 1970); Vol. 5.

GOLDSWORTHY, D.: *Colonial Issues in British Politics, 1945–1961* (London, 1971).

GOLDTHORPE, J. E.: *Outlines of East African Society* (Kampala, 1958).

—— *An African Élite: Makerere College Students, 1922–60* (Nairobi, 1965).

—— 'Social Class and Education in East Africa', *Transactions of the Third World Congress of Sociology*, Vol. 5 1956, pp. 115–22.

GULLIVER, P. H., ed.: *Tradition and Transition in East Africa* (London, 1969).

HAILEY, W. M., LORD ed.: *Native Administration in the British African Territories* (5 volumes), Part I *East Africa*, Part II *Central Africa* (London, 1950).

—— ed.: *An African Survey*, Revised 1956 (London, 1957).

HERSKOVITS, M. J.: *The Human Factor in Changing Africa* (New York, 1961).

HODGKIN, T. H.: *Nationalism in Colonial Africa* (London, 1956).

—— *African Political Parties: an introductory guide* (London, 1961).

HOROWITZ, D.: 'Attitudes of British Conservatives towards Decolonization in Africa', *African Affairs*, 69, 274 (1970) pp. 9–26.

HUNTER, G.: *The New Societies of Tropical Africa: a selective study* (London, 1962).

HUXLEY, ELSPETH: *The Sorcerer's Apprentice* (London, 1951).

—— *A New Earth: an experiment in colonialism* (London, 1960).

INGHAM, K.: *A History of East Africa* (London, 1962).

JEFFRIES, SIR C. J.: *Transfer of Power: the problems of the passing to self-government* (London, 1960).

KIRKMAN, W. P.: *Unscrambling an Empire: a critique of British policy 1956–1966* (London, 1966). Chapters 3–6 concern East Africa.

LEE, J. M.: *Colonial Development and Good Government: a study of the ideas expressed by the British official classes in planning decolonization, 1939–1964* (Oxford, 1967).

LONSDALE, J. M.: 'Some Origins of Nationalism in East Africa', *Journal of African History*, 9, 1 (1968) pp. 119–46.

—— 'The Emergence of African Nations', *African Affairs*, 67, 266 (January 1968) pp. 11–28.

LOWENKOPF, M.: 'Political Parties in Uganda and Tanganyika' (unpublished M.Sc. thesis, London University, 1961).

MACMILLAN, W. M.: *The Road to Self-Rule: a study in colonial evolution* (London, 1959).

MARSH, ZÖE, and KINGSNORTH, G. W.: *An Introduction to the History of East Africa* (Cambridge, 1957).

MIDDLETON, J. F. M., and WINTER, E. H., eds.: *Witchcraft and Sorcery in East Africa* (London, 1963).

MITCHELL, SIR P. E.: *African Afterthoughts* (London, 1954).

NOON, J. A.: 'Political Developments in East Africa', in *Africa in the Modern World*, ed. Calvin W. Stillman (Chicago, 1955), pp. 182–203.

PADMORE, G.: *Pan-Africanism or Communism?: the coming struggle for Africa* (London, 1956).

PERHAM, MARGERY: *Colonial Sequence*, Vol. II, *1949–1969* (London, 1970).

RANGER, T. O.: 'Connexions between "Primary Resistance" Movements and Modern Mass Nationalism in East and Central Africa', 1 and 2, *Journal of African History*, 9, 3, and 4 (1968) pp. 409–36, 631–42.

RICHARDS, AUDREY, ed.: *East African Chiefs: a study of political development in some Uganda and Tanganyika tribes* (London, 1960).

—— *The Multi-cultural States of East Africa* (Montreal, 1970).

ROBINSON, K. E.: *The Dilemmas of Trusteeship* (London, 1965).

ROTBERG, R. I.: 'The Rise of African Nationalism: the case of East and Central Africa', *World Politics*, 15, 1 (October 1962) pp. 75–90.

—— and MAZRUI, A. A., eds.: *Protest and Power in Black Africa* (New York, 1970).

ROTHCHILD, D. S.: 'Majimbo Schemes in Kenya and Uganda', in *Boston University Papers on Africa: transition in African politics*, ed. Butler and Castagno (New York, 1967).

SOUTHALL, A. W.: 'The Growth of Urban Society', in *Tradition and Transition in East Africa*, ed. Gulliver (London, 1969).

TURNER, V., ed.: *Colonialism in Africa, 1870–1960*: Vol. 3, *Profiles of Change* (Stanford, 1971).

WHITELEY, W. H.: 'Language and Politics in East Africa', *Tanganyika Notes and Records*, 47/8 (1957) pp. 159–73.

—— *Swahili: the rise of a national language* (London, 1969).

WILSON, G.: 'The African Elite', in *The Transformation of East Africa*, ed. Diamond and Burke (New York, 1966).

YOUNG, C.: 'Decolonization in Africa', in *Colonialism in Africa*, Vol. 2, ed. Gann and Duignan (Stanford, 1970).

(ii) *Kenya*

AARONOVITCH, S., and AARONOVITCH, K.: *Crisis in Kenya* (London, 1947).

ANDERSON, J. E.: *The Struggle for the School* (London, 1970).

BARNETT, D. L., and NJAMA, KARARI: *Mau Mau from Within: autobiography and analysis of Kenya's peasant revolt* (London, 1966).

BENNETT, G.: 'The Development of Political Organizations in Kenya', *Political Studies*, 5, 2 (June 1957) pp. 113–30.

—— 'Kenya's Frustrated Election', *The World Today*, 17, 6 (June 1961) pp. 254–61.

—— 'Imperial Paternalism: the representation of African interests in the Kenya Legislative Council', in *Essays in Imperial Government*, ed. K. E. Robinson and A. F. Madden, pp. 141–70 (Oxford, 1963).

—— *Kenya, a Political History: the colonial period* (London, 1963).

—— 'Political Realities in Kenya', *World Today*, 19, 7 (July 1963) pp. 294–301.

—— and ROSBERG, C. G.: *The Kenyatta Election: Kenya 1960–1961* (London, 1961).

BERNARDI, B.: *The Mugwe: a failing prophet* (London, 1959).

BLUNDELL, SIR M.: *So Rough a Wind: Kenya memoirs* (London, 1964).

BROWN, J. MURRAY: *Kenyatta* (London, 1972).

BURKE, F. G.: *Political Evolution in Kenya* (Syracuse University, Program of East African Studies, Occasional Paper No. 2, 1964).

CAREY JONES, N. S.: *The Anatomy of Uhuru: an essay on Kenya's independence* (Manchester, 1966).

DELF, G.: *Jomo Kenyatta: towards the truth about the Light of Kenya* (London, 1961).

ENGHOLM, G. F.: 'African Elections in Kenya, March 1957', in *Five Elections in Africa*, ed. W. J. M. Mackenzie and K. E. Robinson, pp. 391–459 (Oxford, 1960).

FABIAN COLONIAL BUREAU: *Opportunity in Kenya* (London, 1953).

FONTAINE, JEAN S. LA: 'Tribalism among the Gisu', in *Tradition and Transition in East Africa*, ed. Gulliver (London, 1969).

FUREDI, F.: 'The African Crowd in Nairobi: popular movements and élite politics', *Journal of African History*, 14, 2 (1973) pp. 275–90.

FURLEY, O. W.: 'The Historiography of Mau Mau', in *Politics and Nationalism in Colonial Kenya*, ed. Ogot (Nairobi, 1972).

GATHERU, R. MUGO: *Child of Two Worlds: a Kikuyu's story* (London, 1964).

GERTZEL, CHERRY: *The Politics of Independent Kenya* (Nairobi, 1970).

—— GOLDSCHMIDT, M., and ROTHCHILD, D., eds.: *Government and Politics in Kenya* (Nairobi, 1970).

HARBESON, J. W.: 'Nationalism and Nation Building in Kenya: The role of land reform' (Ph.D. dissertation, University of Wisconsin, 1970).

—— Land Reforms and Politics in Kenya, 1954–1970', *Journal of Modern African Studies*, 9, 2 (1971), pp. 231–51.

HENDERSON, I., with GOODHART, P.: *The Hunt for Kimathi* (London, 1958).

HUXLEY, ELSPETH, and PERHAM, MARGERY: *Race and Politics in Kenya* (London, 1944; revised edn. 1956).

ITOTE, WARUHIU: *'Mau Mau' General* (Nairobi, 1971).

KARIUKI, J. M.: *'Mau Mau' Detainee* (London and Nairobi, 1963).

KENYATTA, JOMO: *My People of Kikuyu and the Life of Chief Wangombe* (London, 1942).

—— *Kenya: the land of conflict* (Manchester, 1945).

—— *Facing Mount Kenya: the tribal life of the Gikikuyu* (London, 1953).

KIPKORIR, B. E.: 'The Education Élite and Local Society', in *Politics and Nationalism in Colonial Kenya*, ed. Ogot (Nairobi, 1972).

KOINANGE, M.: *The People of Kenya Speak for Themselves* (Detroit, 1955).

LAMBERT, H. E.: *Kikuyu Social and Political Institutions* (London, 1956).

LEAKEY, L. S. B.: *Mau Mau and the Kikuyu* (London, 1952).

—— *Defeating Mau Mau* (London, 1954).

LEVINE, R. A., and LEVINE, BARBARA: *Nyansongo: a community in Kenya* (New York, 1966).

LONSDALE, J. M.: 'Rural Resistance and Mass Political Mobilization amongst the Luo of Western Kenya' (East African History Conference, Dar es Salaam, 1965).

—— 'A Political History of Nyanza, 1883–1945' (University of Cambridge Ph.D. thesis, 1965).

—— 'Political Associations in Western Kenya', in *Protest and Power in Black Africa*, ed. Rotberg and Mazrui (New York, 1970).

MAJDALANY, F.: *State of Emergency: the full story of Mau Mau* (London, 1962).

MANNERS, R. A.: 'The Kipsigis of Kenya: culture change in a "model" East African Tribe', in *Contemporary Change in Traditional Societies*, ed. J. H. Stewart, Vol. 1 (Urbana, Ill., 1967).

MAYER, P.: *Agricultural Co-operation by Neighbourhood Groups among the Gusii: two studies in applied anthropology in Kenya*, Colonial Research Studies No. 3 (London, 1951).

MAZRUI, A.: 'Mau Mau in Two Dimensions' (review article), *Africa Report* (May 1967).

MBOYA, TOM: *The Kenya Question: an African answer* (London, Fabian Colonial Bureau, 1956).

—— *Freedom and After* (London, 1963).

ODINGA, OGINGA: *Not Yet Uhuru: an autobiography* (London, 1967).

OGOT, B. A.: 'British Administration in the Central Nyanza District of Kenya 1900–60', *Journal of African History*, 4, 2 (1963) pp. 249–73.

—— ed.: *Politics and Nationalism in Colonial Kenya* (Nairobi, 1972).

—— 'Revolt of the Elders: an anatomy of the loyalist crowd in the Mau Mau uprising 1952–1956', in *Politics and Nationalism in Colonial Kenya*, ed. Ogot (Nairobi, 1972).

ORCHARDSON, I. Q.: *The Kipsigis*, (Nairobi, 1961).

PADMORE, G.: 'Behind the Mau Mau', *Phylon*, 14, 4 (1953) pp. 355–72.

PANKHURST, RICHARD K. P.: *Kenya: the history of two nations* (London, 1954).

PARKER, MARY: 'Municipal Government and the Growth of African Political Institutions in the Urban Areas of Kenya', *Zaire*, 3, 6 (June 1949) pp. 649–62.

—— *Political and Social Aspects of the Development of Municipal Government in Kenya* (London, Colonial Office, 1949 or 1950).

RAKE, A.: *Tom Mboya: young man of new Africa* (New York, 1962).

RAWCLIFFE, D. H.: *The Struggle for Kenya* (London, 1954).

RENISON, SIR P.: 'Kenya in Transition', *African Affairs*, 62, 249 (October 1963) pp. 341–55.

ROSBERG, C. J.: 'Political Conflict and Change in Kenya', in *Transition in Africa: studies in political adaptation*, ed. Gwendolen Carter and W. O. Brown (Boston, 1958).

—— and NOTTINGHAM, J.: *The Myth of 'Mau Mau': nationalism in Kenya* (New York, London, 1966).

SANGER, CLYDE and NOTTINGHAM, J.: 'The Kenya General Election of 1963', *Journal of Modern African Studies*, 2, 1 (March 1964) pp. 1–40.

SANGREE, W. H.: *Age, Prayer and Politics in Tiriki, Kenya* (London, 1966).

SCHNEIDER, H. K.: 'Pakot Resistance to Change', in *Continuity and Change in African Cultures*, ed. W. R. Bascom and M. J. Herskovits (Chicago, 1959).

SILLITOE, K. K.: 'Local Organization in Nyeri' (East African Institute for Social Research Conference Paper, July 1962).

SINGH, M.: *History of Trade Unions in Kenya* (London, 1969).

—— 'The East African Trade Union Congress, 1949–1950', in *Politics and Nationalism in Colonial Kenya*, ed. Ogot (Nairobi, 1972).

SLATER, M.: *The Trial of Jomo Kenyatta* (London, 1955; revised edn. 1970).

SORRENSON, M. P. K.: *Land Reform in the Kikuyu Country* (London, 1967).

636   SELECT BIBLIOGRAPHY

SPENCER, P.: *The Samburu: a study of gerontocracy in a nomadic tribe* (Berkeley, 1965).
TAMARKIN, M.: 'Tribal Associations, Tribal Solidarity, and Tribal Chauvinism in a Kenya Town [Nakuru]', *Journal of African History*, 14, 2 (1973) pp. 257–74.
TEMU, A. J.: *British Protestant Missions* [Kenya] (London, 1972).
WASSERMAN, G.: 'The Independence Bargain: Kenya Europeans and the Land Issue, 1960–1962', *Journal of Commonwealth Political Studies*, 11, 2 (1973) pp. 99–120.
WELBOURN, F. B.: 'Comment on Corfield', *Race*, 2, 2 (May 1961) pp. 7–27.
WERE, G. S.: 'Politics, Religion and Nationalism in Western Kenya', in *Politics and Nationalism in Colonial Kenya*, ed. Ogot (Nairobi, 1972).
WERLIN, H. H.: 'The Nairobi City Council: a study in comparative local government', *Comparative Studies in Society and History*, 8 (1965).
WILSON, G.: 'Mombasa—A Modern Colonial Municipality', in *Social Change in Modern Africa*, ed. A. Southall (London, 1961).
WOOD, SUSAN: *Kenya: the tensions of progress* (London, 1960).

(iii) *Uganda*

APTER, D. E.: 'Some Problems of Local Government in Uganda', *Journal of African Administration*, 9, 1 (January 1959) pp. 27–37.
—— 'The Role of Traditionalism in the Political Modernization of Ghana and Uganda', *World Politics*, 13, 1 (October 1960) pp. 45–68.
—— *The Political Kingdom in Uganda* (Princeton, 1961, new edn., 1967).
BEATTIE, J. H. M.: 'Democratization in Bunyoro', *Civilizations*, 11, 1 (1961) pp. 8–20.
—— 'Group Aspects of the Nyoro Spirit Mediumship Cult', *Rhodes–Livingstone Journal*, 30 (1961) pp. 11–38.
BELSHAW, D. G. R.: 'An Outline of Resettlement Policy in Uganda, 1945–1963' (EAISR Conference Paper, 1963).
BURKE, F. G.: *Local Government and Politics in Uganda* (Syracuse, 1964).
CARTER, FELICE: 'Education in Uganda' (unpublished Ph.D. thesis, London, 1967).
CARTRY, MICHEL: 'Tradition et changement dans le Royaume du Bouganda', *Revue Française de Science Politique*, 13, 1 (March 1963) pp. 88–119.
DAHYA, B. W.: 'Some Characteristics of Tribal Associations in Kampala' (EAISR Conference Paper, January 1963).
DOORNBUS, M. R.: 'Kumanyana and Rwenzururu: two responses to ethnic inequality', in *Protest and Power in Black Africa*, ed. Rotberg and Mazrui (New York, 1970).
DYSON-HUDSON, N.: *Karimojong Politics* (Oxford, 1966).
EDEL, M. M.: 'African Tribalism: some reflections on Uganda', *Political Science Quarterly*, 80, 3 (1965) pp. 357–72.
ENGHOLM, G. F.: *The Development of Procedure in Uganda's Legislative Council* (London, Chiswick Press, 1956).
—— 'Political Parties and Uganda's Independence', *Transition* (Kampala, 1962).

FALLERS, L. A.: 'The Predicament of the Modern African Chief: an instance from Uganda', *American Anthropologist*, 57, 2 (1955) pp. 290–305.

—— *Bantu Bureaucracy: a study of integration and conflict in the political institutions of an East African people* (Cambridge, 1956).

—— 'Social Class in Modern Buganda' (EAISR Conference Paper, June 1957).

—— 'Despotism, Status, Culture and Social Mobility in an African Kingdom', *Comparative Studies in Society and History*, 2 (1959) pp. 11–32.

—— 'Ideology and Culture in Uganda Nationalism', *American Anthropologist*, 63, 4 (August 1961) pp. 677–86.

—— ed.: *The King's Men: leadership and status in Buganda on the eve of independence* (London, 1964).

FONTAINE, J. S. LA: *The Gisu of Uganda*, Ethnographic Survey of Africa: East Central Africa, Part 10 (London, International African Institute, 1959).

GERTZEL, CHERRY: 'Report from Kampala' and 'How *Kabaka Yekka* Came to Be', *African Report* (October 1964) pp. 3–13.

GHAI, D. P.: 'The Buganda Trade Boycott: a study in tribal, political and economic nationalism', in *Protest and Power in Black Africa*, ed. Rotberg and Mazrui (New York, 1970).

GIRLING, F. K.: *The Acholi of Uganda*, Colonial Research Studies No. 30 (London, HMSO, 1960).

GUTKIND, P. C. W.: 'Some Problems of African Urban Family Life: an example from Uganda, British East Africa', *Zaire*, 15, 1 (1961) pp. 59–74.

—— *The Royal Capital of Buganda* (The Hague, 1963).

INGHAM, K.: *The Making of Modern Uganda* (London, 1958).

LAWRANCE, J. C. D.: *The Iteso: fifty years of change in a Nilo-Hamitic tribe of Uganda* (London, 1957).

LEE, J. M.: 'Buganda's Position in Federal Uganda', *Journal of Commonwealth Political Studies*, 3, 3 (November 1965) pp. 165–81.

LOW, D. A.: *Buganda in Modern History* (London, 1971).

—— *The Mind of Buganda: documents of the modern history of an African Kingdom* (London, 1971).

—— *Lion Rampant: essays in the study of British imperialism* (London, 1973).

—— and PRATT, R. C.: *Buganda and British Overrule, 1900–1955: two studies* (London, 1960).

LOWENKOPF, M.: 'Uganda: prelude to independence', *Parliamentary Affairs* (Winter, 1961/2) pp. 74–80.

McGREGOR, C. P.: *King's College, Budo: the first sixty years* (Nairobi, 1967).

MAIR, LUCY P.: 'Busoga Local Government', *Journal of Commonwealth Political Studies*, 5, 2 (July 1967) pp. 91–108.

MIDDLETON, J. F. M.: 'The Yakan or Allah Water Cult among the Lugbara', *Journal of The Royal Anthropological Institute*, 93, 1 (1963).

—— *The Lugbara of Uganda* (New York, 1965).

—— 'Political Incorporation among the Lugbara of Uganda', in *From Tribe to Nation in Africa*, ed. Cohen and Middleton (Scranton, 1970).

—— 'Some Effects of Colonial Rule among the Lugbara', in *Colonialism in Africa*, Vol. 3, ed. Turner (Stanford, 1971).

MUKHERJEE, R.: *The Problem of Uganda: a study in acculturation* (Berlin, Akademie Verlag, 1956).

MUKWAYA, A. B.: *Land Tenure in Buganda: present day tendencies*, East African Studies No. 1 (Kampala, EAISR, 1953).

MUNGER, E. S.: *Relational Patterns of Kampala, Uganda* (Chicago, 1951).

MUTESA, SIR FREDERICK, Kabaka of Buganda: *Desecration of My Kingdom* (London, 1968).

[OBOTE, A. MILTON] 'Road to the Top: Obote's own story', in *Free Uganda* (Nairobi, 1962).

PARKIN, D. J.: 'Tribe as Fact and Fiction in an East African City' [Kampala] in *Tradition and Transition in East Africa*, ed. Gulliver (London, 1969).

—— *Neighbours and Nationals in an African City Ward* [Kampala] (London, 1969).

PARMA-NTANDA, MUSA K.: *Deposition of His Highness the Kabaka of Buganda* (Kampala, 1954).

PRATT, R. C.: 'Nationalism in Uganda', *Political Studies*, 9, 2 (June 1961) pp. 157–78.

RICHARDS, AUDREY I.: *The Changing Structure of a Ganda Village: Kisozi, 1892–1952* (Nairobi, 1966).

ROTHCHILD, D. S., and ROGIN, M.: 'Uganda', in *National Unity and Regionalism in Eight African States*, ed. G. M. Carter (Ithaca, 1966), pp. 337–440.

SCOTT, R. D.: *The Development of Trade Unions in Uganda* (Nairobi, 1966).

SHEPHERD, G. W.: *They Wait in Darkness* (New York, 1955).

SOFER, C., and SOFER, RHONA: *Jinja Transformed*, East African Studies No. 4 (Kampala, EAISR, 1955).

SOUTHALL, A. W.: *Alur Society: a study in processes and types of domination* (Cambridge, 1956).

—— 'Determinants of the Social Structure of African Urban Populations, with special reference to Kampala (Uganda)', in *Social Implications of Industrialization and Urbanization in Africa South of the Sahara* (Paris, UNESCO, 1956) pp. 578–89.

—— 'Kinship, Friendship, and the Network of Relations in Kisenyi, Kampala', in *Social Change in Modern Africa*, ed. A. Southall (New York, 1961).

—— 'Micropolitics in Uganda: traditional and modern politics', (EAISR Conference Paper, January 1963).

—— 'The Concept of Élites and their Formation in Uganda', in *The New Élites of Tropical Africa*, ed. P. C. Lloyd (London, 1966), pp. 242–66.

—— 'Incorporation among the Alur', in *From Tribe to Nation in Africa*, ed. Cohen and Middleton (Scranton, 1970).

—— and GUTKIND, P. C. W.: *Townsmen in the Making: Kampala and its suburbs*, East African Studies No. 9 (Kampala, EAISR, 1956).

SOUTHWHOLD, M.: *Bureaucracy and Chiefship in Buganda*, East African Studies No. 14 (Kampala, EAISR, n.d.).

TAMUKEDDE, W. P.: *Changes in the Great Lukiko* (EAISR Conference Paper, January 1954).

TWADDLE, M.: 'Tribalism in Eastern Uganda', in *Tradition and Transition in East Africa*, ed. Gulliver (London, 1969).

WELBOURN, F. B.: *Religion and Politics in Uganda, 1952–1962* (Nairobi, 1965).
WINTER, E. H.: *Bwamba: a structural-functional analysis of a patrilineal society* (Cambridge, 1956).
ZAKE, L.: 'New Party enters the Ring in Uganda', *Africa Special Report*, (November 1957).

(iv) *Tanganyika*

ABRAHAMS, R. G.: 'Kahama Township, Western Province, Tanganyika', in *Social Change in Modern Africa*, ed. A. W. Southall (London, 1961).
—— *The Political Organization of Unyamwezi* (Cambridge, 1967).
—— 'The Political Incorporation of non-Nyamwezi Immigrants in Tanzania', in *From Tribe to Nation in Africa*, ed. Cohen and Middleton (Scranton, 1970).
AUSTEN, R. A.: 'Notes on the Pre-history of TANU', *Makerere Journal*, 9 (1964) pp. 1–6.
BARONGO, E. M.: *Tanganyika African National Union* (Swahili) (Dar es Salaam, 1962).
—— *Mkiki ura Siasa Tanganyika* (Dar es Salaam, 1969).
BATES, MARGARET L.: 'Tanganyika: the development of a Trust Territory', *International Organization*, 9, 1 (1955) pp. 32–51.
—— 'Tanganyika under British Administration, 1920–1955' (unpublished D.Phil. thesis, Oxford 1957).
—— 'Tanganyika', in *African One-Party States*, ed. Gwendolen M. Carter (Ithaca, 1962), pp. 395–47.
BENNETT, G.: 'An Outline History of TANU', *Makerere Journal*, 7 (1963) pp. 15–32.
BIENEN, H.: *Tanzania: party transformation and economic development* (Princeton, 1967, expanded edn., 1970).
CHIDZERO, B. T. G.: *Tanganyika and International Trusteeship* (London, 1961).
CLIFFE, L.: 'Nationalism and the Reaction to Enforced Agricultural Improvement in Tanganyika during the Colonial Period', in *Socialism in Tanzania*, ed. Cliffe and Saul (Dar es Salaam, 1973).
—— and SAUL, J. S.: eds.: *Socialism in Tanzania* (2 vols., Dar es Salaam, 1973).
COLE, J. S. R.: 'Progress to Independence: Tanganyika', *Tanganyika Notes and Records*, 58 and 59 (March/September 1962) pp. 179–86.
CORY, H.: *The Indigenous Political System of the Sukuma and Proposals for Political Reform*, East African Studies No. 2 (Nairobi, 1954).
—— 'Reform of Tribal Political Institutions in Tanganyika', *Journal of African Administration*, 12, 2 (April 1960) pp. 77–84.
—— and MALCOLM, W.: *Sukumaland* (London, 1953).
DATTA, A. K.: *Tanganyika: a government in a plural society* (Leiden, 1955).
DRYDEN, S.: *Local Administration in Tanzania* (Nairobi, 1968).
DUDBRIDGE, B. J., and GRIFFITHS, J. E. S.: 'The Development of Local Government in Sukumaland', *Journal of African Administration*, 3, 3 (1951) pp. 141–6.
FLETCHER-COOKE, J.: 'Tanganyika and the Trusteeship Council', *Tanganyika Notes and Records*, 56 (1961) pp. 40–8, reprinted from *International Organization*, 13, 3 (1959).

Fosbrooke, H. A.: 'An Administrative Survey of the Masai Social System', *Tanganyika Notes and Records*, 26 (December 1948) pp. 1–50.

Friedland, W. H.: 'The Evolution of Tanganyika's Political System', in *The Transformation of East Africa*, ed. Diamond and Burke (New York, 1966).

—— 'Co-operation, Conflict and Conscription: TANU–TFL relations 1955–64', in *Boston University Papers on Africa: transition in African politics*, ed. J. Butler and A. A. Castagno (New York, 1967).

—— *Vuta Kamba: the development of trade unions in Tanganyika* (Stanford, 1969).

Gulliver, P. H.: *Land Tenure and Social Change among the Nyakyusa: an essay in applied anthropology in South-West Tanganyika*, East African Studies No. 11 (Kampala, EAISR, 1958).

—— *Social Control in an African Society. A study of the Arusha: agricultural Masai of Northern Tanganyika* (London, 1963).

—— 'The Conservative Commitment in Northern Tanzania', in *Tradition and Change in East Africa*, ed. Gulliver (London, 1969).

—— *Neighbours and Networks: the idiom of kinship in social action among the Ndendeuli of Tanzania* (Berkeley, 1971).

Heussler, R. W.: *British Tanganyika: an essay and documents on district administration* (Durham, N.C., Duke University Press, 1971).

Hyden, G.: *TANU Yajenga Nchi: political development in rural Tanzania* (Lund, 1968).

Iliffe, J.: 'The Age of Improvement and Differentiation', in *The History of Tanzania*, ed. Kimambo and Temu (Nairobi, 1969).

—— 'A History of the Dockworkers of Dar es Salaam', in *Dar es Salaam, City, Port and Region*, ed. J. Sutton (Dar es Salaam, 1970).

Japhet, Kirilo, and Seaton, Earle: *The Meru Land Case* (Nairobi, 1967).

John, C.: 'The Rise of Tanganyikan Nationalism', (unpublished Ph.D. dissertation, Harvard, 1971).

Kifile, H. O.: 'Labour Relations in Tanganyika', *International Labour Review*, 88, 4 (October 1963) pp. 345–65.

Kimambo, I. N.: *Mbiru: popular protest in colonial Tanzania*, Historical Ass. of Tanzania Paper No. 8 (Nairobi, 1971).

Lang, G. O., and Martha, B.: 'Problems of Social and Economic Change in Sukumaland, Tanganyika', *Anthropological Quarterly*, 35 (1962) pp. 86–101.

Leslie, J. A. K.: *A Survey of Dar es Salaam* (London, 1963).

Leys, C. T.: 'Tanganyika: the realities of independence', *International Journal*, 17, 3 (1962) pp. 251–68, reprinted in *Socialism in Tanzania*, ed. Cliffe and Saul (Dar es Salaam, 1972).

Liebenow, J. G.: 'Chieftainship and Local Government in Tanganyika: a study in institutional adaptation' (unpublished Ph.D. thesis, Northwestern University, 1955).

—— 'Responses to Planned Political Change in a Tanganyika Tribal Group', *American Political Science Review*, 50, 2 (June 1956) pp. 442–61.

—— 'Some Problems in Introducing Local Government Reform in Tanganyika', *Journal of African Administration*, 8, 3 (July 1956) pp. 132–9.

—— 'Tribalism, Traditionalism and Modernism in Chagga Local Government', *Journal of African Administration*, 10, 2 (April 1958) pp. 71–82.

—— 'The Chief in Sukuma Local Government', *Journal of African Administration*, 11, 2 (April 1959) pp. 84–92.

—— *Colonial Life and Political Development in Tanzania: the case of the Makonde* (Evanston, 1971).

LISTOWEL, JUDITH: *The Making of Tanganyika* (London, 1965).

LONDSALE, J. M.: 'Some Origins of Nationalism in Tanzania', in *Socialism in Tanzania*, ed. Cliffe and Saul (Nairobi, 1973).

LOWENKOPF, M.: 'Tanganyika Achieves Responsible Government', *Parliamentary Affairs*, 14, 2 (Spring 1960) pp. 244–57.

MACKENZIE, W. J. M.: 'Changes in Local Government in Tanganyika', *Journal of African Administration*, 16, 3 (July 1954) pp. 123–29.

MAGUIRE, G. A.: *Towards 'Uhuru' in Tanganyika: the politics of participation* (Cambridge, 1969).

—— 'The Emergence of the Tanganyika African National Union in the Lake Province', in *Protest and Power in Black Africa*, ed. Rotberg and Mazrui (New York, 1970).

MHANDO, S.: *TANU and the Vote* (Dar es Salaam, 1956).

MIGEYO, ALI: *Portrait of a Nationalist: the life of Ali Migeyo as told to G. R. Mutahaba*, Historical Ass. of Tanzania Paper No. 6 (Nairobi, 1969).

MOFFETT, J. P., ed.: *Handbook of Tanganyika*, 2nd edn. (Dar es Salaam, Government Printer, 1958).

MUSTAFA, SOPHIA: *The Tanganyika Way: a personal story of Tanganyika's growth to independence* (London, 1962).

NELSON, A.: *The Freemen of Meru* (Nairobi, 1967).

NYERERE, JULIUS: *'Uhuru na Umoja', Freedom and Unity: a selection from writings and speeches, 1952–1965* (London, 1967). Contains many speeches etc. originally published separately as pamphlets.

PRATT, R. C.: '"Multi-Racialism" and Local Government in Tanganyika', *Race*, 2, 1 (November 1960) pp. 33–49.

RIGBY, P.: 'Politics and Modern Leadership Roles in Ugogo', in *Colonialism in Africa*, Vol. 3, ed. Turner (Stanford, 1971).

SHAW, J. V.: 'The Development of African Local Government in Sukumaland', *Journal of African Administration*, 6, 4 (1954) pp. 171–8.

STAHL, KATHLEEN M.: *Tanganyika: sail in the wilderness* (The Hague, 1961).

—— 'The Chagga', in *Tradition and Transition in East Africa*, ed. Gulliver (London, 1969).

STEPHENS, H. W.: *The Political Transformation of Tanganyika, 1920–67* (New York, 1968).

SUTTON, J. E. G., ed.: 'Dar es Salaam: city, port and region', *Tanzania Notes and Records*, No. 71 (Dar es Salaam, 1970).

TAYLOR, J. CLAGGETT: *The Political Development of Tanganyika* (Stanford, 1963).

TEMU, A. J.: 'The Rise and Triumph of Nationalism', in *History of Tanzania*, ed. Kimambo and Temu (Nairobi, 1969).

TWINING, SIR E.: 'The Situation of Tanganyika', *African Affairs*, 50, 201 (1951) pp. 297–310.

—— 'Tanganyika's Middle Course in Racial Relations', *Optima*, 8, 4 (December 1958) pp. 211–18.

TWINING, SIR E.: 'The Last Nine Years in Tanganyika', *African Affairs*, 58, 203 (1959) pp. 15–24.

WHITLAMSMITH, G. K.: *Recent Trends in Chagga Political Development* (Moshi, 1958).

WILSON, M.: *Good Company: a study of Nyakyusa age-villages* (London, 1951).

WRIGHT, I. M.: 'The Meru Land Case', *Tanzania Notes and Records*, 66 (1966) pp. 136–46.

YOUNG, A.: 'The Contribution of Missions to Educational Structure and Administrative Policy in Tanganyika, 1918–1961' (unpublished M.A. thesis, Sheffield University, 1963).

YOUNG, R., and FOSBROOKE, H. A.: *Land and Politics among the Luguru of Tanganyika* (published in the US under title *Smoke in the Hills*) (London, 1960).

(v) *Zanzibar*

AYANY, S. G.: *A History of Zanzibar: a study in constitutional development* (Nairobi, 1970).

BATSON, E.: 'The Social Survey of Zanzibar' (unpublished, Cape Town: Dept. of Social Studies, University of Cape Town, n.d., 21 vols.).

CAMPBELL, JANE: 'Multi-racialism and Politics in Zanzibar', *Political Science Quarterly*, 77, 1 (1962).

INSTITUTE OF CURRENT WORLD AFFAIRS: *Zanzibar Arabs* (mimeo., 1954).

—— *The Zanzibar Elections* (mimeo., 1957).

LIENHARDT, P.: 'Behind the Zanzibar Mystery', *New Society* (6 February 1964).

LOFCHIE, M. F.: 'Party Conflict in Zanzibar', *The Journal of Modern African Studies*, 1, 2 (June 1963) pp. 185–207.

—— 'The Transformation of Historic Oligarchies: Zanzibar', in *Political Parties and National Integration in Tropical Africa* (Berkeley, Los Angeles, 1964).

—— *Zanzibar: background to revolution* (Princeton, 1965).

—— 'The Plural Society in Zanzibar', in *Pluralism in Africa*, ed. Kuper and Smith (Berkeley, 1969).

—— 'The Zanzibar Revolution: African protest in a racially plural society', in *Protest and Power in Black Africa*, ed. Rotberg and Mazrui (New York, 1970).

—— 'Was Okello's Revolution a Conspiracy?' in *Socialism in Tanzania*, ed. Cliffe and Saul (Nairobi, 1973).

MIDDLETON, J. F. M.: *Land Tenure in Zanzibar* (London, HMSO, 1961).

—— and CAMPBELL, JANE: *Zanzibar: its society and its politics* (London, 1965).

NATIONALIST, THE: 'The "Official" Version of the Zanzibar Revolution', in *Socialism in Tanzania*, ed. Cliffe and Saul (Nairobi, 1973).

OKELLO, J.: *Revolution in Zanzibar* (Nairobi, 1967).

PENNEY, J. C.: 'Notes on the Election in the Protectorate of Zanzibar', *Journal of African Administration*, 10, 3 (1958) pp. 144–52.

PRINS, A. H. J.: *The Swahili-speaking Peoples of Zanzibar and the East African Coast* (London, IAI, 1961).

REY, L.: 'The Revolution in Zanzibar', in *Socialism in Tanzania*, ed. Cliffe and Saul (Nairobi, 1973).

ROTBERG, R. I.: 'The Political Outlook in Zanzibar', *Africa Report*, 6, 9 (October 1961) pp. 5, 6–12.

SANGER, C.: 'Zanzibar Revisited', *Africa Report* (June 1963) pp. 19–22.

II. EAST AFRICAN CO-OPERATION AND INTEGRATION (POLITICAL AND ECONOMIC), 1939–1963

[See also the *East African Economics Review*, only a few of the articles from which are listed below.]

BANFIELD, JANE: 'Federation in East Africa', *International Journal*, 18 (Spring 1963) pp. 181–93.

BROWNING, P.: 'A Note on the Balance of Payments of East Africa, 1946–1953', *The East African Economics Review*, 2, 1 (July 1955) pp. 39–52.

COX, R.: *Pan-Africanism in Practice: PAFMECSA 1958–1964* (London, 1964).

DUE, J. F., and ROBSON, P.: 'Tax Harmonization in the East African Common Market', Ch. 15 of *Fiscal Harmonization in Common Markets*, ed. C. S. Shoup (New York, 1966).

GLADDEN, E. N.: 'The East African Common Services Organization', *Parliamentary Affairs* (Autumn 1963) pp. 428–39.

HAZLEWOOD, A. D. H.: 'The Territorial Incidence of the East African Common Services', *Bulletin of Oxford University Institute of Economics and Statistics*, 27, 13 (1965) pp. 161–76.

—— 'The "Shiftability" of Industry and the Measurement of Gains and Losses in the East African Common Market', *Bulletin of the Oxford University Institute of Economics and Statistics*, 28, 2 (May 1966) pp. 63–72.

—— 'The East African Common Market: importance and effects', *Bulletin of the Oxford University Institute of Economics and Statistics*, 28, 1 (February 1966) pp. 1–18.

—— 'Economic Integration in East Africa', *African Integration and Disintegration: case studies in economic and political union*, ed. Hazlewood (London, 1967).

HUGHES, A. J.: *East Africa: the search for unity* (Harmondsworth, 1963).

KENNEDY, T. A.: 'The East African Customs Union: some features of its history and operation', *Makerere Journal*, 3 (1959) pp. 19–41.

KIANO, J. G.: 'The Federation Issue in Multi-Racial East and Central Africa' (Doctoral dissertation, University of California, 1956).

LEGUM, C.: *Pan-Africanism: a short political guide* (London, 1962).

LEYS, C., and ROBSON, P., eds.: *Federation in East Africa: opportunities and problems* (London, 1965). Articles by Van Arkadie, Banfield, Ghai, Hazlewood, Lury, Newman, and others.

LURY, D. A.: 'The Trade Statistics of the Countries of East Africa 1945–1964', *Economic and Statistical Review*, 14 (March 1965) pp. viii–xvii.

MCWILLIAM, M.: 'Is there a case for an East African Central Bank?', *East African Economics Review*, 5, 2 (January 1959) pp. 58–68.

MASSELL, B. F.: 'Trade Between East Africa and Neighbouring Countries', *Economic and Statistical Review*, 4 (September 1962) pp. 12–21.

MASSELL, B. F.: 'Industrialization and Economic Union in Greater East Africa', *East African Economics Review*, 9, 2 (December 1962) pp. 108–22.
—— *East African Economic Union: an evaluation and some implications for policy* (Santa Monica, Calif., 1963).
NDEGWA, P.: *The Common Market and Development in East Africa* (Nairobi, 1965, 2nd edn., 1968).
NEWLYN, W. T.: 'Monetary Systems and Integration', *The East African Economics Review*, 11, 1 (June 1964) pp. 41–58.
—— 'Gains and Losses in the East African Common Market', *Yorkshire Bulletin of Economic and Social Research*, 17 (November 1965) pp. 130–8.
—— 'Statistical Analysis of Integration in the East African Banking System', *Economic and Statistical Review*, 21 (December 1966) pp. viii–xii.
NYE, J. S.: 'East African Economic Integration', *Journal of Modern African Studies*, 1, 4 (1963) pp. 475–502.
—— *Pan-Africanism and East African Integration* (Cambridge, Mass., 1965).
ORD, H. W.: 'An Outline of East Africa's Balance of Payments, 1953–1955', *The East African Economics Review*, 3, 2 (January 1957) pp. 253–8.
PROCTOR, J. H.: 'The Effort to Federate East Africa: a post-mortem', *The Political Quarterly*, 27, 1 (January–March 1966) pp. 46–69.
—— and KRISHNA, K. G. V.: 'The East African Common Services Organization: an assessment', *South Atlantic Quarterly*, 64, 4 (1965).
ROBSON, P.: *Economic Integration in Africa* (London, 1968).
ROSBERG, C., and SEGAL, A.: 'An East African Federation', *International Conciliation* (May 1963).
ROTBERG, R. I.: 'The Federation Movement in British East and Central Africa 1889–1953', *Journal of Commonwealth Political Studies*, 2, 2 (May 1964) pp. 141–60.
ROTHCHILD, D. S.: *Toward Unity in Africa: a study of federation in British Africa* (Washington, 1960).
—— *The Politics of Integration: an East African Documentary* (Nairobi, 1968).
SCOTT, R.: 'Labour Legislation and the Federation Issue', *East African Journal*, 1 (November 1964).

III. ECONOMIC DEVELOPMENT AND DEMOGRAPHY, 1945 TO INDE-
PENDENCE

[Relating generally to Chapters V–VIII. See also the *East African Agricultural Journal*, the *East African Economics Review*, and the *Journal of African Administration*, for many short articles which it has not been possible to list individually.]

(i) *The East African economy generally*

[Including a few works which, although not mainly concerned with East Africa, deal with economic issues of special interest in an East African context.]

ARKADIE, B. VAN: 'Gross Domestic Product Estimates for East Africa', *Economic and Statistical Review*, 4 (December 1963) pp. ix–xii.
—— and GHAI, D.: 'The East African Economics', in *The Economics of Africa*, ed. P. Robson and D. A. Lury (London, 1969).

BELSHAW, D. G. R.: *Agricultural Development in East Africa* (Nairobi, 1967).

BLACKER, J. G. C.: 'Population Growth in East Africa', *Economic and Statistical Review*, 8 (September 1963) pp. viii–xii.

—— *Population in East Africa* (Nairobi, 1967).

CHAMBERS, R.: *Settlement Schemes in Tropical Africa* (London, 1969). Concerned in part with East Africa.

CLAYTON, E. S.: *Agrarian Development in Peasant Economies* (New York, 1964). Written from experience of East Africa.

EDEN, T.: 'The Tea Industry of East Africa', *World Crops*, 6, 5 (May 1954) pp. 203–5.

ELKAN, W.: 'Migrant Labour in East Africa: an economist's approach', *The American Economic Review*, 49, 2 (May 1969) p. 197.

—— 'Circular Migration and the Growth of Towns in East Africa', *International and Comparative Law Quarterly* (October 1967) pp. 43–66.

—— and FALLERS, L. A.: 'The Mobility of Labor' in *Labor Commitment and Social Change in Developing Areas*, ed. W. E. Moore and A. S. Feldman, pt. 4: *Competing Status Systems* (New York: Social Science Research Council, 1960).

ENGBERG, H. L.: 'Commercial Banking in East Africa, 1950–1963', *The Journal of Modern African Studies*, 3, 2 (1965) pp. 175–200.

FORD, V. C. R.: *The Trade of Lake Victoria*, East African Studies No. 3 (Kampala, EAISR, 1955).

FRANK, C. R.: 'The Production and Distribution of Sugar in East Africa', *The East African Economics Review*, 10, 2 (December 1963) pp. 96–110.

GHAI, D. P.: 'The Growth of Money Incomes in East Africa: 1946–1960', in *East Africa Past and Present* (Paris, *Présence Africaine*, 1964).

GOLDTHORPE, J. E., and WILSON, F. B.: *Tribal Maps of East Africa and Zanzibar*, East African Studies No. 13 (Kampala, 1960).

HADDON-CAVE, C. P.: 'Real Growth of the East African Territories, 1954–1960', *The East African Economics Review*, 8, 1 (June 1961) pp. 35–53.

HAZLEWOOD, A. D. H.: *Rail and Road in East Africa: transport co-ordination in underdeveloped countries* (Oxford, 1964).

HILL, M. F.: *Permanent Way*, Vol. I: *The Story of the Kenya and Uganda Railway* (Nairobi: East African Railways and Harbours, 1950); Vol. II: *The Story of the Tanganyika Railways* (Nairobi: East African Railways and Harbours, 1958).

HITCHCOCK, E.: 'The Sisal Industry of East Africa', *Tanganyika Notes and Records*, 52 (March 1959) pp. 4–17.

HOYT, E.: 'Economic Sense and the East African', *Africa*, 22, 2 (April 1952) pp. 165–9.

JONES, W. O.: 'Economic Man in Africa', *Food Research Institute Studies*, 1, 2 (Stanford, 1960).

KENNEDY, T. A.: 'Economic Development in British East Africa', *Civilizations*, 6, 3 (1956) pp. 371–89.

—— ORD, H. W., and WALKER, D.: 'On the Calculation and Interpretation of National Accounting Material in East Africa', in *African Studies in Income and Wealth*, ed. L. H. Samuels (London, 1963).

KENNEDY, T. J.: 'A Study of Economic Motivation Involved in Peasant Cultivation of Cotton', *The East African Economics Review*, 10, 2 (1963) pp. 88–95.

KRISHNA, K. G. V.: 'Resources and Problems of Economic Development', in *The Transformation of East Africa*, ed. Diamond and Burke (New York, 1966).

KUCZYNSKI, R. R.: *Demographic Survey of the British Colonial Empire*, Vol. 2, Part 3 (London, 1949).

LEUBUSCHER, CHARLOTTE: *Bulk Buying from the Colonies* (London, 1956).

LIVINGSTONE, I.: 'The Marketing of Crops in Uganda and Tanganyika', in *African Primary Products and International Trade* (Edinburgh, 1965).

LURY, D. A.: 'Population Data in East Africa', in *The Population of Tropical Africa*, ed. J. C. Caldwell and C. Okonjo (London, 1968).

McNEIL, R., and BECHGAARD, K.: *East African Income Tax* (London, 1960).

MARTIN, C. J.: 'The East African Population Census, 1948: planning and enumeration', *Population Studies*, 3, 3 (1949) pp. 303–20.

—— 'Some Estimates of the General Age Distribution, Fertility and Rate of Natural Increase of the African Population of British East Africa', *Population Studies*, 7, 2 (November 1953).

—— 'Estimates of Population Growth in East Africa with Special Reference to Tanganyika and Zanzibar', in *Essays on African Population*, ed. K. M. Barbour and R. M. Prothero (London, 1961) pp. 49–62.

—— 'The Development and Diversity of National Income Series in East Africa since 1947', in *African Studies in Income and Wealth*, ed. L. H. Samuels (London, 1963).

MATHESON, J. K., and BOVILL, E. W.: *East African Agriculture* (London, 1950).

MEAD, D. C.: 'Monetary Analysis in an Under-developed Economy: a case study of three East African territories', *Yale Economic Essays*, 3, 1 (Spring 1963) pp. 56–103.

MEISTER, A.: *Le Développement économique de l'Afrique Orientale (Kenya, Ouganda, Tanzanie)* (Paris, 1966).

MORGAN, W. T. W.: *East Africa, its Peoples and Resources* (Nairobi, 1969).

NEWLYN, W. T.: '"Take-off" considered in an African setting', *Yorkshire Bulletin of Economic and Social Research*, 13, 1 (May 1961) pp. 19–32.

—— and ROWAN, D. C.: *Money and Banking in British Colonial Africa* (Oxford, 1954). Has several sections on East Africa.

O'CONNOR, A. M.: *An Economic Geography of East Africa* (London, 1966).

ORD, H. W.: 'The Employment of Capital in East Africa' (EAISR Conference Paper, mimeo, December 1959).

—— 'East African Companies', *The East African Economics Review*, 7, 1 (June 1960) pp. 35–45.

—— 'The Growth of Money Incomes in East Africa', *The East African Economics Review*, 9, 1 (June 1962) pp. 41–7.

PEARSON, D. S.: *Industrial Development in East Africa* (Nairobi, 1969).

POLLOCK, N. C.: 'Industrial Development in East Africa', *Economic Geography*, 36, 4 (October 1960) pp. 344–54.

POWESLAND, P. G.: *Economic Policy and Labour*, ed. W. Elkan, East African Studies No. 10 (Kampala, EAISR, 1957).

SEIDMAN, ANN: 'The Inherited Dual Economics of East Africa', in *Socialism in Tanzania*, ed. Cliffe and Saul (Nairobi, 1973).

SMITH, T. E., and BLACKER, J. G. C.: *Population Characteristics of the Commonwealth Countries of Tropical Africa* (London, 1963).

SOUTHALL, A. W.: 'Population Movements in East Africa', *Essays on African Population*, ed. Barbour and Prothero (London, 1961).

SWYNNERTON, R. J. M.: 'Agricultural Advances in Eastern Africa', *African Affairs*, 61, 224 (July 1962) pp. 201–15.

USOV, G.: 'The Public Sector in the Economy of East African Countries', *Mirovaya Ekonomika i Mezhdunarodnye Otnosheniya*, 2 (1963) pp. 52–62.

WALKER, D.: 'A Recent Change in East African Company Taxation', *Public Finance*, 15, 2 (1960) pp. 166–88.

—— 'Problems of Economic Development of East Africa', in *Economic Development for Africa South of the Sahara*, ed. E. A. G. Robinson (London, 1964) pp. 89–137.

WARREN, A.: 'East Africa', in *Africa in Transition: geographical essays*, ed. B. W. Hodder and D. R. Harris (London, 1967), pp. 163–217.

YAMEY, B.: 'The Study of Peasant Economic Systems', in *Capital, Saving and Credit in Peasant Societies*, ed. R. Firth and B. S. Yamey (London, 1964).

(ii) *Kenya*

AMSDEN, ALICE: *International Firms and Labour in Kenya: 1945–1970* (London, 1971).

BARWELL, C. W.: 'A Note on Some Changes in the Economy of the Kipsigis Tribe', *Journal of African Administration*, 8, 2 (April 1956) pp. 95–101.

BRANNEY, L.: 'Towards the Systematic Individualization of African Land Tenure', and 'The Kenya Working Party on African Land Tenure', *Journal of African Administration*, 11, 4 (October 1959) pp. 208–24.

BROWN, L. H.: 'Land Consolidation and Better Farming in Kenya', *Empire Journal of Experimental Agriculture*, 30, 120 (1962) pp. 277–85.

—— 'Agricultural Change in Kenya, 1945–1960', *Food Research Studies* (Stanford, 1968) pp. 33–90.

CAVENDISH-BENTINCK, F. W.: *Agricultural Policy in African Areas of Kenya* (Nairobi, 1951).

CLAYTON, E. S.: 'Safeguarding Agrarian Development in Kenya', *Journal of African Administration*, 11, 3 (July 1959) pp. 144–50. [Also other articles in the *J. A. Admin.*]

—— 'Small-Scale Cash Crop Production in a Developing Economy', *Economic Development and Cultural Change*, 4 (1) (July 1961) pp. 618–24.

—— *Agrarian Development in Peasant Economies: some lessons from Kenya* (Oxford, 1964).

—— 'Industrial Development in Kenya' in *Industrial Development in Africa* (New York, United Nations, 1967).

DAVIDSON, B. R.: 'The Economics of Arable Land and Labour Use in African and European Areas of Kenya', *The East African Economics Review*, 7, 1 (June 1960) pp. 5–12.

DAVIDSON, B. R.: and YATES, R. J.: 'Relationship between Population and Potential Arable Land in the African Reserves and the European Highlands', *The East African Economics Review*, 6, 2 (December 1959) pp. 133–6.

FAULKNER, D. E.: *The Development of the Livestock Industry of the Native Areas of Kenya: policy and plans 1949–1958* (Nairobi, 1948).

FEARN, H.: *An African Economy: a study of the development of the Nyanza province of Kenya, 1903–1953* (London, 1961).

FISHER, J.: *The Anatomy of Kikuyu Domesticity and Husbandry* (London, 1964).

HENNINGS, R. O.: 'Some Trends and Problems of African Land Tenure in Kenya', *Journal of African Administration*, 4, 4 (October 1952) pp. 122–34.

—— 'Grazing Management in the Pastoral Areas of Kenya', *Journal of African Administration*, 13, 4 (October 1961) pp. 191–203.

HILL, M. F.: *Cream Country: the story of Kenya Co-Operative Creameries Limited* (Nairobi, 1956).

—— *Planter's Progress: the story of coffee in Kenya* (Nairobi, 1956).

—— *Magadi: the story of the Magadi soda company* (Nairobi and Birmingham, 1964).

HOMAN, F. D.: 'Consolidation Enclosure and Registration of Title in Kenya', *Journal of Local Administration Overseas*, 1, 1 (January 1962) pp. 4–14.

—— 'Land Consolidation and Redistribution of Population in the Imenti Sub-Tribe of the Meru, Kenya', *African Agrarian Systems*, ed. Biebuyck (London, 1963).

HUXLEY, ELSPETH: *No Easy Way: a history of the Kenya Farmers' Association and Unga Limited* (Nairobi, 1957).

INTERNATIONAL BANK FOR RECONSTRUCTION AND DEVELOPMENT: *The Economic Development of Kenya* (Baltimore, 1963).

LEAKEY, L. S. B.: 'The Economics of Kikuyu Tribal Life', *The East African Economics Review*, 3, 1 (July 1956) pp. 165–80.

LEVINE, R.: 'Wealth and Power in Gusiiland', in *Markets in Africa*, ed. Bohannan and Dalton (Evanston, 1962).

LEYS, COLIN: 'Politics in Kenya: the development of peasant society', *British Journal of Political Science*, 1 (1971) pp. 307–37.

MACARTHUR, J. D.: 'Land Tenure Reform and Economic Research into African Farming in Kenya', *The East African Economics Review*, 8, 2 (December 1961) pp. 79–91.

—— 'The Development of Research into the Production Economics of African Peasant Farms in Kenya', *The East African Economics Review*, 9, 2 (December 1962) pp. 95–107.

MACKENZIE, K. W. S.: 'The Development of the Kenya Treasury since 1936', *The East African Economics Review*, 8, 2 (December 1961) pp. 59–73.

McWILLIAM, M. D.: *The East African Tea Industry 1920–1956: a case study in the development of a plantation industry* (Oxford, 1957).

—— 'The Kenya Tea Industry', *The East African Economics Review*, 6, 1 (July 1959) pp. 32–48.

—— 'Economic Problems during the Transfer of Power in Kenya', *The World Today*, 18, 4 (April 1962) pp. 164–75.

—— 'Banking in Kenya, 1950–1960', *The East African Economics Review*, 9, 1 (June, 1962) pp. 16–40.

—— 'Economic Policy and the Kenya Settlers', in *Essays in Imperial Government*, ed. Robinson and Madden (Oxford, 1963).

—— 'Economic Viability and the Race Factor in Kenya', *Economic Development and Cultural Change*, 12, 1 (October 1963) pp. 55–69.

—— 'The World Bank and the Transfer of Power in Kenya', *Journal of Commonwealth Political Studies*, 2, 2 (May 1964) pp. 165–9.

MAHER, C.: 'The People and the Land: some problems, parts 1 and 2', *East African Agricultural Journal*, 7 (October 1941, January 1942) pp. 63–7, 146–51.

MANNERS, R. A.: 'The Kipsigis—Change with Alacrity' in *Markets in Africa*, ed. Bohannan and Dalton (Evanston, 1962).

MARRIS, P., and SOMERSET, A.: *African Businessmen* (London, 1971).

MAXON, R. M.: 'The Early Years of the Gusii Coffee Industry in Kenya, 1933–1946', *Journal of Developing Areas* (April 1972) pp. 365–82.

MIRACLE, M. P.: 'An Economic Appraisal of Kenya's Maize Control', *The East African Economics Review*, 6, 2 (December 1959) pp. 117–25.

OMINDE, S. H.: 'Population Movements to the Main Urban Areas of Kenya', *Cahiers d'Études Africaines*, 5, 20 (1965) pp. 593–617.

—— 'Some Aspects of Population Movements in Kenya', in *The Population of Tropical Africa*, ed. J. C. Caldwell and C. Okonjo (London, 1968).

—— *Land and Population Movements in Kenya* (London, 1968).

RAYMER, J.: 'The Economic Problem and Colonial Policy in an East African Reserve', *Economics*, 1, 4 (1952) pp. 145–9.

RUTHENBERG, H.: *African Agricultural Production Development Policy in Kenya 1952–1965* (Berlin, Springer-Verlag, 1966).

SILLITOE, K. K.: 'Land Use and Community in Nyeri, Kenya' (EAISR Conference Paper, January 1963).

SORRENSON, M. P. K.: *Land Reform in the Kikuyu Country* (London, 1967).

SWYNNERTON, R. J. M.: 'Kenya's Agricultural Planning', *African Affairs*, 56, 224 (July 1957) pp. 209–15.

VASEY, E. A.: 'Economic and Political Trends in Kenya', *African Affairs*, 55, 219 (April 1956) pp. 101–8.

WHISSON, M. G.: *Change and Challenge: a study of the social and economic changes among the Kenya Luo* (Nairobi, 1964).

(iii) *Uganda*

BARNES, J. W., ed.: *The Mineral Resources of Uganda* (Entebbe, 1961).

BARYARUNA, A.: *Factors Affecting Industrial Employment: a study of Ugandan experience 1954–64*, EAISR Occasional Papers No. 1 (Nairobi, 1967).

BELSHAW, D. G. R.: 'Public Investment in Agriculture and the Economic Development of Uganda', *The East African Economics Review*, 2 (December 1962) pp. 69–94.

ECONOMIST INTELLIGENCE UNIT: *Power in Uganda 1957–70: a study of economic growth prospects for Uganda with special reference to the potential demand for electricity* (London, 1957).

EHRLICH, C.: 'The Marketing of Cotton in Uganda, 1900–1950: a case study of colonial government policy' (unpublished Ph.D. thesis, University of London, 1958).

EHRLICH, C.: 'Some Social and Economic Implications of Paternalism in Uganda', *Journal of African History*, 4, 2 (1963) pp. 275–85.

ELKAN, W.: *An African Labour Force*, East African Studies No. 7 (Kampala, EAISR, 1956).

—— 'Central and Local Taxes on Africans in Uganda', *Public Finance*, 13, 4 (1958) pp. 312–22.

—— 'Criteria for Industrial Development in Uganda', *East African Economics Review*, 5, 2 (January 1959) pp. 50–7.

—— 'Regional Disparities in the Incidence of Taxation in Uganda', *The Review of Economic Studies*, 26 (2) 70 (February 1959) pp. 135–47.

—— *Migrants and Proletarians: urban labour in the economic development of Uganda* (London, 1960).

—— and WILSON, G. G.: 'The Impact of the Owen Falls Hydro-electric Project on the Economy of Uganda', *Journal of Development Studies*, 3, 4 (July 1967).

FURLEY, O. W.: 'The Origins of Economic Paternalism in a British Territory: Western Uganda', *Social and Economic Studies*, 11, 1 (March 1962) pp. 57–72.

GOOD, C. M.: *Rural Markets and Trade in East Africa: a study of the functions and development of exchange institutions in Ankole, Uganda* (Chicago, 1970).

HALL, SIR J.: 'Some Aspects of Economic Development in Uganda', *African Affairs*, 51, 203 (April 1952) pp. 124–32.

HAWKINS, E. K.: *Roads and Road Transport in an Underdeveloped Country: a case study of Uganda*, Colonial Research Studies No. 32 (London, HMSO, 1962).

HAZLEWOOD, A. D. H.: 'Trade Balances and Statutory Marketing in Primary Export Economics', *Economic Journal*, 67, 265 (March 1957) pp. 74–82.

HOYLE, B. S.: 'The Economic Expansion of Jinja, Uganda', *Geographical Review*, 53, 3 (1963) pp. 377–88.

INTERNATIONAL BANK FOR RECONSTRUCTION AND DEVELOPMENT: *The Economic Development of Uganda* (Baltimore, 1962).

JOY, J. L.: 'Mechanical Cultivation in Acholi', in *Symposium on Mechanical Cultivation in Uganda*, ed. J. L. Joy (Kampala, 1960).

KAJUBI, W. SENTEZA: 'Coffee and Prosperity in Buganda: some aspects of economic and social change', *Uganda Journal*, 29, 2 (1965) pp. 135–48.

KENDALL, H.: *Town Planning in Uganda* (London, Crown Agents, 1955).

KENNEDY, T. A.: 'An Estimate of Uganda's Balance of Payments, 1949–1957', *The East African Economics Review*, 6, 1 (July 1959) pp. 1–13.

KIBUKAMUSOKE, D. E. B.: 'Competitive Effects of Coffee on Cotton Production in Buganda', *Empire Cotton Growing Review*, 39, 2 (April 1962) pp. 106–13.

KUMALO, C.: 'African Élites in Industrial Bureaucracy' [in Kampala] in *The New Élites of Tropical Africa*, ed. P. C. Lloyd (London, 1966).

LURY, D. A.: 'Cotton and Coffee Growers and Government Development Finance in Uganda 1945–1960', *The East African Economics Review*, 10, 1 (June 1963) pp. 47–53.

MASEFIELD, G. B.: 'Agricultural Change in Uganda: 1945–1960', *Food Research Institute Studies*, 3, 2 (Stanford, 1962) pp. 87–124.

MIDDLETON, J. F. M.: 'Trade and Markets among the Lugbara of Uganda', in *Markets in Africa*, ed. Bohannan and Dalton (Evanston, 1962).

MUKWAYA, A. B.: 'The Marketing of Staple Foodstuffs in Uganda', in *Markets in Africa*, ed. Bohannan and Dalton (Evanston, 1962).

NYHART, J. D.: 'The Uganda Development Corporation and the Promotion of Entrepreneurship' (EAISR Conference Paper, December 1959).

O'CONNOR, A. M.: 'Regional Contrasts in Economic Development in Uganda', *East African Geographic Review*, 1 (1963) pp. 33-43.

—— *Railways and Development in Uganda* (Nairobi, 1965).

POWESLAND, P. G.: *Economic Policy and Labour: a study in Uganda's economic history*, East African Studies No. 10 (Kampala, EAISR, 1957).

RICHARDS, AUDREY I., ed.: *Economic Development and Tribal Change: a study of immigrant labour in Buganda* (Cambridge, 1954).

SOFER, C., and SOFER, RHONA: 'Recent Population Growth in Jinja', *Uganda Journal*, 17, 1 (March 1953) pp. 38-50.

TOTHILL, J. D., ed.: *Agriculture in Uganda* (London, 1940).

WALKER, D.: 'Criteria for Industrial Development in Uganda: a comment', *The East African Economics Review*, 6, 1 (July 1959) pp. 58-66.

WALKER, D., and EHRLICH, C.: 'Stabilization and Development Policy in Uganda: an appraisal', *Kyklos*, 12, 3 (1959) pp. 341-53.

—— and KENNEDY, T. A.: 'Imports and the Uganda Economy', in *Sabens Directory, 1960/61* (Kampala, 1960).

WILSON, GAIL: *Owen Falls: electricity in a developing country* (Nairobi, 1967).

WINTER, E. H.: *Bwamba Economy: the development of a primitive subsistence economy in Uganda*, East African Studies No. 5 (Kampala, EAISR, 1955).

WRIGLEY, C. C.: 'Buganda: an outline economic history', *Economic History Review*, 2nd ser. 10, 1 (August 1957) pp. 69-80.

—— 'African Farming in Buganda' (EAISR Conference Paper 1959).

—— *Crops and Wealth in Uganda*, East African Studies No. 12 (Kampala, EAISR, 1959).

(iv) *Tanganyika*

DE BLIG, HARM: *Dar es Salaam* (Evanston, 1964).

EHRLICH, C.: 'Some Aspects of Economic Policy in Tanganyika, 1945-1960', *Journal of Modern African Studies*, 2 (July 1964) pp. 265-77.

—— 'Some Antecedents of Development Planning in Tanganyika', *The Journal of Development Studies*, 2, 3 (April 1966) pp. 254-67.

FRANKEL, S. H.: 'The Kongwa Experiment: lessons of the East African Groundnut Scheme', in his volume of essays, *The Economic Impact on Underdeveloped Societies* (Oxford, 1953).

FUGGLES-COUCHMAN, N. R.: *Agricultural Change in Tanganyika, 1945-1960* (Stanford, Food Research Institute, 1964).

GRAY, R. F.: 'Economic Exchange in a Sonjo Village', in *Markets in Africa*, ed. Bohannan and Dalton (Evanston, 1962).

GUILLEBAUD, C. W.: *An Economic Survey of the Sisal Industry of Tanganyika* (Welwyn, 1958).

GULLIVER, P. H.: *Labour Migration in a Rural Economy: a study of the Ngoni and Ndendeuli of Southern Tanganyika*, East African Studies No. 6 (Kampala, EAISR, 1955).

—— 'Nyakyusa Labour Migration', *Rhodes–Livingstone Journal*, 21 (1957) pp. 32–63.

—— *Land Tenure and Social Change among the Nyakyusa*, East African Studies No. 11 (Kampala, EAISR, 1958).

—— 'The Evolution of Arusha Trade', in *Markets in Africa*, ed. Bohannan and Dalton (Evanston, 1962).

HALL, R. DE Z.: 'Local Migration in Tanganyika', *African Studies*, 4, 2 (June 1945).

HAWKINS, H. C. G.: *Wholesale and Retail Trade in Tanganyika: a study of distribution in East Africa* (New York, 1965).

HILL, J. F. R., and MOFFETT, J. P., eds.: *Tanganyika: a study of its resources and their development* (Dar es Salaam: Government Printer, 1955).

ILIFFE, J.: *Agricultural Change in Modern Tanganyika*, Historical Assoc. of Tanzania Occasional Paper No. 10 (Nairobi, 1971).

INTERNATIONAL BANK FOR RECONSTRUCTION AND DEVELOPMENT: *The Economic Development of Tanganyika* (Baltimore, 1961).

KIRBY, A.: 'Tanganyika Triumphant', *African Affairs*, 61, 243 (April 1962) pp. 114–25.

LANG, G. O., and LANG, M. B.: 'Problems of Social and Economic Change in Sukumaland, Tanganyika', *Anthropological Quarterly*, 35, 2 (April 1962) pp. 86–101.

LESLIE, J. A. K.: *A Survey of Dar es Salaam* (London, 1963).

LEUBUSCHER, C.: *Tanganyika Territory: a study of economic policy under mandate* (London, 1944).

LITTLE, A. D.: *Tanganyika Industrial Development* (Dar es Salaam, Government Printer, 1961).

LIVINGSTONE, I.: 'The Economic Development of Tanganyika: the World Bank view', *East African Economics Review*, 8, 1 (June 1961) pp. 1–13.

MALCOLM, D. W.: *Sukumaland: an African people and their country: a study of land use in Tanganyika* (London, 1953).

MANN, H. H.: *Tea Cultivation in the Tanganyika Territory and its Development* (Millbank, 1953).

MHALIGA, A.: *Co-operation in Tanganyika* (Tabora, Pontificia Universitas Gregoriana, 1958).

PEACOCK, A. R., and DOSSER, D. G. M.: *The National Income of Tanganyika, 1952–54*, Colonial Research Publication No. 26 (London, HMSO, 1958).

RICHARDS, A. I., and REINING, P.: 'Report on Fertility Surveys in Buganda and Buhaya 1952', in *Culture and Human Fertility*, ed. F. Lorimer (Paris, UNESCO, 1954).

ROUNCE, N. V., and MILNE, G.: 'The Development, Expansion and Rehabilitation of Sukumaland', *Empire Cotton Growing Review* (January 1949).

RUTHENBERG, H.: *Agricultural Development in Tanganyika* (Berlin, Springer-Verlag, 1964).

RUTMAN, G. L.: *The Economy of Tanganyika* (New York, 1968).

SEABROOK, A. T. P.: 'The Groundnut Scheme in Retrospect', *Tanganyika Notes and Records*, 47–8 (June and September 1957) pp. 87–91.

SWYNNERTON, R. J. M.: 'Some Problems of the Chagga on Kilimanjaro', *East African Agricultural Journal*, 14 (October 1949) pp. 117–32.

—— and BENNETT, A. L. B.: *All About K.N.C.U. Coffee* (Moshi, 1948).

WAKEFIELD, A. J.: 'The Groundnut Scheme', *East African Agricultural Journal*, 13 (January 1948) pp. 131–4.

WOOD, A.: *The Groundnut Affair* (London, 1950).

IV. RETROSPECT ON THE ALIEN IMPACT ON EAST AFRICA: THE IMMIGRANT COMMUNITIES, THE INFLUENCE OF WESTERN LAW AND RELIGION

The works listed below are very broadly relevant to Chapters IX–XIII, though there is inevitably some overlap with the subject-matter of the earlier chapters, in particular with the Introduction and with the discussion of Kenya settler politics in Chapter II. A few titles of central importance are repeated from the earlier sections of the bibliography.

The list is of necessity much more selective than the preceding ones, and in drawing it up the emphasis has been on—apart from works dealing directly with the issues defined—(a) the original 'classics' of the main colonial period before the Second World War and (b) studies published since 1965. For fuller guidance on the pre-1945 period, reference should be made to the bibliographies of Volumes I and II of this *History*.

(i) *General*

ABEDI, SHEIKH AMRI (chairman): *African Conference on Local Courts and Customary Law* (University College, Dar es Salaam, 8–18 September 1963).

ALLOTT, A. N., ed.: *The Future of Law in Africa* (Record of the proceedings of the London Conference, 28 December 1959–8 January 1960) (London, 1960).

—— ed.: *Judicial and Legal Systems in Africa* (London, 1962).

ANDERSON, J. N. D.: *Islamic Law in Africa*, Colonial Research Publication No. 16 (London, HMSO, 1954).

BAËTA, C. G., ed.: *Christianity in Tropical Africa* (London, 1968).

BARRETT, D. B.: *Schism and Renewal in Africa: an analysis of six thousand contemporary religious movements* (Nairobi, 1968).

BEATTIE, J. H. M., and MIDDLETON, J., eds.: *Spirit Mediumship and Society in Africa* (London, 1969). Most of the contributions are concerned with East Africa.

BRITISH INSTITUTE OF INTERNATIONAL AND COMPARATIVE LAW: *East African Law Today*, foreword by Lord Denning (London, 1966).

BUELL, R. L.: *The Native Problem in Africa*, 2 vols. (New York, 1928).

COLONIAL OFFICE, AFRICAN STUDIES BRANCH: 'Report of the Judicial Advisers' Conference', *Journal of African Administration*, Special Supplement (1957).

COTRAN, E.: 'The Unification of Laws in East Africa', *Journal of Modern African Studies*, 20, 1, 2 (1963) pp. 209–20.

—— 'Tribal Factors in the Establishment of the East African Legal Systems', in *Tradition and Transition in East Africa*, ed. Gulliver (London, 1969).

DELF, G.: *Asians in East Africa* (London, 1963).

EAST AFRICAN INSTITUTE OF SOCIAL AND CULTURAL AFFAIRS: *Racial and Communal Tensions in East Africa* (Nairobi, 1966).

EGGERT, JOHANNA: *Missionschule und sozialer Wandel in Ostafrika, 1891–1939* (Freiburg, Bertelsmann Universitätslag, 1970).

FRANCK, T. M.: *East African Unity through Law* (New Haven, 1964).

GHAI, D. P., ed.: *Portrait of a Minority: Asians in East Africa* (Nairobi, 1965).

GRAY, J. R.: 'The Missionary Factor in East Africa', in *Africa in the Nineteenth and Twentieth Centuries*, ed. J. C. Anene and G. N. Brown (Ibadan, 1966).

GREGORY, R. G.: *India and East Africa: a history of race relations within the British Empire* (Oxford, 1971).

GROVES, C. P.: *The Planting of Christianity in Africa*, Vol. 2 (London, 1954).

HANCOCK, W. K.: *Survey of British Commonwealth Affairs*, Vol. I: *Problems of Nationality* (London, 1937); Vol. II: *Problems of Economic Policy* (London, 1940).

HARLOW, V. T., CHILVER, E. M., and SMITH, ALISON, eds.: *History of East Africa*, Vol. II (Oxford, 1965).

HARRIES, L. P.: *Islam in East Africa* (London, 1954).

HOLLINGSWORTH, L. W.: *The Asians of East Africa* (London, 1960).

HOPKINS, ELIZABETH: 'Racial Minorities in British East Africa', in *The Transformation of East Africa*, ed. Diamond and Burke (New York, 1966).

HUXLEY, J.: *Africa View* (London, 1931).

IDOWU, E. BOLAJI: *Towards an Indigenous Church* (London, 1965).

JONES, T. JESSE, ed.: *Education in Africa*: Pt. 2, *A Study of East, Central and South Africa by the Second African Education Commission*, Phelps-Stokes Fund (London, 1925).

MANGAT, J. S.: *A History of the Asians of East Africa: c. 1886 to 1945* (Oxford, 1969).

MANNONI, O.: *Prospero and Caliban* (London, 1956), translated from the French, *Psychologie de la colonisation* (Paris, 1950).

MORRIS, H. F.: and READ, J. S.: *Indirect Rule and the Search for Justice: essays in East African legal history* (Oxford, 1972).

OLIVER, R. A.: *The Missionary Factor in East Africa* (London, 1952).

—— *Sir Harry Johnston and the Scramble for Africa* (London, 1957).

—— and MATHEW, G., eds.: *History of East Africa*, Vol. I (Oxford, 1963).

PHILLIPS, A., ed.: *Survey of African Marriage and Family Life* (London, 1953). Sections of this, with updating chapters, were reprinted in 1969 (by L. Mair) and 1971 (by A. Phillips and H. F. Morris).

POCOCK, D.: '"Difference" in East Africa: a study of caste and religion in modern Indian society', *Southwestern Journal of Anthropology*, 13, 4 (Winter 1957) pp. 289–300.

RANGER, T. O.: 'African Reactions to the Imposition of Colonial Rule in East and Central Africa', in *Colonialism in Africa*, Vol. I: *1870–1941*, ed. Gann and Duignan (Cambridge, 1969).

READ, J. S. : 'Crime and Punishment in East Africa : the twilight of customary law', *Howard Law Journal*, 10, 1 (Winter 1964) pp. 164–80.

SAWYER, G. F. A., ed. : *East African Law and Social Change* (Nairobi, 1967).

TAYLOR, J. V. : *Primal Vision : Christian presence amid African religion* (London, 1963).

TRIMINGHAM, J. SPENCER : *Islam in East Africa* (Oxford, 1964).

TWINING, W. : *The Place of Customary Law in the National Legal Systems of East Africa* (Chicago, 1964).

WARREN, M. A. C. : *Revival : an enquiry* (London, 1954).

WATT, W. MONTGOMERY : 'The Political Relevance of Islam in East Africa', *International Affairs* (January 1966) pp. 35–44.

WEIGHT, ERNEST : *Europäer in Ostafrika* (Cologne : Selbstverlag des Geographischen Institute der Universität, 1955).

WELBOURN, F. B. : *East African Rebels : a study of some independent churches* (London, 1961).

—— 'Missionary Stimulus and African Responses', in *Colonialism in Africa*, Vol. 3, ed. Turner (Stanford, 1971).

(ii) *Kenya*

ANDREWS, C. F. : *The Indian Question in Kenya* (The Swift Press, private circulation, Nairobi, 1921).

BEECHER, L. J. : 'African Separatist Churches in Kenya', *World Dominion*, 31, 1 (January–February 1953) pp. 5–12.

BLIXEN, KAREN : *Out of Africa* (London, 1937).

BRETT, E. A. : *Colonialism and Underdevelopment in East Africa : the politics of economic change, 1919–1939* (London, 1973).

CAREY JONES, N. S. : 'The Decolonization of the White Highlands of Kenya', *Geographical Journal*, 131, 2 (June 1965) pp. 186–201.

CHURCH, A. G. : *East Africa : a new dominion* (London, 1927).

CRANWORTH, LORD : *A Colony in the Making : British East Africa* (London, 1912).

DILLEY, MARJORIE R. : *British Policy in Kenya Colony* (New York, 1937).

EAST AFRICAN STANDARD : *The Indian Problem in Kenya : being a selection from speeches, articles and correspondence appearing in the East African press, 1921* (Nairobi, 1922).

ELIOT, SIR CHARLES : *The East Africa Protectorate* (London, 1905).

FROST, R. A. : 'Trusteeship, Discrimination and Attempts to Promote Interracial Co-operation in Kenya, 1945–1963' (unpublished D.Phil. thesis, Oxford, 1972).

GHAI, Y. P., and McAUSLAN, J. P. W. B. : *Public Law and Political Change in Kenya* (Nairobi, London, 1970).

GRIGG, E. W. M. (later LORD ALTRINCHAM) : *Kenya's Opportunity : memories, hopes and ideas* (London, 1955).

HILL, M. F. : 'The White Settler's Role in Kenya', *Foreign Affairs*, 38, 4 (July 1960) pp. 638–45.

HOBLEY, C. W. : *Kenya from Chartered Company to Crown Colony* (London, 1929).

HUXLEY, ELSPETH : *White Man's Country : Lord Delamere and the making of Kenya*, 2 vols. (London, 1935).

SELECT BIBLIOGRAPHY

656   SELECT BIBLIOGRAPHY

656   SELECT BIBLIOGRAPHY

656   SELECT BIBLIOGRAPHY

656   SELECT BIBLIOGRAPHY

656   SELECT BIBLIOGRAPHY

HUXLEY, ELSPETH and PERHAM, MARGERY: *Race and Politics in Kenya* (London, 1944, revised edn. 1956).

KENYATTA, JOMO: *Facing Mount Kenya* (London, 1938).

LEYS, N.: *Kenya* (London, 1925).

—— *The Colour Bar in East Africa* (London, 1941).

LIPSCOMB, J. F.: *White Africans* (London, 1955).

LONSDALE, J. M.: 'European Attitudes and African Pressures: missions and government in Kenya between the wars', *Race*, 10, 2 (1968) pp. 141–51.

MACDERMOTT, P. L.: *British East Africa or IBEA* (London, 1893).

MCWILLIAM, M.: 'Economic Policy and the Kenya Settlers, 1945–1948', in *Essays in Imperial Government*, ed. K. E. Robinson and A. F. Madden (Oxford, 1963).

MORGAN, W. T. W.: 'The "White Highlands" of Kenya', *Geographical Journal*, 129, 2 (June 1963) pp. 140–55.

MUNGEAM, G. H.: *British Rule in Kenya, 1895–1912; the establishment of administration in the East Africa Protectorate* (Oxford, 1966).

REMOLE, R. A.: 'White Settlers, or the Foundation of European Agricultural Settlement in Kenya' (unpublished Ph.D. dissertation, Harvard, 1959).

ROSS, W. McGREGOR: *Kenya from Within* (London, 1927).

RUEL, M. J.: 'Religion and Society among the Kuria of East Africa', *Africa*, 35, 3 (1965) pp. 295–306.

SALVADORI, M.: *La Colonisation européene au Kenya* (Paris, 1938).

SORRENSON, M. P. K.: *Origins of European Settlement in Kenya* (Nairobi, 1968).

WASSERMAN, G.: 'The Adaptation of a Colonial Élite to Decolonization' (unpublished Ph.D. dissertation, Columbia, 1973).

WELBOURN, F. B., and OGOT, B. A.: *A Place to Feel at Home: a study of two independent churches in Western Kenya* (London, 1966).

(iii) *Uganda*

BROWN, D., and ALLEN, P. A. P. J.: *An Introduction to the Law of Uganda* (London, 1968).

ENGHOLM, G. F.: 'The Decline of Immigrant Influence on the Uganda Administration 1945–1952', *Uganda Journal*, 31, 1 (1967) pp. 73–88.

—— 'Immigrant Influences upon the Development of Policy in Uganda, 1902–1952' (unpublished Ph.D. thesis, London, 1968).

FALLERS, L. A.: *Law without Precedent: legal ideas in the courts of colonial Busoga* (Chicago, 1969).

FAUPEL, J. F.: *African Holocaust: the story of the Uganda martyrs* (London, 1962).

GALE, H. P.: *Uganda and the Mill Hill Fathers* (London, 1959).

GEE, T. W.: 'A Century of Muhammadan Influence in Buganda, 1852–1951', *Uganda Journal*, 22, 2 (September 1958) pp. 139–50.

GOLDSCHMIDT, W.: *Sebei Law* (Berkeley, Los Angeles, 1967).

HAYDON, E. S.: *Law and Justice in Buganda* (London, 1960).

HONE, H. R., compiler: *Handbook on Native Courts for the Guidance of Administrative Officers* (Entebbe, 1941).

JOHNSTON, SIR H. H.: *The Uganda Protectorate*, 2 vols. (London, 1902).

KUPER, HILDA, '"Strangers" in Plural Societies: Asians in South Africa and Uganda', in *Pluralism in Africa*, ed. Kuper and Smith (Berkeley, 1969).

LARIMORE, ANN E.: *The Alien Town: patterns of settlement in Busoga, Uganda—an essay in cultural geography* (Chicago, 1958).

LOW, D. A.: *Religion and Society in Buganda, 1875–1900*, East African Studies No. 8 (Kampala, EAISR, 1957).

—— 'Converts and Martyrs in Buganda', in *Christianity in Tropical Africa*, ed. C. G. Baëta (London, 1968).

LUCK, ANNE: *African Saint: the story of Apolo Kivebulaya* (London, 1963).

MORRIS, H. F.: 'Jurisdiction of the Buganda Courts and the Scope of Customary Law in Uganda', *Journal of African Law*, 9, 3 (Autumn 1965) pp. 154–61.

—— 'Two Early Surveys of Native Courts in Uganda', *Journal of African Law*, 11, 3 (Autumn 1967) pp. 159–74.

—— and READ, J. S.: 'Uganda', Vol. 13 in *The British Commonwealth: the development of its laws and constitutions* (London, 1966).

MORRIS, H. S.: 'Indians in East Africa: a study in a plural society', *British Journal of Sociology*, 7 (1956) pp. 194–211.

—— 'Communal Rivalry among Indians in Uganda', *British Journal of Sociology*, 8, 4 (1957) pp. 306–17.

—— 'The Indian Family in Uganda', *American Anthropologist*, 61, 5, Pt. 1 (October 1959) pp. 779–89.

—— *The Indians in Uganda* (London, 1968).

SOFER, C.: 'The Working Groups in a Plural Society', in *Industrial and Labour Relations Review*, 8 (October 1954) p. 70.

SOFER, C., and ROSS, R.: 'Some Characteristics of an East African European Population', *The British Journal of Sociology*, 2, 4 (December 1951) pp. 315–31.

SOUTHALL, A. W.: 'Race and Class in an African Town', *Sociological Journal*, 1 (1963).

STENNING, D. J.: 'Salvation in Ankole', in *African Systems of Thought*, ed. M. Fortes and G. Dieterlen (London, 1965), pp. 258–75.

TAYLOR, J. V.: *The Growth of the Church in Buganda* (London, 1958).

THOMAS, H. B.: '*Imperatrix* v. *Juma and Urzee*', *Uganda Journal*, 7, 2 (October 1939) pp. 70–84.

—— and SCOTT, R.: *Uganda* (London, 1935).

TONGUE, E. DAUNCEY: 'The Contact of Races in Uganda', *British Journal of Psychology*, 25 (1934–5) pp. 356–64.

WELBOURN, F. B.: 'Some Aspects of Kiganda Relgion', *Uganda Journal*, 26, 2 (September 1962) pp. 171–82.

WINTER, E. H.: *Beyond the Mountains of the Moon: the lives of four Africans* (London, 1959).

(iv) *Tanganyika*

ALEXANDER, G.: *Tanganyika Memories: a judge in the red kanzu* (London, 1936).

CAMERON, SIR D.: *My Tanganyika Service and Some Nigeria* (London, 1939).

COLE, J. S. R., and DENISON, W. N.: 'Tanganyika', Vol. 12 in *The British Commonwealth: the development of its laws and constitutions* (London, 1964).

GILLMAN, C.: 'White Colonization in East Africa with Special Regard to Tanganyika Territory', *Geographical Review*, 32, 4 (October 1942) pp. 585–97.

ILIFFE, J.: *Tanganyika under German Rule, 1905–1912* (Cambridge, 1969).

RANGER, T. O.: *The African Churches of Tanzania*, Historical Association of Tanzania Paper No. 5 (Nairobi, n.d.).

REID, E.: *Tanganyika Without Prejudice* (London, 1934).

SCHNEIDER, K.: *Dar es Salaam: Stadtenwicklung unter dem Einfluss der Araber und Inder* (Wiesbaden, Steiner, 1965).

SWANTZ, L. W.: *Church, Mission and State Relations in Pre- and Post-Independent Tanzania, 1955–1964* (New York, Syracuse University, 1965).

TANNER, R. E. S.: 'Conflict within Small European Communities in Tanganyika', *Human Organization*, 23, 4 (1964).

—— *Transition in African Beliefs: traditional religion and Christian change, a study in Sukumaland, Tanzania, East Africa* (Maryknoll, 1967).

WILSON, MONICA: *Communal Rituals of the Nyakyusa* (London, 1959).

(v) *Zanzibar*

GRAY, SIR J. M.: *A History of Zanzibar* (London, 1962).

NICHOLLS, CHRISTINE S.: *The Swahili Coast* (London, 1971).

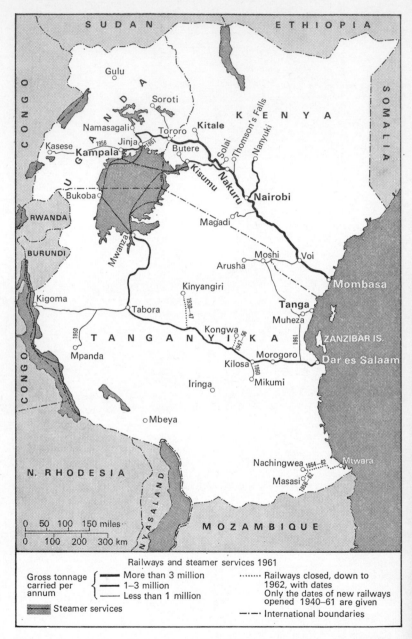

MAP 4. EAST AFRICA: RAILWAYS AND STEAMER SERVICES, 1960–1 [adapted from A. D. Hazlewood, *Rail and Road in East Africa* (Oxford, 1964)].

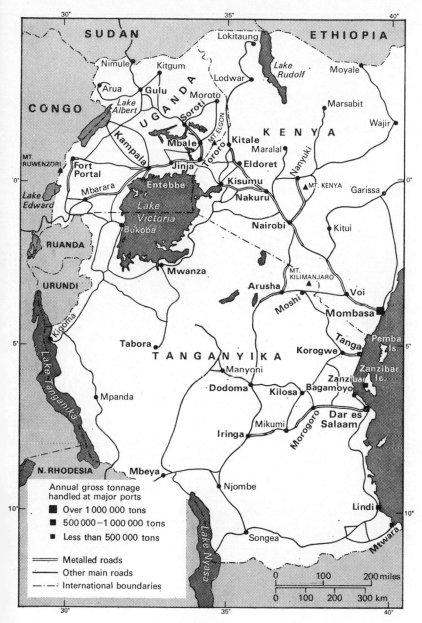

MAP 5. EAST AFRICA: MAIN ROADS, 1961.

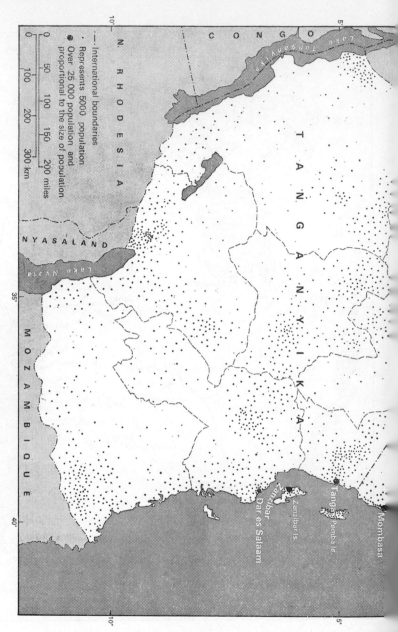

MAP 6. EAST AFRICA: POPULATION, 1961–2 [Based on map accompany...

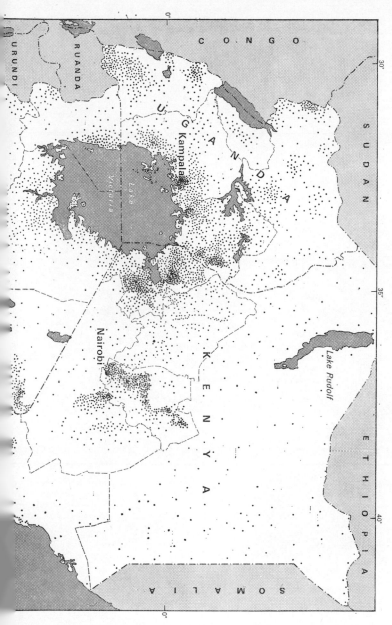

Africa: Its people and resources, ed. W. T. W. Morgan (Nairobi, 1967)].

INDEX